The Western Heritage
Volume B: 1300 to 1815

SIXTH EDITION

DONALD KAGAN

Yale University

STEVEN OZMENT

Harvard University

FRANK M. TURNER

Yale University

Prentice Hall, Upper Saddle River, New Jersey 07458

Library of Congress Cataloging–in–Publication Data

The Library of Congress has catalogued the one volume edition as follows:

Kagan, Donald
The Western Heritage/ Donald Kagan, Steven Ozment, Frank M.
    Turner. —6th ed.
           p.   cm.
     Includes bibliographical references and index.
     ISBN 0-13-617383-7
     1. Civilization, Western.   I. Ozment, Steven E. II. Turner,
Frank M. (Frank Miller). (Date). III. Title
     CB245.K28   1998   97-23706
     909′.09812—dc21   CIP

Editorial Director: Charlyce Jones Owen
Editor-in-Chief, Development: Susanna Lesan
Development Editor: Roberta Meyer
Director of Production and Manufacturing: Barbara Kittle
Production Editor: Barbara DeVries
Executive Manager, New Media: Alison Pendergast
Manufacturing Manager: Nick Sklitsis
Prepress and Manufacturing Buyer: Lynn Pearlman
Marketing Manager: Sheryl Adams

Creative Design Director: Leslie Osher
Interior and Cover Designer: Maria Lange
Supervisor of Production Services: Lori Clinton
Electronic Page Layout: Rosemary Ross
Photo Director: Lorinda Morris-Nantz
Photo Research: Barbara Salz
Cartographer: Maryland Cartographics
Line Art Coordinator: Michele Giusti
Copy Editor: Susan Saslow

Cover Art: Canaletto, *Venice: A Regatta on the Grand Canal.* National Gallery, London/Bridgeman Art
    Library, London.

This book was set in 10/12 Trump Mediaeval by the HSS in-house formatting and
production services group and was printed and bound by RR Donnelley & Sons.
The cover was printed by The Lehigh Press, Inc.

Time Line photo credits appear on page xxxi and constitute a continuation of the copyright page.

 © 1998, 1991, 1987, 1983, 1979 by Prentice-Hall
Simon & Schuster/A Viacom Company
Upper Saddle River, New Jersey 07458

Printed in the United States of America
10 9 8 7 6 5 4 3
ISBN 0-13-617457-4

Prentice-Hall International (UK) Limited, *London*
Prentice-Hall of Australia Pty. Limited, *Sydney*
Prentice-Hall Canada Inc., *Toronto*
Prentice-Hall Hispanoamericana, S.A., *Mexico*
Prentice-Hall of India Private Limited, *New Delhi*
Prentice-Hall of Japan, Inc. *Tokyo*
Simon & Schuster Asia Pte. Ltd., *Singapore*
Editora Prentice-Hall do Brasil, Ltda., *Rio de Janeiro*

BRIEF CONTENTS

DETAILED CONTENTS

Europe in Transition, 1300–1750   **304**

Enlightenment and Revolution 604

Toward the Modern World   796

Global Conflict, Cold War, and New Directions 1028

31 Toward a New Europe and the Twenty-first Century 1122

DOCUMENTS

MAPS

THE WEST & THE WORLD

POLITICAL TRANSFORMATIONS

PREFACE

The heritage of Western civilization has perhaps never been the focus of so much interest and controversy as it is today. Many commentators criticize it, many praise it, but for all it is a subject of intense discussion. *The Western Heritage,* sixth edition, is designed to allow teachers to introduce students to the subject of that discussion. It presents an overview of Western civilization, including its strengths, its weaknesses, and the controversies surrounding it.

On campus after campus, every aspect of Western civilization has become an object of scrutiny and debate. Many participants in this debate fail to recognize that such self-criticism is characteristic of Western civilization and an important part of its heritage. We welcome the debate and hope that this book can help raise its quality.

The collapse of Communism has left the people of half of Europe struggling to reorganize their political institutions and their social and economic lives. The choices they are making and the future they are forging will reflect in large measure their understanding of their heritage. To follow and participate in that process we too need to understand that heritage.

GOALS OF THE TEXT

Since *The Western Heritage* first appeared, we have sought to provide our readers with a work that does justice to the richness and variety of Western civilization. Events since then have only added urgency to our purpose.

Our primary goal has been to present a strong, clear narrative account of the central developments in Western history. We have also sought to call attention to certain critical themes:

- the development of political freedom, constitutional government, and concern for the rule of law and individual rights
- the shifting relations among religion, society, and the state
- the development of science and technology and their expanding impact on thought, social institutions, and everyday life

- the major religious and intellectual currents that have shaped Western culture

We believe that these themes have been fundamental in Western civilization, shaping the past and exerting a continuing influence on the present.

Balanced and Flexible Presentation In this edition as in past editions, our goal has been to present Western civilization fairly, accurately, and in a way that does justice to its great variety. History has many facets, no one of which alone can account for the others. Any attempt to tell the story of the West from a single overarching perspective, no matter how timely, is bound to neglect or suppress some important part of that story.

The Western Heritage, sixth edition, is designed to accommodate a variety of approaches to a course in Western civilization, allowing teachers to stress what is most important to them. Some teachers will ask students to read all the chapters. Others will select among them to reinforce assigned readings and lectures.

We do not believe that a history of the West should be limited to politics and international relations, but we share the conviction that internal and external political events have shaped the Western experience in fundamental and powerful ways. Recent events in central and eastern Europe and the former Soviet Union have strengthened that belief. We have also been told repeatedly by teachers that no matter what their own historical specialization, they believe that a political narrative gives students an effective tool to begin to organize their understanding of the past.

The Western Heritage also provides one of the richest accounts of the social history of the West available today, with strong coverage of family life, the roles of women, and the place of the family in relation to broader economic, political, and social developments. This coverage reflects the explosive growth in social historical research in the past quarter century, which has enriched virtually all areas of historical study.

Finally, no other survey text presents so full an account of the religious and intellectual development of the West. People may be political and social beings, but they are also reasoning and spiritual beings. What they think and believe are among the most important things we can know about them. Their ideas about God, society, law, gender, human nature, and the physical world have changed over the centuries and continue to change. We cannot fully grasp our own approach to the world without understanding the intellectual currents of the past and their influence on our thoughts and conceptual categories.

Clarity and Accessibility Good narrative history requires clear, vigorous prose. As in earlier editions, we have paid careful attention to the quality of our writing, subjecting every paragraph to critical scrutiny. Our goal was to make our presentation fully accessible to students without compromising vocabulary or conceptual level. We hope this effort will benefit both teachers and students.

Recent Scholarship As in previous editions, changes in this edition reflect our determination to incorporate the most recent developments in historical scholarship and the expanding concerns of professional historians.

Pedagogical Features This edition retains the pedagogical features of the last edition, including part-opening comparative timelines, a list of key topics at the beginning of each chapter, chapter review questions, and questions accompanying the more than 200 source documents in the text. Each of these features is designed to make the text more accessible to students and to reinforce key concepts.

- The *part-opening timelines*, which follow the essays that open each of the six parts of the book, summarize major events in politics and government, society and economy, and religion and culture side by side. Appropriate photographs have been added to each timeline.
- *Primary source documents*, more than one third new to this edition, acquaint students with the raw material of history and provide intimate contact with the people of the past and their concerns. *Questions* accompanying the source documents direct students toward important, thought-provoking issues and help them relate the documents to the material in the text. They can

be used to stimulate class discussion or as topics for essays and study groups.

- Each chapter includes an *outline,* a list of *key topics,* and an *introduction.* Together these features provide a succinct overview of each chapter.
- *Chronologies* follow each major section in a chapter, listing significant events and their dates.
- *Concluding sections* summarize the major themes of each chapter and provide a bridge to the next chapter.

- *Chapter review questions* help students review the material in a chapter and relate it to broader themes. They too can be used for class discussion and essay topics.
- *Suggested readings* lists following each chapter have been updated with new titles reflecting recent scholarship.

CHANGES IN THE SIXTH EDITION

The sixth edition retains all of the major content changes that appear in the fifth edition. In addition, Chapter 30, *"Europe and the Soviet-American Rivalry"* has been reorganized to relate the various regional conflicts occurring outside of Europe, including the Mideast, Korea, and Vietnam, more closely to the Cold War conflict between the superpowers. Chapter 31, *"Toward a New Europe and the Twenty-first Century,"* reviews recent events in Eastern Europe. As in the fifth edition, questions appear with each document and after every chapter.

New Features New to the edition are two major features designed to expand students' understanding of the heritage of the West. These are a series of illustrated essays, *The West & the World,* and a series of maps with explanations focusing on key *Political Transformations.*

The West & the World

The students reading this book are drawn from a wide variety of cultures and experiences. They live in a world characterized by highly interconnected economies and instant communication between cultures. In this emerging multicultural society it seems both appropriate and necessary to recognize the ways in which Western civilization has throughout its history interacted with other cultures, influencing other societies and being influenced by them. Examples of this two-way interaction, such as that with Islam, already appear in the main body of the text. In this new feature, we focus on six subjects, comparing Western institutions with those of other parts of the world, or discussing the ways in which developments in the West have influenced cultures in other areas of the globe. Topics for this feature are:

ANCIENT SLAVERY (p. 150)

Slavery has arisen as a social and economic institution in virtually every world culture. This essay compares slavery in the ancient cultures of Mesopotamia, Egypt, China, India, Greece, and Rome. It also describes the role of slavery in the economies of ancient Greece and the ante-bellum American South. The latter comparison seems especially appropriate since in both instances, ancient and modern, the surrounding political structures were democratic.

SOCIAL LIFE IN MALI (1200–1400) (p. 300)

Medieval Europe in many respects constituted an underdeveloped economy. Production was quite limited and was almost entirely agrarian. This essay explores the ways in which that society compares with Mali Society. It discusses Islamic influences on marriage customs, education, and daily life in the African setting, allowing students to draw comparisons with similar European institutions influenced by Christianity, as examined in the preceding chapter.

THE FAMILY IN EUROPE
AND CHINA (1400–1800) (p. 408)

Throughout the human experience, the family has been the most enduring of all institutions. Recent scholarship has greatly improved our understanding of the early modern European family. This essay draws upon that knowledge, enabling students to compare and contrast the European family of the era with family structures in China.

THE ABOLITION OF SLAVERY
IN THE TRANSATLANTIC ECONOMY (p. 754)

The abolition of chattel slavery in the transatlantic economy stands as one of the most remarkable social and economic developments of the eighteenth and nineteenth centuries. Never before had a society abolished slavery. This essay traces the history of that crusade, noting the manner in which it influenced the societies of Africa, Latin America and North America.

IMPERIALISM: ANCIENT AND MODERN (p. 958)

During the past two centuries no interaction of the West with the rest of the world was more important or of more enduring significance than the establishment of colonial empires in Asia and Africa. This essay recalls for students the earlier empires that were part of the Western experience, comparing the imperialism of the ancient world with that of the modern era.

GLOBAL DEMOCRATIZATION (p. 1116)

With the collapse of communism in the past decade, democratization has made enormous gains in Europe and the former Soviet Union. This essay places the recent European experience in the context of the worldwide movement of the past half-century toward greater democratic political participation. It pays particular attention to the civil rights movement in the United States and to the movements toward democracy in Latin America.

Political Transformations

This new map feature concentrates on six highly significant moments of political transformation in the history of the West. As with *The West & the World*, most *Political Transformations* emphasize the interaction of the West with other areas of the world. Each of the features provides a brief overview of the transformation illustrated by a map as well as in an illustrative document. The features will provide opportunities for study not only by individual students, but also for class discussion. The topics for this feature are:

- Greek Colonization from Spain to the Black Sea
- Muslim Conquests and Domination of the Mediterranean to about 750
- Voyages of Discovery and the Colonial Claims of Spain and Portugal
- The Congress of Vienna Redraws the Map of Europe
- The Mandate System: 1919 to World War II
- Decolonization in Asia and Africa

Maps and Illustrations The skillful use of color in the maps greatly improves their clarity and pedagogical usefulness. All 90 maps in the text have been carefully edited for accuracy. The text also contains almost 500 color and black and white illustrations. In this edition, we have added photographs to the timelines preceding each part of the book.

A Note on Dates and Transliterations With this edition of *The Western Heritage* we shift to the use of B.C.E. (before the common era) and C.E. (common era) instead of B.C. (before Christ) and A.D. (*anno domini*, the year of the Lord) to designate dates.

Also, we have followed the most accurate currently accepted English transliterations of Arabic words. For example, today Koran is being replaced by the more accurate *Qur'an*; similarly *Muhammad* is preferable to *Mohammed* and *Muslim* to *Moslem*.

Ancillary Instructional Materials *The Western Heritage* sixth edition comes with an extensive package of ancillary materials.

For the Instructor:

- **Instructor's Manual with Test Items** prepared by Perry M. Rogers, Ohio State University. The manual includes chapter summaries, key points and vital concepts, identification questions, multiple-choice questions, essay questions, and suggested films.
- **Transparency Acetates** of the four-color maps, charts, figures, and graphs in the text provide useful instructional aids for lectures.
- **Prentice Hall Custom Test,** available in Windows, DOS, and Macintosh format, provides the questions from the printed test item file for generating multiple versions of tests.
- **Administrative Handbook** by Jay Boggis provides instructors with resources for using *The Western Heritage* with Annenberg/CPB telecourse, *The Western Tradition.*

For the Student:

- **Study Guide, Volumes I** and **II** includes commentary, definitions, identifications, map exercises, short-answer exercises, and essay questions.
- **Map Workbook** gives the student the opportunity to increase their knowledge of geography through identification exercises.

- **Documents in Western Civilization, Volumes I and II,** provides over 100 additional primary source readings with questions for discussion.
- **Telecourse Study Guide, Volumes I and II,** by Jay Boggis correlates *The Western Heritage* with the Annenberg/CPB telecourse, *The Western Tradition.*

Media Ancillaries:

- **The Western Heritage, Interactive Edition, Version 2.0** takes students on an interactive journey through the evolution of Western civilization and its people. With over 600 study questions, quizzes, and comprehension exercises, this unique CD-ROM provides a highly visual multimedia learning experience that will engage and captivate students' imagination. Available for IBM/Mac.
- **The World Wide Web Companion Study Guide** (*http://www.prenhall.com/kagan*) directly complements *The Western Heritage* and correlates the text to related material on the Internet. Each "chapter" corresponds to the chapter in the textbook and consists of objectives, multiple choice quizzes, essay questions, chapter chat, web destinations, and help.

Acknowledgments We are grateful to the scholars and teachers whose thoughtful and often detailed comments helped shape this revision:

Lenard R. Berlanstein, University of Virginia, Charlottesville
Stephanie Christelow, Idaho State University
Samuel Willard Crompton, Holyoke Community College
Robert L. Ervin, San Jacinto Community College
Joseph Gonzales, Moorpark College
Victor Davis Hanson, California State University, Fresno
William I. Hitchcock, Yale University
Pardaic Kenny, University of Colorado, Boulder
Raymond F. Kierstead, Reed College
Eleanor McCluskey, Palm Beach Atlantic College and Broward Community College
Robert J. Mueller, Hastings College
John Nicols, University of Oregon, Eugene
Sandra J. Peacock, State University of New York, Binghamton
John Powell, Pennsylvania State University

Robert A. Schneider, Catholic University
Hugo Schwyzer, Pasadena City College
Sidney R. Sherter, Long Island University
Roger P. Snow, College of Great Falls

Finally, we would like to thank the dedicated people who helped produce this revision: our development editor, Roberta Meyer; our production editor, Barbara DeVries; Maria Lange who created the handsome new design of this edition; Rosemary Ross who formatted the pages; Lynn Pearlman, our manufacturing buyer; and Barbara Salz, the photo researcher.

D.K.
S.O.
F.M.T.

The New York Times and **Prentice Hall** are sponsoring **Themes of the Times:** a program designed to enhance access to current information of relevance in the classroom.

Through this program, the core subject matter provided in the text is supplemented by a collection of time-sensitive articles from one of the world's most distinguished newspapers, **The New York Times**. These articles demonstrate the vital, ongoing connection between what is learned in the classroom and what is happening in the world around us.

To enjoy the wealth of information of **The New York Times** daily, a reduced subscription rate is available. For information, call toll-free: 1–800–631–1222.

Prentice Hall and **The New York Times** are proud to co-sponsor **Themes of the Times.** We hope it will make the reading of both textbooks and newspapers a more dynamic, involving process.

ABOUT THE AUTHORS

Donald Kagan is Hillhouse Professor of History and Classics at Yale University, where he has taught since 1969. He received the A.B. degree in history from Brooklyn College, the M.A. in classics from Brown University, and the Ph.D. in history from Ohio State University. During 1958–1959 he studied at the American School of Classical Studies as a Fulbright Scholar. He has received three awards for undergraduate teaching at Cornell and Yale. He is the author of a history of Greek political thought, *The Great Dialogue* (1965); a four-volume history of the Peloponnesian war, *The Origins of the Peloponnesian War* (1969); *The Archidamian War* (1974); *The Peace of Nicias and the Sicilian Expedition* (1981); *The Fall of the Athenian Empire* (1987); and a biography of Pericles, *Pericles of Athens and the Birth of Democracy* (1991); and *On the Origins of War* (1995). With Brian Tierney and L. Pearce Williams, he is the editor of *Great Issues in Western Civilization,* a collection of readings.

Steven Ozment is McLean Professor of Ancient and Modern History at Harvard University. He has taught Western Civilization at Yale, Stanford, and Harvard. He is the author of eight books. *The Age of Reform, 1250–1550* (1980) won the Schaff Prize and was nominated for the 1981 American Book Award. *Magdalena and Balthasar: An Intimate Portrait of Life in Sixteenth Century Europe* (1986), *Three Behaim Boys: Growing Up in Early Modern Germany* (1990), and *Protestants: The Birth of a Revolution* (1992) were selections of the History Book Club, as is also his most recent book, *The Bürgermeister's Daughter* (1996).

Frank M. Turner is John Hay Whitney Professor of History at Yale University, where he served as University Provost from 1988 to 1992. He received his B.A. degree at the College of William and Mary and his Ph.D. from Yale. He has received the Yale College Award for Distinguished Undergraduate Teaching. He has directed a National Endowment for the Humanities Summer Institute. His scholarly research has received the support of fellowships from the National Endowment for the Humanities and the Guggenheim Foundation. He is the author of *Between Science and Religion: The Reaction to Scientific Naturalism in Late Victorian England* (1974), *The Greek Heritage in Victorian Britain* (1981), which received the British Council Prize of the Conference on British Studies and the Yale Press Governors Award, and *Contesting Cultural Authority: Essays in Victorian Intellectual Life* (1993). He has also contributed numerous articles to journals and has served on the editorial advisory boards of *The Journal of Modern History, Isis,* and *Victorian Studies.*

TIME LINE PHOTO CREDITS

Time Line I: page 2, (left) Gary Cralle/The Image Bank; (right) Winfield I. Parks, Jr./ National Geographic Image Collection; page 3, The Granger Collection; page 4, Battle of Alexander the Great at Issue. Roman mosaic. Museo Archeologico Nazionale, Naples, Italy. Scala/Art Resource, NY; page 5, Robert Frerck, Woodfin Camp & Associates.

Time Line II: page 198, New York University Institute of Fine Arts; page 199, Bayeux, Musee de l'Eveche. "With special authorization of the City of Bayeux." Giraudon/Art Resource.

Time Line III: page 306, George Gower (1540–96). "Elizabeth I, The Armada Portrait." The Bridgeman Art Library; page 307, The Granger Collection.

Time Line IV: page 607, Musee de la Legion d'Honneur.

Time Line V: page 798, Corbis-Bettmann; page 799, John Christen Johansen, *Signing of the Treaty of Versailles,* 1919, National Portrait Gallery, Smithsonian Institution, Washington, D.C./Art Resource, NY.

Time Line VI: page 1030, Franklin D. Roosevelt Library; page 1031, John Launois/Black Star.

Europe in Transition, 1300–1750

Between the early fourteenth and the mid-eighteenth centuries, Europe underwent many far-reaching changes. These were years of massive physical suffering brought on by disease and war and of new political and cultural construction made possible by better government and growing wealth.

The era began with one of the greatest disasters in European history: a bubonic plague, known as the *Black Death*, that had killed an estimated two-fifths of the population by the mid-fourteenth century. A hundred years of sharp conflicts between popes and secular rulers preceded this demographic crisis and a hundred years of warfare between England and France followed it. The emergence of strong, ruthless monarchs accompanied the decline in papal power during the later Middle Ages. Commanding greater economic and military resources, these new rulers gained control over the church in their lands. By the fourteenth century, the nation-states of Europe were warring with one another, no longer with the armies of the pope.

The fourteenth century also saw the beginning of the great cultural resurgence in Europe known as the *Renaissance*. This rebirth of education and culture was closely associated with the rediscovery of forgotten classical Greek and Latin writings and the rapid growth of colleges and universities throughout western Europe.

The past was not the only previously uncharted region Europeans set out to explore. In the late fifteenth century, they began voyages to America, around Africa, and across the Indian Ocean to Asia that introduced them to exotic cultures and non-Western values. Beginning with Copernicus and culminating with Sir Isaac Newton, scientists charted a new view of the universe. Between them the voyages of discovery and the Scientific Revolution gave Europeans both new confidence in the power of the human mind and a new perspective on their society.

In the sixteenth century, a religious revolt divided Europe spiritually and led to a major restructuring of Western Christendom. The Protestant Reformation began in 1517 when an obscure German professor named Martin Luther challenged the religious teaching and authority of the papacy. Within a quarter century, Europe was permanently divided among a growing variety of Protestant churches and the Roman Catholic Church. For a century and a half, these new religious differences also fueled political conflict. Religious warfare devastated France in the second half of the sixteenth century and wreaked havoc on Germany in the first half of the seventeenth century.

By the middle of the seventeenth century, most religious warfare had ended. The religious turmoil had strengthened the hand of the secular state. For many rulers and their subjects, political stability came to have a higher value than religious allegiance. By the early eighteenth century, Europe's rulers (with the notable exception of the English monarchs, who had the will but not the ability) imitated the French king Louis XIV. Through efficient taxation, a loyal administration, and a powerful standing army, Louis bent France to his will, making it the model of the new absolute state to which rulers everywhere aspired. By the second half of the seventeenth century, the balance of power shifted away from Spain, which had dominated Europe during the sixteenth century. France, Austria, and Prussia joined the new parliamentary monarchy of Great Britain as Europe's new masters. And, for the first time, Russia emerged as a major European power.

With the end of religious conflict, energies turned toward economic expansion. New and more efficient farming methods appeared, and nations took the first steps toward industrialization. In the New World, the colonies grew and were consolidated. By the eighteenth century, competition over trade had replaced religion as the cause of war. The demand for political independence, most notably by the English colonies in America, replaced the earlier demands for religious independence. A new age had dawned, one still believing in the power of God, but increasingly fascinated by human political power. ✦

1300-1750 C.E.

	POLITICS AND GOVERNMENT	SOCIETY AND ECONOMY	RELIGION AND CULTURE
1300–1400	1309–1377 Pope resides in Avignon 1337–1453 Hundred Years' War 1356 *Golden Bull* creates German electoral college	1315–1317 Greatest famine of the Middle Ages 1347–1350 Black Death peaks 1358 *Jacquerie* shakes France 1378 Ciompi Revolt in Florence 1381 English peasants' revolt	1300–1325 Dante Alighieri writes *Divine Comedy* 1302 Boniface VIII issues bull *Unam Sanctam* 1350 Boccaccio, *Decameron* 1375–1527 The Renaissance in Italy 1378–1417 The Great Schism 1380–1395 Chaucer writes *Canterbury Tales* 1390–1430 Christine de Pisan writes in defense of women
1400–1500	1415–1433 Hussite revolt in Bohemia 1428–1519 Aztecs expand in central Mexico 1429 Joan of Arc leads French to victory in Orleans 1434 Medici rule begins in Florence 1453–1471 Wars of the Roses in England 1469 Marriage of Ferdinand and Isabella 1487 Henry Tudor creates Court of Star Chamber	1450 Johann Gutenberg invents printing with movable type 1492 Christopher Columbus encounters the Americas 1498 Vasco da Gama reaches India	1414–1417 The Council of Constance 1425–1450 Lorenzo Valla exposes the *Donation of Constantine* 1450 Thomas à Kempis, *Imitation of Christ* 1492 Expulsion of Jews from Spain
1500–1600	1519 Charles V crowned Holy Roman emperor 1530 *Augsburg Confession* defines Lutheranism 1547 Ivan the Terrible becomes tsar of Russia 1555 *Peace of Augsburg* recognizes the legal principle, *cuius regio, eius religio* 1568–1603 Reign of Elizabeth I of England 1572 Saint Bartholomew's Day Massacre 1588 English defeat of Spanish Armada 1598 Edict of Nantes gives Huguenots religious and civil rights	1519 Hernan Cortes lands in Mexico 1519–1522 Ferdinand Magellan circumnavigates the Earth 1525 German Peasants' Revolt 1531–1533 Francisco Pizarro conquers the Incas 1540 Spanish open silver mines in Peru, Bolivia, and Mexico 1550–1600 The great witch panics	1513 Niccolo Machiavelli, *The Prince* 1516 Erasmus compiles a Greek New Testament 1516 Thomas More, *Utopia* 1517 Martin Luther's Ninety-five theses 1534 Henry VIII declared head of English Church 1540 Jesuit order founded 1541 John Calvin becomes Geneva's reformer 1543 Copernicus, *On the Revolutions* 1545–1563 Council of Trent 1549 English *Book of Common Prayer*

Elizabeth I, The Armada Portrait

1300-1750 C.E.

	POLITICS AND GOVERNMENT	SOCIETY AND ECONOMY	RELIGION AND CULTURE
1600–1700	1624–1642 Era of Richelieu in France	1600–1700 Period of greatest Dutch economic prosperity	1605 Bacon, *The Advancement of Learning*; Shakespeare, *King Lear*; Cervantes, *Don Quixote*
	1629–1640 Charles I's years of personal rule	1600–early Spain maintains 1700s commercial monopoly in Latin America	1609 Kepler, *On the Motion of Mars*
	1640 Long Parliament convenes	1607 English settle Jamestown, Virginia	1611 King James Version of the English Bible
	1642 Outbreak of civil war in England	1608 French settle Quebec	1632 Galileo, *Dialogues on the Two Chief Systems of the World*
	1643–1661 Cardinal Mazarin regent for Louis XIV	1618–1648 Thirty Years' War devastates German economy	
	1648 Peace of Westphalia	1619 African slaves first bought at Jamestown, Virginia	1637 Descartes, *Discourse on Method*
	1649–1652 The *Fronde* in France	1650s– Commercial rivalry 1670s between Dutch and English	1651 Hobbes, *Leviathan*
	1649 Charles I executed		
	1660 Charles II restored to the English throne	1661–1683 Colbert seeks to stimulate French economic growth	
	1661–1715 Louis XIV's years of personal rule		1687 Newton, *Principia Mathematica*
	1682–1725 Reign of Peter the Great		1689 English Toleration Act
	1685 James II becomes king of England	1690 Paris Foundling Hospital established	1690 Locke, *Essay Concerning Human Understanding*
	Louis XIV revokes Edict of Nantes		
	1688 "Glorious Revolution" in Britain		
1700–1789	1700–1721 Great Northern War between Sweden and Russia	1715–1763 Era of major colonial rivalry in the Caribbean	1739 Wesley begins field preaching
	1702–1714 War of Spanish Succession	1719 Mississippi Bubble in France	1748 Montesquieu, *Spirit of the Laws*
	1713 Peace of Utrecht	1733 James Kay's flying shuttle	1750 Rousseau, *Discourse on the Moral Effects of the Arts and Sciences*
	1720–1740 Age of Walpole in England and Fleury in France	1750s Agricultural Revolution in Britain	
		1750–1840 Growth of new cities	1751 First volume Diderot's *Encyclopedia*
	1740 Maria Theresa succeeds to the Habsburg throne	1763 Britain becomes dominant in India	1762 Rousseau, *Social Contract* and *Émile*
	1740–1748 War of the Austrian Succession	1763–1789 Enlightened absolutist rulers seek to spur economic growth	1763 Voltaire, Treatise on Toleration
	1756–1763 Seven Years' War		
	1767 Legislative Commission in Russia	1765 James Hargreaves's spinning jenny	
	1772 First Partition of Poland	1769 Richard Arkwright's waterframe	1774 Goethe, *Sorrow of Young Werther*
	1776 American Declaration of Independence	1771–1775 Pugachev's Rebellion	1775 Smith, *Wealth of Nations*
	1778 France aids the American colonies		1781 Kant, *Critique of Pure Reason*
			Joseph II adopts policy of toleration in Austria

Declaration of Independence

The apparition of the Knight of Death, an allegory of the plague approaching a city, whose defenses against it are all too unsure. From the Tres Riches Heures du Duc de Berry *(1284), [Limbourg Brothers. Ms. 65/1284, fol. 90v. Musee Conde, Chantilly, France. Giraudon/Art Resource, N.Y.]*

The Late Middle Ages (1300–1527):
Centuries of Crisis

Political and Social Breakdown
The Hundred Years' War and the Rise
  of National Sentiment
Progress of the War

The Black Death
Preconditions and Causes
Popular Remedies
Social and Economic Consequences
New Conflicts and Opportunities

**Ecclesiastical Breakdown and Revival:
The Late Medieval Church**
The Thirteenth-Century Papacy
Boniface VIII and Philip the Fair
The Avignon Papacy (1309–1377)
The Great Schism (1378–1417) and the
  Conciliar Movement to 1449

K E Y   T O P I C S

- The Hundred Years' War between England and France
- The effects of the bubonic plague on population and society
- The growing power of secular rulers over the papacy
- Schism, heresy, and reform of the church

The late Middle Ages saw almost unprecedented political, social, and ecclesiastical calamity. France and England grappled with each other in a bitter conflict known as the Hundred Years' War (1337–1453), an exercise in seemingly willful self-destruction that was made even more terrible in its later stages by the introduction of gunpowder and the invention of heavy artillery. Bubonic plague, known to contemporaries as the "Black Death," swept over almost all of Europe, killing as much as one-third of the population in many regions between 1348 and 1350 and transforming many pious Christians into believers in the omnipotence of death. A schism emerged within the church, which lasted thirty-nine years (1378–1417) and led, by 1409, to the election of no fewer than three competing popes and colleges of cardinals. In 1453 the Turks marched seemingly invincibly through Constantinople and toward the West. As their political and religious institutions buckled, as disease, bandits, and wolves attacked their cities in the wake of war, and as

Islamic armies gathered at their borders, Europeans beheld what seemed to be the imminent total collapse of Western civilization.

It was in this period that such scholars as Marsilius of Padua, William of Ockham, and Lorenzo Valla produced lasting criticisms of medieval assumptions about the nature of God, humankind, and society. Kings worked through parliaments and clergy through councils to place lasting limits on the pope's temporal power. The notion, derived from Roman law, that a secular ruler is accountable to the body of which he or she is head had already found expression in documents like Magna Carta. It came increasingly to carry the force of accepted principle and conciliarists (advocates of the judicial superiority of a church council over a pope) sought to extend it to establish papal accountability to the church.

But viewed for their three great calamities—war, plague, and schism—the fourteenth and fifteenth centuries were years in which politics resisted *wisdom, nature strained mercy, and the church was less than faithful to its mandate.*

Political and Social Breakdown

The Hundred Years' War and the Rise of National Sentiment

Medieval governments were by no means all-powerful and secure. The rivalry of petty lords kept localities in turmoil and dynastic rivalries could plunge entire lands into war, especially when power was being transferred to a new ruler, and woe to the ruling dynasty that failed to produce a male heir.

To field the armies and collect the revenues that made their existence possible, late medieval rulers depended on carefully negotiated alliances among a wide range of lesser powers. Like kings and queens in earlier centuries, they too practiced the art of feudal government, but on a grander scale and with greater sophistication. To maintain the order they required, the Norman kings of England and the Capetian kings of France fine-tuned traditional feudal relationships, stressing the duties of lesser to higher power and the unquestioning loyalty noble vassals owed the king. The result was a degree of centralized royal power unseen before in these lands and a nascent "national" consciousness that equipped both France and England for international warfare.

THE CAUSES OF THE WAR   The conflict that came to be known as the Hundred Years' War began in May 1337 and lasted until October 1453. The English king Edward III (r. 1327–1377), the grandson of Philip the Fair of France (r. 1285–1314), may be said to have started the war by asserting a claim to the French throne when the French king Charles IV (r. 1322–1328), the last of Philip the Fair's surviving sons, died without a male heir. The French barons had no intention of placing the then fifteen-year-old Edward on the French throne, choosing instead the first cousin of Charles IV, Philip VI of Valois (r. 1328–1350), the first of a new French dynasty that ruled into the sixteenth century.

But there was more to the war than just an English king's assertion of a claim to the French throne. England and France were then emergent territorial powers in too close proximity to one another. Edward was actually a vassal of Philip's, holding several sizable French territories as fiefs from the king of France, a relationship that went back to the days of the Norman conquest. English possession of any French land was repugnant to the French because it threatened the royal policy of centralization. England and France also quarreled over control of Flanders, which, although a French fief, was subject to political influence from England because its principal industry, the manufacture of cloth, depended on supplies of imported English wool. Compounding these frictions was a long history of prejudice and animosity between the French and English people, who constantly confronted one another on the high seas and in port towns. Taken together, these various factors made the Hundred Years' War a struggle for national identity as well as for control of territory.

Edward III pays homage to his feudal lord Philip VI of France. Legally, Edward was a vassal of the king of France. [Archives Snark International/Art Resource, N.Y.]

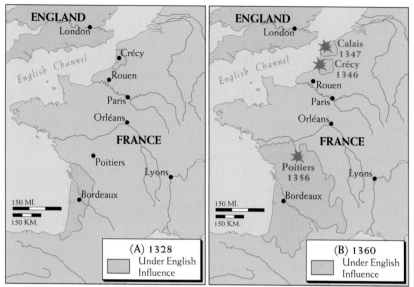

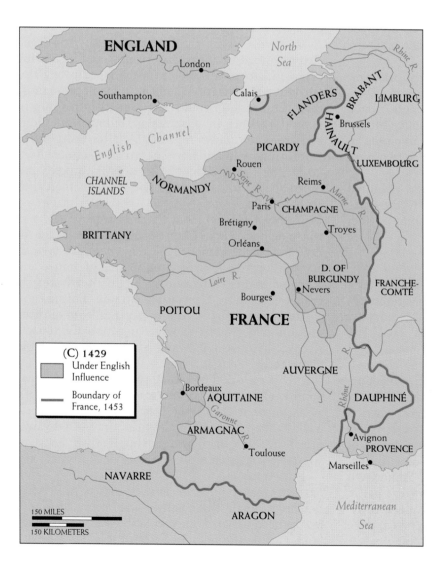

MAP 9–1   THE HUNDRED YEARS' WAR
*The Hundred Years' War went on inter-
mittently from the late 1330s until
1453. These maps show the remarkable
English territorial gains up to the
sudden and decisive turning of the tide
of battle in favor of the French by the
forces of Joan of Arc in 1429.*

FRENCH WEAKNESS   France had three times the population of England, was far the wealthier of the two countries, and fought on its own soil. Yet, for the greater part of the conflict, until after 1415, the major battles ended in often stunning English victories. (See Map 9-1.) The primary reason for these French failures was internal disunity caused by endemic social conflicts. Unlike England, France was still struggling in the fourteenth century to make the transition from a fragmented feudal society to a centralized "modern" state.

Desperate to raise money for the war, French kings resorted to such financial policies as depreciating the currency and borrowing heavily from Italian bankers, which aggravated internal conflicts. In 1355, in a bid to secure funds, the king convened a representative council of townspeople and nobles that came to be known as the Estates General. Although it levied taxes at the king's request, its members also used the king's plight to enhance their own regional rights and privileges, thereby deepening territorial divisions.

France's defeats also reflected English military superiority. The English infantry was more disciplined than the French, and English archers carried a formidable weapon, the longbow, capable of firing six arrows a minute with enough force to pierce an inch of wood or the armor of a knight at two hundred yards.

Finally, French weakness during the Hundred Years' War was due in no small degree to the comparative mediocrity of its royal leadership. English kings were far the shrewder.

Progress of the War

The war had three major stages of development, each ending with a seemingly decisive victory by one or the other side.

THE CONFLICT DURING THE REIGN OF EDWARD III In the first stage of the war, Edward embargoed English wool to Flanders, sparking urban rebellions by merchants and the trade guilds. Inspired by a rich merchant, Jacob van Artevelde, the Flemish cities, led by Ghent, revolted against the French and in 1340 these same cities signed an alliance with England acknowledging Edward as king of France. On June 23 of that same year, in the first great battle of the war, Edward defeated the French fleet in the Bay of Sluys, but his subsequent effort to invade France by way of Flanders failed.

In 1346 Edward attacked Normandy and, after a series of easy victories that culminated at the Battle of Crécy, seized Calais. Exhaustion of both sides and the onset of the Black Death forced a truce in late 1347, and the war entered a brief lull. In 1356, near Poitiers, the English won their greatest victory, routing France's noble cavalry and taking the French king, John II the Good (r. 1350–1364), captive back to England. The defeat brought a complete breakdown of political order to France.

Power in France now lay with the Estates General. Led by the powerful merchants of Paris under Étienne Marcel, it took advantage of royal weakness, demanding and receiving rights similar to those granted the English privileged classes in Magna Carta. But unlike the English Parliament, which represented the interests of a comparatively unified English nobility, the French Estates General was too divided to be an instrument for effective government.

To secure their rights, the French privileged classes forced the peasantry to pay ever-increasing taxes and to repair their war-damaged properties without compensation. This bullying became more than the peasants could bear, and they rose up in several regions in a series of bloody rebellions known as the *Jacquerie* in 1358 (after the peasant revolutionary popularly known as *Jacques Bonhomme* or "simple Jack"). The nobility quickly put down the revolt, matching the rebels atrocity for atrocity.

On May 9, 1360, another milestone of the war was reached when England forced the Peace of Brétigny on the French. This agreement declared an end to Edward's vassalage to the king of France and affirmed his sovereignty over English territories in France (including Gascony, Guyenne, Poitou, and Calais). France also agreed to pay a ransom of three million gold crowns to win King John the Good's release. In return, Edward simply renounced his claim to the French throne.

Such a partition of French territorial control was completely unrealistic, and sober observers on both sides knew it could not last long. France struck back in the late 1360s and by the time of Edward's death in 1377 had beaten the English back to coastal enclaves and the territory of Bordeaux.

FRENCH DEFEAT AND THE TREATY OF TROYES   After Edward's death the English war effort lessened, partly because of domestic problems within England. During the reign of Richard II (r. 1377–1399),

This miniature illustrates two scenes from the English peasant revolt of 1381. On the left, Wat Tyler, one of the leaders of the revolt, is executed in the presence of King Richard II. On the right, King Richard urges armed peasants to end their rebellion. [Arthur Hacker, "The Cloister of the World". Bradford Art Galleries & Museums, Bradford, Great Britain. Bridgeman/Art Resource, NY.]

England had its own version of the *Jacquerie*. In June 1381 long-oppressed peasants and artisans joined in a great revolt of the unprivileged classes under the leadership of John Ball, a secular priest, and Wat Tyler, a journeyman. As in France, the revolt was brutally crushed within the year. But it left the country divided for decades.

The war intensified under Henry V (r. 1413–1422), who took advantage of internal French turmoil created by the rise to power of the duchy of Burgundy. With France deeply divided, Henry V struck hard in Normandy. Happy to see the rest of France besieged, the Burgundians foolishly watched from the sidelines while Henry's army routed the opposition led by the count of Armagnac, who had picked up the royal banner at Agincourt on October 25, 1415. In the years thereafter, belatedly recognizing that the defeat of France would leave them easy prey for the English, the Burgundians closed ranks with French royal forces. This renewed French unity, loose as it was, promised to bring eventual victory over the English, but it was shattered in September 1419 when the duke of Burgundy was assassinated. In the aftermath of this shocking event the duke's son and heir, determined to avenge his father's death, joined forces with the English.

France now became Henry V's for the taking—at least in the short run. The Treaty of Troyes in 1420 disinherited the legitimate heir to the French throne and proclaimed Henry V the successor to the French king, Charles VI. When Henry and Charles died within months of one another in 1422, the infant Henry VI of England was proclaimed in Paris to be king of both France and England. The dream of Edward III that had set the war in motion—to make the ruler of England the ruler also of France—had been realized, at least for the moment.

The son of Charles VI went into retreat in Bourges, where, on the death of his father, he became Charles VII to most of the French people, who ignored the Treaty of Troyes. Displaying unprecedented national feeling inspired by the remarkable Joan of Arc, they soon rallied to his cause and came together in an ultimately victorious coalition.

JOAN OF ARC AND THE WAR'S CONCLUSION Joan of Arc (1412–1431), a peasant from Domrémy, presented herself to Charles VII in March 1429, declaring that the King of Heaven had called her to deliver besieged Orléans from the English. The king was understandably skeptical, but being in retreat from what seemed to be a hopeless war, he was willing to try anything to reverse French fortunes. And the deliverance of Orléans, a city strategic to the control of the territory south of the Loire, would be a godsend. Charles's desperation overcame his skepticism, and he gave Joan his leave.

Circumstances worked perfectly to her advantage. The English force was already exhausted by a six-month siege of Orléans and at the point of withdrawal when Joan arrived with fresh French troops. After repulsing the English from Orléans, the French enjoyed a succession of victories they popularly attributed to Joan. She deserved much of this credit, but not because she was a military genius. She provided the French with something military experts could not: inspiration and a sense of national identity and self-confidence. Within a few months of the liberation of Orléans, Charles VII received his crown in Rheims and ended the nine-year "disinheritance" prescribed by the Treaty of Troyes.

Charles forgot his liberator as quickly as he had embraced her. When the Burgundians captured Joan in May 1430, he was in a position to secure her release but did little for her. The Burgundians and the English wanted her publicly discredited, believing this would also discredit Charles VII and demoralize French resistance. She was turned over to the Inquisition in English-held Rouen. The inquisitors broke the courageous "Maid of Orléans" after ten weeks of interrogation, and she was executed as a relapsed heretic on May 30, 1431. Twenty-five years

Joan of Arc Refuses to Recant Her Beliefs

Joan of Arc, threatened with torture, refused to recent her beliefs and instead defended the instructions she had received from the voices that spoke to her.

✦ *In the following excerpt from her self-defense, do you get the impression that the judges have made up their minds about Joan in advance? How does this judicial process, which was based on intensive interrogation of the accused, differ from a trial today? Why was Joan deemed heretical and not insane when she acknowledged hearing voices?*

On Wednesday, May 9th of the same year [1431], Joan was brought into the great tower of the castle of Rouen before us the said judges. And [she] was required and admonished to speak the truth on many different points contained in her trial which she had denied or to which she had given false replies, whereas we possessed certain information, proofs, and vehement presumptions upon them. Many of the points were read and explained to her, and she was told that if she did not confess them truthfully she would be put to the torture, the instruments of which were shown to her all ready in the tower. There were also present by our instruction men ready to put her to the torture in order to restore her to the way and knowledge of truth, and by this means to procure the salvation of her body and soul which by her lying inventions she exposed to such grave perils.

To which the said Joan answered in this manner: "Truly if you were to tear me limb from limb and separate my soul from my body, I would not tell you anything more: and if I did say anything, I should afterwards declare that you had compelled me to say it by force." Then she said that on Holy Cross Day last she received comfort from St. Gabriel; she firmly believes it was St. Gabriel. She knew by her voices whether she should submit to the Church, since the clergy were pressing her hard to submit. Her voices told her that if she desired Our Lord to aid her she must wait upon Him in all her doings. She said that Our Lord has always been the master of her doings, and the Enemy never had power over them. She asked her voices if she would be burned and they answered that she must wait upon God, and He would aid her.

The Trial of Jeanne D'Arc, trans. by W. P. Barrett (New York: Gotham House, 1932), pp. 303–304.

A contemporary portrait of Joan of Arc (1412–1431) in the National Archives in Paris. [Giraudon/Art Resource, N.Y.]

The Black Death

Preconditions and Causes

later (1456) Charles reopened her trial, and she was declared innocent of all the charges. In 1920 the church declared her a saint.

In 1435 the duke of Burgundy made peace with Charles. France, now unified and at peace with Burgundy, continued progressively to force the English back. By 1453, the date of the war's end, the English held only their coastal enclave of Calais.

The Hundred Years' War, with sixty-eight years of at least nominal peace and forty-four of hot war, had lasting political and social consequences. It devastated France, but it also awakened French nationalism and hastened the transition there from a feudal monarchy to a centralized state. It saw Burgundy become a major European political power. And it encouraged the English, in response to the seesawing allegiance of the Netherlands throughout the conflict, to develop their own clothing industry and foreign markets. In both France and England the burden of the on-again, off-again war fell most heavily on the peasantry, who were forced to support it with taxes and services.

In the late Middle Ages, nine-tenths of the population worked the land. The three-field system, in use in most areas since well before the fourteenth century, had increased the amount of arable land and thereby the food supply. The growth of cities and trade had also stimulated agricultural science and productivity. But as the food supply grew, so also did the population. It is estimated that Europe's population doubled between the years 1000 and 1300 and by 1300 had begun to outstrip food production. There were now more people than there was food available to feed them or jobs to employ them, and the average European faced the probability of extreme hunger at least once during his or her expected thirty-five-year life span.

Between 1315 and 1317 crop failures produced the greatest famine of the Middle Ages. Densely populated urban areas like the industrial towns of the Netherlands experienced great suffering. Decades of overpopulation, economic depression, famine, and bad health progressively weakened Europe's population and made it highly vulnerable to a virulent bubonic plague that struck with full force in 1348.

This "Black Death," so called by contemporaries because of the way it discolored the body, was probably introduced by sea-borne rats from Black Sea areas, and followed the trade routes from Asia into

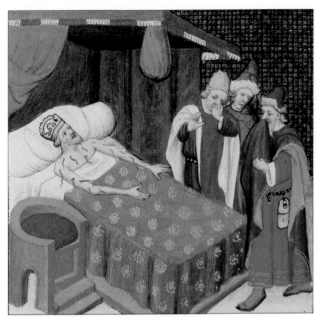

In this scene from an illustrated manuscript of Boccaccio's Decameron, *physicians apply leeches to an emperor. The text says he suffered from a disease that caused a terrible stench, which is why the physicians are holding their noses. Bleeding was the agreed-upon best way to prevent and cure illness and was practiced as late as the nineteenth century. Its popularity was rooted in the belief that a build-up of foul matter in the body caused illness by disrupting the body's four humors (blood, phlegm, yellow bile, and black bile). Bleeding released the foul matter and restored equilibrium among the humors, thus preserving good health by strengthening resistance to disease. [Jean-Loup Charmet/Science Photo Library]*

Europe. Appearing in Sicily in late 1347, it entered Europe through the port cities of Venice, Genoa, and Pisa in 1348, and from there it swept rapidly through Spain and southern France and into northern Europe. Areas that lay outside the major trade routes, like Bohemia, appear to have remained virtually unaffected.

Bubonic plague made numerous reappearances in succeeding decades. By the early fifteenth century, it is estimated that western Europe as a whole had lost as much as two-fifths of its population. There was not a full recovery until the sixteenth century. (See Map 9-2.)

Popular Remedies

The plague, transmitted by rat- or human-borne fleas, often reached a victim's lungs during the course of the disease. From the lungs it could be spread from person to person by the victim's sneezing and wheezing. Contemporary physicians had no understanding of these processes, and so even the most rudimentary prophylaxis against the disease was lacking. To the people of the time the Black Death was a catastrophe with no apparent explanation and against which there was no known defense. Throughout much of western Europe it inspired an obsession with death and dying and a deep pessimism that endured for decades after the plague years.

Popular wisdom held that a corruption in the atmosphere caused the disease. Some blamed poisonous fumes released by earthquakes. Many adopted aromatic amulets as a remedy. According to the contemporary observations of Boccaccio, who recorded the varied reactions to the plague in the *Decameron* (1353), some sought a remedy in moderation and a temperate life; others gave themselves over entirely to their passions (sexual promiscuity within the stricken areas apparently ran high); and still others, "the most sound, perhaps, in judgment," chose flight and seclusion as the best medicine.

Among the most extreme social reactions were processions of flagellants. These religious fanatics beat themselves in ritual penance until they bled, believing that such action would bring divine intervention. The terror created by the flagellants (whose dirty bodies may have actually served to transport the disease) became so socially disruptive and threatening even to established authority that the church finally outlawed such processions.

Jews were cast as scapegoats for the plague. Centuries of Christian propaganda had bred hatred toward them, as had their willing role as society's moneylenders. Pogroms occurred in several cities, sometimes incited by the arrival of flagellants.

Social and Economic Consequences

Whole villages vanished in the wake of the plague. Among the social and economic consequences of this depopulation were a shrunken labor supply and a decline in the value of the estates of the nobility.

FARMS DECLINE   As the number of farm laborers decreased, their wages increased and those of skilled artisans soared. Many serfs now chose to commute their labor services by money payments or to abandon the farm altogether and pursue more interesting and rewarding jobs in skilled craft industries in the cities. Agricultural prices fell because of low-

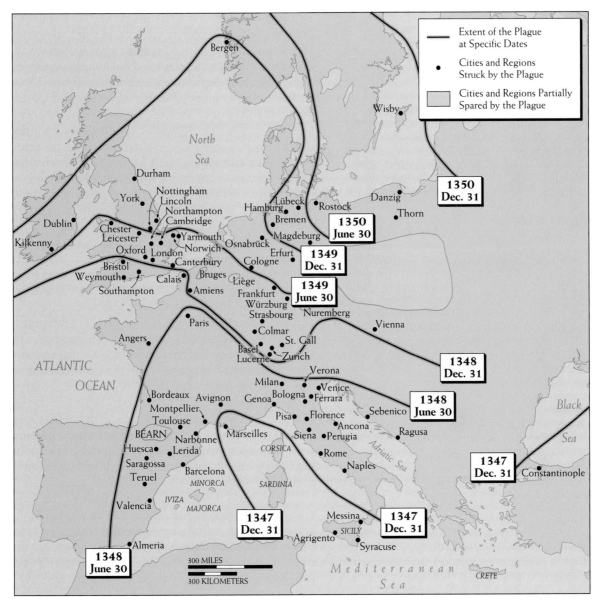

MAP 9–2 SPREAD OF THE BLACK DEATH *Apparently introduced by sea-borne rats from Black Sea areas where plague-infested rodents have long been known, the Black Death brought huge human, social, and economic consequences. One of the lower estimates of Europeans dying is 25,000,000. The map charts the plague's spread in the mid-fourteenth century. Generally following trade routes, the plague reached Scandinavia by 1350, and some believe it then went on to Iceland and even Greenland. Areas off the main trade routes were largely spared.*

ered demand, and the price of luxury and manufactured goods—the work of skilled artisans—rose. The noble landholders suffered the greatest decline in power from this new state of affairs. They were forced to pay more for finished products and for farm labor but received a smaller return on their agricultural produce. Everywhere their rents were in steady decline after the plague.

PEASANTS REVOLT To recoup their losses, some landowners converted arable land to sheep pasture, substituting more profitable wool production for labor-intensive grain crops. Others abandoned the effort to farm their land and simply leased it to the highest bidder. Landowners also sought simply to reverse their misfortune—to close off the new economic opportunities opened for the peasantry by

A Renaissance portrayal of the sixth century (590) procession of St. Gregory to St. Peter's, an effort to end a plague. From the Soane Book of Hours *(c. 1500). [Sir John Soane's Museum. AD590 for removal of placque. E.T. Archive, London.]*

the demographic crisis—through repressive legislation that forced peasants to stay on their farms and froze their wages at low levels. In France the direct tax on the peasantry, the *taille*, was increased, and opposition to it was prominent among the grievances behind the *Jacquerie*. In 1351, the English Parliament passed a Statute of Laborers, which limited wages to preplague levels and restricted the ability of peasants to leave the land of their traditional masters. Opposition to such legislation was also a prominent factor in the English peasants' revolt in 1381.

CITIES REBOUND   Although the plague hit urban populations especially hard, the cities and their skilled industries came, in time, to prosper from its effects. Cities had always been careful to protect their interests; as they grew, they passed legislation to regulate competition from rural areas and to con-

trol immigration. After the plague the reach of such laws was progressively extended beyond the cities to include surrounding lands belonging to impoverished nobles and feudal landlords, many of whom were peacefully integrated into urban life.

The omnipresence of death whetted the appetite for goods that only skilled urban industries could produce. Expensive cloths and jewelry, furs from the north, and silks from the south were in great demand in the second half of the fourteenth century. Faced with life at its worst, people insisted on having the very best. Initially this new demand could not be met. The basic unit of urban industry was the master and apprentices (usually one or two), whose numbers were purposely kept low and whose privileges were jealously guarded. The craft of the skilled artisan was passed from master to apprentice only very slowly. The first wave of plague transformed this already restricted supply of skilled artisans into a shortage almost overnight. As a result, the prices of manufactured and luxury items rose to new heights and this, in turn, encouraged workers to migrate from the countryside to the city and learn the skills of artisans. Townspeople in effect profited coming and going from the forces that impoverished the landed nobility. As wealth poured into the cities and per capita income rose, the cost to urban dwellers of agricultural products from the countryside, now less in demand, declined.

There was also gain as well as loss for the church. Although it suffered losses as a great landholder and was politically weakened, it had received new revenues from the vastly increased demand for religious services for the dead and the dying and from the multiplication of gifts and bequests.

New Conflicts and Opportunities

By increasing the importance of skilled artisans, the plague contributed to new conflicts within the cities. The economic and political power of local artisans and trade guilds grew steadily in the late Middle Ages along with the demand for their goods and services. The merchant and patrician classes found it increasingly difficult to maintain their traditional dominance and grudgingly gave guild masters a voice in city government. As the guilds won political power, they encouraged restrictive legislation to protect local industries. These restrictions, in turn, brought confrontations between master artisans, who wanted to keep their numbers low and expand their industries at a snail's pace, and the many journeymen, who were eager to rise to the rank of master. To the long-existing conflict between the guilds and the urban patriciate was now added a conflict within the guilds themselves.

After 1350 the two traditional "containers" of monarchy—the landed nobility and the church—were politically on the defensive, and to no small degree as a consequence of the plague. Kings took full advantage of the new situation, drawing on growing national sentiment to centralize their governments and economies. As already noted, the plague reduced the economic power of the landed nobility. In the same period the battles of the Hundred Years' War demonstrated the military superiority of paid professional armies over the traditional noble cavalry, thus bringing into question the traditional role of the nobility. The plague also killed many members of the clergy—perhaps one-third of the German clergy fell victim to it as they

Boccaccio Describes the Ravages of the Black Death in Florence

The Black Death provided an excuse to the poet, humanist, and storyteller Giovanni Boccaccio (1313–1375) to assemble his great collection of tales, the Decameron. *Ten congenial men and women flee Florence to escape the plague and while away the time telling stories. In one of the stories, Boccaccio embeds a fine clinical description of plague symptoms as seen in Florence in 1348 and of the powerlessness of physicians and the lack of remedies.*

✦ *What did people do to escape the plague? Was any of it sound medical practice? What does the study of calamities like the Black Death tell us about the people of the past?*

In Florence, despite all that human wisdom and forethought could devise to avert it, even as the cleansing of the city from many impurities by officials appointed for the purpose, the refusal of entrance to all sick folk, and the adoption of many precautions for the preservation of health; despite also humble supplications addressed to God, and often repeated both in public procession and otherwise, by the devout; towards the beginning of the spring of the said year [1348] the doleful effects of the pestilence began to be horribly apparent by symptoms that [appeared] as if miraculous.

Not such were these symptoms as in the East, where an issue of blood from the nose was a manifest sign of inevitable death; but in men and women alike it first betrayed itself by the emergence of certain tumours in the groin or the armpits, some of which grew as large as a common apple, others as an egg, some more, some less, which the common folk called gavoccioli. From the two said parts of the body this deadly gavoccioli soon began to propagate and spread itself in all directions indifferently; after which the form of the malady began to change, spots black or livid making their appearance in many cases on the arm or the thigh or elsewhere, now few and large, now minute and numerous. And as the gavoccioli had been and still were an infallible token of approaching death, such also were these spots on whomsoever they shewed themselves. Which maladies seemed to set entirely at naught both the art of the physician and the virtues of physic; indeed, whether it was that the disorder was of a nature to defy such treatment, or that the physicians were at fault . . . and, being in ignorance of its source, failed to apply the proper remedies; in either case, not merely were those that recovered few, but almost all died within three days of the appearance of the said symptoms . . . and in most cases without any fever or other attendant malady.

The Decameron of Giovanni Boccaccio, *trans. by J. M. Rigg (London: J. M. Dent & Sons, 1930), p. 5.*

A caricature of physicians (early sixteenth century). In the Middle Ages and later, people recognized the shortcomings of physicians and surgeons and visited them only as a last resort. Here a physician carries a uroscope (for collecting and examining urine); cloudy or discolored urine signaled an immediate need for bleeding. The physician/surgeon wears surgical shoes and his assistant carries a flail—a comment on the risks of medical services. [Hacker Art Books]

dutifully ministered to the sick and dying. The reduction in clerical ranks occurred in the same century in which the residence of the pope in Avignon (1309–1377) and the Great Schism (1378–1415) were undermining much of the church's popular support.

Ecclesiastical Breakdown and Revival: The Late Medieval Church

At first glance the popes may appear to have been in a very favorable position in the latter half of the thirteenth century. Frederick II had been van-

quished and imperial pressure on Rome had been removed. The French king, Louis IX, was an enthusiastic supporter of the church, as evidenced by his two disastrous Crusades, which won him sainthood. Although it lasted only seven years, a reunion of the Eastern church with Rome was proclaimed by the Council of Lyons in 1274, when the Western church took advantage of Emperor Michael Palaeologus's request for aid against the Turks. But despite these positive events, the church was not really in as favorable a position as it appeared.

The Thirteenth-Century Papacy

As early as the reign of Pope Innocent III (r. 1198–1216), when papal power reached its height, there were ominous developments. Innocent had elaborated the doctrine of papal plenitude of power and on that authority had declared saints, disposed of *benefices*, and created a centralized papal monarchy with a clearly political mission. Innocent's transformation of the papacy into a great secular power weakened the church spiritually even as it strengthened it politically. Thereafter the church as a papal monarchy and the church as the "body of the faithful" came increasingly to be differentiated. It was against the "papal church" and in the name of the "true Christian Church" that both reformers and heretics raised their voices in protest until the Protestant Reformation.

What Innocent began, his successors perfected. Under Urban IV (r. 1261–1264) the papacy established its own law court, the *Rota Romana*, which tightened and centralized the church's legal proceedings. The latter half of the thirteenth century saw an elaboration of the system of clerical taxation; what had begun in the twelfth century as an emergency measure to raise funds for the Crusades became a fixed institution. In the same period, papal power to determine appointments to many major and minor church offices—the "reservation of *benefices*"—was greatly broadened. The thirteenth-century papacy became a powerful political institution governed by its own law and courts, serviced by an efficient international bureaucracy, and preoccupied with secular goals.

Papal centralization of the church undermined both diocesan authority and popular support. Rome's interests, not local needs, came to control church appointments, policies, and discipline. Discontented lower clergy appealed to the higher authority of Rome against the disciplinary measures of local bishops. In the second half of the thirteenth century, bishops and abbots protested such undercutting of their power. To its critics, the church in Rome was hardly more than a legalized, fiscalized, bureaucratic institution. As early as the late twelfth century, heretical movements of Cathars and Waldensians had appealed to the biblical ideal of simplicity and separation from the world. Other reformers unquestionably loyal to the church, such as Saint Francis of Assisi, would also protest a perceived materialism in official religion.

POLITICAL FRAGMENTATION   The church of the thirteenth century was being undermined by more than internal religious disunity. The demise of imperial power meant that the papacy in Rome was no longer the leader of anti-imperial (Guelf, or propapal) sentiment in Italy. Instead of being the center of Italian resistance to the emperor, popes now found themselves on the defensive against their old allies. That was the ironic price paid by the papacy to vanquish the Hohenstaufens.

Rulers with a stake in Italian politics now directed the intrigue formerly aimed at the emperor toward the College of Cardinals. For example, Charles of Anjou, king of Sicily, managed to create a French–Sicilian faction within the college. Such efforts to control the decisions of the college led Pope Gregory X (r. 1271–1276) to establish the practice of sequestering the cardinals immediately on the death of the pope. The purpose of this so-called conclave of cardinals was to minimize extraneous political influence on the election of new popes, but the college had become so politicized that it proved to be of little avail.

In 1294 such a conclave, in frustration after a deadlock of more than two years, chose a saintly but inept Calabrian hermit as Pope Celestine V. Celestine abdicated under suspicious circumstances after only a few weeks in office. He also died under suspicious circumstances; his successor's critics later argued that he had been murdered for political reasons by the powers behind the papal throne to ensure the survival of the papal office. His tragicomic reign shocked a majority of the College of Cardinals into unified action. He was quickly replaced by his very opposite, Pope Boniface VIII (r. 1294–1303), a nobleman and a skilled politician. His pontificate, however, would augur the beginning of the end of papal pretensions to great power status.

Pope Boniface VIII (r. 1294–1303), depicted here, opposed the taxation of the clergy by the kings of France and England and issued one of the strongest declarations of papal authority over rulers, the bull Unam Sanctam. *This statue is in the Museo Civico, Bologna, Italy. [Scala/Art Resource, N.Y.]*

Boniface VIII and Philip the Fair

Boniface came to rule when England and France were maturing as nation-states. In England a long

Boniface VIII Reasserts the Church's Claim to Temporal Power

Defied by the French and the English, Pope Boniface VIII (r. 1294–1303) boldly reasserted the temporal power of the church in the bull Unam Sanctam *(November 1302). This document claimed that both spiritual and temporal power on earth were under the pope's jurisdiction, because in the hierarchy of the universe spiritual power both preceded and sat in judgment on temporal power.*

✦ *On what does the pope base his claims to supremacy? Is his argument logical, or does he beg the question? On what basis did secular rulers attack his arguments?*

We are taught by the words of the Gospel that in this church and in her power there are two swords, a spiritual one and a temporal one. . . . Certainly anyone who denies that the temporal sword is in the power of Peter has not paid heed to the words of the Lord when he said, "Put up thy sword into its sheath" (Matthew 26:52). Both then are in the power of the church, the material sword and the spiritual. But the one is exercised for the church, the other by the church, the one by the hand of the priest, the other by the hand of kings and soldiers, though at the will and suffrance of the authority subject to the spiritual power. . . . For, according to the blessed Dionysius, it is the law of divinity for the lowest to be led to the highest through intermediaries. In the order of the universe all things are not kept in order in the same fashion and immediately but the lowest are ordered by the intermediate and inferiors by superiors. But that the spiritual power excels any earthly one in dignity and nobility we ought the more openly to confess in proportion as spiritual things excel temporal ones. Moreover we clearly perceive this from the giving of tithes, from benediction and sanctification, from the acceptance of this power and from the very government of things. For, the truth bearing witness, the spiritual power has to institute the earthly power and to judge it if it has not been good. So it is verified the prophecy of Jeremiah (1:10) concerning the church and the power of the church, "Lo, I have set thee this day over the nations and over kingdoms."

As quoted in Brian Tierney, The Crisis of Church and State 1050–1300 *(Englewood Cliffs, N.J.: Prentice-Hall, 1964), pp. 188–189. Used by permission of the publisher.*

---

tradition of consultation between the king and powerful members of English society evolved into formal "parliaments" during the reigns of Henry III (r. 1216–1272) and Edward I (r. 1272–1307), and these meetings helped to create a unified kingdom. The reign of the French king Philip IV the Fair (1285–1314) saw France become an efficient, centralized monarchy. Philip was no Saint Louis, but a ruthless politician. He was determined to end England's continental holdings, control wealthy Flanders, and establish French hegemony within the Holy Roman Empire.

Boniface had the further misfortune of bringing to the papal throne memories of the way earlier popes had brought kings and emperors to their knees. Very painfully he was to discover that the papal monarchy of the early thirteenth century was no match for the new political powers of the late thirteenth century.

THE ROYAL CHALLENGE TO PAPAL AUTHORITY France and England were on the brink of all-out war when Boniface became pope in 1294. Only Edward I's preoccupation with rebellion in Scotland, which the French encouraged, prevented him from invading France and starting the Hundred Years' War a half century earlier than it did start. As both countries mobilized for war, they used the pretext of preparing for a Crusade to tax the clergy heavily. In 1215 Pope Innocent III had decreed that the clergy were to pay no taxes to rulers without prior papal consent. Viewing English and French taxation of the clergy as an assault on traditional clerical rights, Boniface took a strong stand against it. On February 5, 1296, he issued a bull, *Clericis laicos*, which forbade lay taxation of the clergy without prior papal approval and took back all previous papal dispensations in this regard.

In England Edward I retaliated by denying the clergy the right to be heard in royal court, in effect removing from them the protection of the king. But it was Philip the Fair who struck back with a vengeance. In August 1296 he forbade the exportation of money from France to Rome, thereby denying the papacy revenues it needed to operate. Boniface had no choice but to come quickly to terms with Philip. He conceded Philip the right to tax the French clergy "during an emergency," and, not coincidentally, he canonized Louis IX in the same year.

Boniface was then also under siege by powerful Italian enemies, whom Philip did not fail to patronize. A noble family (the Colonnas), rivals of Boniface's family (the Gaetani) and radical followers of Saint Francis of Assisi (the Spiritual Franciscans), were at this time seeking to invalidate Boniface's election as pope on the grounds that Celestine V had resigned the office under coercion. Charges of heresy, simony, and even the murder of Celestine were hurled against Boniface.

Boniface's fortunes appeared to revive in 1300, a "Jubilee year." During such a year, all Catholics who visited Rome and fulfilled certain conditions had the penalties for their unrepented sins remitted. Tens of thousands of pilgrims flocked to Rome in that year, and Boniface, heady with this display of popular religiosity, reinserted himself into international politics. He championed Scottish resistance to England, for which he received a firm rebuke from an outraged Edward I and from Parliament.

But once again a confrontation with the king of France proved the more costly. Philip seemed to be eager for another fight with the pope. He arrested Boniface's Parisian legate, Bernard Saisset, the bishop of Pamiers and also a powerful secular lord, whose independence Philip had opposed. Accused of heresy and treason, Saisset was tried and convicted in the king's court. Thereafter, Philip demanded that Boniface recognize the process against Saisset, something that Boniface could do only if he was prepared to surrender his jurisdiction over the French episcopate. This challenge could not be sidestepped, and Boniface acted swiftly to champion Saisset as a defender of clerical political independence within France. He demanded Saisset's unconditional release, revoked all previous agreements with Philip in the matter of clerical taxation, and ordered the French bishops to convene in Rome within a year. A bull, *Ausculta fili* or "listen, My Son," was sent to Philip in December 1301, pointedly informing him that "God has set popes over kings and kingdoms."

UNAM SANCTAM (1302)   Philip unleashed a ruthless antipapal campaign. Two royal apologists, Pierre Dubois and John of Paris, refuted papal claims to the right to intervene in temporal matters. Increasingly placed on the defensive, Boniface made a last-ditch stand against state control of national churches. On November 18, 1302, he issued the bull *Unam Sanctam*. This famous statement of papal power declared that temporal authority was "subject" to the spiritual power of the church. On its face a bold assertion, *Unam Sanctam* was in truth the desperate act of a besieged papacy.

After *Unam Sanctam* the French and the Colonnas moved against Boniface with force. Guillaume de Nogaret, Philip's chief minister, denounced Boniface to the French clergy as a common heretic and criminal. An army, led by Nogaret and Sciarra Colonna, surprised the pope in mid-August 1303 at his retreat in Anagni. Boniface was badly beaten and almost executed before an aroused populace liberated and returned him safely to Rome. But the ordeal proved too much for him and he died a few months later, in October 1303.

Boniface's immediate successor, Benedict XI (r. 1303–1304), excommunicated Nogaret for his deed, but there was to be no lasting papal retaliation. Benedict's successor, Clement V (r. 1305–1314), was forced into French subservience. A former archbishop of Bordeaux, Clement declared that *Unam Sanctam* should not be understood as in any way diminishing French royal authority. He released Nogaret from excommunication and pliantly condemned the Knights Templars, whose treasure Philip thereafter forcibly expropriated.

In 1309 Clement moved the papal court to Avignon, an imperial city on the southeastern border of France. Situated on land that belonged to the pope, the city maintained its independence from the king. In 1311 Clement made it his permanent residence, to escape both a Rome ridden with strife after the confrontation between Boniface and Philip and further pressure from Philip. There the papacy was to remain until 1377.

After Boniface's humiliation, popes never again seriously threatened kings and emperors, despite continuing papal excommunications and political intrigue. In the future the relation between church and state would tilt in favor of the state and the control of religion by powerful monarchies. Ecclesiastical authority would become subordinate to larger secular political purposes.

The Avignon Papacy (1309–1377)

The Avignon papacy was in appearance, although not always in fact, under strong French influence. During Clement V's pontificate the French came to dominate the College of Cardinals, testing the papacy's agility both politically and economically. Finding itself cut off from its Roman estates, the papacy had to innovate to get needed funds. Clement expanded papal taxes, especially the practice of collecting *annates*, the first year's revenue of a church office or *benefice* bestowed by the pope. Clement VI (r. 1342–1352) began the practice of selling indulgences, or pardons for unrepented sins. To make the purchase of indulgences more compelling, church doctrine on purgatory—a place of punishment where souls would atone for venial sins—also developed during this period. By the fifteenth century the church had extended indulgences to cover the souls of people already dead, allowing the living to buy a reduced sentence in purgatory for their deceased loved ones. Such practices contributed to the Avignon papacy's reputation for materialism and political scheming and gave reformers new ammunition.

POPE JOHN XXII   Pope John XXII (r. 1316–1334), the most powerful Avignon pope, tried to restore papal independence and to return to Italy. This goal led him into war with the Visconti, the most powerful ruling family of Milan, and a costly contest with Emperor Louis IV. John had challenged Louis's election as emperor in 1314 in favor of the rival Habsburg candidate. The result was a minor replay of the confrontation between Philip the Fair and Boniface VIII. When John obstinately and without legal justification refused to recognize Louis's election, the emperor retaliated by declaring John deposed and putting in his place an antipope. As Philip the Fair had also done, Louis enlisted the support of the

Spiritual Franciscans, whose views on absolute poverty had been condemned by John as heretical. Two outstanding pamphleteers wrote lasting tracts for the royal cause: William of Ockham, whom John excommunicated in 1328, and Marsilius of Padua (ca. 1290–1342), whose teaching John declared heretical in 1327.

In his *Defender of Peace* (1324), Marsilius of Padua stressed the independent origins and autonomy of secular government. Clergy were subjected to the strictest apostolic ideals and confined to purely spiritual functions, and all power of coercive judgment was denied the pope. Marsilius argued that spiritual crimes must await an eternal punishment. Transgressions of divine law, over which the pope had jurisdiction, were to be punished in the next life, not in the present one, *unless* the secular ruler declared a divine law also a secular law. This assertion was a direct challenge of the power of the pope to excommunicate rulers and place countries under interdict. The *Defender of Peace* depicted the pope as a subordinate member of a society over which the emperor ruled supreme and in which temporal peace was the highest good.

John XXII made the papacy a sophisticated international agency and adroitly adjusted it to the growing European money economy. The more the *Curia*, or papal court, mastered the latter, however, the more vulnerable it became to criticism. Under John's successor, Benedict XII (r. 1334–1342), the papacy became entrenched in Avignon. Seemingly forgetting Rome altogether, Benedict began construction of the great Palace of the Popes and attempted to reform both papal government and the religious life. His high-living French successor, Clement VI, placed papal policy in lockstep with the French. In this period the cardinals became barely more than lobbyists for policies favorable to their secular patrons.

NATIONAL OPPOSITION TO THE AVIGNON PAPACY   As Avignon's fiscal tentacles probed new areas, monarchies took strong action to protect their interests. The latter half of the fourteenth century saw legislation restricting papal jurisdiction and taxation in France, England, and Germany. In England, where the Avignon papacy was identified with the French enemy after the outbreak of the Hundred Years' War, statutes that restricted payments and appeals to Rome and the pope's power to make high ecclesiastical appointments were several times passed by Parliament between 1351 and 1393.

In France ecclesiastical appointments and taxation were regulated by the so-called Gallican liberties. These national rights over religion had long been exercised in fact and were legally acknowledged by the church in the *Pragmatic Sanction of Bourges*, published by Charles VII (r. 1422–1461) in 1438. This agreement recognized the right of the French church to elect its own clergy without papal interference, prohibited the payment of annates to Rome, and limited the right of appeals from French courts to the *Curia* in Rome. In German and Swiss cities in the fourteenth and fifteenth centuries, local governments also took the initiative to limit and even to overturn traditional clerical privileges and immunities.

JOHN WYCLIFFE AND JOHN HUSS   The popular lay religious movements that most successfully assailed the late medieval church were the Lollards in England and the Hussites in Bohemia. The Lollards looked to the writings of John Wycliffe (d. 1384) to justify their demands, and both moderate and extreme Hussites to the writings of John Huss (d. 1415), although both Wycliffe and Huss would have disclaimed the extremists who revolted in their names.

Wycliffe was an Oxford theologian and a philosopher of high standing. His work initially served the anticlerical policies of the English government. He became within England what William of Ockham and Marsilius of Padua had been at the Bavarian court of Emperor Louis IV: a major intellectual spokesman for the rights of royalty against the secular pretensions of popes. After 1350 English kings greatly reduced the power of the Avignon papacy to make ecclesiastical appointments and collect taxes within England, a position that Wycliffe strongly supported. His views on clerical poverty followed original Franciscan ideals and, more by accident than by design, gave justification to government restriction and even confiscation of church properties within England. Wycliffe argued that the clergy "ought to be content with food and clothing."

Wycliffe also maintained that personal merit, not rank and office, was the only basis of religious authority. This was a dangerous teaching because it raised allegedly pious laypeople above allegedly corrupt ecclesiastics, regardless of the latter's offi-

Marsilius of Padua Denies Coercive Power to the Clergy

According to Marsilius, the Bible gave the pope no right to pronounce and execute sentences on any person. The clergy held a strictly moral and spiritual rule, their judgments to be executed only in the afterlife, not in the present one. Here, on earth, they should be obedient to secular authority. Marsilius argued this point by appealing to the example of Jesus.

✦ *How do Marsilius's arguments compare with those of Pope Boniface in the preceding document? Does Marsilius's argument, if accepted, destroy the worldly authority of the church? Why was his teaching condemned as heretical?*

We now wish . . . to adduce the truths of the holy Scripture . . . which explicitly command or counsel that neither the Roman bishop called pope, nor any other bishop or priest, or deacon, has or ought to have any rulership or coercive judgment or jurisdiction over any priest or nonpriest, ruler, community, group, or individual of whatever condition. . . . Christ himself came into the world not to dominate men, nor to judge them [coercively] . . . not to wield temporal rule, but rather to be subject as regards the . . . present life; and moreover, he wanted to and did exclude himself, his apostles and disciples, and their successors, the bishops or priests, from all coercive authority or worldly rule, both by his example and by his word of counsel or command. . . . When he was brought before Pontius Pilate . . . and accused of having called himself king of the Jews, and [Pilate] asked him whether he had said this . . . [his] reply included these words . . . "My kingdom is not of this world," that is, I have not come to reign by temporal rule or dominion, in the way . . . worldly kings reign. . . . This, then, is the kingdom concerning which he came to teach and order, a kingdom which consists in the acts whereby the eternal kingdom is attained, that is, the acts of faith and the other theological virtues; not however, by coercing anyone thereto.

Marsilius of Padua: The Defender of Peace: The Defensor Pacis, *trans. by Alan Gewirth (New York: Harper, 1967), pp. 113–116.*

cial stature. There was a threat in such teaching to secular as well as to ecclesiastical dominion and jurisdiction. At his posthumous condemnation by the pope, Wycliffe was accused of the ancient heresy of Donatism—the teaching that the efficacy of the church's sacraments did not lie in their true performance but also depended on the moral character of the clergy who administered them. Wycliffe also anticipated certain Protestant criticisms of the medieval church by challenging papal infallibility, the sale of indulgences, the authority of scripture, and the dogma of transubstantiation.

The Lollards, English advocates of Wycliffe's teaching, like the Waldensians, preached in the vernacular, disseminated translations of Holy Scripture, and championed clerical poverty. At first, they came from every social class. Lollards were especially prominent among the groups that had something tangible to gain from the confiscation of clerical properties (the nobility and the gentry) or that had suffered most under the current church system (the lower clergy and the poor people). After the English 1381 peasants' revolt in 1381, an uprising filled with egalitarian notions that could find support in Wycliffe's teaching, Lollardy was officially viewed as subversive. Opposed by an alliance of church and crown, it became a capital offense in England by 1401.

Heresy was not so easily brought to heel in Bohemia, where it coalesced with a strong national movement. The University of Prague, founded in 1348, became the center for both Czech nationalism

Petrarch Describes the Papal Residence at Avignon

Petrarch, the "father of humanism," lived in Avignon and personally observed the papacy there over a long period of time. In this letter written between 1340 and 1353, he describes with deep, pious outrage the ostentation and greed of the Avignon popes.

✦ *Is this criticism realistic? Was it possible for the papacy at this time in its history to live as Petrarch proposes? Can a religious institution survive without real power and its trappings?*

I am now living in [Avignon], in the Babylon of the West. . . . Here reign the successors of the poor fishermen of Galilee [who] have strangely forgotten their origin. I am astounded, as I recall their predecessors, to see these men loaded with gold and clad in purple, boasting of the spoils of princes and nations; to see luxurious palaces and heights crowned with fortifications, instead of a boat turned downwards for [their] shelter. We no longer find the simple nets which were once used to gain a frugal living from the lake of Galilee. . . . One is stupefied nowadays to hear the lying tongues, and to see worthless parchments turned by a leaden seal [i.e., official bulls of the pope] into nets which are used, in Christ's name, but by the arts of Belial [i.e., the devil], to catch hordes of unwary Christians. These fish, too, are dressed and laid on the burning coals of anxiety before they fill the insatiable maw of their captors.

Instead of holy solitude we find a criminal host and crowds . . .; instead of sobriety, licentious banquets . . .; instead of pious pilgrimages . . . foul sloth; instead of the bare feet of the apostles . . . horses decked in gold. . . . In short, we seem to be among the kings of the Persians or Parthians, before whom we must fall down and worship, and who cannot be approached except presents be offered.

James Harvey Robinson, ed., Readings in European History, *vol. 1 (Boston:Athenaeum, 1904).*

---

and a native religious reform movement. The latter began within the bounds of orthodoxy. It was led by local intellectuals and preachers, the most famous of whom was John Huss, the rector of the university after 1403.

The Czech reformers supported vernacular translations of the Bible and were critical of traditional ceremonies and allegedly superstitious practices, particularly those relating to the sacrament of the Eucharist. They advocated lay communion with cup as well as bread, which was traditionally reserved only for the clergy as a sign of the clergy's spiritual superiority over the laity. Hussites taught that bread and wine remained bread and wine after priestly consecration, and questioned the validity of sacraments performed by priests in mortal sin.

Wycliffe's teaching appears to have influenced the movement very early. Regular traffic between England and Bohemia had existed for decades, ever since the marriage in 1381 of Anne of Bohemia to King Richard II. Czech students studied at Oxford, and many returned with copies of Wycliffe's writings.

Huss became the leader of the pro-Wycliffe faction at the University of Prague. In 1410 his activities brought about his excommunication and the placement of Prague under papal interdict. In 1414 Huss won an audience with the newly assembled Council of Constance. He journeyed to the council eagerly, armed with a safe-conduct pass from Emperor Sigismund, naïvely believing that he would convince his strongest critics of the truth of his teaching. Within weeks of his arrival in early November 1414, he was formally accused of heresy and imprisoned. He died at the stake on July 6, 1415, and was followed there less than a year later by his colleague Jerome of Prague.

A portrayal of Jan Huss as he was led to the stake at Constance. After his execution, his bones and ashes were scattered in the Rhine River to prevent his followers from claiming them as relics. This pen-and-ink drawing is from Ulrich von Richenthal's Chronicle of the Council of Constance *(ca. 1450). [The Bettman Archive]*

The reaction in Bohemia to the execution of these national heroes was fierce revolt. Militant Hussites, the Taborites, set out to transform Bohemia by force into a religious and social paradise under the military leadership of John Ziska. After a decade of belligerent protest, the Hussites won significant religious reforms and control over the Bohemian church from the Council of Basel.

The Great Schism (1378–1417) and the Conciliar Movement to 1449

Pope Gregory XI (r. 1370–1378) reestablished the papacy in Rome in January 1377, ending what had come to be known as the "Babylonian Captivity" of the church in Avignon, a reference to the biblical bondage of the Israelites. The return to Rome proved to be short-lived, however.

URBAN VI AND CLEMENT VII On Gregory's death the cardinals, in Rome, elected an Italian archbishop as Pope Urban VI (r. 1378–1389), who immediately announced his intention to reform the *Curia.* This was an unexpected challenge to the car-

dinals, most of whom were French, and they responded by calling for the return of the papacy to Avignon. The French king, Charles V, wanting to keep the papacy within the sphere of French influence, lent his support to a schism, which came to be known as the "Great Schism."

On September 20, 1378, five months after Urban's election, thirteen cardinals, all but one of whom was French, formed their own conclave and elected Pope Clement VII (r. 1378–1397), a cousin of the French king. They insisted that they had voted for Urban in fear of their lives, surrounded by a Roman mob demanding the election of an Italian pope. Be that as it may, the papacy now became a "two-headed thing" and a scandal to Christendom. Allegiance to the two papal courts divided along political lines. England and its allies (the Holy Roman Empire, Hungary, Bohemia, and Poland) acknowledged Urban VI, whereas France and those in its orbit (Naples, Scotland, Castile, and Aragon) supported Clement VII. The Roman line of popes has, however, been recognized de facto in subsequent church history.

Two approaches were initially taken to end the schism. One tried to win the mutual cession of both popes, thereby clearing the way for the election of a new pope. The other sought to secure the resignation of the one in favor of the other. Both approaches proved completely fruitless. Each pope considered himself fully legitimate, and too much was at stake for a magnanimous concession on the part of either. One way remained : the forced deposition of both popes by a special council of the church.

CONCILIAR THEORY OF CHURCH GOVERNMENT Legally a church council could be convened only by a pope, but the competing popes were not inclined to summon a council they knew would depose them. Also, the deposition of a legitimate pope against his will by a council of the church was as serious a matter then as the forced deposition of a monarch by a representative assembly.

The correctness of a conciliar deposition of a pope was thus debated a full thirty years before any direct action was taken. Advocates sought to fashion a church in which a representative council could effectively regulate the actions of the pope. The conciliarists defined the church as the whole body of the faithful, of which the elected head, the pope, was only one part. And the pope's sole purpose was to maintain the unity and well-being of the church—something that the schismatic popes were far from doing. The conciliarists further argued that a council of the church acted with greater authority than the pope alone. In the eyes of the pope(s) such a concept of the church threatened both its political and its religious unity.

THE COUNCIL OF PISA (1409–1410) On the basis of the arguments of the conciliarists, cardinals representing both popes convened a council on their own authority in Pisa in 1409, deposed both the Roman and the Avignon popes, and elected a new pope, Alexander V. To the council's consternation, neither pope accepted its action, and Christendom suddenly faced the spectacle of three contending popes. Although the vast majority of Latin Christendom accepted Alexander and his Pisan successor John XXIII (r. 1410–1415), the popes of Rome and Avignon refused to step down.

THE COUNCIL OF CONSTANCE (1414–1417) This intolerable situation ended when Emperor Sigismund prevailed on John XXIII to summon a new council in Constance in 1414, which the Roman pope Gregory XII also recognized. In a famous declaration entitled *Sacrosancta*, the council asserted their supremacy and proceeded to elect a new pope, Martin V (r. 1417–1431), after the three contending popes had either resigned or been deposed. The council then made provisions for regular meetings of church councils, within five, then seven, and thereafter every ten years.

Despite its role in ending the Great Schism, in the official eyes of the church, Constance was not a legitimate council. Nor have the schismatic popes of Avignon and Pisa been recognized as legitimate (for this reason, another pope could take the name John XXIII in 1958).

THE COUNCIL OF BASEL (R. 1431–1449) Conciliar government of the church peaked at the Council of Basel, when the council negotiated church doctrine with heretics. In 1432 the Hussites of Bohemia presented the *Four Articles of Prague* to the council as a basis for the negotiations. This document contained requests for (1) giving the laity the Eucharist with cup as well as bread; (2) free, itinerant preaching; (3) the exclusion of the clergy from holding secular offices and owning property; and (4) just punishment of clergy who commit mortal sins.

In November 1433 an agreement was reached between the emperor, the council, and the Hussites, giving the Bohemians jurisdiction over their church similar to that held by the French and the English. Three of the four Prague articles were conceded: communion with cup, free preaching by ordained clergy, and like punishment of clergy and laity for mortal sins.

The end of the Hussite wars and the reform legislation curtailing the papal power of appointment and taxation were the high points of the Council of Basel. The exercise of such power by a council did not please the pope, and in 1438 he gained the opportunity to upstage the Council of Basel by negotiating reunion with the Eastern Church. The agreement, signed in Florence in 1439, was short-lived, but it restored papal prestige and signaled the demise of the Conciliar Movement. The Council of Basel collapsed in 1449. A decade later Pope Pius II (r. 1458–1464) issued the papal bull *Execrabilis* (1460) condemning appeals to councils as "erroneous and abominable" and "completely null and void."

Although many who had worked for reform now despaired of ever attaining it, the Conciliar Movement was not a total failure. It planted deep within the conscience of all Western peoples the conviction that the role of a leader of an institution is to provide for the well-being of its members, not just for that of the leader.

A second consequence of the Conciliar Movement was the devolving of religious responsibility onto the laity and secular government. Without papal leadership, secular control of national or territorial churches increased. Kings asserted power over the church in England and France. In German, Swiss, and Italian cities magistrates and city councils reformed and regulated religious life. This development could not be reversed by the powerful popes of the High Renaissance. On the contrary, as the papacy became a limited territorial regime, national control of the church ran apace. Perceived as just one among several Italian states, the Papal States could now be opposed as much on the grounds of "national" policy as for religious reasons.

◆

War, plague, and schism convulsed much of late medieval Europe throughout the fourteenth and into the fifteenth century. Two-fifths of the popu-

lation, particularly along the major trade routes, died from plague in the fourteenth century. War and famine continued to take untold numbers after the plague had passed. The introduction of gunpowder and heavy artillery during the long years of warfare between England and France resulted in new forms of human destruction. Periodic revolts erupted in town and countryside as ordinary people attempted to defend their traditional communal rights and privileges against the new autocratic territorial regimes. Even God's house seemed to be in shambles in 1409, when no fewer than three popes came to rule simultaneously.

There is, however, another side to the late Middle Ages. By the end of the fifteenth century the population losses were rapidly being made up. Between 1300 and 1500, education had become far more accessible, especially to laypeople. The number of universities increased 250 percent, from twenty to seventy, and the rise in the number of residential colleges was even more impressive, especially in France, where sixty-three were built. The fourteenth century saw the birth of Humanism and the fifteenth century gave us the printing press. Most impressive were the artistic and cultural achievements of the Italian Renaissance during the fifteenth century. The later Middle Ages were thus a period of growth and creativity as well as one of waning and decline.

Review Questions

1. What were the underlying and precipitating causes of the Hundred Years' War? What advantages did each side have? Why were the French finally able to drive the English almost entirely out of France?
2. What were the causes of the Black Death and why did it spread so quickly throughout western Europe? Where was it most virulent? What were its effects on European society? How important do you think disease is in changing the course of history?
3. Discuss the struggle between Pope Boniface VIII and King Philip the Fair. Why was Boniface so impotent in the conflict? How had political conditions changed since the reign of Pope Innocent III in the late twelfth century, and what did that mean for the papacy?
4. Briefly trace the history of the church from 1200 to 1450. How did it respond to political threats from the growing power of monarchs? How great an influence did the church have on secular events?
5. What was the Avignon Papacy, and why did it occur? What effect did it have on the state of the papacy? What relation does it have to the Great Schism? How did the church become divided and how was it reunited? Why was the Conciliar Movement a setback for the papacy?
6. Why were kings in the late thirteenth and early fourteenth centuries able to control the church more than the church could control the kings? How did kings attack the church during this period? Contrast these events with earlier ones in which the pope dominated rulers.

Suggested Readings

C. Allmand, *The Hundred Years' War: England and France at War, c. 1300–c. 1450* (1988). Good overview of the war's development and consequences.

P. Ariès, *The Hour of Our Death* (1983). People's familiarity with and philosophy of death in the Middle Ages.

R. Barber (Ed.), *The Pastons: Letters of a Family in the War of the Roses* (1984). Revelations of English family life in an age of crisis.

J. le Goff, *The Birth of Purgatory*, trans. by A. Goldhammer (1984). Cultural impact of the idea.

D. Hay, *Europe in the Fourteenth and Fifteenth Centuries* (1966). Many-sided treatment of political history.

J. Huizinga, *The Waning of the Middle Ages: A Study of the Forms of Life, Thought, and Art in France and the Netherlands in the Dawn of the Renaissance* (1924). A classic study of "mentality" at the end of the Middle Ages; exaggerated, but engrossing.

G. Leff, *Heresy in the Later Middle Ages, I–II* (1967). Magisterial survey of all the major heretical movements.

W. H. McNeill, *Plagues and Peoples* (1976). The Black Death in a broader context.

F. Oakley, *The Western Church in the Later Middle Ages* (1979). Eloquent, sympathetic survey.

S. Ozment, *The Age of Reform, 1250–1550* (1980). Highlights of late medieval intellectual and religious history.

E. Perroy, *The Hundred Years' War*, trans. by W. B. Wells (1965). Still the most comprehensive one-volume account.

C. Platt, *The Castle in Medieval England and Wales* (1982). Has an illustrated chapter on English coastal castles built during the Hundred Years' War.

Y. Renovard, *The Avignon Papacy 1305–1403*, trans. by D. Bethell (1970). The standard narrative account.

M. Spinka, *John Huss's Concept of the Church* (1966). Lucid and authoritative account of Hussite theology.

B. Tierney, *Foundations of the Conciliar Theory* (1955). Important study showing the origins of Conciliar theory in canon law.

B. Tierney, *The Crisis of Church and State 1050–1300* (1964). Part IV provides the major documents in the clash between Boniface VIII and Philip the Fair.

W. Ullmann, *Origins of the Great Schism* (1948). A basic study by a controversial interpreter of medieval political thought.

C. T. Wood, *Philip the Fair and Boniface VIII* (1967). Excerpts from the scholarly debate over the significance of this confrontation.

H. B. Workman, *John Wyclif*, vols. 1 and 2 (1926). Dated but still standard.

P. Ziegler, *The Black Death* (1969). Highly readable account.

Commissioned in 1501, when the artist was 26, Michelangelo's David became the symbol of the Florentine republic and was displayed in front of the Palazzo Vecchio. The detail shown here highlights the restrained emotion and dignity for which the statue is famous. [Michelangelo (1475–1564) David-p. (testa di profilo.) Scala/Art Resource]

Renaissance and Discovery

K E Y   T O P I C S

- The politics, culture, and art of the Italian Renaissance
- Political struggle and foreign intervention in Italy
- The powerful new monarchies of northern Europe
- The thought and culture of the northern Renaissance

If the late Middle Ages saw unprecedented chaos, it also witnessed a rebirth that would continue into the seventeenth century. Two modern Dutch scholars have employed the same word (Herfsttij, or "harvesttide") with different connotations to describe the period. Johan Huizinga has used the word to mean a "waning," or "decline," and Heiko Oberman has used it to mean "harvest." If something was dying away, some ripe fruit was being gathered and seed grain was sown. The late Middle Ages was a time of creative fragmentation.

By the late fifteenth century, Europe was recovering well from two of the three crises of the late Middle Ages: the demographic and the political. The great losses in population were being recaptured, and increasingly able monarchs and rulers

were imposing a new political order. A solution to the religious crisis, however, would have to await the Reformation and Counter-Reformation of the sixteenth century.

Although the opposite would be true in the sixteenth and seventeenth centuries, the city-states of Italy survived the century and a half between 1300 and 1450 better than the territorial states of northern Europe. This was due to Italy's strategic location between East and West and its lucrative Eurasian trade. Great wealth gave rulers and merchants the ability to work their will on both society and culture. They became patrons of government, education, and the arts, always as much for self-aggrandizement as out of benevolence, for whether a patron was a family, a firm, a government, or the church, their endowments enhanced their reputation and power. The result of such patronage was a cultural Renaissance in Italian cities unmatched elsewhere.

With the fall of Constantinople to the Turks in 1453, the shrinkage of Italy's once unlimited trading empire began. City-state soon turned against city-state, and by the 1490s the armies of France invaded Italy. Within a quarter century, Italy's great Renaissance had peaked.

The fifteenth century also saw an unprecedented scholarly renaissance. Italian and northern humanists made a full recovery of classical knowledge and languages and set in motion educational reforms and cultural changes that would spread throughout Europe in the fifteenth and sixteenth centuries. In the process the Italian humanists invented, for all practical purposes, critical historical scholarship and exploited a new fifteenth-century invention, the "divine art" of printing with movable type.

In this period the vernacular—the local language—began to take its place alongside Latin, the international language, as a widely used literary and political language. And European lands progressively superseded the universal Church as the community of highest allegiance, as patriotism and incipient nationalism seized hearts and minds as strongly as religion. Nations henceforth "transcended" themselves not by journeys to Rome but by competitive voyages to the Far East and the Americas, as the age of global exploration opened.

For Europe the late fifteenth and sixteenth centuries were a period of unprecedented territorial expansion and ideological experimentation. Permanent colonies were established within the Americas, and the exploitation of the New World's human and mineral resources was begun. Imported American gold and silver spurred scientific invention and a new weapons industry and touched off an inflationary spiral that produced an escalation in prices by the century's end. The new bullion also helped create an international traffic in African slaves as rival African tribes sold their captives to the Portuguese. These slaves were brought in ever-increasing numbers to work the mines and the plantations of the New World as replacements for faltering American natives. These centuries also saw social engineering and political planning on a large scale. Newly centralized governments began to put long-range economic policies into practice, a development that came to be known as mercantilism.

The Renaissance in Italy (1375–1527)

A Renaissance historian has described the Renaissance as the "prototype of the modern world." In his *Civilization of the Renaissance in Italy* (1860), Jacob Burckhardt argues that in fourteenth- and fifteenth-century Italy, through the revival of ancient learning, new secular and scientific values began to supplant traditional religious beliefs. This was the period in which people began to adopt a rational, objective, and statistical approach to reality and to rediscover the importance of the individual and his or her artistic creativity. The result, in Burckhardt's words, was a release of the "full, whole nature of man."

Other scholars have found Burckhardt's description far too modernizing an interpretation of the Renaissance and have accused him of overlooking the continuity between the Middle Ages and the Renaissance. His critics especially stress the still strongly Christian character of Renaissance humanism. They point out that earlier "renaissances," especially that of the twelfth century, also saw the revival of the ancient classics, interest in Latin language and Greek science, and appreciation of the worth and creativity of individuals.

Despite the exaggeration and bias of Burckhardt's portrayal of the Renaissance, most scholars agree that the Renaissance was a time of transition from the medieval to the modern world. Medieval Europe, especially before the twelfth century, had been a fragmented feudal society with an agricultural economy, and its thought and culture were largely dominated by the church. Renaissance Europe, especially after the fourteenth century, was characterized by growing national consciousness and political centralization, an urban economy based on organized commerce and capitalism, and ever greater lay and secular control of thought and culture, including religion.

The distinctive features and achievements of the Renaissance are most strikingly revealed in Italy from roughly 1375 to 1527, the year of the infamous sack of Rome by imperial soldiers. What was achieved in Italy during the late fourteenth to the early sixteenth centuries also deeply influenced northern Europe.

The Italian City-State

Renaissance society was no simple cultural transformation. It first took distinctive shape within the cities of late medieval Italy. Italy had always had a cultural advantage over the rest of Europe because its geography made it the natural gateway between East and West. Venice, Genoa, and Pisa traded uninterruptedly with the Near East throughout the Middle Ages and maintained vibrant urban societies. When commerce revived on a large scale in the eleventh century, Italian merchants quickly mastered the business skills of organization, bookkeeping, scouting new markets, and securing monopolies. During the thirteenth and fourteenth centuries, trade-rich cities expanded to become powerful city-states, dominating the political and economic life of the surrounding countryside. By the fifteenth century, the great Italian cities had become the bankers of much of Europe.

GROWTH OF CITY-STATES   The growth of Italian cities and urban culture was assisted by the endemic warfare between the emperor and the pope and the Guelf (propapal) and Ghibelline (pro-imperial) factions that this warfare had created. Either of these might have successfully challenged the cities had they permitted each other to concentrate on it. They chose instead to weaken one another and thus strengthened the merchant oligarchies of the cities. Unlike those of northern Europe, which tended to be dominated by kings and territorial princes, the great Italian cities were left free to expand. They became independent states, absorbing the surrounding countryside and assimilating the area's nobility in a unique urban meld of old and new rich. There were five such major, competitive states in Italy: the duchy of Milan; the republics of Florence and Venice; the Papal States; and the kingdom of Naples. (See Map 10–1.)

Social strife and competition for political power were so intense within the cities that most had evolved into despotisms by the fifteenth century—just to survive. Venice was a notable exception. It was ruled by a successful merchant oligarchy with power located in a patrician senate of 300 members and a ruthless judicial body, the Council of Ten, which anticipated and suppressed rival groups. Elsewhere, the new social classes and divisions within society produced by rapid urban growth fueled chronic, near-anarchic conflict.

SOCIAL CLASS AND CONFLICT   Florence was the most striking example. There .were four distinguishable social groups within the city. The first was the old rich, or *grandi*, the nobles and mer-

MAP 10–1   RENAISSANCE ITALY   *The city-states of Renaissance Italy were self-contained principalities whose internal strife was monitored by their despots and whose external aggression was long successfully controlled by treaty.*

chants who traditionally ruled the city. The second group was the emergent new-rich merchant class, capitalists and bankers known as the *popolo grosso*, or "fat people." They began to challenge the old rich for political power in the late thirteenth and early fourteenth centuries. Then there were the middle-burgher ranks of guildmasters, shopowners, and professionals, those smaller businesspeople who, in Florence as elsewhere, tended to take the side of the new rich against the conservative policies of the old rich. Finally, there was the *popolo minuto*, or the "little people," the lower economic classes. In 1457 one-third of the population of Florence, about 30,000 people, were officially listed as paupers, that is, having no wealth at all.

Cosimo de' Medici (1389–1464), Florentine banker and statesman, in his lifetime the city's wealthiest man and most successful politician. This portrait is by Pontormo. [Erich Lessing, Art Resource, N.Y.]

These social divisions produced conflict at every level of society, to which was added the ever-present fear of foreign intrigue. In 1378 there was a great revolt of the poor known as the Ciompi Revolt. It resulted from a combination of three factors that made life unbearable for those at the bottom of society: the feuding between the old and the new rich; the social anarchy that had resulted from the Black Death, which cut the city's population almost in half; and the collapse of the banking houses of Bardi and Peruzzi, which left the poor more economically vulnerable than ever. The successful revolt established a chaotic four-year reign of power by the lower Florentine classes. True stability did not return to Florence until the ascent to power of Cosimo de' Medici (1389–1464) in 1434.

DESPOTISM AND DIPLOMACY   The wealthiest Florentine, Cosimo de' Medici, was an astute statesman. He controlled the city internally from behind the scenes, skillfully manipulating the constitution and influencing elections. Florence was governed by a council, first of six and later of eight members,

known as the *Signoria*. These men were chosen from the most powerful guilds—those representing the major clothing industries (cloth, wool, fur, and silk) and such other groups as bankers, judges, and doctors. Through his informal, cordial relations with the electoral committee, Cosimo was able to keep councillors loyal to him in the *Signoria*. As head of the Office of Public Debt, he was able to favor congenial factions. His grandson Lorenzo the Magnificent (1449–1492, r. 1478–1492) ruled Florence in almost totalitarian fashion during the last quarter of the fifteenth century. The assassination of his brother in 1478 by a rival family, the Pazzi, who plotted with the pope against Medici rule, made Lorenzo a cautious and determined ruler.

Despotism was less subtle elsewhere. To prevent internal social conflict and foreign intrigue from paralyzing their cities, the dominant groups cooperated to install a hired strongman. Known as a *podestà*, his purpose was to maintain law and order. He was given executive, military, and judicial authority. His mandate was direct and simple: to permit, by whatever means required, the normal flow of business activity without which not the old rich, the new rich, nor the poor of a city could long survive. Because these despots could not depend on the divided populace, they operated through mercenary armies, which they obtained through military brokers known as *condottieri*.

It was a hazardous job. Despots were not only subject to dismissal by the oligarchies that hired them, but they were also popular objects of assassination attempts. The spoils of success, however, were very great. In Milan, it was as despots that the Visconti family came to power in 1278 and the Sforza family in 1450. Both ruled without constitutional restraints or serious political competition. The latter produced one of Machiavelli's heroes, Ludovico il Moro.

Political turbulence and warfare gave birth to diplomacy. Consequently, the various city-states could stay abreast of foreign military developments and, if shrewd enough, gain power and advantage short of actually going to war. Most city-states established resident embassies in the fifteenth century. Their ambassadors not only represented them in ceremonies and as negotiators but also became their watchful eyes and ears at rival courts.

Whether within the comparatively tranquil republic of Venice, the strong-arm democracy of Florence, or the undisguised despotism of Milan, the disciplined Italian city proved a most congenial

Florentine women doing needlework, spinning, and weaving. These activities took up much of a woman's time and contributed to the elegance of dress for which Florentine men and women were famed. [Alinari/Art Resource]

climate for an unprecedented flowering of thought and culture. Italian Renaissance culture was promoted as vigorously by despots as by republicans and by secularized popes as enthusiastically as by the more spiritually minded. Such widespread support occurred because the main requirement for patronage of the arts and letters was the one thing that Italian cities of the High Renaissance had in abundance: great wealth.

Humanism

There are several schools of thought on the meaning of "humanism." There are those who see the Italian Renaissance as the birth of modernity, characterized by an un-Christian philosophy that stressed the dignity of humankind and championed individualism and secular values (these are the followers of the nineteenth-century historian Jacob Burckhardt). Others argue that humanists were the very champions of authentic Catholic Christianity, who opposed the pagan teaching of Aristotle and the ineloquent Scholasticism that his writings nurtured. Still others see humanism as a form of scholarship consciously designed to promote a sense of civic responsibility and political liberty.

An authoritative modern commentator on humanism, Paul O. Kristeller, has accused all these views of dealing more with the secondary effects than with the essence of humanism. Humanism,

he believes, was no particular philosophy or value system but simply an educational program that concentrated on rhetoric and sound scholarship for their own sake.

There is truth in each of these definitions. Humanism was the scholarly study of the Latin and Greek classics and of the ancient Church Fathers both for its own sake and in the hope of a rebirth of ancient norms and values. Humanists advocated the *studia humanitatis*, a liberal arts program of study that embraced grammar, rhetoric, poetry, history, politics, and moral philosophy. Not only were these subjects considered a joy in themselves, they were also seen as celebrating the dignity of humankind and preparing people for a life of virtuous action. The Florentine, Leonardo Bruni (ca. 1370–1444), first gave the name *humanitas* or "humanity," to the learning that resulted from such scholarly pursuits. Bruni was a student of Manuel Chrysoloras, a Byzantine scholar who opened the world of Greek scholarship to a generation of young Italian humanists when he taught at Florence between 1397 and 1403.

The first humanists were orators and poets. They wrote original literature, in both the classical and the vernacular languages, inspired by and modeled on the newly discovered works of the ancients. They also taught rhetoric within the universities. When humanists were not employed as teachers of rhetoric, their talents were sought as secretaries, speech writers, and diplomats in princely and papal courts.

The study of classical and Christian antiquity existed before the Italian Renaissance. There were recoveries of ancient civilization during the Carolingian renaissance of the ninth century, within the cathedral school of Chartres in the twelfth century, during the great Aristotelian revival in Paris in the thirteenth century, and among the Augustinians in the early fourteenth century. These precedents, however, only partially compare with the grand achievements of the Italian Renaissance of the late Middle Ages. The latter was far more secular and lay-dominated, had much broader interests, was blessed with far more recovered manuscripts, and possessed far superior technical skills than had been the case in the earlier "rebirths" of antiquity.

Unlike their Scholastic rivals, humanists were less bound to recent tradition; they did not focus all their attention on summarizing and comparing the views of recognized authorities on a text or question, but went directly to the original sources themselves. And their most respected sources were classical and biblical, not the medieval philosophers and theologians. Avidly searching out manuscript collections, Italian humanists made the full sources of Greek and Latin antiquity available to scholars during the fourteenth and fifteenth centuries. Mastery of Latin and Greek was the surgeon's tool of the humanist. There is a kernel of truth—but only a kernel—in the humanists' arrogant assertion that the period between themselves and classical civilization was a "dark middle age."

PETRARCH, DANTE, AND BOCCACCIO Francesco Petrarch (1304–1374) was the "father of humanism." He left the legal profession to pursue letters and poetry. Most of his life was spent in and around Avignon. He was involved in Cola di Rienzo's popular revolt and two-year reign (1347–1349) in Rome as "tribune" of the Roman people. Petrarch also served the Visconti family in Milan in his later years.

Petrarch celebrated ancient Rome in his *Letters to the Ancient Dead*, fancied personal letters to Cicero, Livy, Vergil, and Horace. He also wrote a Latin epic poem (*Africa*, a poetic historical tribute to the Roman general Scipio Africanus), and a set of biographies of famous Roman men (*Lives of Illustrious Men*). Petrarch's most famous contemporary work was a collection of highly introspec-tive love sonnets to a certain Laura, a married woman whom he romantically admired from a safe distance.

His critical textual studies, elitism, and contempt for the allegedly useless learning of the Scholastics were features that many later humanists also shared. Classical and Christian values coexist, not always harmoniously, in his work, an uneasy coexistence that is seen in many later humanists. Medieval Christian values can be seen in Petrarch's imagined dialogues with Saint Augustine and in tracts written to defend the personal immortality of the soul against the Aristotelians.

Petrarch was, however, far more secular in orientation than his famous near-contemporary Dante Alighieri (1265–1321), whose *Vita Nuova* and *Divine Comedy* form, with Petrarch's sonnets, the cornerstones of Italian vernacular literature. Petrarch's student and friend Giovanni Boccaccio (1313–1375) was also a pioneer of humanist studies. His *Decameron*—100 often bawdy tales told by three men and seven women in a country retreat from the plague that ravaged Florence in 1348—is both a stinging social commentary (especially in its exposé of sexual and economic misconduct) and a sympathetic look at human behavior. An avid collector of manuscripts, Boccaccio also assembled an encyclopedia of Greek and Roman mythology.

Dante Alighieri (1265–1321) portrayed with scenes of hell, purgatory, and paradise from the Divine Comedy, *his classic epic poem.* [Scala/Art Resource, N.Y.]

Petrarch's Letter to Posterity

In old age Petrarch wrote a highly personal letter to posterity in which he summarized the lessons he had learned during his lifetime. The letter also summarizes the original values of Renaissance humanists: their suspicion of purely materialistic pleasure, the importance they attached to friendship, and their utter devotion to and love of antiquity.

✦ *Does Petrarch's letter give equal weight to classical and Christian values? Why would he have preferred to live in another age?*

I have always possessed extreme contempt for wealth; not that riches are not desirable in themselves, but because I hate the anxiety and care which are invariably associated with them . . . . I have, on the contrary, led a happier existence with plain living and ordinary fare . . . .

The pleasure of dining with one's friends is so great that nothing has ever given me more delight than their unexpected arrival, nor have I ever willingly sat down to table without a companion . . . .

The greatest kings of this age have loved and courted me . . . . I have fled, however, from many . . . to whom I was greatly attached; and such was my innate longing for liberty that I studiously avoided those whose very name seemed incompatible with the freedom I loved.

I possess a well-balanced rather than a keen intellect—one prone to all kinds of good and wholesome study, but especially to moral philosophy and the art of poetry. The latter I neglected as time went on, and took delight in sacred literature . . . . Among the many subjects that interested me, I dwelt especially upon antiquity, for our own age has always repelled me, so that, had it not been for the love of those dear to me, I should have preferred to have been born in any other period than our own. In order to forget my own time, I have constantly striven to place myself in spirit in other ages, and consequently I delighted in history . . . .

If only I have lived well, it matters little to me how I have talked. Mere elegance of language can produce at best but an empty fame.

Frederic Austen Ogg, ed., A Source Book of Mediaeval History: Documents Illustrative of European Life and Institutions from the German Invasions to the Renaissance *(New York: American Book Company, 1908), pp. 470–473.*

EDUCATIONAL REFORMS AND GOALS Humanists were not bashful scholars. They delighted in going directly to primary sources and refused to be slaves to tradition. Such an attitude not only made them innovative educators, it also kept them constantly in search of new sources of information. Magnificent manuscript collections were assembled with great care, as if they were potent medicines for the ills of contemporary society.

The goal of humanist studies was to be wise and to speak eloquently, to know what is good, and to practice virtue. Learning was not to remain abstract and unpracticed. "It is better to will the good than to know the truth," Petrarch had taught, and this became a motto of many later humanists, who, like Petrarch, believed that learning ennobled people.

Pietro Paolo Vergerio (1349–1420), the author of the most influential Renaissance tract on education, *On the Morals That Befit a Free Man*, left a classic summary of the humanist concept of a liberal education:

We call those studies liberal which are worthy of a free man; those studies by which we attain and practice virtue and wisdom; that education which calls forth, trains, and develops those highest gifts of body and mind which ennoble men and which are rightly judged to rank next in dignity to virtue only, for to a vulgar temper, gain and pleasure are the one aim of existence, to a lofty nature, moral worth and fame.[1]

[1]Cited by De Lamar Jensen, *Renaissance Europe: Age of Recovery and Reconciliation* (Lexington, Mass.: D. C. Health, 1981), p. 111.

The ideal of a useful education and well-rounded people inspired far-reaching reforms in traditional education. Quintilian's *Education of the Orator*, the complete text of which was discovered in 1416, became the basic classical guide for the humanist revision of the traditional curriculum. Vittorino da Feltre (d. 1446) exemplified the ideals of humanist teaching. He not only had his students read the difficult works of Pliny, Ptolemy, Terence, Plautus, Livy, and Plutarch, he also subjected them to vigorous physical exercise and games. Another famous educator, Guarino da Verona (d. 1460), rector of the new University of Ferrara and a student of the age's most renowned Greek scholar, Manuel Chrysoloras, streamlined the study of classical languages and gave it systematic form.

Humanist learning was not confined to the classroom, as Baldassare Castiglione's (1478–1529) famous *Book of the Courtier* illustrates. Written as a practical guide for the nobility at the court of Urbino, it embodies the highest ideals of Italian humanism. It depicts the successful courtier as one who knew how to integrate knowledge of ancient languages and history with athletic, military, and musical skills, while practicing good manners and exhibiting moral character.

Noblewomen also played a role at court in education and culture, and among them none more so than Christine de Pisan (1363?–1434). The Italian-born daughter of the physician and astrologer of the French king Charles V, she received at the French court as fine an education as anyone could have. She became expert in classical, French, and Italian languages and literature. Married at fifteen and the widowed mother of three at twenty-seven, she turned to writing lyric poetry to support herself. She soon became a well-known woman of letters much read throughout the courts of Europe. Her most famous work, *The City of Ladies*, is a chronicle of the accomplishments of the great women of history.

THE FLORENTINE "ACADEMY" AND THE REVIVAL OF PLATONISM Of all the important recoveries of the past made during the Italian Renaissance, none stands out more than the revival of Greek studies, especially the works of Plato, in fifteenth-century Florence. Many factors combined to bring this revival about. An important foundation was laid in 1397 when the city invited Manuel Chrysoloras to come from Constantinople and promote Greek learning. A half century later (1439), the ecumenical Council of Ferrara–Florence, having convened to negotiate the reunion of the Eastern and Western churches, opened the door for many Greek scholars and manuscripts to enter the West. After the fall of Constantinople to the Turks in 1453, Greek scholars fled to Florence for refuge. This was the background against which the Florentine Platonic Academy evolved under the patronage of Cosimo de' Medici and the supervision of Marsilio Ficino (1433–1499) and Pico della Mirandola (1463–1494).

The thinkers of the Renaissance were interested in every variety of ancient wisdom. They were especially attracted, however, to the Platonic tradition and to those Church Fathers who tried to synthesize Platonic philosophy and Christian teaching. The "Florentine Academy" was actually not a formal school, but an informal gathering of influential Florentine humanists devoted to the revival of the works of Plato and the Neoplatonists: Plotinus, Proclus, Porphyry, and Dionysius the Areopagite. To this end, Ficino edited and published the complete works of Plato.

The appeal of Platonism lay in its flattering view of human nature. It distinguished between an eternal sphere of being and the perishable world in which humans actually lived. Human reason was believed to belong to the former, indeed, to have preexisted in this pristine world and to continue to commune with it, as the present knowledge of mathematical and moral truth bore witness.

Strong Platonic influence can be seen in Pico's *Oration on the Dignity of Man*, perhaps the most famous Renaissance statement on the nature of humankind. Pico wrote the *Oration* as an introduction to a pretentious collection of 900 theses. Published in Rome in December 1486, the theses were intended to serve as the basis for a public debate on all of life's important topics. The *Oration* drew on Platonic teaching to depict humans as the only creatures in the world who possessed the freedom to be whatever they chose, able at will to rise to the height of angels or to descend to the level of pigs.

CRITICAL WORK OF THE HUMANISTS: LORENZO VALLA Because they were guided by a scholarly ideal of philological accuracy and historical truthfulness, the humanists could become critics of tradition even when that was not their intention. Dispassionate critical scholarship shook long-standing foundations, not the least of which were those of the medieval church.

The work of Lorenzo Valla (1406–1457), author of the standard Renaissance text on Latin philology, the *Elegances of the Latin Language* (1444), reveals the explosive character of the new learning. Although a good Catholic, Valla became a hero to later Protestants. His popularity among Protestants stemmed from his defense of predestination against the advocates of free will, and especially from his exposé of the *Donation of Constantine* (see Chapter 6).

The fraudulent *Donation*, written in the eighth century, purported to be a grant of vast territories made by the fourth-century Roman emperor Constantine to the pope. Valla did not intend the exposé of the *Donation* to have the devastating force that Protestants later attributed to it. He only proved in a careful, scholarly way what others had long suspected. Using the most rudimentary textual analysis and historical logic, Valla proved that the document was filled with such anachronistic terms as *fief* and that it contained material that could not be in a genuine fourth-century document. In the same dispassionate way Valla also pointed out errors in

---

Christine de Pisan Instructs Women on How to Handle Their Husbands

Renowned Renaissance noblewoman Christine de Pisan has the modern reputation of being perhaps the first feminist, and her book, The Treasure of the City of Ladies *(also known as* The Book of Three Virtues*) has been described as the Renaissance woman's survival manual. Here she gives advice to the wives of artisans.*

✦ *How does Christine de Pisan's image of husband and wife compare with other medieval views? Would the church take issue with her advice in any way? As a noblewoman commenting on the married life of artisans, does her high social standing influence her advice? Would she give similar advice to women of her own social class?*

All wives of artisans should be very painstaking and diligent if they wish to have the necessities of life. They should encourage their husbands or their workmen to get to work early in the morning and work until late . . . . [And] the wife herself should [also] be involved in the work to the extent that she knows all about it, so that she may know how to oversee his workers if her husband is absent, and to reprove them if they do not do well . . . . And when customers come to her husband and try to drive a hard bargain, she ought to warn him solicitously to take care that he does not make a bad deal. She should advise him to be chary of giving too much credit if he does not know precisely where and to whom it is going, for in this way many come to poverty . . . .

In addition, she ought to keep her husband's love as much as she can, to this end: that he will stay at home more willingly and that he may not have any reason to join the foolish crowds of other young men in taverns and indulge in unnecessary and extravagant expense, as many tradesmen do, especially in Paris. By treating him kindly she should protect him as well as she can from this. It is said that three things drive a man from his home: a quarrelsome wife, a smoking fireplace, and a leaking roof. She too ought to stay at home gladly and not go off every day traipsing hither and yon gossiping with the neighbours and visiting her chums to find out what everyone is doing. That is done by slovenly housewives roaming about the town in groups. Nor should she go off on these pilgrimages got up for no good reason and involving a lot of needless expense.

Christine de Pisan, The Treasure of the City of Ladies or The Book of the Three Virtues, *trans. by Sarah Lawson (Penguin Books: New York, 1985), pp. 167–168.*

the Latin Vulgate, still the authorized version of the Bible for the Western church.

Such discoveries did not make Valla any less loyal to the church, nor did they prevent his faithful fulfillment of the office of apostolic secretary in Rome under Pope Nicholas V. Nonetheless, historical criticism of this type served those less loyal to the medieval church. It was no accident that young humanists formed the first identifiable group of Martin Luther's supporters.

CIVIC HUMANISM   Italian humanists were exponents of applied knowledge; their basic criticism of traditional education was that much of it was useless. Education, they believed, should promote individual virtue and public service. This ideal inspired what has been called civic humanism, by which is meant examples of humanist leadership of the political and cultural life. The most striking instance is to be found in Florence. There three humanists served as chancellors: Colluccio Salutati (1331–1406), Leonardo Bruni (ca. 1370–1444), and Poggio Bracciolini (1380–1459). Each used his rhetorical skills to rally the Florentines against the aggression of Naples and Milan. Bruni and Poggio also wrote adulatory histories of the city. Another accomplished humanist scholar, Leon Battista Alberti (1402–1472), was a noted architect and builder in the city. Whether it was humanism that accounted for such civic activity or just a desire to exercise great power remains a debated issue.

On the other hand, many humanists became cliquish and snobbish, an intellectual elite concerned only with pursuing narrow, antiquarian interests and writing pure, classical Latin in the quiet of their studies. It was in reaction against this elitist trend that the humanist historians Niccolò Machiavelli (1469–1527) and Francesco Guicciardini (1483–1540) adopted the vernacular and made contemporary history their primary source and subject matter.

Renaissance Art

In Renaissance Italy, as in Reformation Europe, the values and interests of the laity were no longer subordinated to those of the clergy. In education, culture, and religion the laity assumed a leading role and established models for the clergy to imitate. This was a development due in part to the church's loss of international power during the great crises of the late Middle Ages. It was also encouraged by the rise of national sentiment, the creation of competent national bureaucracies staffed by the laity rather than by clerics, and the rapid growth of lay education during the fourteenth and fifteenth centuries. Medieval Christian values were adjusting to a more this-worldly spirit. Men and women began again to appreciate and even glorify the secular world, secular learning, and purely human pursuits as ends in themselves.

This new perspective on life is prominent in the painting and sculpture of the High Renaissance— the late fifteenth and early sixteenth centuries, when Renaissance art reached its full maturity. Whereas medieval art tended to be abstract and formulaic, Renaissance art was emphatically concerned with the observation of the natural world and the communication of human emotions. Renaissance artists also tried to give their works a greater rational (chiefly mathematical) order, a symmetry and proportionality that reflected pictorially their deeply held belief in the harmony of the universe. The interest of Renaissance artists in ancient Roman art was closely allied to an independent interest in humanity and nature.

Renaissance artists had the advantage of new technical skills developed during the fifteenth century. In addition to the availability of oil paints, two special techniques were perfected: that of using shading to enhance naturalness (*chiaroscuro*) and that of adjusting the size of figures to give the viewer a feeling of continuity with the painting (linear perspective). These techniques permitted the artist to "rationalize" space and paint a more natural world. The result was that, when compared with their flat Byzantine and Gothic counterparts, Renaissance paintings were filled with energy and life and stood out from the canvas in three dimensions.

The new direction was signaled by Giotto (1266–1336), the father of Renaissance painting. An admirer of Saint Francis of Assisi, whose love of nature he shared, Giotto painted a more natural world than his Byzantine and Gothic predecessors. Though still filled with religious seriousness, his work was no longer so abstract and unnatural a depiction of the world. The painter Masaccio (1401–1428) and the sculptor Donatello (1386–1466) continued to portray the world around them more literally and naturally. The heights were reached by the great masters of the High Renaissance: Leonardo da Vinci (1452–1519), Raphael (1483–1520), and Michelangelo Buonarroti (1475–1564).

Giotto's portrayal of the funeral of Saint Francis of Assisi. The saint is surrounded by his admiring brothers and a knight of Assisi (first on the right). Giotto's (1266–1336) work signals the evolution toward Renaissance art. The damaged areas on this fresco resulted from the removal of nineteenth-century restorations. [Scala/Art Resource, N.Y.]

LEONARDO DA VINCI   More than any other person in the period, Leonardo exhibited the Renaissance ideal of the universal person. He was a true master of many skills. One of the greatest painters of all time, he was also a military engineer for Ludovico il Moro in Milan, Cesare Borgia in Romagna, and the French king Francis I. Leonardo advocated scientific experimentation, dissected corpses to learn anatomy, and was an accomplished, self-taught botanist. His inventive mind foresaw such modern machines as airplanes and submarines. Indeed, the variety of his interests was so great that it could shorten his attention span, so that he was constantly moving from one activity to another. His great skill in conveying inner moods through complex facial features can be seen in the most famous of his paintings, the Mona Lisa, as well as in his self-portrait.

RAPHAEL   Raphael, a man of great sensitivity and kindness, was apparently loved by contemporaries as much for his person as for his work. His premature death at thirty-seven cut short his artistic career. He is famous for his tender madonnas, the best known of which graced the monastery of San Sisto in Piacenza and is now in Dresden. Art historians praise his fresco *The School of Athens*, a grandly conceived portrayal of the great masters of Western philosophy, as a virtually perfect example of Renaissance technique. It depicts Plato and Aristotle surrounded by the great philosophers and scientists of antiquity, who are portrayed with features of Raphael's famous contemporaries, including Leonardo and Michelangelo.

MICHELANGELO   The melancholy genius Michelangelo also excelled in a variety of arts and crafts. His eighteen-foot godlike sculpture David, which long stood majestically in the great square of Florence, is a perfect example of the Renaissance artist's devotion to harmony, symmetry, and proportion, as well as the extreme glorification of the human form. Four different popes commissioned works by Michelangelo. The most famous are the frescoes for the Sistine Chapel, painted during the pontificate of Pope Julius II (r. 1503–1513), who also set Michelangelo to work on the pope's own magnificent tomb. The Sistine frescoes originally covered 10,000 square feet and involved 343 figures, over half of which exceeded 10 feet in height. But it is their originality and perfection as works of art that impress most. This labor of love and piety took four years to complete. A person of incredible energy and endurance who lived to be almost ninety, Michelangelo insisted on doing almost everything himself and permitted his assistants only a few of the many chores involved in his work. (For an example of Michelangelo's work, see the photo on page 332.)

His later works are more complex and suggest deep personal changes. They mark, artistically and philosophically, the passing of High Renaissance painting and the advent of a new style known as mannerism, which reached its peak in the late sixteenth and early seventeenth centuries. A reaction

These two works by Donatello, sculpted fifteen years apart, reveal the psychological complexity of Renaissance artists and their work. On the left is a youthful, sexy David, standing awkwardly and seemingly puzzled on the head of the slain Goliath. Created in 1440, it is the earliest free-standing nude made in the West since Roman times. [Art Resource, N.Y.] On the right, sculpted in 1454–1455 from poplar wood, is Mary Magdalen returned from her desert retreat; she is a frightful, toothless old woman, shorn of all dignity. [Scala/Art Resource, N.Y.]

against the simplicity and symmetry of High Renaissance art (which also found expression in music and literature), mannerism made room for the strange and even the abnormal and gave freer reign to the subjectivity of the artist. Mannerism acquired its name because the artist was permitted to express his or her own individual perceptions and feelings, to paint, compose, or write in a "mannered," or "affected," way. Tintoretto (d. 1594) and especially El Greco (d. 1614) became mannerism's supreme representatives.

Slavery in the Renaissance

Throughout Renaissance Italy, slavery flourished as extravagantly as art and culture. A thriving western slave market existed as early as the twelfth century, when the Spanish sold Muslim slaves captured in raids and war to wealthy Italians and other interested buyers. Contemporaries looked on such slavery as a merciful act, since these captives would otherwise have been killed. In addition to widespread household or domestic slavery, collective plantation slavery, following East Asian models, also developed during the High Middle Ages in the eastern Mediterranean. In the savannas of Sudan and on Venetian estates on the islands of Cyprus and Crete, gangs of slaves worked sugar cane plantations, the model for later western Mediterranean and New World slavery.

After the Black Death (1348–1350) had reduced the supply of laborers everywhere in western Europe, the demand for slaves soared. Slaves now began to be imported from Africa, the Balkans, Constantinople, Cyprus, Crete, and the lands surrounding the Black Sea. Because slaves were taken randomly from conquered people, they consisted of many races: Tatars, Circassians, Greeks, Russians, Georgians, and Iranians as well as Asians and Africans. According to one source, "By the end of the fourteenth century, there was hardly a well-to-do household in Tuscany without at least one slave: brides brought them [to their marriages] as

Michelangelo and Pope Julius II

Vasari here describes how Pope Julius, the most fearsome and worldly of the Renaissance popes, forced Michelangelo to complete the Sistine Chapel before Michelangelo was ready to do so.

✦ *Did Michelangelo hold his own with the pope? What does this interchange suggest about the relationship of patrons and artists in the Renaissance? Were great artists like Michelangelo so revered that they could do virtually as they pleased?*

[The pope was very anxious to see the decoration of the Sistine Chapel completed, and constantly inquired when it would be finished.] On one occasion, therefore, Michelangelo replied, "It will be finished when I shall have done all that I believe is required to satisfy Art." "And we command," rejoined the pontiff, "that you satisfy our wish to have it done quickly," adding that if it were not at once completed, he would have Michelangelo thrown headlong from the scaffolding. Hearing this, our artist, who feared the fury of the pope, and with good cause, without taking time to add what was wanting, took down the remainder of the scaffolding to the great satisfaction of the whole city on All Saints' day, when Pope Julius went into that chapel to sing mass. But Michelangelo had much desired to retouch some portions of the work a secco [that is, after the damp plaster upon which the paint had been originally laid al fresco had dried], as had been done by the older

masters who had painted the stories on the walls. He would also have gladly added a little ultramarine to the draperies and gilded other parts, to the end that the whole might have a richer and more striking effect.

The pope, too, hearing that these things were still wanting, and finding that all who beheld the chapel praised it highly, would now fain have had the additions made. But as Michelangelo thought reconstructing the scaffold too long an affair, the pictures remained as they were, although the pope, who often saw Michelangelo, would sometimes say, "Let the chapel be enriched with bright colors and gold; it looks poor." When Michelangelo would reply familiarly, "Holy Father, the men of those days did not adorn themselves with gold; those who are painted here less than any, for they were none too rich; besides which they were holy men, and must have despised riches and ornaments."

James Harvey Robinson, ed., Readings in European History, *vol. 1 (Boston: Athenaeum, 1904), pp. 538–539.*

This portrait of Katharina, by Albrecht Dürer, provides evidence of African slavery in Europe during the sixteenth century. Katharina was in the service of one João Bradao, a Portuguese economic minister living in Antwerp, then the financial center of Europe. Dürer became friends with Bradao during his stay in the Low Countries in the winter of 1520–1521. [Bildarchiv Foto Marburg/Art Resource, N.Y.]

part of their dowry, doctors accepted them from their patients in lieu of fees—and it was not unusual to find them even in the service of a priest."[2]

Owners had complete dominion over their slaves; in Italian law, this meant the "[power] to have, hold, sell, alienate, exchange, enjoy, rent or unrent, dispose of in [their] will[s], judge soul and body, and do with in perpetuity whatsoever may please [them] and [their] heirs and no man may gainsay [them]."[3] A strong, young, healthy slave cost the equivalent of the wages paid a free servant over several years. Considering the lifetime of free service thereafter, slaves could be well worth the cost.

---

[2]Iris Origo, *The Merchant of Prato: Francesco di Marco Datini 1335–1410* (New York: David Godine, 1986), pp. 90–91.

[3]Ibid., p. 209.

The Tatars and Africans appear to have been the worst treated. But as in ancient Greece and Rome, slaves at this time were generally accepted as family members and were integrated into households. Not a few women slaves became mothers of their masters' children. Quite a few children of such unions were adopted and raised as legitimate heirs of their fathers. It was clearly in the interest of their owners to keep slaves healthy and happy; otherwise they were of little use and could even become a threat. Still, slaves remained a foreign and suspected presence in Italian society; they were, as all knew, uprooted and resentful people.

Italy's Political Decline: The French Invasions (1494–1527)

The Treaty of Lodi

As a land of autonomous city-states, Italy's peace and safety from foreign invasion, especially from invasion by the Turks, had always depended on internal cooperation. Such cooperation had been maintained during the latter half of the fifteenth century, thanks to a carefully constructed political alliance known as the Treaty of Lodi (1454–1455). The terms of the treaty brought Milan and Naples, long traditional enemies, into alliance with Florence. These three stood together for decades against Venice, which was frequently joined by the Papal States, to create an internal balance of power. When a foreign enemy threatened Italy, however, the five formed a united front.

Around 1490, following the rise to power of the Milanese despot Ludovico il Moro, hostilities between Milan and Naples resumed. The peace made possible by the Treaty of Lodi ended in 1494 when Naples, supported by Florence and the Borgia Pope Alexander VI (r. 1492–1503), prepared to attack Milan. Ludovico made what proved to be a fatal response in these new political alignments; he appealed for aid to the French. French kings had ruled Naples from 1266 to 1435, before they were driven out by Duke Alfonso of Sicily. Breaking a wise Italian rule, Ludovico invited the French to reenter Italy and revive their dynastic claim to Naples. In his haste to check his rival Naples, Ludovico did not recognize sufficiently that France also had dynastic claims to Milan. Nor did he foresee how insatiable the French appetite for Italian territory would become once French armies had crossed the Alps.

Charles VIII's March Through Italy

The French king Louis XI had resisted the temptation to invade Italy, while nonetheless keeping French dynastic claims in Italy alive. His successor, Charles VIII (r. 1483–1498), an eager youth in his twenties, responded to Ludovico's call with lightning speed. Within five months he had crossed the Alps (August 1495) and raced as conqueror through Florence and the Papal States into Naples. As Charles approached Florence, the Florentine ruler, Piero dé Medici, who had allied with Naples against Milan, tried to placate the French king by handing over Pisa and other Florentine possessions. Such appeasement only brought about Piero's forced exile by a population that was revolutionized then by the radical Dominican preacher Girolamo Savonarola (1452–1498). Savonarola convinced most of the fearful Florentines that the French king's arrival was a long-delayed and fully justified divine vengeance on their immorality.

Charles entered Florence without resistance. Thanks to Savonarola's flattery and the payment of a large ransom, the city was spared a threatened destruction. Savonarola continued to exercise virtual rule over Florence for four years after Charles's departure. The Florentines proved, however, not to be the stuff theocracies are made of. Savonarola's moral rigor and antipapal policies made it impossible for him to survive indefinitely. This became especially true after the Italian cities reunited and the ouster of the French invader, whom Savonarola had praised as a godsend, became national policy. Savonarola was imprisoned and executed in May 1498.

Charles's lightning march through Italy also struck terror in non-Italian hearts. Ferdinand of Aragon, who hoped to expand his own possessions in Italy from his kingdom of Sicily, now found himself vulnerable to a French–Italian axis. He took the initiative to create a counteralliance—the League of Venice, formed in March 1495—in which he joined with Venice, the Papal States, and Emperor Maximilian I against the French. The alliance set the stage for a conflict between France and Spain that would not end until 1559.

Ludovico il Moro meanwhile recognized that he had sown the wind; having desired a French invasion only so long as it weakened his enemies, he now saw Milan threatened by the whirlwind of events that he had himself created. In reaction he joined the League of Venice, and this alliance was able to send Charles into retreat by May. Charles remained thereafter on the defensive until his death in April 1498.

Pope Alexander VI and the Borgia Family

The French returned to Italy under Charles's successor, Louis XII (r. 1498–1515). This time they were assisted by a new Italian ally, the Borgia pope, Alexander VI. Alexander was probably the most corrupt pope who ever sat on the papal throne. He openly promoted the political careers of Cesare and Lucrezia Borgia, the children he had had before he became pope, and he placed papal policy in tandem with the efforts of his powerful family to secure a political base in Romagna.

In Romagna several principalities had fallen away from the church during the Avignon papacy. And Venice, the pope's ally within the League of Venice, continued to contest the Papal States for their loyalty. Seeing that a French alliance could give him the opportunity to reestablish control over the region, Alexander took steps to secure French favor. He annulled Louis XII's marriage to Charles VIII's sister so Louis could marry Charles's widow, Anne of Brittany—a popular political move designed to keep Brittany French. The pope also bestowed a cardinal's hat on the archbishop of Rouen, Louis's favorite cleric. Most important, Alexander agreed to abandon the League of Venice; this withdrawal of support made the league too weak to resist a French reconquest of Milan. In exchange, Cesare Borgia received the sister of the king of Navarre, Charlotte d'Albret, in marriage, a union that greatly enhanced Borgia military strength. Cesare also received land grants from Louis XII and the promise of French military aid in Romagna.

All in all it was a scandalous trade-off, but one that made it possible for both the French king and the pope to realize their ambitions within Italy. Louis successfully invaded Milan in August 1499. Ludovico il Moro, who had originally opened the Pandora's box of French invasion, spent his last years languishing in a French prison. In 1500 Louis and Ferdinand of Aragon divided Naples between them, while the pope and Cesare Borgia conquered the cities of Romagna without opposition. Alexander awarded his victorious son the title "duke of Romagna."

Pope Julius II

Cardinal Giuliano della Rovere, a strong opponent of the Borgia family, succeeded Alexander VI as Pope Julius II (r. 1503–1513). He suppressed the Borgias and placed their newly conquered lands in Romagna under papal jurisdiction. Julius came to be known as the "warrior pope" because he brought the Renaissance papacy to a peak of military prowess and diplomatic intrigue. Shocked, as were other contemporaries, by this thoroughly secular papacy, the humanist Erasmus (1466?–1536), who had witnessed in disbelief a bullfight in the papal palace during a visit to Rome, wrote a popular anonymous satire entitled *Julius Excluded from Heaven*. This humorous account purported to describe the pope's unsuccessful efforts to convince Saint Peter that he was worthy of admission to heaven.

Assisted by his powerful allies, Pope Julius succeeded in driving the Venetians out of Romagna in 1509. Thus he ended Venetian claims in the region and fully secured the Papal States. Having realized this long-sought papal goal, Julius turned to the second major undertaking of his pontificate: ridding Italy of his former ally, the French invader. Julius, Ferdinand of Aragon, and Venice formed a second Holy League in October 1511, and within a short period Emperor Maximilian I and the Swiss joined them. By 1512 the league had the French in full retreat, and they were soundly defeated by the Swiss in 1513 at Novara.

The French were nothing if not persistent. They invaded Italy a third time under Louis's successor, Francis I (r. 1515–1547). French armies massacred Swiss soldiers of the Holy League at Marignano in September 1515, revenging the earlier defeat at Novara. The victory won from the pope the Concordat of Bologna in August 1516. This agreement gave the French king control over the French clergy in exchange for French recognition of the pope's superiority over church councils and his right to collect annates in France. This was an important compromise that helped keep France Catholic after the outbreak of the Protestant Reformation. But the new French entry into Italy also led to the first of four major wars with Spain in the first half of the sixteenth century: the Habsburg–Valois wars, none of which France won.

Niccolò Machiavelli

The period of foreign invasions made a shambles of Italy. The same period that saw Italy's cultural peak in the work of Leonardo, Raphael, and Michelangelo also witnessed Italy's political tragedy. One who watched as French, Spanish, and German armies wreaked havoc on this country was Niccolò Machiavelli (1469–1527). The more he saw, the more convinced he became that Italian political unity and independence were ends that justified any means.

A humanist and a careful student of ancient Rome, Machiavelli was impressed by the way Roman rulers and citizens had then defended their homeland. They possessed *Virtù*, the ability to act decisively and heroically for the good of their country. Stories of ancient Roman patriotism and self-sacrifice were Machiavelli's favorites, and he lamented the absence of such traits among his compatriots. Such romanticizing of the Roman past caused some exaggeration of both ancient virtue and contemporary failings. His Florentine contemporary, Francesco Guicciardini, a more sober historian less given to idealizing antiquity, wrote truer chronicles of Florentine and Italian history.

Machiavelli also held deep republican ideals, which he did not want to see vanish from Italy. He believed that a strong and determined people could struggle successfully with fortune. He scolded the

---

Major Political Events of the Italian Renaissance (1375–1527)

1378–1382	The Ciompi Revolt in Florence
1434	Medici rule in Florence established by Cosimo de' Medici
1454–1455	Treaty of Lodi allies Milan, Naples, and Florence (in effect until 1494)
1494	Charles VIII of France invades Italy
1494–1498	Savonarola controls Florence
1495	League of Venice unites Venice, Milan, the Papal States, the Holy Roman Empire, and Spain against France
1499	Louis XII invades Milan (the second French invasion of Italy)
1500	The Borgias conquer Romagna
1512–1513	The Holy League (Pope Julius II, Ferdinand of Aragon, Emperor Maximilian, and Venice) defeats the French
1513	Machiavelli writes *The Prince*
1515	Francis I leads the third French invasion of Italy
1516	Concordat of Bologna between France and the papacy
1527	Sack of Rome by imperial soldiers

Machiavelli Discusses the Most Important Trait for a Ruler

Machiavelli believed that the most important personality trait of a successful ruler was the ability to instill fear in his subjects.

✦ *Why did Machiavelli maintain that rulers must be feared? Do American politicians of today appear to embrace Machiavelli's theory?*

Here the question arises; whether it is better to be loved than feared or feared than loved. The answer is that it would be desirable to be both but, since that is difficult, it is much safer to be feared than to be loved, if one must choose. For on men in general this observation may be made: they are ungrateful, fickle, and deceitful, eager to avoid dangers, and avid for gain, and while you are useful to them they are all with you, offering you their blood, their property, their lives, and their sons so long as danger is remote, as we noted above, but when it approaches they turn on you. Any prince, trust-ing only in their words and having no other preparations made, will fall to his ruin, for friendships that are bought at a price and not by greatness and nobility of soul are paid for indeed, but they are not owned and cannot be called upon in time of need. Men have less hesitation in offending a man who is loved than one who is feared, for love is held by a bond of obligation which, as men are wicked, is broken whenever personal advantage suggests it, but fear is accompanied by the dread of punishment which never relaxes.

Niccolò Machiavelli, *The Prince* (1513), trans. and ed. by Thomas G. Bergin (New York: Appleton-Century-Crofts, 1947), p. 48.

Italian people for the self-destruction their own internal feuding was causing. He wanted an end to that behavior above all, so that a reunited Italy could drive all foreign armies out.

But were his fellow citizens up to such a challenge? The juxtaposition of what Machiavelli believed the ancient Romans had been with the failure of his contemporaries to attain such high ideals made him the famous cynic whose name—in the epithet *Machiavellian*—has become synonymous with ruthless political expediency. Only a strongman, he concluded in the end, could impose order on so divided and selfish a people; the salvation of Italy required, for the present, a cunning dictator.

It has been argued that Machiavelli wrote *The Prince* in 1513 as a cynical satire on the way rulers actually did behave and not as a serious recommendation of unprincipled despotic rule. To take his advocacy of tyranny literally, it is argued, contradicts both his earlier works and his own strong family tradition of republican service. But Machiavelli seems to have been in earnest when he advised rulers to discover the advantages of fraud and brutality, at least as a temporary means to the higher end of a unified Italy. He apparently hoped to see a strong ruler emerge from the Medici family, which had captured the papacy in 1513 with the pontificate of Leo X (r. 1513–1521). At the same time, the Medici family retained control over the powerful territorial state of Florence. The situation was similar to that of Machiavelli's hero Cesare Borgia and his father Pope Alexander VI, who had earlier brought factious Romagna to heel by placing secular family goals and religious policy in tandem. *The Prince* was pointedly dedicated to Lorenzo de' Medici, duke of Urbino and grandson of Lorenzo the Magnificent.

Whatever Machiavelli's hopes may have been, the Medicis were not destined to be Italy's deliverers. The second Medici pope, Clement VII (r. 1523–1534), watched helplessly as Rome was sacked by the army of Emperor Charles V in 1527, also the year of Machiavelli's death.

Revival of Monarchy in Northern Europe

After 1450 there was a progressive shift from divided feudal to unified national monarchies as "sovereign" rulers emerged. This is not to say that the dynastic and chivalric ideals of feudal monarchy vanished. Territorial princes did not pass from the scene; representative bodies persisted and in some areas even grew in influence. But in the late fifteenth and early sixteenth centuries, the old problem of the one and the many was decided in favor of the interests of monarchy.

The feudal monarchy of the High Middle Ages was characterized by the division of the basic powers of government between the king and his semiautonomous vassals. The nobility and the towns had acted with varying degrees of unity and success through evolving representative assemblies such as the English Parliament, the French Estates General, and the Spanish *Cortes* to thwart the centralization of royal power. Because of the Hundred Years' War and the Great Schism in the church, the nobility and the clergy were in decline by the late Middle Ages and less able to contain expanding monarchies.

The increasingly important towns began to ally with the king. Loyal, business-wise townspeople, not the nobility and the clergy, increasingly staffed the royal offices and became the king's lawyers, bookkeepers, military tacticians, and foreign diplomats. This new alliance between king and town broke the bonds of feudal society and made possible the rise of sovereign states.

In a sovereign state, the powers of taxation, war making, and law enforcement no longer belong to semiautonomous vassals but are concentrated in the monarch and are exercised by his or her chosen agents. Taxes, wars, and laws become national rather than merely regional matters. Only as monarchs became able to act independently of the nobility and representative assemblies could they overcome the decentralization that had been the basic obstacle to nation building. Ferdinand and Isabella of Spain rarely called the *Cortes* into session. The French Estates General did not meet at all from 1484 to 1560. Henry VII (r. 1485–1509) of England managed to raise revenues without going begging to Parliament after Parliament voted him customs revenues for life in 1485. Monarchs were also assisted by brilliant theorists, from Marsilius of Padua in the fourteenth century to Machiavelli to Jean Bodin in the sixteenth, who eloquently argued the sovereign rights of monarchy.

The many were, of course, never totally subjugated to the one. But in the last half of the fifteenth century, rulers demonstrated that the law was their creature. They appointed civil servants whose vision was no longer merely local or regional. In Castile, they were the *corregidores*, in England, the justices of the peace, and in France, bailiffs operating through well-drilled lieutenants. These royal ministers and agents could become closely attached to the localities they administered in the ruler's name. And regions were able to secure congenial royal appointments. Throughout England, for example, local magnates served as representatives of the Tudors. Nonetheless these new executives remained royal executives, bureaucrats whose outlook was "national" and whose loyalty was to the "state."

Monarchies also began to create standing national armies in the fifteenth century. The noble cavalry receded as the infantry and the artillery became the backbone of royal armies. Mercenary soldiers were recruited from Switzerland and Germany to form the major part of the "king's army." Professional soldiers who fought for pay and booty proved far more efficient than feudal vassals who fought simply for honor's sake. Monarchs who failed to meet their payrolls, however, faced a new danger of mutiny and banditry on the part of foreign troops.

The growing cost of warfare in the fifteenth and sixteenth centuries increased the need of monarchs for new national sources of income, but their efforts to expand royal revenues were hampered by the stubborn belief among the highest classes that they were immune from government taxation. The nobility guarded their properties and traditional rights and despised taxation as an insult and a humiliation. Royal revenues accordingly grew at the expense of those least able to resist, and least able to pay.

The monarchs had several options when it came to raising money. As feudal lords they could collect rents from their royal domain. They could also levy national taxes on basic food and clothing, such as the *gabelle*, or "salt tax," in France and the *alcabala*, or 10 percent sales tax on commercial transactions, in Spain. The rulers could also levy direct taxes on the peasantry. This they did through agreeable representative assemblies of the privileged classes in which the peasantry did not sit. The *taille*, which the French kings independently determined from year to year after the Estates General was suspended in 1484, was such a tax. Innovative fund-raising devices in the fifteenth century included the sale of public offices and the issuance of high-interest government bonds. But rulers did not levy taxes on the powerful nobility. Rather, they borrowed from rich nobles and the great bankers of Italy and Germany. In money matters, the privileged classes remained as much the kings' creditors and competitors as their subjects.

France

Charles VII (r. 1422–1461) was a king made great by those who served him. His ministers created a permanent professional army, which—thanks initially to the inspiration of Joan of Arc—drove the English out of France. And largely because of the enterprise of an independent merchant banker named Jacques Coeur, the French also developed a strong economy, diplomatic corps, and national administration during Charles's reign. These were the sturdy tools with which Charles's son and successor, the ruthless Louis XI (r. 1461–1483), made France a great power.

There were two cornerstones of French nation building in the fifteenth century. The first was the collapse of the English Empire in France following the Hundred Years' War. The second was the defeat of Charles the Bold and his duchy of Burgundy. Perhaps Europe's strongest political power in the mid-fifteenth century, Burgundy aspired to dwarf both France and the Holy Roman Empire as the leader of a dominant middle kingdom. It might have done so had not the continental powers joined in opposition.

When Charles the Bold died in defeat in a battle at Nancy in 1477, the dream of Burgundian Empire died with him. Louis XI and Habsburg emperor Maximilian I divided the conquered Burgundian lands between them, with the treaty-wise Habsburgs getting the better part. The dissolution of Burgundy ended its constant intrigue against the French king and left Louis XI free to secure the monarchy. The newly acquired Burgundian lands and his own Angevin inheritance permitted the king to end his reign with a kingdom almost twice the size of that with which he had started. Louis successfully harnessed the nobility, expanded the trade and industry so carefully nurtured by Jacques Coeur, created a national postal system, and even established a lucrative silk industry at Lyons (later transferred to Tours).

A strong nation is a two-edged sword. Because Louis's successors inherited a secure and efficient government, they felt free to pursue what proved ultimately to be a debilitating foreign policy. Conquests in Italy in the 1490s and a long series of losing wars with the Habsburgs in the first half of the sixteenth century left France by the mid-sixteenth century again a defeated nation almost as divided internally as during the Hundred Years' War.

Spain

Spain, too, became a strong country in the late fifteenth century. Both Castile and Aragon had been poorly ruled and divided kingdoms in the mid-fifteenth century. The union of Isabella of Castile (r. 1474–1504) and Ferdinand of Aragon (r. 1479–1516) changed that situation. The two future sovereigns married in 1469, despite strong protests from neighboring Portugal and France, both of whom foresaw the formidable European power the marriage would create. Castile was by far the richer and more populous of the two, having an estimated five million inhabitants to Aragon's population of under one million. Castile was also distinguished by its lucrative sheep-farming industry, run by a government-backed organization called the Mesta, another example of developing centralized economic planning. Although the marriage of Ferdinand and Isabella dynastically united the two kingdoms, they remained constitutionally separated. Each retained its respective government agencies—separate laws, armies, coinage, and taxation—and cultural traditions.

Ferdinand and Isabella could do together what neither was able to accomplish alone: subdue their realms, secure their borders, venture abroad militarily, and Christianize the whole of Spain. Between 1482 and 1492 they conquered the Moors in Granada. Naples became a Spanish possession in 1504. By 1512 Ferdinand had secured his northern borders by conquering the kingdom of Navarre. Internally, Ferdinand and Isabella won the allegiance of the *Hermandad*, a powerful league of cities and towns, which served them against stubborn landowners. Townspeople allied themselves with the crown and progressively replaced the nobility within the royal administration. The crown also extended its authority over the wealthy chivalric orders, a further circumscription of the power of the nobility.

Spain had long been remarkable among European lands as a place where three religions—Islam, Judaism, and Christianity—co-existed with a certain degree of toleration. This toleration was to end dramatically under Ferdinand and Isabella, who made Spain the prime exemplar of state-controlled religion.

Ferdinand and Isabella exercised almost total control over the Spanish church as they placed religion in the service of national unity. They appointed the higher clergy and the officers of the Inquisition. The Inquisition, run by Tomás de Torquemada (d. 1498), Isabella's confessor, was a key national agency established in 1479 to monitor the activity of converted Jews (*conversos*) and Muslims (*Moriscos*) in Spain. In 1492 the Jews were exiled and their properties were confiscated. In 1502 non-converting Moors in Granada were driven into exile by Cardinal Francisco Jiménez de Cisneros (1437–1517), under whom Spanish spiritual life remained largely uniform and successfully controlled. This was a major reason Spain remained a loyal Catholic country throughout the sixteenth century and provided a base of operation for the European Counter-Reformation.

Despite a certain internal narrowness, Ferdinand and Isabella were rulers with wide horizons. They contracted anti-French marriage alliances that came to determine a large part of European history in the sixteenth century. In 1496 their eldest daughter, Joanna, later known as "the Mad," married Archduke Philip, the son of Emperor Maximilian I. The fruit of this union, Charles I of Spain, was the first ruler over a united Spain; by his inheritance and election as emperor in 1519, he came to rule over a European kingdom almost equal in size to that of Charlemagne. A second daughter, Catherine of Aragon, wed Arthur, the son of the English king Henry VII. After Arthur's premature death, she was betrothed to his brother, the future King Henry VIII (r. 1509–1547), whom she married eight years later in 1509. The failure of this marriage became the key factor in the emergence of the Anglican church and the English Reformation.

The new power of Spain was also revealed in Ferdinand and Isabella's promotion of overseas exploration. They sponsored the Genoese adventurer Christopher Columbus (1451–1506), who arrived at the islands of the Caribbean while sailing west in search of a shorter route to the spice markets of the Far East. This patronage led to the creation of the Spanish Empire in Mexico and Peru, whose gold and silver mines helped to make Spain Europe's dominant power in the sixteenth century.

England

The latter half of the fifteenth century was a period of especially difficult political trial for the English. Following the Hundred Years' War, a defeated England was subjected to internal warfare between two rival branches of the royal family, the House of York and the House of Lancaster. This conflict, known to us today as the Wars of the Roses (because York's symbol, according to legend, was a white rose, and Lancaster's a red rose), kept England in turmoil from 1455 to 1485.

The Lancastrian monarchy of Henry VI (r. 1422–1461) was consistently challenged by the duke of York and his supporters in the prosperous southern towns. In 1461 Edward IV (r. 1461–1483), son of the duke of York, successfully seized power and instituted a strong-arm rule that lasted more than twenty years; it was only briefly interrupted in 1470–1471 by Henry VI's short-lived restoration. Assisted by loyal and able ministers, Edward effectively increased the power and finances of the monarchy.

His brother, Richard III (r. 1483–1485), usurped the throne from Edward's son, and after Richard's death, the new Tudor dynasty portrayed him as an unprincipled villain who had also murdered Edward's sons in the Tower of London to secure his hold on the throne. The best-known version of this characterization—unjust according to some—is found in Shakespeare's *Richard III*. Be that as it may, Richard's reign saw the growth of support for the exiled Lancastrian Henry Tudor, who returned to England to defeat Richard on Bosworth Field in August 1485.

Henry Tudor ruled as Henry VII (r. 1485–1509), the first of the new Tudor dynasty that would dominate England throughout the sixteenth century. To bring the rival royal families together and to make the hereditary claim of his offspring to the throne uncontestable, Henry married Edward IV's daughter, Elizabeth of York. He succeeded in disciplining the English nobility through a special instrument of the royal will known as the *Court of Star Chamber*. Created with the sanction of Parliament in 1487, the court was intended to end the perversion of English justice by "over-mighty subjects," that is, powerful nobles who used intimidation and bribery to win favorable verdicts in court cases. In the Court of Star Chamber, the king's councillors sat as judges and were not swayed by such tactics. The result was a more equitable court system.

It was also a court more amenable to the royal will. Henry shrewdly construed legal precedents to the advantage of the crown, using English law to further the ends of monarchy. He managed to confiscate noble lands and fortunes with such success that he was able to govern without dependence on Parliament for royal funds, always a cornerstone of strong monarchy. In these ways, Henry began to shape a monarchy that would develop into one of early modern Europe's most exemplary governments during the reign of his granddaughter, Elizabeth I.

The Holy Roman Empire

Germany and Italy were the striking exceptions to the steady development of politically centralized lands in the last half of the fifteenth century. Unlike England, France, and Spain, the Holy Roman Empire saw the many thoroughly repulse the one. In Germany territorial rulers and cities resisted every effort at national consolidation and unity. As in Carolingian times, rulers continued to partition their kingdoms, however small, among their sons. By the late fifteenth century, Germany was hopelessly divided into some 300 autonomous political entities.

The princes and the cities did work together to create the machinery of law and order, if not of union, within the divided empire. The emperor and the major German territorial rulers reached an agreement in 1356, the *Golden Bull*. It established a seven-member electoral college consisting of the archbishops of Mainz, Trier, and Cologne; the duke of Saxony; the margrave of Brandenburg; the count Palatine; and the king of Bohemia. This group also functioned as an administrative body. They elected the emperor and, in cooperation with him, provided what transregional unity and administration existed.

The figure of the emperor gave the empire a single ruler in law, if not in fact. The conditions of his rule and the extent of his powers over his subjects, especially the seven electors, were renegotiated with every imperial election. Therefore, the rights of the many (the princes) were always balanced against the power of the one (the emperor).

In the fifteenth century an effort was made to control incessant feuding by the creation of an imperial diet (*Reichstag*). This was a national assembly of the seven electors, the nonelectoral princes, and the sixty-five imperial free cities. The cities were the weakest of the three bodies represented in the diet. During such an assembly in Worms in 1495, the members won from Emperor Maximilian I (r. 1493–1519) an imperial ban on private warfare and the creation of a Supreme Court of Justice to enforce internal peace, and an imperial Council of Regency to coordinate imperial and internal German policy. The latter was very grudgingly conceded by the emperor because it gave the princes a share in executive power.

Although important, these reforms were still a poor substitute for true national unity. In the sixteenth and seventeenth centuries, the territorial princes became virtually sovereign rulers in their various domains. Such disunity aided religious dissent and conflict. It was in the cities and territories of still-feudal, fractionalized, backward Germany that the Protestant Reformation broke out in the sixteenth century.

The Northern Renaissance

The scholarly works of northern humanists created a climate favorable to religious and educational reforms on the eve of the Reformation. Northern humanism was initially stimulated by the importation of Italian learning through such varied intermediaries as students who had studied in Italy, merchants who traded there, and the Brothers of the Common Life. This last was an influential lay religious movement that began in the Netherlands and permitted men and women to live a shared religious life without making formal vows of poverty, chastity, and obedience.

The northern humanists, however, developed their own distinctive culture. They tended to come from more diverse social backgrounds and to be more devoted to religious reforms than their Italian counterparts. They were also more willing to write for lay audiences as well as for a narrow intelligentsia. Thanks to the invention of printing with movable type, it became possible for humanists to convey their educational ideals to laypeople and clerics alike. Printing gave new power and influence to elites in both church and state, who now could popularize their viewpoints freely and widely.

The Printing Press

A variety of forces converged in the fourteenth and fifteenth centuries to give rise to the invention of the printing press. Since the days of Charlemagne,

The printing press made possible the diffusion of Renaissance learning. But no book stimulated thought more at this time than did the Bible. With Gutenberg's publication of a printed Bible in 1454, scholars gained access to a dependable, standardized text, so that Scripture could be discussed and debated as never before. [Huntington Library]

kings and princes had encouraged schools and literacy to help provide educated bureaucrats to staff the offices of their kingdoms. Without people who could read, think critically, and write reliable reports, no kingdom, large or small, could be properly governed. By the fifteenth century, a new literate lay public had been created, thanks to the enormous expansion of schools and universities during the late Middle Ages (the number of universities more than tripled between 1300 and 1500, growing from twenty to seventy).

The invention of a process of cheap paper manufacture also helped to make books economical and to broaden their content. Manuscript books had been inscribed on vellum, a cumbersome and expensive medium. (It required 170 calfskins or 300 sheepskins to make a single vellum Bible.) Single-sheet woodcuts had long been printed. This involved carving a block of wood and inking it, then stamping out as many copies as one could make before the wood deteriorated. The end product was much like a modern poster.

In response to the demand for books created by the expansion of lay literacy, Johann Gutenberg (d. 1468) invented printing with movable type in the mid-fifteenth century in the German city of Mainz, the center of printing for the whole of western Europe. Thereafter, books were rapidly and handsomely produced on topics both profound and practical, and intended for ordinary lay readers, scholars,

and clerics alike. Especially popular in the early decades of print were books of piety and religion, calendars and almanacs, and "how-to" books (for example, on child rearing, making brandies and liquors, curing animals, and farming successfully).

The new technology proved enormously profitable to printers, whose numbers exploded. By 1500, within a scant fifty years of Gutenberg's press, printing presses operated in at least sixty German cities and in more than 200 cities throughout Europe. The printing press was a boon to the careers of humanists, who now gained international audiences.

Literacy deeply affected people everywhere, nurturing self-esteem and a critical frame of mind. By standardizing texts, the print revolution made anyone who could read an instant authority. Rulers in church and state now had to deal with a less credulous and docile laity. Print was also a powerful tool for political and religious propaganda as well. Kings could now indoctrinate people as never before, and the clergy found themselves able to mass produce both indulgences and pamphlets.

Erasmus

The far-reaching influence of Desiderius Erasmus (1466?–1536), the most famous of the northern humanists and the "prince of the humanists," illustrates the impact of the printing press. Erasmus gained fame both as an educational and as a religious reformer. His life and work make clear that many loyal Catholics wanted major reforms long before the Reformation made them a reality.

Erasmus earned his living by tutoring when patrons were scarce. He prepared short Latin dialogues for his students that were intended to teach them how to speak and live well, inculcating good manners and language by encouraging them to imitate what they read.

These dialogues were published under the title *Colloquies*; they grew in number and length in consecutive editions, coming also to embrace anticlerical dialogues and satires on popular religious superstition. Erasmus collected ancient and contemporary proverbs as well, which he published under the title *Adages*. Beginning with about 800 examples, he increased his collection to more than 5,000 in the final edition of the work. Among the sayings that the *Adages* popularized are such common modern expressions as "to leave no stone unturned" and "where there is smoke, there is fire."

Erasmus aspired to unite the classical ideals of humanity and civic virtue with the Christian ideals of love and piety. He believed that disciplined study of the classics and the Bible, if begun early enough, was the best way to reform both individuals and society. He summarized his own beliefs with the phrase *philosophia Christi*, a simple, ethical piety in imitation of Christ. He set this ideal in starkest contrast to what he believed to be the dogmatic, ceremonial, and factious religious practice of the later Middle Ages. What most offended him about the Scholastics, both those of the late Middle Ages and, increasingly, the new Lutheran ones, was their letting doctrine and disputation overshadow humble piety and Christian practice.

To promote his own religious beliefs, Erasmus labored to make the ancient Christian sources available in their original versions. He believed that only as people drank from the pure, unadulterated sources could moral and religious health result. He edited the works of the Church fathers and produced a Greek edition of the New Testament (1516), which became the basis for his new, more accurate Latin translation (1519).

These various enterprises did not please church authorities. They were unhappy with both Erasmus's "improvements" on the Vulgate, Christendom's Bible for over a thousand years, and his popular anticlerical satires. At one point in the mid-sixteenth century, all of Erasmus's works were placed on the *Index of Forbidden Books*. Erasmus also received Luther's unqualified condemnation for his views on the freedom of human will. Still, Erasmus's works became basic tools of reform in the hands of both Protestant and Catholic reformers.

Humanism and Reform

In France, Spain, England, and Germany, humanism stirred both educational and religious reform.

GERMANY Rudolf Agricola (1443–1485), the "father of German humanism," spent ten years in Italy and he introduced Italian learning to Germany when he returned. Conrad Celtis (d. 1508), the first German poet laureate, and Ulrich von Hutten (1488–1523), a fiery knight, gave German humanism a nationalist coloring hostile to non-German cultures, especially Roman. Von Hutten especially illustrates the union of humanism, German nationalism, and Luther's religious reform. A poet who admired Erasmus, he attacked indulgences and published an edition of Valla's exposé of the Donation of Constantine (see the earlier section on Valla). He died in 1523 the victim of a hopeless knights' revolt against the princes.

The *cause célèbre* that brought von Hutten onto the historical stage and unified reform-minded German humanists was the Reuchlin affair. Johann Reuchlin (1455–1522) was Europe's foremost Christian authority on Hebrew and Jewish learning. He wrote the first reliable Hebrew grammar by a Christian scholar and was personally attracted to Jewish mysticism. Around 1506 a Christian who had converted from Judaism, supported by the Dominican order in Cologne, began a movement to suppress Jewish writings. When this man, whose name was Pfefferkorn, attacked Reuchlin, many German humanists, in the name of academic freedom and good scholarship and not for any pro-Jewish sentiment, rushed to Reuchlin's defense. The controversy lasted several years and produced one of the great satires of the period, the *Letters of Obscure Men* (1515), a merciless satire of monks and Scholastics to which von Hutten contributed. When Martin Luther came under attack in 1517 for his famous ninety-five theses against indulgences, many German humanists saw a repetition of the Scholastic attack on Reuchlin and rushed to his side.

Thomas More (1478–1535), painted by Hans Holbein the Younger in 1527. The English statesman and author was beheaded by Henry VIII for his refusal to recognize the king's sovereignty over the English church. [The Frick Collection]

ENGLAND   Italian learning came to England by way of English scholars and merchants and visiting Italian prelates. Lectures by William Grocyn (d. 1519) and Thomas Linacre (d. 1524) at Oxford and those of Erasmus at Cambridge marked the scholarly maturation of English humanism. John Colet (1467–1519), dean of Saint Paul's Cathedral, patronized humanist studies for the young and promoted religious reform as well.

Thomas More (1478–1535), a close friend of Erasmus, is the best known English humanist. His *Utopia* (1516), a conservative criticism of contemporary society, rivals the plays of Shakespeare as the most-read sixteenth-century English work. Utopia depicted an imaginary society based on reason and tolerance that overcame social and political injustice by holding all property and goods in common and requiring everyone to earn their bread by their own work.

More became one of Henry VIII's most trusted diplomats. But his repudiation of the Act of Supremacy (1534), which made the king of England head of the English church in place of the pope (see Chapter 11), and his refusal to recognize the king's marriage to Anne Boleyn led to his execution in July 1535. Although More remained Catholic, humanism in England, as also in Germany, played an important role in preparing the way for the English Reformation.

FRANCE   The French invasions of Italy made it possible for Italian learning to penetrate France, stirring both educational and religious reform. Guillaume Budé (1468–1540), an accomplished Greek scholar, and Jacques Lefèvre d'Étaples (1454–1536), a biblical authority, were the leaders of French humanism. Lefèvre's scholarly works exemplified the new critical scholarship and influenced Martin Luther. Guillaume Briçonnet (1470–1533), the bishop of Meaux, and Marguerite d'Angoulême (1492–1549), sister of King Francis I, the future queen of Navarre, and a successful spiritual writer in her own right, cultivated a generation of young reform-minded humanists. The future Protestant reformer John Calvin was a product of this native reform circle.

SPAIN   Whereas in England, France, and Germany, humanism prepared the way for Protestant reforms, in Spain it entered the service of the Catholic Church. Here the key figure was Francisco Jiménez de Cisneros (1437–1517), a confessor to Queen Isabella, and after 1508 the "Grand Inquisitor"—a position that allowed him to enforce the strictest religious orthodoxy. Jiménez founded the University of Alcalá near Madrid in 1509, printed a Greek edition of the New Testament, and translated many religious tracts designed to reform clerical life and better direct lay piety. His great achievement, taking fifteen years to complete, was the *Complutensian Polyglot Bible*, a six-volume work that placed the Hebrew, Greek, and Latin versions of the Bible in parallel columns. Such scholarly projects and internal church reforms joined with the repressive measures of Ferdinand and Isabella to keep Spain strictly Catholic throughout the Age of Reformation.

Voyages of Discovery and the New Empire in the West

On the eve of the Reformation, the geographical as well as the intellectual horizons of Western people were changing. The fifteenth century saw the beginning of western Europe's global expansion and the transference of commercial supremacy from the Mediterranean and the Baltic to the Atlantic seaboard.

Gold and Spices

Mercenary motives, reinforced by traditional missionary ideals, inspired the Portuguese prince Henry the Navigator (1394–1460) to sponsor the Portuguese exploration of the African coast. His main object was the gold trade, which for centuries Muslims had monopolized. By the last decades of the fifteenth century, gold from Guinea was entering Europe by way of Portuguese ships calling at the port cities of Lisbon and Antwerp, rather than by the traditional Arab land routes. Antwerp became the financial center of Europe, a commercial crossroads where the enterprise and derring-do of the Portuguese, the Spanish, and especially the Flemish met the capital funds of the German banking houses of Fugger and Welser.

The rush for gold quickly expanded into a rush for the spice markets of India. In the fifteenth century the diet of most Europeans was a dull combination of bread and gruel, cabbage, turnips, peas, lentils, and onions, together with what meat became available during seasonal periods of slaughter. Spices, especially pepper and cloves, were in great demand both to preserve and to enhance the taste of food.

Bartholomew Dias (d. 1500) opened the Portuguese Empire in the East when he rounded the Cape of Good Hope at the tip of Africa in 1487. A decade later, in 1498, Vasco da Gama (d. 1524) reached the coast of India. When he returned to Portugal, he brought with him a cargo worth sixty times the cost of the voyage. Later, the Portuguese established themselves firmly on the Malabar Coast with colonies in Goa and Calcutta and successfully challenged the Arabs and the Venetians for control of the European spice trade. (See Political Transformations, pp. 360.)

While the Portuguese concentrated on the Indian Ocean, the Spanish set sail across the Atlantic. They did so in the hope of establishing a shorter route to the rich spice markets of the East Indies. But rather than beating the Portuguese at their own game, Christopher Columbus (1451–1506) came upon the Americas instead.

Amerigo Vespucci (1451–1512) and Ferdinand Magellan (1480–1521) showed that these new lands were not the outermost territory of the Far East, as

Columbus died believing. Their travels proved the lands to be an entirely new continent that opened on the still greater Pacific Ocean. Magellan, in search of a westward route to the East Indies, died in the Philippines.

The Spanish Empire in the New World

Columbus's voyage of 1492 marked, unknowingly to those who undertook and financed it, the beginning of more than three centuries of Spanish conquest, exploitation, and administration of a vast American empire. That imperial venture produced important results for the cultures of both the European and the American continents. The gold and silver extracted from its American possessions financed Spain's major role in the religious and political conflicts of the age and contributed to European inflation of the sixteenth century.

In large expanses of both South and North America, Spanish government set an imprint of Roman Catholicism, economic dependence, and hierarchical social structure that has endured to the present day. Such influence was already clear with Columbus. On October 12, 1492, after a thirty-three day voyage from the Canary Islands, Columbus landed in San Salvador (Watlings Island) in the eastern Bahamas. He thought that he was on an outer island of Japan (or what he called Cipangu); he had undertaken his journey in the mistaken notion that the island of Japan would be the first land mass he would reach as he sailed west. This belief was based on Marco Polo's accounts of his years in China in the thirteenth century and the first globe map of the world, by Martin Behaim. That map, published in 1492, showed only ocean between the west coast of Europe and the east coast of Asia. Not until his third voyage to the Caribbean did Columbus realize that the island of Cuba was not Japan and that the South American continent beyond it was not China.

When Columbus landed in San Salvador, his three ships were met on the beach by naked and extremely friendly natives. Like all the natives Columbus met on his first voyage, they were Taino Indians, who spoke a variant of a language known as Arawak. From the start, the natives' generosity amazed Columbus. They freely gave his men all the corn and yams they desired and many sexual favors as well. "They never say no," Columbus marveled. At the same time Columbus observed how very easily they could be enslaved.

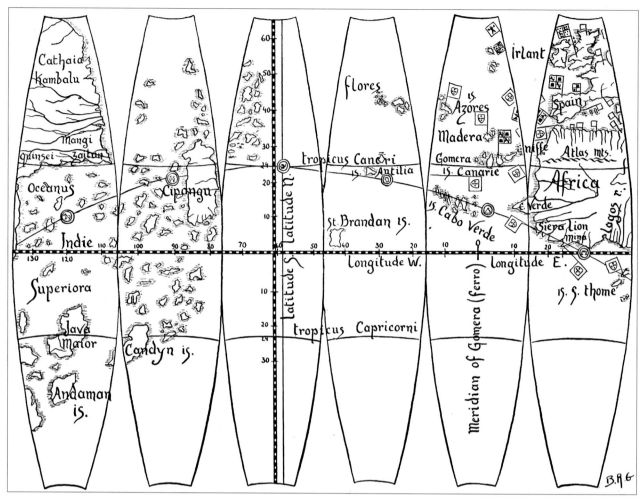

What Columbus knew of the world in 1492 was contained in this map by the Nuremberg geographer Martin Behaim, creator of the first spherical globe of the Earth. The ocean section of Behaim's globe is reproduced here. Departing the Canary Islands (in the second section from the right), Columbus expected his first major landfall to be Japan (Cipangu, in the second section from the left). When he landed at San Salvador, he thought he was on the outer island of Japan. And when he arrived in Cuba, he thought he was in Japan. [Reprinted from Samuel Eliot Morison, Admiral of the Ocean Sea. *Little, Brown and Company, Boston. 1942]*

A Conquered World

Mistaking the islands where he landed for the East Indies, Columbus called the native peoples whom he encountered "Indians." That name persisted even after it had become clear that this was new continent and not the East Indies. These native peoples had migrated across the Bering Straits from Asia onto the American landmass many thousands of years before the European voyages of discovery, creating communities all the way from Alaska to South America. The islands that Columbus mistakenly believed to be the East Indies came to be known as the West Indies.

Native Americans had established advanced civilizations going back to as early as the first millennium B.C.E. in two parts of what is today known as Latin America: Mesoamerica, which stretches from central Mexico into the Yucatan and Guatemala, and the Andean region of South America, primarily modern-day Peru and Bolivia. The earliest civilization in Mesoamerica, that of the Olmec, dates to about 1200 B.C.E. By the early centuries of the first millennium C.E. much of the region was dominated by the powerful city of Teotihuacán, which at the time was one of the largest urban centers in the world. The first millennium C.E. saw the flowering of the remarkable civilization of the Mayas in the

Yucatan region. The Mayans built large cities with immense pyramids and achieved considerable skills in mathematics and astronomy.

The first great interregional civilization in Andean South America, that of Chavín, emerged during the first millennium B.C.E. Regional cultures of the succeeding Early Intermediate Period (100–600 C.E.) included the Nazca on the south coast of Peru and the Moche on the north coast. The Huari-Tiahuanco culture again imposed interregional conformity during the Middle Horizon (600–1000). In the Late Intermediate Period, the Chimu Empire (800–1400) dominated the valleys of the Peruvian north coast. These early Andean societies built major ceremonial centers throughout the Andes, constructed elaborate irrigation systems, canals, and highways, and created exquisite pottery, textiles, and metalwork.

At the time of the arrival of the first Spanish explorers, the Aztec Empire dominated Mesoamerica and the Inca Empire dominated Andean South America. (See Map 10–3.) Both were very rich, and their conquest promised the Spanish the possibility of acquiring large quantities of gold.

THE AZTECS IN MEXICO The forebears of the Aztecs had arrived in the Valley of Mexico early in the twelfth century, where they lived as a subservient people. In 1428, under the leadership of Chief Itzcoatl, they rebelled against their rulers. That rebellion opened a period of Aztec conquest that reached its climax just after 1500. Their capital, Tenochtitlán (modern-day Mexico City), was located on an island in the center of a lake. By the time the Spanish conquerors arrived, the Aztecs governed many smaller tribes harshly, forcing labor and tribute from them. Believing that the gods must literally be fed with human bodies to guarantee continuing sunshine and soil fertility, the Aztecs also demanded and received thousands of captives each year to be sacrificed to their gods. Such policies left the Aztecs surrounded by terrorized tribes that felt no loyalty to them and longed for a liberator.

In 1519, Hernán Cortés landed on the coast of Mexico with a force of about 600 men. He opened communication with tribes nearby and then with Montezuma, the Aztec ruler. Montezuma initially believed Cortés to be a god. Aztec religion contained the legend of a priest named Quetzalcoatl who had been driven away four centuries earlier and had promised to return in the very year in which Cortés arrived. Montezuma initially attempted to

appease Cortés with gifts of gold. The Indians had recently been ravaged by epidemic diseases of European origin, principally smallpox, and were in no position to oppose him. After several weeks of negotiations and the forging of alliances with subject tribes, Cortés's forces marched on Tenochtitlán, conquered it, and imprisoned Montezuma, who later died under unexplained circumstances. The Aztecs tried to drive the Spanish out, but by late 1521 they were defeated after great loss of life. Cortés proclaimed the former Aztec Empire to be New Spain.

THE INCAS IN PERU The second great Native American civilization conquered by the Spanish was that of the Incas, located in the highlands of Peru. Like the Aztecs, they had conquered many neighboring states and tribes and by the early sixteenth century ruled harshly over several million subject people, whom they compelled to build their roads and cities, farm their lands, and fight their wars.

In 1531, largely inspired by Cortés's example in Mexico, Francisco Pizarro sailed from Panama and landed on the western coast of South America to undertake a campaign against the Inca Empire. His force included perhaps 200 men armed with guns and swords and equipped with horses, the military power of which the Incas did not fathom.

In late 1531, Pizarro lured the Inca chief Atahualpa into a conference, where he captured him and killed many of his followers. Atahualpa attempted to ransom himself by having a vast horde of gold transported from all over Peru to Pizarro. Discovering that he could not turn Atahualpa into a puppet ruler, Pizarro executed him in 1533. Division within the ranks of the Spanish conquerors prevented effective royal control of the sprawling Inca civilization until the late 1560s.

The conquests of Mexico and Peru stand among the most brutal episodes in modern Western history. One civilization armed with advanced weaponry subdued, in a remarkably brief time, two powerful peoples. Beyond the drama and bloodshed, these conquests made it very difficult for these Native American cultures to have a major impact on Western civilization. Some scholars believe, however, that the Iroquois tribes of North America set examples of freedom of speech, assembly, and religion that may have influenced the framers of the American Constitution.

The Spanish and the Native Americans made some accommodations to each other, but in the end

POLITICAL TRANSFORMATIONS

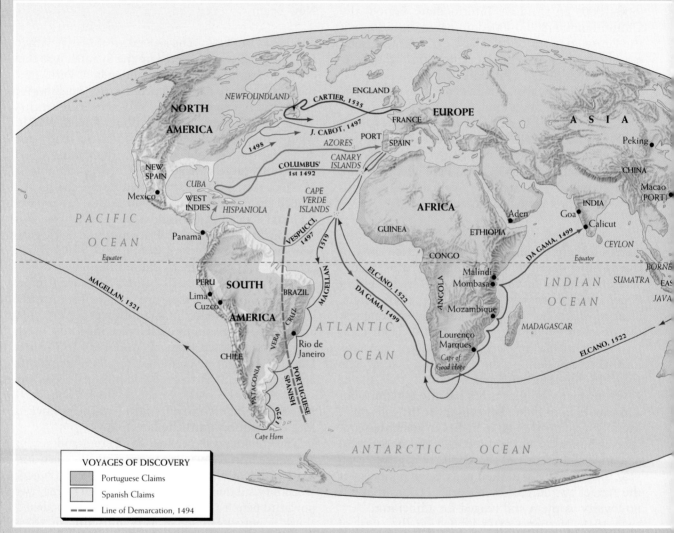

VOYAGES OF DISCOVERY

- Portuguese Claims
- Spanish Claims
- – – – Line of Demarcation, 1494

MAP 10–2

Voyages of Discovery and the Colonial Claims of Spain and Portugal

In 1487, Bartholew Diaz began a voyage around the Cape of Good Hope. His mission was benign—to map the geography of the African coast and assess the political stability of the people there with an eye to the possibilities for Western trade. Later voyages east and west would become increasingly less exploratory and benign. That was especially true of the voyages to the West Indies, Central America, and Mexico, where European settlement of the coastal regions drove native populations inland and established an aggressive Western rule and culture. By the late sixteenth and seventeenth centuries, European diseases greatly reduced native populations, causing planters and developers to import Europeans as indentured servants to replace native workers on the plantations of the new colonies. When the Europeans proved inadequate to the job, African slaves were brought across the ocean by the tens of thousands.

The transition from reconnaissance to settlement and exploitation of the world beyond Europe began with Vasco da Gama's voyage east in 1497. Focused strictly on commerce and carrying well-armed troops with an eye to establishing a Western trading empire, da Gama made the first passage across the southern Atlantic, arriving in Calcutta in 1498. En route, he had both peaceful and hostile confrontations with natives. Arriving at the Bay of São Braz (also called Mossel Bay and the site of Seal Island) while rounding the Cape of Good Hope in early December, 1497, he encountered the natives of South Africa for the first time. The journal that describes this encounter, written by an unidentified sailor, portrays the good intentions of the Portuguese visitors and the friendliness of most of the natives. It also makes clear the Europeans' condescension.

On Saturday [December 2] about two hundred negroes came, both young and old. They brought with them about a dozen oxen and cows and four or five sheep. As soon as we saw them we went ashore. They forthwith began to play on four or five flutes [known as "goras"], some producing high notes and others low ones, thus making a pretty harmony for negroes who are not expected to be musicians; and they danced in the style of negroes. The captain-major [da Gama] then ordered the trumpets to be sounded, and we, in the boats, danced, and the captain-major did so likewise. . . .

A Journal of the First Voyage of Vasco da Gama, 1497–1499, translated and edited by E.G. Ravenstein (London, Hakluyt Society, 1898), p. 11.

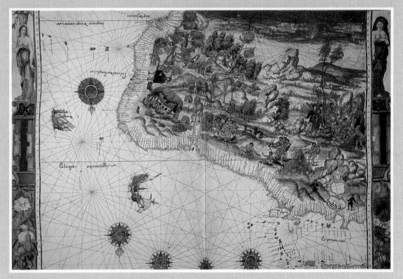

This map of Brazil, c1547, was drawn "upside-down," as if viewed from North America. Note Spanish cruelties to Indians, as well as scenes from daily life. [The Granger Collection, N.Y.]

European values, religion, economic goals, and language dominated. No group that retained indigenous religion, language, or values could become part of the new dominant culture or of the political power elite. In that sense, the Spanish conquests of the early sixteenth century marked the beginning of the process whereby South America was transformed into Latin America.

The Economy of Exploitation

From the beginning, the native peoples of America and their lands were drawn into the Atlantic economy and the world of competitive European commercialism. For the Indians of Latin America and somewhat later the blacks of Africa, that drive for gain meant various arrangements of forced labor.

There were three major components in the colonial economy of Latin America: mining, agriculture, and shipping. Each of them involved either labor or servitude or a relationship of dependence of the New World economy on that of Spain.

MINING The early *conquistadores*, or "conquerors," were primarily interested in gold, but by the middle of the sixteenth century, silver mining provided the chief source of metallic wealth. The great mining centers were Potosí in Peru and somewhat smaller sites in northern Mexico. The Spanish crown was particularly interested in mining because it received one-fifth (the *quinto*) of all mining revenues. For this reason, the crown maintained a monopoly over the production and sale of mercury, required in the silver-mining process. Exploring for silver never lost predominance during the colonial era. Its production by forced labor for the benefit of Spaniards and the Spanish crown epitomized the wholly extractive economy that stood at the foundation of colonial life.

AGRICULTURE The major rural and agricultural institution of the Spanish colonies was the *hacienda*. This was a large landed estate owned by persons originally born in Spain (*peninsulares*) or persons of Spanish descent born in America (*creoles*). Laborers on the hacienda usually stood in some relation of formal servitude to the owner and were rarely free to move from the services of one landowner to another.

The *hacienda* economy produced two major products: foodstuffs for mining areas and urban cen-

A sixteenth-century Aztec drawing depicts the Spanish conquest of Mexico. [The Bettmann Archive]

ters and leather goods used in mining machinery. Both farming and ranching were subordinate to the mine economy.

In the West Indies, the basic agricultural unit was the plantation. In Cuba, Hispaniola, Puerto Rico, and other islands, the labor of black slaves from Africa produced sugar to supply an almost insatiable demand for the product in Europe.

A final major area of economic activity in the Spanish colonies was urban service occupations. These included government offices, the legal profession, and shipping. Their practitioners were either *peninsulares* or *creoles*, with the former dominating more often than not.

LABOR SERVITUDE All of this extractive and exploitive economic activity required labor, and the Spanish in the New World decided very early that the native population would supply that labor. A series of social devices was used to draw them into the new economic life imposed by the Spanish.

The first of these was the *encomienda*. This was a formal grant of the right to the labor of a specific number of Indians, usually a few hundred, but sometimes thousands, for a particular period of time. The institution stood in decline by the middle of the sixteenth century because the Spanish monarchs feared that the holders of *encomienda* might become a powerful independent nobility in the New World. They were also persuaded on humani-

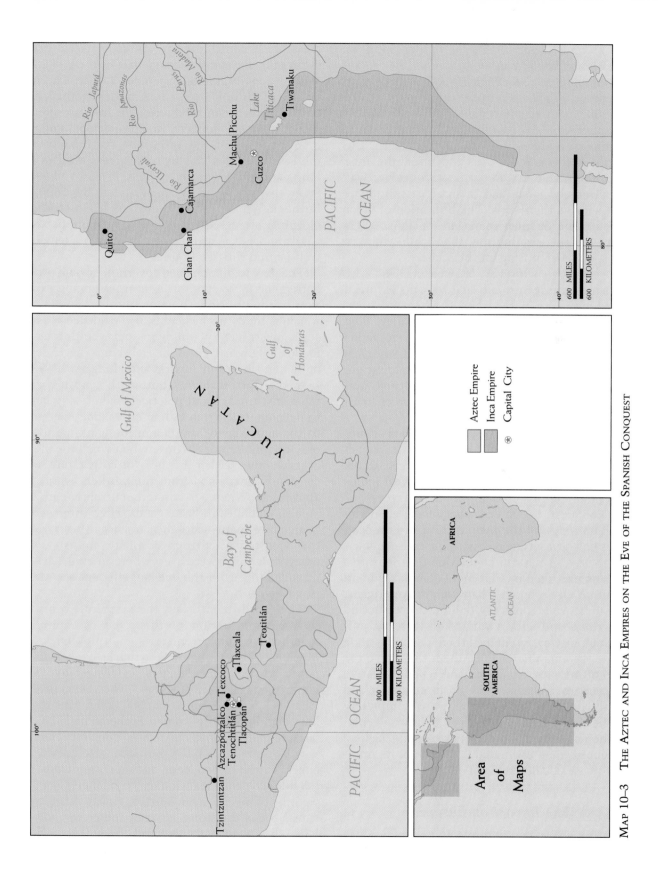

MAP 10–3   The Aztec and Inca Empires on the Eve of the Spanish Conquest

Aztec Empire
Inca Empire
⊛ Capital City

Area
of
Maps

tarian grounds against this particular kind of exploitation of the Indians.

The passing of the *encomienda* led to a new arrangement of labor servitude, the *repartimiento*. This device required adult male Indians to devote a certain number of days of labor annually to Spanish economic enterprises. In the mines of Peru, the *repartimiento* was known as the *mita*, the Inca term for their labor tax. *Repartimiento* service was often extremely harsh, and in some cases Indians did not survive their stint. The limitation of labor time led some Spanish managers to abuse their workers on the assumption that fresh workers would soon be appearing on the scene.

The eventual shortage of workers and the crown's pressure against extreme versions of forced labor led to the use of free labor. The freedom, however, was more in appearance than reality. Free Indian laborers were required to purchase goods from the land or mine owner, to whom they became forever indebted. This form of exploitation, known as *debt peonage*, continued in Latin America long after the nineteenth-century wars of liberation.

Black slavery was the final mode of forced or subservient labor in the New World. Both the Spanish and the Portuguese had earlier used African slaves in Europe. The sugar plantations of the West Indies now became the major center of black slavery.

The conquest, the forced labor of the economy of exploitation, and the introduction of European diseases had devastating demographic consequences for the Native American population. For centuries Europeans had lived in a far more complex human and animal environment than Native Americans. They had frequent contact with different ethnic and racial groups and with a variety of domestic animals. Such interaction helped them develop strong immune systems that enabled them to survive the ravages of measles, smallpox, and typhoid. Native Americans, by contrast, grew up in a simpler and more sterile environment and were completely defenseless against these diseases. Within a generation the native population of New Spain (Mexico) was reduced to an estimated 8 percent of its numbers, from 25,000,000 to 2,000,000.

The Impact on Europe

The influx of spices and precious metals into Europe from the new Spanish Empire was a mixed blessing. It contributed to a steady rise in prices during the sixteenth century that created an inflation rate estimated at 2 percent a year. The new supply of bullion from the Americas joined with enlarged European production to increase greatly the amount of coinage in circulation, and this increase in turn fed inflation. Fortunately, the increase in prices was by and large spread over a long period and was not sudden. Prices doubled in Spain by mid-century, quadrupled by 1600. In Luther's Wittenberg, the cost of basic food and clothing increased almost 100 percent between 1519 and 1540. Generally wages and rents remained well behind the rise in prices.

The new wealth enabled governments and private entrepreneurs to sponsor basic research and expansion in the printing, shipping, mining, textile, and weapons industries. There is also evidence of large-scale government planning in such ventures as the French silk industry and the Habsburg–Fugger development of mines in Austria and Hungary.

In the thirteenth and fourteenth centuries capitalist institutions and practices had already begun to develop in the rich Italian cities (one may point to the activities of the Florentine banking houses of Bardi and Peruzzi). Those who owned the means of production, either privately or corporately, were clearly distinguished from the workers who operated them. Wherever possible, entrepreneurs created monopolies in basic goods. High interest was charged on loans—actual, if not legal, usury. And the "capitalist" virtues of thrift, industry, and orderly planning were everywhere in evidence—all intended to permit the free and efficient accumulation of wealth.

The late fifteenth and the sixteenth centuries saw the maturation of this type of capitalism together with its attendant social problems. The Medicis of Florence grew very rich as bankers of the pope, as did the Fuggers of Augsburg, who bankrolled Habsburg rulers. The Fuggers lent Charles I of Spain more than 500,000 florins to buy his election as Holy Roman Emperor in 1519, and boasted that they had created the emperor. The new wealth and industrial expansion also raised the expectations of the poor and the ambitious and heightened the reactionary tendencies of the wealthy. This effect, in turn, aggravated the traditional social divisions between the clergy and the laity, the urban patriciate and the guilds, and the landed nobility and the agrarian peasantry.

Montaigne on "Cannibals" in Foreign Lands

The French philosopher Michel de Montaigne (1533–1592) had seen a Brazilian native in Rouen in 1562, an alleged cannibal brought to France by the explorer Villegagnon. The experience gave rise to an essay on the subject of what constitutes a "savage." Montaigne concluded that no people on earth were more barbarous than Europeans who take natives of other lands captive.

♦ *Is Montaigne romanticizing New World natives? Is he being too hard on Europeans? Had the Aztecs or Incas had the ability to discover and occupy Europe, would they have enslaved and exploited Europeans?*

Now, to return to my subject, I think there is nothing barbarous and savage in that nation [Brazil], from what I have been told . . . . Each man calls barbarism whatever is not his own practice; for indeed it seems we have no other test of truth and reason than the example and pattern of the opinions and customs of the country we live in. There [we] always [find] the perfect religion, the perfect government, the perfect and accomplished manners in all things. Those [foreign] people are wild, just as we call wild the fruits that Nature has produced by herself and in her normal course; where really it is those that we have changed artificially and led astray from the common order that we should rather call wild. The former retain alive and vigorous their genuine virtues and properties, which we have debased in the latter by adapting them to gratify our corrupted taste. And yet for all that, the savor and delicacy of some uncultivated fruits of those countries is quite as excellent, even to our taste, as that of our own. It is not reasonable that [our human] art should win the place of honor over our great and powerful mother Nature. We have so overloaded the beauty and richness of her works by our inventions that we have quite smothered her. Yet wherever her purity shines forth, she wonderfully puts to shame our vain and frivolous attempts: "Ivy comes readier without our care;/In lonely caves the arbutus grows more fair;/No art with artless bird song can compare."[1] All our efforts cannot even succeed in reproducing the nest of the tiniest little bird, its contexture, its beauty and convenience; or even the web of the puny spider. All things, says Plato,[2] are produced by nature, by fortune, or by art; the greatest and most beautiful by one or the other of the first two, the least and most imperfect by the last.

These nations, then, seem to me "barbarous" in this sense, that they have been fashioned very little by the human mind, and are still very close to their original naturalness. The laws of nature still rule them, very little corrupted by ours; and they are in such a state of purity that I am sometimes vexed that they were unknown earlier, in the days when there were men able to judge them better than we.

[1]*Propertius, 1.11.10*
[2]*Laws, 10*

The Complete Essays of Montaigne, trans. by Donald M. Frame (Stanford: Stanford University Press, 1958), pp. 153–154.

These divisions may indirectly have prepared the way for the Reformation as well by making many people critical of traditional institutions and open to new ideas—especially those that seemed to promise greater freedom and a chance at a better life.

♦

As it recovered from national wars during the late Middle Ages, Europe saw the establishment of permanent centralized states and regional governments. The foundations of modern France, Spain,

England, Germany, and Italy were laid at this time. As rulers imposed their will on regions outside their immediate domains, the "one" progressively took control of the "many," and previously divided lands came together as nations.

Thanks to the work of Byzantine and Islamic scholars, ancient Greek science and scholarship found their way into the West in these centuries. Europeans had been separated from their classical cultural heritage for almost eight centuries. No other world civilization had experienced such a disjunction from its cultural past. The discovery of classical civilization occasioned a rebirth of intellectual and artistic activity in both southern and northern Europe. One result was the splendor of the Italian Renaissance, whose scholarship, painting, and sculpture remain among western Europe's most impressive achievements.

Ancient learning was not the only discovery of the era. New political unity spurred both royal greed and national ambition. By the late fifteenth century, Europeans were in a position to venture far away to the shores of Africa, the southern and eastern coasts of Asia, and to the New World of the Americas. European discovery was not the only outcome of these voyages; the exploitation of the peoples and lands of the New World revealed a dark side of Western civilization. Some penalties were paid even then. The influx of New World gold and silver created new human and economic problems on the European mainland. In some circles Europeans even began to question their civilization's traditional values.

Review Questions

1. Discuss Jacob Burkhardt's interpretation of the Renaissance. What criticisms have been leveled against it? How would you define the term *Renaissance* in the context of fifteenth- and sixteenth-century Italy?

2. How would you define *Renaissance humanism*? In what ways was the Renaissance a break with the Middle Ages, and in what ways did it owe its existence to medieval civilization?

3. Who were some of the famous literary and artistic figures of the Italian Renaissance? What did they have in common that might be described as "the spirit of the Renaissance"?

4. Why did the French invade Italy in 1494? How did this event trigger Italy's political decline?

How do the actions of Pope Julius II and the ideas of Niccolò Machiavelli signify a new era in Italian civilization?

5. A common assumption is that creative work proceeds best in periods of calm and peace. Given the combination of political instability and cultural productivity in Renaissance Italy, do you think this assumption is valid?

6. How did the Renaissance in the north differ from the Italian Renaissance? In what ways was Erasmus the embodiment of the northern Renaissance?

7. What factors led to the voyages of discovery? How did the Spanish establish their empire in the Americas? Why was the conquest so violent? What was the experience of native peoples during and after the conquest?

Suggested Readings

L. B. ALBERTI, *The Family in Renaissance Florence*, trans. by R. N. Watkins (1962). A contemporary humanist, who never married, explains how a family should behave.

M. ASTON, *The Fifteenth Century: The Prospect of Europe* (1968). Crisp social history, with pictures.

R. H. BAINTON, *Erasmus of Christendom* (1960). Charming presentation.

H. BARON, *The Crisis of the Early Italian Renaissance*, vols. 1 and 2 (1966). A major work, setting forth the civic dimension of Italian humanism.

B. BERENSON, *Italian Painters of the Renaissance* (1957). Eloquent and authoritative.

C. BOXER, *Four Centuries of Portuguese Expansion, 1415–1825* (1961). Comprehensive survey by the leading authority.

G. A. BRUCKER, *Renaissance Florence* (1969). Comprehensive survey of all facets of Florentine life.

G. A. BRUCKER, *Giovanni and Lusanna: Love and Marriage in Renaissance Florence* (1986). Love in the Renaissance shown to be more Bergman than Fellini.

J. BURCKHARDT, *The Civilization of the Renaissance in Italy* (1867). The old classic that still has as many defenders as detractors.

R. E. CONRAD, *Children of God's Fire: A Documentary History of Black Slavery in Brazil* (1983). Not for the squeamish.

A. W. CROSBY, *The Columbian Exchange: Biological and Cultural Consequences of 1492* (1973). A study of the epidemiological disaster that Columbus visited upon Native Americans.

E. L. EISENSTEIN, *The Printing Press As an Agent of Change: Communications and Cultural Transformations in Early Modern Europe*, 2 vols. (1979). Bold, stimulating account of the centrality of printing to all progress in the period.

W. K. Ferguson, *Europe in Transition, 1300–1520* (1962). A major survey that deals with the transition from medieval society to Renaissance society.

C. Gibson, *Spain in America* (1956). A splendidly clear and balanced narrative.

C. Gibson, *The Aztecs Under Spanish Rule: A History of the Indians of the Valley of Mexico* (1964). Exceedingly interesting book.

F. Gilbert, *Machiavelli and Guicciardini* (1984). The two great Renaissance historians lucidly compared.

M. Gilmore, *The World of Humanism, 1453–1517* (1952). A comprehensive survey, especially strong in intellectual and cultural history.

W. L. Gundersheimer (ED.), *French Humanism, 1470–1600* (1969). Essays summarizing research and provoking further study.

J. R. Hale, *Renaissance Europe: The Individual and Society, 1480–1520* (1971). A galloping social history.

L. Hanke, *Bartholome de Las Casas: An Interpretation of His Life and Writings* (1951). Biography of the great Dominican critic of Spanish exploitation of Native Americans.

J. Hankins, *Plato in the Renaissance* (1992). A magisterial study of how Plato was read and interpreted by Renaissance scholars.

D. Herlihy, *The Family in Renaissance Italy* (1974). Excellent on family structure and general features.

D. Herlihy and C. Klapisch-Zuber, *Tuscans and Their Families* (1985). Important work based on unique demographic data that gives the reader a new appreciation of quantitative history.

D. L. Jensen, *Renaissance Europe: Age of Recovery and Reconciliation* (1981). Up-to-date and comprehensive survey.

F. Katz, *The Ancient American Civilizations* (1972). An excellent introduction.

B. Keen and M. Wasserman, *A Short History of Latin America* (1984). A good survey with very helpful bibliographical guides.

R. Kelso, *Doctrine of the Lady of the Renaissance* (1978). Noblewomen in the Renaissance.

C. Klapisch-Zuber, *Women, Family, and Ritual in Renaissance Italy* (1985). Provocative, wide-ranging essays documenting Renaissance Italy as very much a man's world.

P. O. Kristeller, *Renaissance Thought: The Classic, Scholastic, and Humanist Strains* (1961). A master shows the many sides of Renaissance thought.

I. Maclean, *The Renaissance Notion of Women* (1980). An account of the views of Renaissance intellectuals and their sources in antiquity.

R. Marius, *Thomas More: A Biography* (1984). Eloquent analysis of the man as well as of the saint.

L. Martines, *Power and Imagination: City States in Renaissance Italy* (1980). Stimulating account of cultural and political history.

H. A. Miskimin, *The Economy of Early Renaissance Europe, 1300–1460* (1975). Shows interaction of social, political, economic, and cultural change.

S. E. Morrison, *Admiral of the Ocean Sea: A Life of Christopher Columbus* (1946). Still the authoritative biography.

E. Panofsky, *Meaning in the Visual Arts* (1955). Eloquent treatment of Renaissance art.

J. H. Parry, *The Age of Reconnaissance* (1964). A comprehensive account of exploration in the years 1450–1650.

P. Partner, *Renaissance Rome, 1500–1559: A Portrait of a Society* (1976). A description of the city from an insider's perspective.

M. M. Phillips, *Erasmus and the Northern Renaissance* (1956). A learned, rewarding account of the man and the movement.

J. B. A. Pocock, *The Machiavellian Moment in Florentine Political Thought and the Atlantic Republican Tradition* (1975). Traces the influence of Florentine political thought in early modern Europe.

I. A. Richter (ED.), *The Notebooks of Leonardo da Vinci* (1985). The master in his own words.

Q. Skinner, *The Foundations of Modern Political Thought I: The Renaissance* (1978). Broad survey, including absolutely every known political theorist, major and minor.

*Luther and the Wittenberg reformers with Elector John Frederick of Saxony (1532–1547),
painted about 1543. Luther is on the far left, Philip Melanchthon in the front on the far right.
[Lucas Cranach the Younger, German, 1515–1586, "Martin Luther and the Wittenberg
Reformers," (1926.55), oil on panel, 27⅝ x 15⅝ in. The Toledo Museum of Art, Toledo, Ohio;
Purchased with funds from the Libbey Endowment, Gift of Edward Drummond Libbey.]*

The Age of Reformation

K E Y   T O P I C S

- The social and religious background to the Reformation
- Martin Luther's challenge to the church and the course of the
  Reformation in Germany
- The Reformation in Switzerland, France, and England
- Transitions in family life between medieval and modern times

In the second decade of the sixteenth century, a
powerful religious movement began in Saxony in
Germany and rapidly spread throughout northern
Europe, deeply affecting society and politics as well
as the spiritual lives of men and women. Attacking what they believed to be burdensome superstitions that robbed people of both their money
and their peace of mind, Protestant reformers led a broad revolt against the
medieval church. In a short span of
time, hundreds of thousands of people
from all social classes set aside the

beliefs of centuries and adopted a more simplified
religious practice.

The Protestant Reformation challenged aspects
of the Renaissance, especially its tendency to follow
classical sources in glorifying human nature and its
loyalty to traditional religion. Protestants were
more impressed by the human potential for evil
than by the inclination to do good; they
encouraged parents, teachers, and magistrates to be firm disciplinarians. On the
other hand, Protestants also embraced
many Renaissance values, especially in

the sphere of educational reform and particularly with regard to training in ancient languages. Like the Italian humanists, the Protestant reformers prized the tools that allowed them to go directly to the original sources. For them this meant the study of the Hebrew and Greek scriptures, enabling them to root their consequent challenges to traditional institutions in biblical authority.

Society and Religion

The Protestant Reformation occurred at a time of sharp conflict between the emerging nation-states of Europe, bent on conformity and centralization within their realms, and the self-governing small towns and regions, long accustomed to running their own affairs. Since the fourteenth century, the king's law and custom had progressively overridden local law and custom almost everywhere. Many towns and territories were keenly sensitive to the loss of traditional rights and freedoms. Many townspeople and village folk perceived in the religious revolt an ally in their struggle to remain politically free and independent. The Reformation came to be closely identified in the minds of its supporters with what we today might call states' rights or local control.

Social and Political Conflict

The Reformation broke out first in the free imperial cities of Germany and Switzerland. There were about sixty-five such cities, and each was in a certain sense a little kingdom unto itself. The great majority had Protestant movements, but with mixed success and duration. Some quickly turned Protestant and remained so. Some were Protestant only for a short time. Others developed mixed confessions, frowning on sectarianism and aggressive proselytizing, and letting Catholics and Protestants live side by side with appropriate barriers.

What seemed a life-and-death struggle with higher princely or royal authority was not the only conflict cities were experiencing. They also suffered deep internal social and political divisions. Certain groups favored the Reformation more than others. In many places, guilds whose members were economically prospering and socially rising were in the forefront of the Reformation. The printers' guild is a prominent example. Its members were literate, sophisticated about the world, in a rapidly growing industry, and economically very ambitious. They also had an economic stake in fanning religious conflict with Protestant propaganda, which many of course also sincerely believed. Guilds with a history of opposition to reigning governmental authority also stand out among early Protestant supporters, regardless of whether their members were literate.

There is, in brief, evidence to suggest that people who felt pushed around and bullied by either local or distant authority—a guild by an autocratic local government, an entire city or region by a powerful prince or king—often perceived in the Protestant movement an ally, at least initially.

The Reformation broke out against a background of deep social and political divisions that bred resentment against authority. This early sixteenth-century woodcut by Georg Pencz presents a warning against tyranny. It shows a world turned upside down, with the hunted becoming the hunters. The rabbits capture the hunters and their dogs and subject them to the same brutal treatment—skinning, butchering, and cooking—that the hunters and dogs routinely inflict on rabbits. The message: tyranny eventually begets rebellion. [Hacker Art Books]

Injustice. This woodcut by an unknown artist compares the law, represented by the court scene in the center, to a spider's web, shown in the window on the right. Just as the web traps small, weak insects, the law ensnares the poor, seen hanging on the gallows and the wheel through the window on the left. And just as the large bee flies easily through the web, the rich and powerful escape punishment for their crimes. [Hacker Art Books]

Social and political experience thus coalesced with the larger religious issues in both town and countryside. A Protestant sermon or pamphlet seemed directly relevant, for example, to the townspeople of German and Swiss cities who faced incorporation into the territory of a powerful local prince, who looked on them as obedient subjects rather than as free citizens. When Martin Luther and his comrades wrote, preached, and sang about a priesthood of all believers, scorned the authority of ecclesiastical landlords, and ridiculed papal laws as arbitrary human inventions, they touched political as well as religious nerves. And this was as true in the villages as in the towns. Like city dwellers, the peasants on the land also heard in the Protestant sermon and pamphlet a promise of political liberation and even a degree of social betterment. More than the townspeople, the peasants found their traditional liberties—from fishing and hunting rights to representation at local diets—progressively being chipped away by the great secular and ecclesiastical landlords who ruled over them.

Popular Religious Movements and Criticism of the Church

The Protestant Reformation could also not have occurred without the monumental crises of the medieval church during the "exile" in Avignon, the Great Schism, the Conciliar period, and the Renaissance papacy. For increasing numbers of people, the medieval church had ceased to provide a viable foundation for religious piety. Many intellectuals and laypeople felt a sense of crisis about the traditional teaching and spiritual practice of the church. Between the secular pretensions of the papacy and the dry teaching of Scholastic theologians, laity and clerics alike began to seek a more heartfelt, idealistic, and—often, in the eyes of the pope—increasingly heretical religious piety. The late Middle Ages were marked by independent lay and clerical efforts to reform local religious practice and by widespread experimentation with new religious forms.

A variety of factors contributed to the growth of lay criticism of the church. The laity in the cities were becoming increasingly knowledgeable about the world and those who controlled their lives. They traveled widely—as soldiers, pilgrims, explorers, and traders. New postal systems and the printing press increased the information at their disposal. The new age of books and libraries raised literacy and heightened curiosity. Laypeople were increasingly able to take the initiative in shaping the cultural life of their communities.

From the Albigensians, Waldensians, Beguines, and Beghards in the thirteenth century to the Lollards and Hussites in the fifteenth, lay religious movements shared a common goal of religious simplicity in imitation of Jesus. Almost without exception they were inspired by an ideal of apostolic poverty in religion; that is, all wanted a religion of true self-sacrifice like that of Jesus and the first disciples. The laity sought a more egalitarian church, one that gave the members as well as the head of the church a voice, and a more spiritual church, one that lived manifestly according to its New Testament model.

THE MODERN DEVOTION   One of the most constructive lay religious movements in northern Europe on the eve of the Reformation was that of the Brothers of the Common Life, or what came to be known as the Modern Devotion. The brothers

fostered religious life outside formal ecclesiastical offices and apart from formal religious vows. Established by Gerard Groote (1340–1384), the Modern Devotion was centered at Zwolle and Deventer in the Netherlands. The brother and (less numerous) sister houses of the Modern Devotion, however, spread rapidly throughout northern Europe and influenced parts of southern Europe as well. In these houses clerics and laity came together to share a common life, stressing individual piety and practical religion. Lay members were not expected to take special religious vows or to wear special reli-

gious dress, nor did they abandon their ordinary secular vocations.

The brothers were also active in education. They worked as copyists, sponsored many religious and a few classical publications, ran hospices for poor students, and conducted schools for the young, especially for boys preparing for the priesthood or a monastic vocation. As youths, Nicholas of Cusa, Johann Reuchlin, and Desiderius Erasmus were looked after by the brothers. Thomas à Kempis (d. 1471) summarized the philosophy of the brothers in what became the most popular religious book of the period, the *Imitation of Christ*. This semimystical guide to the inner life was intended primarily for monks and nuns, but was widely appropriated by laity who also wanted to pursue the ascetic life.

The Modern Devotion has been seen as the source of humanist, Protestant, and Catholic reform movements in the sixteenth century. Some scholars, however, believe that it represented an individualistic approach to religion, indifferent and even harmful to the sacramental piety of the church. It was actually a very conservative movement. The brothers retained the old clerical doctrines and values, while placing them within the new framework of an active common life. Their practices clearly met a need for a more personal piety and a better-informed religious life. Their movement appeared at a time when the laity were demanding good preaching in the vernacular and were even taking the initiative to endow special preacherships to ensure it. The Modern Devotion permitted laypeople to practice a full religious life without surrendering their life in the world.

LAY CONTROL OVER RELIGIOUS LIFE   On the eve of the Reformation, Rome's international network of church offices, which had unified Europe religiously during the Middle Ages, began to fall apart in many areas. This collapse was hurried along by a growing sense of regional identity—incipient nationalism—and local secular administrative competence. The long-entrenched *benefice* system of the medieval church had permitted important ecclesiastical posts to be sold to the highest bidders and had left residency requirements in parishes unenforced. Such a system did not result in a vibrant local religious life. The substitutes hired by nonresident holders of *benefices* lived elsewhere, mostly in Rome. They milked the revenues of their offices, often performed their chores mechanically, and had neither firsthand knowledge of nor much sympathy with local needs and problems. Rare was the late medieval German town that did not have complaints about the maladministration, concubinage, or fiscalism of their clergy, especially the higher clergy (bishops, abbots, and prelates).

Communities had protested loudly the financial abuses of the medieval church long before Luther published his famous summary of economic grievances in 1520 in the *Address to the Christian Nobility of the German Nation*. The sale of indulgences in particular had been repeatedly attacked before Luther came on the scene. On the eve of the

Reformation, this practice had expanded to permit people to buy release from time in purgatory for both themselves and their deceased loved ones. Rulers and magistrates had little objection to their sale, and might even encourage it so long as a generous portion of the income they generated remained in the local coffers. But when an indulgence was offered primarily for the benefit of distant interests, as with the Saint Peter's indulgence protested by Luther, resistance arose for strictly financial reasons, because their sale drained away local revenues.

The sale of indulgences would not end until rulers found new ways to profit from religion, and the laity found a more effective popular remedy for religious anxiety. The Reformation provided the former by sanctioning the secular dissolution of monasteries and the confiscation of ecclesiastical properties. It held out the latter in its new theology of justification by faith.

City governments also undertook to improve local religious life on the eve of the Reformation by endowing preacherships. These positions, supported by *benefices*, provided for well-trained and dedicated pastors who could provide regular preaching and pastoral care that went beyond the routine performance of the mass and traditional religious functions. In many instances these preacherships became platforms for Protestant preachers.

Magistrates also carefully restricted the growth of ecclesiastical properties and clerical privileges. During the Middle Ages, canon and civil law had come to recognize special clerical rights in both property and person. Because they were holy places, churches and monasteries had been exempted from the taxes and laws that affected others. They were treated as special places of "sacral peace" and asylum. It was considered inappropriate for holy persons (clergy) to be burdened with such "dirty jobs" as military service, compulsory labor, standing watch at city gates, and other obligations of citizenship. Nor was it thought right that the laity, of whatever rank, should sit in judgment on those who were their shepherds and intermediaries with God. The clergy, accordingly, came to enjoy an immunity of place (which exempted ecclesiastical properties from taxes and recognized their right of asylum) and an immunity of person (which exempted the clergy from the jurisdiction of civil courts).

On the eve of the Reformation measures were passed to restrict these privileges and to end their abuses. Among them we find efforts to regulate ecclesiastical acquisition of new property, to circumvent the right of asylum in churches and monasteries (a practice that posed a threat to the normal administration of justice), and to bring the clergy under the local tax code. Governments had understandably tired of ecclesiastical interference in what to them were strictly political spheres of competence and authority.

Martin Luther and German Reformation to 1525

Unlike France and England, late medieval Germany lacked the political unity to enforce "national" religious reforms during the late Middle Ages. There were no lasting Statutes of Provisors and *Praemunire*, as in England, nor a Pragmatic Sanction of Bourges, as in France, limiting papal jurisdiction and taxation on a national scale. What happened on a unified national level in England and France occurred only locally and piecemeal within German territories and towns. As popular resentment of clerical immunities and ecclesiastical abuses, especially over the selling of indulgences, spread among German cities and towns, an unorganized "national" opposition to Rome formed. German humanists had long given voice to such criticism, and by 1517 it was pervasive enough to provide a solid foundation for Martin Luther's reform.

Luther (1483–1546) was the son of a successful Thüringian miner. He was educated in Mansfeld, Magdeburg (where the Brothers of the Common Life were his teachers), and Eisenach. Between 1501 and 1505 he attended the University of Erfurt, where the nominalist teachings of William of Ockham and Gabriel Biel (d. 1495) prevailed. After receiving his master of arts degree in 1505, Luther registered with the Law Faculty following his parents' wishes. But he never began the study of law. To the disappointment of his family, he instead entered the Order of the Hermits of Saint Augustine in Erfurt on July 17, 1505. This decision had apparently been building for some time and was resolved during a lightning storm in which Luther, terrified, crying out to Saint Anne for assistance (Saint Anne was the patron saint of travelers in distress), promised to enter a monastery if he escaped death.

Ordained in 1507, Luther pursued a traditional course of study. In 1510 he journeyed to Rome on the business of his order, finding there justification for the many criticisms of the church he had heard in Germany. In 1511 he moved to the Augustinian monastery in Wittenberg, where he earned his doctorate in theology in 1512. Thereafter, he became a leader within the monastery, the new university, and the spiritual life of the city.

Justification by Faith Alone

Reformation theology grew out of a problem then common to many of the clergy and the laity: the failure of traditional medieval religion to provide either full personal or intellectual satisfaction. Luther was especially plagued by the disproportion between his own sense of sinfulness and the perfect righteousness that medieval theology taught that God required for salvation. Traditional church teaching and the sacrament of penance proved to be of no consolation. Luther wrote that he came to despise the phrase "righteousness of God," for it seemed to demand of him a perfection he knew neither he nor any other human being could ever achieve. His insight into the meaning of "justification by faith alone" was a gradual process that extended between 1513 and 1518. The righteousness that God demands, he concluded, did not result from many religious works and ceremonies but was given in full measure to those who believe and trust in Jesus Christ, who alone is the perfect righteousness satisfying to God. To believe in Christ meant to stand before God clothed in Christ's sure righteousness.

The Attack on Indulgences

An indulgence was a remission of the temporal penalty imposed by priests on penitents as a "work of satisfaction" for their mortal sins. According to medieval theology, after the priest absolved a penitent of guilt for the sins, the penitent remained under an eternal penalty, a punishment God justly imposed for sin. After absolution, however, this eternal penalty was said to be transformed into a temporal penalty, a manageable "work of satisfaction" that the penitent might perform here and now (for example, prayers, fasting, almsgiving, retreats, and pilgrimages). Penitents who defaulted on such prescribed works of satisfaction could expect to suffer for them in purgatory.

At this point, indulgences, which had earlier been given to Crusaders who did not complete their penances because they had fallen in battle, became

Lutherans made Jesus' blessing of infants and small children (Mark 10:13) a new theme in art and a forceful polemic both against Catholics, who believed good works to be a condition of salvation, and Anabaptists, who rejected infant baptism. Lucas Cranach the Elder painted over twenty versions of this scene. Here he portrays Jesus directly accessible to those with simple childlike faith, who do no special good works and have nothing to recommend them except God's grace. [Elke Walford, Hamburger Kunsthalle]

an aid to laity, made genuinely anxious by their belief in a future suffering in purgatory for neglected penances or unrepented sins. In 1343 Pope Clement VI (r. 1342–1352) had proclaimed the existence of a "treasury of merit," an infinite reservoir of good works in the church's possession that could be dispensed at the pope's discretion. On the basis of this declared treasury the church sold "letters of indulgence," which covered the works of satisfaction owed by penitents. In 1476 Pope Sixtus IV (r. 1471–1484) extended indulgences also to purgatory.

Originally, indulgences had been given only for the true self-sacrifice of going on a Crusade to the Holy Land. By Luther's time, they were regularly dispensed for small cash payments (very modest sums that were regarded as a good work of alms-giving). They were presented to the laity as remitting not only their own future punishments, but also those of their dead relatives presumed to be suffering in purgatory.

In 1517 a Jubilee indulgence was proclaimed during the pontificate of Pope Julius II (r. 1503–1513) to raise funds for the rebuilding of Saint Peter's in Rome. It was preached on the borders of Saxony in the territories of Archbishop Albrecht of Mainz. Albrecht was much in need of revenues because of the large debts he had incurred in order to hold, contrary to church law, three ecclesiastical appointments. The selling of the indulgence was a joint venture by Albrecht, the Augsburg banking-house of Fugger, and Pope Leo X, half the proceeds going to the pope and half to Albrecht and his cred-

A contemporary caricature depicts John Tetzel, the famous indulgence preacher. The last lines of the jingle read: "As soon as gold in the basin rings, right then the soul to Heaven springs." It was Tetzel's preaching that spurred Luther to publish his ninety-five theses.[Courtesy Staatliche Lutherhalle]

Johannes Tezelus Dominicaner Münch/mit sei-
nen Römischen Ablaßkram/welchen er im Jahr Christi 1517. in Deutsch-
landen zu marckt gebracht/wie er in der Kirchen zu Pirn in seinem
Vaterland abgemahlet ist.

O ihr deutschen mercket mich recht/
Des heiligen Vaters Papstes Knecht/
Bin ich/vnd br in euch ist allein/
Zehn taufent vnd neun hundert carein/
Gnad vnd Ablaß von einer Sünd/
Vor euch/ewer Eltern/Weib vnd Rind/
Sol ein jeder gewehret sein
So viel ihr legt ins Kästelein/
So bald der Gülden im Becken klingt/
Im huy die Seel im Himel springt/

itors. The famous indulgence preacher John Tetzel (d. 1519) was enlisted to preach the indulgence in Albrecht's territories because he was a seasoned professional who knew how to stir ordinary people to action. As he exhorted on one occasion:

Don't you hear the voices of your dead parents and other relatives crying out, "Have mercy on us, for we suffer great punishment and pain. From this you could release us with a few alms. . . . We have created you, fed you, cared for you, and left you our temporal goods. Why do you treat us so cruelly and leave us to suffer in the flames, when it takes only a little to save us?"[1]

When on October 31, 1517, Luther, according to tradition, posted his ninety-five theses against indulgences on the door of Castle Church in Wittenberg, he protested especially against the impression created by Tetzel that indulgences actually remitted sins and released the dead from punishment in purgatory. Luther believed these claims went far beyond

[1]*Die Reformation in Augenzeugen berichten*, ed. by Helmar Junghaus (Düsseldorf: Karl Rauch Verlag, 1967), p. 44.

the traditional practice and seemed to make salvation something that could be bought and sold.

Election of Charles V

The ninety-five theses were embraced by humanists and other proponents of reform. The theses made Luther famous overnight and prompted official proceedings against him. In October he was called before the general of the Dominican order in Augsburg. But as sanctions were being prepared against Luther, Emperor Maximilian I died (January 12, 1519), and this event, fortunate for the Reformation, turned attention away from heresy in Saxony to the contest for a new emperor.

The pope backed the French king, Francis I. However, Charles I of Spain, a youth of nineteen, succeeded his grandfather and became Emperor Charles V. (See Map 11–1.) Charles was assisted by both a long tradition of Habsburg imperial rule and a massive Fugger campaign chest, which secured the votes of the seven electors. The electors, who

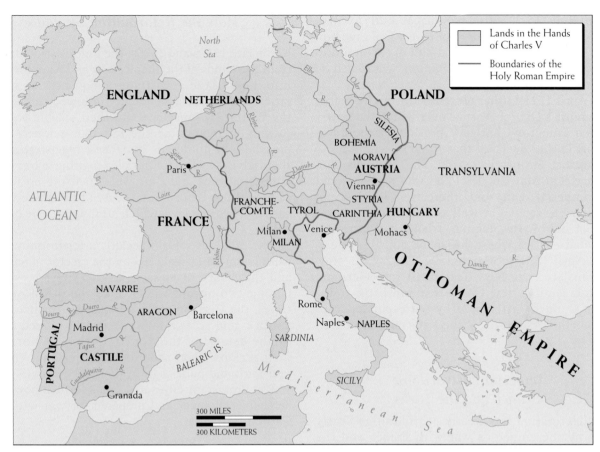

MAP 11–1 THE EMPIRE OF CHARLES V *Dynastic marriages and simple chance concentrated into Charles's hands rule over the lands shown here, plus Spain's overseas possessions. Crowns and titles rained down on him; election in 1519 as emperor gave him new distractions and responsibilities.*

traditionally enhanced their power at every opportunity, wrung new concessions from Charles for their votes. The emperor agreed to a revival of the Imperial Supreme Court and the Council of Regency and promised to consult with a diet of the empire on all major domestic and foreign affairs that affected the empire. These measures also helped the development of the Reformation by preventing unilateral imperial action against the Germans, something Luther could be thankful for in the early years of the Reformation.

Luther's Excommunication and the Diet of Worms

In the same month in which Charles was elected emperor, Luther entered a debate in Leipzig (June 27, 1519) with the Ingolstadt professor John Eck. During this contest, Luther challenged the infalli-

bility of the pope and the inerrancy of church councils, appealing, for the first time, to the sovereign authority of Scripture alone. He burned all his bridges to the old church when he further defended certain teachings of John Huss that had been condemned by the Council of Constance.

In 1520 Luther signaled his new direction with three famous pamphlets. The *Address to the Christian Nobility of the German Nation* urged the German princes to force reforms on the Roman church, especially to curtail its political and economic power in Germany. The *Babylonian Captivity of the Church* attacked the traditional seven sacraments, arguing that only two, Baptism and the Eucharist, were biblical, and exalted the authority of Scripture, church councils, and secular princes over that of the pope. The eloquent *Freedom of a Christian* summarized the new teaching of salvation by faith alone.

On June 15, 1520, Leo's papal bull *Exsurge Domine* condemned Luther for heresy and gave him sixty days to retract. The final bull of excommunication, *Decet Pontificem Romanum*, was issued on January 3, 1521.

In April 1521 Luther presented his views before the empire's Diet of Worms, over which the newly elected Emperor Charles V presided. Ordered to recant, Luther declared that to do so would be to act against Scripture, reason, and his own conscience. On May 26, 1521, he was placed under the imperial ban and thereafter became an "outlaw" to secular as well as to religious authority. For his own protection, friends hid him in a secluded castle, where he spent almost a year, from April 1521 to March 1522. During his stay, he translated the New Testament into German, using Erasmus's new Greek text and Latin translation , and he attempted by correspondence to oversee the first stages of the Reformation in Wittenberg.

Imperial Distractions: France and the Turks

The Reformation was greatly helped in these early years by the emperor's war with France and the advance of the Ottoman Turks into eastern Europe. Against both adversaries Charles V, who also remained a Spanish king with dynastic responsibilities outside the empire, needed German troops, and to that end he promoted friendly relations with the German princes. Between 1521 and 1559 Spain (the Habsburg dynasty) and France (the Valois dynasty) fought four major wars over disputed territories in Italy and along their borders. In 1526 the Turks overran Hungary at the Battle of Mohacs, while in western Europe the French-led League of Cognac formed against Charles for the second Habsburg–Valois war.

Thus preoccupied, the emperor agreed through his representatives at the German Diet of Speyer in 1526 that each German territory was free to enforce the Edict of Worms (1521) against Luther "so as to be able to answer in good conscience to God and the emperor." That concession, in effect, gave the German princes territorial sovereignty in religious matters and the Reformation time to put down deep roots. Later (in 1555) the Peace of Augsburg would enshrine such local princely control over religion in imperial law.

How the Reformation Spread

In the late 1520s and 1530s, the Reformation passed from the hands of the theologians and pamphleteers into those of the magistrates and princes. In many cities, the magistrates quickly followed the lead of the Protestant preachers and their sizable congregations in mandating the religious reforms they preached. In numerous instances, magistrates had themselves worked for decades to bring about basic church reforms and thus welcomed the preachers as new allies. Reform now ceased to be merely slogans and became laws which all townspeople had to obey.

The religious reform became a territorial political movement as well, led by the elector of Saxony and the prince of Hesse, the two most powerful German Protestant rulers. Like the urban magistrates, the German princes quickly recognized the political and economic opportunities offered them by the demise of the Roman Catholic Church in their regions. Soon they too were pushing Protestant faith and politics onto their neighbors. By the 1530s, Protestant cities and lands formed powerful defensive alliances and prepared for war with the Catholic emperor.

The Peasants' Revolt

In its first decade the Protestant movement suffered more from internal division than from imperial interference. By 1525 Luther had become as much an object of protest within Germany as was the pope. Original allies, sympathizers, and fellow travelers declared their independence from him.

Like the German humanists, the German peasantry also had at first believed Luther to be an ally. The peasantry had been organized since the late fifteenth century against efforts by territorial princes to override their traditional laws and customs and to subject them to new regulations and taxes. Peasant leaders, several of whom were convinced Lutherans, saw in Luther's teaching about Christian freedom and his criticism of monastic landowners a point of view close to their own. They openly solicited Luther's support of their political and economic rights, including their revolutionary request for release from serfdom.

Luther and his followers sympathized with the peasants. Indeed, for several years Lutheran pamphleteers made Karsthans, the burly, honest peasant

The peasant revolt of 1524–1525 frightened both Protestant and Catholic rulers, who united to suppress it. Many peasants died in the revolt, but in its early stages the peasant armies inflicted substantial casualties and committed atrocities of their own. Here Albrecht Dürer (1471–1528) portrays three armed peasants conversing. [Sachsische Landesbibliothek, Abteilung Deutsche Fotothek]

who earned his bread by the sweat of his brow and sacrificed his own comfort and well-being for others, a symbol of the simple life that God desired all people to live. The Lutherans, however, were not social revolutionaries. When the peasants revolted against their masters in 1524–1525, Luther, not surprisingly, condemned them in the strongest possible terms as "un-Christian" and urged the princes to crush their revolt without mercy. Tens of thousands of peasants (estimates run between 70,000 and 100,000) died by the time the revolt was put down.

For Luther, the freedom of the Christian was to be found in an inner release from guilt and anxiety, not in a right to restructure society by violent revolution. Had Luther supported the peasants' revolt, he would not only have contradicted his own teaching, but would probably also have ended any chance of the survival of his reform beyond the 1520s. Still, many believe that his decision

German Peasants Protest Rising Feudal Exactions

In the late fifteenth and early sixteenth centuries, German feudal lords, both secular and ecclesiastical, tried to increase the earnings from their lands by raising demands on their peasant tenants. As the personal freedoms of peasants were restricted, their properties confiscated, and their traditional laws and customs overridden, massive revolts occurred in southern Germany in 1525. Some historians see this uprising and the social and economic conditions that gave rise to it as the major historical force in early modern history. The following is the most representative and well-known statement of peasant grievances.

✦ *Are the peasants' demands reasonable given the circumstances of the sixteenth century? Are the peasants more interested in material than in spiritual freedom? Which of the demands are the most revolutionary?*

1. It is our humble petition and desire . . . that in the future . . . each community should choose and appoint a pastor, and that we should have the right to depose him should he conduct himself improperly. . . .

2. We are ready and willing to pay the fair tithe of grain. . . . The small tithes [of cattle], whether [to] ecclesiastical or lay lords, we will not pay at all, for the Lord God created cattle for the free use of man. . . .

3. We . . . take it for granted that you will release us from serfdom as true Christians, unless it should be shown us from the Gospel that we are serfs.

4. It has been the custom heretofore that no poor man should be allowed to catch venison or wildfowl or fish in flowing water, which seems to us quite unseemly and unbrotherly as well as selfish and not agreeable to the Word of God. . . .

5. We are aggrieved in the matter of woodcutting, for the noblemen have appropriated all the woods to themselves. . . .

6. In regard to the excessive services demanded of us which are increased from day to day, we ask that this matter be properly looked into so that we shall not continue to be oppressed in this way. . . .

7. We will not hereafter allow ourselves to be further oppressed by our lords, but will let them demand only what is just and proper according to the word of the agreement between the lord and the peasant. The lord should no longer try to force more services or other dues from the peasant without payment. . . .

8. We are greatly burdened because our holdings cannot support the rent exacted from them. . . . We ask that the lords may appoint persons of honor to inspect these holdings and fix a rent in accordance with justice. . . .

9. We are burdened with a great evil in the constant making of new laws. . . . In our opinion we should be judged according to the old written law. . . .

10. We are aggrieved by the appropriation . . . of meadows and fields which at one time belonged to a community as a whole. These we will take again into our own hands. . . .

11. We will entirely abolish the due called Todfall [that is, heriot or death tax, by which the lord received the best horse, cow, or garment of a family upon the death of a serf] and will no longer endure it, nor allow widows and orphans to be thus shamefully robbed against God's will, and in violation of justice and right. . . .

12. It is our conclusion and final resolution, that if any one or more of the articles here set forth should not be in agreement with the Word of God, as we think they are, such article we will willingly retract.

Translations and Reprints from the Original Sources of European History, *vol. 2 (Philadelphia: Department of History, University of Pennsylvania, 1897).*

ended the promise of the Reformation as a social revolution.

The Reformation Elsewhere

Although Luther's was the first, Switzerland and France had their own independent church reform movements almost simultaneously with Germany's. From them developed new churches as prominent and lasting as the Lutheran.

Zwingli and the Swiss Reformation

Switzerland was a loose confederacy of thirteen autonomous cantons, or states, and allied areas. (See MAP 11–2.) SOME cantons became Protestant, some remained Catholic, and a few other cantons and regions managed to effect a compromise. There were two main preconditions of the Swiss Reformation. First was the growth of national sentiment occasioned by popular opposition to foreign mercenary service (providing mercenaries for Europe's warring nations was a major source of Switzerland's livelihood). Second was a desire for church reform that had persisted in Switzerland since the councils of Constance (1414–1417) and Basel (1431–1449).

THE REFORMATION IN ZURICH Ulrich Zwingli (1484–1531), the leader of the Swiss Reformation, had been humanistically educated in Bern, Vienna, and Basel. He was strongly influenced by Erasmus, whom he credited with having set him on the path to reform. He served as a chaplain with Swiss mercenaries during the disastrous Battle of Marignano in Italy in 1515 and thereafter became an eloquent critic of mercenary service. Zwingli believed that this service threatened both the political sovereignty and the moral well-being of the Swiss confederacy. By 1518 Zwingli was also widely known for opposition to the sale of indulgences and to religious superstition.

In 1519 he entered the competition for the post of people's priest in the main church of Zurich. His candidacy was contested because of his acknowledged fornication with a barber's daughter, an affair he successfully minimized in a forcefully written self-defense. Actually, his conduct was less scandalous to his contemporaries, who sympathized with the plight of the celibate clergy, than it may be to the modern reader. One of Zwingli's first acts as a reformer was to petition for an end to clerical celibacy and for the right of all clergy to marry, a practice that quickly became accepted in all Protestant lands.

From his new position as people's priest in Zurich, Zwingli engineered the Swiss Reformation. In March 1522 he was party to the breaking of the Lenten fast—an act of protest analogous to burning one's national flag today. Zwingli's reform guideline was very simple and very effective. Whatever lacked literal support in Scripture was to be neither believed nor practiced. As had also happened with Luther, that test soon raised questions about such honored traditional teachings and practices as fasting, transubstantiation, the worship of saints, pilgrimages, purgatory, clerical celibacy, and certain sacraments. A disputation held on January 29, 1523, concluded with the city government granting its sanction to Zwingli's Scripture test. Thereafter Zurich became to all intents the center of the Swiss Reformation. The new regime imposed a harsh discipline that made the city one of the first examples of puritanical Protestantism.

THE MARBURG COLLOQUY Landgrave Philip of Hesse (1504–1567) sought to unite Swiss and German Protestants in a mutual defense pact, a potentially significant political alliance. His efforts were spoiled, however, by theological disagreements between Luther and Zwingli over the nature of Christ's presence in the Eucharist. Zwingli maintained a symbolic interpretation of Christ's words, "This is my body"; Christ, he argued, was only spiritually, not bodily, present in the bread and wine of the Eucharist. Luther, to the contrary, insisted that Christ's human nature could share the properties of his divine nature; hence, where Christ was spiritually present, he could also be bodily present, for his was a special nature. Luther wanted no part of an abstract, spiritualized Christ. Zwingli, on the other hand, feared that Luther had not broken sufficiently with medieval sacramental theology.

Philip of Hesse brought the two Protestant leaders together in his castle in Marburg in early October 1529, but they were unable to work out their differences on this issue. Luther left thinking Zwingli a dangerous fanatic. Although cooperation between the two sides did not cease, the disagreement splintered the Protestant movement theologically and politically. Separate defense leagues formed, and semi-Zwinglian theological views came to be embodied in the *Tetrapolitan Confession*. This confession of faith was prepared by the

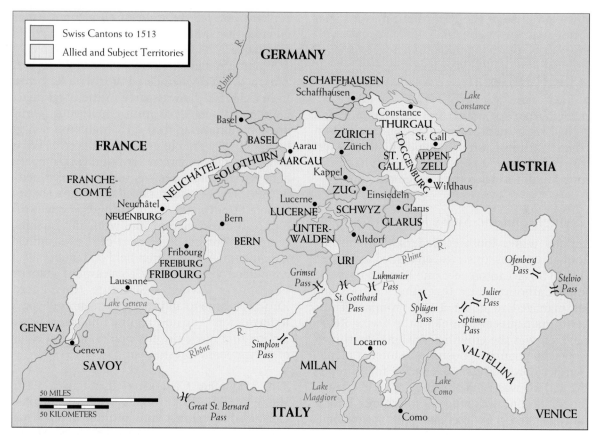

MAP 11–2   THE SWISS CONFEDERATION   *While nominally still a part of the Holy Roman Empire, Switzerland grew from a loose defensive union of the central "forest cantons" in the thirteenth century into a fiercely independent association of regions with different languages, histories, and, finally, religions.*

Strasbourg reformers Martin Bucer and Caspar Hedio for presentation to the Diet of Augsburg (1530) as an alternative to the Lutheran *Augsburg Confession.*

SWISS CIVIL WARS   As the Swiss cantons divided between Protestantism and Catholicism, civil wars began. There were two major battles, both at Kappel, one in June 1529 and a second in October 1531. The first ended in a Protestant victory, which forced the Catholic cantons to break their foreign alliances and to recognize the rights of Swiss Protestants. During the second battle Zwingli was found wounded on the battlefield and was unceremoniously executed, his remains scattered to the four winds so his followers would have no relics to console and inspire them. The subsequent treaty confirmed the right of each canton to determine its own religion. Heinrich Bullinger (1504–1575), who was Zwingli's protégé and later married his daugh-

ter, became the new leader of the Swiss Reformation and guided its development into an established religion.

Anabaptists and Radical Protestants

The moderate pace and seemingly low ethical results of the Lutheran and Zwinglian reformations discontented many people, among them some of the original followers of Luther and Zwingli. They desired a more rapid and thorough implementation of apostolic Christianity—that is, a more visible moral transformation—and accused the major reformers of going only halfway. The most important of these radical groups were the Anabaptists, the sixteenth-century ancestors of the modern Mennonites and Amish. The Anabaptists were especially distinguished by their rejection of infant baptism and their insistence on only adult baptism (Anabaptism derives from the Greek word meaning "to rebaptize"). They believed that baptism performed on a consenting adult conformed to Scripture and was more respectful of human freedom.

CONRAD GREBEL AND THE SWISS BRETHREN   Conrad Grebel (1498–1526), with whom Anabaptism originated, performed the first adult rebaptism in Zurich in January 1525. Initially a co-worker with Zwingli and an even greater biblical literalist, Grebel broke openly with Zwingli. In a religious disputation in October 1523, Zwingli supported the city government's plea for a very gradual removal of traditional religious practices.

The alternative of the Swiss Brethren, as Grebel's group came to be called, was embodied in the *Schleitheim Confession* of 1527. This document distinguished Anabaptists not only by their practice of adult baptism but also by their refusal to go to war, to swear oaths, and to participate in the offices of secular government. Anabaptists physically separated from society to form a more perfect community in imitation of what they believed to be the example of the first Christians. Because of the close connection between religious and civic life in this period, the political authorities viewed such separatism as a threat to basic social bonds.

THE ANABAPTIST REIGN IN MÜNSTER   At first, Anabaptism drew its adherents from all social classes. But as Lutherans and Zwinglians joined with Catholics in opposition to the Anabaptists and persecuted them within the cities, a more rural, agrarian class came to make up the great majority. In 1529, rebaptism became a capital offense throughout the Holy Roman Empire. Estimates are that between 1525 and 1618 at least 1,000 and perhaps as many as 5,000 men and women were executed for rebaptizing themselves as adults. Brutal measures were universally applied against nonconformists after Anabaptist extremists came to power in the German city of Münster in 1534–1535.

Led by two Dutch emigrants, a baker, Jan Matthys of Haarlem, and a tailor, Jan Beukelsz of Leiden, the Anabaptist majority in this city forced Lutherans and Catholics either to convert or to emigrate. The Lutherans and Catholics left and the city was blockaded by besieging armies. Münster transformed itself into an Old Testament theocracy, replete with charismatic leaders and the practice of polygamy. The latter was undertaken as a measure of social control because there were so many more women, recently widowed or deserted, than men in the city. Many women revolted against the practice and were allowed to leave the resented polygynous marriages.

The outside world was deeply shocked by such developments in Münster. Protestant and Catholic armies united to crush the radicals. The skeletons of their leaders long hung in public view as a warning to all who would so offend traditional Christian sensitivities. After this episode, moderate, pacifistic Anabaptism became the norm among most nonconformists. The moderate Anabaptist leader Menno Simons (1496–1561), the founder of the Mennonites, set the example for the future.

SPIRITUALISTS   Another radical movement, that of the Spiritualists, was made up mostly of isolated individuals distinguished by their disdain of all traditions and institutions. They believed that the only religious authority was God's spirit, which spoke here and now to every individual. Among them were several former Lutherans. Thomas Müntzer (d. 1525), who had close contacts with Anabaptist leaders in Germany and Switzerland, died as a leader of a peasants' revolt. Sebastian Franck (d. 1541), a freelance critic of all dogmatic religion, proclaimed the religious autonomy of every individual soul. Caspar Schwenckfeld (d. 1561) was a prolific writer and wanderer after whom the Schwenckfeldian Church is named.

ANTITRINITARIANS   A final group of radical Protestants was the Antitrinitarians, exponents of a commonsense, rational, and ethical religion. Chief among this group were the Spaniard Michael Servetus (1511–1553), executed in 1553 in Geneva for "blasphemies against the Holy Trinity," and the Italians Lelio (d. 1562) and Faustus Sozzini (d. 1604), the founders of Socinianism. These thinkers were the strongest opponents of Calvinism, especially its belief in original sin and predestination, and have a deserved reputation as defenders of religious toleration.

John Calvin and the Genevan Reformation

In the second half of the sixteenth century, Calvinism replaced Lutheranism as the dominant Protestant force in Europe. Calvinism was the religious ideology that inspired or accompanied massive political resistance in France, the Netherlands, and

A portrait of the young John Calvin. [Bibliothèque Publique et Universitaire, Geneva]

Scotland. It established itself within the geographical region of the Palatinate during the reign of Elector Frederick III (r. 1559–1576). Calvinists believed strongly in both divine predestination and the individual's responsibility to reorder society according to God's plan. They became zealous reformers determined to transform and order society so that men and women would act externally as they believed, or should believe, internally and were presumably destined to live eternally.

In his famous study, *The Protestant Ethic and the Spirit of Capitalism* (1904), the German sociologist Max Weber argues that this peculiar combination of religious confidence and self-disciplined activism produced an ethic that stimulated and reinforced the spirit of emergent capitalism. According to this argument, there was thus a close association between Calvinism and other later forms of Puritanism and the development of modern capitalist societies.

The founder of Calvinism, John Calvin (1509–1564), was born into a well-to-do family, the son of the secretary to the bishop of Noyon in Picardy. He received church *benefices* at age twelve, which financed the best possible education at Parisian colleges and a law degree at Orléans. In the 1520s, he

associated with the indigenous French reform party. Although he would finally reject this group as ineffectual, its members contributed to his preparation as a religious reformer.

It was probably in the spring of 1534 that Calvin experienced that conversion to Protestantism by which he said his "long stubborn heart" was "made teachable" by God. His own experience became a personal model of reform that he would later apply to the recalcitrant citizenry of Geneva. His mature theology stressed the sovereignty of God over all creation and the necessity of humankind's conformity to his will. In May 1534 he dramatically surrendered the *benefices* he had held for so long and at such profit and joined the Reformation.

POLITICAL REVOLT AND RELIGIOUS REFORM IN GENEVA
Whereas in Saxony religious reform paved the way for a political revolution against the emperor, in Geneva a political revolution against the local prince-bishop laid the foundation for the religious change. Genevans successfully revolted against their resident prince-bishop in the late 1520s, and the city council assumed his legal and political powers in 1527.

In late 1533 the Protestant city of Bern dispatched two reformers to Geneva: Guillaume Farel (1489–1565) and Antoine Froment (1508–1581). In the summer of 1535, after much internal turmoil, the Protestants triumphed, and the traditional mass and other religious practices were removed. On May 21, 1536, the city voted officially to adopt the Reformation: "to live according to the Gospel and the Word of God . . . without . . . any more masses, statues, idols, or other papal abuses."

Calvin arrived in Geneva after these events, in July 1536. He was actually en route to a scholarly refuge in Strasbourg, in flight from the persecution of Protestants in France, when warring between France and Spain forced him to turn sharply south to Geneva. Farel successfully pleaded with him to stay in the city and assist the Reformation, threatening Calvin with divine vengeance if he turned away from this task.

Before a year had passed, Calvin had drawn up articles for the governance of the new church as well as a catechism to guide and discipline the people. Both were presented for approval to the city councils in early 1537. Because of the strong measures they proposed to govern Geneva's moral life, many suspected the reformers were intent upon creating a "new papacy." Opponents attacked Calvin and Farel, fearing that they were going too far too fast. Geneva's powerful Protestant ally, Bern, which had adopted a more moderate Protestant reform, pressured Geneva's magistrates to restore traditional religious ceremonies and holidays that Calvin and Farel had abolished. When the reformers opposed these actions, they were exiled from the city.

Calvin went to Strasbourg, a model Protestant city, where he became pastor to French exiles and wrote biblical commentaries. He also produced a second edition of his masterful *Institutes of the Christian Religion*, which many consider the definitive theological statement of the Protestant faith. Most important, he learned from the Strasbourg reformer Martin Bucer how to implement his goals successfully.

CALVIN'S GENEVA   In 1540 Geneva elected syndics who were both favorable to Calvin and determined to establish full Genevan political and religious independence from Bern. They knew Calvin would be a valuable ally in this project and invited him to return. This he did in September 1540, never to leave the city again. Within months of his return, the city implemented new ecclesiastical ordinances that provided for cooperation between the magistrates and the clergy in matters of internal discipline.

Following the Strasbourg model, the Genevan Church was organized into four offices: (1) pastors, of whom there were five; (2) teachers or doctors to instruct the populace in and to defend true doctrine; (3) elders, a group of twelve laypeople chosen by and from the Genevan councils and empowered to "oversee the life of everybody"; and (4) deacons to dispense church goods and services to the poor and the sick.

Calvin and his followers were motivated above all by a desire to transform society morally. Faith, Calvin taught, did not sit idly in the mind but conformed one's every action to God's law. The "elect" should live in a manifestly God-pleasing way, if they were truly God's "elect." In the attempted realization of this goal, Calvin spared no effort. The *consistory*, or regulatory court, became his instrument of power. This body was composed of the elders and the pastors and was presided over by one of the four syndics. It enforced the strictest moral discipline.

Among the many personal conflicts in Geneva that gave Calvin his reputation as a stern moralist, none proved more damaging than his active role in

A caricature of drunkenness by Hans Weidt, The Winebag and His Wheelbarrow *addressed the very serious problem of alcoholism that plagued the sixteenth century. Both Catholic and Protestant clergy railed against it. [Hacker Art Books]*

the capture and execution of the Spanish physician and amateur theologian Michael Servetus in 1553. Servetus had earlier been condemned by the Inquisition. He died at the stake in Protestant Geneva for denying the doctrine of the Trinity, a subject on which he had written a scandalous book.

After 1555, the city's syndics were all devout Calvinists, greatly strengthening Calvin's position and Geneva became home to thousands of exiled Protestants who had been driven out of France, England, and Scotland. Refugees (more than 5,000), most of them utterly loyal to Calvin, eventually made up more than one-third of the population of Geneva.

To the thousands of persecuted Protestants who flocked to Geneva in mid-century, the city was a beacon and a refuge, Europe's only free city. During Calvin's lifetime Geneva also gained the reputation of being a "woman's paradise" because the laws there severely punished men who beat their wives.

Theodore Beza Describes
John Calvin's Final Days

Calvin's ceaseless labor to make Geneva a bulwark of Protestantism left him an ill and worn-out man at age fifty-five. He remained nonetheless a model of discipline to the end. The following description comes from an admiring biography by Calvin's successor, Theodore Beza.

✦ *Is Calvin's self-denial reminiscent of the fasting and mortification of the flesh practiced by earlier Christian mystics and fanatics? Compare the extreme discipline Calvin imposed on himself to that which he and his followers imposed upon the citizens of Geneva. Does his suffering indicate that he was "elect"?*

On the 6th of February, 1564, . . . he delivered his last sermon. . . . From this period he taught no more in public, except that he was carried at different times, until the last day of March, to the meeting of the congregation, and addressed them in a few words. His diseases, contracted by incredible labours of mind and body, were various and complicated. . . . He was naturally of a spare and feeble frame, tending to consumption. During sleep he seemed almost awake, and spent a great part of the year in preaching, teaching, and dictating. For at least ten years, the only food he [had taken] was at supper, so that it is astonishing how he could so long escape consumption. He frequently suffered from migraine, which he cured only by fasting, so as occasionally to refrain from food for thirty-six hours. But by overstraining his voice and . . . by an immoderate use of aloes, he suffered from hemorrhoids, which degenerated into ulcers, and five years before his death he was occasionally attacked by a spitting of blood. [He also suffered from] gout in the right leg, frequently returning pains of colic, and stone, which he had only felt a few months before his death. . . . The physicians neglected no remedies, and he observed the directions of his medical attendants with a strictness which none could surpass. . . . Though tormented by so many diseases, no one ever heard him utter a word unbecoming a man of bravery, much less a Christian. Only lifting up his eyes to heaven, he used to say, "How long, O Lord!" for even in health he often had this sentence on his lips, when he spoke of the calamities of his brethren, with whose sufferings he was both day and night more afflicted than with any of his own. When admonished and entreated by us to forbear, at least in his sickness, from the labour of dictating, or at least of writing, "What, then," he said, "would you have my Lord find me idle when he cometh?"

Theodore Beza, The Life of John Calvin, *trans. by Francis Gibson (Philadelphia: Westminster, 1836), pp. 78–79.*

Political Consolidation of the Lutheran Reformation

By 1530, the Reformation was in Europe to stay. It would, however, take several decades and major attempts to eradicate it, before all would recognize this fact. With the political triumph of Lutheranism in the empire by the 1550s, Protestant movements elsewhere gained a new lease on life.

The Diet of Augsburg

Emperor Charles V, who spent most of his time on politics and military maneuvers outside the empire, especially in Spain and Italy, returned to the empire in 1530 to direct the Diet of Augsburg. This meeting of Protestant and Catholic representatives assembled to impose a settlement of the religious divisions. With its terms dictated by the Catholic emperor, the diet adjourned with a blunt order to all Lutherans to revert to Catholicism.

The Reformation was by this time too firmly established for that to occur. In February 1531 the Lutherans responded with the formation of their own defensive alliance, the Schmalkaldic League. The league took as its banner the *Augsburg Confession*, a moderate statement of Protestant beliefs that had been spurned by the emperor at the Diet of Augsburg. In 1538 Luther drew up a more strongly worded Protestant confession known as the *Schmalkaldic Articles*. Under the leadership of Landgrave Philip of Hesse and Elector John Frederick of Saxony, the league achieved a stalemate with the emperor, who was again distracted by renewed war with France and the ever-resilient Turks.

The Expansion of the Reformation

In the 1530s German Lutherans formed regional consistories, judicial bodies composed of theologians and lawyers, which oversaw and administered the new Protestant churches. These consistories replaced the old Catholic episcopates. Philip Melanchthon, the "praeceptor of Germany," oversaw the enactment of educational reforms that provided for compulsory primary education, schools for girls, a humanist revision of the traditional curriculum, and catechetical instruction of the laity in the new religion.

The Reformation also entrenched itself elsewhere. Introduced into Denmark by Christian II (r. 1513–1523), Lutheranism thrived there under Frederick I (r. 1523–1533), who joined the Schmalkaldic League. Under Christian III (r. 1536–1559), Lutheranism became the official state religion.

In Sweden, King Gustavus Vasa (r. 1523–1560), supported by a Swedish nobility greedy for church lands, embraced Lutheranism, confiscated church property, and subjected the clergy to royal authority at the Diet of Vesteras (1527).

In politically splintered Poland, Lutherans, Anabaptists, Calvinists, and even Antitrinitarians found room to practice their beliefs. Poland, primarily because of the absence of a central political authority, became a model of religious pluralism and toleration in the second half of the sixteenth century.

Reaction Against Protestants: The Interim

Charles V made abortive efforts in 1540–1541 to enforce a compromise agreement between Protestants and Catholics. As these and other conciliar efforts failed, he turned to a military solution. In 1547 imperial armies crushed the Protestant Schmalkaldic League, defeating John Frederick of Saxony in April and taking Philip of Hesse captive shortly thereafter.

The emperor established puppet rulers in Saxony and Hesse and issued as imperial law the Augsburg Interim, a new order that Protestants everywhere must readopt old Catholic beliefs and practices. Protestants were granted a few cosmetic concessions, for example, clerical marriage (with papal approval of individual cases) and communion in both kinds (that is, bread and wine). Although the Interim met only surface acceptance within Germany, it forced many Protestant leaders into exile. The Strasbourg reformer Martin Bucer, for example, departed to England, where he would play an important role in drafting the religious documents of the English Reformation during the reign of Edward VI. In Germany, the city of Magdeburg became a refuge for persecuted Protestants and the center of Lutheran resistance.

The Peace of Augsburg

The Reformation was too entrenched by 1547 to be ended even by brute force. Maurice of Saxony, handpicked by Charles V to rule Saxony, recognized the inevitable and shifted his allegiance to the Protes-

Rules Governing Genevan Moral Behavior

During Calvin's lifetime, Geneva gained the reputation of being a model evangelical city. Persecuted Protestants in the outside world considered it Europe's freest and most godly city. Strict moral enforcement conformed faith and practice. It also gave the city and the new church the order they needed to survive against their enemies. The following selections are from ordinances governing the village churches around Geneva.

✦ *Are Calvin's rules designed primarily to protect the Reformation? What do these rules suggest that he fears most? Are the penalties heavy or slaps on the wrist? Is it a sign of the failure of his reform that the Genevan people never stopped doing these things?*

Concerning the Time of Assembling at Church

That the temples be closed for the rest of the time [when religious services are not being held] in order that no one shall enter therein out of hours, impelled thereto by superstition; and if any one be found engaged in any special act of devotion therein or near by he shall be admonished for it: if it be found to be of a superstitious nature for which simple correction is inadequate, then he shall be chastised.

Blasphemy

Whoever shall have blasphemed, swearing by the body or by the blood of our Lord, or in similar manner, he shall be made to kiss the earth for the first offence; for the second to pay 5 sous, and for the third 6 sous, and for the last offence be put in the pillory for one hour.

Drunkenness

1. That no one shall invite another to drink under penalty of 3 sous.
2. That taverns shall be closed during the sermon, under penalty that the tavern-keeper shall pay 3 sous, and whoever may be found therein shall pay the same amount.

3. If any one be found intoxicated he shall pay for the first offence 3 sous and shall be remanded tot he consistory; for the second offence he shall be held to pay the sum of 6 sous, and for the third 10 sous and be put in prison.
4. That no one shall make *roiaumes* [great feasts] under penalty of 10 sous.

Songs and Dances

If any one sing immoral, dissolute or outrageous songs, or dance the *virollet* or other dance, he shall be put in prison for three days and then sent to the Consistory.

Usury

That no one shall take upon interest or profit more than five per cent upon penalty of confiscation of the principal and of being condemned to make restitution as the case may demand.

Games

That no one shall play at any dissolute game or at any game whatsoever it may be, neither for gold nor silver nor for any excessive stake, upon penalty of 5 sous and forfeiture of stake played for.

Translations and Reprints from the Original Sources of European History, Vol. 3 (Philadelphia Department of History, University of Pennsylvania, 1909), pp. 10–11.

tants. Confronted by fierce resistance and weary from three decades of war, the emperor was forced to relent. After suffering a defeat by Protestant armies in 1552, Charles reinstated the Protestant leaders and guaranteed Lutheran religious freedoms in the Peace of Passau (August 1552). With this declaration he effectively surrendered his lifelong quest for European religious unity.

The Peace of Augsburg in September 1555 made the division of Christendom permanent. This agreement recognized in law what had already been well established in practice: *cuius regio, eius religio,* meaning that the ruler of a land would determine the religion of the land. Lutherans were permitted to retain all church lands forcibly seized before 1552. An "ecclesiastical reservation" was added, however, that was intended to prevent high Catholic prelates who converted to Protestantism from taking their lands, titles, and privileges with them. Those discontented with the religion of their region were permitted to migrate to another.

The Peace of Augsburg did not extend official recognition to Calvinism and Anabaptism as legal forms of Christian belief and practice. Anabaptists had long adjusted to such exclusion by forming their own separatist communities. Calvinists, however, were not separatists and could not choose that route. They remained determined not only to secure the right to worship publicly as they pleased but also to shape society according to their own religious convictions. While Anabaptists retreated and Lutherans enjoyed the security of an established religion, Calvinists organized to lead national revolutions throughout northern Europe in the second half of the sixteenth century.

The English Reformation to 1533

Late medieval England had a well-earned reputation for maintaining the rights of the crown against the pope. Edward I (r. 1272–1307) had rejected efforts by Pope Boniface VIII to prevent secular taxation of the clergy. Parliament passed the first Statutes of Provisors and *Praemunire* in the mid-fourteenth century curtailing payments and judicial appeals to Rome as well as papal appointments in England. Lollardy, humanism, and widespread anticlerical sentiment prepared the way religiously and intellectually for Protestant ideas, which entered England in the early sixteenth century.

The Preconditions of Reform

In the early 1520s future English reformers met at the White Horse Inn in Cambridge to discuss Lutheran writings smuggled into England by merchants and scholars. One of these future reformers was William Tyndale (ca. 1492–1536), who translated the New Testament into English in 1524–1525, while in Germany. Printed in Cologne and

Progress of Protestant Reformation on the Continent	
1513–1517	Fifth Lateran Council fails to bring about reform in the church
1517	Luther posts ninety-five theses against indulgences
1519	Charles I of Spain elected Holy Roman Emperor (as Charles V)
1519	Luther challenges authority of pope and inerrancy of church councils at Leipzig Debate
1521	Papal bull excommunicates Luther for heresy
1521	Diet of Worms condemns Luther
1521–1522	Luther translates the New Testament into German
1524–1525	Peasants' revolt in Germany
1527	The *Schleitheim Confession* of the Anabaptists
1529	Marburg Colloquy between Luther and Zwingli
1530	Diet of Augsburg fails to settle religious differences
1531	Formation of Protestant Schmalkaldic League
1534–1535	Anabaptists assume political power in city of Münster
1536	Calvin arrives in Geneva
1540	Jesuits, founded by Ignatius of Loyola, recognized as order by pope
1546	Luther dies
1547	Armies of Charles V crush Schmalkaldic League
1548	Augsburg Interim outlaws Protestant practices
1555	Peace of Augsburg recognizes rights of Lutherans to worship as they please
1545–1563	Council of Trent institutes reforms and responds to the Reformation

Worms, Tyndale's New Testament began to circulate in England in 1526.

Cardinal Thomas Wolsey (ca. 1475–1530), the chief minister of King Henry VIII (r. 1509–1547), and Sir Thomas More (1478–1535), Wolsey's successor, guided royal opposition to incipient English Protestantism. The king himself defended the seven sacraments against Luther, receiving as a reward the title "Defender of the Faith" from Pope Leo X. Following Luther's intemperate reply to Henry's amateur theological attack, More wrote a lengthy *Response to Luther* in 1523.

The King's Affair

While Lollardy and humanism may be said to have provided the native seeds for religious reform, it was Henry's unhappy marriage that broke the soil and allowed the seeds to take root. In 1509 Henry had married Catherine of Aragon (d. 1536), daughter of Ferdinand and Isabella of Spain, and the aunt of Emperor Charles V. By 1527 the union had produced no male heir to the throne and only one surviving child, a daughter, Mary. Henry was justifiably concerned about the political consequences of leaving only a female heir. In this period, people believed it unnatural for women to rule over men. At best, a woman ruler meant a contested reign; at worst, turmoil and revolution.

Henry even came to believe that his union with Catherine, who had many miscarriages and stillbirths, had been cursed by God, because Catherine had first been the wife of his brother, Arthur. Henry's father, King Henry VII, had betrothed Catherine to Henry after Arthur's untimely death to keep the English alliance with Spain intact. They were officially married in 1509, a few days before Henry VIII received his crown. Because marriage to the wife of one's brother was prohibited by both canon and biblical law (see Leviticus 18:16, 20:21), the marriage had required a special dispensation from Pope Julius II.

By 1527 Henry was thoroughly enamored of Anne Boleyn, one of Catherine's ladies in waiting. He determined to put Catherine aside and take Anne as his wife. This he could not do in Catholic England, however, without papal annulment of the marriage to Catherine. And therein lay a special problem. The year 1527 was also the year when soldiers of the Holy Roman Empire mutinied and sacked Rome. The reigning pope, Clement VII, was at the time a prisoner of Charles V, who happened also to be Catherine's nephew. Even if this had not been the case, it would have been virtually impossible for the pope to grant an annulment of a marriage that not only had survived for eighteen years but had been made possible in the first place by a special papal dispensation.

Cardinal Wolsey, who aspired to become pope, was placed in charge of securing the royal annulment. Lord Chancellor since 1515 and papal legate-at-large since 1518, Wolsey had long been Henry's

"heavy" and the object of much popular resentment. When he failed to secure the annulment through no fault of his own, he was dismissed in disgrace in 1529. Thomas Cranmer (1489–1556) and Thomas Cromwell (1485–1540), both of whom harbored Lutheran sympathies, thereafter became the king's closest advisers. Finding the way to a papal annulment closed, Henry's new advisers struck a different course. Why not simply declare the king supreme in English spiritual affairs as he was in English temporal affairs? Then the king could settle the king's affair himself.

The "Reformation Parliament"

In 1529 Parliament convened for what would be a seven-year session that earned it the title the "Reformation Parliament." During this period, it passed a flood of legislation that harassed and finally placed royal reins on the clergy. In doing so, it established a precedent that would remain a feature of English government: whenever fundamental changes are made in religion, the monarch must consult with and work through Parliament. In January 1531 the clergy in Convocation (a legislative assembly representing the English clergy) publicly recognized Henry as head of the church in England "as far as the law of Christ allows." In 1532 Parliament published official grievances against the church, ranging from alleged indifference to the needs of the laity to an excessive number of religious holidays. In the same year Parliament passed the Submission of the Clergy, which effectively placed canon law under royal control and thereby the clergy under royal jurisdiction.

In January 1533 Henry wed the pregnant Anne Boleyn, with Thomas Cranmer officiating. In February 1533 Parliament made the king the highest court of appeal for all English subjects. In March 1533 Cranmer became archbishop of Canterbury and led the Convocation in invalidating the king's marriage to Catherine. In 1534 Parliament ended all payments by the English clergy and laity to Rome and gave Henry sole jurisdiction over high ecclesiastical appointments. The Act of Succession in the same year made Anne Boleyn's children legitimate heirs to the throne, and the Act of Supremacy declared Henry "the only supreme head in earth of the Church of England."

When Thomas More and John Fisher, bishop of Rochester, refused to recognize the Act of Succession and the Act of Supremacy, Henry had them

The Execution of Fisher and More

In 1535 Bishop John Fisher, a long-time pamphleteer for Queen Catherine's cause, and Sir Thomas More, famed humanist and former lord chancellor, were beheaded for refusing to recognize the king's supremacy. They were the most distinguished of Henry VIII's adversaries and victims. As reported by Hall's Chronicle, More managed to find humor in the proceedings.

✦ *How could More die so boldly? What does the author mean by asking whether he was a foolish wise man or a wise foolish man? Is the description propaganda? What impact did More's execution have on Henry's reign?*

The twenty-second day of the same month John Fisher, bishop of Rochester, was beheaded, and his head set upon London Bridge. This bishop was of very many men lamented; for he was reported to be a man of great learning, and a man of very good life, but therein wonderfully deceived, for he maintained the pope to be supreme head of the Church, and very maliciously refused the king's title of supreme head. . . .

Also the sixth day of July was Sir Thomas More beheaded for the like treason before rehearsed, which, as you have heard, was for the denying of the king's Majesty's supremacy. This man was also counted learned, and, as you have heard before, he was lord chancellor of England, and in that time a great persecutor of such as detested the supremacy of the bishop of Rome, which he himself so highly favored that he stood to it until he was brought to the scaffold on the Tower Hill, where on a block his head was stricken from his shoulders and had no more harm.

I cannot tell whether I should call him a foolish wise man or a wise foolish man, for undoubtedly he, beside his learning, had a great wit, but it was so mingled with taunting and mocking, that it seemed to them that best knew him that he thought nothing to be well spoken except he had ministered some mock in the communication, insomuch as at his coming to the Tower one of the officers demanded his upper garment for his fee, meaning his gown, and he answered he should have it and took him his cap, saying that it was the uppermost garment that he had. . . .

Also the hangman kneeled down to him asking him forgiveness of his death (as the manner is), to whom he said, "I forgive thee, but I promise thee that thou shalt never have honesty of the striking of my head, my neck is so short." Also even when he should lay down his head on the bock he, having a great gray beard, struck out his beard, and said to the hangman, "I pray you let me lay my beard over the block lest ye should cut it." Thus with a mock he ended his life.

James Harvey Robinson, ed., *Readings in European History*, Vol. 2 (Boston, Athenaeum: 1906), pp. 142–143.

executed, making clear his determination to have his way regardless of the cost. In 1536 and 1538 Parliament dissolved England's monasteries and nunneries.

Wives of Henry VIII

Henry's domestic life proved to lack the consistency of his political life. In 1536 Anne Boleyn was executed for alleged treason and adultery, and her daughter, Elizabeth, was declared illegitimate. Henry had four further marriages. His third wife, Jane Seymour, died in 1537 shortly after giving birth to the future Edward VI. Henry wed Anne of Cleves sight unseen on the advice of Cromwell, the purpose being to create by the marriage an alliance with the Protestant princes. Neither the alliance nor the marriage proved worth the trouble; the marriage was annulled by Parliament, and Cromwell was dismissed and eventually executed. Catherine

An allegorical depiction of the Tudor succession by the painter Lucas de Heere (1534–1584). On Henry VIII's right stands his Catholic daughter Mary (1533–1558) and her husband Philip II of Spain. They are accompanied by Mars, the god of war. Henry's son, Edward VI (r. 1547–1553), kneels at the king's left. Elizabeth I (1558–1603) is shown standing in the foreground attended by Peace and Plenty, allegorical figures of what her reign brought to England. [Sudeley Castle] [National Museums & Galleries of Wales]

Howard, Henry's fifth wife, was beheaded for adultery in 1542. His last wife, Catherine Parr, a patron of humanists and reformers, for whom Henry was the third husband, survived him to marry still a fourth time—obviously she was a match for the English king.

The King's Religious Conservatism

Henry's boldness in politics and his domestic affairs did not extend to religion. True, because of Henry's actions the pope had ceased to be head of the English Church and English Bibles were placed in English churches, but despite the break with Rome, Henry remained decidedly conservative in his religious beliefs. With the Ten Articles of 1536, he made only mild concessions to Protestant tenets, otherwise maintaining Catholic doctrine in a country filled with Protestant sentiment. Despite his many wives and amorous adventures, Henry absolutely forbade the English clergy to marry and threatened any clergy who were twice caught in concubinage with execution.

Angered by the growing popularity of Protestant views, even among his chief advisers, Henry struck directly at them in the Six Articles of 1539. These reaffirmed transubstantiation, denied the Eucharistic cup to the laity, declared celibate vows inviolable, provided for private masses, and ordered the continuation of auricular confession. (Protestants referred to the articles as the "whip with six stings.") Although William Tyndale's English New Testament grew into the Coverdale Bible (1535) and the Great Bible (1539), and the latter was mandated for every English parish, England had to await Henry's death before it could become a genuinely Protestant country.

The Protestant Reformation Under Edward VI

When Henry died, his son and successor, Edward VI (r. 1547–1553), was only ten years old. Edward reigned under the successive regencies of Edward Seymour, who became the duke of Somerset (1547–1550), and the earl of Warwick, who became known as the duke of Northumberland (1550–1553). During this time England fully enacted the Protestant Reformation. The new king and Somerset corresponded directly with John Calvin. During Somerset's regency, Henry's Six Articles and laws against heresy were repealed, and clerical marriage and communion with cup were sanctioned.

In 1547 the chantries, places where endowed masses had traditionally been said for the dead, were dissolved. In 1549 the Act of Uniformity imposed Thomas Cranmer's *Book of Common Prayer* on all English churches. Images and altars were removed from the churches in 1550. After Charles V's victory over the German princes in 1547, German Protestant leaders had fled to England for refuge. Several of these refugees now directly assisted the completion of the English Reformation, Martin Bucer prominent among them.

The Second Act of Uniformity, passed in 1552, imposed a revised edition of the *Book of Common Prayer* on all English churches. A forty-two-article confession of faith, also written by Thomas Cranmer, was adopted, setting forth a moderate Protestant doctrine. It taught justification by faith and the supremacy of Holy Scripture, denied transubstantiation (although not real presence), and recognized only two sacraments.

All these changes were short-lived, however. In 1553 Catherine of Aragon's daughter succeeded Edward (who had died in his teens) to the English throne as Mary I (r. 1553–1558) and proceeded to restore Catholic doctrine and practice with a singlemindedness that rivaled that of her father. It was not until the reign of Anne Boleyn's daughter, Eliz- abeth I (r. 1558–1603), that a lasting religious settlement was worked out in England.

Catholic Reform and Counter-Reformation

The Protestant Reformation did not take the medieval church completely by surprise. There were many internal criticisms and efforts at reform before there was a Counter-Reformation in reaction to Protestant successes.

Sources of Catholic Reform

Before the Reformation began, ambitious proposals had been made for church reform. But sixteenth-century popes, ever mindful of how the councils of Constance and Basel had stripped the pope of his traditional powers, quickly squelched such efforts to bring about basic changes in the laws and institutions of the church. They preferred the charge

Main Events of the English Reformation

1529	Reformation Parliament convenes
1532	Parliament passes the Submission of the Clergy
1533	Henry VIII weds Anne Boleyn; Convocation proclaims marriage to Catherine of Aragon invalid
1534	Act of Succession makes Anne Boleyn's children legitimate heirs to the English throne
1534	Act of Supremacy declares Henry VIII "the only supreme head of the Church of England"
1535	Thomas More executed for opposition to Acts of Succession and Supremacy
1535	Publication of Coverdale Bible
1539	Henry VIII imposes the Six Articles
1547	Edward VI succeeds to the throne under protectorships of Somerset and Northumberland
1549	First Act of Uniformity imposes *Book of Common Prayer* on English churches
1553–1558	Mary Tudor restores Catholic doctrine
1558–1603	Elizabeth I fashions an Anglican religious settlement

given to the Fifth Lateran Council (1513–1517) in the key-note address by the superior general of the Hermits of Saint Augustine: "Men are to be changed by, not to change, religion."

Despite such papal foot-dragging, the church was not without its reformers. Many new religious orders also sprang up in the sixteenth century to lead a broad revival of piety within the church. The first of these orders was the Theatines, founded in 1524 to groom devout and reform-minded leaders at the higher levels of the church hierarchy. One of the co-founders was Bishop Gian Pietro Carafa, who would be Pope Paul IV. Another new order, whose mission pointed in the opposite direction, was the Capuchins. Recognized by the pope in 1528, they sought to return to the original ascetic and charitable ideals of Saint Francis and became very popular among the ordinary people to whom they directed their ministry. The Somaschi, who became active in the mid-1520s, and the Barnabites, founded in 1530, directed their efforts at repairing the moral, spiritual, and physical damage done to people in war-torn areas of Italy.

For women, there was the new order of Ursulines, founded in 1535. It established convents in Italy and France for the religious education of girls from all social classes and became very influential. Another new religious order, the Oratorians, officially recognized in 1575, was an elite group of secular clerics who devoted themselves to the promotion of religious literature and church music. Among their members was the great Catholic hymnist and musician Giovanni Perluigi da Palestrina (1526–1594).

In addition to these lay and clerical movements the Spanish mystics Saint Teresa of Avila (1515–1582) and Saint John of the Cross (1542–1591) revived and popularized the mystical piety of medieval monasticism.

Ignatius of Loyola and the Jesuits

Of the various reform groups, none was more instrumental in the success of the Counter-Reformation than the Society of Jesus, the new order of Jesuits. Organized by Ignatius of Loyola in the 1530s, it was officially recognized by the church in 1540. The society grew within the space of a century from its original 10 members to more than 15,000 members scattered throughout the world, with thriving missions in India, Japan, and the Americas.

The Ecstasy of Saint Teresa of Avila, *by Gianlorenzo Bernini (1598–1680). Mystics like Saint Teresa and Saint John of the Cross helped revive the traditional piety of medieval monasticism. [Scala/Art Resource, N.Y.]*

The founder of the Jesuits, Ignatius of Loyola (1491–1556), was a heroic figure. A dashing courtier and *caballero* in his youth, he began his spiritual pilgrimage in 1521 after he had been seriously wounded in the legs during a battle with the French. During a lengthy and painful convalescence, he passed the time by reading Christian classics. So impressed was he with the heroic self-sacrifice of the church's saints and their methods of overcoming mental anguish and pain that he underwent a profound religious conversion. Henceforth, he, too, would serve the church as a soldier of Christ.

After recuperating, Ignatius applied the lessons he had learned during his convalescence to a program of religious and moral self-discipline that came to be embodied in the *Spiritual Exercises*. This psychologically perceptive devotional guide contained mental and emotional exercises designed to teach one absolute spiritual self-mastery over

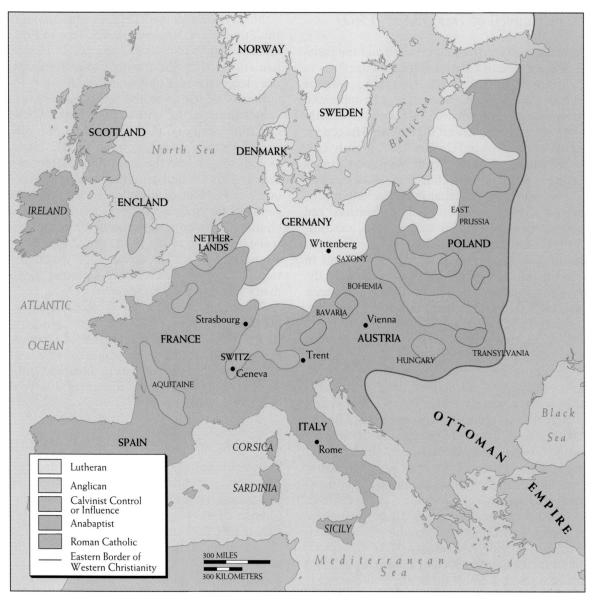

MAP 11–3 THE RELIGIOUS SITUATION ABOUT 1560   *By 1560 Luther, Zwingli, and Loyola were dead, Calvin near the end of his life, the English break from Rome fully accomplished, and the last session of the Council of Trent about to assemble. Here is the religious geography of western Europe then.*

one's feelings. It taught that a person could shape his or her own behavior, even create a new religious self, through disciplined study and regular practice.

Whereas in Jesuit eyes Protestants had distinguished themselves by disobedience to church authority and religious innovation, the exercises of Ignatius were intended to teach good Catholics to deny themselves and submit without question to higher church authority and spiritual direction.

Perfect discipline and self-control were the essential conditions of such obedience. To these were added the enthusiasm of traditional spirituality and mysticism and uncompromising loyalty to the church's cause above all else. This was a potent combination that helped counter the Reformation and win many Protestants back to the Catholic fold, especially in Austria and Bavaria and along the Rhine.

The Council of Trent (1545–1563)

The broad success of the Reformation and the insistence of the Emperor Charles V forced Pope Paul to call a general council of the church to reassert church doctrine. In anticipation, the pope appointed a reform commission, chaired by Caspar Contarini (1483–1542), a leading liberal theologian. His report, presented to the pope in February 1537, bluntly criticized the fiscality and simony of the papal *Curia* as the primary source of the church's loss of esteem. The report was so critical that Pope Paul attempted unsuccessfully to suppress its publication and Protestants reprinted and circulated it as justification of their criticism.

The long-delayed council of the church met in 1545 in the imperial city of Trent in northern Italy. There were three sessions, spread over eighteen years, with long interruptions due to war, plague, and imperial and papal politics. The council met from 1545 to 1547, from 1551 to 1552, and from 1562 to 1563, a period that spanned the careers of four different popes.

Unlike the general councils of the fifteenth century, Trent was strictly under the pope's control, with high Italian prelates very prominent in the proceedings. Initially four of the five attending archbishops and twenty-one of the twenty-three attending bishops were Italians. Even at its final session in 1562, more than three-quarters of the council fathers were Italians. Voting was limited to the high levels of the clergy; university theologians, the lower clergy, and the laity were not permitted to share in the council's decisions.

The council's most important reforms concerned internal church discipline. Steps were taken to curtail the selling of church offices and other religious goods. Many bishops who resided in Rome rather than within their dioceses were forced to move to their appointed seats of authority. Trent strengthened the authority of local bishops so they could effectively discipline popular religious practice. The bishops were also subjected to new rules that required them not only to reside in their dioceses, but also to be highly visible by preaching regularly and conducting annual visitations. Trent also sought to give the parish priest a brighter image by requiring him to be neatly dressed, better educated, strictly celibate, and active among his parishioners. To this end, Trent also called for the construction of a seminary in every diocese.

Not a single doctrinal concession was made to the Protestants, however. In the face of Protestant criticism the Council of Trent gave a ringing reaffirmation to the traditional Scholastic education of the clergy; the role of good works in salvation; the authority of tradition; the seven sacraments; transubstantiation; the withholding of the Eucharistic cup from the laity; clerical celibacy; the reality of purgatory; the veneration of saints, relics, and sacred images; and the granting of letters of indulgence. The council resolved medieval Scholastic quarrels in favor of the theology of Saint Thomas Aquinas, further enhancing his authority within the church. Thereafter, the church offered its strongest resistance to groups like the Jansenists, who strongly endorsed the medieval Augustinian tradition, a source of alternative Catholic as well as many Protestant doctrines.

Rulers initially resisted Trent's reform decrees, fearing a revival of papal political power within their lands. But with the passage of time and the pope's assurances that religious reforms were his sole intent, the new legislation took hold and parish life revived under the guidance of a devout and better-trained clergy.

The Church in Spanish America

Roman Catholic priests had accompanied the earliest explorers and the conquerors of the Native Americans. Because of internal reforms within the Spanish church at the turn of the sixteenth century, these first clergy tended to be imbued with many of the social and religious ideals of Christian humanism. They believed that they could foster Erasmus's concept of the "philosophy of Christ" in the New World. Consequently these missionary priests were filled with zeal not only to convert the inhabitants to Christianity but also to bring to them learning and civilization of a European kind.

A very real tension existed between the early Spanish conquerors and the mendicant friars who sought to minister to the Indians. Without conquest, the church could not convert the Indians, but the priests often deplored the harsh labor conditions imposed on them. During the first three-quarters of a century of Spanish domination, priests were among the most eloquent and persuasive defenders of the rights of native peoples in the New World.

Bartolomé de Las Casas, a Dominican, contended that conquest was not necessary for con-

A Defense of American Natives

Bartolomé de Las Casas (1474–1566), a Dominican missionary to the New World, describes the native people of the islands of the Caribbean and their systematic slaughter by the Spanish.

◆ *Is Las Casas romanticizing the American natives? Does he truly respect their native culture and beliefs?*

This infinite multitude of people was so created by God that they were without fraud . . . subtilty or malice. . . . Toward the Spaniards whom they serve, patient, meek, and peaceful, [they] lay aside all contentious and tumultuous thoughts, and live without any hatred or desire of revenge. The people are most delicate and tender, enjoying such a feeble constitution of body as does not permit them to endure labour. . . . The[ir] nation [the West Indies] is very poor and indigent, possessing little, and by reason that they gape not after temporal goods, [being] neither proud nor ambitious. Their diet is such that the most holy hermit cannot feed more sparingly in the wildernesse. They go naked . . . and a poor shag mantle . . . is their greatest and their warmest covering. They lie upon mats; only those who have larger fortunes lie upon a kind of net which is tied at the four corners and so fasten'd to the roof, which the Indians in their natural language call Hamecks [hammocks]. They are of a very apprehensive and docile wit, and capable of all good learning, and very apt to receive our Religion, which when they have but once tasted [it], they are carried [off] with a very ardent and zealous desire to make fur-

ther progress in it; so that I have heard divers Spaniards confess that they had nothing else to hinder them from enjoying heaven, but the ignorance of the true God.

To these quiet Lambs, endued with such blessed qualities, came the Spaniards like most cruel Tygres, Wolves, and Lions . . . for these forty years, minding nothing else but the slaughter of these unfortunate wretches . . . [whom] they have so cruelly and inhumanely butchered, [so] that of three millions of people which Hispaniola [modern Haiti and Dominican Republic] itself did contain, there are left remaining alive scarce three hundred persons. And the island of Cuba . . . lies wholly desert, untilled and ruined. The islands of St. John and Jamaica lie waste and desolate. The Lycayan islands neighboring to the north upon Cuba and Hispaniola . . . are now totally unpeopled and destroyed; the inhabitants thereof amounting to above 500,000 souls, partly killed, and partly forced away to work in other places. . . . Other islands there were near the island of St. John more than thirty in number, which were totally made desert. All which islands . . . lie now altogether solitary without any people or inhabitant.

Bartolomé de Las Casas, The Tears of the Indians, *trans. by John Phillips (1656), from reprint of original edition (Academic Reprints, Stanford, Calif., n.d.), pp. 2–4.*

Bartolomé de Las Casas (1474–1566) was the most outspoken and effective defender of the Native Americans against Spanish exploitation. [Bildarchiv Preussischer Kulturbesitz]

version. One result of his campaign was new royal regulation of conquest after 1550. Another result was the "Black Legend," which portrayed all Spanish treatment of Indians as unprincipled and inhumane. Those who held this point of view drew heavily on Las Casas's writings. Although largely true, the "Black Legend" nonetheless exaggerated the case against Spain and has been exploited by Spanish critics. Many of the Indian rulers had also been exceedingly cruel, as witnessed by the Aztec demands for human sacrifice, and both the Aztecs and the Incas enslaved other peoples. Had the Aztecs discovered Spain and held the upper hand there, the persecution of native Europeans would likely have been as great as that of native Americans at the hands of the Spanish.

By the end of the sixteenth century, the church in Spanish America had become largely an institution upholding the colonial status quo. On many occasions, individual priests did defend the communal rights of Indian tribes, but the colonial church also prospered as the Spanish elite prospered. The church became a great landowner through crown grants and through bequests from Catholics who died in the New World. The monasteries took on an economic as well as a spiritual life of their own. Whatever its concern for the spiritual welfare of the Indians, the church remained one of the indications that

Spanish America was a conquered world. And those who spoke for the church did not challenge Spanish domination or any but the most extreme modes of Spanish economic exploitation. By the end of the colonial era in the late eighteenth century, the Roman Catholic Church had become one of the most conservative forces in Latin America.

The Social Significance of the Reformation in Western Europe

It was a common trait of the Lutheran, Zwinglian, and Calvinist reformers to work within the framework of reigning political power. Luther, Zwingli, and Calvin saw themselves and their followers as subject to definite civic responsibilities and obligations. Their conservatism in this regard has led scholars to characterize them as "magisterial reformers," meaning not only that they were the leaders of the major Protestant movements but also that they succeeded by the force of the magistrate's sword. Some have argued that this willingness to resort to coercion led the reformers to compromise their principles. They themselves, however, never contemplated reform outside or against the societies of which they were members. They wanted it to take shape within the laws and institutions of the sixteenth century. To that end, they remained highly sensitive to what was politically and socially possible in their age. Some scholars believe that the reformers were too conscious of the historically possible, that their reforms went forward with such caution that they changed late medieval society very little and actually encouraged acceptance of the sociopolitical status quo.

The Revolution in Religious Practices and Institutions

The Reformation may have been politically conservative, but by the end of the sixteenth century it had brought about radical changes in traditional religious practices and institutions in those lands where it succeeded.

RELIGION IN FIFTEENTH-CENTURY LIFE   In the fifteenth century, on the streets of the great cities of central Europe that later turned Protestant (for example, Zurich, Strasbourg, Nuremberg, or Geneva), the clergy and the religious were everywhere. They made up 6 to 8 percent of the total urban population, and they exercised considerable political as well as spiritual power. They legislated and taxed; they tried cases in special church courts; and they enforced their laws with threats of excommunication.

The church calendar regulated daily life. About one-third of the year was given over to some kind of religious observance or celebration. There were frequent periods of fasting. On almost a hundred days out of the year a pious Christian could not, without special dispensation, eat eggs, butter, fat, or meat.

Monasteries and especially nunneries were prominent and influential institutions. The children of society's most powerful citizens resided there. Local aristocrats were closely identified with particular churches and chapels, whose walls recorded their lineage and proclaimed their generosity. On the streets, friars from near and far begged alms from passersby. In the churches the mass and liturgy were read entirely in Latin. Images of saints were regularly displayed, and on certain holidays their relics were paraded about and venerated.

There was a booming business at local religious shrines. Pilgrims gathered there by the hundreds, even thousands, many sick and dying, all in search of a cure or a miracle, but also for diversion and entertainment. Several times during the year special preachers arrived in the city to sell letters of indulgence.

Many clergy walked the streets with concubines and children, although they were sworn to celibacy and forbidden marriage. The church tolerated such relationships upon payment of penitential fines.

People everywhere could be heard complaining about the clergy's exemption from taxation and, in many instances, also from the civil criminal code. People also grumbled about having to support church offices whose occupants actually lived and worked elsewhere. Townspeople also expressed concern that the church had too much influence over education and culture.

RELIGION IN SIXTEENTH-CENTURY LIFE   In these same cities after the Reformation had firmly established itself, few changes in politics and society were evident. The same aristocratic families governed as before, and the rich generally got richer and the poor poorer. But overall numbers of clergy fell by two-thirds and religious holidays shrunk by one-third. Cloisters were nearly gone, and many that remained were transformed into hospices for the sick and poor or into educational institutions, their endowments also turned over to these new purposes. A few cloisters remained for very devout old monks and nuns, who could not be pensioned off or who lacked families and friends to care for them. But these remaining cloisters died out with their inhabitants.

In the churches, which had also been reduced in number by at least one-third, worship was conducted almost completely in the vernacular. In some, particularly those in Zwinglian cities, the walls were stripped bare and whitewashed to make sure the congregation meditated only on God's word. The laity observed no obligatory fasts. Indulgence preachers no longer appeared. Local shrines were closed down, and anyone found openly venerating saints, relics, and images was subject to fine and punishment.

Copies of Luther's translation of the New Testament or, more often, excerpts from it could be found in private homes, and meditation on them was encouraged by the new clergy. The clergy could marry, and most did. They paid taxes and were punished for their crimes in civil courts. Domestic moral life was regulated by committees composed of roughly equal numbers of laity and clergy, over whose decisions secular magistrates had the last word.

The Instructions of a Father to His Youngest Son

At age fourteen, in the year 1539, Christoph Ravensburg departed Augsburg, Germany, for an apprenticeship in Lyons, France, bearing with him these words of advice from his father.

✦ *What are the father's overriding concerns as his son leaves home for the first time? What does his father consider to be the traits of a "true man"? On what is Christoph to rely in time of temptation and danger?*

Dear son Christoph, . . . If you heed the instructions that follow, you will become a true man.

Love God and be mindful of Him, and see to the keeping of His commandments. Attend the traditional religious service in the land where you will be, as other devout and honorable people there do. And argue neither little nor much over any matter of faith, for that will put you at a disadvantage and even threaten your life.

Sebastian Weyer and his brother [the father's business associates in Lyons] will try to place you with a proper master. . . . They will also look after your basic needs, be it clothing or something else. Therefore, try your best to do what they tell you. And when you are with your master, do what he and his wife tell you, and do it with the utmost diligence, always willingly and obediently.

Above all else, take care that you do not lie and steal. Should you have the merchants' money in your hand or see their many wares lying before you, take none of it for yourself. For it often happens that money or something else is purposefully placed before one such as

you as a test. So as dear to you as your life and my favor are, for the sake of life and limb, be false to no one about anything.

Avoid bad company, and when you sometimes hear it said, or actually see other Germans acting improperly and wanting to be Junkers [wealthy noblemen indulging themselves], let it be an example and a warning to you that you not do so.

Do not let your master's other servants or maids with whom you will be living teach you to steal anything in the house, be it food, drink, or anything else that it is wrong to take, for this may bring you great misfortune. They will tempt one such as you to see if he lets himself be led astray.

When bathing or swimming, avoid the great threatening waters of the Saone and the Rhone [which meet in Lyons]. Do not enter them; if you are tempted to do so, resist, as I have told you many times before. Use other waters for your needs, so that you do not drown. . . .

Avoid strong drink by mixing a lot of water in with the wine. Resolve not to get drunk

---

Not all Protestant clergy remained enthusiastic about this new lay authority in religion. And the laity themselves were also ambivalent about certain aspects of the Reformation. Over half of the original converts returned to the Catholic fold before the end of the sixteenth century. Whereas one-half of Europe could be counted in the Protestant camp in the mid-sixteenth century, only one-fifth would be there by the mid-seventeenth century.[2]

[2]Geoffrey Parker, *Europe in Crisis, 1598–1648* (Ithaca, N.Y.: Cornell University Press, 1979), p. 50.

The Reformation and Education

Another important cultural achievement of the Reformation was its implementation of many of the educational reforms of humanism in the new Protestant schools and universities. Many Protestant reformers in Germany, France, and England were humanists. Even when their views on Church doctrine and humankind separated them from the humanist movement, the Protestant reformers continued to share with the humanists a common opposition to Scholasticism and a belief in the unity

either during your journey or upon your arrival. When you are thirsty, drink only water or well-watered wine, because your natural disposition is to eat and drink a lot. Take care of yourself in this way so that you become all the less susceptible to illness.

Avoid gambling, whoring, partying, cursing, and other bad associations and vices. Place yourself in the company of honest people, whom you know to be good and accomplished, and from whom you can learn something good yourself. And when you can find the time, be sure to practice your writing and arithmetic so that you do not forget them . . . .

Keep yourself and your clothes clean, and take good care of your clothes. Be always ready and willing, not argumentative. And do not give up too soon when someone reproaches you for something, for they do it for your own good.

Concentrate on your needs and be frugal and sparing. Don't spend money needlessly, because when you are larger and older, you will want and need it. Do not take comfort in [any expected] wealth [from me]; resolve to learn how to earn [your own] money and to spend it wisely.

As you well know, great expenditures are now being made on your behalf and they will also be made on behalf of your brothers and sisters, so that after my death, you will discover all the less [money for yourself]. Therefore, look to your own needs; plan well now to support yourself and also to be in a position to help the children of your brothers and sisters as well.

Take care that in your innocence you not let yourself be talked into entering a marriage on your own or become entangled [with some woman]. Stay away from dishonest women so that you do not get the pox [syphilis] and other maladies that flow from them.

Keep your feet warm and dry, for the world is an unholy bath; this will make you less vulnerable to foot ailments.

Do not go about the streets at night unless your master sends you out. He will instruct you and arrange things so that you may go safely. Many corrupt youth hang out on the bridge over the Saone and villainy often occurs there.

. . .

Write often to me and your mother, and let me know what kind of master you have there, what his name is and what he does, also how many servants he has and how he treats you.

Finally, as I said at the beginning and as has long been your custom, above all else be god-fearing with your reading, prayer, etc. and act as other devout people there do. Buy yourself a Latin prayerbook like the others there have so that almighty God may help you and you suffer no want. May the Lord God care for you.

Written by your father in Augsburg,
26 March, 1539.
Leo Ravenspurg

Friedrich Beyschlag, ed., "Ein Vater an seinen Sohn (1539)," *Archiv für Kulturgeschichte* 4 (1906): 296–302, trans. by S. Ozment.

of wisdom, eloquence, and action. The humanist program of studies, which provided the language skills to deal authoritatively with original sources, proved to be a more appropriate tool for the elaboration of Protestant doctrine than did scholastic dialectic, which remained ascendant in the Counter-Reformation.

The Catholic counterreformers recognized the close connections between humanism and the Reformation. Ignatius of Loyola observed the way in which the new learning had been embraced by and served the Protestant cause. In his *Spiritual Exercises*, he insisted that when the Bible and the Church Fathers were read directly, they be read under the guidance of the authoritative scholastic theologians: Peter Lombard, Bonaventure, and Thomas Aquinas. The latter, Ignatius argued, being "of more recent date," had the clearer understanding of what Scripture and the Fathers meant and therefore should guide the study of the past.

When in August 1518 Philip Melanchthon (1497–1560), a young humanist and professor of Greek, arrived at the University of Wittenberg, his first act was to implement curricular reforms on the

A village wedding as portrayed by Pieter Bruegel the Younger (1564–1638).
[Scala/Art Resource, N.Y.]

humanist model. In his inaugural address, entitled *On Improving the Studies of the Young*, Melanchthon presented himself as a defender of good letters and classical studies against "barbarians who practice barbarous arts." By the latter he meant the scholastic theologians of the later Middle Ages, whose methods of juxtaposing the views of conflicting authorities and seeking to reconcile them by disputation had, he believed, undermined both good letters and sound biblical doctrine. Scholastic dominance in the universities was seen by Melanchthon as having bred contempt for the Greek language and learning and as having encouraged neglect of the study of mathematics, sacred studies, and the art of oratory. Melanchthon urged the careful study of history, poetry, and other humanist disciplines.

Together Luther and Melanchthon restructured the University of Wittenberg's curriculum. Commentaries on Lombard's *Sentences* were dropped, as

was canon law. Straightforward historical study replaced old Scholastic lectures on Aristotle. Students read primary sources directly, not by way of accepted Scholastic commentators. Candidates for theological degrees defended the new doctrine on the basis of their own exegesis of the Bible. New chairs of Greek and Hebrew were created. Luther and Melanchthon also pressed for universal compulsory education so both boys and girls could reach vernacular literacy in the Bible.

In Geneva, John Calvin and his successor, Theodore Beza, founded the Genevan Academy, which later evolved into the University of Geneva. That institution, created primarily for training Calvinist ministers, pursued ideals similar to those set forth by Luther and Melanchthon. Calvinist refugees trained in the academy carried Protestant educational reforms to France, Scotland, England, and the New World. Through such efforts a working knowledge of Greek and Hebrew became commonplace in educated circles in the sixteenth and seventeenth centuries.

Some contemporaries decried what they saw as a narrowing of the original humanist program as Protestants took it over. Erasmus, for example, came to fear the Reformation as a threat to the liberal arts and good learning. Sebastian Franck pointed to parallels between Luther's and Zwingli's debates over Christ's presence in the Eucharist and such old scholastic disputations as that over the Immaculate Conception of the Virgin.

Humanist culture and learning nonetheless remained indebted to the Reformation. The Protestant endorsement of the humanist program of studies remained as significant for the humanist movement as the latter had been for the Reformation. Protestant schools and universities consolidated and preserved for the modern world many of the basic pedagogical achievements of humanism. There the *studia humanitatis*, although often as little more than a handmaiden to theological doctrine, found a permanent home, one that remained hospitable even in the heyday of Conservative Protestantism.

The Reformation and the Changing Role of Women

The Protestant reformers took a positive stand on clerical marriage and strongly opposed monasticism and the celibate life. From this position they challenged the medieval tendency alternately to degrade women as temptresses (following the model of Eve) and to exalt them as virgins (following the model of Mary). Protestants opposed the popular antiwoman and antimarriage literature of the Middle Ages. They praised woman in her own right, but especially in her biblical vocation as mother and housewife. Although from a modern perspective, women remained subject to men, new marriage laws gave them greater security and protection.

Relief of sexual frustration and a remedy of fornication were prominent in Protestant arguments for marriage. But the reformers also viewed their wives as indispensable companions in their work, and this not solely because they took domestic cares off their husbands' minds. Luther, who married in 1525 at the age of forty-two, wrote of women:

Imagine what it would be like without women. The home, cities, economic life, and government would vir-

Albrecht Dürer's portrait of a young girl (1515). The Protestant movement encouraged girls to be literate in their native languages. [Kupferstichkabinett Staatliche Museen, Preussischer Kulturbesitz, Berlin]

tually disappear. Men cannot do without women. Even if it were possible for men to beget and bear children, they still could not do without women.[3]

John Calvin wrote at the death of his wife:

I have been bereaved of the best companion of my life, of one who, had it been so ordered, would not only have been the willing sharer of my indigence, but even of my death. During her life she was the faithful helper of my ministry.[4]

Such tributes were intended in part to overcome Catholic criticism that marriage distracted the cleric from his ministry. They were primarily the

[3]*Luther's Works, Vol. 54: Table Talk*, ed. and trans. by Theodore G. Tappert (Philadelphia: Fortress Press, 1967), p. 161.
[4]*Letters of John Calvin*, Vol. 2, trans. by J. Bonnet (Edinburgh: T. Constable, 1858), p. 216.

The family of Hans Holbein the Younger (1497–1534), as painted by the artist himself. [Via Foto Hans Hinz, Basel]

expression of a new value placed on the estate of marriage and family life. In opposition to the celibate ideal of the Middle Ages, Protestants stressed as no religious movement before them the sacredness of home and family. This attitude contributed to a more respectful and sharing relationship between husbands and wives and between parents and children.

The ideal of the companionate marriage—that is, of husband and wife as co-workers in a special God-ordained community of the family, sharing authority equally within the household—led to an important expansion of the grounds for divorce in Protestant cities as early as the 1520s. Women now had an equal right with men to divorce and remarry in good conscience—unlike in Catholicism, where only a separation from bed and table,

not divorce and remarriage, was permitted a couple in a failed marriage. The reformers were actually more willing to permit divorce and remarriage on grounds of adultery and abandonment than were secular magistrates, who feared liberal divorce laws would lead to social upheaval.

Protestant doctrines were as attractive to women as they were to men. Renegade nuns wrote exposés of the nunnery in the name of Christian freedom and justification by faith, declaring that the nunnery was no special woman's place at all and that supervisory male clergy (who alone could hear the nuns' confessions and administer sacraments to them) made their lives as unpleasant and burdensome as any abusive husband. Women in the higher classes, who enjoyed new social and political freedoms during the Renaissance, found in Protestant theology a religious complement to their greater independence in other walks of life. Some cloistered noblewomen, however, protested the closing of nunneries. They believed the cloister provided them a more interesting and independent way of life than they would have known in the secular world.

Because they wanted women to become pious housewives, Protestants encouraged the education of girls to literacy in the vernacular, with the expectation that they would thereafter model their lives on the Bible. During their studies, however, women found biblical passages that suggested they were equal to men in the presence of God. Education also gave some women a role as independent authors in the Reformation. From a modern perspective, these may seem like small advances, but they were significant, if indirect, steps in the direction of the emancipation of women.

Changes in the timing and duration of marriage, in family size, and in infant and child care suggest that family life was under a variety of social and economic pressures in the sixteenth and seventeenth centuries. The Reformation was a factor in these changes, but not the only or even the major one. [For a comparison of the family in western Europe and China, see The West & the World essay on p. 408.]

◆

During the early Middle Ages, Christendom had been divided into Western and Eastern churches with irreconcilable theological differences. When, in 1517, Martin Luther posted ninety-five theses questioning the selling of indulgences and the traditional sacrament of penance that lay behind them, he created a division within Western Christendom itself—an internal division between Protestants and Catholics.

The Lutheran protest came at a time of political and social discontent with the church. Not only princes and magistrates, but many ordinary people as well resented traditional clerical rights and privileges. In many instances the clergy were exempted from secular laws and taxes, while remaining powerful landowners whose personal lifestyles were not all that different from those of the laity. Spiritual and secular protest combined to make the Protestant Reformation a successful assault on the old

church. In town after town and region after region within Protestant lands, the major institutions and practices of traditional piety were significantly transformed.

It soon became clear, however, that the division would not stop with the Lutherans. Making Scripture the only arbiter in religion had opened a Pandora's box. People proved to have very different ideas about what Scripture taught. Indeed, there seemed to be as many points of view as there were readers. Rapidly the Reformation created Lutheran, Zwinglian, Anabaptist, Spiritualist, Calvinist, and Anglican versions of biblical religion—a splintering of Protestantism that still endures.

Catholics had been pursuing reform before the Reformation broke out in Germany, although without papal enthusiasm, and certainly not along clear Protestant lines. When major reforms finally came in the Catholic Church around the mid-sixteenth century, they were doctrinally reactionary but administratively and spiritually flexible. The church enforced strict obedience and conformity to its teaching, but it also provided the laity with a better educated and disciplined clergy. For laity who wanted a deeper and more individual piety, experimentation with proven spiritual practices was now permitted. By century's end, such measures had successfully countered and in some areas even spectacularly reversed Protestant gains.

After the Reformation, pluralism steadily became a fact of Western religious life. It did so at first only by sheer force, since no one religious body was then prepared to concede the validity of alternative Christian beliefs and practices. During the sixteenth and seventeenth centuries, only those groups that fought doggedly for their faith gained the right to practice it freely. Despite these struggles, religious pluralism endured. Never again would there be only a Catholic Christian Church in Europe.

Review Questions

1. What were the main problems of the church that contributed to the Protestant Reformation? Why was the church unable to suppress dissent as it had earlier?

2. What were the basic similarities and differences between the ideas of Luther and Zwingli? Between Luther and Calvin? Did the differences

tend to split the Protestant ranks and thereby lessen the effectiveness of the movement?

3. Why did the Reformation begin in Germany? What political factors contributed to the success of the Reformation there as opposed to France or Italy?

4. What was the Catholic reformation and what principal decisions and changes were instituted by the Council of Trent? Was the Protestant Reformation a healthy movement for the Catholic Church?

5. Why did Henry VIII finally break with the Catholic Church? Was the "new" religion he established really Protestant? What problems did his successors face as a result of Henry's move?

6. What impact did the Reformation have on women in the sixteenth and seventeenth centuries? What new factors and pressures affected relations between men and women, family size, and child care during this period?

Suggested Readings

W. BOUWSMA, *John Calvin: A Sixteenth Century Portrait* (1988). Interpretation of Calvin against background of Renaissance intellectual history.

J. DELUMEAU, *Catholicism Between Luther and Voltaire: A New View of the Counter Reformation* (1977). Programmatic essay for a social history of the Counter-Reformation.

A. G. DICKENS, *The Counter Reformation* (1969). Brief narrative with pictures.

A. G. DICKENS, *The English Reformation* (1974). The best one-volume account.

A. G. DICKENS AND JOHN M. TONKIN, *The Reformation in Historical Thought* (1985). The standard critical guide to the main developments in Reformation studies.

G. DONALDSON, *The Scottish Reformation* (1960). Dependable, comprehensive narrative.

G. ELTON, *Reform and Reformation: England, 1509–1558* (1977). Standard political narrative.

H. O. EVENNETT, *The Spirit of the Counter Reformation* (1968). Essay on the continuity of Catholic reform and its independence from the Protestant Reformation.

J. FLANDRIN, *Families in Former Times* (1979). Family life in France.

B. GOTTLIEB, *The Family in the Western World* (1992). Accessible overview with up-to-date annotated bibliographies.

R. HOULBROOKE, *English Family Life, 1450–1716. An Anthology from Diaries* (1988). A rich collection of documents illustrating family relationships.

R. P. HSIA (ED.), *The German People and the Reformation* (1988). Substantial excerpts from the latest research.

J. L. IRWIN (ED.), *Womanhood in Radical Protestantism, 1525–1675* (1979). Sources illustrating images of women in sectarian Protestant thought.

H. JEDIN, *A History of the Council of Trent*, vols. 1 and 2 (1957–1961). Comprehensive, detailed, authoritative.

D. L. JENSEN, *Reformation Europe, Age of Reform and Revolution* (1981). Excellent, up-to-date survey.

W. K. JORDAN, *Edward VI: The Young King* (1968). The basic biography.

R. M. KINGDON (ED.), *Transition and Revolution: Problems and Issues of European Renaissance and Reformation History* (1974). Covers politics, printing, theology, and witchcraft.

A. MACFARLANE, *The Family Life of Ralph Josselin: A Seventeenth Century Clergyman* (1970). A model study of Puritan family life!

J. F. MCNEILL, *The History and Character of Calvinism* (1954). The most comprehensive account and very readable.

E. W. MONTER, *Calvin's Geneva* (1967). Dependable sketch derived from authoritative studies.

H. A. OBERMAN, *Luther: Man Between God and the Devil* (1989). Perhaps the best account of Luther's life, by a Dutch master.

J. O'MALLEY, *The First Jesuits* (1993). Extremely detailed account of the creation of the Society of Jesus and its original purposes.

S. OZMENT, *The Age of Reform 1250–1550: An Intellectual and Religious History of Late Medieval and Reformation Europe* (1980). A broad survey of major religious ideas and beliefs.

S. OZMENT, *When Fathers Ruled: Family Life in Reformation Europe* (1983). A survey of sixteenth-century attitudes toward marriage and parenthood.

S. OZMENT, *Three Behaim Boys: Growing Up in Early Modern Germany* (1990). The lives of three boys in their late teens and early adulthood told in their own words.

S. OZMENT, *Protestants: The Birth of a Revolution* (1992). The Reformation in Germany as a religious and cultural movement.

R. R. POST, *The Modern Devotion* (1968). Currently the authoritative interpretation.

E. F. RICE, JR., *The Foundations of Early Modern Europe 1460–1559* (1970). Broad, succinct narrative.

J. G. RIDLEY, *Thomas Cranmer* (1962). The basic biography.

J. J. SCARISBRICK, *The Reformation and the English People* (1990). Eloquent argument that the Reformation changed little religiously, and that it was a political, not a spiritual, triumph.

Q. SKINNER, *The Foundations of Modern Political Thought II: The Age of Reformation* (1978). A comprehensive survey that treats every political thinker and tract.

L. W. Spitz, *The Protestant Reformation 1517–1559* (1985). Sweeping survey with rich bibliographies.

D. Starkey, *The Reign of Henry VIII* (1985). Portrayal of the king as in control of neither his life nor his court.

J. Stayer, *Anabaptists and the Sword* (1972). The political philosophies of sectarians.

L. Stone, *The Family, Sex and Marriage in England 1500–1800* (1977). Controversial but in many respects still reigning view of English family history.

G. Strauss (ED. and Trans.), *Manifestations of Discontent in Germany on the Eve of the Reformation* (1971). Rich collection of sources for both rural and urban scenes.

G. Strauss, *Luther's House of Learning: The Indoctrination of the Young in the German Reformation* (1978). Account of Protestant efforts to rear children in the new faith, stressing the negative side.

R. H. Tawney, *Religion and the Rise of Capitalism* (1947). Advances beyond Max Weber's arguments relating Protestantism and capitalist economic behavior.

E. Troeltsch, *The Social Teaching of the Christian Churches*, vols. 1 and 2, trans. by O. Wyon (1960). Old, liberal account of the Reformation and its critics with fondness for the latter.

M. Weber, *The Protestant Ethic and the Spirit of Capitalism*, trans. by T. Parsons (1958). First appeared in 1904–1905 and has continued to stimulate debate over the relationship between religion and society.

F. Wendel, Calvin: *The Origins and Development of His Religious Thought*, trans. by P. Mairet (1963). The best treatment of Calvin's theology.

G. H. Williams, *The Radical Reformation* (1962). Broad survey of the varieties of dissent within Protestantism.

The West & the World

THE FAMILY IN EUROPE AND CHINA (1400–1800)

A family has a certain internal force and logic of its own. Time, place, and culture, however, are also important in making it what it is. A person raised in a twelfth-century household is different from one raised in a twentieth-century household, and growing up in Europe is not the same as growing up in Asia. The differences do not, however, lie in the ability of husbands and wives to love one another, or of parents to love their children. Rather, they result from the different ways in which a society or a culture infuses its larger communal values, shaped by politics, economics, and religious beliefs, into family life.

THE WESTERN EUROPEAN FAMILY

Later Marriages. Between 1500 and 1800, men and women in western Europe and England married at later ages than they had in previous centuries. Men tended to be in their mid- to late twenties rather than in their late teens and early twenties, and women in their early to mid-twenties rather than in their teens. The canonical, or church-sanctioned, age for marriage remained fourteen for men and twelve for women, and engagements might occur at these young ages, especially among royalty and nobility. As it had done throughout the high and later Middle Ages, the church also recognized as valid the free, private exchange of vows between a man and a woman at these minimal ages. However, after the Reformation, which condemned such clandestine unions, the church increasingly required both

parental agreement and public vows in church before a marriage could be recognized as fully licit—procedures it had always actually preferred.

Late marriage in the West reflected the difficulty couples had supporting themselves independently. The difficulty arose because of the population growth that occurred during the late fifteenth and early sixteenth centuries, when western Europe recovered much of the population loss incurred during the plague. Larger families meant more heirs and hence a grater division of resources. In Germanic and Scandinavian countries, the custom of a fair sharing of inheritance among all male children worked to delay marriages, for divided inheritances often meant small incomes for the recipients. It simply took the average couple a longer time than previously to prepare themselves materially for marriage. In the sixteenth century, one in five women never married, and these, combined with the estimated 15 percent who were unmarried widows, constituted a sizable unmarried female population.

A later marriage meant a marriage of shorter duration because couples who married in their thirties would not spend as much time together as couples who married in their twenties. Such marriages also contributed to more frequent remarriage for men because women who bore children for the first time at advanced ages had higher mortality rates than younger mothers. Moreover, as growing church condemnation and the rapid growth of orphanages and foundling homes between 1600 and 1800 confirm, delayed marriage

A sixteenth century French tribute to the happiness of a peaceful, productive marriage and loving children. "La Famille de Berchem," by Frans Floris (ca. 1516–1570). [Corbis-Bettmann]

increased premarital sex and raised the number of illegitimate children.

Arranged Marriages. Marriage tended to be "arranged" in the sense that the parents customarily met and discussed the terms of the marriage. By the fifteenth century, the wealth and social standing of the bride and the bridegroom were not the only things considered when parents arranged a marriage. The two involved people may have known each other in advance and even to have had some prior relationship. Also, emotional feeling for one another was increasingly respected by parents. Parents did not force total strangers to live together, and children had a legal right to resist an unwanted marriage. A forced marriage was by definition invalid, and parents understood that unwanted marriages could fail. The best marriage was one desired by both the couple and their families.

Family Size. The western European family was conjugal, or nuclear; that is, it consisted of a father

and a mother and two to four children who survived into adulthood. This nuclear family lived within a larger household, consisting of in-laws, servants, laborers, and boarders. The average husband and wife had seven or eight children, a birth about every two years. Of these, however, an estimated one-third died by age five, and one-half by their teens. Rare is the family, at any social level, that did not experience infant mortality and child death.

Birth Control. Artificial birth control has existed since antiquity. The ancient Egyptians used alligator dung and other acidic sperm killers, and sponges were also popular. In the West, the church's condemnation of *coitus interruptus* (male withdrawal before ejaculation) during the thirteenth and fourteenth centuries suggests that a contraceptive mentality—that is, a conscious and regular effort at birth control—may have been developing at this time. But early birth control measures, when applied, were not very effective,

A young couple in love (ca. 1480) by an anonymous artist. [Bildarchiv Preussischer Kulturbesitz]

Wet nurses were women who had recently had a baby or were suckling a child of their own, and who, for a fee, agreed also to suckle another child. The practice appears to have increased the risk of infant mortality, exposing infants to a strange and shared milk supply from women who were usually not as healthy as the infants' own mothers and who often lived under less sanitary conditions. But nursing an infant was a chore some upper-class women found distasteful, and their husbands also preferred that they not do it. Among women, vanity and convenience appear to have been motives for turning to wet nurses. For husbands, more was at stake in the practice. Because the church forbade sexual intercourse while a woman was lactating, and sexual intercourse was also believed to spoil a lactating woman's milk (pregnancy, of course, eventually ended her milk supply), a nursing wife was often a reluctant lover. In addition, nursing had a contraceptive effect (about 75 percent effective). Some women prolonged nursing their children precisely to delay a new pregnancy, and some husbands understood and cooperated in this form of family planning. For other husbands, however, especially noblemen and royalty who desired an abundance of male heirs, nursing seemed to rob them of offspring and to jeopardize the patrimony; hence, their support of wet nursing.

Loving Families?   The traditional western European family had features that may seem cold and unloving. When children were between the ages of eight and thirteen, parents routinely sent them out of their homes into apprenticeships, off to school, or into employment in the homes and businesses of relatives, friends, and even strangers. In addition, the emotional ties between spouses seem to have been as tenuous as those between parents and children. Widowers and widows often married again within a few months of their spouses' deaths, and marriages with extreme disparity in age—between older men and younger women and between older women and younger men—also suggest limited affection.

In response to such modern-day criticism, an early modern parent would surely have asked, "What greater love can parents have for their children than to equip them to make their way vocationally in the world?" An apprenticed child was a self-supporting child, and hence a child with a

and for both historical and moral reasons the church firmly opposed them. During the eleventh century it suppressed an extreme ascetic sect, the Cathars, whom it accused of practicing birth control. The church also opposed (and still opposes) contraception on moral grounds. According to Saint Thomas Aquinas, a moral act must always aid and abet, never frustrate, the natural end of the being or thing in question, and he believed that the natural end of sex could be only the birth of children and their godly rearing within the bounds of holy matrimony and the community of the church.

Wet Nursing.   The church allied with the physicians of early modern Europe on another intimate family matter: the condemnation of women who hired nurses to suckle their newborn children, sometimes for as long as a year and a half. The practice was popular among upper-class women, who looked on it as a symbol of their high rank.

future. Considering primitive living conditions, contemporaries could also appreciate the purely utilitarian and humane side of marriage and understand when widowers and widows quickly married again. On the other hand, marriages with extreme disparity in age were no more the norm in early modern Europe than the practice of wet nursing, and they received just as much criticism and ridicule.

THE TRADITIONAL CHINESE FAMILY[1]

The Meaning of Family. In Chinese the word for "family" and "home" is the same: all who live together under one roof. For the Chinese, as for the European family, the child–parent unit (the "nuclear family") distinguished itself from its kin by marriage, and both groups separated themselves from servants, boarders, and/or workers, who circulated or lived within the household. And both cultures recognized the family as society's fundamental unit.

In addition to its many relatives by blood and marriage, the Chinese family also thought of itself as part of the ruling regime, or "state," another group identity beyond the immediate family, village, and clan that rulers, attempting to unify their lands, encouraged. They did this primarily by exalting patrilineage, or membership in a group that traced its history over untold generations of males. During the later Middle Ages, patrilineage played a similar role in Europe: With matrilineal lines ignored, the maternal side of a family's history was suppressed. Despite the effects of their rulers, the Chinese never felt as close to the state as they did to their families and kin. In Europe, by contrast, a quasi "national" consciousness—that is, a sense of being "German," "French," or "English" as well as a member of a particular family, village, or clan—was more successful inculcated.

The Chinese family also counted its dead ancestors as intimate family members, their spirits said to roam the earth and scrutinize the conduct of their kin, a belief that encouraged good behavior

[1]The sources for the following are Maurice Freedman, *The Study of Chinese Society: Essays by Maurice Freedman* (Stanford, CA: Stanford University Press, 1979); Martin C. Yang, *A Chinese Village: Taitou, Shantung Province* (New York: Columbia University Press, 1965); and Margery Wolf, "Child Training and the Chinese Family," in Maurice Freedman, ed., *Family and Kinship in Chinese Society* (Stanford, CA: Stanford University Press, 1970), pp. 37–62.

and achievement. As in Western Christendom, the Chinese believed that the world of the living communed with that of the dead. Children were admonished to act in ways that pleased and honored the spirits of their ancestors, lest the latter bring misfortune upon their families. In Europe, by contrast, the living were thought to be of more help to the dead than the dead to the living. By special prayers and masses, people believed they could help their deceased relatives pass through purgatory and into heaven.

Family Size. The average Chinese family was slightly smaller than the average European family, numbering five or six members instead of seven or eight. Like Western Christianity, Confucianism exalted the authority of the father over the family and stressed the virtues of order and obedience within it. No religious virtue was said to be greater than loyalty to one's family.

Family Relationships. For the family of the bride, a wedding was a costly affair and arranged with the greatest of care. Whereas in Europe, fathers usually took the lead in finding husbands for their daughters, mothers played that role in China. This actually worked to the bride's favor, for a mother better understood what marriage involved for a woman and probably got her daughter the best possible mate. Also unlike in Europe, where by 1500 a couple's emotional compatibility had become almost as important a consideration in the making of a marriage as wealth and social standing, a prospective Chinese bride and bridegroom had both less to say about whom they married and a smaller role in the arrangements.

The life of a new daughter-in-law was not completely enviable. Her new family often looked on her as an unnatural member, an alien artificially incorporated by marriage. A bride's transition into her husband's family was often traumatic. After the wedding, she became the sole legal responsibility of her husband's family, breaking her ties with her own family to a degree unheard of in Europe. No longer able to count on her own family for security and affection, she often found her husband's household stressful, especially during the first years. Confucianism contributed to this state of affairs by stressing family solidarity against foreign influence, including that of daughters-in-law, whom it instructed families to isolate.

A Chinese Merchant's Family, ca. 1856. In a pose reflecting the gender divisions within the traditional Chinese family, the father sits with his sons on the right, his wife and daughter sit on the left. [Mark Sexton/Courtesy Peabody & Essex Museum, Salem, MA]

Particularly in well-ordered, high-status families, a new wife came immediately under the authority of her mother-in-law, who, with her son's concurrence (Chinese sons did not challenge their mothers), regulated and supervised her every activity within the new household. A daughter-in-law also could not protest this situation because of her dependence on the good will of her mother-in-law. Regardless of the disagreement, a daughter-in-law who found herself at odds with her mother-in-law faced a difficult life. In the end, it often became a simple choice between capitulation or misery. Only with the passage of time and the bearing of children did the bride gain grater respect and freedom within her new household.

A daughter-in-law also faced an up-hill battle with her mother-in-law for the loyalty and affection of her husband. Deeply committed to both, he found himself in a delicate situation, having to treat each in such a way that the other would not be offended.

Child Rearing. The goal of Chinese parents was to raise loyal and obedient children who would support them in their old age. That was also true of European parents in rural society, while the urban upper classes also looked on worldly success and family honor as equally important goals. As in Europe, Chinese parents treated their children differently after they had reached six or seven years of age. Boys especially came under the strict discipline of their fathers, who henceforth dealt with them in a consciously aloof and formal manner, the best way, it was believed, to render children dutiful and loyal. Fear and shame were also employed to discourage behavior that displeased or dishonored parents. As among European, Chinese parents now resisted overly generous displays of affection and indulgence, fearing such treatment might spoil their children and make them unreliable in later life, when the parents' survival and well-being would depend totally on their loyalty and devotion.

Mothers took a different approach to child rearing. Along with the promise of future security, bearing a child gave a woman a greater importance within the family. Whereas fathers sought to retain the loyalty of a child by inculcating fear and shame, mothers attempted a friendlier relationship, often becoming their children's advocate and mediator with the father. Both parents beat disobedient children, but as a child matured, corporal punishment became almost wholly the responsibility of the father, another feature the Chinese family shared with the European. The mother was the parent in whom a child might trustingly confide and with whom a joke might be shared.

On the whole, daughters were treated more affectionately than sons. This was because Chinese parents knew that a daughter would never be theirs again once she had married and joined her husband's household. Not being dependent on their daughters for their future well-being, parents had less need to drill loyalty and obedience into them, and could thus treat a daughter with greater informality and affection than they could a son. The result was a shorter, but comparatively happier relationship between parents and daughters.

✦ *What did Western European and Chinese families consider to be the most important factors in a successful marriage?*
✦ *Why was a new wife more harmoniously integrated into a Western European family than into a Chinese family?*
✦ *Did Western European and Chinese parents have the same goals in child-rearing?*
✦ *Did Western European and Chinese parents express pride in and affection for their children in the same way?*
✦ *In which culture do you think the family had greater independence from outside influences (religion, politics, and mass culture)?*

The massacre of worshiping Protestants at Vassy, France (March 1, 1562), which began the French wars of religion. An engraving by an unidentified seventeenth century artist. [The Granger Collection, N.Y.]

The Age of Religious Wars

K E Y   T O P I C S

- The war between Calvinists and Catholics in France
- The Spanish occupation of the Netherlands
- The struggle for supremacy between England and Spain
- The devastation of central Europe during the Thirty Years' War

The late sixteenth century and the first half of the seventeenth century are described as the "age of religious wars" because of the bloody opposition of Protestants and Catholics across Europe. Both genuine religious conflict and bitter dynastic rivalries fueled the wars. In France, the Netherlands, England, and Scotland in the second half of the sixteenth century, Calvinists fought Catholic rulers for the right to govern their own territories and to practice their chosen religion openly. In the first half of the seventeenth century, Lutherans, Calvinists, and Catholics marched against one another in central and northern Europe during the Thirty Years' War. By the middle of the seventeenth century, English Puritans had successfully revolted against the Stuart monarchy and the Anglican Church.

Renewed Religious Struggle

During the first half of the sixteenth century, religious conflict had been confined to central Europe and was primarily a struggle by Lutherans to secure rights and freedoms for themselves. In the second half of the sixteenth century, the focus shifted to western Europe—to France, the Netherlands, England, and Scotland—and became a struggle by Calvinists for recognition. After the Peace of Augsburg (1555), and with it acceptance of the principle that a region's ruler would determine its religion (*cuius regio, eius religio*), Lutheranism became a legal religion in the Holy Roman Empire. The Peace of Augsburg did not, however, extend recognition to non-Lutheran Protestants. Both Catholics and Lutherans scorned Anabaptists and other sectarians as anarchists, and Calvinists were not yet strong enough to demand legal standing.

Outside the empire the struggle for Protestant religious rights had intensified in most countries by the mid-sixteenth century. After the Council of Trent adjourned in 1563, Catholics began a Jesuit-led international counteroffensive against Protestants. At the time of John Calvin's death in 1564, Geneva had become both a refuge for Europe's persecuted Protestants and an interna-

The religious conflicts of the sixteenth and seventeenth centuries are reflected in the art and architecture of the period. This eighteenth-century cloister-church in Ottobeuren in Bavaria, designed by Johann Michael Fischer, is in the baroque style congenial to the Catholic Counter-Reformation. The interior explodes with energy and is filled with sculptures and paintings and magnificent woodwork that catch the eye. The intent was to inspire and move the worshiper to self-transcendence. [Bildarchiv Preussicscher Kulturbesitz]

tional school for Protestant resistance, producing leaders fully equal to the new Catholic challenge.

Genevan Calvinism and Catholicism as revived by the Council of Trent were two equally dogmatic, aggressive, and irreconcilable church systems. Calvinists may have looked like "new papists" to critics when they dominated cities like Geneva. Yet when, as minorities, they found their civil and religious rights denied, they became true firebrands and revolutionaries. Calvinism adopted a presbyterian organization that magnified regional and local religious authority. Boards of presbyters, or elders, rep-

resenting the many individual congregations of Calvinists, directly shaped the policy of the church at large.

By contrast, the Counter-Reformation sponsored a centralized episcopal church system, hierarchically arranged from pope to parish priest, that stressed absolute obedience to the person at the top. The high clergy—the pope and his bishops—not the synods of local churches, ruled supreme. Calvinism proved attractive to proponents of political decentralization who opposed totalitarian rulers, whereas Catholicism remained congenial to proponents of absolute monarchy determined to maintain "one king, one church, one law."

The opposition between the two religions can be seen even in the art and architecture that each came to embrace. The Catholic Counter-Reformation found the baroque style congenial. A successor to mannerism, baroque art is a grandiose, three-dimensional display of life and energy. Great baroque artists like Peter Paul Rubens (1571–1640) and Gianlorenzo Bernini (1598–1680) were Catholics. Protestants by contrast opted for a simpler and more restrained art and architecture, as can be seen in the English churches of Christopher Wren (1632–1723) and the gentle, searching portraits of the Dutch Mennonite, Rembrandt van Rijn (1606–1669).

As religious wars engulfed Europe, the intellectuals perceived the wisdom of religious pluralism and toleration more quickly than did the politi-

cians. A new skepticism, relativism, and individualism in religion became respectable in the sixteenth and seventeenth centuries. (See Chapter 14.) Sebastian Castellio's (1515–1563) pithy censure of John Calvin for his role in the execution of the anti-Trinitarian Michael Servetus summarized a growing sentiment: "To kill a man is not to defend a doctrine, but to kill a man."[1] The French essayist Michel de Montaigne (1533–1592) asked in scorn of the dogmatic mind: "What do I know?" And the Lutheran Valentin Weigel (1533–1588), surveying a half century of religious strife in Germany, advised people to look within themselves for religious truth and no longer to churches and creeds.

Such skeptical views gained currency in larger political circles only at the cost of painful experi-

[1]*Contra libellum Calvini* (N.P., 1562), p. E 2 a.

In stark contrast to the baroque style, this seventeenth-century Calvinist church in the Palatinate has no interior decoration to distract the worshiper from the Word of God. The intent was to create an atmosphere of quiet introspection and reflection on one's spiritual life and God's Word. [German National Museum, Nuremburg]

ence. Religious strife and civil war were best held in check where rulers tended to subordinate theological doctrine to political unity, urging tolerance, moderation, and compromise—even indifference—in religious matters. Rulers of this kind came to be known as *politiques*, and the most successful among them was Elizabeth I of England. By contrast, such rulers as Mary I of England, Philip II of Spain, and Oliver Cromwell, who took their religion with the utmost seriousness and refused every compromise, did not in the long run achieve their political goals.

As we shall see, the wars of religion were both internal national conflicts and truly international wars. Catholic and Protestant subjects struggled against one another for control of the crown of France, the Netherlands, and England. The Catholic governments of France and Spain conspired and finally sent armies against Protestant regimes in England and the Netherlands. The outbreak of the Thirty Years' War in 1618 made the international dimension of the religious conflict especially clear; before it ended in 1648, the war drew every major European nation directly or indirectly into its deadly net.

The French Wars of Religion (1562–1598)

Anti-Protestant Measures and the Struggle for Political Power

French Protestants are known as *Huguenots*, a term derived from Besançon Hugues, the leader of Geneva's political revolt against the House of Savoy in the 1520s, a prelude to that city's Calvinist Reformation. Huguenots were under surveillance in France already in the early 1520s, when Lutheran writings and doctrines began to circulate in Paris. The capture of the French king Francis I by the forces of Emperor Charles V at the Battle of Pavia in 1525 provided a motive for the first wave of Protestant persecution in France. The French government hoped thereby to pacify their Habsburg conqueror, a fierce opponent of German Protestants, and to win their king's swift release.

A second major crackdown came a decade later. When Protestants plastered Paris and other cities with anti-Catholic placards on October 18, 1534, mass arrests of suspected Protestants followed. The government retaliation drove John Calvin and other members of the French reform party into exile. In 1540 the Edict of Fontainebleau subjected French Protestants to the Inquisition. Henry II (r. 1547–1559) established new measures against Protestants in the Edict of Chateaubriand in 1551. Save for a few brief interludes, the French monarchy remained a staunch foe of the Protestants until the ascension to the throne of Henry of Navarre in 1589.

The Habsburg–Valois wars (see Chapter 11) had ended with the Treaty of Cateau-Cambrésis in 1559, after which Europe experienced a moment of peace. But the same year marked the beginning of internal French conflict and the shift of the European balance of power away from France to Spain. The shift began with an accident. During a tournament held to celebrate the marriage of his thirteen-year-old daughter to Philip II, the son of Charles V and heir to the Spanish Habsburg lands, the French king, Henry II, was mortally wounded when a lance pierced his visor. This unforeseen event brought to the throne his sickly fifteen-year-old son, Francis II, under the regency of the queen mother, Catherine de Médicis. With the monarchy so weakened by Henry's death, three powerful families saw their chance to control France and began to compete for the young king's ear. They were the Bourbons, whose power lay in the south and west; the Montmorency-Chatillons, who controlled the center of France; and the Guises, who were dominant in eastern France.

The Guises were by far the strongest and had little trouble establishing firm control over the young king. Francis, duke of Guise, had been Henry II's general, and his brothers, Charles and Louis, were cardinals of the church. Mary Stuart, Queen of Scots and wife of Francis II, was their niece. Throughout the latter half of the sixteenth century, the name of Guise remained interchangeable with militant, reactionary Catholicism.

The Bourbon and Montmorency-Chatillon families, in contrast, developed strong Huguenot sympathies, largely for political reasons. The Bourbon Louis I, prince of Condé (d. 1569), and the Montmorency-Chatillon Admiral Gaspard de Coligny (1519–1572) became the political leaders of the French Protestant resistance. They collaborated early in an abortive plot to kidnap Francis II from his Guise advisers in the Conspiracy of Amboise in 1560. This conspiracy was strongly condemned by John Calvin, who considered such tactics a disgrace to the Reformation.

Appeal of Calvinism

Often for quite different reasons ambitious aristocrats and discontented townspeople joined Calvinist churches in opposition to the Guise-dominated French monarchy. In 1561 more than 2,000 Huguenot congregations existed throughout France. Yet Huguenots were a majority of the population in only two regions: Dauphiné and Languedoc. Although they made up only about one fifteenth of the population, Huguenots were in important geographic areas and were heavily represented among the more powerful segments of French society. More than two-fifths of the French aristocracy became Huguenots. Many apparently hoped to establish within France a principle of territorial sovereignty akin to that secured within the Holy Roman Empire by the Peace of Augsburg. In this way, Calvinism indirectly served the forces of political decentralization.

John Calvin and Theodore Beza consciously sought to advance their cause by currying favor with powerful aristocrats. Beza converted Jeanne d'Albert, the mother of the future Henry IV. The prince of Condé was apparently converted in 1558 under the influence of his Calvinist wife. For many aristocrats—Condé probably among them—Calvinist religious convictions were attractive primarily as aids to long-sought political goals.

The military organization of Condé and Coligny progressively merged with the religious organization of the French Huguenot churches, creating a potent combination that benefitted both political and religious dissidents. Calvinism gave political resistance justification and inspiration, and the forces of political resistance made Calvinism a viable religious alternative in Catholic France. Each side had much to gain from the other. The confluence of secular and religious motives, although beneficial to aristocratic resistance and Calvinist religion alike, tended to cast suspicion on the religious appeal of Calvinism. Clearly religious conviction was neither the only nor always the main reason for becoming a Calvinist in France in the second half of the sixteenth century.

Catherine de Médicis and the Guises

Following Francis II's death in 1560, Catherine de Médicis continued as regent for her minor son, Charles IX (r. 1560–1574). At a colloquy in Poissy, she tried unsuccessfully to reconcile the Protestant

Catherine de Médicis (1519–1589) exercised power in France during the reigns of her three sons Francis II (r. 1559–1560), Charles IX (r. 1560–1574), and Henry III (r. 1574–1589). [H. Roger Viollet]

and Catholic factions. Fearing the power and guile of the Guises, Catherine, whose first concern was always to preserve the monarchy, sought allies among the Protestants. In 1562, after conversations with Beza and Coligny, she issued the January Edict, a measure that granted Protestants freedom to worship publicly outside towns—although only privately within them—and to hold synods. In March this royal toleration came to an abrupt end when the duke of Guise surprised a Protestant congregation at Vassy in Champagne and proceeded to massacre several score. That event marked the beginning of the French wars of religion (March 1562).

Had Condé and the Huguenot armies rushed immediately to the queen's side after this attack, Protestants might well have secured an alliance with the crown. The queen mother's fear of Guise power was great at this time. But the hesitation of the Protestant leaders, due primarily to indecision on the part of Condé, placed the young king and the queen mother, against their deepest wishes, in firm Guise control. Cooperation with the Guises became the only alternative to capitulation to the Protestants.

THE PEACE OF SAINT-GERMAIN-EN-LAYE   During the first French war of religion, fought between April 1562 and March 1563, the duke of Guise was assassinated. It is a measure of the international character of the struggle in France that troops from Hesse and the Palatinate fought alongside the Huguenots. A brief resumption of hostilities in 1567–1568 was followed by the bloodiest of all the conflicts, between September 1568 and August 1570. In this period, Condé was killed and Huguenot leadership passed to Coligny. This was actually a blessing in disguise for the Protestants because Coligny was far the better military strategist. In the Peace of Saint-Germain-en-Laye (1570), which ended the third war, the crown, acknowledging the power of the Protestant nobility, granted the Huguenots religious freedoms within their territories and the right to fortify their cities.

Perpetually caught between fanatical Huguenot and Guise extremes, Queen Catherine had always sought to balance one side against the other. Like the Guises, she wanted a Catholic France; she did not, however, desire a Guise-dominated monarchy. After the Peace of Saint-Germain-en-Laye the crown tilted manifestly toward the Bourbon faction and the Huguenots, and Coligny became Charles IX's most trusted adviser. Unknown to the king, Catherine began to plot with the Guises against the ascendant Protestants. As she had earlier sought Protestant support when Guise power threatened to subdue the monarchy, she now sought Guise support as Protestant influence grew.

There was reason for Catherine to fear Coligny's hold on the king. Louis of Nassau, the leader of Protestant resistance to Philip II in the Netherlands, had gained Coligny's ear. Coligny used his position of influence to win the king of France over to a planned French invasion of the Netherlands in support of the Dutch Protestants. Such a course of action would have placed France squarely on a collision course with mighty Spain. Catherine recognized far better than her son that France stood little chance in such a contest. She and her advisers had been much sobered in this regard by news of the stunning Spanish victory over the Turks at Lepanto in October 1571 (to be discussed later).

The Saint Bartholemew's Day Massacre, as depicted by the contemporary Protestant painter François Dubois. In this notorious event, 3,000 Protestants were slaughtered in Paris and an estimated 20,000 others died throughout France. The massacre transformed the religious struggle in France from a contest for political power into a war for survival between Protestants and Catholics. [Musée Cantonal des Beaux Arts, Palais de Rumine, Lausanne]

THE SAINT BARTHOLOMEW'S DAY MASSACRE When Catherine lent her support to the infamous Saint Bartholomew's Day Massacre of Protestants, she did so out of a far less reasoned judgment. Her decision appears to have been made in a state of near panic. On August 22, 1572, four days after the Huguenot Henry of Navarre had married the king's sister, Marguerite of Valois—still another sign of growing Protestant power—Coligny was struck down, although not killed, by an assassin's bullet. Catherine had apparently been party to this Guise plot to eliminate Coligny. After its failure, she feared both the king's reaction to her complicity with the Guises and the Huguenot response under a recovered Coligny. Catherine convinced Charles that a Huguenot coup was afoot, inspired by Coligny, and that only the swift execution of Protestant leaders could save the crown from a Protestant attack on Paris.

On Saint Bartholomew's Day, August 24, 1572, Coligny and 3,000 fellow Huguenots were butchered in Paris. Within three days an estimated 20,000 Huguenots were executed in coordinated attacks throughout France. It is a date that has ever since lived in infamy for Protestants.

Pope Gregory XIII and Philip II of Spain reportedly greeted the news of the Protestant massacre with special religious celebrations. Philip especially had good reason to rejoice. By throwing France into civil war, the massacre ended for the moment any planned French opposition to his efforts to subdue his rebellious subjects in the Netherlands. But the massacre of thousands of Protestants also gave the discerning Catholic world cause for new alarm. The event changed the nature of the struggle between Protestants and Catholics both within and beyond the borders of France. It was thereafter no longer an internal contest between Guise and Bourbon factions for French political influence, nor was it simply a Huguenot campaign to win basic religious freedoms. Henceforth, in Protestant eyes, it became an international struggle to the death for sheer survival against an adversary whose cruelty now justified any means of resistance.

PROTESTANT RESISTANCE THEORY Only as Protestants faced suppression and sure defeat did they begin to sanction active political resistance. At first, they tried to practice the biblical precept of obedient subjection to worldly authority (Romans 13:1). Luther had only grudgingly approved resistance to the emperor after the Diet of Augsburg in 1530. In 1550 Lutherans in Magdeburg had published a highly influential defense of the right of lower authorities to oppose the emperor's order that all Lutherans return to the Catholic fold.

Calvin, who never faced the specter of total political defeat after his return to Geneva in September 1540, had always condemned willful disobedience and rebellion against lawfully constituted governments as un-Christian. But he also taught that lower magistrates, as part of the lawfully constituted government, had the right and duty to oppose tyrannical higher authority.

The exiled Scottish reformer John Knox, who had seen his cause crushed by Mary of Guise, the Regent of Scotland, and Mary I of England, laid the groundwork for later Calvinist resistance. In his famous *First Blast of the Trumpet Against the Terrible Regiment of Women* (1558), he declared that the removal of a heathen tyrant was not only permissible, but a Christian duty. He had the Catholic queen of England in mind.

After the great massacre of French Protestants on Saint Bartholomew's Day, 1572, Calvinists everywhere came to appreciate the need for an active defense of their religious rights. Classical Huguenot theories of resistance appeared in three major works of the 1570s. The first was the *Franco-Gallia* of François Hotman (1573), a humanist argument that the representative Estates General of France historically held higher authority than the French king. The second was Theodore Beza's *On the Right of Magistrates over Their Subjects* (1574), which, going beyond Calvin's views, justified the correction and even the overthrow of tyrannical rulers by lower authorities. Finally, Philippe du Plessis Mornay's *Defense of Liberty Against Tyrants* (1579) admonished princes, nobles, and magistrates beneath the king, as guardians of the rights of the body politic, to take up arms against tyranny in other lands.

The Rise to Power of Henry of Navarre

Henry III (r. 1574–1589) was the last of Henry II's sons to wear the French crown. He found the monarchy wedged between a radical Catholic League, formed in 1576 by Henry of Guise, and vengeful Huguenots. Neither group would have been reluctant to assassinate a ruler whom they considered heretical and a tyrant. Like the queen mother, Henry sought to steer a middle course. In this effort he received support from a growing body

Theodore Beza Defends the Right to Resist Tyranny

One of the oldest problems in political and social theory has been that of knowing when resistance to repression in matters of conscience is justified. Since Luther's day, Protestant reformers had urged their followers to obey established political authority. After the 1572 Saint Bartholomew's Day Massacre, however, Protestant pamphleteers urged Protestants to resist tyrants and persecutors with armed force. In 1574 Theodore Beza pointed out the obligation of rulers to act in the best interests of their subjects and the latter's right to resist them when they did not.

✦ *When does a ruler go too far according to Beza? To whom may subjects appeal against a tyrant? Does Beza believe that individuals may take the law into their own hands?*

It is apparent that there is a mutual obligation between the king and the officers of a kingdom; that the government of the kingdom is not in the hands of the king in its entirety, but only the sovereign degree; that each of the officers has a share in accord with his degree; and that there are definite conditions on either side. If these conditions are not observed by the inferior officers, it is the part of the sovereign to dismiss and punish them. . . . If the king, hereditary or elective, clearly goes back on the conditions without which he would not have been recognized and acknowledged, can there be any doubt that the lesser magistrates of the kingdom, of the cities, and of the provinces, the administration of which they have received from the sovereignty itself, are free of their oath, at least to the extent that they are entitled to resist flagrant oppression of the realm which they swore to defend and protect according to their office and their particular jurisdiction? . . .

We must now speak of the third class of subjects, which though admittedly subject to the sovereign in a certain respect, is, in another respect, and in cases of necessity the protector of the rights of the sovereignty itself, and is established to hold the sovereign to his duty, and even, if need be, constrain and punish him. . . . The people is prior to all the magistrates, and does not exist for them, but they for it. . . . Whenever law and equity prevailed, nations neither created nor accepted kings except upon definite conditions. From this it follows that when kings flagrantly violate these terms, those who have the power to give them their authority have no less power to deprive them of it.

Constitutionalism and Resistance in the Sixteenth Century: Three Treatises by Hotman, Beza, and Mornay, trans. and ed. by Julian H. Franklin (New York: Pegasus, 1969), pp. 111–114.

of neutral Catholics and Huguenots, who put the political survival of France above its religious unity. Such *politiques* were prepared to compromise religious creeds as might be required to save the nation.

The Peace of Beaulieu in May 1576 granted the Huguenots almost complete religious and civil freedom. France, however, was not ready then for such sweeping toleration. Within seven months of the Peace of Beaulieu, the Catholic League forced Henry to return to the illusory quest for absolute religious unity in France. In October 1577 the king truncated the Peace of Beaulieu and once again circumscribed areas of permitted Huguenot worship. Thereafter Huguenot and Catholic factions quickly returned to their accustomed anarchical military solutions. The Protestants were led by Henry of Navarre, now heir to the French throne by virtue of his marriage to Margaret of Valois, Henry III's sister.

In the mid-1580s the Catholic League, supported by the Spanish, became completely dominant in Paris. In what came to be known as the Day of the

Barricades, Henry III attempted to rout the league with a surprise attack in 1588. The effort failed badly, and the king had to flee Paris. Forced by his weakened position into unkingly guerilla tactics, and also emboldened by news of the English victory over the Spanish Armada in 1588, Henry successfully plotted the assassinations of both the duke and the cardinal of Guise. These assassinations sent France reeling once again. Led by still another Guise brother, the Catholic League reacted with a fury that matched the earlier Huguenot response to the Massacre of Saint Bartholomew's Day. The king now had only one course of action. He struck an alliance with the Protestant Henry of Navarre in April 1589.

As the two Henrys prepared to attack the Guise stronghold of Paris, however, a fanatical Jacobin friar stabbed and killed Henry III. Thereupon the Bourbon Huguenot Henry of Navarre succeeded the childless Valois king to the French throne as Henry IV (r. 1589–1610). Pope Sixtus V and Philip II stood aghast at the sudden prospect of a Protestant France. They had always wanted France to be religiously Catholic and politically weak, and they now acted to achieve that end. Spain rushed troops to support the besieged Catholic League. Philip II apparently even harbored hopes of placing his eldest daughter, Isabella, the granddaughter of Henry II and Catherine de Médicis, on the French throne.

Direct Spanish intervention in the affairs of France seemed only to strengthen Henry IV's grasp on the crown. The French people viewed his right to hereditary succession more seriously than his espoused Protestant confession. Henry was also widely liked. Notoriously informal in dress and manner—a factor that made him especially popular with the soldiers—Henry also had the wit and charm to neutralize the strongest enemy in a face-to-face confrontation. He came to the throne as a *politique*, long weary with religious strife and fully prepared to place political peace above absolute religious unity. He believed that a royal policy of tolerant Catholicism would be the best way to achieve such peace. On July 25, 1593, he publicly abjured the Protestant faith and embraced the traditional and majority religion of his country. "Paris is worth a mass," he is reported to have said.

It was, in fact, a decision he had made only after a long period of personal agonizing. The Huguenots were understandably horrified by this turnabout, and Pope Clement VIII remained skeptical of Henry's sincerity. But most of the French church and people, having known internal strife too long, rallied to the king's side. By 1596 the Catholic League was dispersed, its ties with Spain were broken, and the wars of religion in France, to all intents, had ground to a close.

Henry IV of France (r. 1589–1610) on horseback, painted in 1594. [Giraudon/Art Resource, N.Y.]

Henry IV Recognizes Huguenot Religious Freedom

By the Edict of Nantes (April 13, 1598) Henry IV recognized Huguenot religious freedoms and the rights of Protestants to participate in French public institutions. Here are some of its provisions.

✦ *Are Huguenots given equal religious standing with Catholics? Are there limitations on their freedoms?*

We have by this perpetual and irrevocable Edict pronounced, declared, and ordained and we pronounce, declare and ordain:

Art. I. Firstly, that the memory of everything done on both sides from the beginning of the month of March, 1585, until our accession to the Crown and during the other previous troubles, and at the outbreak of them, shall remain extinct and suppressed, as if it were something which had never occurred. . . .

Art. II. We forbid all our subjects, of whatever rank and quality they may be, to renew the memory of these matters, to attack, be hostile to, injure or provoke each other in revenge for the past, whatever may be the reason and pretext . . . but let them restrain themselves and live peaceably together as brothers, friends, and fellow-citizens. . . .

Art. III. We ordain that the Catholic, Apostolic, and Roman religion shall be restored and reestablished in all places and districts of this our kingdom and the countries under our rule, where its practice has been interrupted. . . .

Art. VI. And we permit those of the so-called Reformed religion to live and dwell in all the towns and districts of this our kingdom and the countries under our rule, without being annoyed, disturbed, molested or constrained to do anything against their conscience, or for this cause to be sought out in their houses and districts where they wish to live, provided that they conduct themselves in other respects to the provisions of our present Edict. . . .

Art. XXI. Books dealing with the matters of the aforesaid so-called Reformed religion shall not be printed and sold publicly, except in the towns and districts where the public exercise of the said religion is allowed. . . .

Art. XXII. We ordain that there shall be no difference or distinction, because of the aforesaid religion, in the reception of students to be instructed in Universities, Colleges, and schools, or of the sick and poor into hospitals, infirmaries, and public charitable institutions. . . .

Art. XXVII. In order to reunite more effectively the wills of our subjects, as is our intention, and to remove all future complaints, we declare that all those who profess or shall profess the aforesaid so-called Reformed religion are capable of holding and exercising all public positions, honours, offices, and duties whatsoever . . . in the towns of our kingdom . . . notwithstanding all contrary oaths.

Church and State Through the Centuries: A Collection of Historic Documents, *trans. and ed. by S. Z. Ehler and John B. Morrall (New York: Biblo and Tannen, 1967), pp. 185–187.*

The Edict of Nantes

On April 13, 1598, Henry IV's famous Edict of Nantes proclaimed a formal religious settlement. The following month, on May 2, 1598, the Treaty of Vervins ended hostilities between France and Spain.

In 1591 Henry IV had already assured the Huguenots of at least qualified religious freedoms. The Edict of Nantes made good that promise. It rec-

Titian's portrait of Philip II of Spain (r. 1556–1598), the most powerful ruler of his time. [Alinari/Art Resource]

ognized and sanctioned minority religious rights within what was to remain an officially Catholic country. This religious truce—and it was never more than that—granted the Huguenots, who by this time numbered well over one million, freedom of public worship, the right of assembly, admission to public offices and universities, and permission to maintain fortified towns. Most of the new freedoms, however, were to be exercised within their own towns and territories. Concession of the right to fortify their towns reveals the continuing distrust between French Protestants and Catholics. As significant as it was, the edict only transformed a long hot war between irreconcilable enemies into a long cold war. To its critics it had only created a state within a state.

A Catholic fanatic assassinated Henry IV in May 1610. Although he is best remembered for the Edict of Nantes, the political and economic policies Henry IV put in place were equally important. They laid the foundations for the transformation of France into the absolute state it would become under Cardinal Richelieu and Louis XIV. Ironically, in pursuit of the political and religious unity that had escaped Henry IV, Louis XIV, calling for "one king, one church, one law," would revoke the Edict of Nantes in 1685 (see Chapter 13). This action would force France and Europe to learn again by bitter experience the hard lessons of the wars of religion. Rare is the politician who learns from the lessons of history rather than repeating its mistakes.

Imperial Spain and the Reign of Philip II (r. 1556–1598)

Pillars of Spanish Power

Until the English defeated the mighty Spanish Armada in 1588, no one person stood larger in the second half of the sixteenth century than Philip II of Spain. Philip was heir to the intensely Catholic and militarily supreme western Habsburg kingdom.

The battle of Lepanto occurred off the coast of Greece on October 7, 1571. In the largest naval engagement of the sixteenth century, the Spanish and their Italian allies under Don John of Austria smashed the Turkish fleet and ended the Ottoman threat in the western Mediterranean. [National Maritime Museum, London]

The eastern Habsburg lands of Austria, Bohemia, and Hungary had been given over by his father, Charles V, to Philip's uncle, the emperor Ferdinand I. These lands, together with the imperial title, remained in the possession of the Austrian branch of the family.

NEW WORLD RICHES   Populous and wealthy Castile gave Philip a solid home base. The regular arrival in Seville of bullion from the Spanish colonies in the New World provided additional wealth. In the 1540s great silver mines had been opened in Potosí in present-day Bolivia and in Zacatecas in Mexico. These gave Philip the great sums needed to pay his bankers and mercenaries. He nonetheless never managed to erase the debts left by his father nor to finance his own foreign adventures fully. He later contributed to the bankruptcy of the Fuggers when, at the end of his life, he defaulted on his enormous debts.

INCREASED POPULATION   The new American wealth brought dramatic social change to the peoples of Europe during the second half of the sixteenth century. As Europe became richer, it was also becoming more populous. In the economically and politically active towns of France, England, and the Netherlands, populations had tripled and quadrupled by the early seventeenth century. Europe's population exceeded 70 million by 1600.

The combination of increased wealth and population triggered inflation. A steady 2 percent a year rise in prices in much of Europe had serious cumulative effects by mid-century. There were more people than before and greater coinage in circulation, but less food and fewer jobs; wages stagnated while prices doubled and tripled in much of Europe.

This was especially the case in Spain. Because the new wealth was concentrated in the hands of a few, the traditional gap between the "haves"—the propertied, privileged, and educated classes—and the "have-nots" greatly widened. Nowhere did the unprivileged suffer more than in Spain, where the Castilian peasantry, the backbone of Philip II's great empire, became the most heavily taxed people of Europe. Those whose labor contributed most to making possible Spanish hegemony in Europe in the second half of the sixteenth century prospered least from it.

EFFICIENT BUREAUCRACY AND MILITARY A subjugated peasantry and wealth from the New World were not the only pillars of Spanish strength. Philip II shrewdly organized the lesser nobility into a loyal and efficient national bureaucracy. A reclusive man, he managed his kingdom by pen and paper rather than by personal presence. He was also a learned and pious Catholic, although some popes suspected that he used religion as much for political as for devotional purposes. That he was a generous patron of the arts and culture can be seen in his unique retreat outside Madrid, the Escorial, a combination palace, church, tomb, and monastery. Philip also knew personal sorrows. His mad and treacherous son, Don Carlos, died under suspicious circumstances in 1568—some contemporaries suspected that Philip had him quietly executed—only three months before the death of the queen.

SUPREMACY IN THE MEDITERRANEAN During the first half of Philip's reign, attention focused almost exclusively on the Mediterranean and the Turkish threat. By history, geography, and choice, Spain had traditionally been Catholic Europe's champion against Islam. During the 1560s the Turks advanced deep into Austria, while their fleets dominated the Mediterranean. Between 1568 and 1570 armies under Philip's half-brother, Don John of Austria, the illegitimate son of Charles V, suppressed and dispersed the Moors in Granada.

In May 1571 a Holy League of Spain, Venice, and the pope, again under Don John's command, formed to check Turkish belligerence in the Mediterranean. In what was the largest naval battle of the sixteenth century, Don John's fleet engaged the Ottoman navy under Ali Pasha off Lepanto in the Gulf of Corinth on October 7, 1571. Before the engagement ended, over one-third of the Turkish fleet had been sunk or captured and 30,000 Turks had died. The Mediterranean for the moment belonged to Spain, and the Europeans were left to fight each other. Philip's armies also succeeded in putting down resistance in neighboring Portugal, which Spain annexed in 1580. The conquest of Portugal not only added to Spanish seapower but also brought the magnificent Portuguese overseas empire in Africa, India, and the Americas into the Spanish orbit.

The Revolt in the Netherlands

The spectacular Spanish military success in southern Europe was not repeated in northern Europe. When Philip attempted to impose his will within the Netherlands and on England and France, he learned the lessons of defeat. The resistance of the Netherlands especially proved the undoing of Spanish dreams of world empire. (See Map 12–1.)

CARDINAL GRANVELLE The Netherlands was not only the richest area of Philip's Habsburg kingdom, but of Europe as well. In 1559 Philip had departed the Netherlands for Spain, never again to return. His half-sister, Margaret of Parma, assisted by a special council of state, became regent in his absence. The council was headed by Philip's hand-picked lieutenant, the extremely able Antoine Perrenot (1517–1586), after 1561 known as Cardinal Granvelle. Granvelle hoped to check Protestant gains by internal church reforms. He planned to break down the traditional local autonomy of the seventeen Netherlands provinces by stages and establish in its place a centralized royal government directed from Madrid. A politically docile and religiously uniform country was the goal.

The merchant towns of the Netherlands were, however, Europe's most independent; many, like magnificent Antwerp, were also Calvinist strongholds. By tradition and habit the people of the Netherlands inclined far more toward variety and toleration than toward obeisant conformity and hierarchical order. Two members of the council of state formed a stubborn opposition to the Spanish overlords, who now sought to reimpose their traditional rule with a vengeance. They were the Count of Egmont (1522–1568) and William of Nassau, the Prince of Orange (1533–1584), known as "the Silent" because of his extremely small circle of confidants.

Like other successful rulers in this period, William of Orange placed the Netherlands' political autonomy and well-being above religious creeds. He personally passed through successive Catholic, Lutheran, and Calvinist stages. In 1561 he married Anne of Saxony, the daughter of the Lutheran elector Maurice and the granddaughter of the late Landgrave Philip of Hesse. He maintained his Catholic practices until 1567, when he turned Lutheran. After the Saint Bartholomew's Day Massacre (1572), Orange (as he was called) became an avowed Calvinist.

In 1561 Cardinal Granvelle proceeded with a planned ecclesiastical reorganization of the Netherlands. It was intended to tighten the control of the Catholic hierarchy over the country and to acceler-

MAP 12–1   THE NETHERLANDS DURING THE REFORMATION   *The northern and southern provinces of the Netherlands. The former, the United Provinces, were mostly Protestant in the second half of the sixteenth century, while the southern Spanish Netherlands made peace with Spain and remained largely Catholic.*

ate its consolidation as a Spanish ward. Orange and Egmont, organizing the Dutch nobility in opposition, succeeded in gaining Granvelle's removal from office in 1564. Aristocratic control of the country after Granvelle's departure, however, proved woefully inefficient. Popular unrest continued to grow, especially among urban artisans, who joined the congregations of radical Calvinist preachers in increasing numbers.

THE COMPROMISE   The year 1564 also saw the first fusion of political and religious opposition to Regent Margaret's government. This opposition resulted from Philip II's unwise insistence that the decrees of the Council of Trent be enforced throughout the Netherlands. William of Orange's younger brother, Louis of Nassau, who had been raised a Lutheran, led the opposition, and it received support from the Calvinist-inclined lesser nobility and

A view of the Escorial, Philip II's massive palace-monastery-mausoleum northwest of Madrid. Built between 1563 and 1584, it was a monument to the piety and power of the king. Philip vowed to build the complex after the Spanish defeated the French at Saint-Quentin on Saint Lawrence's day in 1577. The floor plan of the Escorial resembles a grill, the symbol of Saint Lawrence (who, according to legend, was martyred by being roasted alive on a grill). [Robert Frerck/Odyssey Productions]

townspeople. A national covenant was drawn up called the *Compromise*, a solemn pledge to resist the decrees of Trent and the Inquisition. Grievances were loudly and persistently voiced. When Regent Margaret's government spurned the protesters as "beggars" in 1566, Calvinists rioted through the country. Louis called on French Huguenots and German Lutherans to send aid to the Netherlands, and a full-scale rebellion against the Spanish regency appeared imminent.

THE DUKE OF ALBA   The rebellion failed to materialize, however, because the Netherlands' higher nobility would not support it. Their shock at Calvinist iconoclasm and anarchy was as great as their resentment of Granvelle's more subtle repression. Philip, determined to make an example of the Protestant rebels, dispatched the duke of Alba to suppress the revolt. His army of 10,000 journeyed northward from Milan in 1567 in a show of combined Spanish and papal might. A special tribunal, known to the Spanish as the Council of Troubles and among the Netherlanders as the Council of

Blood, reigned over the land. The counts of Egmont and Horn and several thousand suspected heretics were publicly executed before Alba's reign of terror ended.

The Spanish levied new taxes, forcing the Netherlands to pay for the suppression of its own revolt. One of these taxes, the "tenth penny," a 10 percent sales tax, met such resistance from merchants and artisans that it remained uncollectible in some areas even after a reduction to 3 percent. Combined persecution and taxation sent tens of thousands fleeing from the Netherlands during Alba's cruel six-year rule. Alba came to be more hated than Granvelle or the radical Calvinists had ever been.

RESISTANCE AND UNIFICATION   William of Orange was an exile in Germany during these turbulent years. He now emerged as the leader of a broad movement for the Netherlands' independence from Spain. The northern, Calvinist-inclined provinces of Holland, Zeeland, and Utrecht, of which Orange was the *stadholder*, or governor, became his base. As in France, political resistance in the Netherlands

The Milch Cow, *a sixteenth-century satirical painting depicting the Netherlands as a cow in whom all the great powers of Europe have an interest. Elizabeth of England is feeding her (England had longstanding commercial ties with Flanders); Philip II of Spain is attempting to ride her (Spain was trying to reassert its control over the entire area); William of Orange is trying to milk her (he was the leader of the anti-Spanish rebellion); and the king of France holds her tail (France hoped to profit from the rebellion at Spain's expense). [Rijksmuseum, Amsterdam]*

NOT LONGE TIME SINCE I SAWE A COWE.
DID FLAVNDERS REPRESENTE
VPON WHOSE BACKE KINGE PHILIP RODE
AS BEING MALECONTNT.

THE QUEENE OF ENGLAND GIVING HAY
WHEARE ON THE COW DID FEEDE
A ONE THAT WAS HER GREATEST HELPE
IN HER DISTRESSE AND NEEDE.

THE PRINCE OF ORANGE MILKT THE CO
AND MADE HIS PVRSE THE PAYLE
THE COW DID SHYT IN MONSIEVR HAND
WHILE HE DID HOLD HER TAYLE.

gained both organization and inspiration by merging with Calvinism.

The early victories of the resistance attest to the popular character of the revolt. A case in point is the capture of the port city of Brill by the "Sea Beggars," an international group of anti-Spanish exiles and criminals, among them many Englishmen. William of Orange did not hesitate to enlist their services. Their brazen piracy, however, had forced Queen Elizabeth to disassociate herself from them and to bar their ships from English ports. In 1572 the Beggars captured Brill and other seaports in Zeeland and Holland. Mixing with the native population, they quickly sparked rebellions against Alba in town after town and spread the resistance southward. In 1574 the people of Leiden heroically resisted a long Spanish siege. The Dutch opened the dikes and flooded their country to repulse the hated Spanish. The faltering Alba had by that time ceded power to Don Luis de Requesens, who replaced him as commander of Spanish forces in the Netherlands in November 1573.

THE PACIFICATION OF GHENT   The greatest atrocity of the war came after Requesens's death in 1576. Spanish mercenaries, leaderless and unpaid, ran amok in Antwerp on November 4, 1576, leaving 7,000 people dead in the streets. The event came to be known as the Spanish Fury.

These atrocities accomplished in four short days what neither religion nor patriotism had previously been able to do. The ten largely Catholic southern provinces (what is roughly modern Belgium) now came together with the seven largely Protestant northern provinces (what is roughly the modern Netherlands) in unified opposition to Spain. This union, known as the Pacification of Ghent, was accomplished on November 8, 1576. It declared internal regional sovereignty in matters of religion, a key clause that permitted political cooperation among the signatories, who were not agreed over religion. It was a Netherlands version of the territorial settlement of religious differences brought about in the Holy Roman Empire in 1555 by the Peace of Augsburg. Four provinces initially held out, but they soon made the resistance unanimous by joining the all-embracing Union of Brussels in January 1577. For the next two years the Spanish faced a unified and determined Netherlands.

Don John, the victor over the Turks at Lepanto in 1571, had taken command of Spanish land forces in November 1576. He now experienced his first defeat. Confronted by unified Netherlands resistance, he signed the humiliating Perpetual Edict in February 1577. This edict provided for the removal of all Spanish troops from the Netherlands within twenty days. This withdrawal of troops gave the country to William of Orange and effectively ended

Philip II Declares William of Orange an Outlaw (1580)

In the following proclamation the king of Spain accused William of Orange of being the "chief disturber of the public peace" and offered his captors, or assassins, generous rewards.

◆ *Why was William of Orange perceived by Philip II as such a threat? Why was it important that Spain gain control over the Netherlands?*

Philip, by the grace of God king of Castile, etc. to all to whom these presents may come, greeting:

It is well known to all how favorably the late emperor, Charles V, . . . treated William of Nassau. . . . Nevertheless, as everyone knows, we had scarcely turned our back on the Netherlands before the said William . . . (who had become . . . prince of Orange) began . . . by sinister arts, plots, and intrigues . . . to gain [control] over those whom he believed to be malcontents, or haters of justice, or anxious for innovations, and . . . above all, those who were suspected in the matter of religion. . . . With the knowledge, advice, and encouragement of the said Orange, the heretics commenced to destroy the images, altars, and churches. . . . So soon as the said Nassau was received into the government of the provinces, he began, through his agents and satellites, to introduce heretical preaching. . . . Then he introduced liberty of conscience . . . which soon brought it about that the Catholics were openly persecuted and driven out. . . . Moreover he obtained such a hold upon our poor subjects of Holland and Zee-land . . . that nearly all the towns, one after the other, have been besieged. . . .

Therefore, for all these just reasons, for his evil doings as chief disturber of the public peace . . . we outlaw him forever and forbid our subjects to associate with him . . . in public or in secret. We declare him an enemy of the human race, and in order the sooner to remove our people from his tyranny and oppression, we promise, on the word of a king and as God's servant, that if one of our subjects be found so generous of heart and so desirous of doing us a service and advantaging the public that he shall find the means of executing this decree and of ridding us of the said pest, either by delivering him to us dead or alive, or by depriving him at once of life, we will give him and his heirs landed estates or money, as he will, to the amount of twenty-five thousand gold crowns. If he has committed any crime, of any kind whatsoever, we will pardon him. If he be not noble, we will ennoble him for his valor; and should he require other persons to assist him, we will reward them according to the service rendered, pardon their crimes, and ennoble them too.

James Harvey Robinson, ed., Readings in European History, *vol. 2 (Boston: Athenaeum, 1906), pp. 174–177.*

for the time being whatever plans Philip may have had for using the Netherlands as a staging area for an invasion of England.

THE UNION OF ARRAS AND THE UNION OF UTRECHT The Spanish, however, were nothing if not persistent. Don John and Alessandro Farnese of Parma, the regent Margaret's son, revived Spanish power in the southern provinces, where constant fear of Calvinist extremism had moved the leaders to break the Union of Brussels. In January 1579 the southern provinces formed the Union of Arras, and within five months they made peace with Spain. These provinces later served the cause of the Counter-Reformation. The northern provinces responded with the formation of the Union of Utrecht.

NETHERLANDS INDEPENDENCE   Seizing what now appeared to be a last opportunity to break the back of Netherlands resistance, Philip II declared William of Orange an outlaw and placed a bounty of 25,000 crowns on his head. The act predictably stiffened the resistance of the northern provinces. In a famous defiant speech to the Estates General of Holland in December 1580, known as the Apology, Orange publicly denounced Philip as a heathen tyrant whom the Netherlands need no longer obey.

On July 22, 1581, the member provinces of the Union of Utrecht met in The Hague and formally declared Philip no longer their ruler. They turned instead to the French duke of Alençon, Catherine de Médici's youngest son. The southern provinces had also earlier looked to him as a possible middle way between Spanish and Calvinist overlordship. All the northern provinces save Holland and Zeeland accepted Alençon as their "sovereign" (Holland and Zeeland distrusted him almost as much as they did Philip II), but with the understanding that he would be only a titular ruler. But Alençon, an ambitious failure, saw this as his one chance at greatness. When he rashly attempted to take actual control of the provinces in 1583, he was deposed and returned to France.

Spanish efforts to reconquer the Netherlands continued into the 1580s. William of Orange, assassinated in July 1584, was succeeded by his seventeen-year-old son, Maurice (1567–1625), who, with the assistance of England and France, continued Dutch resistance. Fortunately for the Netherlands, Philip II began now to meddle directly in French and English affairs. He signed a secret treaty with the Guises (the Treaty of Joinville in December 1584) and sent armies under Farnese into France in 1590. Hostilities with the English, who had openly aided the Dutch rebels, also increased. Gradually they built toward a climax in 1588, when Philip's great Armada was defeated in the English Channel.

These new fronts overextended Spain's resources, strengthening the Netherlands. Spanish preoccupation with France and England permitted the northern provinces to drive out all Spanish soldiers by 1593. In 1596 France and England formally recognized the independence of these provinces. Peace was not, however, concluded with Spain until 1609, when the Twelve Years' Truce gave the northern provinces virtual independence. Full recognition came finally in the Peace of Westphalia in 1648.

England and Spain (1553–1603)

Mary I

Before Edward VI died in 1553, he agreed to a device to make Lady Jane Grey, the teenage daughter of a powerful Protestant nobleman and, more important, the granddaughter on her mother's side of Henry VIII's younger sister Mary, his successor in place of the Catholic Mary Tudor (r. 1553–1558). But popular support for the principle of hereditary monarchy was too strong to deprive Mary of her rightful rule. Popular uprisings in London and elsewhere led to Jane Grey's removal from the throne within days of her crowning, and she was eventually beheaded.

Once enthroned, Mary proceeded to act even beyond the worst fears of the Protestants. In 1554 she entered a highly unpopular political marriage with Prince Philip (later Philip II) of Spain, a symbol

Portrait of Mary I (r. 1553–1558), Queen of England. By Sir Anthony Mor (Antonio Moro) (1517/20–76/7), Prado, Madrid. [The Bridgeman Art Library, London/Index.]

A Description of Mary Tudor

In 1557 the Venetian Ambassador reported to his government on the state of England, including a description of Mary I. At the time he wrote, she was receiving widespread criticism of her rule, particularly of her foreign policy, which the critics felt tied England too closely to the interests of Spain.

✦ *Does the gender of its subject color this description? Would a king be similarly described? What does the ambassador see as Mary's weaknesses and strengths?*

Queen Mary, the daughter of Henry VIII and of his queen Catherine, daughter of Ferdinand the Catholic, king of Aragon, is a princess of great worth. In her youth she was rendered unhappy by the event of her mother's divorce; by the ignominy and threats to which she was exposed after the change of religion in England, she being unwilling to unbend to the new one; and by the dangers to which she was exposed by the duke of Northumberland, and the riots among the people when she ascended the throne.

She is of short stature, well made, thin and delicate, and moderately pretty; her eyes are so lively that she inspires reverence and respect, and even fear, wherever she turns them; nevertheless she is very shortsighted. Her voice is deep, almost like that of a man. She understands five languages—English, Latin, French, Spanish, and Italian, in which last, however, she does not venture to converse. She is also much skilled in ladies' work, such as producing all sorts of embroidery with the needle. She has a knowledge of music, chiefly on the lute, on which she plays exceedingly well. As to the qualities of her mind, it may be said of her that she is rash, disdainful, and parsimonious rather than liberal. She is endowed with great humility and patience, but withal high-spirited, courageous, and resolute, having during the whole course of her adversity not been guilty of the least approach to meanness of deportment; she is, moreover, devout and staunch in the defense of her religion.

Some personal infirmities under which she labors are the causes to her of both public and private affliction; to remedy these recourse is had to frequent bloodletting, and this is the real cause of her paleness and the general weakness of her frame. These have also given rise to the unfounded rumor that the queen is in a state of pregnancy. The cabal she has been exposed to, the evil disposition of the people toward her, the present poverty and the debt of the crown, and her passion for King Philip, from whom she is doomed to live separate, are so many other causes of the grief with which she is overwhelmed. She is, moreover, a prey to the hatred she bears my Lady Elizabeth, and which has its source in the recollection of the wrongs she experienced on account of her mother, and in the fact that all eyes and hearts are turned towards my Lady Elizabeth as successor to the throne. . . .

James Harvey Robinson, ed., Readings in European History, *vol. 2 (Boston: Athenaeum, 1906), pp. 149–150.*

of militant Catholicism to English Protestants. At his direction she pursued a foreign policy that in 1558 cost England its last enclave on the Continent, Calais.

Mary's domestic measures were equally shocking to the English people and even more divisive. During her reign, Parliament repealed the Protestant statutes of Edward and reverted to the Catholic religious practice of her father, Henry VIII. The great Protestant leaders of the Edwardian Age—John Hooper, Hugh Latimer, and Thomas Cranmer—were executed for heresy. Hundreds of Protestants either joined them in martyrdom (282 were burned at the stake during Mary's reign) or took flight to the Continent. These "Marian exiles" settled in Germany and Switzerland, forming especially large communities in Frankfurt, Strasbourg, and Geneva. (John Knox, the future leader of the Reformation in Scotland, was prominent among these exiles.) There they worshiped in their own congregations, wrote tracts justifying armed resistance, and waited for the time when a Protestant counteroffensive could be launched in their homelands. They were also exposed to religious beliefs more radical than any set forth during Edward VI's reign. Many of these exiles later held positions in the Church of England during Elizabeth I's reign.

Elizabeth I

Mary's successor was her half-sister, Elizabeth I (r. 1558–1603), the daughter of Henry VIII and Anne Boleyn. Elizabeth had remarkable and enduring successes in both domestic and foreign policy. Assisted by a shrewd adviser, Sir William Cecil (1520–1598),

Elizabeth I (r. 1558–1603) standing on a map of England in 1592. An astute politician in both foreign and domestic policy, Elizabeth was perhaps the most successful ruler of the sixteenth century. [National Portrait Gallery, London]

she built a true kingdom on the ruins of Mary's reign. Between 1559 and 1563, she and Cecil guided a religious settlement through Parliament that prevented England from being torn asunder by religious differences in the sixteenth century, as the Continent was. Another ruler who subordinated religious to political unity, Elizabeth merged a centralized episcopal system, which she firmly controlled, with broadly defined Protestant doctrine and traditional Catholic ritual. In the resulting Anglican Church inflexible religious extremes were not permitted.

In 1559 an Act of Supremacy passed Parliament repealing all the anti-Protestant legislation of Mary Tudor and asserting Elizabeth's right as "supreme governor" over both spiritual and temporal affairs. An Act of Uniformity in the same year mandated a revised version of the second *Book of Common Prayer* (1552) for every English parish. The issuance of the *Thirty-Nine Articles on Religion* in 1563—which were a revision of Thomas Cranmer's original forty-two—made a moderate Protestantism the official religion within the Church of England.

CATHOLIC AND PROTESTANT EXTREMISTS Elizabeth hoped to avoid both Catholic and Protestant extremism at the official level by pursuing a middle way. Her first archbishop of Canterbury, Matthew Parker (d. 1575), represented this ideal. But Elizabeth could not prevent the emergence of subversive Catholic and Protestant zealots. When she ascended the throne, Catholics were in the majority in England. The extremists among them, encouraged by the Jesuits, plotted against her. Catholic radicals were also encouraged and later directly assisted by the Spanish, who were piqued both by Elizabeth's Protestant sympathies and by her refusal to follow the example of her half-sister Mary and take Philip II's hand in marriage. Elizabeth remained unmarried throughout her reign, using the possibility of a marriage alliance very much to her diplomatic advantage.

Catholic extremists hoped eventually to replace Elizabeth with Mary Stuart, Queen of Scots. Unlike Elizabeth, who had been declared illegitimate during the reign of her father, Mary Stuart had an unblemished claim to the throne by way of her grandmother Margaret, the sister of Henry VIII. Elizabeth acted swiftly against Catholic assassination plots and rarely let emotion override her political instincts. Despite proven cases of Catholic treason and even attempted regicide, she executed

An Unknown Contemporary Describes Queen Elizabeth

No sixteenth-century ruler governed more effectively than Elizabeth I of England (r. 1558–1603), who was both loved and feared by her subjects. An unknown contemporary has left the following description, revealing not only her intelligence and political cunning but also something of her immense vanity.

♦ *How does this description compare with that of Mary I? How do their personal qualities and political skills differ?*

I will proceed with the description of the queen's disposition and natural gifts of mind and body, wherein she either matched or exceeded all the princes of her time, as being of a great spirit yet tempered with moderation, in adversity never dejected, in prosperity rather joyful than proud; affable to her subjects, but always with due regard to the greatness of her estate, by reason whereof she was both loved and feared.

In her later time, when she showed herself in public, she was always magnificent in apparel; supposing haply thereby that the eyes of her people (being dazzled by the glittering aspect of her outward ornaments) would not so easily discern the marks of age and decay of natural beauty; and she came abroad the more seldom, to make her presence the more grateful and applauded by the multitude, to whom things rarely seen are in manner as new.

She suffered not, at any time, any suitor to depart discontented from her, and though ofttimes he obtained not that he desired, yet he held himself satisfied with her manner of speech, which gave hope of success in the second attempt. . . .

Latin, French, and Italian she could speak very elegantly, and she was able in all those languages to answer ambassadors on the sudden. . . . Of the Greek tongue she was also not altogether ignorant. She took pleasure in reading of the best and wisest histories, and some part of Tacitus's *Annals* she herself turned into English for her private exercise. She also translated Boethius's *On the Consolation of Philosophy* and a treatise of Plutarch, *On Curiosity*, with divers others. . . .

It is credibly reported that not long before her death, she had a great apprehension of her own age and declination by seeing her face (then lean and full of wrinkles) truly represented to her in a glass, which she a good while very earnestly beheld; perceiving thereby how often she had been abused by flatterers (whom she held in too great estimation) that had informed her the contrary.

James Harvey Robinson, ed., Readings in European History, vol. 2 (Boston: Athenaeum, 1906), pp. 191–193.

---

fewer Catholics during her forty-five years on the throne than Mary Tudor had executed Protestants during her brief five-year reign. She showed little mercy, however, to separatists and others who threatened the unity of her rule.

Elizabeth dealt cautiously with the Puritans, who were Protestants working within the national church to "purify" it of every vestige of "popery" and to make its Protestant doctrine more precise. The Puritans had two special grievances:

(1) the retention of Catholic ceremony and vestments within the Church of England, which made it appear to the casual observer that no Reformation had occurred,

(2) the continuation of the episcopal system of Church governance, which conceived of the English church theologically as the true successor to Rome, while placing it politically under the firm hand of the queen and her compliant archbishop.

Elizabeth I before Parliament. The artist shows the Queen small and in the background, and places Parliament prominently in the foreground, suggesting that England, despite the enormous power of the Queen, is a land where parliamentary government reigns supreme. [Folger Shakespeare Library]

Sixteenth-century Puritans were not separatists. They enjoyed wide popular support and were led by widely respected men like Thomas Cartwright (d. 1603). They worked through Parliament to create an alternative national church of semiautonomous congregations governed by representative presbyteries (hence, "Presbyterians"), following the model of Calvin and Geneva. Elizabeth dealt firmly but subtly with this group, conceding absolutely nothing that lessened the hierarchical unity of the Church of England and her control over it.

The more extreme Puritans wanted every congregation to be autonomous, a law unto itself, with neither higher episcopal nor presbyterian control. They came to be known as Congregationalists. Elizabeth and her second archbishop of Canterbury, John Whitgift (d. 1604), refused to tolerate this group, whose views on independence they found patently subversive. The Conventicle Act of 1593 gave such separatists the option of either conforming to the practices of the Church of England or facing exile or death.

DETERIORATION OF RELATIONS WITH SPAIN A series of events led inexorably to war between England and Spain, despite the sincerest desires on the part of both Philip II and Elizabeth to avoid a confrontation. In 1567 the Spanish duke of Alba marched his mighty army into the Netherlands, which was, from the English point of view, simply a convenient staging area for a Spanish invasion of England. Pope Pius V (r. 1566–1572), who favored a military conquest of Protestant England, "excommunicated" Elizabeth for heresy in 1570. This mischievous act only encouraged both internal resistance and international intrigue against the queen. Two years later, as already noted, the piratical Sea Beggars, many of whom were Englishmen, occupied the port city of Brill in the Netherlands and aroused the surrounding countryside against the Spanish.

Following Don John's demonstration of Spain's awesome seapower at the famous naval battle of Lepanto in 1571, England signed a mutual defense pact with France. Also in the 1570s, Elizabeth's famous seamen, John Hawkins (1532–1595) and Sir Francis Drake (1545?–1596), began to prey regularly on Spanish shipping in the Americas. Drake's circumnavigation of the globe between 1577 and 1580 was one in a series of dramatic demonstrations of English ascendancy on the high seas.

After the Saint Bartholomew's Day Massacre, Elizabeth was the only protector of Protestants in France and the Netherlands. In 1585 she signed the Treaty of Nonsuch, which provided English soldiers and cavalry to the Netherlands. Funds that had previously been funneled covertly to support Henry of Navarre's army in France now flowed openly.

MARY, QUEEN OF SCOTS These events made a tinderbox of English–Spanish relations. The spark that finally touched it off was Elizabeth's execution of Mary, Queen of Scots (1542–1587).

Mary Stuart was the daughter of King James V of Scotland and Mary of Guise and had resided in France from the time she was six years old. This

In 1588 Philip II sent a massive naval armada to invade England. The English, however, with the help of the weather and the Dutch, dispersed and destroyed the Spanish fleet. Spain never fully recovered from this defeat. [Giraudon/Art Resource, N.Y.]

thoroughly French and Catholic queen had returned to Scotland after the death of her husband, the French king Francis II, in 1561. There she found a successful, fervent Protestant Reformation that had won legal sanction the year before in the Treaty of Edinburgh (1560). As hereditary heir to the throne of Scotland, Mary remained queen by divine and human right. She was not intimidated by the Protestants who controlled her realm. She established an international French court culture, the gaiety and sophistication of which impressed many Protestant nobles whose religion often made their lives exceedingly dour.

Mary was closely watched by the ever-vigilant Scottish reformer John Knox. He fumed publicly and always with effect against the queen's private mass and Catholic practices, which Scottish law made a capital offense for everyone else. Knox won support in his role of watchdog from Elizabeth and Cecil. Elizabeth personally despised Knox and never forgave him for writing the *First Blast of the Trumpet Against the Terrible Regiment of Women*, a work aimed at provoking a revolt against Mary

Tudor but published in the year of Elizabeth's ascent to the throne. Elizabeth and Cecil tolerated Knox because he served their foreign policy, never permitting Scotland to succumb to the young Mary and her French and Catholic ways.

In 1568 a public scandal forced Mary's abdication and flight to her cousin Elizabeth in England. Mary's reputed lover, the earl of Bothwell, was, with cause, suspected of having killed her legal husband, Lord Darnley. When a packed court acquitted Bothwell, he subsequently married Mary. The outraged reaction from Protestant nobles forced Mary to surrender the throne to her one-year-old son, who became James VI of Scotland (and, later, Elizabeth's successor as King James I of England). Because of Mary's clear claim to the English throne, she remained an international symbol of a possible Catholic England, and she was consumed by the desire to be queen of England. Her presence in England, where she resided under house arrest for nineteen years, was a constant discomfort to Elizabeth.

In 1583 Elizabeth's vigilant secretary, Sir Francis Walsingham, uncovered a plot against Elizabeth involving the Spanish ambassador Bernardino de Mendoza. After Mendoza's deportation in January 1584, popular antipathy toward Spain and support for Protestant resistance in France and the Netherlands became massive throughout England.

In 1586 Walsingham uncovered still another plot against Elizabeth, the so-called Babington plot (after Anthony Babington, who was caught seeking Spanish support for an attempt on the queen's life). This time he had uncontestable proof of Mary's complicity. Elizabeth believed that the execution of a sovereign, even a dethroned sovereign, weakened royalty everywhere. She was also aware of the outcry that Mary's execution would create throughout the Catholic world, and Elizabeth sincerely wanted peace with English Catholics. But she really had no choice in the matter and consented to Mary's execution on February 18, 1587. This event dashed all Catholic hopes for a bloodless reconversion of Protestant England. After the execution of the Catholic queen of Scotland, Pope Sixtus V (r. 1585–1590), who feared Spanish domination almost as much as he abhorred English Protestantism, could no longer withhold public support for a Spanish invasion of England. Philip II ordered his Armada to make ready.

THE ARMADA   Spain's war preparations were interrupted in the spring of 1587 by Sir Francis Drake's successful shelling of the port city of Cadiz, an attack that inflicted heavy damage on Spanish ships and stores. After "singeing the beard of Spain's king," Drake raided the coast of Portugal, further incapacitating the Spanish. The success of these strikes forced the Spanish to postpone their planned invasion of England until the spring of 1588.

On May 30 of that year, a mighty fleet of 130 ships bearing 25,000 sailors and soldiers under the command of the duke of Medina-Sidonia set sail for England. In the end, however, the English won a stunning victory. The invasion barges that were to transport Spanish soldiers from the galleons onto English shores were prevented from leaving Calais and Dunkirk. The swifter English and Netherlands ships, helped by what came to be known as an "English wind," dispersed the waiting Spanish fleet, over one-third of which never returned to Spain.

The news of the Armada's defeat gave heart to Protestant resistance everywhere. Although Spain continued to win impressive victories in the 1590s,

it never fully recovered from this defeat. Spanish soldiers faced unified and inspired French, English, and Dutch armies. By the time of Philip's death on September 13, 1598, his forces had been successfully rebuffed on all fronts. His seventeenth-century successors were all inferior leaders who never knew responsibilities equal to Philip's. Nor did Spain ever again know such imperial grandeur. The French soon dominated the Continent, while in the New World the Dutch and the English progressively whittled away Spain's once glorious overseas empire.

Elizabeth died on March 23, 1603, leaving behind her a strong nation poised to expand into a global empire.

The Thirty Years' War (1618–1648)

The Thirty Years' War in the Holy Roman Empire was the last and most destructive of the wars of religion. Religious and political differences had long set Catholics against Protestants and Calvinists against Lutherans. What made the Thirty Years' War so devastating was the now-entrenched hatred of the various sides and their seeming determination to sacrifice all for their religious beliefs. As the conflicts multiplied, virtually every major European land, especially Lutheran Denmark and Sweden, became involved either directly or indirectly. When the hostilities ended in 1648, the peace terms shaped much of the map of northern Europe as we know it today.

Preconditions for War

FRAGMENTED GERMANY   In the second half of the sixteenth century, Germany was an almost ungovernable land of about 360 autonomous political entities. There were independent secular principalities (duchies, landgraviates, and marches); ecclesiastical principalities (archbishoprics, bishoprics, and abbeys); numerous free cities; and castle regions dominated by knights. The Peace of Augsburg (1555) had given each a significant degree of sovereignty within its own borders. Each levied its own tolls and tariffs and coined its own money, practices that made land travel and trade between the various regions difficult, where not impossible. In addition, many of these little lands were filled with great

The horror of the Thirty Year's War is captured in this painting by Jan Brueghel (1568–1625) and Sebastien Vranx (1573–1647). During the breaks in fighting, marauding armies ravaged the countryside, destroying villages and massacring the rural population. [Kunsthistorisches Museum, Vienna]

power pretensions. Political decentralization and fragmentation characterized Germany as the seventeenth century opened; it was not a unified nation like Spain, England, or even strife-filled France.

Because of its central location, Germany had always been Europe's highway for merchants and traders going north and south and east and west. During the Thirty Years' War it became its stomping ground. Europe's rulers pressed in on Germany both for reasons of trade and because some of them held lands or legal privileges within certain German principalities. German princes, in their turn, looked to import and export markets beyond German borders. They opposed any efforts to consolidate the Holy Roman Empire, lest their territorial rights, confirmed by the Peace of Augsburg, be overturned. German princes were not loath to turn to Catholic France or to the kings of Denmark and Sweden for allies against the Habsburg emperor. The princes

perceived the emperor's dynastic connections with Spain, and the policies he generated as a result, to be against their territorial interests. Even the pope found political reasons for supporting Bourbon France against the menacing international kingdom of the Habsburgs.

After the Council of Trent, Protestants in the empire suspected the existence of an imperial and papal conspiracy to recreate the Catholic Europe of pre-Reformation times. The imperial diet, which was controlled by the German princes, demanded strict observance of the constitutional rights of Germans, as set forth in agreements with the emperor since the mid-fourteenth century. Consequently, it effectively countered every move by the emperor to impose his will in the empire. In the late sixteenth century, the emperor ruled only to the degree to which he was prepared to use force of arms against his subjects.

RELIGIOUS DIVISION   Religious conflict accentuated the international and internal political divisions. (See Map 12–2.) During this period the population within the Holy Roman Empire was about equally divided between Catholics and Protestants, the latter having perhaps a slight numerical edge by 1600. The terms of the Peace of Augsburg had attempted to freeze the territorial holdings of the Lutherans and the Catholics. In the intervening years, however, the Lutherans had gained political control in some Catholic areas, as had the Catholics in a few previously Lutheran areas. Such territorial reversals, or the threat of them, only increased the suspicion and antipathy between the two sides.

The Lutherans had been far more successful in securing their rights to worship in Catholic lands than the Catholics had been in securing such rights in Lutheran lands. The Catholic rulers, who were in a weakened position after the Reformation, had no choice but to make concessions to Protestant communities within their territories. These communities remained a sore point. Also, the Catholics wanted strict enforcement of the "Ecclesiastical Reservation" of the Peace of Augsburg, which Protestants had made little effort to recognize. The

MAP 12–2   RELIGIOUS DIVISIONS ABOUT 1600   *By 1600 few could seriously expect Christians to return to a uniform religious allegiance. In Spain and southern Italy, Catholicism remained relatively unchallenged, but note the existence elsewhere of large religious minorities, both Catholic and Protestant.*

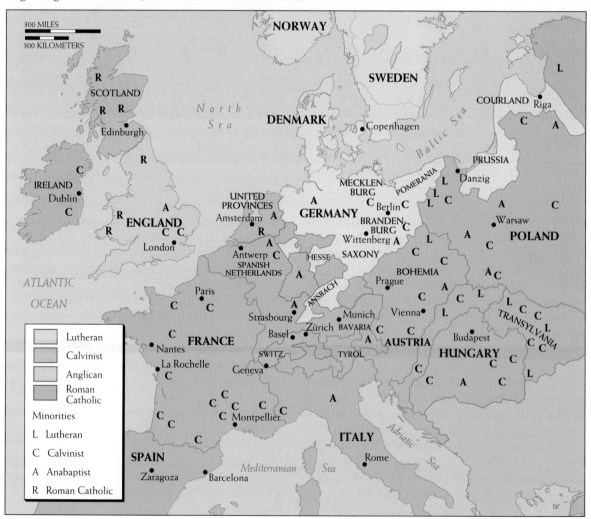

Catholics demanded that all ecclesiastical princes, electors, archbishops, bishops, and abbots who had deserted the Catholic for the Protestant side be immediately deprived of their religious offices and positions and that their ecclesiastical principalities be promptly returned to Catholic control. The Lutherans, and especially the Calvinists in the Palatinate, ignored this stipulation at every opportunity.

There was religious strife in the empire not only between Protestants and Catholics but also between liberal and conservative Lutherans and between Lutherans and the growing numbers of Calvinists. The last half of the sixteenth century was a time of warring Protestant factions within German universities. In addition to the heightened religious strife, the challenge of the new scientific and material culture that was becoming ascendant in intellectual and political circles increased the anxiety of religious people of all persuasions.

CALVINISM AND THE PALATINATE   As elsewhere in Europe, Calvinism was the political and religious leaven within the Holy Roman Empire on the eve of the Thirty Years' War. Calvinism was unrecognized as a legal religion by the Peace of Augsburg. It gained a strong foothold within the empire, however, when Frederick III (r. 1559–1576), a devout convert to Calvinism, became elector Palatine (ruler within the Palatinate) and made it the official religion of his domain. Heidelberg became a German Geneva in the 1560s: both a great intellectual center of Calvinism and a staging area for Calvinist penetration into the empire. By 1609 Palatine Calvinists headed a Protestant defensive alliance that received outside support from Spain's sixteenth-century enemies: England, France, and the Netherlands.

The Lutherans came to fear the Calvinists almost as much as they did the Catholics. Palatine Calvinists seemed to the Lutherans directly to threaten the Peace of Augsburg—and hence the legal foundation of the Lutheran states—by their bold missionary forays into the empire. Also, outspoken Calvinist criticism of the doctrine of Christ's real presence in the Eucharist shocked the more religiously conservative Lutherans. The elector Palatine once expressed his disbelief in transubstantiation by publicly shredding the host and mocking it as a "fine God." To Lutherans, such religious disrespect and aggressiveness disgraced the Reformation.

MAXIMILIAN OF BAVARIA AND THE CATHOLIC LEAGUE
If the Calvinists were active within the Holy Roman Empire, so also were their Catholic counterparts, the Jesuits. Staunchly Catholic Bavaria, supported by Spain, became militarily and ideologically for the Counter-Reformation what the Palatinate was for Protestantism. From there, the Jesuits launched successful missions throughout the empire, winning such major cities as Strasbourg and Osnabrück back to the Catholic fold by 1600. In 1609 Maximilian, duke of Bavaria, organized a Catholic League to counter a new Protestant alliance that had been formed in the same year under the leadership of the Calvinist Elector Palatine, Frederick IV (r. 1583–1610). When the league fielded a great army under the command of Count Johann von Tilly, the stage was set, both internally and internationally, for the worst of the religious wars, the Thirty Years' War. (See Map 12–3.)

Four Periods of War

The war went through four distinguishable periods. During its course it drew in every major western European nation—at least diplomatically and financially if not by direct military involvement. The four periods were the Bohemian (1618–1625); the Danish (1625–1629); the Swedish (1630–1635); and the Swedish–French (1635–1648).

THE BOHEMIAN PERIOD   The war broke out in Bohemia after the ascent to the Bohemian throne in 1618 of the Habsburg Ferdinand, the archduke of Styria, who was also in the line of succession to the imperial throne. Educated by the Jesuits and a fervent Catholic, Ferdinand was determined to restore the traditional faith throughout Austria, Bohemia, and Poland—the eastern Habsburg lands.

No sooner had Ferdinand become king of Bohemia than he revoked the religious freedoms of Bohemian Protestants. In force since 1575, these freedoms had even been recently broadened by Emperor Rudolf II (r. 1576–1612) in his Letter of Majesty in 1609. The Protestant nobility in Prague responded to Ferdinand's act in May 1618 by literally throwing his regents out the window. The event has ever since been known as the "defenestration of Prague." The three officials fell fifty feet into a dry moat that, fortunately, was padded with manure, which cushioned their fall and spared their

MAP 12–3 THE HOLY ROMAN EMPIRE ABOUT 1618 *On the eve of the Thirty Years'*
War, the Holy Roman Empire was politically and religiously fragmented, as
revealed by this somewhat simplified map. Lutherans dominated the north and
Catholics the south, while Calvinists controlled the United Provinces and the
Palatinate and were important in Switzerland and Brandenburg.

lives. In the following year Ferdinand became Holy Roman Emperor as Ferdinand II, by the unanimous vote of the seven electors. The Bohemians, however, defiantly deposed him in Prague and declared the Calvinist elector Palatine, Frederick V (r. 1616–1623), their overlord.

What had begun as a revolt of the Protestant nobility against an unpopular king of Bohemia thereafter escalated into an international war. Spain sent troops to Ferdinand, who found more immediate allies in Maximilian of Bavaria and the opportunistic Lutheran elector John George I of Saxony (r. 1611–1656). John George saw a sure route to territorial gain by joining in an easy victory over the weaker elector Palatine. This was not the only time politics and greed would overshadow religion during this long conflict, although Lutheran–Calvinist religious animosity also overrode a common Protestantism.

Ferdinand's army under Tilly routed Frederick V's troops at the Battle of White Mountain in 1620. By 1622 Ferdinand had managed not only to subdue and re-Catholicize Bohemia but to conquer the Palatinate as well. While he and his allies enjoyed the spoils of these victories, the fighting extended into northwestern Germany as the duke of Bavaria pressed the conflict. Laying claim to land as he went, he continued to pursue Ernst von Mansfeld, one of Frederick's surviving mercenary generals, into the north.

THE DANISH PERIOD   The emperor's subjugation of Bohemia and the Palatinate and Maximilian's forays into northwestern Germany raised new fears that a reconquest and re-Catholicization of the whole empire now loomed. This was in fact precisely Ferdinand II's design. The Lutheran King Christian IV (r. 1588–1648) of Denmark, who already held territory within the empire as the duke of Holstein, was eager to extend Danish influence over the coastal towns of the North Sea. Encouraged by the English, the French, and the Dutch, he picked up the Protestant banner of resistance, opening the Danish period of the conflict (1625–1629). Christian's forces were not, however, up to the challenge. Entering Germany with his army in 1626, he was quickly humiliated by Maximilian and forced to retreat into Denmark.

As military success made Maximilian stronger and more difficult to control, Ferdinand II sought a more pliant tool for his policies by hiring a powerful, complex mercenary, Albrecht of Wallenstein (1583–1634). Wallenstein was another opportunistic Protestant who had gained a great deal of territory by joining Ferdinand during the conquest of Bohemia. A brilliant and ruthless military strategist, Wallenstein not only completed Maximilian's work by bringing the career of the elusive Ernst von Mansfeld to an end but also penetrated Denmark with an occupying army. By 1628 Wallenstein commanded a crack army of more than 100,000 and became a law unto himself within the empire, completely outside the emperor's control. Pandora's box had now been fully opened.

Wallenstein broke Protestant resistance so successfully that Ferdinand issued the Edict of Restitution in 1629. This proclamation dramatically reasserted the Catholic safeguards of the Peace of Augsburg (1555). It reaffirmed the illegality of Calvinism—a completely unrealistic move in 1629. It also ordered the return of all church lands acquired by the Lutherans since 1552, an equally unrealistic mandate. Compliance would have involved the return of no less than sixteen bishoprics and twenty-eight cities and towns to Catholic allegiance. Although based on legal precedent and certainly within Ferdinand's power to command, the expectations of the edict were not adjusted to the political realities of 1629. It struck panic in the hearts of Protestants and Habsburg opponents everywhere, who now saw clearly the emperor's plan to recreate a Catholic Europe. Resistance quickly reignited.

THE SWEDISH PERIOD   Gustavus Adolphus of Sweden (r. 1611–1632), a deeply pious king of a unified Lutheran nation, became the new leader of Protestant forces within the empire, opening the Swedish period of the war (1630–1635). He was handsomely bankrolled by two very interested bystanders: the French minister Cardinal Richelieu, whose foreign policy was to protect French interests by keeping Habsburg armies tied down in Germany, and the Dutch, who had not forgotten Spanish Habsburg domination in the sixteenth century. The Swedish king found ready allies in the electors of Brandenburg and Saxony and soon won a smashing victory at Breitenfeld in 1630. The Protestant victory at Breitenfeld so dramatically reversed the course of the war that it has been regarded as the most decisive, although far from the final, engagement of the long conflict.

One of the reasons for the overwhelming Swedish victory at Breitenfeld was the military genius of Gustavus Adolphus. The Swedish king brought a new mobility to warfare by having both his infantry and his cavalry employ fire and charge tactics. At six deep, his infantry squares were smaller than the traditional ones, and he filled them with equal numbers of musketeers and pikemen. His cavalry also alternated pistol shot with sword charges. His artillery was lighter and more mobile in battle. Each unit of his army—infantry, cavalry, and artillery—had both defensive and offensive capability and could quickly change from one to the other.

Gustavus Adolphus died at the hands of Wallenstein's forces during the Battle of Lützen (November 1632)—a very costly engagement for both sides that created a brief standstill. Ferdinand had long been resentful of Wallenstein's independence,

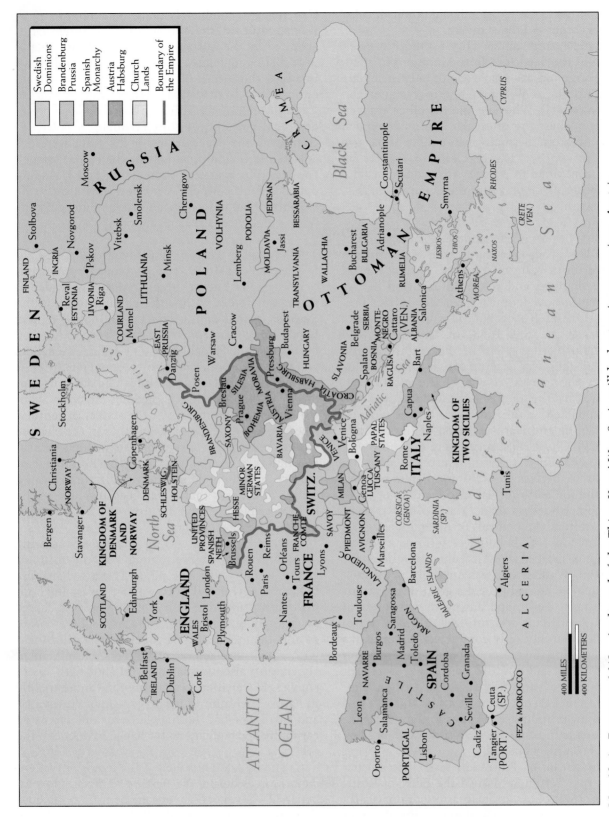

Legend:
- Swedish Dominions
- Brandenburg Prussia
- Spanish Monarchy
- Austria Habsburg
- Church Lands
- Boundary of the Empire

RUSSIA

Moscow

Stolbova
FINLAND
Novgorod
INGRIA
Reval
ESTONIA
Pskov
Vitebsk
Smolensk
Chernigov

SWEDEN

Bergen
Christiania
NORWAY
Stavanger
Stockholm

Baltic Sea

LIVONIA
Riga
COURLAND
Memel
LITHUANIA
Minsk
POLAND
VOLHYNIA
PODOLIA
Lemberg
JEDISAN
BESSARABIA

Black Sea

CRIMEA

Constantinople
Scutari

OTTOMAN EMPIRE

Smyrna

RHODES

CYPRUS

LESBOS
CHIOS
NAXOS
CRETE (VEN.)

Athens
MOREA

Salonica
RUMELIA
ALBANIA
Adrianople

Copenhagen
DENMARK
SCHLESWIG
HOLSTEIN
KINGDOM OF DENMARK AND NORWAY

North Sea

SCOTLAND
Edinburgh
York
ENGLAND
Bristol London
WALES
Plymouth
Belfast
IRELAND
Dublin
Cork

EAST PRUSSIA
Danzig
Posen
Warsaw
Cracow
BRANDENBURG
Breslau
SILESIA
Prague
BOHEMIA MORAVIA
SAXONY
Pressburg
Budapest
HUNGARY
AUSTRIA HABSBURG
Vienna

MINOR GERMAN STATES
HESSE
BAVARIA
SWITZ.
FRANCHE COMTE

UNITED PROVINCES
SPANISH NETH.
Brussels
Reims
Rouen
Paris
Orléans
Tours
FRANCE
Nantes
Lyons
LANGUEDOC
Bordeaux
Toulouse
Marseilles
AVIGNON
PIEDMONT
SAVOY
Genoa
MILAN
VENICE
Venice
Bologna
PAPAL STATES
LUCCA TUSCANY
Rome
ITALY
Capua
Naples
KINGDOM OF TWO SICILIES

CROATIA
SLAVONIA
Belgrade
SERBIA
MONTE-NEGRO
BOSNIA
Spalato
RAGUSA
Cattaro (VEN.)
Bart

Adriatic Sea

TRANSYLVANIA
WALLACHIA
BULGARIA
Bucharest
MOLDAVIA
Jassy

Mediterranean Sea

CORSICA (GENOA)
SARDINIA (SP.)
BALEARIC ISLANDS
Barcelona
Saragossa
ARAGON
Madrid
Toledo
CASTILE
SPAIN
Cordoba
Granada
Seville
Cadiz
Ceuta (SP.)
Tangier (PORT.)
FEZ & MOROCCO
Leon
NAVARRE
Burgos
Salamanca
PORTUGAL
Lisbon
Oporto

ALGERIA
Algiers
Tunis

ATLANTIC OCEAN

400 MILES
400 KILOMETERS

MAP 12–4 *At the end of the Thirty Years' War, Spain still had extensive possessions. Austria and Brandenburg–Prussia were prominent, the independence of the United Provinces and Switzerland was recognized, and Sweden held important river mouths in northern Germany.*

although he was the major factor in imperial success. In 1634 Ferdinand had Wallenstein assassinated. By that time, Wallenstein had not only served his purpose for the emperor, but, ever opportunistic, he was even trying openly to strike bargains with the Protestants for his services. The Wallenstein episode is a telling commentary on this war without honor. Despite the deep religious motivations, greed and political gain were the real forces at work in the Thirty Years' War. Even allies that owed one another their success were not above treating each other as mortal enemies.

In the Peace of Prague in 1635 the German Protestant states, led by Saxony, reached a compromise agreement with Ferdinand. The Swedes, however, received continued support from France and the Netherlands. Desiring to maximize their investment in the war, they refused to join the agreement. Their resistance to settlement plunged the war into its fourth and most devastating phase, the Swedish–French period (1635–1648).

THE SWEDISH–FRENCH PERIOD The French openly entered the war in 1635, sending men and munitions as well as financial subsidies. After their entrance the war dragged on for thirteen years, with French, Swedish, and Spanish soldiers looting the length and breadth of Germany—warring, it seemed, simply for the sake of warfare itself. The Germans, long weary of the devastation, were too disunited to repulse the foreign armies; they simply watched and suffered. By the time peace talks began in the Westphalian cities of Münster and Osnabrück in 1644, an estimated one-third of the German population had died as a direct result of the war. It has been called the worst European catastrophe since the Black Death of the fourteenth century.

The Treaty of Westphalia

The Treaty of Westphalia in 1648 brought all hostilities within the Holy Roman Empire to an end. (See Map 12–4.) It rescinded Ferdinand's Edict of Restitution and firmly reasserted the major feature of the religious settlement of the Peace of Augsburg, as the ruler of each land was again permitted to determine the religion of his or her land. The treaty also gave the Calvinists their long-sought legal recognition. The independence of the Swiss Confederacy and the United Provinces of Holland, long recognized in fact, was now proclaimed in law. And

the treaty elevated Bavaria to the rank of an elector state. The provisions of the treaty made the German princes supreme over their principalities. Yet, as guarantors of the treaty, Sweden and France found many occasions to meddle in German affairs until the century's end, France to considerable territorial gain. Brandenburg–Prussia emerged as the most powerful northern German state. Because the treaty broadened the legal status of Protestantism, the pope opposed it altogether, but he had no power to prevent it.

France and Spain remained at war outside the empire until 1659, when French victories forced on the Spanish the humiliating Treaty of the Pyrenees. Thereafter France became Europe's dominant power, and the once vast Habsburg kingdom waned.

By confirming the territorial sovereignty of Germany's many political entities, the Treaty of Westphalia perpetuated German division and political weakness into the modern period. Only two German states attained any international significance during the seventeenth century: Austria and Brandenburg–Prussia. The petty regionalism within the empire also reflected on a small scale the drift of larger European politics. In the seventeenth century, distinctive nation-states, each with its own political, cultural, and religious identity, reached maturity and firmly established the competitive nationalism of the modern world.

◆

Both religion and politics played major roles in each of the great conflicts of the Age of Religious Wars—the internal struggle in France, Spain's unsuccessful effort to subdue the Netherlands, England's successful resistance of Spain, and the steady march of virtually every major European power through the hapless empire during the first half of the seventeenth century. Parties and armies of different religious persuasions are visible in each conflict, and in each we also find a life-or-death political struggle.

The wars ended with the recognition of minority religious rights and a guarantee of the traditional boundaries of political sovereignty. In France, the Edict of Nantes (1598) brought peace by granting Huguenots basic religious and civil freedoms and by recognizing their towns and territories. Peace and sovereignty came to the Netherlands with the departure of the Spanish, guaranteed initially by the Twelve Years' Truce

(1609) and secured fully by the Peace of West-phalia (1648). The conflict between England and Spain ended with the removal of the Spanish threat to English sovereignty in politics and religion, which resulted from the execution of Mary, Queen of Scots (1587), and the English victory over the Armada (1588). In the Holy Roman Empire, peace came with the reaffirmation of the political principle of the Peace of Augsburg (1555), as the Peace of Westphalia brought the Thirty Years' War to an end by again recognizing the sovereignty of rulers within their lands and their right to determine the religious beliefs of their subjects. Europe at mid-century had real, if brief, peace.

Review Questions

1. What part did politics play in the religious positions of the French leaders? How did the king (or his regent) decide which side to favor? What led to the infamous Saint Bartholomew's Day Massacre, and what did it achieve?

2. How did Spain achieve a position of dominance in the sixteenth century? What were its strengths and weaknesses as a nation? What were Philip II's goals? Which was he unable to achieve and why?

3. Henry of Navarre (Henry IV of France), Elizabeth I, and William of Orange were all *politiques*. Define the term and explain why it applies to these three rulers.

4. Discuss the background to the establishment of the Anglican church in England. What were the politics of Mary I? What was Elizabeth I's settlement, and how difficult was it to impose on all of England? Who were her detractors and what were their criticisms?

5. Why was the Thirty Years' War fought? To what extent did politics determine the outcome of the war? Discuss the Treaty of Westphalia in 1648. Could matters have been resolved without war?

6. It has been said that the Thirty Years' War is the outstanding example in European history of meaningless conflict. Evaluate this statement and provide specific reasons.

Suggested Readings

F. Braudel, *The Mediterranean and the Mediterranean World in the Age of Philip the Second*, vols. 1 and 2 (1976). Widely acclaimed work of a French master historian.

N. Z. Davis, *Society and Culture in Early Modern France* (1975). Essays on popular culture.

R. Dunn, *The Age of Religious Wars 1559–1689* (1979). Excellent brief survey of every major conflict.

J. H. Elliott, *Europe Divided 1559–1598* (1968). Direct, lucid narrative account.

G. R. Elton, *England Under the Tudors* (1955). Masterly account.

J. H. Franklin (ED. and Trans.), *Constitutionalism and Resistance in the Sixteenth Century: Three Treatises by Hotman, Beza, and Mornay* (1969). Three defenders of the right of people to resist tyranny.

P. Geyl, *The Revolt of the Netherlands, 1555–1609* (1958). The authoritative survey.

J. Guy, *Tudor England* (1990). The standard history and good synthesis of recent scholarship.

C. Haigh, *Elizabeth I* (1988). Elizabeth portrayed as a magnificent politician and propagandist.

D. Loades, *Mary Tudor* (1989). Authoritative and good storytelling.

J. Lynch, *Spain Under the Habsburg I: 1516–1598* (1964). Political narrative.

W. MacCaffrey, *Queen Elizabeth and the Making of Policy 1572–1588* (1985). Very good on the intricacy of Elizabethan religious policy.

G. Mattingly, *The Armada* (1959). A masterpiece and novel-like in style.

J. E. Neale, *Queen Elizabeth I* (1934). Superb biography.

J. E. Neale, *The Age of Catherine de Médicis* (1962). Short, concise summary.

G. Parker, *Philip II* (1978). Readable, admiring account.

G. Parker, *Europe in Crisis, 1598–1648* (1979). The big picture at a gallop.

T. K. Rabb (ED.), *The Thirty Years' War* (1972). Excerpts from the scholarly debate over the war's significance.

J. G. Ridley, *John Knox* (1968). Large, detailed biography.

J. H. M. Salmon (ED.), *The French Wars of Religion: How Important Were the Religious Factors?* (1967). Scholarly debate over the relation between politics and religion.

J. H. M. Salmon, *Society in Crisis: France in the Sixteenth Century* (1976). Standard narrative account.

A. Soman (ED.), *The Massacre of St. Bartholomew's Day: Reappraisals and Documents* (1974). Results of an international symposium on the anniversary of the massacre.

K. Thomas, *Religion and the Decline of Magic* (1971). Provocative, much acclaimed work focused on popular culture.

C. V. WEDGWOOD, *The Thirty Years' War* (1939). Extremely detailed account that downplays the war's achievements.

C. V. WEDGWOOD, *William the Silent* (1944). Excellent political biography of William of Orange.

J. WORMALD, *Mary, Queen of Scots: A Study in Failure* (1991). Mary portrayed as a queen who did not understand her country and was out of touch with the times.

Charles I governed England from 1625 to 1649. His attempts to establish an absolutist government in matters of both church and state provoked clashes with the English Parliament and the outbreak of the Civil War in 1642. He was executed in 1649. [Daniel Mytens/The Granger Collection]

Paths to Constitutionalism and Absolutism:
England and France in the Seventeenth Century

K E Y   T O P I C S

- The factors behind the divergent political paths of England and France in the seventeenth century
- The conflict between Parliament and the king over taxation and religion in early Stuart England, the English Civil War, and the abolition of the monarchy
- The Restoration and the development of Parliament's supremacy over the monarchy after the "Glorious Revolution"
- The establishment of an absolutist monarchy in France under Louis XIV
- The wars of Louis XIV

During the seventeenth century England and France moved in two very different political directions. By the close of the century, after decades of fierce civil and religious conflict that pitted Parliament and monarch against each other, England had developed into a parliamentary monarchy with a policy of religious toleration. Parliament, composed of the House of Lords and the House of Commons, shared responsibility for government with the monarch. It met regularly and the Commons, composed primarily of wealthy landed gentry, had to stand for election every three years. By contrast, France developed an abso-

lutist, centralized form of government dominated by a monarchy that shared little power with any other national institutions. Its authority resided rather in a complex set of relationships with local nobility, guilds, and towns and in its ability to support the largest standing army in Europe. In the seventeenth century France also abandoned Henry IV's policy of religious toleration and proscribed all but the Roman Catholic church.

These English and French forms of government became models for other nations. The French model, termed absolutism in the nineteenth century, would be imitated by other monarchies across the continent during the eighteenth century. The English model would later inspire the political creed known in the nineteenth century as liberalism. Like all such political labels, these terms, although useful, can conceal considerable complexity. English "parliamentary monarchs" did not share all power with Parliament; they controlled the army, foreign policy, and much patronage. Likewise the "absolute monarchs" of France and their later imitators elsewhere in Europe were not truly absolute; laws, traditions, and many local institutions and customs limited their power.

Two Models of European Political Development

In the second half of the sixteenth century, changes in military organization, weapons, and tactics sharply increased the cost of warfare. Because traditional sources of revenue were inadequate to finance these growing costs—as well as the costs of government—monarchs sought new sources. Only monarchies that succeeded in building a secure financial base that was not deeply dependent on the support of noble estates, diets, or assemblies achieved absolute rule. The French monarchy succeeded in this effort after mid-century, whereas the English monarchy failed. The paths to that success and failure led to the two models of government—absolutism in France and parliamentary monarchy in England—that shaped subsequent political development in Europe.

In their pursuit of adequate income, English monarchs of the seventeenth century threatened the local political interests and economic well-being of the country's nobility and others of great landed and commercial wealth. These politically active groups, invoking traditional English liberties in their defense, effectively resisted the monarchs' attempted intrusions throughout the century.

The experience of Louis XIV, the French king, was different. During the second half of the seventeenth century, he would make the French nobility dependent upon his goodwill and patronage. In turn, he would support their local influence and their place in a firm social hierarchy. But even the French king's dominance of the nobility was not wholly complete. Louis accepted the authority of the noble-dominated *Parlement* of Paris to register royal decrees before they officially became law, and he permitted regional *parlements* to exercise considerable author-

ity over local administration and taxation. Funds from taxes levied by the central monarchy found their way into many local pockets.

Religious factors also affected the political destinies of England and France. A strong Protestant religious movement known as Puritanism arose in England and actively opposed the Stuart monarchy. Puritanism represented a nonpolitical force that sought at first to limit and eventually to overturn the English monarchy. Louis XIV, in contrast, crushed the Protestant communities of France. He was generally supported in these efforts by Roman Catholics, who saw religious uniformity enforced by the monarchy working to their advantage.

There were also major institutional differences between the two countries. In Parliament, England possessed a political institution that had long bargained with the monarch over political issues. In the early seventeenth century, to be sure, Parliament did not meet regularly and was not the strong institution it would become by the close of the century. Nor was there anything certain or inevitable about the transformation it underwent over the course of the century. The institutional basis for it, however, was in place. Parliament was there and expected to be consulted from time to time. Its members—nobility and gentry—had experience organizing and speaking, writing legislation, and criticizing royal policies. Furthermore, the English had a legal and political tradition based on concepts of liberty to which members of Parliament and their supporters throughout the country could and did appeal in their conflict with the monarchy.

For all intents, France lacked a similarly strong tradition of broad liberties, representation, and bargaining between the monarchy and other national institutions. The Estates General had met from time to time to grant certain revenues to the monarch, but it played no role after the early seventeenth century. It met in 1614, but thereafter the monarchy was able to find other sources of income, and the Estates General was not called again until the eve of the French Revolution in 1789. Consequently, whatever political forces might have wished to oppose or limit the monarchy lacked both an institutional base from which to operate and a tradition of meetings during which the necessary political skills might have been developed.

Finally, personalities played an important role. During the first half of the century, France profited from the guidance of two of its most able statesmen, Cardinals Richelieu and Mazarin. Mazarin trained Louis XIV to be a hard-working, if not always wise, monarch. Louis drew strong and capable ministers about himself. The four Stuart monarchs of England, on the other hand, had trouble simply making people trust them. They did not always keep their word. They acted on whim. They often displayed faulty judgment. In a political situation that demanded compromise, they rarely offered any. They offended significant groups of their subjects unnecessarily. In a nation that saw itself as strongly Protestant, they were suspected, sometimes accurately, of Catholic sympathies. Many of Charles's opponents in Parliament, of course, had flaws of their own, but the nature of the situation focused attention and criticism on the king.

In both England and France, the nobility and large landowners stood at the top of the social hierarchy and sought to protect their privileges and local interests. Important segments of the British nobility and landed classes came to distrust the Stuart monarchs, whom they believed sought to undermine their local political control and social standing. Parliamentary government was the result of the efforts of these English landed classes to protect their concerns and limit the power of the monarchy to interfere with life on the local level. The French nobility under Louis XIV, in contrast, eventually concluded that the best way to secure their own interests was to support his monarchy. He provided them with many forms of patronage, and he protected their tax exemptions, their wealth, and their local social standing.

The divergent developments of England and France in the seventeenth century would have surprised most people in 1600. It was not inevitable that the English monarchy would have to govern through Parliament or that the French monarchy would avoid dealing with national political institutions that could significantly limit its authority. The Stuart kings of England certainly aspired to the autocracy Louis XIV achieved, and some English political philosophers eloquently defended the divine right of kings and absolute rule. At the beginning of the seventeenth century, the English monarchy was strong. Queen Elizabeth, after a reign of almost forty-five years, was much revered. Parliament met only when called to provide financial support to the monarch. France, on the other hand, was emerging from the turmoil of its religious wars. The strife of that conflict had torn the society asunder. The monarchy was relatively weak. Henry IV, who had become king in 1589, pursued a policy of religious toleration. The French nobles had significant military forces at their disposal and in the middle of the seventeenth century confronted the king with rebellion. These conditions would change dramatically in both nations by the late seventeenth century.

Constitutional Crisis and Settlement in Stuart England

James I

In 1603 James VI of Scotland (r. 1603–1625), the son of Mary Stuart, Queen of Scots, without opposition or incident succeeded the childless Elizabeth as James I of England. His was a difficult situation. The elderly queen had been very popular and was totally identified with the nation. James was not well known, would never be popular, and, as a Scot, was an outsider. He inherited not only the crown but also a large royal debt and a fiercely divided church—problems that his politically active subjects expected him to address. The new king strongly advocated the divine right of kings, a subject on which he had written a book—*A Trew Law of Free Monarchies*—in 1598. He expected to rule with a minimum of consultation beyond his own royal court.

James quickly managed to anger many of his new subjects, but he did not wholly alienate them. In this period Parliament met only when the monarch summoned it, which James hoped to do rarely. Its chief business was to grant certain sources of income. The real value of these revenues, however, had been falling during the past half century, limiting their importance and thus the importance of Parliament to the king. To meet his needs, James developed other sources of income, largely by levying—solely on the authority of ill-defined privileges claimed to be attached to the office of king—new custom duties known as *impositions*. These were a version of the older customs duties known as *tonnage* and *poundage*. Members of Parliament resented these independent efforts to raise revenues as an affront to their authority over the royal purse, but they did not seek a serious confrontation. Rather, throughout James's reign they wrangled and negotiated behind the scenes.

The religious problem also festered under James. Puritans within the Church of England had hoped

This elegant painting portrays a very quiet London of the mid-1630s. During the next sixty years it would suffer wrenching political turmoil and the devastation of a great fire. [Yale Center for British Art]

that James's experience with the Scottish Presbyterian church and his own Protestant upbringing would incline him to favor their efforts to further the reformation of the English church. Since the days of Elizabeth, they had sought to eliminate elaborate religious ceremonies and replace the hierarchical episcopal system of church governance with a more representative Presbyterian form like that of the Calvinist churches on the Continent.

In January 1604, the Puritans had their first direct dealing with the new king. James responded in that month to a statement of Puritan grievances, the so-called Millenary Petition, at a special religious conference at Hampton Court. The political implications of the demands in this petition concerned him, and their tone offended him. To the dismay of the Puritans, he firmly declared his intention to maintain and even enhance the Anglican episcopacy. "A Scottish presbytery," he snorted, "agreeth as well with monarchy as God and the devil. No bishops, no king." James was not simply being arbitrary. Elizabeth also had not accommodated the Puritan demands. To have done so would have created strife within the Church of England.

Both sides left the conference with their suspicions of one another largely confirmed. The Hampton Court conference did, however, sow one fruitful seed. A commission was appointed to render a new translation of the Bible. That mission was fulfilled in 1611 with the publication of the eloquent Authorized, or King James, Version.

James also offended the Puritans with his opposition to their narrow view of human life and social activities. The Puritans believed that Sunday should be a day taken up largely with religious observances and little leisure or recreation. James believed recreation and sports were innocent activities and good for his people. He also believed Puritan narrowness discouraged Roman Catholics from converting to the Church of England. Consequently, in 1618 he issued the *Book of Sports*, which permitted games on Sunday for people who attended Church of England services. The clergy refused to read his order from the pulpit, and he had to rescind it.

It was during James's reign that some religious dissenters began to leave England. In 1620 Puritan separatists founded Plymouth Colony in Cape Cod Bay in North America, preferring flight from England to Anglican conformity. Later in the 1620s, a larger, better financed group of Puritans left England to found the Massachusetts Bay Colony. In each case, the colonists believed that reformation

King James I Defends Popular Recreation Against the Puritans

The English Puritans believed in strict observance of the Sabbath, disapproving any sports, games, or general social conviviality on Sunday. James I thought these strictures prevented many Roman Catholics from joining the Church of England. In 1618 James ordered the clergy of the Church of England to read the Book of Sports *from their pulpits. In this declaration, he permitted people to engage in certain sports and games after church services. His hope was to allow innocent recreations on Sunday while encouraging people to attend the Church of England. Despite the king's good intentions, the order offended the Puritans. The clergy resisted his order and he had to withdraw it.*

✦ *What motives of state might have led James I to issue this declaration? How does he attempt to make it favorable to the Church of England? Why might so many clergy have refused to read this statement to their congregations?*

With our own ears we heard the general complaint of our people, that they were barred from all lawful recreation and exercise upon the Sunday's afternoon, after the ending of all divine service, which cannot but produce two evils: the one the hindering of the conversion of many [Roman Catholic subjects], whom their priests will take occasion hereby to vex, persuading them that no honest mirth or recreation is lawful or tolerable in our religion, which cannot but breed a great discontentment in our people's hearts, especially as such as are peradventure upon the point of turning [to the Church of England]: the other inconvenience is, that this prohibition barreth the common and meaner sort of people from using such exercises as may make their bodies more able for war, when we or our successors shall have occasion to use them; and in place thereof sets up filthy tipplings and drunkenness, and breeds a number of idle and discontented speeches in their ale-houses. For when shall the common people have leave to exercise, if not upon the Sundays and holy days, seeing they must apply their labor and win their living in all working days? . . .

[A]s for our good people's lawful recreation, our pleasure likewise is, that after the end of divine service our good people be not disturbed, . . . or discouraged from any lawful recreation, such as dancing, either men or women; archery for men, leaping, vaulting, or any other such harmless recreation, or from having of Hay-games, Whitsun-ales, and Morris-dances; and the setting up of May-poles and other sports therewith used; . . . but withal we do here account still as prohibited all unlawful games to be used upon Sundays only, as bear and bull-baitings . . . and at all times in the meaner sort of people by law prohibited, bowling.

And likewise we bar from this benefit and liberty all such known as recusants [Roman Catholics], either men or women, as will abstain from coming to church or divine service, being therefore unworthy of any lawful recreation after the said service, that will not first come to the church and serve God; prohibiting in like sort the said recreations to any that, though [they] conform in religion [i.e., members of the Church of England], are not present in the church at the service of God, before their going to the said recreations.

Henry Bettenson, ed., Documents of the Christian Church, *2nd ed. (London: Oxford University Press, 1963), pp. 400–403.*

had not gone far enough in England and that only in America could they worship freely and organize a truly reformed church.

Although James inherited a difficult situation, he also created special problems for himself. His court became a center of scandal and corruption. He governed by favorites, the most influential of whom was the duke of Buckingham, whom rumor made the king's homosexual lover. Buckingham controlled royal patronage and openly sold peerages and titles to the highest bidders—a practice that angered the nobility because it cheapened their rank. There had always been court favorites, but never before had a single person so controlled access to the monarch.

James's foreign policy also roused opposition. He regarded himself as a peacemaker. Peace reduced pressures on royal revenues and the need for larger debts. The less his demands for money, the less the king had to depend on the goodwill of Parliament. In 1604 he concluded a much-needed peace with Spain, England's chief adversary during the second half of the sixteenth century. His subjects viewed this peace as a sign of pro-Catholic sentiment. James further increased suspicions when he tried unsuccessfully to relax the penal laws against Catholics. The English had not forgotten the brutal reign of Mary Tudor and the acts of treason by Catholics during Elizabeth's reign. In 1618 James hesitated, not unwisely, to rush English troops to the aid of Protestants in Germany at the outbreak of the Thirty Years' War. This hesitation caused some to question his loyalty to the Anglican Church. These suspicions increased when he tried to arrange a marriage between his son Charles and the Spanish *Infanta* (the daughter of the king of Spain). In the king's last years, as his health failed and the reins of government passed increasingly to his son Charles and to Buckingham, parliamentary opposition and Protestant sentiment combined to undo his pro-Spanish foreign policy. In 1624, shortly before James's death, England entered a continental war against Spain largely in response to the pressures of members of Parliament.

Charles I

Parliament had favored the war with Spain but would not adequately finance it because its members distrusted Buckingham. Unable to gain adequate funds from Parliament, Charles I (r. 1625–1649), like his father, resorted to extraparliamentary measures. He levied new tariffs and duties and attempted to collect discontinued taxes. He even subjected the English people to a so-called forced loan (a tax theoretically to be repaid), imprisoning those who refused to pay. The government quartered troops in transit to war zones in private homes. All these actions intruded on life at the local level and challenged the power of the local nobles and landowners to control their districts.

When Parliament met in 1628, its members were furious. Taxes were being illegally collected for a war that was going badly for England and that now, through royal blundering, involved France as well as Spain. Parliament expressed its displeasure by making the king's request for new funds conditional on his recognition of the Petition of Right. This important declaration of constitutional freedom required that henceforth there should be no forced loans or taxation without the consent of Parliament, that no freeman should be imprisoned without due cause, and that troops should not be billeted in private homes. It was thus an expression of resentment and resistance to the intrusion of the monarchy on the local level. Though Charles agreed to the petition, there was little confidence that he would keep his word.

YEARS OF PERSONAL RULE In August 1628, Charles's chief minister, Buckingham, with whom Parliament had been in open dispute since 1626, was assassinated. His death, while sweet to many, did not resolve the hostility between the king and Parliament. In January 1629, Parliament further underscored its resolve to limit royal prerogative. It declared that religious innovations leading to "popery"—by this it meant Charles's high-church policies—and the levying of taxes without parliamentary consent were acts of treason. Perceiving that things were getting out of hand, Charles promptly dissolved Parliament and did not recall it again until 1640, when war with Scotland forced him to do so.

To conserve his limited resources, Charles made peace with France in 1629 and Spain in 1630. This policy again roused fears among some of his subjects that he was too friendly to Roman Catholic powers. The French and Roman Catholic background of Charles's wife furthered these suspicions. Part of her marriage contract permitted her to hear mass daily at the English court. Charles's attitude toward the Church of England also raised suspicions. He supported a group within the church, known as Arminians, who rejected many Puritan

Parliament Presents Charles I
with the Petition of Right

After becoming monarch in 1625 Charles I (1625–1649) had imposed unparliamentary taxes, coerced freemen, and quartered troops in transit in private homes. These actions deeply offended Parliament, which in 1628 refused to grant him any funds until he rescinded those practices by recognizing the Petition of Right (June, 1628). The Petition constituted a general catalog of the offenses associated with the exercise of arbitrary royal authority.

✦ *What limits does the Petition attempt to place on royal taxation? How did the Petition criticize arbitrary arrest? Why was the quartering of soldiers in private homes so offensive?*

[The Lords Spirit and Temporal, and commons in Parliament assembled] do humbly pray your Most Excellent Majesty, that no man hereafter be compelled to make or yield any gift, loan, benevolence, tax, or such like charge, without common consent by Act of parliament; and that none be called to make answer, to take such oath, or to give attendance, or be confined, or otherwise molested or disquieted concerning the same, or for refusal thereof; and that no freeman, in any such manner as in before-mentioned, be imprisoned or detained; and that your Majesty will be pleased to remove the said soldiers and mariners [who have been quartered in private homes], and that your people may not be so burdened in time to come; and that the foresaid commissions for proceeding by martial law, may be revoked and annulled; and that

hereafter no commissions of like nature may issue forth to any person or persons whatsoever, to be executed as aforesaid, lest by colour of them any of your Majesty's subjects be destroyed or put to death, contrary to the laws and franchise of the land

All which they most humble pray of your Most Excellent Majesty, as their rights and liberties according to the laws and statues of this realm.

The King's Reply: The King willeth that right be done according to the laws and customs of the realm; and that the statues be put in due execution, that his subjects may have no cause to complain of any wrong or oppressions, contrary to their just rights and liberties, to the preservation whereof he holds himself as well obliged as of his prerogative.

Samuel R. Gardiner, ed., The Constitutional Documents of the Puritan Revolution (Oxford: Clarendon Press, 1889), pp. 4–5.

doctrines and favored elaborate, high-church practices. The Puritans were convinced these practices would bring a return to Roman Catholicism.

To allow Charles to rule without renegotiating financial arrangements with Parliament, his chief minister, Thomas Wentworth (after 1640, earl of Stafford), instituted a policy known as *thorough.* This policy imposed strict efficiency and administrative centralization in government. Its goal was absolute royal control of England. Its success depended on the king's ability to operate independently of Parliament, which no law required him to summon.

Charles's ministers exploited every legal fundraising device. They enforced previously neglected laws and extended existing taxes into new areas. For example, starting in 1634, they gradually extended inland to the whole of England a tax called *ship money,* normally levied only on coastal areas to pay for naval protection. A great landowner named John Hampden mounted a legal challenge to the extension of this tax. Although the king prevailed in what was a close legal contest, his victory was costly. It deepened the animosity toward him among the powerful landowners, who would elect and sit in Parliament should he need to summon it.

During these years of personal rule, Charles surrounded himself with an elaborate court and patronized some of the greatest artists of the day. Like his father, he sold noble titles and knighthoods, lessening their value and the social exclusiveness conferred on those who already possessed them. Nobles and great landowners feared that the growth of the court, the king's relentless pursuit of revenue, and the inflation of titles and honors would reduce their local influence and social standing. They also feared that the monarch might actually succeed in governing without ever again calling Parliament into session.

Charles might very well have ruled indefinitely without Parliament had not his religious policies provoked war with Scotland. James I had allowed a wide variety of religious observances in England, Scotland, and Ireland. Charles by contrast hoped to impose religious conformity at least within England and Scotland. William Laud (1573–1645), who was first Charles's religious advisor and, after 1633, archbishop of Canterbury, held a high-church view of Anglicanism. He favored powerful bishops, elaborate liturgy, and personal religious observance and devotion rather than the preaching and listening favored by the Puritans. As a member of the Court of High Commission, Laud had already radicalized the English Puritans by denying them the right to publish and preach. In 1637 Charles and Laud, against the opposition of the English Puritans as well as the Scots, tried to impose on Scotland the English episcopal system and a prayerbook almost identical to the Anglican *Book of Common Prayer*.

The Scots rebelled, and Charles, with insufficient resources for a war, was forced to call Parliament. The members of Parliament opposed his policies almost as much as they wanted to crush the rebellion. Led by John Pym (1584–1643), they refused even to consider funds for war until the king agreed to redress a long list of political and religious grievances. The king, in response, immediately dissolved Parliament—hence its name, the Short Parliament (April–May 1640). When the Presbyterian Scots invaded England and defeated an English army at the Battle of Newburn in the summer of 1640, Charles reconvened Parliament, this time on its terms, for a long and most fateful duration.

THE LONG PARLIAMENT   The landowners and the merchant classes represented by Parliament had resented the king's financial measures and paternalistic rule for some time. The Puritans in Parliament resented his religious policies and deeply distrusted the influence of the Roman Catholic queen. The Long Parliament (1640–1660) thus acted with widespread support and general unanimity when it convened in November 1640.

The House of Commons impeached both the earl of Stafford and Archbishop Laud. Disgraced and convicted by a parliamentary bill of attainder (a judgment of treason entailing loss of civil rights), Stafford was executed in 1641. Laud was imprisoned and also later executed (1645). Parliament abolished the Court of Star Chamber and the Court of High Commission, royal instruments of political and religious *thorough*, respectively. The levying of new taxes without consent of Parliament and the inland extension of ship money now became illegal. Finally, Parliament resolved that no more than three years should elapse between its meetings and that it could not be dissolved without its own consent. Parliament was determined that neither Charles nor any future English king could again govern without consulting it.

Despite its cohesion on these initial actions, Parliament was divided over the precise direction to take on religious reform. Both moderate Puritans (the Presbyterians) and more extreme Puritans (the Independents) wanted the complete abolition of the episcopal system and the *Book of Common Prayer*. The majority Presbyterians sought to reshape England religiously along Calvinist lines, with local congregations subject to higher representative governing bodies (presbyteries). Independents wanted a much more fully decentralized church with every congregation as its own final authority. Finally, many conservatives in both houses of Parliament were determined to preserve the English church in its current form. Their numbers fell dramatically after 1642, however, when many of them left the House of Commons with the outbreak of civil war.

These divisions further intensified in October 1641, when a rebellion erupted in Ireland and Parliament was asked to raise funds for an army to suppress it. Pym and his followers, loudly reminding the House of Commons of the king's past behavior, argued that Charles could not be trusted with an army and that Parliament should become the commander-in-chief of English armed forces. Parliamentary conservatives, on the other hand, were appalled by such a bold departure from tradition.

ERUPTION OF CIVIL WAR   Charles saw the division within Parliament as a chance to reassert his power.

On December 1, 1641, Parliament presented him with the "Grand Remonstrance," a more-than-200-article summary of popular and parliamentary grievances against the crown. In January 1642, he invaded Parliament with his soldiers. He intended to arrest Pym and the other leaders, but they had been forewarned and managed to escape. The king then withdrew from London and began to raise an army. Shocked by his action, a majority of the House of Commons passed the Militia Ordinance, which gave Parliament authority to raise an army of its own. The die was now cast. For the next four years (1642–1646), civil war engulfed England.

Charles assembled his forces at Nottingham, and the war began in August. It was fought over two main issues:

- Would an absolute monarchy or a parliamentary government rule England?
- Would English religion be controlled by the king's bishops and conform to high Anglican practice or adopt a decentralized, Presbyterian system of church governance?

Charles's supporters, known as Cavaliers, were located in the northwestern half of England. The parliamentary opposition, known as Roundheads because of their close-cropped hair, had its stronghold in the southeastern half of the country. Supporters of both sides included nobility, gentry, and townspeople. The chief factor distinguishing them was religion; the Puritans tended to favor Parliament.

Oliver Cromwell and the Puritan Republic

Two factors led finally to Parliament's victory. The first was an alliance with Scotland consummated in 1643 when John Pym persuaded Parliament to accept the terms of the Solemn League and Covenant, an agreement that committed Parliament, with the Scots, to a Presbyterian system of church government. This policy meant for the Scots that they would never again be confronted with an attempt to impose the English prayerbook on their religious services. The second factor was the reorganization of the parliamentary army under Oliver Cromwell (1599–1658), a middle-aged country squire of iron discipline and strong Independent religious sentiment. Cromwell and his "godly men" favored neither the episcopal system of the king nor the pure Presbyterian system of the Solemn League and Covenant. They were willing to tolerate an

Oliver Cromwell's New Model Army defeated the royalists in the English Civil War. After the execution of Charles I in 1649, Cromwell dominated the short-lived English republic, conquered Ireland and Scotland, and ruled as Lord Protector from 1653 until his death in 1658. [Historical Pictures/Stock Montage, Inc.]

established majority church, but only if it also permitted Protestant dissenters to worship outside it.

The allies won the Battle of Marston Moor in 1644, the largest engagement of the war. In June 1645, Cromwell's newly reorganized forces, known as the New Model Army, fighting with disciplined fanaticism, won a decisive victory over the king at Naseby. (See Map 13–1.)

Defeated militarily, Charles tried again to take advantage of divisions within Parliament, this time seeking to win the Presbyterians and the Scots over to the royalist side. But Cromwell and his army firmly foiled him. In December 1648, Colonel Thomas Pride physically barred the Presbyterians, who made up a majority of Parliament, from taking

The English Civil War 1642-1646

Controlled by the Parliamentarians, Beginning of 1645.

Controlled by the Royalists, Beginning of 1645.

Conquered by the Parliamentarians, in 1645.

✴ Battle Site

SCOTLAND

North Sea

Glasgow
Edinburgh
Philiphaugh 1645

Belfast

Marston Moor 1644

IRELAND

ENGLAND

Dublin

Lichfield 1643

Naseby 1645

WALES

Edge Hill 1642

Cambridge

Turnham Green 1643

London

Newbury 1643 & 1644

Langport 1645

100 MILES

100 KILOMETERS

English Channel

MAP 13–1 THE ENGLISH CIVIL WAR *This map shows the rapid deterioration of the royalist position in 1645.*

their seats. After "Pride's Purge," only a "rump" of fewer than fifty members remained. Though small in numbers, this Independent Rump Parliament did not hesitate to use its power. On January 30, 1649, after a trial by a special court, the Rump Parliament executed Charles as a public criminal and thereafter abolished the monarchy, the House of Lords, and the Anglican Church. What had begun as a civil war had at this point become a revolution.

From 1649 to 1660, England became officially a Puritan republic, although for much of that time it was dominated by Cromwell. During this period, Cromwell's army conquered Ireland and Scotland, creating the single political entity of Great Britain. Cromwell, however, was a military man and no

politician. He was increasingly frustrated by what seemed to him to be pettiness and dawdling on the part of Parliament. When in 1653 the House of Commons entertained a motion to disband his expensive army of 50,000, Cromwell responded by marching in and disbanding Parliament. He ruled thereafter as Lord Protector.

This military dictatorship, however, proved no more effective than Charles's rule had been and became just as harsh and hated. Cromwell's great army and foreign adventures inflated his budget to three times that of Charles. Near chaos reigned in many places, and commerce suffered throughout England. Cromwell was as intolerant of Anglicans as Charles had been of Puritans. People deeply resented his Puritan prohibitions of drunkenness, theatergoing, and dancing. Political liberty vanished in the name of religious liberty.

Cromwell's challenge had been to devise a political structure to replace that of monarch and Parliament. He tried various arrangements, none of which worked. He quarreled with the various Parliaments elected while he was Lord Protector. By the time of his death in 1658, most of the English were ready to end the Puritan religious experiment and the republican political experiment and return to their traditional institutions of government. Negotiations between leaders of the army and the exiled Charles II (r. 1660–1685), son of Charles I, led to the restoration of the Stuart monarchy in 1660.

Charles II and the Restoration of the Monarchy

Charles II returned to England amid great rejoicing. A man of considerable charm and political skill, Charles set a refreshing new tone after eleven years of somber Puritanism. His restoration returned England to the status quo of 1642, with a hereditary monarch once again on the throne, no legal requirement that he summon Parliament regularly, and the Anglican Church, with its bishops and prayerbook, supreme in religion.

The king, however, had secret Catholic sympathies and favored a policy of religious toleration. He wanted to allow all those outside the Church of England, Catholics as well as Puritans, to worship freely so long as they remained loyal to the throne. But in Parliament, even the ultraroyalist Anglicans did not believe patriotism and religion could be separated. Between 1661 and 1665, through a series of laws known as the Clarendon Code, Parliament

The bleeding head of Charles I is exhibited to the crowd after his execution on a cold day in January 1649. The contemporary Dutch artist also professed to see the immediate ascension of Charles's soul to heaven. In fact, many saw the king as a martyr. [DYCK, Sir Anthony van (1599–1641) (after) The Execution of King Charles I of England (1600-49) *(oil on canvas), by Weesop (an eyewitness), 1649. Private Collection. The Bridgeman Art Library, London.]*

excluded Roman Catholics, Presbyterians, and Independents from the religious and political life of the nation. These laws imposed penalties for attending non-Anglican worship services, required strict adherence to the *Book of Common Prayer* and the *Thirty-Nine Articles*, and demanded oaths of allegiance to the Church of England from all persons serving in local government.

At the time of the Restoration, England adopted Navigation Acts that required all imports to be carried either in English ships or in ships registered to the country from which the cargo originated. Dutch ships carried cargo from many nations, and such laws struck directly at Dutch dominance in the shipping industry. A series of naval wars between England and Holland ensued. Charles also attempted to tighten his grasp on the rich English colonies in North America and the Caribbean, many of which had been settled and developed by separatists who desired independence from English rule.

Although Parliament strongly supported the monarchy, Charles, following the pattern of his predecessors, required greater revenues than Parliament appropriated. These he obtained in part by increased customs duties. Because England and France were both at war with Holland, he also received aid from France. In 1670 England and France formally allied against the Dutch in the Treaty of Dover. In a secret portion of this treaty, Charles pledged to announce his conversion to Catholicism as soon as conditions in England permitted. In return for this announcement (which was never made), Louis XIV of France promised to pay a substantial subsidy to England.

In an attempt to unite the English people behind the war with Holland, and as a sign of good faith to Louis XIV, Charles issued a Declaration of Indulgence in 1672. This document suspended all laws against Roman Catholics and Protestant nonconformists. But again, the conservative Parliament proved less generous than the king and refused to grant money for the war until Charles rescinded the measure. After he did, Parliament passed the Test Act, which required all officials of the crown, civil and military, to swear an oath against the doctrine of transubstantiation—a requirement that no loyal Roman Catholic could honestly meet.

A Portrait of Oliver Cromwell

Oliver Cromwell was one of the most powerful and controversial personalities of seventeenth-century Britain. He became Lord Protector through his command of the army which had first championed the parliamentary cause and later disbanded Parliament. Royalist statesman and historian Edward Hyde, the earl of Clarendon (1609–1674) was an enemy of Cromwell. Yet, his portrait of Cromwell mixed criticism with grudging admiration for the Puritan leader.

✦ *According to the earl of Clarendon, what were the chief features of Cromwell's personality? What was the character of his methods of governing? How did his position at home and abroad depend upon his military standing?*

He was one of those men whom his enemies cannot condemn without at the same time also praising. For he could never have done half that mischief without great parts of courage and industry and judgment. And he must have had a wonderful understanding of the nature and humours of men and a great dexterity in applying them . . . [to] raise himself to such a height. . . .

When he first appeared in the Parliament, he seemed to have a person in no degree gracious, no ornament of discourse, none of those talents which reconcile the affections of the standers-by; yet as he grew into his place and authority, his parts seemed to be renewed, as if he concealed faculties till he had occasion to use them. . . .

After he was confirmed and invested Protector . . . he consulted with very few . . . nor communicated any enterprise he resolved upon with more than those who were to have principal parts in the execution of it; nor to them sooner than was absolutely necessary. What he once resolved . . . he would not be dissuaded from, nor endure any contradiction. . . .

In all other matters which did not concern . . . his jurisdiction, he seemed to have great reverence for the law. . . . and as he proceeded with . . . indignation and haughtiness with those who were refractory and dared to contend with his greatness, so towards those who complied with his good pleasure, and courted his protection, he used a wonderful civility, generosity, and bounty.

To three nations [England, Ireland, and Scotland], which perfectly hated him, to an entire obedience to all his dictates; to awe and govern those nations by an army that was not devoted to him and wished his ruin; this was an instance of a very prodigious address. But his greatness at home was but a shadow of the glory he had abroad. It was hard to discover which feared him most, France, Spain, or the Netherlands. . . . As they did all sacrifice their honour and their interest to his pleasure, so there is nothing he could have demanded that any of them would have denied him.

James Harvey Robinson, ed., Readings in European History, *vol. 2 (Boston: Atheneum, 1906), pp. 248–250.*

Parliament had aimed the Test Act largely at the king's brother, James, duke of York, heir to the throne and a recent, devout convert to Catholicism. In 1678 a notorious liar named Titus Oates swore before a magistrate that Charles's Catholic wife, through her physician, was plotting with Jesuits and Irishmen to kill the king so James could assume the throne. The matter was taken before Parliament, where Oates was believed. In the ensuing hysteria, known as the Popish Plot, several people were tried and executed. Riding the crest of anti-Catholic sentiment and led by the earl of Shaftesbury (1621–1683), opposition members of Parliament, called Whigs, made an impressive but unsuccessful effort to enact a bill excluding James from succession to the throne.

Charles II (r. 1660–1685) was a person of considerable charm and political skill. Here he is portrayed as the founder of the Royal Society. [Robert Harding Picture Library, London]

More suspicious than ever of Parliament, Charles II turned again to increased customs duties and the assistance of Louis XIV for extra income. By these means he was able to rule from 1681 to 1685 without recalling Parliament. In these years, Charles suppressed much of his opposition. He drove the earl of Shaftesbury into exile, executed several Whig leaders for treason, and bullied local corporations into electing members of Parliament submissive to the royal will. When Charles died in 1685 (after a deathbed conversion to Catholicism), he left James the prospect of a Parliament filled with royal friends.

James II and Renewed Fears of a Catholic England

James II (r. 1685–1688) did not know how to make the most of a good thing. He alienated Parliament by insisting on the repeal of the Test Act. When Parliament balked, he dissolved it and proceeded openly to appoint known Catholics to high posi-

tions in both his court and the army. In 1687 he issued a Declaration of Indulgence, which suspended all religious tests and permitted free worship. Local candidates for Parliament who opposed the declaration were removed from their offices by the king's soldiers and were replaced by Catholics. In June 1688, James went so far as to imprison seven Anglican bishops who had refused to publicize his suspension of laws against Catholics. Each of these actions represented a direct royal attack on the local power and authority of nobles, landowners, the church, and other corporate bodies whose members believed they possessed particular legal privileges. James was attacking English liberty and challenging all manner of social privileges and influence.

Under the guise of a policy of enlightened toleration, James was actually seeking to subject all English institutions to the power of the monarchy. His goal was absolutism, and even conservative, loyalist Tories, as the royal supporters were called, could not abide this policy. The English feared, with reason, that James planned to imitate the religious intolerance of Louis XIV, who had, in 1685, revoked the Edict of Nantes (which had protected French Protestants for almost a century) and imposed Catholicism on the entire nation, using his dragoons against those who protested or resisted.

James soon faced united opposition. When his Catholic second wife gave birth to a son and Catholic male heir to the throne on June 20, 1688, opposition turned to action. The English had hoped that James would die without a male heir so the throne would pass to Mary, his Protestant eldest daughter. Mary was the wife of William III of Orange, *stadtholder* of the Netherlands, great-grandson of William the Silent, and the leader of European opposition to Louis XIV's imperial designs. Within days of the birth of James's son, Whig and Tory members of Parliament formed a coalition and invited Orange to invade England to preserve "traditional liberties," that is, the Anglican Church and parliamentary government.

The "Glorious Revolution"

William of Orange arrived with his army in November 1688 and was received without opposition by the English people. In the face of sure defeat, James fled to France and the protection of Louis XIV. With James gone, Parliament declared the throne vacant and on its own authority in 1689 proclaimed

William and Mary became the monarchs of England in 1689. Their accession brought England's economic and military resources into the balance against the France of Louis XIV. [Robert Harding Picture Library, London]

William and Mary the new monarchs, completing the successful bloodless "Glorious Revolution." William and Mary, in turn, recognized a Bill of Rights that limited the powers of the monarchy and guaranteed the civil liberties of the English privileged classes. Henceforth, England's monarchs would be subject to law and would rule by the consent of Parliament, which was to be called into session every three years. The Bill of Rights also pointedly prohibited Roman Catholics from occupying the English throne. The Toleration Act of 1689 permitted worship by all Protestants and outlawed Roman Catholics and anti-Trinitarians (those who denied the Christian doctrine of the Trinity).

The measure closing this century of strife was the Act of Settlement in 1701. This bill provided for the English crown to go to the Protestant House of Hanover in Germany if none of the children of Queen Anne (r. 1702–1714), the second daughter of James II and the last of the Stuart monarchs, was alive at her death. She outlived all of her children, and so in 1714, the elector of Hanover became King George I of England, the third foreign monarch to occupy the English throne in just over a century.

The Glorious Revolution of 1688 established a framework of government by and for the governed that seemed to bear out the arguments of John Locke's *Second Treatise of Government* (1690). In this work, Locke described the relationship of a king and his people as a bilateral contract. If the king broke that contract, the people, by whom Locke meant the privileged and powerful, had the right to depose him. Locke had written the essay before the revolution, but it came to be read as a justification for it. Although neither in fact nor in theory a "popular" revolution such as would occur in America and France a hundred years later, the Glorious Revolution did establish in England a permanent check on monarchical power by the classes represented in Parliament. At the same time, as will be seen in Chapter 15, in its wake the English government had achieved a secure financial base that would allow it to pursue a century of warfare.

Rise of Absolute Monarchy in France

Seventeenth-century France, in contrast to England, saw both discontent among the nobility and religious pluralism smothered by the absolute monarchy and the closed Catholic state of Louis XIV (r. 1643–1715). An aggressive ruler who sought glory (*la gloire*) in foreign wars, Louis XIV subjected his subjects at home to "one king, one law, one faith."

Historians once portrayed Louis XIV's reign as a time when the rising central monarchy exerted far-reaching, direct control of the nation at all levels. A somewhat different picture has now emerged. Louis's predecessors and their chief ministers in the half century before his reign had already tried to impose direct rule, arousing discontent and, at mid-century, a rebellion among the nobility. Louis's genius was to make the monarchy the most important and powerful political institution in France while also assuring the nobles and other wealthy groups of their social standing and political and social influence on the local level. Rather than destroying existing local social and political institutions, Louis largely worked through them. Once nobles understood the king would support their local authority, they supported his central royal authority. In other words, the king and the nobles came to recognize that they needed each other. Nevertheless, Louis made it clear to all concerned that he was the senior partner in the relationship.

Louis's royal predecessors laid the institutional foundations for absolute monarchy and also taught him certain practices to avoid. Just as the emergence of a strong Parliament was not inevitable in England, neither was the emergence of an absolute monarchy in France.

Henry IV and Sully

Coming to the throne after the French wars of religion, Henry IV (r. 1589–1610; see Chapter 12) sought to curtail the privileges of the French nobility. His targets were the provincial governors and the regional *parlements*, especially the powerful *Parlement* of Paris, where a divisive spirit lived on. Here were to be found the old privileged groups, tax-exempt magnates who were largely preoccupied with protecting their self-interests. During the reign of Louis XIII (r. 1610–1643), royal civil servants known as *intendants* subjected these privileged groups to stricter supervision, implementing the king's will with some success in the provinces. An important function of the *intendants* was to prevent abuses from the sale of royal offices that conferred the right to collect revenues, sell licenses, or carry out other remunerative forms of administration. It was usually nobles who acquired these lucrative offices, which was one reason for their ongoing influence.

After decades of religious and civil war, an economy more amenable to governmental regulation emerged during Henry IV's reign. Henry and his finance minister, the duke of Sully (1560–1641), established government monopolies on gunpowder, mines, and salt, preparing the way for the mercantilist policies of Louis XIV and his minister, Colbert. They began a canal system to link the Atlantic and the Mediterranean by joining the Saône, the Loire, the Seine, and the Meuse rivers. They introduced the royal *corvée*, a labor tax that created a national force of drafted workers used to improve roads and the conditions of internal travel. Sully even dreamed of organizing the whole of Europe politically and commercially into a kind of common market.

Louis XIII and Richelieu

Henry IV was assassinated in 1610, and the following year Sully retired. Because Henry's son and successor, Louis XIII, was only nine years old at his father's death, the task of governing fell to the queen mother, Marie de Médicis (d. 1642). Finding herself in a vulnerable position, she sought security abroad by signing a ten-year mutual defense pact with France's archrival Spain in the Treaty of Fontainebleau (1611). This alliance also arranged for the later marriage of Louis XIII to the Spanish *Infanta* as well as for the marriage of the queen's daughter Elizabeth to the heir to the Spanish throne. The queen sought internal security against pressures from the French nobility by promoting the career of Cardinal Richelieu (1585–1642) as the king's chief adviser. Richelieu, loyal and shrewd, aspired to make France a supreme European power. He, more than any other person, was the secret of French success in the first half of the seventeenth century.

An apparently devout Catholic who also believed that the church best served both his own ambition

Cardinal Richelieu laid the foundations for the political ascendancy of the French monarchy. ["Cardinal Richelieu" by Philippe de Champaigne. The National Gallery, London]

and the welfare of France, Richelieu pursued a strongly anti-Habsburg policy. Although he supported the Spanish alliance of the queen and Catholic religious unity within France, he was determined to contain Spanish power and influence, even when that meant aiding and abetting Protestant Europe. It is an indication both of Richelieu's awkward political situation and of his diplomatic agility that he could, in 1631, pledge funds to the Protestant army of Gustavus Adolphus, the king of Sweden, while also insisting that Catholic Bavaria be spared from attack and that Catholics in conquered countries be permitted to practice their religion. One measure of the success of Richelieu's foreign policies can be seen in France's substantial gains in land and political influence when the Treaty of Westphalia (1648) ended hostilities in the Holy Roman Empire (see Chapter 12) and the Treaty of the Pyrenees (1659) sealed peace with Spain.

At home, Richelieu pursued centralizing policies utterly without qualm. Supported by the king, who let his chief minister make most decisions of state,

Richelieu stepped up the campaign against separatist provincial governors and parlements. He made it clear that there was only one law, that of the king, and none could stand above it. When disobedient nobles defied his edicts, they were imprisoned and even executed. Such treatment of the nobility won Richelieu much enmity, even from the queen mother, who, unlike Richelieu, was not always willing to place the larger interests of the state above the pleasure of favorite nobles.

Richelieu started the campaign against the Huguenots that would end in 1685 with Louis XIV's revocation of the Edict of Nantes. Royal armies conquered major Huguenot cities in 1629. The subsequent Peace of Alais (1629) truncated the Edict of Nantes by denying Protestants the right to maintain garrisoned cities, separate political organizations, and independent law courts. Only Richelieu's foreign policy, which involved France in ties with Protestant powers, prevented the earlier implementation of the policy of extreme intolerance that marked the reign of Louis XIV. In the same year that Richelieu rescinded the independent political status of the Huguenots in the Peace of Alais, he also entered negotiations to make Gustavus Adolphus his counterweight to the expansion of Habsburg power within the Holy Roman Empire. By 1635 the Catholic soldiers of France were fighting openly with Swedish Lutherans against the emperor's army in the final phase of the Thirty Years' War (see Chapter 12).

Richelieu employed the arts and the printing press to defend his actions and to indoctrinate the French people in the meaning of *raison d'état* ("reason of state"). This also set a precedent for Louis XIV, who made elaborate use of royal propaganda and spectacle to assert and enhance his power.

Young Louis XIV and Mazarin

Although Richelieu helped lay the foundations for a much expanded royal authority, his immediate legacy was strong resentment of the monarchy among the French nobility and wealthy commercial groups. The crown's steady multiplication of royal offices, its replacement of local authorities by "state" agents, and its reduction of local sources of patronage undermined the traditional position of the privileged groups in French society. Among those affected were officers of the crown in the law courts and other royal institutions.

This medallion shows Anne of Austria, the wife of Louis XIII, with her son, Louis XIV. She wisely placed political authority in the hands of Cardinal Mazarin, who prepared Louis to govern France. [Giraudon/Art Resource, N.Y.]

When Louis XIII died in 1643, Louis XIV was only five years old. During his minority, the queen mother, Anne of Austria (d. 1666), placed the reins of government in the hands of Cardinal Mazarin (1602–1661), who continued Richelieu's determined policy of centralization. During Cardinal Mazarin's regency, long-building resentment produced a backlash. Between 1649 and 1652, in a series of widespread rebellions known as the *Fronde* (after the slingshot used by street boys), segments of the nobility and townspeople sought to reverse the drift toward absolute monarchy and to preserve local autonomy.

The *Parlement* of Paris initiated the revolt in 1649, and the nobility at large soon followed. Urging them on were the influential wives of princes whom Mazarin had imprisoned for treason. The many (the nobility) briefly triumphed over the one (the monarchy) when Mazarin released the imprisoned princes in February 1651. He and Louis XIV thereafter entered a short exile (Mazarin leaving France, Louis fleeing Paris). They returned in October 1652 after an interlude of inefficient and nearly anarchic rule by the nobility. The period of the Fronde convinced most French people that the rule of a strong king was preferable to the rule of many regional powers with competing and irreconcilable claims. At the same time, Louis XIV and his later advisors learned that heavy-handed policies like those of Richelieu and Mazarin could endanger the monarchy. Louis would ultimately concentrate unprecedented authority in the monarchy, but his means would be more clever than those of his predecessors.

The Years of Louis's Personal Rule

On the death of Mazarin, Louis XIV assumed personal control of the government. Unlike his royal predecessors, he appointed no single chief minister. One result was to make revolt more difficult. Rebellious nobles would now be challenging the king directly; they could not claim to be resisting only a bad minister.

Mazarin prepared Louis XIV well to rule France. The turbulent events of his youth also made an indelible impression on the king. Louis wrote in his memoirs that the *Fronde* caused him to loathe "kings of straw," and he followed two strategies to assure he would never become one.

First, Louis and his advisors became masters of propaganda and political image creation. Indoctrinated with a strong sense of the grandeur of his crown, Louis never missed an opportunity to impress it on the French people. When the *dauphin* (the heir to the French throne) was born in 1662, for example, Louis appeared for the celebration dressed as a Roman emperor.

Second, Louis made sure the French nobles and other major social groups would benefit from the growth of his own authority. Although he maintained control over foreign affairs and limited the influence of noble institutions on the monarchy, he never tried to abolish those institutions or limit their authority at the local level. The crown, for example, usually conferred informally with regional *parlements* before making rulings that would affect them. Likewise, the crown would rarely enact economic regulations without consulting local opinion. Local *parlements* enjoyed considerable latitude in all regional matters. In an exception to this pattern, Louis did clash with the *Parlement* of Paris, with which he had to register laws, and eventually in 1673 he curtailed much of its power. Many regional *parlements* and other regional authorities, however, had resented the power of that body.

Employing these strategies of propaganda and cooperation, Louis set out to anchor his rule in the principle of the divine right of kings, to domesticate the French nobility by binding them to the court rituals of Versailles, and to crush religious dissent.

King by Divine Right

Reverence for the king and the personification of government in his person had been nurtured in France since Capetian times. It was a maxim of French law and popular opinion that "the king of France is emperor in his realm" and the king's wish the law of the land. Building on this reverence, Louis XIV defended absolute royal authority on the grounds of divine right.

An important source for Louis's concept of royal authority was his devout tutor, the political theorist Bishop Jacques-Bénigne Bossuet (1627–1704).

Bishop Bossuet Defends the Divine Right of Kings

The revolutions of the seventeenth century caused many to fear anarchy far more than tyranny, among them the influential French bishop Jacques-Bénigne Bossuet (1627–1704), the leader of French Catholicism in the second half of the seventeenth century. Louis XIV made him court preacher and tutor to his son, for whom Bossuet wrote a celebrated Universal History. In the following excerpt, Bossuet defends the divine right and absolute power of kings. He depicts kings as embracing in their person the whole body of the state and the will of the people they govern and, as such, as being immune from judgment by any mere mortal.

✦ *Why might Bossuet have wished to make such extravagant claims for absolute royal power? How might these claims be transferred to any form of government? What are the religious bases for Bossuet's argument? How does this argument for absolute royal authority lead also to the need for a single uniform religion in France?*

The royal power is absolute. . . . The prince need render account of his acts to no one. "I counsel thee to keep the king's commandment, and that in regard of the oath of God. Be not hasty to go out of his sight; stand not on an evil thing for he doeth whatsoever pleaseth him. Where the word of a king is, there is power; and who may say unto him, What doest thou? Whoso keepeth the commandment shall feel no evil thing" [Eccles. 8:2–5]. Without this absolute authority the king could neither do good nor repress evil. It is necessary that his power be such that no one can hope to escape him, and finally, the only protection of individuals against the public authority should be their innocence. This confirms the teaching of St. Paul: "Wilt thou then not be afraid of the power? Do that which is good" [Rom. 13:3].

God is infinite, God is all. The prince, as prince, is not regarded as a private person: he is a public personage, all the state is in him; the will of all the people is included in his. As all perfection and all strength are united in God, so all the power of individuals is united in the person of the prince. What grandeur that a single man should embody so much! . . .

Behold an immense people united in a single person; behold this holy power, paternal and absolute; behold the secret cause which governs the whole body of the state, contained in a single head: you see the image of God in the king, and you have the idea of royal majesty. God is holiness itself, goodness itself, and power itself. In these things lies the majesty of God. In the image of these things lies the majesty of the prince.

From Politics Drawn from the Very Words of Holy Scripture, *as quoted in James Harvey Robinson, ed.,* Readings in European History, *vol. 2 (Boston: Athenaeum, 1906), pp. 275–276.*

An ardent champion of the Gallican liberties—the traditional rights of the French king and church in matters of ecclesiastical appointments and taxation—Bossuet defended what he called the "divine right of kings." In support of his claims he cited examples of Old Testament rulers divinely appointed by and answerable only to God. As medieval popes had insisted that only God could judge a pope, so Bossuet argued that none save God could judge the king. Kings may have remained duty-bound to reflect God's will in their rule—in this sense, Bossuet considered them always subject to a higher authority. Yet as God's regents on Earth they could not be bound to the dictates of mere princes and parliaments. Such assumptions lay behind Louis XIV's alleged declaration: *L'état, c'est moi* ("I am the state").

Versailles

More than any other monarch of the day, Louis XIV used the physical setting of his royal court to exert political control. The palace court at Versailles on the outskirts of Paris became Louis's permanent residence after 1682. It was a true temple to royalty, architecturally designed and artistically decorated to proclaim the glory of the Sun King, as Louis was known. A spectacular estate with magnificent fountains and acres of orange groves, it became home to thousands of the more important nobles, royal officials, and servants. Although its physical maintenance and new additions, which continued throughout Louis's lifetime, consumed over half his annual revenues, Versailles paid significant political dividends.

Because Louis ruled personally, he was the chief source of favors and patronage in France. To emphasize his prominence, he organized life at court around every aspect of his own daily routine. He encouraged nobles to approach him directly, but required them to do so through elaborate court etiquette. Polite and fawning nobles sought his attention, entering their names on waiting lists to be in attendance at especially favored moments. The king's rising and dressing in particular were times of rare intimacy, when nobles could whisper their special requests in his ear. Fortunate nobles held his night candle as they accompanied him to his bed.

Although only five feet four inches in height, the king had presence and was always engaging in conversation. He turned his own sexuality to political

Louis XIV of France (r. 1643–1715) was the dominant European monarch in the second half of the seventeenth century. The powerful centralized monarchy he created established the prototype for the mode of government later termed absolutism. *[Giraudon/Art Resource, N.Y.]*

ends and encouraged the belief at court that it was an honor to lie with him. Married to the Spanish *Infanta* Marie Thérèse for political reasons in 1660, he kept many mistresses. After Marie's death in 1683, he settled down in a secret marriage to Madame de Maintenon and apparently became much less the philanderer.

Court life was a carefully planned and successfully executed effort to domesticate and trivialize the nobility. Barred by law from high government positions, the ritual and play kept them busy and dependent so they had little time to plot revolt. Dress codes and high-stakes gambling contributed to their indebtedness and dependency on the king. Members of the court spent the afternoons hunting, riding, or strolling about the lush gardens of Versailles. Evenings were given over to planned entertainment in the large salons (plays, concerts, gambling, and the like), followed by supper at 10:00

p.m. Even the king's retirement was part of the day's spectacle.

Moments near the king were important to most court nobles because they were effectively excluded from the real business of government. Louis ruled through powerful councils that controlled foreign affairs, domestic relations, and economic regulations. Each day after morning mass, which Louis always observed, he spent hours with the chief ministers of these councils, whom he chose from families long in royal service or from among people just beginning to rise in the social structure. Unlike the nobles at court, they had no real or potential power bases in the provinces and depended solely on the king for their standing in both government and society.

Some nobles, of course, did not attend Versailles. Some tended to their local estates and cultivated their local influence. Many others were simply too poor to cut a figure at court. All the nobility understood, however, that Louis, unlike Richelieu and Mazarin, would not threaten their local social standing. Louis supported France's traditional social structure and the social privileges of the nobility.

Suppression of the Jansenists

Like Richelieu before him, Louis believed that political unity and stability required religious conformity. His first move in this direction, which came early in his personal reign, was against the Roman Catholic Jansenists.

The French crown and the French church had by long tradition—originating with the so-called Gallican liberties in the fourteenth century—jealously guarded their independence from Rome. A great influx of Catholic religious orders, the Jesuits prominent among them, followed Henry IV's conversion to Catholicism. Because of their leadership at the Council of Trent and their close connections

Versailles, as painted in 1668 by Pierre Patel the Elder (1605–1676). The central building is the hunting lodge built for Louis XII earlier in the century. The wings that appear here were some of Louis XIV's first expansions. [Giraudon/Art Resource, N.Y.]

to Spain, the Jesuits had been banned from France by Catherine de Médicis. Henry IV, however, lifted the ban in 1603, with certain conditions: He required members of the order to swear an oath of allegiance to the king, he limited the number of new colleges they could open, and he required them to have special licenses for public activities.

The Jesuits were not, however, easily harnessed. They rapidly monopolized the education of the upper classes, and their devout students promoted the religious reforms and doctrine of the Council of Trent throughout France. In a measure of their success, Jesuits served as confessors to Henry IV, Louis XIII, and Louis XIV.

Jansenism arose in the 1630s as part of an intra-Catholic opposition to the theology and the political influence of the Jesuits. Jansenists adhered to the Augustinian tradition that had also spawned many Protestant teachings. Serious and uncompromising, they particularly opposed Jesuit teachings about free will. They believed with Saint Augustine that original sin so corrupted humankind that individuals could do nothing good nor secure their own salvation without divine grace. The namesake of the movement, Cornelius Jansen (d. 1638), was a Flemish theologian and the bishop of Ypres. His posthumously published *Augustinus* (1640) assailed Jesuit teaching on grace and salvation.

A prominent Parisian family, the Arnaulds, became Jansenist allies, adding a political element to the Jansenists' theological objections to the Jesuits. Like many other French people, the Arnaulds believed the Jesuits had been behind the assassination of Henry IV in 1610.

The Arnaulds dominated Jansenist communities at Port-Royal and Paris during the 1640s. In 1643 Antoine Arnauld published a work entitled *On Frequent Communion*, in which he criticized the Jesuits for confessional practices that permitted the easy redress of almost any sin. The Jesuits, in turn, condemned the Jansenists as "crypto-Calvinists."

On May 31, 1653, Pope Innocent X declared heretical five Jansenist theological propositions on grace and salvation. In 1656 the pope banned Jansen's *Augustinus* and the Sorbonne censured Antoine Arnauld. In this same year, Antoine's friend, Blaise Pascal (1623–1662), the most famous of Jansen's followers, published the first of his *Provincial Letters* in defense of Jansenism. A deeply religious man, Pascal tried to reconcile the "reasons of the heart" with growing seventeenth-century reverence for the clear and distinct ideas of the mind

(see Chapter 14). He objected to Jesuit moral theology not only as being lax and shallow, but also because he felt its rationalism failed to do full justice to the religious experience.

In 1660 Louis permitted the papal bull *Ad Sacram Sedem* (1656) to be enforced in France, thus banning Jansenism. He also closed down the Port-Royal community. Thereafter, Jansenists either retracted their views or went underground. Much later, in 1710, Louis lent his support to a still more thorough purge of Jansenist sentiment.

Jansenism had offered the prospect of a Catholicism broad enough to appeal to France's Protestant Huguenots. By suppressing it, Louis also eliminated the best hope for bringing peaceful religious unity to his country.

Louis's Early Wars

Louis's France was in many ways like much of the rest of contemporary Europe. It had a largely subsistence economy and its cities enjoyed only limited commercial prosperity. It did not, in other words, achieve the economic strength of a modern industrial economy. By the 1660s, however, France was superior to any other European nation in administrative bureaucracy, armed forces, and national unity. Louis had sufficient resources at his disposal to raise and maintain a large and powerful army, and by every external measure he was in a position to dominate Europe. He spent most of the rest of his reign attempting to do so.

GOVERNING FOR WARFARE Three remarkable French ministers established and supported Louis XIV's great war machine: Colbert, Louvois, and Vauban.

Jean-Baptiste Colbert (1619–1683), controller general of finances and Louis's most brilliant minister, created the economic base Louis needed to finance his wars. Colbert worked to centralize the French economy with the same rigor that Louis had worked to centralize the French government. Colbert tried, with modest success, to organize much economic activity under state supervision and, through tariffs, carefully regulated the flow of imports and exports. He sought to create new national industries and organized factories around a tight regimen of work and ideology. He simplified the administrative bureaucracy, abolished unnecessary positions, and reduced the number of tax-exempt nobles. He also increased the *taille*, a direct

The policies of Jean-Baptiste Colbert (1619–1683) transformed France into a major commercial power. [Erich Lessing/Art Resource, N.Y.]

tax on the peasantry and a major source of royal income.

This kind of close government control of the economy came to be known as *mercantilism* (a term invented by later critics of the policy). Its aim was to maximize foreign exports and internal reserves of bullion, the gold and silver necessary for making war. Modern scholars argue that Colbert overcontrolled the French economy and cite his "paternalism" as a major reason for the failure of French colonies in the New World. Be that as it may, his policies unquestionably transformed France into a major commercial power, with foreign bases in Africa, in India, and in the Americas, from Canada to the Caribbean.

Louis's army, about a quarter of a million strong, was the creation of Michel Tellier and his more famous son, the marquis of Louvois (1641–1691). Louis's war minister from 1677 to 1691, Louvois was a superior military tactician.

Before Louvois, the French army had been an amalgam of local recruits and mercenaries, uncoordinated groups whose loyalty could not always be

counted on. Without regular pay or a way to supply their everyday needs, troops often lived by pillage. Louvois instituted good salaries and improved discipline, making soldiering a respectable profession. He limited military commissions and introduced a system of promotion by merit, bringing dedicated fighters into the ranks. Enlistment was for four years and was restricted to single men. *Intendants*, the king's ubiquitous civil servants, monitored conduct at all levels.

Because it was well disciplined, this new, large, and powerful standing army had considerable public support. Unlike its undisciplined predecessor, the new army no longer threatened the lives, homes, or well-being of the people it was supposed to protect. It thus provides an excellent example of the kinds of benefits many saw in the growing authority of the central monarchy.

What Louvois was to military organization, Sebastien Vauban (1633–1707) was to military engineering. He perfected the arts of fortifying and besieging towns. He also devised the system of trench warfare and developed the concept of defensive frontiers that remained basic to military tactics through World War I.

THE WAR OF DEVOLUTION   Louis's first great foreign adventure was the War of Devolution (1667–1668). It was fought, as would be the later and more devastating War of the Spanish Succession, over Louis's claim to the Spanish Belgian provinces through his wife, Marie Thérèse (1638–1683). According to the terms of the Treaty of the Pyrenees (1659), Marie had renounced her claim to the Spanish succession on condition that a 500,000-crown dowry be paid to Louis within eighteen months of the marriage, a condition that was not met. When Philip IV of Spain died in September 1665, he left all his lands to his sickly four-year-old son by a second marriage, Charles II (r. 1665–1700), and explicitly denied any lands to his daughter. Louis had always harbored the hope of turning the marriage to territorial gain and even before Philip's death had argued that Marie was entitled to a portion of the inheritance.

Louis had a legal argument on his side, which gave the war its name. He maintained that in certain regions of Brabant and Flanders, which were part of the Spanish inheritance, property "devolved" to the children of a first marriage rather than to those of a second. Therefore, Marie had a higher claim than Charles II to these regions. Although

Throughout the age of the splendor at the court of Louis XIV millions of French peasants lived lives of poverty and hardship, as depicted in this 1640 painting, Peasant Family *by Louis LeNain. [Erich Lessing/Art Resource, N.Y.]*

such regional laws could hardly bind the king of Spain, Louis was not deterred from sending his armies, under the viscount of Turenne, into Flanders and the Franche-Comté in 1667. In response to this aggression, England, Sweden, and the United Provinces of Holland formed the Triple Alliance, a force sufficient to compel Louis to agree to peace under the terms in the Treaty of Aix-la-Chapelle (1668). According to the treaty, he gained control of certain towns bordering the Spanish Netherlands. (See Map 13–2.)

INVASION OF THE NETHERLANDS   In 1670, with the signing of the Treaty of Dover, England and France became allies against the Dutch. Without the English, the Triple Alliance crumbled. This left Louis in a stronger position to invade the Netherlands for a second time, which he did in 1672. This time he aimed directly at Holland, which had organized the Triple Alliance in 1667, foiling French designs in Flanders. Dutch gloating after the Treaty of Aix-la-Chapelle had mightily offended Louis. Such cartoons as one depicting the sun (Louis was called the "Sun King") eclipsed by a great moon of Dutch cheese distressed him. Without neutralizing Holland, he knew he could never hope to acquire land in the Spanish Netherlands, much less fulfill his dreams of European hegemony.

Louis's successful invasion of the United Provinces in 1672 brought the downfall of Dutch statesmen Jan and Cornelius De Witt. Replacing them was the twenty-seven-year-old Prince of Orange, destined after 1689 to become King

William III of England. Orange was the great-grandson of William the Silent, who had repulsed Philip II and dashed Spanish hopes of dominating the Netherlands in the sixteenth century.

Orange, an unpretentious Calvinist, who was in almost every way Louis's opposite, galvanized the seven provinces into a fierce fighting unit. In 1673 he united the Holy Roman Emperor, Spain, Lorraine, and Brandenburg in an alliance against Louis. His enemies now saw the French king as a "Christian Turk," a menace to the whole of western Europe, Catholic and Protestant alike. In the ensuing warfare, both sides experienced gains and losses. Louis lost his ablest generals, Turenne and Condé, in 1675, but a victory by Admiral Duquesne over the Dutch fleet in 1676 gave France control of the Mediterranean. The Peace of Nijmwegen, signed with different parties in successive years (1678, 1679), ended the hostilities of this second war. There were various minor territorial adjustments but no clear victor except the United Netherlands, which retained all of its territory.

Revocation of the Edict of Nantes

In the decade after his invasion of the Netherlands, Louis made his second major move to assure religious conformity. Following the proclamation of the Edict of Nantes in 1598, relations between the great Catholic majority (nine-tenths of the French population) and the Protestant minority remained hostile. There were about 1.75 million Huguenots in France in the 1660s, but their numbers were declin-

ing in the second half of the seventeenth century. The French Catholic Church had long denounced Calvinists as heretical and treasonous and had supported their persecution as both pious and patriotic.

Following the Peace of Nijmwegen in 1678–1679, which halted for the moment his aggression in Europe, Louis launched a methodical government campaign against the French Huguenots in a determined effort to unify France religiously. He hounded the Huguenots out of public life, banning them from government office and excluding them from such professions as printing and medicine. He

Louis XIV Revokes the Edict of Nantes

Believing that a country could not be under one king and one law unless it was also under one religious system, Louis XIV stunned much of Europe in October 1685 by revoking the Edict of Nantes, which had protected the religious freedoms and civil rights of French Protestants since 1598. Compare this document to the one in Chapter 15 in which the elector of Brandenburg welcomes displaced French Protestants into his domains.

✦ *What specific actions does this declaration order against Protestants? Does it offer any incentives for Protestants to convert to Catholicism? How does this declaration compare with the English Test Act?*

Art. 1. Know that we . . . with our certain knowledge, full power and royal authority, have by this present, perpetual and irrevocable edict, suppressed and revoked the edict of the aforesaid king our grandfather, given at Nantes in the month of April, 1598, in all its extent . . . together with all the concessions made by [this] and other edicts, declarations, and decrees, to the people of the so-called Reformed religion, of whatever nature they be . . . and in consequence we desire . . . that all the temples of the people of the aforesaid so-called Reformed religion situated in our kingdom . . . should be demolished forthwith.

Art. 2. We forbid our subjects of the so-called Reformed religion to assemble any more for public worship of the above-mentioned religion. . . .

Art. 3. We likewise forbid all lords, of whatever rank they may be, to carry out heretical services in houses and fiefs . . . the penalty for . . . the said worship being confiscation of their body and possessions.

Art. 4. We order all ministers of the aforesaid so-called Reformed religion who do not wish to be converted and to embrace the Catholic, Apostolic, and Roman religion, to depart from our kingdom and the lands subject to us within fifteen days from the publication of our present edict . . . on pain of the galleys.

Art. 5. We desire that those among the said [Reformed] ministers who shall be converted [to the Catholic religion] shall continue to enjoy during their life, and their wives shall enjoy after their death as long as they remain widows, the same exemptions from taxation and billeting of soldiers, which they enjoyed while they fulfilled the function of ministers. . . .

Art. 8. With regard to children who shall be born to those of the aforesaid so-called Reformed religion, we desire that they be baptized by their parish priests. We command the fathers and mothers to send them to the churches for that purpose, on penalty of a fine of 500 livres or more if they fail to do so; and afterwards, the children shall be brought up in the Catholic, Apostolic, and Roman religion. . . .

Art. 10. All our subjects of the so-called Reformed religion, with their wives and children, are to be strongly and repeatedly prohibited from leaving our aforesaid kingdom . . . or of taking out . . . their possessions and effects. . . .

The members of the so-called Reformed religion, while awaiting God's pleasure to enlighten them like the others, can live in the towns and districts of our kingdom . . . and continue their occupation there, and enjoy their possessions . . . on condition . . . that they do not make public profession of [their religion].

S. Z. Ehler and John B. Morrall, ed. and trans., Church and State Through the Centuries: A Collection of Historic Documents *(New York: Biblo and Tannen, 1967), pp. 209–213.*

used subsidies and selective taxation to encourage Huguenots to convert to Catholicism. And in 1681 he bullied them by quartering his troops in their towns. In the final stage of the persecution, Louis revoked the Edict of Nantes in October 1685. As a result, Protestant churches and schools were closed, Protestant ministers exiled, nonconverting laity forced to be galley slaves, and Protestant children ceremonially baptized by Catholic priests.

The revocation of the Edict of Nantes was a major blunder. Louis was afterwards viewed in Protestant countries as a new Philip II, intent on a Catholic reconquest of the whole of Europe, who must be resisted at all costs. The revocation prompted the voluntary emigration of more than a quarter million French people, who formed new communities and joined the resistance to France in England, Germany, Holland, and the New World. Thousands of French Huguenots served in the army of Louis's archfoe, William of Orange, later King William III of England. Many of those who remained in France became part of an uncompromising guerilla resistance to the king. Despite the many domestic and foreign liabilities it brought him, Louis, to his death, considered the revocation to be his most pious act, one that placed God in his debt.

Louis's Later Wars

THE LEAGUE OF AUGSBURG AND THE NINE YEARS' WAR   After the Treaty of Nijmwegen, Louis maintained his army at full strength and restlessly probed beyond his perimeters. In 1681 his forces conquered the free city of Strasbourg, prompting new defensive coalitions to form against him. One of these, the League of Augsburg, created in 1686 to resist French expansion into Germany, had grown by 1689 to include England, Spain, Sweden, the United Provinces, and the electorates of Bavaria, Saxony, and the Palatinate. It also had the support of the Austrian emperor Leopold. Between 1689 and 1697, the league and France battled each other in the Nine Years' War. During the same period, England and France struggled for control of North America in what came to be known as King William's War.

The Nine Years' War ended when stalemate and exhaustion forced both sides to accept an interim settlement. The Peace of Ryswick, signed in September 1697, was a triumph for William of Orange, now William III of England, and Emperor Leopold. It secured Holland's borders and thwarted Louis's expansion into Germany.

WAR OF THE SPANISH SUCCESSION: TREATIES OF UTRECHT AND RASTADT   After Ryswick, Louis, who seemed to thrive on partial success, made still a fourth attempt to realize his grand design to dominate Europe. This time an unforeseen turn of events helped him. On November 1, 1700, Charles II of Spain, known as "the Sufferer" because of his genetic deformities and lingering illnesses, died.

Both Louis and the Austrian emperor Leopold had claims to the Spanish inheritance through their grandsons: Louis through his marriage to Marie Thérèse and Leopold through his marriage to her younger sister, Margaret Thérèse. Although Louis's grandson, Philip of Anjou, had the better claim (because Marie Thérèse was Margaret Thérèse's older sister), Marie Thérèse had renounced her right to the Spanish inheritance in the Treaty of the Pyrenees (1659), and the inheritance was expected to go to Leopold's grandson.

Louis nurtured fears that the Habsburgs would dominate Europe should they gain control of Spain as well as the Holy Roman Empire. Most of the nations of Europe, however, feared France more than the Habsburgs and determined to prevent a union of the French and Spanish crowns. As a result, before Charles II's death, negotiations began among the nations involved to partition his inheritance in a way that would preserve the existing balance of power.

Charles II upset these negotiations by leaving his entire inheritance to Philip of Anjou, Louis's grandson. At a stroke, Spain and its possessions had fallen to France. Although Louis had been party to the partition agreements that preceded Charles's death, he now saw God's hand in Charles's will; he chose to enforce its terms over those of the partition agreement. Philip of Anjou moved to Madrid and became Philip V of Spain. Louis, in what was interpreted as naked French aggression, sent his troops again into Flanders, this time to remove Dutch soldiers from Spanish territory in the name of the new French king of Spain. Louis also declared Spanish America open to French ships.

In September 1701, England, Holland, and the Holy Roman Empire formed the Grand Alliance to counter Louis. They sought to preserve the balance of power by once and for all securing Flanders as a neutral barrier between Holland and France and by gaining for the emperor his fair share of the Spanish inheritance. After the formation of the Grand Alliance, Louis increased the stakes of battle by recognizing the claim of James Edward, the son of James II of England, to the English throne.

In 1701 the thirteen-year War of the Spanish Succession (1701–1714) began, and once again total war enveloped western Europe. France, for the first time, went to war with inadequate finances, a poorly equipped army, and mediocre military leadership. The English, in contrast, had advanced weaponry (flintlock rifles, paper cartridges, and ring bayonets) and superior tactics (thin, maneuverable troop columns rather than the traditional deep ones). John Churchill, the duke of Marlborough, who succeeded William of Orange as military leader of the alliance, bested Louis's soldiers in every major engagement. He routed French armies at Blenheim in August 1704 and on the plain of Ramillies in 1706—two decisive battles of the war. In 1708–1709 famine, revolts, and uncollectible taxes tore France apart internally. Despair pervaded the French court. Louis wondered aloud how God could forsake one who had done so much for him.

Though ready to make peace in 1709, Louis could not bring himself to accept the stiff terms of the alliance. These included a demand that he transfer all Spanish possessions to the emperor's grandson Charles and remove Philip V from Madrid. Hostilities continued, and a clash of forces at Malplaquet (September 1709) left carnage on the battlefield unsurpassed until modern times.

France finally signed an armistice with England at Utrecht in July 1713 and concluded hostilities with Holland and the emperor in the Treaty of Rastadt in March 1714. This agreement confirmed Philip V as king of Spain but gave Gibraltar to England, making it a Mediterranean power. (See Map 13–3.) It also won Louis's recognition of the right of the House of Hanover to accede to the English throne.

Politically, the eighteenth century would belong to England as the sixteenth had belonged to Spain and the seventeenth to France. Although France remained intact and strong, the realization of Louis XIV's territorial ambitions had to await the rise of Napoleon Bonaparte. On his deathbed on September 1, 1715, Louis fittingly warned his heir, the *dauphin*, not to imitate his love of buildings and his liking for war.

Louis XIV's Legacy

Louis XIV left France a mixed legacy. His wars had brought widespread death and destruction, and his

The Reign of Louis XIV (1643–1715)	
1643	Louis ascends the French throne at the age of 5
1643–1661	Cardinal Mazarin directs the French government
1648	Peace of Westphalia
1649–1652	The *Fronde* revolt
1653	The pope declares Jansenism a heresy
1659	Treaty of Pyren´ees between France and Spain
1660	Papal ban on Jansenists enforced in France
1661	Louis commences personal rule
1667–1668	War of Devolution
1670	Secret Treaty of Dover between France and Great Britain
1672–1679	French war against the Netherlands
1685	Louis revokes the Edict of Nantes
1689–1697	War of the League of Augsburg
1701	Outbreak of the War of the Spanish Succession
1713	Treaty of Utrecht between France and Great Britain
1714	Treaty of Rastatt between France and Spain
1715	Death of Louis XIV

armies had shelled civilian populations. Although the monarchy was still strong at his death, it was more feared than admired. Its finances were insecure and dependent on debt. Continued warfare in the eighteenth century would weaken its finances further, leading eventually to the crises that sparked the French Revolution. Louis's policies of centralization would later make it difficult for France to develop effective institutions of representation and self-government. The aristocracy, after its years of domestication at Versailles, would have difficulty providing the nation with effective leaders and ministers.

Yet Louis's reign also had a positive side. He may have loved war too much, but he also built the magnificent palace of Versailles and brought a new majesty to France. He skillfully manipulated the fractious French aristocracy and bourgeoisie, he elevated skilled and trustworthy ministers, councillors, and *intendants*, and he created a new French Empire by expanding trade into Asia and colonizing North America.

Louis's rule was not so absolute as to exert oppressive control over the daily lives of his sub-

MAP 13–3 EUROPE IN 1714 *The War of the Spanish Succession ended in the year before the death of the aged Louis XIV. By then France and Spain, although not united, were both ruled by members of the Bourbon family, and Spain had lost its non-Iberian possessions.*

jects as in the police states of the nineteenth and twentieth centuries. His absolutism functioned primarily in the classic areas of European state action—the making of war and peace, the regulation of religion, and the oversight of economic activity. Even at the height of his power, local institutions, some controlled by townspeople and others by nobles, continued to exert administrative authority at the local level. The king and his min-

isters supported the high status and tax exemptions of these local elites. But in contrast to the Stuart kings of England, Louis firmly prevented them from capturing or significantly limiting his authority on the national level. Not until the French monarchy was so weakened by financial crisis at the end of the eighteenth century would it succumb to demands for a more representative form of government.

The foreign policy of Louis XIV brought warfare to all of Europe. This eighteenth-century painting by Benjamin West memorializes the British victory over France in the battle of La Hogue in 1692. [Benjamin West, "The Battle of La Hogue". © 1778, oil on canvas, 1.527 x 2.143 (60 1/8 x 84 3/8); framed: 1.803 x 2.410 (71 x 94 7/8). Andrew W. Mellon Fund. © 1993 National Gallery of Art, Washington.]

✦

In the seventeenth century, England and France developed divergent forms of government. England became the model for parliamentary monarchy, France for absolute monarchy.

The politically active English elite—the nobility along with the wealthy landowning and commercial classes—struggled throughout the century to limit the authority of rulers—including Oliver Cromwell as well as the Stuart monarchs—over local interests. In the process, they articulated a political philosophy that stressed the need to prevent the central concentration of political power. The Bill of Rights of 1689 and the Toleration Act following the Glorious Revolution of William and Mary seemed to achieve the goals of this philosophy. These acts brought neither democracy nor full religious freedom in a modern sense; the Bill of Rights protected only the privileged, not all the English people, and the Toleration Act outlawed Catholics and Unitarians. Still, they firmly established representative government in England and extended legal recognition, at least in principle, to a variety of religious beliefs. The Bill of Rights required the monarch to call Parliament regularly.

In France, by contrast, the monarchy remained supreme. Although the king had to mollify privileged local elites, by considering the interests of the nobility and the traditional rights of towns and regions, France had no national institution like Parliament through which he had to govern. Louis XIV was able, on his own authority, to fund the largest army in Europe. He could and did crush *religious dissent. His own propaganda and the fear of his adversaries may have led to an exaggerated view of Louis's power, but his reign nonetheless provided a model of effective centralized power that later continental rulers tried to follow.*

Review Questions

1. By the end of the seventeenth century, England and France had different systems of government with different religious policies. What were the main differences? Similarities? Why did each nation develop as it did? How much did the particular personalities of the rulers of each nation determine the manner in which their political institutions emerged?

2. Why did the English king and Parliament come into conflict in the 1640s? What were the most important issues behind the war between them and who bears more responsibility for it? What role did religion play in the conflict?

3. What was the Glorious Revolution and why did it take place? What were James II's mistakes and what were the issues involved in the events of 1688? What kind of settlement emerged from the revolution? How did England in 1700 differ from England in 1600?

4. Discuss the development of absolutism in France. What policies of Henry IV and Louis XIII were essential in creating the absolute monarchy?

5. What were the chief ways Louis XIV consolidated his monarchy? What limits were there on his authority? What was Louis's religious policy?

6. Assess the success of Louis XIV's foreign policy. What were his aims? Were they realistic? To what extent did he attain them?

Suggested Readings

M. ASHLEY, *England in the Seventeenth Century* (1980). Readable survey.

ROBERT ASHTON, *Counter-Revolution: The Second Civil War and Its Origins, 1646–1648* (1995). A major examination of the resumption of civil conflict in England that ended with the abolition of the monarchy, House of Lords, and established church.

W. BEIK, *Absolutism and Society in Seventeenth-Century France* (1985). An important study that questions the extent of royal power.

J. BERGIN, *Cardinal Richelieu: Power and the Pursuit of Wealth* (1985). Considers the role of finance and private wealth in the rise of Richelieu.

R. BONNEY, *Political Change in France Under Richelieu and Mazarin, 1624–1661* (1978). A careful examination of how these two cardinals lay the foundation for Louis XIV's absolutism.

R. BRIGGS, *Early Modern France, 1560–1715* (1977). A useful brief survey.

G. BURGESS, *Absolute Monarchy and the Stuart Constitution* (1996). A new study that challenges many of the traditional interpretive categories.

P. BURKE, *The Fabrication of Louis XIV* (1992). Examines the manner in which the public image of Louis XIV was forged in art.

P. COLLINSON, *The Religion of Protestants: The Church in English Society 1559–1625* (1982). The best introduction to Puritanism.

B. COWARD, *Cromwell* (1991). A brief biography.

R. S. DUNN, *The Age of Religious Wars, 1559–1715* (1979). Lucid survey setting the conflicting political systems of France and England in larger perspective.

D. HIRST, *Authority and Conflict: England 1603–1658* (1986). Scholarly survey integrating history and historiography.

R. HUTTON, *Charles the Second, King of England, Scotland, and Ireland* (1989). Replaces all previous biographies.

P. LAKE, *Anglicans and Puritans: Presbyterianism and English Conformist Thought from Whitgift to Hooker* (1988). An important study of religious thought.

R. LOCKYER, *Buckingham* (1984). Biography of the English court favorite.

R. METTAM, *Power and Faction in Louis XIV's France* (1988). Examines the political intricacies of the reign and suggests the limits to absolutism.

G. PARKER, *Europe in Crisis 1598–1648* (1979). Examines the entire scope of early seventeenth-century Europe.

O. RANUM, *The Fronde: A French Revolution, 1648–1652* (1993). The best recent work on the subject.

D. L. RUBIN (ED.), *The Sun King: The Ascendancy of French Culture During the Reign of Louis XIV* (1992). A collection of useful essays.

C. RUSSELL, *The Fall of the English Monarchies, 1637–1642* (1991). A major revisionist account, which should be read with Stone's book.

K. SHARPE, *The Personal Rule of Charles I* (1992). A major narrative work.

J. SPUR, *The Restoration Church of England, 1646–1689* (1992). Now the standard work on this subject.

L. STONE, *The Causes of the English Revolution 1529–1642* (1972). Brief survey stressing social history and ruminating over historians and historical method.

V. TAPIÉ, *France in the Age of Louis XIII and Richelieu* (1984). A narrative account.

G. Treasure, *Mazarin: The Crisis of Absolutism in France* (1996). An examination not only of Mazarin, but also of the larger national and international background.

N. Tyacke, *Anti-Calvinists: The Rise of English Arminianism c. 1590–1640* (1987). The most important recent study of Archbishop Laud's policies and his predecessors.

D. Underdown, *Fire from Heaven: Life in an English Town in the Seventeenth Century* (1992). A lively account of the manner in which a single English town experienced the religious and political events of the century.

M. Walzer, *The Revolution of the Saints: A Study in the Origins of Radical Politics* (1965). Effort to relate ideas and politics that depicts Puritans as true revolutionaries.

J. B. Wolf, *Louis XIV* (1968). Very detailed political biography.

Nicolaus Copernicus's revolutionary view of the universe, with the sun in the center, is summarized in this diagram from his De Revolutionibus Orbium Coelestium (On the Revolutions of Heavenly Bodies), *published in 1543. [Library of the Collegium Maius. Collegium Maius, Cracow, Poland. Erich Lessing/Art Resource]*

New Directions in Thought and Culture in the Sixteenth and Seventeenth Centuries

The Scientific Revolution
Nicolaus Copernicus: Rejection of an Earth-Centered Universe
Tycho Brahe and Johannes Kepler: New Scientific Observations
Galileo Galilei: A Universe of Mathematical Laws
Isaac Newton: The Laws of Gravitation
Newton's Reconciliation of Science and Faith

Continuing Superstitions: Witch Hunts and Panic
Village Origins
Influence of the Clergy
Role of Women
Witch Panics
End of the Witch Hunts

Literary Imagination in Transition
Miguel de Cervantes Saavedra: Rejection of Idealism
William Shakespeare: Dramatist of the Age
John Milton: Puritan Poet
John Bunyan: Visions of Christian Piety

Philosophy in the Wake of Changing Science
Francis Bacon: Empirical Method
René Descartes: The Method of Rational Deduction
Blaise Pascal: Reason and Faith
Baruch Spinoza: The World as Divine Substance
Thomas Hobbes: Apologist for Absolutism
John Locke: Defender of Moderate Liberty

KEY TOPICS

- The astronomical theories of Copernicus, Brahe, Kepler, Galileo, and Newton and the emergence of the scientific worldview
- Witchcraft and witch hunts
- The literary imagination in a changing world
- The philosophical foundations of modern thought

The sixteenth and seventeenth centuries witnessed a sweeping change in the scientific view of the universe. An Earth-centered picture gave way to one in which the Earth was only another planet orbiting about the sun. The sun itself became one of millions of stars. This transformation of humankind's perception of its place in the larger scheme of things led to a profound rethinking of moral and religious matters as well as of scientific theory. Faith and reason needed new modes of reconciliation, as did faith and science. The new ideas and methods of science challenged modes of thought associated with medieval times and Scholasticism. The new outlook on physical nature touched the literary imagination, and religious thinkers had to reconsider many traditional ideas. Philosophers applied rational, scientific thought to the realm of politics. Some supported absolutism; others, parliamentary systems.

The new scientific concepts and the methods of their construction were so impressive that they set the standard for assessing the validity of knowledge in the Western world thereafter. Perhaps no single intellectual development proved to be more significant for the future of European and Western civilization.

Side by side with enlightenment and science, however, came a new wave of superstition and persecution. The *changing world of religion and politics also created profound fear and anxiety among both the simple and the learned, resulting in Europe's worst witch hunts.*

The Scientific Revolution

The process by which the new view of the universe and of scientific knowledge came to be established is normally termed the *Scientific Revolution*. This metaphor must be used carefully, however. The word *revolution* normally denotes rapid political change involving large numbers of people. The Scientific Revolution was not rapid, nor did it involve more than a few hundred human beings. It was a complex movement with many false starts and many brilliant people with wrong as well as useful ideas. It took place in the studies and the crude laboratories of thinkers in Poland, Italy, Bohemia, France, and Great Britain.

The Scientific Revolution stemmed from two major tendencies. The first, illustrated by Nicolaus Copernicus, was the imposition of important small changes on existing models of thought. The second, embodied by Francis Bacon, was the desire to pose new kinds of questions and to use new methods of investigation. In both cases, scientific thought changed current and traditional opinions in other fields.

Nicolaus Copernicus: Rejection of an Earth-Centered Universe

Nicolaus Copernicus (1473–1543) was a Polish astronomer who enjoyed a high reputation throughout his life. He had been educated in Italy and corresponded with other astronomers throughout Europe. He had not been known, however, for strikingly original or unorthodox thought. In 1543, the year of his death, Copernicus published *On the Revolutions of the Heavenly Spheres*. Because he died near the time of publication, the fortunes of his work are not the story of one person's crusade for progressive science. Copernicus's book was "a revolution-making rather than a revolutionary text."[1] What Copernicus did was to provide an intellectual springboard for a complete criticism of

---

[1] Thomas S. Kuhn, *The Copernican Revolution: Planetary Astronomy in the Development of Western Thought* (New York: Vintage, 1959), p. 135.

the then-dominant view of the position of the Earth in the universe.

THE PTOLEMAIC SYSTEM   At the time of Copernicus, the standard explanation of the place of the Earth in the heavens was that associated with Ptolemy and his work entitled the *Almagest* (150 C.E.). Commentators on the original work had developed several alternative Ptolemaic systems over the centuries. Most of these assumed that the Earth was the center of the universe. Above the Earth lay a series of crystalline spheres, one of which contained the moon, another the sun, and still others the planets and the stars. This was the astronomy found in such works as Dante's *Divine Comedy*. At the outer regions of these spheres lay the realm of God and the angels. Aristotelian physics provided the intellectual underpinnings of the Ptolemaic systems. The Earth had to be the center because of its heaviness. The stars and the other heavenly bodies had to be enclosed in the crystalline spheres so that they could move. Nothing could move unless something was actually moving it. The state of rest was natural; motion was the condition that required explanation.

Numerous problems were associated with this system, and these had long been recognized. The most important was the observed motions of the planets, which included noncircular patterns around the Earth. At certain times the planets actually appeared to be going backward. The Ptolemaic systems explained these strange motions primarily through epicycles. An epicycle is an orbit upon an orbit, like a spinning jewel on a ring. The planets were said to make a second revolution in an orbit tangent to their primary orbit around the Earth. Other intellectual but nonobservational difficulties related to the immense speed at which the spheres had to move around the Earth. To say the least, the Ptolemaic systems were cluttered. They were effective, however, as long as one assumed Aristotelian physics and the Christian belief that the Earth rested at the center of the created universe.

COPERNICUS'S UNIVERSE   Copernicus's *On the Revolutions of the Heavenly Spheres* challenged this picture in the most conservative manner possible. It suggested that if the Earth were assumed to move about the sun in a circle, many of the difficulties with the Ptolemaic systems would disappear or become simpler. Although not wholly eliminated, the number of epicycles would be somewhat fewer. The motive behind this shift away from the Earth-centered universe was to find a solution to the problems of planetary motion. By allowing the Earth to move around the sun, Copernicus was able to construct a more mathematically elegant basis for astronomy. He had been discontented with the traditional system because it was mathematically clumsy and inconsistent. The primary appeal of his new system was its mathematical aesthetics. With

Copernicus Ascribes Movement to the Earth

Copernicus published De Revolutionibus Orbium Caelestium *(On the Revolutions of the Heavenly Spheres) in 1543. In his preface, addressed to Pope Paul III, he explained what had led him to think that the Earth moved around the sun and what he thought were some of the scientific consequences of the new theory.*

✦ *How does Copernicus justify his argument to the pope? How important was historical precedent and tradition to the pope? Might Copernicus have thought that the pope would be especially susceptible to such argument, even though what Copernicus proposed (the movement of the Earth) contradicted the Bible?*

I may well presume, most Holy Father, that certain people, as soon as they hear that in this book about the Revolutions of the Spheres of the Universe I ascribe movement to the Earthly globe, will cry out that, holding such views, I should at once be hissed off the stage. . . .

So I should like your Holiness to know that I was induced to think of a method of computing the motions of the spheres by nothing else than the knowledge that the Mathematicians [who had previously considered the problem] are inconsistent in these investigations.

For, first, the mathematicians are so unsure of the movements of the Sun and Moon that they cannot even explain or observe the constant length of the seasonal year. Secondly, in determining the motions of these and of the other five planets, they use neither the same principles and hypotheses nor the same demonstrations of the apparent motions and revolutions. . . . Nor have they been able thereby to discern or deduce the principal thing—namely the shape of the Universe and the unchangeable symmetry of its parts. . . .

I pondered long upon this uncertainty of mathematical tradition in establishing the motions of the system of the spheres. At last I began to chafe

that philosophers could by no means agree on any one certain theory of the mechanism of the Universe, wrought for us by a supremely good and orderly Creator. . . . I therefore took pains to read again the works of all the philosophers on whom I could lay hand to seek out whether any of them had ever supposed that the motions of the spheres were other than those demanded by the [Ptolemaic] mathematical schools. I found first in Cicero that Hicetas [of Syracuse, fifth century B.C.] had realized that the Earth moved. Afterwards I found in Plutarch that certain others had held the like opinion. . . .

Thus assuming motions, which in my work I ascribe to the Earth, by long and frequent observations I have at last discovered that, if the motions of the rest of the planets be brought into relation with the circulation of the Earth and be reckoned in proportion to the circles of each planet, not only do their phenomena presently ensue, but the orders and magnitudes of all stars and spheres, nay the heavens themselves, become so bound together that nothing in any part thereof could be moved from its place without producing confusion of all the other parts of the Universe as a whole.

As quoted in Thomas S. Kuhn, The Copernican Revolution: Planetary Astronomy in the Development of Western Thought *(New York: Vintage Books, 1959), pp. 137–139, 141–142.*

the sun at the center of the universe, mathematical astronomy would make more sense. A change in the conception of the position of the Earth meant that the planets were actually moving in circular orbits and only seemed to be doing otherwise because of the position of the observers on Earth.

Except for this modification in the position of the Earth, Copernicus retained Ptolemaic ideas in most of the other parts of his book. The path of the planets remained circular. Genuine epicycles still existed in the heavens. His system was no more accurate than the existing ones for predicting the location of the planets. He had used no new evidence. The major impact of his work was to provide another way of confronting some of the difficulties inherent in Ptolemaic astronomy. It did not immediately replace the old astronomy, but it allowed other people who were also discontented with the Ptolemaic systems to think in new directions.

Copernicus's concern about the relationship between mathematics and the observed behavior of planets is an example of the single most important factor in the developing new science: the fusion of mathematics with empirical data and observation. Mathematics provided the model to which the new scientific thought would conform; new empirical evidence helped persuade the learned public of its validity.

Tycho Brahe and Johannes Kepler: New Scientific Observations

The next major step toward the conception of a sun-centered system was taken by Tycho Brahe (1546–1601). He actually spent most of his life opposing Copernicus and advocating a different kind of Earth-centered system. He suggested that the moon and the sun revolved around the Earth and that the other planets revolved around the sun. In attacking Copernicus, however, he gave the latter's ideas more publicity. More important, this Danish astronomer's major weapon against Copernican astronomy was a series of new naked-eye astronomical observations. Brahe constructed the most accurate tables of observations that had been drawn up for centuries.

When Brahe died, these tables came into the possession of Johannes Kepler (1571–1630), a German astronomer. Kepler was a convinced Copernican, but his reasons for taking that position were not scientific. Kepler was deeply influenced by Renais-

Tycho Brahe in the Uranienburg observatory on the Danish island of Hven (1587). Brahe made the most important observations of the stars since antiquity. Kepler used his data to solve the problem of planetary motion in a way that supported Copernicus's sun-centered view of the universe. Ironically, Brahe himself had opposed Copernicus's view. [Bildarchiv Preussischer Kulturbesitz]

sance Neoplatonism, which held the sun in special honor. He was determined to find mathematical harmonies in Brahe's numbers that would support a sun-centered universe. After much work Kepler discovered that to keep the sun at the center of things, he must abandon the Copernican concept of circular orbits. The mathematical relationships that emerged from a consideration of Brahe's observations suggested that the orbits of the planets were elliptical. Kepler published his findings in his 1609 book, entitled *On the Motion of Mars*. He had solved the problem of planetary orbits by using Copernicus's sun-centered universe and Brahe's empirical data.

Kepler had also defined a new problem. None of the available theories could explain why the planetary orbits were elliptical. That solution awaited the work of Sir Isaac Newton.

Galileo Galilei: A Universe of Mathematical Laws

From Copernicus to Brahe to Kepler, there had been little new information about the heavens that might not have been known to Ptolemy. In the same year that Kepler published his volume on Mars, however, an Italian scientist named Galileo Galilei (1564–1642) first turned a telescope on the heavens. Through that recently invented instrument he saw stars where none had been known to exist, mountains on the moon, spots moving across the sun, and moons orbiting Jupiter. The heavens were far more complex than anyone had formerly suspected. None of these discoveries proved that the Earth orbited the sun, but they did suggest the complete inadequacy of the Ptolemaic system. It simply could not accommodate itself to all these new phenomena. Some of Galileo's colleagues at the University of Padua were so unnerved that they refused to look through the telescope.

Galileo publicized his findings and arguments for the Copernican system in numerous works, the most famous of which was his *Dialogues on the Two Chief Systems of the World* (1632). This book brought down on him the condemnation of the Roman Catholic Church. He was compelled to recant his opinions. He is reputed, however, to have muttered after the recantation, *"E pur si muove,"* or "it [the Earth] still moves."

Galileo's discoveries and his popularization of the Copernican system were of secondary importance in his life work. His most important achievement was to articulate the concept of a universe totally subject to mathematical laws. More than any other writer of the century, he argued that nature in its most minute details displayed mathematical regularity:

Philosophy is written in that great book which ever lies before our eyes—I mean the universe—but we cannot understand it if we do not first learn the language and grasp the symbols in which it is written. This book is written in the mathematical language, and the symbols are triangles, circles, and other geometrical figures, without whose help it is impossible to comprehend a single

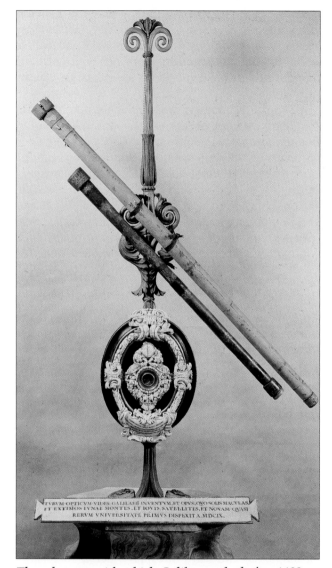

The telescope with which Galileo worked after 1609. He observed Earth's moon and the cyclical phases of the planet Venus and discovered the most prominent moons of Jupiter. These observations had revolutionary intellectual and theological implications in the seventeenth century. [Istituto e Museo de Storia della Scienza, Scala/Art Resource, N.Y.]

word of it; without which one wanders through a dark labyrinth.[2]

The universe was rational; however, its rationality was not that of scholastic logic but of mathe-

[2]Quoted in E. A. Burtt, *The Metaphysical Foundations of Modern Physical Science* (Garden City, N.Y.: Anchor-Double-day, 1954), p. 75.

matics. Copernicus had thought that the heavens conformed to mathematical regularity; Galileo saw this regularity throughout all physical nature. He believed that the smallest atom behaved with the same mathematical precision as the largest heavenly sphere.

A world of quantity was replacing one of qualities. All aspects of the world—including color, beauty, and taste—would increasingly be described in terms of the mathematical relationships among quantities. Mathematical models would eventually be applied even to social relations. Nature was cold, rational, mathematical, and mechanistic. What was real and lasting was what was mathematically measurable. Few intellectual shifts have wrought such momentous changes for Western civilization.

Isaac Newton: The Laws of Gravitation

Englishman Isaac Newton (1642–1727) drew on the work of his predecessors and his own brilliance to solve the major remaining problem of planetary motion and to establish a basis for physics that endured more than two centuries. The question that continued to perplex seventeenth-century scientists who accepted the theories of Copernicus, Kepler, and Galileo was how the planets and other heavenly bodies moved in an orderly fashion. The Ptolemaic and Aristotelian answer had been the crystalline spheres and a universe arranged in the order of the heaviness of its parts. Many unsatisfactory theories had been set forth to deal with the question.

In 1687 Newton published *The Mathematical Principles of Natural Philosophy*, better known by its Latin title of *Principia Mathematica*. Much of the research and thinking for this great work had taken place more than fifteen years earlier. Newton was heavily indebted to the work of Galileo and particularly to the latter's view that inertia applied to bodies both at rest and in motion. Galileo's mathematical bias permeated Newton's thought. Newton reasoned that the planets and all other physical objects in the universe moved through mutual attraction, or gravity. Every object in the universe affected every other object through gravity. The attraction of gravity explained why the planets moved in an orderly rather than a chaotic manner. He had found that "the force of gravity towards the whole planet did arise from and was compounded of the forces of gravity towards all its parts, and towards every one part was in the inverse

Sir Isaac Newton discovered the mathematical and physical laws governing the force of gravity. Newton believed that religion and science were compatible and mutually supportive, and that the study of nature gave one a better understanding of the Creator. This portrait of Newton is by Sir Godfrey Kneller. [Bildarchiv Preussischer Kulturbesitz]

proportion of the squares of the distances from the part."[3] Newton proved this relationship mathematically. He made no attempt to explain the nature of gravity itself.

Newton was a great mathematical genius, but he also upheld the importance of empirical data and observation. Like Francis Bacon (see pages 499–501), he believed that one must observe phenomena before attempting to explain them. The final test of any theory or hypothesis for him was whether it described what could actually be observed. He was a great opponent of the rationalism of the French philosopher Descartes (see pages 501–502), which he believed included insufficient guards against error. As Newton's own theory of universal gravi-

[3]Quoted in A. Rupert Hall, *From Galileo to Newton, 1630–1720* (London: Fontana, 1970), p. 300.

Galileo Discusses the Relationship of Science and the Bible

The religious authorities were often critical of the discoveries and theories of sixteenth- and seventeenth-century science. For years before his condemnation by the Roman Catholic Church in 1633, Galileo had contended that scientific theory and religious piety were compatible. In his Letter to the Grand Duchess Christiana *(of Tuscany), written in 1615, he argued that God had revealed truth in both the Bible and physical nature and that the truth of physical nature did not contradict the Bible if the latter were properly understood.*

✦ *Is Galileo's argument based on science or theology? Did the church believe that nature was as much a revelation of God as the Bible? As Galileo describes them, which is the surer revelation of God, nature or the Bible? Why might the pope reject Galileo's argument?*

The reason produced for condemning the opinion that the Earth moves and the sun stands still is that in many places in the Bible one may read that the sun moves and the Earth stands still. . . .

With regard to this argument, I think in the first place that it is very pious to say and prudent to affirm that the holy Bible can never speak untruth—whenever its true meaning is understood. But I believe nobody will deny that it is often very abstruse, and may say things which are quite different from what its bare words signify. . . .

This being granted, I think that in discussions of physical problems we ought to begin not from the authority of scriptural passages, but from sense-experiences and necessary demonstrations; for the holy Bible and the phenomena of nature proceed alike from the divine Word, the former as the dictate of the Holy Ghost and the latter as the observant executrix of God's commands. It is necessary for the Bible, in order to be accommodated to the understanding of every man, to speak many things which appear to differ from the absolute truth so far as the bare meaning of the words is concerned. But Nature, on the other hand, is inexorable and immutable; she never transgresses the laws imposed upon her, or cares a whit whether her abstruse reasons and methods of operation are understandable to men. For that reason it appears that nothing physical which sense-experience sets

before our eyes, or which necessary demonstrations prove to us, ought to be called in question (much less condemned) upon the testimony of biblical passages which may have some different meaning beneath their words. For the Bible is not chained in every expression to conditions as strict as those which govern all physical effects; nor is God any less excellently revealed in Nature's actions than in the sacred statements of the Bible. . . .

From this I do not mean to infer that we need not have an extraordinary esteem for the passages of holy Scripture. On the contrary, having arrived at any certainties in physics, we ought to utilize these as the most appropriate aids in the true exposition of the Bible and in the investigation of those meanings which are necessarily contained therein for these must be concordant with demonstrated truths. I should judge the authority of the Bible was designed to persuade men of those articles and propositions which, surpassing all human reasoning, could not be made credible by science, or by any other means than through the very mouth of the Holy Spirit. . . .

But I do not feel obliged to believe that the same God who has endowed us with senses, reason, and intellect has intended to forgo their use and by some other means to give us knowledge which we can attain by them.

Discoveries and Opinions of Galileo, *trans. and ed. by Stillman Drake (Garden City, N.Y.: Doubleday Anchor Books, 1957), pp. 181–183.*

Major Works of the Scientific Revolution	
1543	*On the Revolutions of the Heavenly Spheres* (Copernicus)
1605	*The Advancement of Learning* (Bacon)
1609	*On the Motion of Mars* (Kepler)
1620	*Novum Organum* (Bacon)
1632	*Dialogues on the Two Chief Systems of the World* (Galileo)
1637	*Discourse on Method* (Descartes)
1687	*Principia Mathematica* (Newton)

tation became increasingly accepted, so too was Baconian empiricism.

Newton's Reconciliation of Science and Faith

With the work of Newton, the natural universe became a realm of law and regularity. Beliefs in spirits and divinities were no longer necessary to explain its operation. Thus, the Scientific Revolution liberated human beings from the fear of a chaotic or haphazard universe. Most of the scientists were very devout people. They saw in the new picture of physical nature a new picture also of God. The Creator of this rational, lawful nature must also be rational. To study nature was to come to a better understanding of that Creator. Science and religious faith were not only compatible but mutually supporting. As Newton wrote, "The main Business of Natural Philosophy is to argue from Phaenomena without feigning Hypothesis, and to deduce Causes from Effects, till we come to the very first Cause, which certainly is not mechanical."[4]

This reconciliation of faith and science allowed the new physics and astronomy to spread rapidly. At the very time when Europeans were finally tiring of the wars of religion, the new science provided the basis for a view of God that might lead away from irrational disputes and wars over religious doctrine. Faith in a rational God encouraged faith in the rationality of human beings and in their capacity to improve their lot once liberated from the traditions of the past. The Scientific Revolution provided the great model for the desirability of

[4]Quoted in Franklin Baumer, *Main Currents of Western Thought*, 4th ed. (New Haven: Yale, 1978) p. 323.

change and of criticism of inherited views. The new science, however, caused some people to feel that the mystery had been driven from the universe and that the rational Creator was less loving and less near to humankind than the God of earlier ages.

Continuing Superstition: Witch Hunts and Panics

The new science by no means swept away all other thought. Traditional beliefs and fears long retained their hold on the culture. During the sixteenth and seventeenth centuries many Europeans remained preoccupied with sin, death, and the Devil. Religious people, including many among the learned and many who were sympathetic to the emerging scientific ideas, continued to believe in the power of magic and the occult. Until the end of the seventeenth century almost all Europeans in one way or another believed in the power of demons.

Nowhere is the dark side of early modern thought and culture better seen than in the witch hunts and panics that erupted in almost every Western land. Between 1400 and 1700, courts sentenced an estimated 70,000–100,000 people to death for harmful magic (*maleficium*) and diabolical witchcraft. In addition to inflicting harm on their neighbors, these witches were said to attend mass meetings known as *sabbats*, to which they were believed to fly. They were also accused of indulging in sexual orgies with the Devil, who appeared at such gatherings in animal form, most often as a he-goat. Still other charges against them were cannibalism (they were alleged to be especially fond of small Christian children) and a variety of ritual acts and practices designed to insult every Christian belief and value.

Where did such beliefs come from, and how could seemingly enlightened people believe them? Their roots were in both popular and elite cultures, especially in clerical culture.

Village Origins

In village societies, so-called cunning folk played a positive role in helping people cope with calamity. People turned to them for help when such natural disasters as plague and famine struck or when such physical disabilities as lameness or inability to conceive offspring befell either humans or animals. The cunning folk provided consolation and gave people

Newton Contemplates the Nature of God

Isaac Newton believed there was a close relationship between his scientific theory and the truths of religion. He and many other scientists of his generation were convinced that the investigation of physical nature would lead to proofs of the existence of God. In this passage, taken from comments he added to later editions of the Principia Mathematica, *Newton explains how the character of planetary motion leads one to conclude that God exists.*

✦ *How do Newton's arguments for God's existence compare with those of Thomas Aquinas (see Chapter 8, page 292)? If the pope could accept Aquinas's arguments, why not also those of Galileo and Newton? Why is Newton, like Copernicus and Galileo before him, so convinced that science and religion are in harmony? Are they still "medieval" men, or did the times in which they lived force them to argue this way to justify their work?*

The six primary planets are revolved about the sun in circles concentric with the sun. . . . Ten moons are revolved about the earth, Jupiter, and Saturn in circles concentric with them . . .; but it is not to be conceived that mere mechanical causes could give birth to so many regular motions. . . . This most beautiful system of sun, planets, and comets could only proceed from the counsel and dominion of an intelligent and powerful Being. And if the fixed stars are the centers of other like systems, these, being formed by the like wise counsel, must be all subject to the dominion of One, especially since the light of the fixed stars is of the same nature with the light of the sun and from every system light passes into all the other systems; and lest the systems of the fixed stars should, by their gravity, fall on each other, he hath placed those systems at immense distances from one another.

This Being governs all things, not as the soul of the world, but as Lord over all; and on account of his dominion he is wont to be called "Lord God." . . . The word "God" usually signifies "Lord," but every lord is not a God. It is the domin-ion of a spiritual being which constitutes a God: a true, supreme, or imaginary dominion makes a true, supreme, or imaginary god. And from his true dominion it follows that the true God is a living, intelligent, and powerful Being; and, from his other perfections, that he is supreme or most perfect. He is eternal and infinite, omnipotent, and omniscient; that is, his duration reaches from eternity to eternity; his presence from infinity to infinity; he governs all things and knows all things that are or can be done. He is not eternity and infinity, but eternal and infinite; he is not duration or space, but he endures and is present. He endures forever and is everywhere present; and, by existing always and everywhere, he constitutes duration and space. . . . We have ideas of his attributes, but what the real substance of anything is we know not. . . . We know him only by his most wise and excellent contrivances of things and final causes; we admire him for his perfections, but we reverence and adore him on account of his dominion, for we adore him as his servants; and a god without dominion, providence, and final causes is nothing else but Fate and Nature.

H. S. Thayer, ed., Newton's Philosophy of Nature: Selections from His Writings *(New York: Hafner Press, 1974), pp. 42–44.*

hope that such natural calamities might be averted or reversed by magical means. In this way they provided an important service and kept village life moving forward.

Possession of magical powers, for good or ill, made one an important person within village society. Not surprisingly, claims to such powers most often were made by the people most in need of security and influence, namely, the old and the impoverished, especially single or widowed women. Witch beliefs in village society may also have been a way of defying urban Christian society's attempts to impose its laws and institutions on the countryside. From this perspective, village Satanism became a fanciful substitute for an impossible social revolt, a way of spurning the values of one's new masters. It is also possible, although unlikely, that witch beliefs in rural society had a foundation in local fertility cults, whose semipagan practices, designed to ensure good harvests, may have acquired the features of diabolical witchcraft under church persecution.

Influence of the Clergy

Popular belief in magic was the essential foundation of the great witch hunts of the sixteenth and seventeenth centuries. Had ordinary people not believed that certain gifted individuals could aid or harm others by magical means, and had they not been willing to make accusations, the hunts could never have occurred. Yet the contribution of learned

Three witches suspected of practicing harmful magic are burned alive on a pyre in Baden. On the left, two of them are shown feasting and cavorting with demons at a sabbat. [Bildarchiv Preussischer Kulturbesitz]

society was equally great. The Christian clergy also practiced magic, that of the holy sacraments, and the exorcism of demons had been one of their traditional functions within society. Fear of demons and the Devil, which the clergy actively encouraged, allowed the clergy to assert their moral authority over people and to enforce religious discipline and conformity.

In the late thirteenth century the church declared that only its priests possessed legitimate magical power. Since such power was not human, theologians reasoned, it had to come either from God or from the Devil. If it came from God, then it was properly confined to and exercised only on behalf of the church. Those who practiced magic outside the church evidently derived their power from the Devil. From such reasoning grew accusations of "pacts" between non-Christian magicians and Satan. This made the witch hunts a life-and-death struggle against Christian society's worst heretics and foes, those who had directly sworn allegiance to the Devil himself.

The church based its intolerance of magic outside its walls on sincere belief in and fear of the Devil. But attacking witches was also a way for established Christian society to extend its power and influence into new areas. To accuse, try, and execute witches was also a declaration of moral and political authority over a village or territory. As the cunning folk were local spiritual authorities, revered and feared by people, their removal became a major step in establishing a Christian beachhead in village society.

Role of Women

A good 80 percent of the victims of witch hunts were women, the vast majority between forty-five and sixty years of age and single. This fact has suggested to some that misogyny fueled the witch hunts. Based in male hatred and sexual fear of women, and occurring at a time when women threatened to break out from under male control, witch hunts, it is argued, were simply woman hunts. Older single women may, however, have been vulnerable for more basic social reasons. They were a largely dependent social group in need of public assistance and natural targets for the peculiar "social engineering" of the witch hunts. Some accused witches were women who sought to protect and empower themselves within their communities by claiming supernatural powers.

It may be, however, that gender played a largely circumstantial role. Because of their economic straits, more women than men laid claim to the supernatural powers that made them influential in village society. For this reason, they found themselves on the front lines in disproportionate numbers when the church declared war against all who practiced magic without its blessing. Also, the involvement of many of these women in midwifery associated them with the deaths of beloved wives and infants and thus made them targets of local resentment and accusations. Both the church and midwives' neighbors were prepared to think and say the worst about these women. It was a deadly combination.

Witch Panics

Why did the great witch panics occur in the second half of the sixteenth and early seventeenth centuries? The misfortune created by religious division and warfare were major factors. The new levels of violence exacerbated fears and hatreds and encouraged scapegoating. But political self-aggrandizement also played a role. As governments expanded and attempted to control their realms, they, like the Church, wanted to eliminate all competition for the loyalty of their subjects. Secular rulers as well as the pope could pronounce their competitors "devilish."

Some argue that the Reformation was responsible for the witch panics. Having weakened the traditional religious protections against demons and the Devil, while at the same time portraying them as still powerful, the Reformation is said to have forced people to protect themselves by executing perceived witches.

End of the Witch Hunts

Why did the witch hunts come to an end in the seventeenth century? Many factors played a role. The emergence of a new, more scientific worldview made it difficult to believe in the powers of witches. When in the seventeenth century mind and matter came to be viewed as two independent realities, words and thoughts lost the ability to affect things. A witch's curse was merely words. With advances in medicine and the beginning of insurance companies, people learned to rely on themselves when faced with natural calamity and physical affliction

Why More Women Than Men Are Witches

A classic of misogyny, The Hammer of Witches *(1486), written by two Dominican monks, Heinrich Krämer and Jacob Sprenger, was sanctioned by Pope Innocent VIII as an official guide to the church's detection and punishment of witches. Here Krämer and Sprenger explain why they believe that the great majority of witches are women rather than men.*

✦ *Why would two Dominican monks say such things about women? What are the biblical passages that they believe justify them? Do their descriptions have any basis in the actual behavior of women then? What is the rivalry between married and unmarried people that they refer to?*

Why are there more superstitious women than men? The first [reason] is that they are more credulous; and since the chief aim of the devil is to corrupt faith, therefore he rather attacks them. . . . The second reason is that women are naturally more impressionable and ready to receive the influence of a disembodied spirit. . . . The third reason is that they have slippery tongues and are unable to conceal from their fellow-women those things which by evil arts they know; and since they are weak, they find an easy and secret manner of vindicating themselves by witchcraft. . . . [Therefore] since women are feebler both in mind and body, it is not surprising that they should come more under the spell of witchcraft. For as regards intellect, or the understanding of spiritual things, they seem to be of a different nature from men, a fact which is vouched for by the logic of the authorities, backed by various examples from the Scriptures. . . .

But the natural reason [for woman's proclivity to witchcraft] is that she is more carnal than a man, as is clear from her many carnal abominations. And it should be noted that there was a defect in the formation of the first woman, since she was formed from a bent rib, that is, a rib of the breast, which is bent as it were in a contrary direction to a man. And since through this defect she is an imperfect animal, she always deceives. . . .

As to her other mental quality, her natural will, when she hates someone whom she formerly loved, then she seethes with anger and impatience in her whole soul, just as the tides of the sea are always heaving and boiling. . . .

Truly the most powerful cause which contributes to the increase of witches is the woeful rivalry between married folk and unmarried women and men. This [jealousy or rivalry exists] even among holy women, so what must it be among the others . . . ?

Just as through the first defect in their intelligence women are more prone [than men] to abjure the faith, so through their second defect of inordinate affections and passions they search for, brood over, and inflict various vengeances, either by witchcraft or by some other means. Wherefore it is no wonder that so great a number of witches exist in this sex. . . . [Indeed, witchcraft] is better called the heresy of witches than of wizards, since the name is taken from the more powerful party [that is, the greater number, who are women]. Blessed be the Highest who has so far preserved the male sex from so great a crime.

Malleus Maleficarum, *trans. by Montague Summers (Bungay, Suffolk: John Rodker, 1928), pp. 41–47.*

and no longer searched for supernatural causes and solutions. Witch hunts also tended to get out of hand. Accused witches sometimes alleged that important townspeople had also attended sabbats; even the judges could be so accused. At this point the trials ceased to serve the purposes of those who were conducting them. They not only became dysfunctional but threatened anarchy as well.

Although Protestants, like Catholics, hunted witches, the Reformation may also have contributed to an attitude of mind that put the Devil in a more manageable perspective. Protestants ridiculed the sacramental magic of the old church as superstition and directed their faith to a sovereign God absolutely supreme over time and eternity. Even the Devil was believed to serve God's purposes and acted only with his permission. Ultimately God was the only significant spiritual force in the universe. This belief made the Devil a less fearsome creature. "One little word can slay him," Luther wrote of the Devil in the great hymn of the Reformation.

Finally, the imaginative and philosophical literature of the sixteenth and seventeenth centuries (see below), while continuing to display concern for religion and belief in the supernatural, also suggested that human beings have a significant degree of control over their own lives and need not be constantly fearing demons and resorting to supernatural aid.

Literary Imagination in Transition

The world of the new science developed in the midst of a society where medieval outlooks and religious values remained very much alive. Literary figures of the same period often reflected both the new and the old. In Cervantes one sees a brilliant writer raising questions about the adequacy of medieval values of chivalry and honor and probing the nature of human perceptions of reality. Shakespeare's dramas provide an insight into virtually the entire range of late sixteenth- and early seventeenth-century English worldviews. John Milton could attempt to justify the ways of the Christian God to doubting human beings and in the same work have characters debate the adequacy of the Ptolemaic and Copernican systems. During the same years that Newton reached his deepest insights about nature, John Bunyan could write one of the classic works of simple Christian piety. It is the combination of past and future worldviews that makes the thought of the seventeenth century so remarkable and rich.

Miguel de Cervantes Saavedra: Rejection of Idealism

Spanish literature of the sixteenth and seventeenth centuries reflects the peculiar religious and politi-

Miguel de Cervantes Saavedra (1547–1616), the author of Don Quixote, *considered by many to be Spain's greatest writer. [Art Resource, N.Y.]*

cal history of Spain in this period. Spain was a deeply Catholic country, and this was a major influence on its literature. Since the joint reign of Ferdinand and Isabella (1479–1504), the church had received the unqualified support of reigning political power. Although there was religious reform in Spain, a Protestant Reformation never occurred, thanks largely to the entrenched power of the church and the Inquisition.

A second influence on Spanish literature was the aggressive piety of Spanish rulers, and this intertwining of Catholic piety and political power underlay a third influence: preoccupation with medieval chivalric virtues—in particular, questions of honor and loyalty. The novels and plays of the period almost invariably focus on a special decision involving a character's reputation as his honor or loyalty is tested. In this regard Spanish literature may be said to have remained more Catholic and medieval than that of England and France, where major Protestant movements had occurred. Two of the most important Spanish writers in this period became priests (Lope de Vega and Pedro Calderón de la Barca). The one generally acknowledged to be the greatest Spanish writer of all time, Cervantes, was preoccupied in his work with the strengths and weaknesses of religious idealism.

Cervantes (1547–1616) had only a smattering of formal education. He educated himself by wide reading in popular literature and immersion in the "school of life." As a young man he worked in Rome for a Spanish cardinal. As a soldier he was decorated for gallantry in the Battle of Lepanto (1571). He also spent five years as a slave in Algiers after his ship was pirated in 1575. Later, while working as a tax collector, he was several times imprisoned for padding his accounts, and it was in prison that he began, in 1603, to write his most famous work, *Don Quixote*.

The first part of *Don Quixote* appeared in 1605. The intent of this work seems to have been to satirize the chivalric romances then popular in Spain. But Cervantes could not conceal his deep affection for the character he created as an object of ridicule, Don Quixote. The work is satire only on the surface and has remained as much an object of study by philosophers and theologians as by students of Spanish literature. Cervantes presented Don Quixote as a none-too-stable middle-aged man. Driven mad by reading too many chivalric romances, he had come to believe he was an aspiring knight who had to prove his worthiness by brave deeds. To this end, he donned a rusty suit of armor and chose for his inspiration a quite unworthy peasant girl (Dulcinea), whom he fancied to be a noble lady to whom he could, with honor, dedicate his life.

Don Quixote's foil—Sancho Panza, a clever, worldly-wise peasant who serves as his squire—watched with bemused skepticism as his lord did battle with a windmill (which he mistook for a dragon) and repeatedly made a fool of himself as he galloped across the countryside. The story ends tragically with Don Quixote's humiliating defeat by a well-meaning friend, who, disguised as a knight, bests Don Quixote in combat and forces him to renounce his quest for knighthood. The humiliated Don Quixote does not, however, come to his senses as a result. He returns sadly to his village to die a shamed and broken-hearted old man.

Throughout *Don Quixote*, Cervantes juxtaposes the down-to-Earth realism of Sancho Panza with the old-fashioned religious idealism of Don Quixote. The reader perceives that Cervantes admired the one as much as the other and meant to portray both as representing attitudes necessary for a happy life.

William Shakespeare: Dramatist of the Age

There is much less factual knowledge about Shakespeare (1564–1616) than one would expect of the greatest playwright in the English language. He married at the early age of eighteen, in 1582, and he and his wife, Anne Hathaway, were the parents of three children (including twins) by 1585. He apparently worked as a schoolteacher for a time and in this capacity gained his broad knowledge of Renaissance learning and literature. His own reading and enthusiasm for the learning of his day are manifest in the many literary allusions that appear in his plays.

Shakespeare lived the life of a country gentleman. There is none of the Puritan distress over worldliness in his work. He took the new commercialism and the bawdy pleasures of the Elizabethan Age in stride and with amusement. He was a radical neither in politics nor religion. The few allusions in his works to the Puritans seem more critical than complimentary.

That Shakespeare was interested in politics is apparent from his historical plays and the references to contemporary political events that fill all his plays. He viewed government through the character of the individual ruler, whether Richard III or Elizabeth Tudor, not in terms of ideal systems or social goals. By modern standards he was a political conservative, accepting the social rankings and the power structure of his day and demonstrating unquestioned patriotism.

Shakespeare knew the theater as one who participated in every phase of its life—as a playwright, an actor, and part owner of a theater. He was a member and principal writer of a famous company of actors known as the King's Men. Between 1590 and 1610, many of his plays were performed at court, where he moved with comfort and received both Queen Elizabeth's and King James's enthusiastic patronage.

Elizabethan drama was already a distinctive form when Shakespeare began writing. Unlike French drama of the seventeenth century, which was dom-

A view of London indicating the Swan Theatre, where many of Shakespeare's plays were performed. [Folger Shakespeare Library]

inated by classical models, English drama developed in the sixteenth and seventeenth centuries as a blending of many forms: classical comedies and tragedies, medieval morality plays, and contemporary Italian short stories.

Two contemporaries, Thomas Kyd and Christopher Marlowe, influenced Shakespeare's tragedies. Kyd (1558–1594) wrote the first dramatic version of Hamlet. The tragedies of Marlowe (1564–1593) set a model for character, poetry, and style that only Shakespeare among the English playwrights of the period surpassed. Shakespeare synthesized the best past and current achievements. A keen student of human motivation and passion, he had a unique talent for getting into people's minds.

Shakespeare wrote histories, comedies, and tragedies. *Richard III* (1593), a very early play, stands out among the histories, although the picture it presents of Richard as an unprincipled villain has been characterized by some scholars as "Tudor propaganda." Shakespeare's comedies, although not attaining the heights of his tragedies, surpass his history plays in originality.

Shakespeare's tragedies are considered his unique achievement. Four of these were written within a three-year period: *Hamlet* (1603), *Othello* (1604), *King Lear* (1605), and *Macbeth* (1606). The most original of the tragedies, *Romeo and Juliet* (1597), transformed an old popular story into a moving drama of "star-cross'd lovers." Both Romeo and Juliet, denied a marriage by their warring families, die tragic deaths. Romeo, believing Juliet to be dead when she has merely taken a sleeping potion, poisons himself. When Juliet awakes to find Romeo dead, she kills herself with his dagger.

Throughout his lifetime and ever since, Shakespeare was immensely popular with both the playgoer and the play reader. The works of no other dramatist from his age are performed in theaters, and even on the screen, more regularly today.

John Milton: Puritan Poet

John Milton (1608–1674) was the son of a devout Puritan father. As a student, he avidly read the Christian and pagan classics. In 1638 he traveled to Italy, where he found in the lingering Renaissance a very congenial intellectual atmosphere. The Phlegraean Fields near Naples, a volcanic region, later became the model for hell in *Paradise Lost*, and it is suspected by some scholars that the Villa d'Este provided the model for paradise in *Paradise Regained*. Milton remained throughout his life a man more at home in the Italian Renaissance, with its high ideals and universal vision, than in the war-torn England of the seventeenth century.

A man of deep inner conviction and principle, Milton believed that standing a test of character was the most important thing in a person's life. This belief informed his own personal life and is the subject of much of his literary work.

In 1639 Milton joined the Puritan struggle against Charles I and Archbishop Laud. Employing his writing talent, he defended the Presbyterian form of church government against the episcopacy and supported other Puritan reforms. After a month-long unsuccessful marriage in 1642 (a marriage later reconciled), he wrote several tracts in defense of the right to divorce. These writings became targets of a Parliamentary censorship law in 1643, against which Milton wrote an eloquent defense of freedom of the press entitled *Areopagitica* (1644).

Until the upheavals of the civil war moderated his views, Milton believed that government should have the least possible control over the private lives of individuals. When Parliament divided into Presbyterians and Independents, he took the side of the latter, who wanted to dissolve the national church altogether in favor of the local autonomy of individual congregations. He also defended the execution of Charles I in a tract entitled *On the Tenure of Kings and Magistrates*. After his intense labor on this tract, his eyesight failed. Milton was totally blind when he wrote his masterpieces.

Paradise Lost, completed in 1665 and published in 1667, is a study of the destructive qualities of pride and the redeeming possibilities of humility. It elaborates in traditional Christian language and concept the revolt of Satan in heaven and the fall of Adam on Earth. The motives of Satan and all who rebel against God intrigued Milton. His proud but

John Milton (1608–1674). [Courtesy of the Prints Division, Library of Congress]

tragic Satan, who preferred to reign in hell than to serve in heaven, is one of the great figures in world literature and represented for Milton the absolute corruption of potential greatness.

Milton wanted *Paradise Lost* to be for England what Homer's *Iliad* was for Greece and Vergil's *Aeneid* for Rome. In choosing biblical subject matter, he revealed the great influence of contemporary theology on his mind. Milton tended to agree with the Arminians, followers of the Dutch Protestant theologian Arminius (1560–1609), who, unlike the extreme Calvinists, did not believe that all worldly events, including the Fall of Man, were immutably fixed in the eternal decree of God. Milton shared the Arminian belief that human beings must take responsibility for their fate and that human efforts to improve character could, with God's grace, bring salvation.

Perhaps his own blindness, joined with the hope of making the best of the failed Puritan revolution, inclined Milton to sympathize with those who urged people to make the most of what they had, even in the face of defeat. That is a manifest concern of his last works, *Samson Agonistes*, which

John Milton Defends Freedom to Print Books

During the English Civil War, the Parliament passed a very strict censorship measure. In Areopagitica *(1644), John Milton attacked this law and contributed one of the major defenses for the freedom of the press in the history of Western culture. In the following passage, he compares the life of a book with the life of a human being.*

✦ *Why does Milton think that it may be more dangerous and harmful to attack a book than to attack a person? Was life cheaper and intelligence rarer in his time? Does he have particular kinds of books in mind? What can a book do for society that people cannot?*

I deny not but that it is of greatest concern in the Church and Commonwealth to have a vigilant eye how books demean themselves as well as men; and thereafter to confine, imprison, and do sharpest justice on them as [if they were criminals]; for books are not absolutely dead things, but do contain a progeny of life in them to be as active as that soul was whose progeny they are; nay, they do preserve as in a vial the purest efficacy and extraction of that living intellect that bred them. . . . He who kills a man kills a reasonable creature, God's Image; but he who destroys a good book, kills reason itself, kills the Image of God, as it were. . . . Many a man lives [as] a burden to the Earth; but a good book is the precious life-blood of a master spirit, embalmed and treasured up on purpose to a life beyond life. It is true, no age can restore a life, whereof, perhaps there is no great loss; and revolutions of ages do not oft recover the loss of a rejected truth, for the want of which whole nations fare the worse. We should be wary, therefore, what persecution we raise against the living labours of public men, how we spill that seasoned life of man preserved and stored up in books; since we see a kind of homicide may be thus committed, sometimes a martyrdom, and if it extends to the whole impression, a kind of massacre, whereof the execution ends not in the slaying of an elemental life, but strikes at that ethereal . . . essence, the breath of reason itself; slays an immortality rather than a life.

J. A. St. John, ed., The Prose Works of John Milton *(London: H. G. Bohn, 1843–1853), 2:8–9.*

recounts the biblical story of Samson, and *Paradise Regained*, the story of Christ's temptation in the wilderness, both published in 1671.

John Bunyan: Visions of Christian Piety

Bunyan (1628–1688) was the English author of two classics of sectarian Puritan spirituality: *Grace Abounding* (1666) and *The Pilgrim's Progress* (1678). A Bedford tinker, his works speak especially for the seventeenth-century working people and popular religious culture. He received only the most basic education before taking up his father's craft, and he served in Oliver Cromwell's revolutionary army for two years. The visionary fervor of the New Model Army influenced his work, which is filled with the language of battle.

After the restoration of the monarchy in 1660, Bunyan went to prison for his fiery preaching and remained there for twelve years. During these years, he wrote his famous autobiography, *Grace Abounding*, both a very personal statement and a model for the faithful. Like *The Pilgrim's Progress*, Bunyan's later masterpiece, *Grace Abounding* is Puritan piety at its most fervent. Puritans believed that individuals could do absolutely nothing to save themselves, and this made them extremely restless and introspective. People could only trust that God had placed them among the elect and try each day to live a life that reflected such favored status. So long as men and women struggled successfully against the flesh and the world, they had presumptive evidence that they were among God's elect. To falter or to become complacent in the face of temptation was to cast doubt on one's faith and salvation and even to raise the specter of eternal damnation.

This anxious questing for salvation is the subject of *The Pilgrim's Progress*, a work unique in its contribution to Western religious symbolism and imagery. It is the story of the journey of Christian and his friends Hopeful and Faithful to the Celestial City. It teaches that one must deny spouse, children, and all Earthly security and go in search of "Life, life, eternal life." During the long journey, the travelers must resist the temptations of Worldly-Wiseman and Vanity Fair, pass through the Slough of Despond, and endure a long dark night in Doubting Castle, their faith being tested at every turn. Bunyan later wrote a work tracing the progress of Christian's opposite, *The Life and Death of Mr. Badman* (1680), which told the story of a man so addicted to the bad habits of Restoration society, of which Bunyan strongly disapproved, that he journeyed steadfastly not to heaven but to hell.

Philosophy in the Wake of Changing Science

By the end of the sixteenth century, many people, weary of religious strife, no longer embraced either the old Catholic or the new Protestant absolutes. The century that followed was a period of intellectual as well as political transition. The thinkers of the Renaissance, reacting against the dogmatic thinking of medieval Scholasticism, had laid the groundwork for this change.

The revolution in scientific thought contributed directly to a major reconsideration of Western philosophy. Several of the most important figures in the Scientific Revolution, such as Descartes and

The microscope of Robert Hooke (1635–1703). The microscope became the telescope's companion as a major optical instrument in the seventeenth century. Several scientists, including Galileo, had a hand in its development, but the Englishman Hooke and the Dutchman Anton von Leeuwenhoek (1632–1723) did the most to perfect it. [Historical Collections, National Museum of Health and Medicine, Armed Forces Institute of Pathology]

Bacon, were also philosophers discontented with the scholastic heritage. Bacon stressed the importance of empirical research. Descartes attempted to find certainty through the exploration of his thinking processes. Newton's interests likewise extended to philosophy; he wrote broadly on many topics, including scientific method and theology.

The new methods of science had a broad impact on philosophers. The emphasis that Galileo placed on mathematics spread to other areas of thought. Pascal, a gifted mathematician, became concerned about the issue of certain knowledge and religious faith. Spinoza would write his ethical discourses in the form of geometrical theorems. Hobbes produced a great political treatise through a mode of rational reasoning resembling mathematics. Locke would attempt to explore the human mind in a fashion that he believed resembled Newton's approach to the physical universe. Virtually all of these writers found a tension that they hoped to resolve between the new science and religious belief.

Francis Bacon: Empirical Method

Bacon (1561–1626) was an Englishman of almost universal accomplishment. He was a lawyer, a high royal official, and the author of histories, moral essays, and philosophical discourses. Traditionally, he has been regarded as the father of empiricism and of experimentation in science. Much of this reputation is unearned. Bacon was not a scientist except in the most amateur fashion. His accomplishment was setting a tone and helping to create a climate conducive to scientific work.

In books such as *The Advancement of Learning* (1605), the *Novum Organum* (1620), and the *New Atlantis* (1627), Bacon attacked the scholastic belief that most truth had already been discovered and only required explanation, as well as the scholastic reverence for intellectual authority in general. He believed that scholastic thinkers paid too much attention to tradition and to the knowledge of the ancients. He urged contemporaries to strike out on their own in search of a new understanding of nature. He wanted seventeenth-century Europeans to have confidence in themselves and their own abilities rather than in the people and methods of the past. Bacon was one of the first major European writers to champion the desirability of innovation and change.

Bacon believed that human knowledge should produce useful results. In particular, knowledge of

Sir Francis Bacon (1561–1626), champion of the inductive method of gaining knowledge. [By courtesy of the National Portrait Gallery, London]

nature should be brought to the aid of the human condition. These goals required the modification or abandonment of scholastic modes of learning and thinking. Bacon contended, "The [scholastic] logic now in use serves more to fix and give stability to the errors which have their foundation in commonly received notions than to help the search after truth."[5] Scholastic philosophers could not escape from their syllogisms to examine the foundations of their thought and intellectual presuppositions. Bacon urged that philosophers and investigators of nature examine the evidence of their senses before constructing logical speculations. In a famous passage, he divided all philosophers into

[5]Quoted in Baumer, p. 281.

Bacon Attacks the Idols That Harm Human Understanding

Francis Bacon wanted the men and women of his era to have the courage to change the way they thought about physical nature. In this famous passage from the Novum Organum *(1620), he attempted to explain why it is so difficult to ask new questions and seek new answers.*

◆ *Is Bacon's view of human nature pessimistic? Are people hopelessly trapped in overlapping worlds of self-interest and fantasy imposed by their nature and cultural traditions? How did Bacon expect people to overcome such formidable barriers?*

The idols and false notions which are now in possession of the human understanding and have taken deep root therein. . . . so beset men's minds that truth can hardly find entrance. . . . There are four classes of Idols which beset men's minds. To these for distinction's sake I have assigned names,—calling the first class *Idols of the Tribe;* the second, *Idols of the Cave;* the third, *Idols of the Marketplace;* the fourth, *Idols of the Theatre.*

. . . .

The Idols of the Tribe have their foundation in human nature itself; and in the tribe or race of men. For it is a false assertion that the sense of man is the measure of things. On the contrary, all perceptions as well as the sense as of the mind are according to the measure of the universe. And the human understanding is like a false mirror, which, receiving rays irregularly, distorts and discolours the nature of things by mingling its own nature with it.

The Idols of the Cave are the idols of the individual man. For every one (besides the errors common to human nature in general) has a cave or den of his own, which refracts and discolours the light of nature; owing either to his own proper and peculiar nature; or to his education and conversation with others; or to the reading of books, and the authority of those whom he esteems and admires. . . .

There are also Idols formed by the intercourse and association of men with each other, which I call Idols of the Marketplace, on account of the commerce and consort of men there. For it is by discourse that men associate; and words are imposed according to the apprehension of the vulgar. And therefore the ill and unfit choice of words wonderfully obstructs the understanding. . . .

Lastly, there are Idols which have immigrated into men's minds from the various dogmas of philosophies, and also from wrong laws of demonstration. These I call Idols of the Theatre; because in my judgment all the received systems are but so many stage plays, representing worlds of their own creation after an unreal and scenic fashion.

Francis Bacon, Essays, Advancement of Learning, New Atlantis, and Other Pieces, *ed. by Richard Foster Jones (New York: Odyssey, 1937), pp. 278–280.*

"men of experiment and men of dogmas." He observed:

The men of experiment are like the ant, they only collect and use; the reasoners resemble spiders, who make cobwebs out of their own substance. But the bee takes a middle course: it gathers its material from the flowers of the garden and of the field, but transforms and digests it by a power of its own. Not unlike this is the true business of philosophy.[6]

[6]Quoted in Baumer, p. 288.

By directing scientists toward an examination of empirical evidence, Bacon hoped that they would achieve new knowledge and thus new capabilities for humankind.

Bacon compared himself with Columbus, plotting a new route to intellectual discovery. The comparison is significant, because it displays the consciousness of a changing world that appears so often in writers of the late sixteenth and early seventeenth centuries. They were rejecting the past not from simple hatred but rather from a firm understanding that the world was much more complicated than their medieval forebears had thought.

Neither Europe nor European thought could remain self-contained. Like the new worlds on the globe, new worlds of the mind were also emerging. Most of the people in Bacon's day, including the intellectuals, thought that the best era of human history lay in antiquity. Bacon dissented vigorously from that view. He looked to a future of material improvement achieved through the empirical examination of nature. His own theory of induction from empirical evidence was quite unsystematic, but his insistence on appeal to experience influenced others whose methods were more productive.

Bacon believed that science had a practical purpose and its goal was human improvement. Some scientific investigation does have this character. Much pure research does not. Bacon, however, linked science and material progress in the public mind. This was a powerful idea and has continued to influence Western civilization to the present day. It has made science and those who can appeal to the authority of science major forces for change and innovation. Thus, though not making any major scientific contribution himself, Bacon directed investigators of nature to a new method and a new purpose.

René Descartes: The Method of Rational Deduction

Descartes (1596–1650) was a gifted mathematician who invented analytic geometry. His most important contribution, however, was to develop a scientific method that relied more on deduction than empirical observation and induction.

In 1637 he published his *Discourse on Method*, in which he attempted to provide a basis for all thinking founded on a mathematical model. The work appeared in French rather than in Latin because he wanted it to have wide circulation and

René Descartes (1596–1650) believed that because the material world operated according to mathematical laws, it could be accurately understood by the exercise of human reason. [Erich Lessing/Art Resource, N.Y.]

application. He began by saying that he would doubt everything except those propositions about which he could have clear and distinct ideas. This approach rejected all forms of intellectual authority except the conviction of his own reason. He concluded that he could not doubt his own act of thinking and his own existence. From this base he proceeded to deduce the existence of God. The presence of God was important to Descartes because God guaranteed the correctness of clear and distinct ideas. Because God was not a deceiver, the ideas of God-given reason could not be false.

On the basis of such assumptions, Descartes concluded that human reason could fully comprehend the world. He divided existing things into two basic categories: things thought and things occupying space—mind and body. Thinking was characteristic of the mind, and extension (things occupying space) was characteristic of the body. Within the material world, the world of extension, mathematical laws reigned supreme and could be grasped by reason. Because they were mathematical, they could be deduced from each other and constituted a complete system. The world of extension was the world of the scientist. It had no place for spirits, divinity, or anything nonmaterial. Descartes separated mind from body to banish such things from the realm of scientific speculation. Reason was to be applied only to the mechanical and mathematical realm of matter.

Descartes's emphasis on deduction and rational speculation exercised broad influence. His deductive methodology, however, eventually lost favor to scientific induction, in which the scientist draws generalizations from data derived from empirical observations.

Blaise Pascal: Reason and Faith

Pascal (1623–1662) was a French mathematician and a physical scientist who surrendered all his

Pascal Meditates on Human Beings as Thinking Creatures

Pascal was both a religious and a scientific writer. Unlike other scientific thinkers of the seventeenth century, he was not overly optimistic about the ability of science to improve the human condition. But science and philosophy might help human beings to understand their situation better. In these passages from his Pensées *(Thoughts), he ponders the uniqueness of human beings as thinking creatures.*

✦ *Is this an intellectual's view of human nature? Does the idea that man is a rational creature come from the belief that human reason is more noble than the universe? Does Pascal ignore human will and emotion, selfishness, and destructiveness?*

339

I can well conceive a man without hands, feet, head (for it is only experience which teaches us that the head is more necessary than feet). But I cannot conceive man without thought; he would be a stone or a brute.

344

Reason commands us far more imperiously than a master; for in disobeying the one we are unfortunate, and in disobeying the other we are fools.

346

Thought constitutes the greatness of man.

347

Man is but a reed, the most feeble thing in nature; but he is a thinking reed. The entire universe need

not arm itself to crush him. A vapour, a drop of water suffices to kill him. But, if the universe were to crush him, man would still be more noble than that which killed him, because he knows that he dies and the advantage which the universe has over him; the universe knows nothing of this.

All our dignity consists, then, in thought. By it we must elevate ourselves, and not by space and time which we cannot fill. Let us endeavour, then, to think well; this is the principle of morality.

348

A thinking reed—It is not from space that I must seek my dignity, but from the government of my thought. I shall have no more if I possess worlds. By space the universe encompasses and swallows me up like an atom; by thought I comprehend the world.

Blaise Pascal, Pensées and The Provincial Letters *(New York: Modern Library, 1941), pp. 115–116.*

Pascal invented this adding machine, the ancestor of mechanical calculators, around 1644. It has eight wheels with ten cogs each, corresponding to the numbers 0–9. The wheels move forward for addition, backward for subtract. [Bildarchiv Preussischer Kulturbesitz]

wealth to pursue an austere, self-disciplined life. He aspired to write a work that would refute both dogmatism (which he saw epitomized by the Jesuits) and skepticism. Pascal considered the Jesuits' casuistry (i.e., arguments designed to minimize and excuse sinful acts) a distortion of Christian teaching. He rejected the skeptics of his age because they either denied religion altogether (atheists) or accepted it only as it conformed to reason (deists). He never produced a definitive refutation of the two sides. Rather he formulated his views on these matters in piecemeal fashion in a provocative collection of reflections on humankind and religion published posthumously under the title *Pensées*.

Pascal allied himself with the Jansenists, seventeenth-century Catholic opponents of the Jesuits. His sister was a member of the Jansenist community of Port-Royal, near Paris. The Jansenists shared with the Calvinists Saint Augustine's belief in human beings' total sinfulness, their eternal predestination by God, and their complete dependence on faith and grace for knowledge of God and salvation.

Pascal believed that reason and science were of no avail in matters of religion. Here only the reasons of the heart and a "leap of faith" could prevail. He saw two essential truths in the Christian religion: that a loving God, worthy of human attainment, exists, and that human beings, because they are corrupt by nature, are utterly unworthy of God. He believed that the atheists and the deists of his age had spurned the clear lesson of reason. For him rational analysis of the human condition revealed utter mortality and corruption and exposed the weakness of reason itself in resolving the problems of human nature and destiny. Reason properly drove those who truly heed it to faith in God and reliance on divine grace.

Pascal made a famous wager with the skeptics. It is a better bet, he argued, to believe that God exists and to stake everything on his promised mercy than not to do so. This is because if God does exist, everything will be gained by the believer, whereas, should he prove not to exist, the loss incurred by having believed in him is by comparison very slight.

Convinced that belief in God improved life psychologically and disciplined it morally (regardless of whether God proved in the end to exist), Pascal worked to strengthen traditional religious belief. He urged his contemporaries to seek self-understanding by "learned ignorance" and to discover humankind's greatness by recognizing its misery. He hoped thereby to counter what he believed to be the false optimism of the new rationalism and science.

Baruch Spinoza: The World as Divine Substance

The most controversial thinker of the seventeenth century may have been Baruch Spinoza (1632–1677), the son of a Jewish merchant of Amsterdam. His philosophy caused his excommunication by his own synagogue in 1656. During his lifetime, both Jews and Protestants attacked him as an atheist.

Spinoza's most influential writing, the *Ethics*, appeared after his death in 1677. Religious leaders universally condemned it for its apparent espousal of pantheism (a doctrine equating God and nature). Spinoza so closely identified God and nature that little room seemed left either for divine revelation in scripture or for the personal immortality of the soul—a position equally repugnant to Jews and to Christians. The *Ethics* was written, in the spirit of the new science, as a geometrical system of definitions, axioms, and propositions. Spinoza divided the work into five parts, which dealt with God, the mind, emotions, human bondage, and human freedom.

The most controversial part of the *Ethics* deals with the nature of substance and of God. According to Spinoza, there is only one substance, which is self-caused, free, and infinite, and that substance is God. From this definition it follows that everything that exists is in God and cannot even be conceived

of apart from him. Such a doctrine was not literally pantheistic because God was still seen to be more than the created world that he, as primal substance, embraced. But in Spinoza's view, statements about the natural world were also statements about divine nature. Mind and matter are thus seen to be extensions of the infinite substance of God; what transpires in the world of people and nature is also an expression of the divine.

Such teaching seemed to portray the world as eternal and human actions as unfree and inevitable. Jews and Christians had traditionally condemned such teachings because they deny the creation of the world by God in time and destroy any voluntary basis for personal reward and punishment.

Although his contemporaries condemned him, Spinoza found enthusiastic supporters among many nineteenth-century thinkers who, unable to accept traditional religious language and doctrines, found in his teaching a congenial rational religion.

Thomas Hobbes: Apologist for Absolutism

Thomas Hobbes (1588–1679) was the most original political philosopher of the seventeenth century. Although he never broke with the Church of England, he embraced basic Calvinist beliefs, particularly their low view of human nature and the ideal of a commonwealth based on a divine–human covenant.

An urbane and much-traveled man, Hobbes enthusiastically supported the new scientific movement. During the 1630s, he visited Paris, where he came to know Descartes, and he spent time with Galileo in Italy as well. He took special interest in the works of William Harvey (1578–1657), famous for his discovery of the circulation of blood through the body. Hobbes was also a superb classicist. His first published work was a translation of Thucydides' *History of the Peloponnesian War*, the first English translation of this work, still reprinted today.

The English civil war made Hobbes a political philosopher and inspired his *Leviathan* (1651). Written as the concluding part of a broad philosophical system that analyzed physical bodies and human nature, the work established Hobbes as a major European thinker.

Hobbes viewed people and society in a thoroughly materialistic and mechanical way. All psychological processes begin with and are derived

A portrait of Thomas Hobbes (1588–1679), whose political treatise, Leviathan, portrayed rulers as absolute lords over their lands, incorporating in their persons the individual wills of all their people. [Bildarchiv Preussischer Kulturbesitz]

from bare sensation, and all motivations are egoistical, intended to increase pleasure and minimize pain. The human power of reasoning, which Hobbes defined as the process of adding and subtracting the consequences of agreed-upon general names of things, develops only after years of concentrated industry. Human will he defined as simply "the last appetite before choice."

Despite this mechanistic view of human nature, Hobbes believed people could accomplish much by the reasoned use of science. Such progress, however, was contingent on their prior correct use of that greatest of human creations, the commonwealth, in which people were freely united by mutual agreement in one all-powerful sovereign government.

The key to Hobbes's political philosophy can be found in a brilliant myth he created about the original state of humankind. According to this account, people in their natural state are inclined to "perpetual and restless desire" for power. Because all people want and, in their natural state, possess a natural right to everything, their equality breeds enmity, competition, diffidence, and perpetual quarreling—"a way of every man against every man." As Hobbes put it in a famous summary:

In such condition there is no place for industry, because the fruit thereof is uncertain; and consequently no culture of the Earth; no navigation nor use of the commodities that may be imported by sea; no commodious building; no instruments of moving and removing such things as require much force; no knowledge of the face of the Earth; no account of time; no arts; no letters; no society; and, which is worst of all, continual fear and danger of violent death; and the life of man solitary, poor, nasty, brutish, and short.[7]

Whereas earlier and later philosophers saw the original human state as a paradise from which humankind had fallen, Hobbes saw it as a corruption from which only society could deliver people. Contrary to Aristotle and Christian thinkers like Thomas Aquinas, Hobbes did not believe human beings were naturally sociable; they were self-centered beasts and utterly without a master until one was imposed by force.

People escape this terrible state of nature, according to Hobbes, only by entering a social contract, that is, by agreeing to live in a commonwealth tightly ruled by a recognized sovereign. They are driven to this solution by their desire for "commodious living" and fear of death. The social contract obliges every person, for the sake of peace and self-defense, to agree to set aside personal rights to all things and to be content with as much liberty against others as he or she would allow others against himself or herself. All agree to live according to a secularized version of the golden rule: "Do not that to another which you would not have done to yourself."[8]

Because words and promises are insufficient to guarantee this state, the social contract also establishes the coercive use of force to compel compliance. Believing the dangers of anarchy to be always

[7]Thomas Hobbes, *Leviathan* Parts I and II, ed. by H. W. Schneider (Indianapolis: Bobbs-Merrill, 1958), pp. 86, 106–107.
[8]Hobbes, p. 130.

greater than those of tyranny, Hobbes thought that rulers should be absolute and unlimited in their power, once established in office. There is no room in Hobbes's political philosophy for protest in the name of individual conscience, nor for resistance to legitimate authority by private individuals. Contemporary Catholics and Puritans alike criticized these features of the *Leviathan*. To his critics, Hobbes pointed out the alternative:

The greatest that in any form of government can possibly happen to the people in general is scarce sensible in respect of the miseries and horrible calamities that accompany a civil war or that dissolute condition of masterless men, without subjection to laws and a coercive power to tie their hands from rapine and revenge.[9]

[9]Hobbes, p. 152.

It is puzzling why Hobbes believed that absolute rulers would be more benevolent and less egoistic than all other people. He simply placed the highest possible value on a strong, efficient ruler who could save human beings from the chaos attendant on the state of nature. In the end, it mattered little to Hobbes whether that ruler was Charles I, Oliver Cromwell, or Charles II, each of whom received Hobbes's enthusiastic support—once he was established in power.

John Locke: Defender of Moderate Liberty

Locke (1632–1704) has proved to be the most influential political thinker of the seventeenth century. Although he was not as original as Hobbes, his political writings became a major source of the later

The famous title page illustration for Hobbes's Leviathan. *The ruler is pictured as absolute lord of his lands, but note that the ruler incorporates the mass of individuals whose self-interests are best served by their willing consent to accept him and cooperate with him.* [*Rare Books Division, The New York Public Library. Astor, Lenox and Tilden Foundation.*]

Enlightenment criticism of absolutism. They gave inspiration to both the American and the French revolutions.

Locke's sympathies lay with the Puritans and the parliamentary forces that challenged the Stuart monarchy. His father fought with the parliamentary army during the English civil war. Locke read deeply in the works of Francis Bacon, René Descartes, and Isaac Newton and was a close friend of the English physicist and chemist Robert Boyle (1627–1691). Some view Locke as synthesizing the rationalism of Descartes and the experimental science of Bacon, Newton, and Boyle.

Locke came for a brief period also under the influence of Hobbes. This ended, however, after his association with Anthony Ashley Cooper, the earl of Shaftesbury. Shaftesbury was considered by his contemporaries to be a radical in both religion and politics. He organized an unsuccessful rebellion against Charles II in 1682, after which both he and Locke, who lived with him, were forced to flee to Holland.

In his *Essay Concerning Human Understanding* (1690), Locke explored the function of the human mind. He portrayed it at birth as a blank tablet. There are no innate ideas, he argued; all knowledge is derived from direct sensual experience. What people know is not the external world in itself but the results of the interaction of the mind with the outside world.

Locke also denied the existence of innate moral norms. Moral ideas are the product of people's subordination of self-love to reason—a free act of self-discipline so that conflict in conscience may be avoided and happiness attained. Locke also believed the teachings of Christianity to be identical to what uncorrupted reason taught. A rational person would therefore always live according to Christian moral precepts. Although Locke firmly denied toleration to Catholics and atheists—both of whom were considered subversive in England—he otherwise sanctioned a variety of Protestant religious practice.

During the reign of Charles II, Locke wrote *Two Treatises of Government.* Here he opposed the argument, set forth by Sir Robert Filmer and Thomas Hobbes, that rulers are absolute in their power. Filmer was the author of *Patriarcha, or the Natural Power of Kings* (1680), which compared the rights of kings over their subjects to those of fathers over their children. Locke devoted his entire first treatise

John Locke (1632–1704), defender of the rights of the people against rulers who think their power absolute. [By courtesy of the National Portrait Gallery, London]

to a refutation of this argument, maintaining that both fathers and rulers were bound to the law of nature. The voice of reason teaches that "all mankind [are] equal and independent, [and] no one ought to harm another in his life, health, liberty, or possessions,"[10] inasmuch as all humans are made in the image of God. According to Locke, people enter into social contracts, empowering legislatures and monarchs to "umpire" their disputes, precisely to preserve their natural rights, not to give rulers an absolute power over them. Rulers are "entrusted" with the preservation of the law of nature and transgress it at their peril:

[10]John Locke, *The Second Treatise of Government*, ed. by T. P. Peardon (Indianapolis: Bobbs-Merrill, 1952), Ch. 2, secs. 4–6, pp. 4–6.

John Locke Explores the Sources of Human Knowledge

An Essay Concerning Human Understanding (1690) was probably the most influential philosophical work ever written in English. Locke's fundamental idea, which is explicated in the passage below, was that human knowledge is grounded in the experiences of the senses and in the reflection of the mind on those experiences. He rejected any belief in innate ideas. His emphasis on experience led to the wider belief that human beings are creatures of their environment. After Locke, numerous writers argued that human beings could be improved if the political and social environments in which they lived were reformed.

✦ *How does Locke explain the manner in which the human mind comes to be furnished? What does Locke mean by* experience? *How does reflection deal with external sensations? What is the role that external environment plays in Locke's psychology?*

Let us then suppose the mind to be, as we say, white paper void of all characters, without any ideas. Whence comes it to be furnished? Whence comes it by that vast store which the busy and boundless fancy of man has painted on it with an almost endless variety? Whence has it all the materials of reason and knowledge? To this I answer, in one word, from experience; in that all our knowledge is founded, and from that it ultimately derives itself. Our observation, employed either about external sensible objects, or about the internal operations of our minds perceived and reflected on by ourselves, is that which supplies our understanding with all the materials of thinking. These two are the fountains of knowledge, from whence all the ideas we have, or can naturally have, do spring.

First, our senses, conversant about particular sensible objects, do convey into the mind several distinct perceptions of things, according to those various ways wherein those objects do affect them. And thus we come by those ideas we have of yellow, white, heat, cold, soft, hard, bitter, sweet, and all those which we call sensible qualities. . . . This great source of most of the ideas we have, depending wholly upon our senses, and derived by them to the understanding, I call SENSATION.

Secondly, the other fountain from which experience furnisheth the understanding with ideas is the perception of the operations of our own minds within us, as it is employed about the ideas it has got . . . and such are perception, thinking, doubting, believing, reasoning, knowing, willing, and all the different actings of our own minds. . . . I call this REFLECTION, the ideas it affords being such only as the mind gets by reflecting on its own operations within itself. . . . These two, I say, viz., external material things as the objects of SENSATION, and the operations of our own minds within as the objects of REFLECTION, are to me the only originals from whence all our ideas take their beginnings. . . .

The understanding seems to me not to have the least glimmering of any ideas which it doth not receive from one of these two.

John Locke, An Essay Concerning Human Understanding, *vol. 1 (London: Everyman's Library, 1961), pp. 77–78.*

Whenever that end [the preservation of life, liberty, and property] is manifestly neglected or opposed, the trust must necessarily be forfeited and the power devolve into the hands of those that gave it, who may place it anew where they think best for their safety and security.[11]

From Locke's point of view, absolute monarchy was "inconsistent" with civil society and can be "no form of civil government at all."

Locke's main differences with Hobbes stemmed from the latter's negative views of human nature. Locke believed that the natural human state was one of perfect freedom and equality in which everyone enjoyed, in unregulated fashion, the natural rights of life, liberty, and property. Contrary to Hobbes, human beings in their natural state were creatures not of monomaniacal passion but of extreme goodwill and rationality. And they did not surrender their natural rights unconditionally when they entered the social contract. Rather they established a means whereby these rights could be better preserved. The warfare that Hobbes believed characterized the state of nature emerged for Locke only when rulers failed to preserve people's natural freedom and attempted to enslave them by absolute rule. The preservation and protection of human freedom, not its suppression, was government's mandate.

◆

The Scientific Revolution and the thought of writers whose work was contemporaneous with it mark a major turning point in the history of Western thought and eventually had a worldwide impact. The scientific and political ideas of the late sixteenth and seventeenth centuries gradually overturned many of the most fundamental premises of the medieval worldview. The sun replaced the Earth as the center of the solar system. The solar system itself came to be viewed as one of many possible systems in the universe. The new knowledge of the physical universe provided occasions for challenges to the authority of the church and of scripture. Mathematics began to replace theology and metaphysics as the tool for understanding nature.

Parallel to these developments and sometimes related to them, political thought became much

less concerned with religious issues. Hobbes generated a major theory of political obligation with virtually no reference to God. Locke theorized about politics with a recognition of God but with little attention to scripture. Both Locke and Spinoza championed greater freedom of religious and political expression. Locke produced a psychology that emphasized the influence of environment on human character and action. All of these new ideas gradually displaced or reshaped theological and religious modes of thought and placed humankind and life on Earth at the center of Western thinking. Intellectuals in the West consequently developed greater self-confidence in their own capacity to shape the world and their own lives.

None of this came easily, however. The new science and enlightenment were accompanied by new anxieties that were reflected in a growing preoccupation with sin, death, and the Devil. The worst expression of this preoccupation was a succession of witch hunts and trials that took the lives of as many as 100,000 people between 1400 and 1700.

Review Questions

1. Discuss the contributions of Copernicus, Brahe, Kepler, Galileo, and Newton to the Scientific Revolution. Which do you think made the most important contributions and why? What did Francis Bacon contribute to the foundation of scientific thought?
2. How would you define the term *Scientific Revolution*? In what ways was it truly revolutionary? Which is more enduring, a political revolution or an intellectual one?
3. How did Isaac Newton reconcile his scientific discoveries with his faith in God? Compare his experience with that of Galileo or Pascal. Are reason and faith compatible?
4. Compare and contrast the political philosophies of Thomas Hobbes and John Locke. How did each view human nature? Would you rather live under a government designed by Hobbes or by Locke? Why?
5. How do you explain the phenomenon of witchcraft and witch hunts in an age of scientific enlightenment? Why did the witch panics occur in the late sixteenth and early seventeenth centuries? How might the Reformation have contributed to them?

[11]Locke, Ch. 13, sec. 149, p. 84.

6. How do the literary works of Cervantes, Shakespeare, and Milton reflect concern about the adequacy of past values and how did they shape the worldview of their own seventeenth century society?

Suggested Readings

R. ASHCRAFT, *Revolutionary Politics and Locke's Two Treatises of Government* (1986). A major study emphasizing the radical side of Locke's thought.

M. BIAGIOLI, *Galileo Courtier: The Practice of Science in the Culture of Absolutism* (1993). A major revisionist work that emphasizes the role of the political setting on Galileo's career and thought.

H. BUTTERFIELD, *The Origins of Modern Science 1300–1800* (1949). A classic survey.

J. CAIRD, *Spinoza* (1971). Intellectual biography by a philosopher.

H. F. COHEN, *The Scientific Revolution: A Historiographical Inquiry* (1994). Supplants all previous discussions of the history and concept of the Scientific Revolution.

J. DUNN, *The Political Thought of John Locke; An Historical Account of the "Two Treatises of Government"* (1969). An excellent introduction.

M. DURAN, *Cervantes* (1974). Detailed biography.

M. A. FINOCCHIARO, *The Galileo Affair: A Documentary History* (1989). A collection of all the relevant documents and introductory commentary.

S. GAUKROGER, *Descartes: An Intellectual Biography* (1995). A major work that explores both the science and philosophy in Descartes's work.

A. GOLDGAR, *Impolite Learning: Conduct and Community in the Republic of Letters, 1680–1750* (1995). A lively survey of the structure of the European intellectual community.

A. R. HALL, *The Scientific Revolution 1500–1800: The Formation of the Modern Scientific Attitude* (1966). Traces undermining of traditional science and rise of new sciences.

I. HARRIS, *The Mind of John Locke: A Study of Political Theory in Its Intellectual Setting* (1994). The most comprehensive recent treatment.

C. HILL, *Milton and the English Revolution* (1977). A major biography.

M. HUNTER, *Science and Society in Restoration England* (1981). Examines the social relations of scientists and scientific societies.

M. JACOB, *The Newtonians and the English Revolution* (1976). A controversial book that attempts to relate science and politics.

D. JOHNSTON, *The Rhetoric of Leviathan: Thomas Hobbes and the Politics of Cultural Transformation* (1986). An important study that links Hobbes's thought to the rhetoric of the Renaissance.

R. KIECKHEFER, *European Witch Trials: Their Foundations in Popular and Learned Culture 1300–1500* (1976). Excellent background for understanding the great witch panic.

A. KORS AND E. PETERS (EDS.), *European Witchcraft, 1100–1700* (1972). Collection of major documents.

A. KOYRÉ, *From the Closed World to the Infinite Universe* (1957). Treated from perspective of the historian of ideas.

T. S. KUHN, *The Copernican Revolution* (1957). Remains the leading work on the subject.

C. LARNER, *Enemies of God: The Witchhunt in Scotland* (1981). Perhaps the most exemplary local study of the subject.

P. LASLETT, *Locke's Two Treatises of Government*, 2nd ed. (1970). Definitive texts with very important introductions.

B. LEVACK, *The Witch Hunt in Early Modern Europe* (1986). Lucid, up-to-date survey of research.

D. LINDBERG AND R. L. NUMBERS (EDS.), *God and Nature: Historical Essays on the Encounter Between Christianity and Science* (1986). The best collection of essays on the subject.

D. LINDBERG AND R. S. WESTMAN (EDS.), *Reappraisals of the Scientific Revolution* (1990). Important essays pointing the way toward new understandings of the subject.

J. MARTIN, *Francis Bacon, The State, and the Reform of Natural Philosophy* (1992). Relates Bacon's thought to his political goals.

O. MAYER, *Authority, Liberty, and Automatic Machinery in Early Modern Europe* (1986). A lively study that seeks to relate thought about machinery to thought about politics.

R. POPKIN, *The History of Scepticism from Erasmus to Spinoza* (1979). A classic study of the fear of loss of intellectual certainty.

P. REDONDI, *Galileo: Heretic* (1987). A controversial work that examines the relationship of Galileo's thought to the church's teaching on the Eucharist rather than to planetary motion.

S. SHAPIN AND S. SCHAFFER, *Leviathan and the Air-Pump: Hobbes, Boyle, and the Experimental Life* (1985). A study of the debate over the validity of scientific experiment during the age of the Scientific Revolution.

Q. SKINNER, *Reason and Rhetoric in the Philosophy of Hobbes* (1996). A major study by one of the leading scholars of Hobbes and early modern political thought.

L. STEWART, *The Rise of Public Science: Rhetoric, Technology, and Natural Philosophy in Newtonian Britain, 1660–1750* (1992). Examines the manner in which science became related to public life and economic development.

K. THOMAS, *Religion and the Decline of Magic* (1971). Provocative, much acclaimed work focused on popular culture.

R. S. WESTFALL, *Never at Rest: A Biography of Isaac Newton* (1981). The major study.

B. H. G. WORMALD, *Francis Bacon: History, Politics, and Science, 1561–1626* (1993). The most extensive recent study.

Peter the Great (r. 1682–1725) seeking to make Russia a major military power, reorganized the country's political and economic structures. His reign saw Russia enter fully into European power politics. [The Apotheosis of Tsar Peter the Great 1682–1725 by unknown artist, 1710. Historical Museum, Moscow./E.T. Archive]

Successful and Unsuccessful Paths to Power (1686–1740)

The Maritime Powers
Spain
The Netherlands
France After Louis XIV
Great Britain: The Age of Walpole

Central and Eastern Europe
Sweden: The Ambitions of Charles XII
The Ottoman Empire

Poland: Absence of Strong Central Authority
The Habsburg Empire and the Pragmatic
    Sanction
Prussia and the Hohenzollerns

**The Entry of Russia into the European
Political Arena**
Birth of the Romanov Dynasty
Peter the Great

K E Y   T O P I C S

- The decline of Spain and the Netherlands relative to France and England among the maritime powers
- French aristocratic resistance to the monarchy
- Early eighteenth-century British political stability
- The efforts of the Habsburgs to secure their holdings
- The emergence of Prussia as a major power under the Hohenzollerns
- The efforts of Peter the Great to transform Russia into a powerful centralized nation along Western lines

The late seventeenth and early eighteenth centuries witnessed significant shifts of power and influence among the states of Europe. Nations that had been strong lost their status as significant military and economic units. Other countries that in some cases had figured only marginally in international relations came to the fore. Great Britain, France, Austria, Russia, and Prussia emerged during this period as the powers that would dominate Europe until at least World War I. Their political and economic dominance occurred at the expense of Spain, the United Netherlands, Poland, Sweden, and the Ottoman Empire. Equally essential to their rise was the weakness of the Holy Roman Empire after the Treaty of Westphalia (1648), which ended the Thirty Years' War.

The successful competitors for international power were those states that created strong central political authorities. Far-sighted observers in the late seventeenth century already understood that in the future those domains that would become or remain great powers must imitate the political and military organization of Louis XIV's France. Strong monarchy alone could impose unity of purpose on the state. The turmoil of seventeenth-century civil wars and aristocratic revolts had impressed people with the value of a strong monarch as the guarantor of minimum domestic tranquility.

Imitation of French absolutism involved more than belief in a strong monarchy. It usually required building a standing army, organizing an efficient tax structure to support the army, and establishing a bureaucracy to collect the taxes. Moreover, the political classes of the country, especially the nobles, had to be converted to a sense *of duty and loyalty to the central government that was more intense than their loyalty to other competing political and social institutions.*

The waning powers were those that failed to achieve such effective organization. They were unable to employ their political, economic, and human resources to resist external aggression or to overcome the forces of domestic dissolution. Internal and external failures were closely related. If a state did not maintain or establish a central political authority with sufficient power over the nobility, the cities, the guilds, and the church, it could not raise a strong army to defend its borders or its economic interests. More often than not, the key element leading to success or failure was the character, personality, and energy of the monarch.

The Maritime Powers

In western Europe, Britain and France emerged as the dominant powers. This development represented a shift of influence away from Spain and the United Netherlands. Both the latter countries had been strong and important during the sixteenth and seventeenth centuries, but they became politically and militarily marginal during the eighteenth century. Neither, however, disappeared from the map, and both retained considerable economic vitality and influence. The difference was that France and Britain attained so much more power and economic strength.

Spain

Spanish power had depended on the influx of wealth from the Americas and on the capacity of the Spanish monarchs to rule the still largely autonomous provinces of the Iberian Peninsula. The economic life of Spain was never healthy. Except for wool, it had virtually no exports to pay for its imports. Instead of promoting domestic industries, the Spanish government financed imports by using the gold and silver mined in its New World empire. This external source of wealth was uncertain because the treasure fleets from the New World (discussed more fully in Chapter 17) could be and sometimes were captured by pirates or hostile navies.

The political life of Spain was also weak. Within its divisions of Castile, Aragon, Navarre, the Basque provinces, and other districts, the royal government could not operate without the cooperation of strong local nobles and the church. From the defeat of the Armada in 1588 to the Treaty of the Pyrenees in 1659 after Spain's defeat by France, Spain suffered a series of foreign policy reverses that harmed the domestic prestige of the monarchy. Furthermore, between 1665 and 1700, the physically malformed, dull-witted, and sexually impotent Charles II was monarch. Throughout his reign, the provincial estates and the nobility increased their power. After his death, the other powers of Europe fought over who would succeed him in the War of the Spanish Succession (1701–1714).

The Treaty of Utrecht (1713), which ended the war, gave the Spanish crown to Philip V (r. 1700–1746), a grandson of Louis XIV. The new king should have tried to consolidate his internal power and protect Spanish overseas trade. However, his second wife, Elizabeth Farnese, used Spanish power to secure thrones for her two sons in Italy. Such diversions of government resources allowed the nobility and the provinces to continue to assert their privileges against the monarchy. Not until the reign of Charles III (r. 1759–1788) did Spain have a monarch concerned with efficient domestic and imperial administration and internal improvement. By the third quarter of the century, Spain was better governed, but it could no longer compete effectively in great power politics.

The Netherlands

The decline of the United Provinces of the Netherlands occurred wholly within the eighteenth century. After the death of William III of Britain in 1702, the various local provinces successfully prevented the emergence of another strong *stadtholder*. Unified political leadership therefore vanished. During the earlier long wars of the Netherlands with Louis XIV and Britain, naval supremacy had slowly but steadily passed to the British. The fishing industry declined, and the Dutch lost their technological superiority in shipbuilding. Countries between which Dutch ships had once carried goods now traded directly with each other. For example, the British began to use their own vessels in the Baltic traffic with Russia.

Similar stagnation overtook the Dutch domestic industries, such as textile finishing, paper making, and glass blowing. The disunity of the provinces and the absence of vigorous leadership hastened this economic decline and prevented action that might have slowed or halted it.

In the mid-eighteenth century, when this picture of the Amsterdam Exchange was painted, Amsterdam had replaced the cities of Italy and south Germany as the leading banking center of Europe. Amsterdam retained this position until the late eighteenth century. [Museum Boymans-van Beuningen, Rotterdam]

What saved the United Provinces from becoming completely insignificant in European matters was their continued financial dominance. Well past the middle of the century, their banks continued to provide loans and financing for European trade.

France After Louis XIV

Despite its military reverses in the War of the Spanish Succession, France remained a great power. It was less strong in 1715 than in 1680, but it still possessed the largest European population, an advanced if troubled economy, and the administrative structure bequeathed it by Louis XIV. Moreover, even if France and its resources had been drained by the last of Louis's wars, the other major states of Europe were similarly debilitated. What France required was economic recovery and consolidation, wiser political leadership, and a less ambitious foreign policy. It did enjoy a period of recovery, but its leadership was at best indifferent. Louis XIV was succeeded by his five-year-old great-grandson Louis XV (r. 1715–1774). The young boy's uncle, the duke of Orléans, became regent and remained so until his death in 1720. The regency, marked by financial and moral scandals, further undermined the faltering prestige of the monarchy.

The impending collapse of John Law's bank triggered a financial panic throughout France. Desperate investors, such as those shown here in the city of Rennes, sought to exchange their paper currency for gold and silver before the bank's supply of precious metals was exhausted. [Musée de Bretagne, Rennes]

JOHN LAW AND THE MISSISSIPPI BUBBLE   The duke of Orléans was a gambler, and for a time he turned over the financial management of the kingdom to John Law (1671–1729), a Scottish mathematician and fellow gambler. Law believed that an increase in the paper-money supply would stimulate France's economic recovery. With the permission of the regent, he established a bank in Paris that issued paper money. Law then organized a monopoly, called the Mississippi Company, on trading privileges with the French colony of Louisiana in North America.

The Mississippi Company also took over the management of the French national debt. The company issued shares of its own stock in exchange for government bonds, which had fallen sharply in value. To redeem large quantities of bonds, Law encouraged speculation in Mississippi Company stock. In 1719 the price of the stock rose handsomely. Smart investors, however, took their profits by selling their stock in exchange for paper money from Law's bank, which they then sought to exchange for gold. The bank, however, lacked enough gold to redeem all the paper money brought to it.

In February 1720, all gold payments were halted in France. Soon thereafter Law himself fled the country. The Mississippi Bubble, as the affair was called, had burst. The fiasco brought disgrace on the government that had sponsored Law. The Mississippi Company was later reorganized and functioned profitably, but fear of paper money and speculation marked French economic life for decades.

RENEWED AUTHORITY OF THE *PARLEMENTS* The duke of Orléans made a second decision that also lessened the power of the monarchy. He attempted to draw the French nobility once again into the decision-making processes of the government. Louis XIV had filled his ministries and bureaucracies with persons from nonnoble families. The regent, under pressure from the nobility, tried to restore a balance. He set up a system of councils on which nobles were to serve along with bureaucrats. The years of idle noble domestication at Versailles, however, had worked too well, and the nobility seemed to lack both the talent and the desire to govern. The experiment failed.

Despite this failure, the great French nobles did not surrender their ancient ambition to assert their rights, privileges, and local influence over those of the monarchy. The chief feature of eighteenth-century French political life was the attempt of the nobility to use its authority to limit the power of the monarchy. The most effective instrument in this process was the *parlements*, or courts dominated by the nobility.

The French *parlements* were different from the English Parliament. These French courts, the most important of which was the *Parlement* of Paris, could not legislate. Rather, they had the power to recognize or not to recognize the legality of an act or law promulgated by the monarch. By long tradition their formal approval had been required to make a royal law valid. Louis XIV had often restricted stubborn, uncooperative *parlements*. In another major political blunder, however, the duke of Orléans had formally approved the full reinstitution of the *parlements'* power to allow or disallow laws. Thereafter the growing financial and moral weakness of the monarchy allowed these aristocratic judicial institutions to reassert their authority. This situation meant that until the revolution in 1789 the *parlements* became natural centers for aristocratic resistance to royal authority.

ADMINISTRATION OF CARDINAL FLEURY In 1726 Cardinal Fleury (1653–1743) became the chief minister of the French court. He was the last of the great clerics who loyally and effectively served the French monarchy. Like his seventeenth-century pre-

Cardinal Fleury (1653–1743) was the tutor and chief minister of Louis XV from 1726 to 1743. Fleury gave France a period of peace and prosperity, but was unable to solve the state's long-term financial problems. This portrait is by Hyacinthe Rigaud

decessors, the cardinals Richelieu and Mazarin, Fleury was a realist. He understood the political ambition and incapacity of the nobility and worked quietly to block their undue influence. He was also aware of the precarious financial situation of the royal treasury.

The cardinal, who was seventy-three years old when he came to office, was determined to give the country a period of peace. He surrounded himself with able assistants who tried to solve France's financial problems. Part of the national debt was repudiated. New industries enjoying special privileges were established, and roads and bridges built. On the whole the nation prospered, but Fleury could never draw from the nobles or the church sufficient tax revenues to put the state on a stable financial footing.

Fleury died in 1743, having unsuccessfully attempted to prevent France from intervening in the

Madame de Pompadour (1721–1764) was the mistress of Louis XV. She exercised considerable political influence at the court and was a notable patron of artists, craftspeople, and writers. This 1763 portrait is by Hubert Drouais (1727–1775) [H. Roger Viollet]

war then raging between Austria and Prussia. The cost of this intervention was to undo all his financial pruning and planning.

Another failure must also be credited to this elderly cleric. Despite his best efforts, he had not trained Louis XV to become an effective monarch. Louis XV possessed most of the vices and almost none of the virtues of his great-grandfather Louis XIV. He wanted to hold on to absolute power but was unwilling to work the long hours required. He did not choose many wise advisers after Fleury. He was tossed about by the gossip and intrigues of the court. His personal life was scandalous. Louis XV was not an evil person but a mediocre one. And in a monarch, mediocrity was unfortunately often a greater fault than vice.

Despite this political drift, France remained a great power. France's army at mid-century was still the largest and strongest military force on the Continent. Its commerce and production expanded. Its colonies produced wealth and spurred domestic industries. Its cities grew and prospered. The wealth of the nation waxed as the absolutism of the monarchy waned. France did not lack sources of power and strength, but the political leadership could not organize, direct, or inspire its people.

Great Britain: The Age of Walpole

In 1713 Britain had emerged as a victor over Louis XIV, but the nation required a period of recovery. As an institution, the British monarchy was not in the degraded state of the French monarchy, yet its stability was not certain.

THE HANOVERIAN DYNASTY   In 1714 the Hanoverian dynasty, as designated by the Act of Settlement (1701), came to the throne. Almost immediately, George I (r. 1714–1727) faced a challenge to his new title. The Stuart pretender James Edward (1688–1766), the son of James II, landed in Scotland in December 1715. His forces marched southward but met defeat less than two months later. Although militarily successful against the pretender, the new dynasty and its supporters saw the need for consolidation.

WHIGS AND TORIES   During the seventeenth century, England had been one of the most politically restive countries in Europe. The closing years of Queen Anne's reign (1702–1714) had seen sharp clashes between the political factions of Whigs and Tories over whether to end the war with France. The Tories had urged a rapid peace settlement and after 1710 had opened negotiations with France. During the same period, the Whigs were seeking favor from the elector of Hanover, the future George I, who would soon be their monarch. His concern for his domains in Hanover made him unsympathetic to the Tory peace policy. In the final months of Anne's reign, some Tories, fearing that they would lose power under the waiting Hanoverian dynasty, opened channels of communication with the Stuart pretender; and a few even rallied to his cause.

Under these circumstances, George I, on his arrival in Britain, clearly favored the Whigs. Previously the differences between the Whigs and the Tories had been vaguely related to principle. The Tories emphasized a strong monarchy, low taxes for landowners, and firm support of the Anglican Church. The Whigs supported monarchy but wanted Parliament to retain final sovereignty. They favored urban commercial interests as well as the prosperity of the landowners. They encouraged a policy of religious toleration toward the Protestant nonconformists in England. Socially both groups supported the status quo.

Neither group was organized like a modern political party. Outside Parliament, each party consisted of political networks based on local connections and economic influence. Each group acknowledged a few national spokespeople, who articulated positions and principles. After the Hanoverian accession and the eventual Whig success in achieving the firm confidence of George I, the chief difference for

almost forty years between the Whigs and the Tories was that one group had access to public office and patronage and the other did not. This early Hanoverian proscription of Tories from public life was one of the most prominent features of the age.

THE LEADERSHIP OF ROBERT WALPOLE   The political situation after 1715 remained in flux, until Robert Walpole (1676–1745) took over the helm of government. Walpole had been active in the House of Commons since the reign of Queen Anne and had been a cabinet minister. What gave him special prominence under the new dynasty was a British financial scandal similar to the French Mississippi Bubble.

Management of the British national debt had been assigned to the South Sea Company, which exchanged government bonds for company stock. As in the French case, the price of the stock soared,

Sir Robert Walpole (1676–1745), far left, is shown talking with the Speaker of the House of Commons. Walpole, who dominated British political life from 1721 to 1742, is considered the first prime minister of Britain. [Mansell Collection]

Lady Mary Wortley Montagu Advises Her Husband on Election to Parliament

In this letter of 1714, Lady Mary Wortley Montagu discussed with her husband the various paths that he might follow to gain election to the British House of Commons. Note her emphasis on knowing the right people and on having large amounts of money to spend on voters. Eventually, her husband was elected to Parliament in a borough that was controlled through government patronage.

✦ *What are the various ways in which candidates and their supporters used money to campaign? What role did friendships play in the campaigning? How important do the political ideas or positions of the candidates seem to be? Women could not vote in eighteenth-century parliamentary elections. Is there some other influence they exert?*

You seem not to have received my letters, or not to have understood them: you had been chose undoubtedly at York, if you had declared in time; but there is not any gentleman or tradesman disengaged at this time; they are treating every night. Lord Carlisle and the Thompsons have given their interest to Mr. Jenkins. I agree with you of the necessity of your standing this Parliament, which, perhaps, may be more considerable than any that are to follow it; but, as you proceed, 'tis my opinion, you will spend your money and not be chose. I believe there is hardly a borough unengaged. I expect every letter should tell me you are sure of some place; and, as far as I can perceive you are sure of none. As it has been managed, perhaps it will be the best way to deposit a certain sum in some friend's hands, and buy some little Cornish borough: it would, undoubtedly, look better to be chose for a considerable town; but I take it to be now too late. If you have any thoughts of Newark, it will be absolutely necessary for you to enquire after Lord Lexington's interest; and your best way to apply yourself to Lord Holdernesse, who is both a Whig and an honest man. He is now in town, and you may enquire of him if Brigadier Sutton stands there; and if not, try to engage him for you. Lord Lexington is so ill at the Bath, that it is a doubt if he will live 'till the elections; and if he dies, one of his heiresses, and the whole interest of his estate, will probably fall on Lord Holdernesse.

'Tis a surprize to me, that you cannot make sure of some borough, when a number of your friends bring in so many Parliament-men without trouble or expense. 'Tis too late to mention it now, but you might have applied to Lady Winchester, as Sir Joseph Jekyl did last year, and by her interest the Duke of Bolton brought him in for nothing; I am sure she would be more zealous to serve me, than Lady Jekyl.

Lord Wharncliffe, ed., Letters and Works of Lady Mary Wortley Montagu, 3rd ed., vol. 1 (London, 1861), p. 211.

only to crash in 1720 when prudent investors sold their holdings and took their speculative profits. Parliament intervened and, under Walpole's leadership, adopted measures to honor the national debt. To most contemporaries, Walpole had saved the financial integrity of the country and had thus proved himself a person of immense administrative capacity and political ability.

George I gave Walpole his full confidence. For this reason Walpole has often been regarded as the first prime minister of Great Britain and the originator of the cabinet system of government. Walpole generally demanded that all the ministers in the cabinet agree on policy, but he could not prevent frequent public differences among them. Unlike a modern English prime minister, he was not chosen by the majority of the House of Commons. The real sources of his power were the personal support of the king, George I and later George II (r. 1727–1760), his ability to handle the House of Commons, and his iron-fisted control of government patronage. To oppose Walpole meant the almost certain loss of government patronage for oneself, one's family, or one's friends. Through the skillful use of patronage, Walpole bought support for himself and his policies from people who wanted to receive jobs, appointments, favors, and government contracts. Such corruption supplied the glue of political loyalty.

Walpole's favorite slogan was *"Quieta non movere"* (roughly, "Let sleeping dogs lie"). To that end, he pursued peace abroad and supported the status quo at home. In this regard he much resembled Cardinal Fleury.

Lady Mary Wortley Montagu (1689–1762) was a famous writer of letters and an extremely well-traveled woman of the eighteenth century. As the previous document suggests, she was also a shrewd and toughminded political advisor to her husband. [National Portrait Gallery, London]

This series of four Hogarth etchings satirizes the notoriously corrupt English electoral system. Hogarth shows the voters going to the polls after having been bribed and intoxicated with free gin. (Voting was then in public. The secret ballot was not introduced in England until 1872.) The fourth etching, "Chairing the Member," shows the triumphal procession of the victorious candidate, which is clearly turning into a brawl. [Hogarth, "Election". The Metropolitan Museum of Art, Harris Brisbane Dick Fund, 1932. Acc. #32.35.(212).]

[Hogarth, "Canvassing for Votes". The Metropolitan Museum of Art, Harris Brisbane Dick Fund, 1932. Acc.]

[Hogarth, "Election Scene". The Metropolitan Museum of Art, Harris Brisbane Dick Fund, 1932. Acc. #91.1.75.]

[Hogarth, "Chairing the Members". The Metropolitan Museum of Art, Harris Brisbane Dick Fund, 1932. Acc. #32.35(214).]

THE STRUCTURE OF PARLIAMENT   The structure of the eighteenth-century British House of Commons aided Walpole in his pacific policies. It was neither a democratic nor a representative body. Each of the counties into which Britain was divided elected two members. But if the more powerful landed families in a county agreed on the candidates, there was no contest. Most members, however, were elected from a variety of units called boroughs. A few boroughs were large enough for elections to be relatively democratic, but most had few electors. For example, a local municipal corporation or council of only a dozen members might have the right to elect a member of Parliament. In Old Sarum, one of the most famous corrupt, or "rotten," boroughs, the Pitt family simply bought up those pieces of property to which a vote was attached and thus in effect owned a seat in the House of Commons. Through proper electoral management, which involved favors to the electors, the House of Commons could be controlled.

The structure of Parliament and the manner in which the House of Commons was elected meant that the owners of property, especially wealthy nobles, dominated the government of England. They did not pretend to represent people and districts or to be responsive to what would later be called public opinion. They regarded themselves as representing various economic and social interests, such as the West Indian interest, the merchant interest, or the landed interest. These owners of property were suspicious of an administrative bureaucracy controlled by the crown or its ministers. To diminish royal influence, they or their agents served as local government administrators, judges, militia commanders, and tax collectors. In this sense, the British nobility and large landowners actually did govern the nation. And because they regarded the Parliament as the political sovereign, there was no absence of central political authority and direction. Consequently, the supremacy of Parliament gave Britain the unity that absolute monarchy provided elsewhere in Europe.

These parliamentary structures also helped to strengthen the financial position of the British government. The British monarch could not raise taxes the way his continental counterparts could, but the British government consisting of the monarch and Parliament could and did raise vast sums of tax revenue and loans to wage war throughout the eighteenth century. All Britons paid

France and Great Britain in the Early Eighteenth Century	
1713	Treaty of Utrecht ends the War of the Spanish Succession
1714	George I becomes king of Great Britain and establishes the Hanoverian dynasty
1715	Louis XV becomes King of France
1715–1720	Regency of the duke of Orléans in France
1720	Mississippi Bubble bursts in France and South Sea Bubble bursts in Great Britain
1720–1742	Robert Walpole dominates British politics
1726–1743	Cardinal Fleury serves as Louis XV's chief minister
1727	George II becomes king of Great Britain
1733	Excise tax crisis in Britain

taxes. There were virtually no exemptions. The British credit market was secure through the regulation of the Bank of England, founded in 1693. This strong system of finance and tax collection was one of the cornerstones of eighteenth-century British power.

FREEDOM OF POLITICAL LIFE   British political life was genuinely more free than that on the Continent. There were real limits on the power of Robert Walpole. Parliament could not wholly ignore popular political pressure. Even with the extensive use of patronage, many members of Parliament maintained independent views. Newspapers and public debate flourished. There was freedom of speech and association. There was no large standing army. Those Tories barred from political office and the Whig enemies of Walpole could and did openly oppose his policies—which would have been impossible on the Continent.

For example, in 1733 Walpole presented to the House of Commons a scheme to expand the scope of the excise tax, a tax that resembled a modern sales tax. The outcry in the press, on the public platform, and in the streets was so great that he eventually withdrew the measure. What the British regarded as their traditional political rights raised a real and potent barrier to the power of the government. Again in 1739 the public outcry over the alleged Spanish treatment of British merchants in the Caribbean pushed Britain into a war that Walpole opposed and deplored.

Walpole's ascendancy, which lasted until 1742, did little to raise the level of British political morality, but it brought a kind of stability that Britain had not enjoyed for a century. Its foreign trade grew steadily and spread from New England to India. Agriculture became more productive. All forms of economic enterprise seemed to prosper. The navy became stronger. As a result of this political stability and economic growth, Great Britain became a European power of the first order and stood at the beginning of its era as a world power. Its government and economy during the next generation became a model for all progressive Europeans.

Central and Eastern Europe

The major factors in the shift of political influence among the maritime nations were naval strength, economic progress, foreign trade, and sound domestic administration. The conflicts among them occurred less in Europe than on the high seas and in their overseas empires. These nations existed in well-defined geographical areas with established borders. Their populations generally accepted the authority of the central government.

Central and eastern Europe were different. Except for the Baltic ports, the economy was agrarian. There were fewer cities and many more large estates populated by serfs. The states in this region did not possess overseas empires. Changes in the power structure normally involved changes in borders or, at least, in which prince ruled a particular area. Military conflicts took place at home rather than overseas.

The political structure of this region, which lay largely east of the Elbe River, was very "soft." The almost constant warfare of the seventeenth century had led to a habit of temporary and shifting political loyalties. The princes and aristocracies of small states and principalities were unwilling to subordinate themselves to a central monarchical authority. Consequently, the political life of the region and the kind of state that emerged there were different from those of western Europe.

Beginning in the last half of the seventeenth century, eastern and central Europe began to assume the political and social contours that would characterize it for the next two centuries. After the Peace of Westphalia, the Austrian Habsburgs rec-

Charles XII of Sweden (r. 1697–1718) led his nation into a number of disastrous wars. These conflicts exhausted the country's resources, preventing Sweden from playing a major role in later eighteenth-century power politics. [H. Roger Viollet]

ognized the basic weakness of the position of Holy Roman Emperor and began to consolidate their power outside Germany. At the same time, Prussia emerged as a factor in North German politics and as a major challenger to Habsburg domination of Germany. Most important, Russia at the opening of the eighteenth century became a military power of the first order. These three states (Austria, Prussia, and Russia) achieved their new status largely as a result of the political decay or military defeat of Sweden, Poland, and the Ottoman Empire.

Sweden: The Ambitions of Charles XII

Under Gustavus Adolphus II (r. 1611–1632), Sweden had played an important role as a Protestant combatant in the Thirty Years' War. During the rest of the seventeenth century, Sweden had consolidated its control of the Baltic, thus preventing Russian possession of a Baltic port and permitting Polish and German access to the sea only on Swedish terms. The Swedes also possessed one of the better armies in Europe. Sweden's economy, however, based primarily on the export of iron, was not strong enough to ensure continued political success.

In 1697 Charles XII (r. 1697–1718) came to the throne. He was headstrong, to say the least, and perhaps insane. In 1700 Russia began a drive to the west against Swedish territory. The Russian goal was a foothold on the Baltic. In the resulting Great Northern War (1700–1721), Charles XII led a vigorous and often brilliant campaign, but one that eventually resulted in the defeat of Sweden. In 1700 he defeated the Russians at the Battle of Narva, but then he turned south to invade Poland. The conflict dragged on, and the Russians were able to strengthen their forces.

In 1708 the Swedish monarch began a major invasion of Russia but became bogged down in the harsh Russian winter. The next year his army was decisively defeated at the Battle of Poltava. Thereafter the Swedes could maintain only a holding action against their enemies. Charles himself sought refuge in Turkey and did not return to Sweden until 1714. He was killed four years later while fighting the Norwegians.

The Great Northern War came to a close in 1721. Sweden had exhausted its military and economic resources and had lost its monopoly on the Baltic coast. Russia had conquered a large section of the eastern Baltic, and Prussia had gained a part of Pomerania. Internally, after the death of Charles XII, the Swedish nobles were determined to reassert their power over the monarchy. They did so but then quarreled among themselves. Sweden played a very minor role in European affairs thereafter.

The Ottoman Empire

At the southeastern extreme of Europe, the Ottoman Empire was a barrier to the territorial ambitions of the Austrian Habsburgs, Poland, and Russia. The empire in the late seventeenth century still controlled most of the Balkan Peninsula and the entire coastline of the Black Sea. In theory the empire existed to enhance the spread of Islam. Its population, however, was exceedingly diverse both ethnically and religiously. The empire ruled these people not on a territorial but on a religious basis. That is, it created units, called *millets*, that included all persons of a particular religious faith. Various laws and regulations applied to the per-

sons who belonged to a particular millet rather than to a particular administrative territory. Non-Islamic persons in the empire were known as *zimmis*. They could practice their religion, but they were second class citizens who could not rise in the service of the empire or profit much from its successes. This mode of government maintained the self-identity of these various peoples and allowed for little religious integration or interaction.

From the fifteenth century onward, the Ottoman Empire had tried to push further westward in Europe. The empire made its greatest military invasion into Europe in 1683, when it unsuccessfully besieged Vienna. In addition, many Christians in the Balkans and on the Aegean islands had converted to Islam. Many of these people had earlier been forced to convert to Roman Catholicism by the Venetians and welcomed the Turks and their faith as vehicles for political liberation. Much of the Islamic presence in the Balkans today dates to these conversions.

By the last third of the seventeenth century, however, the Ottomans had overextended themselves politically, economically, and militarily. From the mid-sixteenth century, the Ottoman rulers spent so much time at war that they could not attend to meetings of governmental bodies in Constantinople. As time passed, political groups in the capital resisted any substantial strengthening of the central government or of the role of the sultan. Rivalries for power among army leaders and nobles, as well as their flagrant efforts to enrich themselves, weakened the effectiveness of the government. In the outer provinces, such as Transylvania, Wallachia, and Moldavia (all parts of modern Romania), the empire depended on the goodwill of local rulers, who paid tribute but never submitted themselves fully to the imperial power. The empire's economy was weak, and its exports were primarily raw materials. Moreover, the actual conduct of most of its trade had been turned over to representatives of other nations.

By the early eighteenth century, the weakness of the Ottoman Empire meant that a political vacuum that would grow during the next two centuries had come into existence on the southeastern perimeter of Europe. The various European powers who had created strong armies and bureaucracies would begin to probe and eventually dismember the Ottoman Empire. In 1699 the Turks

John III Sobieski (1624–1696) was elected king of Poland in 1764. Sobieski led the Polish Army in repulsing the Turkish siege of Vienna in 1683, an event discussed in one of the documents in this chapter. Despite this victory Sobieski failed to establish a strong central monarchy in Poland. [Erich Lessing/Art Resource, N.Y.]

concluded a treaty with their longtime Habsburg enemy and surrendered all pretensions of control over and consequent receipt of revenues from Hungary, Transylvania, Croatia, and Slavonia. From this time onward, Russia also attempted to extend its territory and influence at the expense of the empire. By the early nineteenth century, many of the peoples who lived in the Balkans and around the Black Sea would seek to create their own national states. The retreat and decay of the Ottoman Empire and the scramble of other states and regional peoples to assume control of southeastern Europe would cause political and ethnic turmoil there from the eighteenth century to our own day.

Poland: Absence of Strong Central Authority

In no other part of Europe was the failure to maintain a competitive political position so complete as in Poland. In 1683 King John III Sobieski (r. 1674–1696) had led a Polish army to rescue Vienna from the Turkish siege. Following that spectacular effort, however, Poland became a byword for the dangers of aristocratic independence. In Poland as nowhere else on the Continent, the nobility became the single most powerful political factor in the country. Unlike the British nobility and landowners, the Polish nobility would not even submit to a central authority of their own making. There was

The King of Poland Frees Vienna from the Turks

In 1683 the Ottoman Empire had laid siege to Vienna. The Habsburg monarchy found itself under enormous military pressure. The military forces of John III Sobieski, the king of Poland, rescued the city and repulsed the last great Turkish advance upon central Europe.

✦ *What role did religious sentiments and prejudice play in this description? In that regard, how was the battle portrayed as a conflict between two different religions and two different cultures? How is the ruler of Austria portrayed so as to make the king of Poland the hero of the account? What factors appear to have led the leader of the Ottoman forces to retreat? What were the physical fruits of battle for the victors?*

The Victory which the King of Poland hath obtained over the Infidels, is so great and so compleat that past Ages can scarce parallel the fame; and perhaps future Ages will never see any thing like it. . . . On the one hand we see Vienna besieged by three hundred thousand Turks; reduced to the last extremity; its Outworks taken; the Enemy fixed to the Body of the Place; . . . : We see an Emperor [the Habsburg ruler] chased from his Capital; retired to a Corner of his Dominions; all his Country at the mercy of the Tartars, who have filled the Camp with an infinite Number of unfortunate Slaves that had been forcibly carried away out of Austria. On the other hand, we see the King of Poland, who goes out of his Kingdom, with part of his Army, and hastens to succour his . . . Allies, . . . to march against the Enemies of the Christian Religion willing to act in Person on this Occasion, as a true Buckler of Religion. . . .

The Battle was fought on the 12th, it lasted 14 or 15 Hours; the slaughter was horrible, and the loss of the Turks inestimable, for they left the Field of Battle, besides the Dead and Prisoners, all their Canon, Equipage, Tents and infinite Riches that they had been six Years gathering together throughout the whole Ottoman Empire. . . .

The Night was spent in slaughter, and the unhappy Remnant of this Army saved their Lives by flight, having abandoned all to the Victors; even an infinite Number of Waggons, loaden with Ammunition, and some Field pieces, that designed to have carried with them; and which were found the next Day upon the Road they had taken; which makes us suspect that they'll not be able to rally again, . . .

The King [of Poland] understood afterwards by Deserters, who come every hour in Troops to surrender themselves to him, as well as the Renegadoes, that the Visier [the Turkish leader], seeing the defeat of the Army, called his Sons to him, embraced them, bitterly bewailed their Misfortune, and turned towards the Han of the Tartars [an ally of the Turks], and said, 'And thou, wilt not thou succour me?' To whom the Tartar Prince replied, That he knew the King of Poland by more than one Proof, and that the Visier would be very happy if he could save himself by flight, as having no other way for his Security, and that he was going to show him Example.

The Grand Visier being thus abandoned, took the same way, and retired in Disorder with only one Horse. . . . The Booty that was taken in this Action is infinite and inestimable; The Field of Battle was sowed with Gold Sabres, . . . and such a prodigious Quantity of other things that the Pillage which has already lasted three Days, will scarce be over in a whole Week. . . .

From Polish Manuscripts: or the Secret History of the Reign of John Sobieski, the III of That Name, King of Poland, *trans. by M. Delerac (London: D. Rhodes, 1700), pp. 355–364, as quoted in Alfred J. Bannan and Achilles Edelenyi, eds.,* Documentary History of Eastern Europe *(New York: Twayne Publishers, Inc., 1970), pp. 112–116.*

no effective central authority in the form of either a king or a parliament.

The Polish monarchy was elective, but the deep distrust and divisions among the nobility prevented their electing a king from among themselves. Sobieski was a notable exception. Most of the Polish monarchs were foreigners and were the tools of foreign powers. The Polish nobles did have a central legislative body called the *Sejm*, or Diet. It included only the nobles and specifically excluded representatives from corporate bodies, such as the towns. In the Diet, however, there existed a practice known as the *liberum veto*, whereby the staunch opposition of any single member could require the body to disband. Such opposition was termed "exploding the Diet." This practice was most often the work of a group of dissatisfied nobles rather than of one person. Nonetheless, the requirement of unanimity was a major stumbling block to effective government.

Government as it was developing elsewhere in Europe simply was not tolerated in Poland. Localism reminiscent of the Middle Ages continued to hold sway as the nobles used all their energy to maintain their traditional "Polish liberties." There was no way to collect enough taxes to build up an army. The price of this noble liberty would eventually be the disappearance of Poland from the map of Europe during the latter half of the eighteenth century.

The Habsburg Empire and the Pragmatic Sanction

The close of the Thirty Years' War marked a fundamental turning point in the history of the Austrian Habsburgs. Previously, in alliance with the Spanish branch of the family, they had hoped to dominate all of Germany and to return it to the Catholic fold. They did not achieve either goal, and the decline of Spanish power meant that in future diplomatic relations the Austrian Habsburgs were on their own. The Treaty of Westphalia in 1648 permitted Protestantism within the Holy Roman Empire and also recognized the political autonomy of more than 300 corporate German political entities within the empire. These included large units (such as Saxony, Hanover, Bavaria, and Brandenburg) and scores of small cities, bishoprics, principalities, and petty territories of independent knights.

After 1648 the Habsburgs retained a firm hold on the title of Holy Roman Emperor, but the effectiveness of the title depended less on force of arms than on the cooperation that the emperor could elicit from the various political bodies in the empire. The Diet of the empire sat at Regensburg from 1663 until the empire was dissolved in 1806. The Diet and the emperor generally regulated the daily economic and political life of Germany. The post-Westphalian Holy Roman Empire resembled Poland in its lack of central authority. Unlike its Polish neighbor, however, the Holy Roman Empire was reorganized from within as the Habsburgs attempted to regain their authority. As will be seen shortly, Prussia set out on its course toward European power at the same time.

CONSOLIDATION OF AUSTRIAN POWER   While concentrating on their hereditary Austrian holdings among the German states, the Habsburgs also began to consolidate their power and influence within their other hereditary possessions. (See Map 15–1.) These included, first, the Crown of Saint Wenceslas, encompassing the kingdom of Bohemia (in the modern Czech Republic and Slovakia) and the duchies of Moravia and Silesia and, second, the Crown of Saint Stephen, which included Hungary, Croatia, and Transylvania. In the middle of the seventeenth century, much of Hungary remained occupied by the Turks and was liberated only at the end of the century.

In the early eighteenth century, the family further extended its domains, receiving the former Spanish (thereafter Austrian) Netherlands, Lombardy in northern Italy, and briefly, the kingdom of Naples in southern Italy through the Treaty of Utrecht in 1713. During the eighteenth and nineteenth centuries, the Habsburgs' power and influence in Europe were based primarily on their territories outside Germany.

In the second half of the seventeenth century and later, the Habsburgs faced immense problems in these hereditary territories. In each they ruled by virtue of a different title and had to gain the cooperation of the local nobility. The most difficult province was Hungary, where the Magyar nobility seemed ever ready to rebel. There was almost no common basis for political unity among peoples of such diverse languages, customs, and geography. Even the Habsburg zeal for Roman Catholicism no longer proved a bond for unity as they confronted the equally zealous Calvinism of many of the Magyar nobles. The Habsburgs established various central councils to chart common policies for their

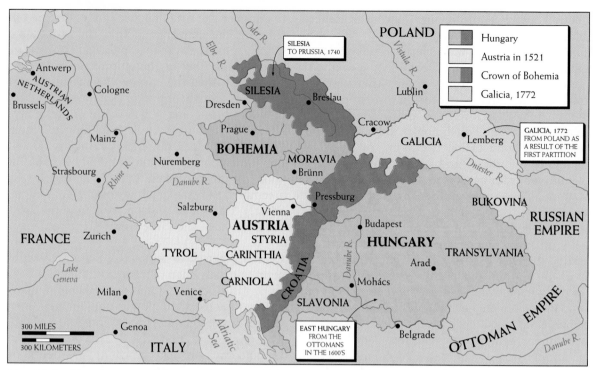

MAP 15–1   THE AUSTRIAN HABSBURG EMPIRE, 1521–1772   *The empire had three main units—Austria, Bohemia, and Hungary. Expansion was mainly eastward: East Hungary from the Ottomans (seventeenth century) and Galicia from Poland (1772). Meantime, Silesia was lost, but the Habsburgs retained German influence as Holy Roman emperors.*

far-flung domains. Virtually all of these bodies dealt with only part of the Habsburgs' holdings. Repeatedly, the Habsburgs had to bargain with nobles in one part of Europe to maintain their position in another.

Despite all these internal difficulties, Leopold I (r. 1657–1705) rallied his domains to resist the advances of the Turks and the aggression of Louis XIV. He achieved Ottoman recognition of his sovereignty over Hungary in 1699 and began the suppression of a long rebellion by his new Magyar subjects that lasted from 1703 to 1711. He also conquered much of the Balkan Peninsula and western Romania. These southeastward extensions allowed the Habsburgs to hope to develop Mediterranean trade through the port of Trieste. The expansion at the cost of the Ottoman Empire also helped them to compensate for their loss of domination over the Holy Roman Empire. Strength in the East gave them greater political leverage in Germany. Leopold I was succeeded by Joseph I (r. 1705–1711), who continued his policies.

THE HABSBURG DYNASTIC PROBLEM   When Charles VI (r. 1711–1740) succeeded Joseph, he had no male heir, and there was only the weakest of precedents for a female ruler of the Habsburg domains. Charles feared that on his death the Austrian Habsburg lands might fall prey to the surrounding powers, as had those of the Spanish Habsburgs in 1700. He was determined to prevent that disaster and to provide his domains with the semblance of legal unity. To those ends, he devoted most of his reign to seeking the approval of his family, the estates of his realms, and the major foreign powers for a document called the Pragmatic Sanction.

This instrument provided the legal basis for a single line of inheritance within the Habsburg dynasty through Charles VI's daughter Maria Theresa (r. 1740–1780). Other members of the Habsburg family recognized her as the rightful heir. The nobles of the various Habsburg domains did likewise after extracting various concessions from Charles. So, when Charles VI died in October 1740, he believed that he had secured legal unity for the Habsburg Empire and a safe succession for his daughter.

Charles VI had indeed established a permanent line of succession and the basis for future legal bonds within the Habsburg holdings. He had failed, however, to protect his daughter from foreign aggression, either through the Pragmatic Sanction or, more important, by leaving her a strong army and a full treasury. Less than two months after his death, the fragility of the foreign agreements became apparent. In December 1740, Frederick II of Prussia invaded the Habsburg province of Silesia. Maria Theresa had to fight to defend her inheritance.

Prussia and the Hohenzollerns

The Habsburg achievement had been to draw together into an uncertain legal unity a collection of domains possessed through separate feudal titles. The achievement of the Hohenzollerns of Brandenburg-Prussia was to acquire a similar collection of titular holdings and then to forge them into a centrally administered unit. Despite the geographical separation of their territories and the paucity of their natural economic resources, they transformed feudal ties and structures into bureaucratic ones. They subordinated every social class and most economic pursuits to the strengthening of the institution that united their far-flung realms: the army. They thus made the term "Prussian" synonymous with administrative rigor and military discipline.

A STATE OF DISCONNECTED TERRITORIES The rise of Prussia occurred within the German power vacuum created after 1648 by the Peace of Westphalia. It is the story of the extraordinary Hohenzollern family, which had ruled the German territory of Brandenburg since 1417. (See Map 15–2.) Through inheritance the family had acquired the duchy of Cleves and the counties of Mark and Ravensburg in 1609, the duchy of East Prussia in 1618, and the duchy of Pomerania in 1637. Except for Pomerania, none of these lands was contiguous with Brandenburg. East Prussia lay inside Poland and outside the authority of the Holy Roman Emperor. All of the territories lacked good natural resources, and many of them were devastated during the Thirty Years' War. At Westphalia the Hohenzollerns lost part of Pomerania to Sweden but were compensated by receiving three more bishoprics and the promise of the archbishopric of Magdeburg when it became vacant, as it did in

1680. By the late seventeenth century, the scattered Hohenzollern holdings represented a block of territory within the Holy Roman Empire second in size only to that of the Habsburgs.

Despite its size, the Hohenzollern conglomerate was weak. The areas were geographically separate, with no mutual sympathy or common concern among them. In each, local noble estates limited the power of the Hohenzollern prince. The various areas were also exposed to foreign aggression.

FREDERICK WILLIAM, THE GREAT ELECTOR The person who began to forge these areas and nobles into a modern state was Frederick William (r. 1640–1688), who became known as the Great Elector (the ruler of Brandenburg was called an elector because he was one of the princes who elected the Holy Roman Emperor). He established himself and his successors as the central uniting power by breaking the local noble estates, organizing a royal bureaucracy, and establishing a strong army.

Between 1655 and 1660, Sweden and Poland engaged in a war that endangered the Great Elector's holdings in Pomerania and East Prussia. Frederick William had neither the military nor the financial resources to confront this threat. In 1655 the Brandenburg estates refused to grant his new taxes; however, he proceeded to collect the required taxes by military force. In 1659 a different grant of taxes, originally made in 1653, elapsed; Frederick William continued to collect them as well as those he had imposed by his own authority. He used the money to build up an army that allowed him to continue to enforce his will without the approval of the nobility. Similar threats and coercion took place against the nobles in his other territories.

There was, however, a political and social trade-off between the elector and his various nobles. These *Junkers*, or German noble landlords, were allowed almost complete control over the serfs on their estates. In exchange for their obedience to the Hohenzollerns, the Junkers received the right to demand obedience from their serfs. Frederick William also tended to choose as the local administrators of the tax structure men who would normally have been members of the noble estates. He thus co-opted potential opponents into his service. The taxes fell most heavily on the backs of the peasants and the urban classes.

As the years passed, sons of Junkers increasingly dominated the army officer corps, and this practice

The Great Elector Welcomes Protestant Refugees from France

The Hohenzollern dynasty of Brandenburg-Prussia pursued a policy of religious toleration. The family itself was Calvinist, whereas most of its subjects were Lutherans. When Louis XIV of France revoked the Edict of Nantes in 1685 (see the document in Chapter 13), Frederick William, the Great Elector, seized the opportunity to invite into his realms French Protestants. As his proclamation indicates, he wanted to attract persons with productive skills who could aid the economic development of his domains.

✦ *In reading this document, do you believe religious or economic concerns more nearly led the Elector of Brandenburg to welcome the French Protestants? What specific privileges did the Elector extend to them? To what extent were these privileges a welcoming measure and to what extent were they inducements to emigrate to Brandenburg? In what kind of economic activity does the elector expect the French refugees to engage?*

We, Friedrich Wilhelm, by Grace of God Margrave of Brandenburg. . . .

Do hereby proclaim and make known to all and sundry that since the cruel persecutions and rigorous ill-treatment in which Our co-religionists of the Evangelical-Reformed faith have for some time past been subjected in the Kingdom of France, have caused many families to remove themselves and to betake themselves out of the said Kingdom into other lands, We now . . . have been moved graciously to offer them through this Edict . . . a secure and free refuge in all Our Lands and Provinces. . . .

Since Our Lands are not only well and amply endowed with all things necessary to support life, but also very well-suited to the reestablishment of all kinds of manufactures and trade and traffic by land and water, We permit, indeed, to those settling therein free choice to establish themselves where it is most convenient for their profession and way of living. . . .

The personal property which they bring with them, including merchandise and other wares, is to be totally exempt from any taxes, customs dues, licenses, or other imposts of any description, and not detained in any way. . . .

As soon as these Our French co-religionists of the Evangelical-Reformed faith have settled in any town or village, they shall be admitted to the domiciliary rights and craft freedoms customary there, gratis and without payments of any fee; and shall be entitled to the benefits, rights, and privileges enjoyed by Our other, native, subjects, residing there. . . .

Not only are those who wish to establish manufacture of cloth, stuffs, hats, or other objects in which they are skilled to enjoy all necessary freedoms, privileges and facilities, but also provision is to be made for them to be assisted and helped as far as possible with money and anything else which they need to realize their intention. . . .

Those who settle in the country and wish to maintain themselves by agriculture are to be given a certain plot of land to bring under cultivation and provided with whatever they need to establish themselves initially. . . .

C. A. Macartney, ed., The Habsburg and Hohenzollern Dynasties in the Seventeenth and Eighteenth Centuries *(New York: Walker, 1970), pp. 270–273.*

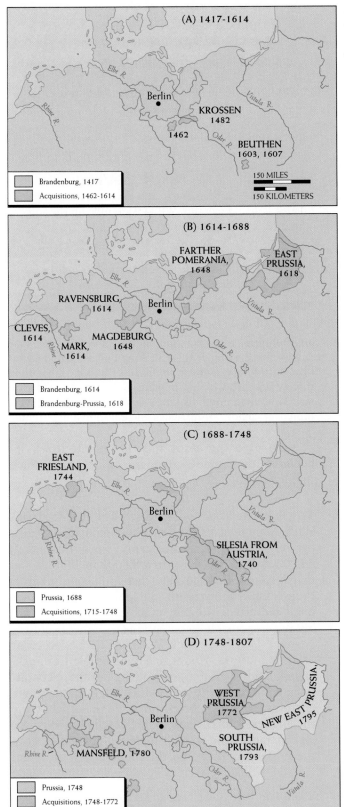

MAP 15–2 EXPANSION OF BRANDENBURG-PRUSSIA
In the seventeenth-century, Brandenburg-Prussia expanded mainly by acquiring dynastic titles in geographically separated lands. In the eighteenth century, it expanded through aggression to the east, seizing Silesia in 1740 and various parts of Poland in 1772, 1793, and 1795.

became even more pronounced during the eighteenth century. All officials and army officers took an oath of loyalty directly to the elector. The army and the elector thus came to embody the otherwise absent unity of the state. The existence of the army made Prussia a valuable potential ally and a state with which other powers needed to curry favor.

FREDERICK WILLIAM I, KING OF PRUSSIA   Yet, even with the considerable accomplishments of the Great Elector, the house of Hohenzollern did not possess a crown. The achievement of a royal title was one of the few state-building accomplishments of Frederick I (r. 1688–1713). This son of the Great Elector was the least "Prussian" of his family during these crucial years. He built palaces, founded Halle University (1694), patronized the arts, and lived luxuriously. In 1701, however, at the outbreak of the War of the Spanish Succession, he put his army at the disposal of the Habsburg Holy Roman Emperor. In exchange for this loyal service, the emperor permitted Frederick to assume the title of "King in Prussia." Thereafter Frederick became Frederick I, and he passed the much-desired royal title to his son Frederick William I in 1713.

Frederick William I (r. 1713–1740) was both the most eccentric and one of the most effective Hohenzollerns. After giving his father a funeral that matched the luxury of his life, Frederick William I immediately imposed strict austerity. Some jobs were abolished, and other salaries lowered. His political aims seem to have been the consolidation of an obedient, compliant bureaucracy and a bigger army. He initiated a policy of *Kabinett* government, which meant that lower officials submitted all relevant documents to him in his office, or *Kabinett*. Then he alone examined the papers, made his decisions, and issued his orders. He thus skirted the influence of ministers and ruled alone.

Frederick William I organized the bureaucracy along military lines. He united all departments under the *General-Ober Finanz-Kriegs-und-Domänen-Direktorium*, more happily known to us as the General Directory. He imposed taxes on the nobility and changed most remaining feudal dues into money payments. He sought to transform feudal and administrative loyalties into a sense of duty to the monarch as a political institution rather than as a person. He once described the perfect royal servant as

Austria and Prussia in the Late Seventeenth and Early Eighteenth Centuries	
1640–1688	Reign of Frederick William, the Great Elector
1657–1705	Leopold I rules Austria and resists the Turkish invasions
1683	Turkish siege of Vienna
1688–1713	Reign of Frederick I of Prussia
1699	Peace treaty between Turks and Habsburgs
1711–1740	Charles VI rules Austria and secures agreement to the Pragmatic Sanction
1713–1740	Frederick William I builds up the military power of Prussia
1740	Maria Theresa succeeds to the Habsburg throne
1740	Frederick II violates the Pragmatic Sanction by invading Silesia

an intelligent, assiduous, and alert person who after God values nothing higher than his king's pleasure and serves him out of love and for the sake of honor rather than money and who in his conduct solely seeks and constantly bears in mind his king's service and interests, who, moreover, abhors all intrigues and emotional deterrents.[1]

Service to the state and the monarch was to become impersonal, mechanical, and, in effect, unquestioning.

THE PRUSSIAN ARMY   The discipline that Frederick William applied to the army was fanatical. During his reign the size of the army grew from about 39,000 in 1713 to more than 80,000 in 1740. It was the third or fourth largest army in Europe, whereas Prussia ranked thirteenth in population. Rather than using recruiters, the king made each canton or local district responsible for supplying a quota of soldiers.

After 1725 Frederick William always wore an officer's uniform. He formed one regiment from the tallest soldiers he could find in Europe. Separate laws applied to the army and to civilians. Laws, customs, and royal attention made the officer corps the highest social class of the state. Military service attracted the sons of Junkers. Thus, the army, the Junker nobility, and the monarchy were forged

[1]Quoted in Hans Rosenberg, *Bureaucracy, Aristocracy, and Autocracy* (Boston: Beacon Press, 1958), p. 93.

into a single political entity. Military priorities and values dominated Prussian government, society, and daily life as in no other state of Europe. It has often been said that whereas other nations possessed armies, the Prussian army possessed its nation.

Although Frederick William I built the best army in Europe, he avoided conflict. He wanted to drill his soldiers but not to order them into battle. Although he terrorized his family and associates and on occasion knocked out teeth with his walking stick, he was not militarily aggressive. The army was for him a symbol of Prussian power and unity, not an instrument to be used for foreign adventures or aggression.

At his death in 1740, he passed to his son Frederick II "the Great" (r. 1740–1786) this superb military machine, but he could not also pass on the wisdom to refrain from using it. Almost immediately on coming to the throne, Frederick II upset the Pragmatic Sanction and invaded Silesia. He thus crystallized the Austrian–Prussian rivalry for control of Germany that would dominate central European affairs for over a century.

Though economically weak and with a small population, Prussia became an important state because it developed a large, well-trained army. Prussian troops were known for their discipline, the result of constant drill and harsh punishment. In this mid-eighteenth-century engraving one soldier is being whipped while another is about to run a gauntlet of other soldiers. [Bildarchiv Preussischer Kulturbesitz]

The Entry of Russia into the European Political Arena

Though ripe with consequences for the future, the rise of Prussia and the new consolidation of the Austrian Habsburg domains seemed to many at the time only another shift in the long-troubled German scene. The emergence of Russia, however, as an active European power was a wholly new factor in European politics. Previously Russia had been considered part of Europe only by courtesy. Geographically and politically it lay on the periphery. Hemmed in by Sweden on the Baltic and by the Ottoman Empire on the Black Sea, the country had no warm-water ports. Its chief outlet to the west was Archangel on the White Sea, which was ice free for only part of the year. There was little trade. What Russia did possess was a vast reserve of largely undeveloped natural and human resources.

Birth of the Romanov Dynasty

The reign of Ivan the Terrible, which had begun so well and closed so frighteningly, was followed by anarchy and civil war known as the "Time of Troubles." In 1613, hoping to restore stability, an assembly of nobles elected as tsar a seventeen-year-old boy named Michael Romanov (r. 1613–1654). Thus began the dynasty that despite palace revolutions, military conspiracies, assassinations, and family strife ruled Russia until 1917.

Michael Romanov and his two successors, Alexis I (r. 1654–1676) and Theodore III (r. 1676–1682), brought stability and some bureaucratic centralization to Russia. The country remained, however, weak and impoverished. The bureaucracy after years of turmoil was still largely controlled by the *boyars*, the old nobility. This administrative apparatus could barely suppress a revolt of peasants and Cossacks (horsemen who lived on the steppe frontier) under Stepan Razin in 1670–1671. Furthermore, the government and the tsars faced the danger of mutiny from the *streltsy*, or guards of the Moscow garrison.

Peter the Great

In 1682 another boy—ten years old at the time—ascended the fragile Russian throne as co-ruler with his half brother. His name was Peter (r. 1682–1725), and Russia would never be the same after him. He and the ill Ivan V had come to power on the shoulders of the *streltsy*, who expected to be rewarded for their support. Much violence and bloodshed had surrounded the disputed succession. Matters became even more confused when the boys' sister, Sophia, was named regent. Peter's followers overthrew her in 1689. From that date onward, Peter ruled personally, although in theory he shared the crown until Ivan died in 1696. The dangers and turmoil of his youth convinced Peter of two things. First, the power of the tsar must be made secure from the jealousy of the *boyars* and the greed of the *streltsy*. Second, the military power of Russia must be increased. In that respect he resembled Louis XIV of France, who had experienced the turmoil of the *Fronde* during his youth and resolved to establish a strong monarchy.

Western Europe, particularly its military resources, fascinated Peter I, who became known as Peter the Great. He was an imitator of the first

---

Rise of Russian Power

1533–1584	Reign of Ivan the Terrible
1584–1613	"Time of Troubles"
1613	Michael Romanov becomes tsar
1682	Peter the Great, age ten, becomes tsar
1689	Peter assumes personal rule
1696	Russia captures Azov on the Black Sea from the Turks
1697	European tour of Peter the Great
1698	Peter returns to Russia to put down the revolt of the *streltsy*
1700	The Great Northern War opens between Russia and Sweden; Russia defeated at Narva by Swedish Army of Charles XII
1703	Saint Petersburg founded
1709	Russia defeats Sweden at the Battle of Poltava
1718	Charles XII of Sweden dies
1718	Son of Peter the Great dies in prison under mysterious circumstances
1721	Peace of Nystad ends the Great Northern War
1721	Peter establishes a synod for the Russian church
1722	Peter issues the Table of Ranks
1725	Peter dies leaving an uncertain succession

After Peter the Great of Russia returned from his journey to western Europe, he personally cut off the traditional and highly prized long sleeves and beards of the Russian nobles. His action symbolized his desire to see Russia become more powerful and more modern. [The Granger Collection]

order. The products and workers from the West who had filtered into Russia impressed and intrigued him. In 1697 he made a famous visit in transparent disguise to western Europe. There he dined and talked with the great and the powerful, who considered this almost seven-foot-tall ruler both crude and rude. His happiest moments on the trip were spent inspecting shipyards, docks, and the manufacture of military hardware.

Peter returned to Moscow determined to copy what he had seen abroad, for he knew that warfare would be necessary to make Russia a great power. The tsar's drive toward westernization, though unsystematic, had four general goals: taming the *boyars* and the *streltsy*, achieving secular control of the church, reorganizing the internal administration, and developing the economy. Peter pursued each of these goals ruthlessly. His effort was unprecedented in Russian history in both its intensity and scope.

TAMING THE *BOYARS* AND *STRELTSY* Peter made a sustained attack on the *boyars*. In 1698, immediately on his return from abroad, he personally shaved the long beards of the court *boyars* and sheared off the customary long, hand-covering sleeves of their shirts and coats, which had made them the butt of jokes throughout Europe. More important, he demanded that the nobles serve his state.

In 1722 Peter published a Table of Ranks that equated a person's social position and privileges with his rank in the bureaucracy or the army rather than with his position in the nobility. Peter thus intended to make the social standing of individual *boyars* a function of their willingness to

Peter the Great Establishes Building Requirements in Saint Petersburg

By constructing Saint Petersburg on the Gulf of Finland, Peter the Great tried to consolidate his military efforts in the Great Northern War. The city was to provide Russia with a permanent outlet to the West and to be the site of its new capital. The construction of this city consequently served symbolic political ends as well as military and economic ones. In this document, Peter explains how he expected the city to be constructed.

✦ *Why might Peter have been so concerned that the work on the city progress rapidly? What are the difficulties in construction in Russia that this document reveals? What do those difficulties tell you about Russia's society and its economic resources? Why might Peter have been concerned that only houses face on the streets of the new city.*

1. On the City Island and the Admiralty Island in Saint Petersburg, as likewise on the banks of the greater Neva and its more important arms, wood buildings are forbidden, only adobe houses being allowed. The two above-mentioned islands and the embankments excepted, wood may be used for buildings, the plans to be obtained from the architect. . . . The roofs are to be covered either with two thicknesses of turf laid on rafters with cross-ribs (not on laths or boards), or with tiles. No other roof covering is allowed under penalty of severe fines. The streets should be bordered directly by the houses, not with fences or stables.

2. The most illustrious and mighty Peter the Great, Emperor and Autocrat of all Russia, has commanded his imperial decree to be proclaimed to people of all ranks. Whereas stone construction here is advancing very slowly, it being difficult to obtain stonemasons and other artisans of this craft even for good pay; for this reason all stone buildings of any description are forbidden in the whole state for a few years, until construction has suffi-ciently progressed here, under penalty of confiscation of the offender's property and exile. This decree is to be announced in all the cities and districts of the Saint Petersburg province, except this city, so that none may plead ignorance as an excuse.

3. The following is ordered: no building shall be undertaken in Petersburg on the grounds of houses, between neighboring back yards, until all the main and side streets are entirely built up. However, if after this any person needs more buildings, he may build on his grounds, along the neighbor's lot. No stables or barns may be built facing the street, but only inside the grounds. Along the streets and side streets all the space must be filled by residences, as ordered. In the locations where, as ordered by previous decrees, wooden houses may be built, they must be made of squared logs. If the logs are used as they are, the walls must be faced with boards and coated with red, or painted to look like brick.

From Marthe Blinoff, ed., Life and Thought in Old Russia, *(University Park: The Pennsylvania State University Press, 1961), pp. 16–17.*

Peter the Great built Saint Petersburg on the Gulf of Finland to provide Russia with better contact with western Europe. He moved Russia's capital there from Moscow in 1703. This is an eighteenth-century view of the city. [John R. Freeman]

serve the central state. Unlike Prussian Junkers, however, the Russian nobility never became perfectly loyal to the state. They repeatedly sought to reassert their independence and their control of the Russian imperial court and to bargain with later tsars over local authority and the nobles' dominance of the serfs.

The *streltsy* fared less well than the *boyars*. In 1698 they had rebelled while Peter was on his European tour. On his return, he brutally suppressed the revolt. There were private tortures and public executions, in which Peter's own ministers took part. Almost 1,200 of the rebels were put to death, and their corpses remained on public display to discourage future disloyalty.

ACHIEVING SECULAR CONTROL OF THE CHURCH Peter dealt with the potential independence of the Russian Orthodox Church with similar ruthlessness. Here again, he had to confront a problem that had arisen in the turbulent decades that had pre-

ceded his reign. The Russian church had long opposed the scientific as well as the theological thought of the West. In the mid-seventeenth century, a reformist movement led by Patriarch Nikon introduced certain changes into church texts and ritual. These reforms caused great unrest among the Old Believers, a group of Russian Christians who strongly opposed these changes. Although condemned by the hierarchy, the Old Believers persisted in their opposition. Thousands of them committed suicide rather than submit to the new rituals. The Old Believers represented a rejection of change and innovation; their opposition discouraged the church hierarchy from making any further substantial accommodations with modern thought.

In the future Peter wanted to avoid two kinds of difficulties with the church. First, the clergy must not be able to oppose change and westernization. Second, the hierarchy of the church must not be permitted to cause again the kind of controversy that had inspired the Old Believers. Consequently,

Bishop Burnet Recalls the Visit of Peter the Great to England

In 1797 and 1798 Peter the Great of Russia toured western Europe to discover how Russia must change its society and economy in order to become a great power. As this description indicates, English Bishop Gilbert Burnet found the tsar a curious person. He was deeply impressed by the tsar's difficult personality and by his determination to have his subjects learn the ways of western Europe.

✦ *What qualities did Burnet admire and criticize in Peter the Great? How had some of these qualities been manifested in Peter's behavior as ruler of Russia? Why might Peter the Great have been so interested in ships and shipbuilding? What steps did the tsar take to allow his subjects to become familiar with other nations?*

He came this winter over to England, and stayed some months among us. . . . I had good interpreters, so I had much free discourse with him; he is a man of a very hot temper, soon inflamed, and very brutal in his passion; he raises his natural heat, by drinking much brandy, . . . he is subject to convulsive motions all over his body, and his head seems to be affected with these; he wants not capacity, and has a larger measure of knowledge, than might be expected from his education, which was very indifferent; a want of judgment, with an instability of temper, appear in him too often and too evidently; he is mechanically turned, and seems designed by nature rather to be a ship-carpenter, than a great prince. This was his chief study and exercise, while he stayed here: he wrought much with his own hands, and made all about him work at the models of ships. . . . He was . . . resolved to encourage learning, and to polish his people, by sending some of them to travel in other countries, and to draw strangers to come and live among them. . . . After I had seen him often, and had conversed much with him, I could not but adore the depth of the providence of God, that had raised up such a furious man to so absolute an authority over so great a part of the world.

Bishop Burnet's History of His Own Time *(Oxford: Clarendon Press, 1823), vol. 4, pp. 396–397.*

---

in 1721, Peter simply abolished the position of patriarch. In its place he established a synod headed by a layman, called the Procurator General, to rule the church in accordance with secular requirements. So far as transforming a traditional institution was concerned, this action toward the church was the most radical policy of Peter's reign. It produced still further futile opposition from the Old Believers, who saw the tsar as leading the church into new heresy.

REORGANIZING DOMESTIC ADMINISTRATION In his reorganization of domestic administration, Peter looked to institutions then used in Sweden. These were "colleges," or bureaus, of several persons rather than departments headed by a single minister. These colleges, which he imposed on Russia, were to look after matters such as the collection of taxes, foreign relations, war, and economic affairs. This new organization was an attempt to breathe life into Russia's stagnant and inefficient administration.

In 1711 Peter created a central senate of nine members who were to direct the Moscow government when the tsar was away with the army. The purpose of these and other local administrative reforms was to establish a bureaucracy that could support an efficient army.

DEVELOPING THE ECONOMY AND WAGING WAR   The economic development advocated by Peter the Great was closely related to his military needs. He encouraged the establishment of an iron industry in the Ural Mountains, and by mid-century Russia had become the largest iron producer in Europe. He sent promising young Russians abroad to acquire technical and organizational skills. He tried to attract West European craftspeople to live and work in Russia. Except for the striking growth of the iron industry, which nevertheless later languished, these efforts had only marginal success.

The goal of these internal reforms and political departures was to support a policy of warfare. Peter was determined to secure warm-water ports that would allow Russia to trade with the West and to have a greater impact on European affairs. This policy led him into wars with the Ottoman Empire and Sweden. His armies began fighting the Turks in 1695 and captured Azov on the Black Sea in 1696. It was a temporary victory, for in 1711 he was compelled to return the port.

Peter had more success against Sweden, where the inconsistency and irrationality of Charles XII were no small aid. In 1700 Russia invaded the Swedish Baltic possessions. The Swedish king's failure to follow up his victory at Narva in 1700 allowed Peter to regroup his forces and reserve his resources. In 1709, when Charles XII returned to fight Russia again, Peter was ready, and the Battle of Poltava sealed the fate of Sweden. In 1721 the Peace of Nystad, which ended the Great Northern War, confirmed the Russian conquest of Estonia, Livonia, and part of Finland. Henceforth Russia possessed warm-water ports and a permanent influence on European affairs.

At one point the domestic and foreign policies of Peter the Great literally intersected. This was at the spot on the Gulf of Finland where he founded his new capital city of Saint Petersburg. There he built government structures and compelled the *boyars* to construct town houses. He thus imitated those European monarchs who had copied Louis XIV by constructing smaller versions of Versailles. The founding of Saint Petersburg went beyond establishing a central imperial court, however. It symbolized a new Western orientation of Russia and Peter's determination to hold his position on the Baltic coast. He had begun the construction of the city and had moved the capital there in 1703, even before his victory over Sweden was assured.

Despite his notable success on the Baltic, Peter's reign ended with a great question mark. He had long quarreled with his only son, Alexis. Peter was jealous of the young man and feared he might undertake sedition. In 1718 Peter had his son imprisoned, and during this imprisonment, Alexis died mysteriously. Thereafter Peter claimed for himself the right to name a successor, but he could never bring himself to designate one either orally or in writing. Consequently, when he died in 1725, there was no firm policy on the succession to the throne. For more than thirty years, soldiers and nobles again determined who ruled Russia. Peter had laid the foundations of a modern Russia, but he had failed to lay the foundations of a stable state.

By the second quarter of the eighteenth century, the major European powers were not yet nation-states in which the citizens felt themselves united by a shared sense of community, culture, language, and history. They were still monarchies in which the personality of the ruler and the personal relationships of the great noble families exercised considerable influence over public affairs. The monarchs, except in Great Britain, had generally succeeded in making their power greater than the nobility's. The power of the aristocracy and its capacity to resist or obstruct the policies of the monarch were not destroyed, however. In Britain, of course, the nobility had tamed the monarchy, but even there tension between nobles and monarchs would continue throughout the rest of the century.

In foreign affairs the new arrangement of military and diplomatic power established early in the century prepared the way for two long conflicts. The first was a commercial rivalry for trade and overseas empire between France and Great Britain. During the reign of Louis XIV, these two nations had collided over the French bid for dominance in Europe. During the eighteenth century, they dueled for control of commerce on other continents. The second arena of warfare was in central Europe, where Austria and Prussia fought for the leadership of the German states.

Behind these international conflicts and the domestic rivalry of monarchs and nobles, however, the society of eighteenth-century Europe began to change. The character and the structures of the societies over which the monarchs ruled were beginning to take on some features associated with the modern age. These economic and social developments would eventually transform the life of Europe to a degree beside which the state building of the early eighteenth-century monarchs paled.

Review Questions

1. Explain why Britain and France remained leading powers in western Europe while Spain and the United Netherlands declined.

2. How did the structure of British government change under the political leadership of Robert Walpole? What were the chief sources of Walpole's political strength?

3. How was the Hohenzollern family able to forge a conglomerate of diverse land holdings into the state of Prussia? Who were the major personalities involved in this process and what were their individual contributions? Why was the military so important in Prussia?

4. Compare and contrast the varying success with which the Hohenzollerns and Habsburgs each handled their problems. Which family was more successful and why? Why were Sweden, the Ottoman Empire, and Poland each less successful?

5. How and why did Russia emerge as a great power? Discuss the character of Peter the Great. What were Russia's domestic problems before Peter came to power? What were his methods of reform? To what extent did he succeed? How were his reforms related to his military ambitions?

6. It has been said that Peter the Great was a rational ruler, interested in the welfare of his people. Do you agree with this statement? Why? Can you make a case for Peter as a bloody tyrant, concerned only with promoting his own glory?

Suggested Readings

T. M. BARKER, *Army, Aristocracy, Monarchy: Essays in War, Society and Government in Austria, 1618–1780* (1982). Examines the intricate power relationships among these major institutions.

J. BLACK, *Eighteenth-Century Europe 1700–1789* (1990). An excellent survey.

J. BREWER, *The Sinews of Power: War, Money and the English State, 1688–1783* (1989). An extremely important study of the financial basis of English power.

R. BROWNING, *Political and Constitutional Ideas of the Court Whigs* (1982). An excellent overview of the ideology of Walpole's supporters.

F. L. CARSTEN, *The Origins of Prussia* (1954). Discusses the groundwork laid by the Great Elector in the seventeenth century.

J. C. D. CLARK, *English Society: 1688–1832: Social Structure and Political Practice during the Ancien Régime* (1985). An important, controversial work that emphasizes the role of religion in English political life.

A. COBBAN, *A History of Modern France*, 2nd ed., vol. 1 (1961). A lively and opinionated volume.

L. COLLEY, *In Defiance of Oligarchy: The Tory Party, 1714–60* (1982). An important study that challenges much conventional opinion about eighteenth-century British politics.

N. DAVIS, *God's Playground*, vol. 1 (1991). Excellent on prepartition Poland.

P. M. G. DICKSON, *Finance and Government Under Maria Theresa* (1987). A definitive work.

W. DOYLE, *The Old European Order, 1660–1800* (1992). The most thoughtful treatment of the subject.

P. DUKES, *The Making of Russian Absolutism: 1613–1801* (1982). An overview based on recent scholarship.

R. R. ERGANG, *The Potsdam Führer* (1941). The biography of Frederick William I.

R. J. W. EVANS, *The Making of the Habsburg Monarchy, 1550–1700: An Interpretation* (1979). Places much emphasis on intellectual factors and the role of religion.

F. FORD, *Robe and Sword: The Regrouping of the French Aristocracy After Louis XIV* (1953). An important book for political, social, and intellectual history.

J. M. HITTLE, *The Service City: State and Townsmen in Russia, 1600–1800* (1979). Examines the relationship of cities in Russia to the growing power of the central government.

H. HOLBORN, *A History of Modern Germany, 1648–1840* (1966). The most comprehensive survey in English.

R. A. KANN AND Z. V. DAVID, *The Peoples of the Eastern Habsburg Lands, 1526–1918* (1984). A helpful overview of the subject.

D. MCKAY AND H. M. SCOTT, *The Rise of the Great Powers 1648–1815* (1983). Now the standard survey.

W. H. MCNEIL, *Europe's Steppe Frontier, 1500–1800* (1964). An interpretive essay on the history of southeastern Europe.

R. K. MASSIE, *Peter the Great: His Life and His World* (1980). A good popular biography.

L. B. NAMIER AND J. BROOKE, *The History of Parliament: The House of Commons, 1754–1790*, 3 vols. (1964). A detailed examination of the unreformed British House of Commons and electoral system.

J. B. OWEN, *The Eighteenth Century* (1974). An excellent introduction to England in this period.

G. Parker, *The Military Revolution: Military Innovation and the Rise of the West (1500–1800)* (1988). A major work in every respect.

J. H. Plumb, *Sir Robert Walpole*, 2 vols. (1956, 1961). A masterful biography ranging across the sweep of European politics.

J. H. Plumb, *The Growth of Political Stability in England, 1675–1725* (1969). An important interpretive work.

N. V. Riasanovsky, *The Image of Peter the Great in Russian History and Thought* (1985). Examines the legacy of Peter in Russian history.

N. V. Riasanovsky, *A History of Russia*, 5th ed. (1992). The best one-volume introduction.

H. Rosenberg, *Bureaucracy, Aristocracy, and Autocracy: The Prussian Experience, 1660–1815* (1960). Emphasizes the organization of Prussian administration.

P. F. Sugar, *Southeastern Europe Under Ottoman Rule, 1354–1804* (1977). An extremely clear presentation.

E. N. Williams, *The Ancien Régime in Europe* (1972). A state-by-state survey of very high quality.

"The Iron Forge", 1772 (oil on canvas). During the eighteenth century, most goods were produced in small workshops such as this iron forge painted by Joseph Wright of Derby (1734–1797), or in the homes of artisans. Not until very late in the century,with the early stages of industrialization, did a few factories appear. In the small early workshops it would not have been uncommon for the family of the owner to visit, as portrayed in this painting. [The Bridgeman Art Library, London/Broadlands Trust, Hants]

Society and Economy
Under the Old Regime
in the Eighteenth Century

K E Y   T O P I C S

- The varied privileges and powers of Europe's aristocracies in the Old Regime and their efforts to increase their wealth
- The plight of rural peasants
- Family structure and family economy
- The transformation of Europe's economy by the agricultural and industrial revolutions
- Urban growth and the social tensions that accompanied it
- The strains on the institutions of the Old Regime brought about by social change

During the French Revolution and the turmoil spawned by that upheaval, it became customary to refer to the patterns of social, political, and economic relationships that had existed in France before 1789 as the *ancien régime*, or the "old regime." The term has come to be applied generally to the life and institutions of prerevolutionary Europe. Politically, it meant the rule of theo-retically absolute monarchies with growing bureaucracies and aristocratically led armies. Economically, scarcity of food, predominance of agriculture, slow transport, a low level of iron production, comparatively unsophisticated financial institutions, and, in some cases, competitive commercial overseas empires characterized the Old Regime. Socially, men and women living during *the period saw themselves less as individuals than as members of distinct corporate bodies that possessed certain privileges or rights as a group.*

Tradition, hierarchy, corporateness, and privilege were the chief social characteristics of the Old Regime. Yet it was by no means a static society. Change and innovation were fermenting in its midst. Farming became more commercialized, and both food production and the size of the population increased. The early stages of the Industrial Revolution made more consumer goods available, and domestic consumption expanded throughout the century. The colonies in the Americas provided strong demand for European goods and manufactures. Merchants in seaports and other cities were expanding their businesses. By preparing their states for war, European governments put new demands on the resources and the economic organizations of their nations. The spirit of rationality that had been so important to the Scientific Revolution of the seventeenth century continued to manifest itself in the economic life of the eighteenth century. The Old Regime itself fostered the changes that eventually transformed it into a different kind of society.

Major Features of Life in the Old Regime

Socially, prerevolutionary Europe was based on (1) aristocratic elites possessing a wide variety of inherited legal privileges; (2) established churches intimately related to the state and the aristocracy; (3) an urban labor force usually organized into guilds; and (4) a rural peasantry subject to high taxes and feudal dues. Of course, the men and women living during this period did not know it as the "Old Regime." Most of them earned their livelihoods and passed their lives as their forebears had done for generations before them and as they expected their children to do after them.

Maintenance of Tradition

During the eighteenth century, the past weighed more heavily on people's minds than did the future. Few persons outside the government bureaucracies, the expanding merchant groups, and the movement for reform called the Enlightenment (see Chapter 18) considered change or innovation desirable. This was especially true of social relationships. Both nobles and peasants, for different reasons, repeatedly called for the restoration of traditional, or customary, rights. The nobles asserted what they considered their ancient rights against the intrusion of the expanding monarchical bureaucracies. The peasants, through petitions and revolts, called for the revival or the maintenance of the customary manorial rights that allowed them access to particular lands, courts, or grievance procedures.

Except for the early industrial development in Britain and the accompanying expansion of personal consumption, the eighteenth-century economy was also predominantly traditional. The quality and quantity of the grain harvest remained the most important fact of life for most of the population and the gravest concern for governments.

Hierarchy and Privilege

Closely related to this traditional social and economic outlook was the hierarchical structure of the society. The medieval sense of rank and degree not only persisted but became more rigid during the century. In several continental cities, sumptuary laws regulating the dress of the different classes remained on the books. These laws forbade persons in one class or occupation to wear clothes like those worn by their social superiors. These laws, which sought to make the social hierarchy easily visible, were largely ineffective by this time. What really enforced the hierarchy was the corporate nature of social relationships.

Each state or society was considered a community composed of numerous smaller communities. Eighteenth-century Europeans did not enjoy what Americans regard as "individual rights." Instead a person enjoyed such rights and privileges as were guaranteed to the particular communities or groups of which she or he was a part. The "community" might include the village, the municipality, the nobility, the church, the guild, a university, or the parish. In turn, each of these bodies enjoyed certain privileges, some great, some small. The privileges might involve exemption from taxation or from some especially humiliating punishment, the right to practice a trade or craft, the right of one's children to pursue a particular occupation, or, for the church, the right to collect the tithe.

The Aristocracy

The eighteenth century was the great age of the aristocracy. The nobility constituted approximately 1 to 5 percent of the population of any given country. In every country, the nobility was the single wealthiest sector of the population, had the widest degree of social, political, and economic power, and set the tone of polite society. In most countries, the nobility had their own separate house in the parliament, estates, or diet. Only nobles had any kind of representation in Hungary and Poland. Land continued to provide the aristocracy with its largest source of income, but aristocrats did not merely own estates. Their influence was felt throughout social and economic life. In much of Europe, however, it was felt that manual labor was regarded as beneath a noble. In Spain, it was assumed that even the poorer nobles would lead lives of idleness. In other nations, however, the nobility often fostered economic innovation and embraced the commercial spirit. Such willingness to change helped protect the nobility's wealth.

Varieties of Aristocratic Privilege

To be an aristocrat was a matter of birth and legal privilege. This much the aristocracy had in common across the Continent. In almost every other respect, they differed markedly from country to country.

BRITISH NOBILITY The smallest, wealthiest, best-defined, and most socially responsible aristocracy resided in Great Britain. It consisted of about 400 families, and the eldest male members of each family sat in the House of Lords. Through the corruptions of the electoral system, these families also controlled many seats in the House of Commons. The estates of the British nobility ranged from a few thousand to fifty thousand acres, from which they received rents. The nobles owned about one-fourth of all the arable land in the country. Increasingly the British aristocracy invested its wealth in commerce, canals, urban real estate, mines, and even industrial ventures. Because only the eldest son inherited the title and the land, younger sons moved into commerce, the army, the professions, and the church. British landowners in both houses of Parliament levied taxes and also paid them. They had few significant legal privileges, but their direct or indirect control of local government gave them immense political power and social influence. The aristocracy dominated the society and politics of the English counties. Their country houses, many of which were built in the eighteenth century, were centers for local society.

FRENCH NOBILITY The situation of the continental nobilities was less clear-cut. In France, the approximately 400,000 nobles were divided between nobles "of the sword," or those whose nobility was derived from military service, and those "of the robe," or those who had either acquired their titles by serving in the bureaucracy or had purchased them. The two groups had quarreled in the past but often cooperated during the eighteenth century to defend their common privileges.

The foundation of aristocratic life was the possession of land. English aristocrats and large landowners controlled local government as well as the English Parliament. This painting of Robert Andrews and his wife by Thomas Gainsborough (1728–1788) shows an aristocratic couple on their estate. The gun and the hunting dog in this portrait suggest the importance landowners assigned to the virtually exclusive hunting privileges they enjoyed on their land. [The National Gallery, London]

Eighteen-century France had some of the best roads in the world, but they were often built with forced labor. French peasants were required to work part of each year on such projects. This system, called the corvée, *was not abolished until the French Revolution in 1789. [Giraudon/Art Resource, N.Y.]*

The French nobles were also divided between those who held office or favor with the royal court at Versailles and those who did not. The court nobility reaped the immense wealth that could be gained from holding high office. The nobles' hold on such offices intensified during the century. By the late 1780s, appointments to the church, the army, and the bureaucracy, as well as other profitable positions, tended to go to the nobles already established in court circles. Whereas these well-connected aristocrats were rich, the provincial nobility, called *hobereaux*, were often little better off than wealthy peasants.

Despite differences in rank, origin, and wealth, certain hereditary privileges set all French aristocrats apart from the rest of society. They were exempt from many taxes. For example, most French nobles did not pay the *taille*, or land tax, the basic tax of the Old Regime. The nobles were technically liable for payment of the *vingtième*, or the "twentieth," which resembled an income tax, but they rarely had to pay it in full. The nobles were not liable for the royal *corvées*, or forced labor on public works, which fell on the peasants. In addition to these exemptions, French nobles could collect feudal dues from their tenants and enjoyed exclusive hunting and fishing privileges.

EASTERN EUROPEAN NOBILITIES East of the Elbe River, the character of the nobility became even more complicated and repressive. Throughout the area, the military traditions of the aristocracy remained important. In Poland, there were thousands of nobles, or *szlachta*, who after 1741 were entirely

exempt from taxes. Until 1768 these Polish aristocrats possessed the right of life and death over their serfs. Most of the Polish nobility were relatively poor. A few rich nobles who had immense estates exercised political power in the fragile Polish state.

In Austria and Hungary, the nobility continued to possess broad judicial powers over the peasantry through their manorial courts. They also enjoyed various degrees of exemption from taxation. The wealthiest of them, Prince Esterhazy of Hungary, owned ten million acres of land.

In Prussia, after the accession of Frederick the Great in 1740, the position of the Junker nobles became much stronger. Frederick's various wars required their full support. He drew his officers almost wholly from the Junker class. Nobles also increasingly made up the bureaucracy. As in other parts of eastern Europe, the Prussian nobles had extensive judicial authority over the serfs.

In Russia, the eighteenth century saw what amounted to the creation of the nobility. Peter the Great's (r. 1682–1725) linking of state service and noble social status through the Table of Ranks (1722) established among Russian nobles a self-conscious class identity that had not previously existed. Thereafter they were determined to resist compulsory state service. In 1736 Empress Anna (r. 1730–1740) reduced such service to twenty-five years. In 1762 Peter III (r. 1762) exempted the greatest nobles entirely from compulsory service. In 1785, in the Charter of the Nobility, Catherine the Great (r. 1762–1796) legally defined noble rights and privileges in exchange for the assurance that the nobility would serve the state voluntarily. Noble privileges included the right of transmitting noble status to a nobleman's wife and children, the judicial protection of noble rights and property, considerable power over the serfs, and exemption from personal taxes.

Aristocratic Resurgence

The Russian Charter of the Nobility constituted one aspect of the broader European-wide development termed the "aristocratic resurgence." The aristocratic resurgence was the nobility's reaction to the threat to their social position and privileges that they felt from the expanding power of the monarchies. This resurgence took several forms in the eighteenth century. First, all nobilities tried to preserve their exclusiveness by making it more difficult to become a noble. Second, they pushed to reserve appointments to the officer corps of the armies, the bureaucracies, the government ministries, and the church exclusively for nobles. By doing this, they hoped to control the power of the monarchies.

Third, the nobles attempted to use the authority of existing aristocratically controlled institutions against the power of the monarchies. These institutions included the British Parliament, the French courts, or *parlements*, and the local aristocratic estates and provincial diets in Germany and the Habsburg Empire. Fourth, the nobility sought to improve its financial position by gaining further exemptions from taxation or by collecting higher rents or long-forgotten feudal dues from the peasantry. The nobility tried to shore up its position by various appeals to traditional and often ancient privileges that had lapsed over time. This aristocratic challenge to the monarchies was a fundamental political fact of the day.

The Land and Its Tillers

Land was the economic basis of eighteenth-century life and the foundation of the status and power of the nobility. Well over three-fourths of all Europeans lived in the country, and few of them ever traveled more than a few miles from their birthplace. Except for the nobility and the wealthier nonaristocratic landowners, most people who dwelled on the land were poor. They lived in various states of economic and social dependency, exploitation, and vulnerability.

Peasants and Serfs

Rural social dependency related directly to the land. The nature of the dependency differed sharply for free peasants, such as English tenants and most French cultivators, and for the serfs of Germany, Austria, and Russia, who were legally bound to a particular plot of land and a particular lord. But everywhere, the class that owned most of the land also controlled the local government and the courts. For example, in Great Britain, all farmers and smaller tenants had the legal rights of English citizens. The justices of the peace, however, who presided over the county courts and who could call out the local militia, were always substantial landowners, as were the members of Parliament, who made the laws. In eastern Europe, the landowners presided over the manorial courts. On the Continent, the burden of taxation fell on the tillers of the soil.

OBLIGATIONS OF PEASANTS Landlord power increased as one moved across Europe from west to east. Most French peasants owned some land, but there were a few serfs in eastern France. Nearly all French peasants were subject to certain feudal dues, called *banalités*. These included the required use-for-payment of the lord's, or *seigneur*'s, mill to grind grain and his oven to bake bread. The *seigneur* could also require a certain number of days each year of the peasant's labor. This practice of forced labor was termed the *corvée*. Because even landowning French peasants rarely possessed enough land to support their families, they had to rent more land from the *seigneur* and were also subject to feudal dues attached to those plots. In Prussia and Austria, despite attempts by the monarchies late in the century to improve the lot of the serfs, the landlords continued to exercise almost complete control over them. In many of the Habsburg lands, law and custom required the serfs to provide service, or *robot*, to the lords.

Serfs were worst off in Russia. There nobles reckoned their wealth by the number of "souls," or, male serfs, owned rather than by the acreage the landlord possessed. Russian landlords, in effect, regarded serfs merely as economic commodities. They could demand as many as six days a week of labor, known as *barshchina*, from the serfs. Like Prussian and Austrian landlords, they enjoyed the right to punish their serfs. On their own authority, Russian landlords could even exile a serf to Siberia.

An English Traveler Describes Serfdom in Eighteenth-Century Russia

William Coxe was an Englishman who traveled widely in eastern Europe. His description of Russian serfdom portrays the brutality of the institution. It also illustrates his amazement at the absence in Russia of civil liberties such as he and more humble citizens enjoyed in England.

✦ *What are the examples of a Russian master not being restrained by law in his treatment of his serfs? What rights did the serfs have in regard to possessing property acquired through their own industry? How did Russian masters improve the skills of their serfs for their own economic benefit?*

Peasants belonging to individuals are the private property of the landholders, as much as implements of agriculture, or herds of cattle; and the value of an estate is estimated, as in Poland, by the number of boors [serfs], and not by the number of acres. ... If the Polish boor is oppressed, and he escapes to another master, the latter is liable to no pecuniary penalty for harboring him; but in Russia the person who receives another's vassal is subject to a heavy fine. With respect to his own demands upon his peasants, the lord is restrained by no law, either in the exaction of any sum, or in the mode of employing them. He is absolute master of their time and labour: some he employs in agriculture: a few he makes his menial servants, and perhaps without wages; and from others he exacts an annual payment.

Each vassal, therefore, is rated according to the arbitrary will of his master. Some contribute four or five shillings a year; others, who are engaged in traffic or trade, are assessed proportion to their supposed profits. ... With regard to any capital which they may have acquired by their industry, it may be seized, and there can be no redress. ...

... [S]ome of the Russian nobility send their vassals to Moscow or Petersburg for the purpose of learning various handcraft trades: they either employ them on their own estates; let them out for hire; sell them at an advanced price; or receive from them an annual compensation for the permission of exercising trade for their own advantage.

William Coxe, Travels into Poland, Russia, Sweden, and Denmark, *4th ed., vol. 3 (London: T. Cadell, 1972, first printed 1784), pp. 174–181.*

Serfs had no legal recourse against the orders and whims of their lords. There was little difference between Russian serfdom and slavery.

In southeastern Europe, where the Ottoman Empire held sway, peasants were free though landlords tried to exert authority in every way. The domain of the landlords was termed a çift. The landlord was often an absentee who managed the estate through an overseer. During the seventeenth and eighteenth centuries, these landlords, like those elsewhere in Europe, often became more commercially oriented and turned to the production of commercial crops, such as cotton, vegetables, potatoes, and maize.

Scarcity of labor rather than recognition of legal rights supported the independence of the southeastern European peasants. A peasant might migrate from one landlord to another. Because the second landlord needed the peasant's labor, he had no reason to return him to the original landlord. During the seventeenth and eighteenth centuries, however, disorder originating in the capital of Constantinople (now Istanbul) spilled over into the Balkan Peninsula. In this climate, landlords increased their authority by offering their peasants protection from bandits or rebels who might destroy peasant villages. As in medieval times, the manor house or armed enclosure of a local landlord became the peasants' refuge. These landlords also owned all the housing and tools required by the peasants and furnished their seed grain. Consequently, despite legal independence, Balkan peasants under the Ottoman Empire became largely dependent upon the landlords, though never to the extent of serfs in eastern Europe or Russia.

PEASANT REBELLIONS   The Russian monarchy itself contributed to the further degradation of the serfs.

Peter the Great gave whole villages to favored nobles. Later in the century, Catherine the Great confirmed the authority of the nobles over their serfs in exchange for the landowners' political cooperation. Russia experienced vast peasant unrest with well over fifty peasant revolts occurring between 1762 and 1769. These culminated between 1773 and 1775 in Pugachev's Rebellion, when Emelyan Pugachev (1726–1775) promised the serfs land of their own and freedom from their lords. All

---

Catherine the Great Issues a Proclamation Against Pugachev

Against a background of long-standing human degradation and increasing landowner authority, a Don Cossack named Emelyan Pugachev led the greatest serf rebellion in Russian history from 1773 to 1775. Empress Catherine the Great's proclamation of 1773 argues that he was alienating the serfs from their natural and proper allegiance to her and their masters.

◆ *How does the language of this proclamation seek to denigrate as well as to condemn Pugachev and his followers? What does the proclamation claim that Pugachev has been promising? On what grounds did Catherine expect her loyal subjects to resist Pugachev?*

By the grace of God, we Catherine II . . . make known to our faithful subjects, that we have learnt, with the utmost indignation and extreme affliction, that a certain Cossack, a deserter and fugitive from the Don, named Emelyan Pugachev, after having traversed Poland, has been collecting, for some time past, in the districts that border on the river Irghis, in the government of Orenburg, a troop of vagabonds like himself; that he continues to commit in those parts all kinds of excesses, inhumanly depriving the inhabitants of their possessions, and even of their lives. . . .

In a word, there is not a man deserving of the Russian name, who does not hold in abomination the odious and insolent like by which Pugachev fancies himself able to seduce and to deceive persons of a simple and credulous disposition, by promising to free them from the bonds of submission, and obedience to their sovereign, as if the Creation of the universe had established human

societies in such a manner as that they can subsist without an intermediate authority between the sovereign and the people.

Nevertheless, as the insolence of this vile refuse of the human race is attended with consequences pernicious to the provinces adjacent to that district; as the report of the flagrant enormities which he has committed, may affright those persons who are accustomed to imagine the misfortunes of others as ready to fall upon them, and as we watch with indefatigable care over the tranquillity of our faithful subjects, we inform them . . . that we have taken . . . such measures as are the best adapted to stifle the sedition . . .

We trust . . . that every true son of the country will unremittedly fulfill his duty, of the contributing to the maintenance of good order and of public tranquillity, by preserving himself from the snares of seduction, and by discharging his obedience to his lawful sovereign.

William Tooke, Life of Catherine II, Empress of Russia, *4th ed., vol. 2 (London: T. N. Longman and O. Rees, 1800), pp. 460–461 (spelling modernized).*

of southern Russia was in turmoil until the government brutally suppressed the rebellion. Thereafter, any thought of liberalizing or improving the condition of the serfs was set aside for a generation.

Pugachev's was the largest peasant uprising of the eighteenth century, but smaller peasant revolts or disturbances took place in Bohemia in 1775, in Transylvania in 1784, in Moravia in 1786, and in Austria in 1789. There were almost no revolts in western Europe, but England experienced many rural riots. Rural rebellions were violent, but the peasants and serfs normally directed their wrath against property rather than persons. The rebels usually sought to reassert traditional or customary rights against practices that they perceived as innovations. Their targets were carefully chosen and included unfair pricing, onerous new or increased feudal dues, changes in methods of payment or land use, unjust officials, or extraordinarily brutal overseers and landlords. Peasant revolts were thus conservative in nature.

Aristocratic Domination of the Countryside: The English Game Laws

One of the clearest examples of aristocratic domination of the countryside and of aristocratic manipulation of the law to its own advantage was English legislation on hunting.

Between 1671 and 1831, English landowners had the exclusive legal right to hunt game animals. These specifically included hares, partridges, pheasants, and moorfowl. Similar legislation covered other animals such as deer, the killing of which by an unauthorized person became a capital offense in the eighteenth century. By law, only persons owning a particular amount of landed property could hunt these animals. Excluded from the right to hunt were all persons renting land, wealthy city merchants who did not own land, and poor people in cities, villages, and the countryside. The poor were excluded because the elite believed that allowing the poor to enjoy the sport of hunting would undermine their work habits. The city merchants were excluded because the landed gentry in Parliament wanted to demonstrate visibly and legally the superiority of landed wealth over commercial wealth. Thus, the various game laws upheld the superior status of the aristocracy and the landed gentry.

The game laws represent a prime example of class legislation. The gentry who benefitted from the laws and whose parliamentary representatives had passed them also served as the local justices of the peace who administered the laws and punished their violation. The justices of the peace could levy fines and even have poachers impressed into the army. Gentry could also take civil legal action against wealthier poachers, such as rich farmers who rented land, and thus saddle them with immense legal fees. The gentry also employed gamekeepers to protect game from poachers. The gamekeepers were known to kill the dogs belonging to people suspected of poaching. By the middle of the century, gamekeepers had devised trapguns to shoot poachers who tripped their hidden levers.

A small industry arose to circumvent the game laws, however. Many poor people living either on an estate or in a nearby village would kill game for food. They believed that the game actually belonged to the community, and this poaching increased during hard times. Poaching was thus one way for the poor to find food.

Even more important was the black market in game animals sustained by the demand of urban people for this kind of luxury meat. Here arose the possibility of poaching for profit, and indeed, poaching technically meant the stealing or killing of game for sale. Local people from both the countryside and the villages would steal the game and then sell it to intermediaries called *higglers*. Later, coachmen took over this function. The higglers and the coachmen would smuggle the game into the cities, where poulterers would sell it at a premium price. Everyone involved made a bit of money along the way. During the second half of the century, English aristocrats began to construct large game preserves. The rural poor, who had lost their rights to communal land as a result of its enclosure by the large landowners, deeply resented these preserves, which soon became hunting grounds to organized gangs of poachers.

Penalties against poaching increased in the 1790s after the outbreak of the French Revolution, but so did the amount of poaching as the economic hardships caused by Britain's participation in the wars of the era put a greater burden on poor people and as the demand for food in English cities grew along with their population. By the 1820s, both landowners and reformers called for a change in the law. In 1831 Parliament rewrote the game laws, retaining the landowners' possession of the game but permitting them to allow other people to hunt it. Poaching continued, but the exclusive right of the landed classes to hunt game had ended.

Family Structures and the Family Economy

In preindustrial Europe, the household was the basic unit of production and consumption. Few productive establishments employed more than a handful of people not belonging to the family of the owner, and those rare exceptions were in cities. The overwhelming majority of Europeans, however, lived in rural areas. There, as well as in small towns and cities, the household mode of organization predominated on farms, in artisans' workshops, and in small merchants' shops. With that mode of economic organization, there developed what is known as the *family economy*. Its structure as described here had prevailed over most of Europe for centuries.

Households

What was a household in the preindustrial Europe of the Old Regime? There were two basic models, one characterizing northwestern Europe and the other eastern Europe.

NORTHWESTERN EUROPE In northwestern Europe, the household almost invariably consisted of a married couple, their children through their early teenage years, and their servants. Except for the few wealthy people, households were small, usually consisting of not more than five or six members. Furthermore, in these households, more than two generations of a family rarely lived under the same roof. High mortality and late marriage prevented families of three generations. In other words, grandparents rarely lived in the same household as their grandchildren and families consisted of parents and children. The family structure of northwestern Europe was thus nuclear rather than extended.

This particular characteristic of the northwestern European household is one of the major discoveries of recent research into family history. Previously historians had assumed that before industrialization Europeans lived in extended familial settings with several generations living together in a household. Recent demographic investigation has sharply reversed this picture. Children lived with their parents only until their early teens. Then they normally left home, usually to enter the work force of young servants who lived and worked in another household. A child of a skilled artisan might remain with his or her parents to learn a valuable skill; but only rarely would more than one child do so because children's labor was more remunerative outside the home.

These young men and women who had left home would eventually marry and form an independent household of their own. This practice of moving away from home is known as *neolocalism*. These young people married relatively late. Men were usually over twenty-six, and women over twenty-three. The new couple usually had children as soon after marriage as possible. Frequently, the woman was already pregnant at marriage. Family and community pressure often compelled the man to marry her. In any case, premarital sexual relations were common, though illegitimate births were rare. The new couple would soon employ a servant, who, together with their growing children, would undertake whatever form of livelihood the household used to support itself.

The word *servant* in this context may be confusing. It does not refer to someone looking after the needs of wealthy people. Rather, in preindustrial Europe, a servant was a person—either male or female—who was hired, often under a clear contract, to work for the head of the household in exchange for room, board, and wages. The servant was usually young and by no means always socially inferior to his or her employer. Normally, the servant was an integral part of the household and ate with the family.

Young men and women became servants when their labor was no longer needed in their parents' household or when they could earn more money for their family outside the parental household. Being a servant for several years—often as many as eight or ten—allowed young people to acquire the productive skills and the monetary savings necessary to begin their own household. These years spent as servants largely account for the late age of marriage in northwestern Europe.

EASTERN EUROPE As one moved eastward across the continent, the structure of the household and the pattern of marriage changed. There both men and women usually married before the age of twenty. Consequently, children were born to much younger parents. Often, especially among Russian serfs, wives were older than their husbands. Eastern European households were generally larger than those in the West. Often a rural Russian household consisted of more than nine and possibly more than twenty members, with three or perhaps even four generations of the same family living together. Early marriage made this situation more likely. In Russia, marrying involved not starting a new household but remaining in and expanding one already established.

The landholding structure in eastern Europe accounts, at least in part, for these patterns of marriage and the family. The lords of the manor who owned land wanted to ensure that it would be cultivated so they could receive their rents. Thus, for example, in Poland, landlords might forbid marriage between their own serfs and those from another estate. They might also require widows and widowers to remarry to assure adequate labor for a particular plot of land. Polish landlords also frowned on the hiring of free laborers—the equivalent of servants in the West—to help cultivate land. The landlords preferred to use other serfs. This practice inhibited the formation of independent households. In Russia, landlords ordered the families of young people in their villages to arrange marriages within a short, set time. These lords discouraged single-generation family households because the death or serious illness of one person in such a household might mean that the land assigned to it would go out of cultivation.

The Family Economy

Throughout Europe, most people worked within the family economy. That is to say, the household was the basic unit of production and consumption. Almost everyone lived within a household of some kind because it was virtually impossible for ordinary people to support themselves independently. Indeed, except for members of religious orders, people living outside a household were viewed with great suspicion. They were considered potentially criminal or disruptive or, at least, potentially dependent on the charity of others. Everywhere beggars met deep hostility.

Depending on their ages and skills, everyone in the household worked. The need to survive poor harvests or economic slumps meant that no one could be idle. Within this family economy, all goods and income produced went to the benefit of the household rather than to the individual family member. On a farm much of the effort went directly into raising food or producing other agricultural goods that could be exchanged for food. Few western Europeans, however, had enough land to support their household from farming alone. Thus one or more family members might work elsewhere and send wages home. For example, the father and older children might work as harvest pickers or might fish or might engage in other labor, either in the neighborhood or farther from home. If the father was such a migrant worker, the burden of farm work would fall on his wife and their younger children. This was not an uncommon pattern.

The family economy also dominated the life of skilled urban artisans. The father was usually the chief artisan. He normally employed one or more servants, but would expect his children to work in the enterprise also. His eldest child was usually trained in the trade. His wife often sold his wares or opened a small shop of her own. Wives of merchants also often ran their husbands' businesses, especially when the husband traveled to purchase new goods. In any case, everyone in the family was involved. If business was poor, family members would look for employment elsewhere, not to support themselves as individuals but to ensure the survival of the family unit.

In western Europe, the death of a father often brought disaster to the economy of the household. The continuing economic life of the family usually depended on his land or skills. The widow might take on the farm or the business, or his children might do so. The widow usually sought to remarry quickly to restore the labor and skills of a male to the household and to prevent herself from becoming dependent on relatives or charity.

The high mortality rate of the time meant that many households were reconstituted second family groups that included stepchildren. Because of the advanced age of the widow or economic hard times, however, some households might simply dissolve. The widow became dependent on charity or relatives. The children became similarly dependent or entered the workforce of servants earlier than they would otherwise. In other cases, the situation could be so desperate that they would resort to crime or to begging. The personal, emotional, and economic vulnerability of the family economy cannot be overemphasized.

In eastern Europe, the family economy functioned in the context of serfdom and landlord domination. Peasants clearly thought in terms of their families and expanding the land available for cultivation. The village structure may have mitigated the pressures of the family economy, as did the multigenerational family. Dependence on the available land was the chief fact of life. There were many fewer

Rules Are Established for the Berlin Poor House

Poverty was an enormous problem in eighteenth-century Europe, often forcing family members to work away from home and creating thousands of migrant workers and beggars. Governments were hostile to beggars and sometimes migrant workers, whom they regarded as a potential source of crime and disorder. Many of these concerns are evident in the regulations for the Berlin Poor House.

✦ *What were the distinctions made between the poor who deserved sympathy and those who did not? How would such a distinction affect social policy? Why might beggars have been regarded as dangers to public order? What attitudes toward work are displayed in these regulations?*

Whereas His Majesty . . . has renewed the prohibition of begging in the streets and in houses and has made all giving of alms punishable; it is decided to inform the public of the present measures for the relief of the poor, and to acquaint it with the main outlines of the above order:

1. In the new workhouse, . . . the genuinely needy and the poor deserving sympathy shall be cared for better than hitherto, but the deliberate beggars shall more resolutely be made to work.

2. The past organization of this house has therefore been totally altered, so that all persons to be received in it shall be divided into two entirely separate main classes, differentiated both in the status of their work and its location, in their dormitory and in their board.

3. The first class is meant for the old and for other persons deserving help and sympathy, who cannot entirely live by their work and do not wish to beg. Those report to the Poor's Chest in the Town Hall of Berlin, with a certificate from the Minister of their Church, showing their hitherto unblemished character, and after their references have been checked, they shall be accepted. They spin in the house as much wool as their age and health permits, and if they spin more than the cost of their keep, the surplus shall be paid out to them. . . .

5. The second main class is destined for those who do not wish to make use of this benefaction, but would rather live by begging. These deliberate beggars will be arrested by the Poor Law Constables, if necessary with the assistance of the Police, irrespective of age or status, whether they be vagabonds, journeymen, citizens, discharged soldiers, their wives or children, and will be sent to the workhouse.

6. Those who are caught begging for the first time shall be put into this class for three months at least, for the second time, for a year, and for the third and later times for several years, according to circumstances, for life.

7. Similarly, this class is destined for those who after due process of law have been sent for punishment as runaway servants and apprentices, for a period of time determined by the Court.

8. All the persons under numbers 5, 6, and 7 shall be forced to spin and prepare wool, and shall be kept on a minimum standard, clearly differentiated from the first class, both in the status and quantity of their work in their board and their lodging.

9. The children shall be cared for separately, . . . and shall receive education for several hours a day. . . .

10. Before a beggar is discharged, he must, in order that he shall not again become a public nuisance, prove an occupation in prospect or the existence of relations or of other persons, who will look after him and will put him up at once. . . .

Kruegeger, Geschichte der Manufacturen . . . , as quoted and translated in S. Pollard and C. Holmes, eds., Documents of European Economic History, vol. I *(London: Edward Arnold, 1968),* pp. 166–167.

(a)

(b)

These four scenes were painted by the English artist Francis Wheatley (1747–1801) near the close of the eighteenth century. They illustrate in a very idealized manner the life of a farm family in the morning (a), at noon (b), in the evening (c), and at night (d). Note the artist's assumptions about the division of labor by gender. Men work in the fields, women work in the home or look after the needs of men and children. As other illustrations in this chapter show, many eighteenth-century women in fact worked outside the home, but considerable social pressure was developing at this time to restrict them to domestic roles. These paintings are thus more prescriptive than descriptive, intended in part to persuade their viewers that women belonged in their separate family sphere. Many, perhaps most, families living in the countryside could not maintain the closeness that these paintings extol. To survive, many had to send members to work on other farms or even in other regions of the country following the harvest. [Yale Center for British Art, Paul Mellon Collection]

(c)

(d)

Priscilla Wakefield Demands More Occupations Be Opened to Women

At the end of the eighteenth century, several English women writers began to demand a wider life for women. Priscilla Wakefield was among such authors. She was concerned that women found themselves only able to pursue occupations that paid poorly. Often they were excluded from work on the grounds of their alleged physical weakness. She also believed that women should receive equal wages for equal work. Many of the issues she raised have yet to be adequately addressed on behalf of women.

✦ *From reading this passage, what do you understand to have been the arguments at the end of the eighteenth century to limit the kinds of employment that women might enter? Why did women receive lower wages for work similar to or the same as that done by men? What occupations traditionally filled by men does Wakefield believe women might also pursue?*

Another heavy discouragement to the industry of women, is the inequality of the reward of their labor, compared with that of men; an injustice which pervades every species of employment performed by both sexes.

In employments which depend on bodily strength, the distinction is just; for it cannot be pretended that the generality of women can earn as much as men, when the produce of their labor is the result of corporeal exertion; but it is a subject of great regret, that this inequality should prevail even where an equal share of skill and application is exerted. Male stay-makers, mantua-makers, and hair-dressers, are better paid than female artists of the same professions; but surely it will never be urged as an apology for this disproportion, that women are not as capable of making stays, gowns, dressing hair, and similar arts, as men; if they are not superior to them, it can only be accounted for upon this principle, that the prices they receive for their labor are not sufficient to repay them for the expense of qualifying themselves for their business; and that they sink under the mortification of being regarded as artisans of inferior estimation. . . .

Besides these employments which are commonly performed by women, and those already shown to be suitable for such persons as are above the condition of hard labor, there are some pro-fessions and trades customarily in the hands of men, which might be conveniently exercised by either sex.—Watchmaking requiring more ingenuity than strength, seems peculiarly adapted to women; as do many parts of the business of stationer, particularly, ruling account books or making pens. The compounding of medicines in an apothecary's shop, requires no other talents than care and exactness; and if opening a vein occasionally be a indispensable requisite, a woman may acquire the capacity of doing it, for those of her own sex at least, without any reasonable objection. . . . Pastry and confectionery appear particularly consonant to the habits of women, though generally performed by men; perhaps the heat of the ovens, and the strength requisite to fill and empty them, may render male assistants necessary; but certain women are most eligible to mix up the ingredients, and prepare the various kinds of cakes for baking.—Light turnery and toy-making depend more upon dexterity and invention than force, and are therefore suitable work for women and children. . . .

Farming, as far as respects the theory, is commensurate with the powers of the female mind: nor is the practice of inspecting agricultural processes incompatible with the delicacy of their frames if their constitution be good.

Priscilla Wakefield, Reflections on the Present Condition of the Female Sex *(1798), (London, 1817), pp. 125–127, as quoted in Bridget Hill, ed.,* Eighteenth-Century Women: An Anthology *(London: George Allen & Unwin, 1984), pp. 227–228.*

artisan and merchant households, and there was far less geographical mobility than in western Europe.

Women and the Family Economy

The family economy established many of the chief constraints on the lives and personal experiences of women in preindustrial society. Most of the historical research that has been undertaken on this subject relates to western Europe. There, a woman's life experience was largely the function of her capacity to establish and maintain a household. For women, marriage was an economic necessity as well as an institution that fulfilled sexual and psychological needs. Outside a household a woman's life was vulnerable and precarious. Some women succeeded in becoming economically independent. They were the exception. Normally, unless she were an aristocrat or a member of a religious order, a woman probably could not support herself solely by her own efforts. Consequently, a woman devoted much of her life first to maintaining her parents' household and then to devising some means of getting her own household to live in as an adult. Bearing and rearing children were usually subordinate to these goals.

By the age of seven, a girl would have begun to help with the household work. On a farm, this might mean looking after chickens, watering animals, or carrying food to adults working the land. In an urban artisan's household, she would do light work, perhaps cleaning or carrying and later sewing or weaving. The girl would remain in her parents' home as long as she made a real contribution to the family enterprise or as long as her labor elsewhere was not more remunerative to the family.

An artisan's daughter might not leave home until marriage because at home she could learn increasingly valuable skills associated with the trade. The situation was different for the much larger number of girls growing up on farms. Their parents and brothers could often do all the necessary farm work, and a girl's labor at home quickly became of little value to her family. She would then leave home, usually between the ages of twelve and fourteen. She might take up residence on another farm, but more likely she would migrate to a nearby town or city. She would rarely travel more than thirty miles from her parents' household. She would then normally become a servant, once again living in a household, but this time in the household of an employer.

Having migrated from home, the young woman's chief goal was to accumulate enough capital for a dowry. Her savings would make her eligible for marriage because they would allow her to make the necessary contribution to form a household with her husband. Marriage within the family economy was a joint economic undertaking, and the wife was expected to make an immediate contribution of capital for establishing the household. A young woman might well work for ten years or more to accumulate a dowry. This practice meant that marriage was usually postponed until her mid- to late twenties.

Within marriage, earning enough money or producing enough farm goods to ensure an adequate food supply dominated women's concerns. Domestic duties, childbearing, and child rearing were subordinate to economic pressures. Consequently, couples tried to limit the number of children, usually through the practice of *coitus interruptus*, the withdrawal of the male before ejaculation. Parents often placed young children with wet nurses so the mother could continue to make her economic contribution to the household. The wet nurse, in turn, contributed to the economic welfare of her own household. The child would be fully reintegrated into its own family when it was weaned and would then be expected to aid the family at an early age.

The work of married women differed markedly between city and country and was in many ways a function of their husbands' occupations. If the peasant household had enough land to support itself, the wife spent much of her time quite literally carrying things for her husband—water, food, seed, harvested grain, and the like. There were few such adequate landholdings, however. If the husband had to do work besides farming, such as fishing or migrant labor, the wife might actually be in charge of the farm and do the ploughing, planting, and harvesting. In the city, the wife of an artisan or a merchant might well be in charge of the household finances and actively participate in managing the trade or manufacturing enterprise. When her husband died, she might take over the business and perhaps hire an artisan. Finally, if economic disaster struck the family, it was usually the wife who organized what Olwen Hufton has called the "economy of expedients,"[1] within which family members might be sent off to find work elsewhere or even to beg in the streets.

Through all this economic activity women found many occupations and professions closed to them

---

[1] Olwen Hufton, "Women and the Family Economy in Eighteenth-Century France," *French Historical Studies*, 9 (1976): 19.

An Edinburgh Physician Describes
the Dangers of Childbirth

Death in childbirth was a common occurrence throughout Europe until the twentieth century. This brief letter from an Edinburgh physician illustrates how devastating infectious diseases could be to women at the time of childbirth.

✦ *How does this passage illustrate a health danger that only women confronted? How might the likelihood of the death of oneself or a spouse in childbirth have affected one's attitudes toward children? How does this passage illustrate limitations on knowledge about disease in the eighteenth century?*

We had puerperal fever in the infirmary last winter. It began about the end of February, when almost every woman, as soon as she was delivered, or perhaps about twenty-four hours after, was seized with it; and all of them died, though every method was tried to cure the disorder. What was singular, the women were in good health before they were brought to bed, though some of them had been long in the hospital before delivery. One woman had been dismissed from the ward before she was brought to bed; came into it some days after with her labor upon her; was easily delivered, and remained perfectly well for twenty-four hours, when she was seized with a shivering and the other symptoms of the fever. I caused her to be removed to another ward; yet notwithstanding all the care that was taken of her she died in the same manner as the others.

From a letter to Mr. White from a Dr. Young of Edinburgh, 21 November, 1774, cited in C. White, Treatise on the Management of Pregnant and Lying-In Women (London, 1777), pp. 45–46, as quoted in Bridget Hill, ed., Eighteenth-Century Women: An Anthology (London: George Allen & Unwin, 1984), p. 102.

because they were women. They labored with less education than men, because in this society women in all levels of life consistently found fewer opportunities for education than men. They often received lower wages than men for the same work.

Children and the World of the Family Economy

For women of all social ranks, childbirth was a time of fear and personal vulnerability. Contagious diseases endangered both mother and child. Puerperal fever was frequent, as were other infections from unsterilized medical instruments. Not all midwives were skillful practitioners. Furthermore, most mothers and children immediately encountered immense poverty and wretched housing. Assuming that both mother and child survived, the mother might nurse the infant, but often the child would be sent to a wet nurse. Convenience may have led to this practice among the wealthy, but economic necessity dictated it for the poor. The structures and customs of the family economy did not permit a woman to devote herself entirely to rearing a child. The wet-nursing industry was well organized, with urban children being frequently transported to wet nurses in the country, where they would remain for months or even years.

Throughout Europe, the birth of a child was not always welcome. The child might represent another economic burden on an already hard-pressed household. Or it might be illegitimate. The number of illegitimate births seems to have increased during the eighteenth century, possibly because increased population migration led to fleeting romances.

Through at least the end of the seventeenth century, unwanted or illegitimate births could lead to infanticide, especially among the poor. The parents might smother the infant or expose it to the elements. These practices were one result of both the ignorance and the prejudice surrounding contraception.

The late seventeenth and the early eighteenth centuries saw a new interest in preserving the lives of abandoned children. Although foundling hospitals established to care for abandoned children had existed before, their size and number expanded during these years. Two of the most famous were the Paris Foundling Hospital (1670) and the London Foundling Hospital (1739). Such hospitals cared for thousands of European children, and the demands for their services increased during the eighteenth century. For example, early in the century, an average of 1,700 children a year were admitted to the Paris Foundling Hospital. In the peak year of 1772, however, that number rose to 7,676 children. Not all of those children came from Paris. Many had been brought to the city from the provinces, where local foundling homes and hospitals were overburdened. The London Foundling Hospital lacked the income to deal with all the children brought to it. In the middle of the eighteenth century, the hospital found itself compelled to choose children for admission by a lottery system.

Sadness and tragedy surrounded abandoned children. Most of them were illegitimate infants from across the social spectrum. Many, however, were left with the foundling hospitals because their parents could not support them. There was a close relationship between rising food prices and increasing numbers of abandoned children in Paris. Parents would sometimes leave personal tokens or saints' medals on the abandoned baby in the vain hope that they might one day be able to reclaim the child. Few children were reclaimed. Leaving a child at a foundling hospital did not guarantee its survival. In Paris, only about 10 percent of all abandoned children lived to the age of ten.

Despite all of these perils of early childhood, children did grow up and come of age across Europe. The world of the child may not have received the kind of attention that it does today, but during the eighteenth century, the seeds of that modern sensibility were sown. Particularly among the upper classes, new interest arose in the education of children. In most areas education remained firmly in the hands of the churches. As economic skills became more demanding, literacy became more valuable, and literacy rates rose during the century. Yet most Europeans remained illiterate. Not until the late nineteenth century was the world of childhood inextricably linked to the process of education. Then children would be reared to become members of a national citizenry. In the Old Regime, they were reared to make their contribution to the economy of their parents' family and then to set up their own households.

The Revolution in Agriculture

Thus far this chapter has examined those groups who sought stability and who, except for certain members of the nobility, resisted change. Other groups, however, wished to pursue significant new directions in social and economic life. The remainder of this chapter will consider those forces and developments that would during the next century transform European life. These developments first appeared in agriculture.

The main goal of traditional peasant society was a stability that would ensure the local food supply. Despite differences in rural customs throughout Europe, the tillers resisted changes that might endanger the sure supply of food, which they generally believed that traditional cultivation would provide. The food supply was never certain, and the farther east one traveled, the more uncertain it became. Failure of the harvest meant not only hardship but death from either outright starvation or protracted debility. Often, people living in the countryside had more difficulty finding food than did city dwellers, whose local government usually stored reserve supplies of grain.

Poor harvests also played havoc with prices. Smaller supplies or larger demand raised grain prices. Even small increases in the cost of food could exert heavy pressure on peasant or artisan families. If prices increased sharply, many of those families fell back on poor relief from their local municipality or county or the Church.

Historians now believe that during the eighteenth century, bread prices slowly but steadily rose, spurred largely by population growth. Since bread was their main food, this inflation put pressure on all of the poor. Prices rose faster than urban wages and brought no appreciable advantage to the small peasant producer. On the other hand, the rise in grain prices benefitted landowners and those wealthier peasants who had surplus grain to sell.

The rising grain prices gave landlords an opportunity to improve their incomes and lifestyle. To achieve those ends, landlords in western Europe began a series of innovations in farm production that became known as the *Agricultural Revolution*.

Landlords commercialized agriculture and thereby challenged the traditional peasant ways of production. Peasant revolts and disturbances often resulted. The governments of Europe, hungry for new taxes and dependent on the goodwill of the nobility, used their armies and militias to smash peasants who defended the past.

NEW CROPS AND NEW METHODS The drive to improve agricultural production began during the sixteenth and seventeenth centuries in the Low Countries, where the pressures of the growing population and the shortage of land required changes in cultivation. Dutch landlords and farmers devised better ways to build dikes and to drain land, so that they could farm more extensive areas. They also experimented with new crops, such as clover and turnips, that would increase the supply of animal fodder and restore the soil. These improvements became so famous that early in the seventeenth century English landlords hired Cornelius Vermuyden, a Dutch drainage engineer, to drain thousands of acres of land around Cambridge.

English landlords provided the most striking examples of eighteenth-century agricultural improvement. They originated almost no genuinely new farming methods, but they popularized ideas developed in the previous century either in the Low Countries or in England. Some of these landlords and agricultural innovators became famous. For example, Jethro Tull (1674–1741) was willing to experiment himself and to finance the experiments of others. Many of his ideas, such as the rejection of manure as fertilizer, were wrong. Others, however, such as using iron plows to turn earth more deeply and planting wheat by a drill rather than by casting, were excellent. His methods permitted land to be cultivated for longer periods without having to be left fallow.

Turgot Describes French Landholding

The economy of Europe until the nineteenth century was overwhelmingly rural. That meant that economic growth and political stability depended largely on agricultural production. During the eighteenth century, many observers became keenly aware that different kinds of landholding led to different attitudes toward work and to different levels of production. Robert Jacques Turgot (1727–1781), who later became finance minister of France, analyzed these differences in an effort to reform French agriculture. He was especially concerned with arrangements that encouraged long-term investment. The métayer system, discussed by Turgot, was an arrangement whereby landowners arranged to have land farmed by peasants who received part of the harvest as payment for their working the land. The peasant had no long-term interest in improving the land. Virtually all observers regarded the system as inefficient.

✦ *Why does Turgot clearly favor those farmers who can make investments in the land they rent from a proprietor? What are the structures of the métayer system? Why did it necessarily lead to poor investments and lesser harvests? What is Turgot's attitude toward work and entrepreneurship?*

1. What really distinguishes the area of large-scale farming from the areas of small-scale production is that in the former areas the proprietors find farmers who provide them with a permanent revenue from the land and who buy from them the right to cultivate it for a certain number of years. These farmers undertake all the expenses of cultivation, the ploughing, the sowing and the stocking of the farm with cattle, animals and tools. They are really agricultural entrepreneurs, who possess, like the entrepreneurs in all other branches of commerce, considerable funds, which they employ in the cultivation of land. . . .

Charles "Turnip" Townsend (1674–1738) encouraged other important innovations. He learned from the Dutch how to cultivate sandy soil with fertilizers. He also instituted crop rotation, using wheat, turnips, barley, and clover. This new system of rotation replaced the fallow field with one sown with a crop that both restored nutrients to the soil and supplied animal fodder. The additional fodder meant that more livestock could be raised. These fodders allowed animals to be fed during the winter and assured a year-round supply of meat. The larger number of animals increased the quantity of manure available as fertilizer for the grain crops. Consequently, in the long run, there was more food for both animals and human beings.

A third British agricultural improver was Robert Bakewell (1725–1795), who pioneered new methods of animal breeding that produced more and better animals and more milk and meat.

These and other innovations received widespread discussion in the works of Arthur Young (1741–1820), who edited the *Annals of Agriculture*. In 1793 he became secretary of the British Board of Agriculture. Young traveled widely across Europe, and his books are among the most important documents of life during the second half of the eighteenth century.

ENCLOSURE REPLACES OPEN-FIELD METHOD   Many of the agriculture innovations, which were adopted only slowly, were incompatible with the existing organization of land in England. Small cultivators who lived in village communities still farmed most of the soil. Each farmer tilled an assortment of unconnected strips. The two- or three-field systems of rotation left large portions of land fallow and unproductive each year. Animals grazed on the common land in the summer and on the stubble of

---

They have not only the brawn but also the wealth to devote to agriculture. They have to work, but unlike workers they do not have to earn their living by the sweat of their brow, but by the lucrative employment of their capital, just as the shipowners of Nantes and Bordeaux employ theirs in maritime commerce.

2. *Métayer* System   The areas of small-scale farming, that is to say at least 4/7ths of the kingdom, are those where there are no agricultural entrepreneurs, where a proprietor who wishes to develop his land cannot find anyone to cultivate it except wretched peasants who have no resources other than their labor, where he is obliged to make, at his own expense, all the advances necessary for tillage, beasts, tools, sowing, even to the extent of advancing to his *métayer* the wherewithal to feed himself until the first harvest, where consequently a proprietor who did not have any property other than his estate would be obliged to allow it to lie fallow.

After having deducted the costs of sowing and feudal dues with which the property is burdened, the proprietor shares with the *métayer* what remains of the profits, in accordance with the agreement they have concluded. The proprietor runs all the risks of harvest failure and any loss of cattle:

he is the real entrepreneur. The *métayer* is nothing more than a mere workman, a farm hand to whom the proprietor surrenders a share of his profits instead of paying wages. But in his work the proprietor enjoys none of the advantages of the farmer who, working on his own behalf, works carefully and diligently; the proprietor is obliged to entrust all his advances to a man who may be negligent or a scoundrel and is answerable for nothing.

This *métayer*, accustomed to the most miserable existence and without the hope and even the desire to obtain a better living for himself, cultivates badly and neglects to employ the land for valuable and profitable production; by preference he occupies himself in cultivating those things whose growth is less troublesome and which provide him with more foodstuffs, such as buck wheat and chestnuts which do not require any attention. He does not worry very much about his livelihood; he knows that if the harvest fails, his master will be obliged to feed him in order not to see his land neglected.

A. M. R. Turgot, Oeuvres, et documents les concernant, ed. by F. Schelle, 5 vols. (Paris, 1914), vol. II, pp. 448–450, as quoted and translated in S. Pollard and C. Holmes, eds., Documents of European Economic History, vol. I *(London: Edward Arnold, 1968), pp. 38–39.*

the harvest in the winter. Until at least the middle of the eighteenth century, the decisions about what crops would be planted were made communally. The entire system discouraged improvement and favored the poorer farmers, who needed the common land and stubble fields for their animals. The village method precluded expanding the pasture land to raise more animals that would, in turn, produce more manure, which could be used for fertilizer. Thus, the methods of traditional production aimed at a steady, but not a growing, supply of food.

In 1700 approximately half the arable land in England was farmed by this open-field method. By the second half of the century, the rising price of wheat encouraged landlords to consolidate or enclose their lands to increase production. The enclosures were intended to use land more rationally and to achieve greater commercial profits. The process involved the fencing of common lands, the reclamation of previously untilled waste, and the transformation of strips into block fields. These procedures brought turmoil to the economic and social life of the countryside. Riots often ensued.

Because many English farmers either owned their strips or rented them in a manner that amounted to ownership, the larger landlords usually resorted to parliamentary acts to legalize the enclosure of the land, which they owned but rented to the farmers. Because the large landowners controlled Parliament, such measures passed easily. Between 1761 and 1792, almost 500,000 acres were enclosed through parliamentary act, compared with 75,000 acres between 1727 and 1760. In 1801 a general enclosure act streamlined the process.

The enclosures were controversial at the time and have remained so among historians. They permitted the extension of both farming and innovation and thus increased food production on larger agricultural units. They also disrupted small traditional communities; they forced off the land independent farmers, who had needed the common pasturage, and poor cottagers, who had lived on the reclaimed waste land. The enclosures, however, did not depopulate the countryside. In some counties where the enclosures took place, the population increased. New soil had come into production, and services subsidiary to farming also expanded.

The enclosures did not create the labor force for the British Industrial Revolution. What the enclosures most conspicuously displayed was the introduction of the entrepreneurial or capitalistic attitude of the urban merchant into the countryside.

This commercialization of agriculture, which spread from Britain slowly across the Continent during the next century, strained the paternal relationship between the governing and governed classes. Previously, landlords often had looked after the welfare of the lower orders through price controls or waiving rents during depressed periods. As the landlords became increasingly concerned about profits, they began to leave the peasants to the mercy of the marketplace.

LIMITED IMPROVEMENTS IN EASTERN EUROPE Improving agriculture tended to characterize farm production west of the Elbe. Dutch farming was quite efficient. In France, despite the efforts of the government to improve agriculture, enclosures were restricted. Yet there was much discussion in France about improving agricultural methods. These new procedures benefitted the ruling classes because better agriculture increased their incomes and assured a larger food supply, which discouraged social unrest.

In Prussia, Austria, Poland, and Russia, agricultural improvement was limited. Nothing in the relationship of the serfs to their lords encouraged innovation. In eastern Europe, the chief method of increasing production was to bring previously untilled lands under the plow. The landlords or their agents rather than the villages normally directed farm management. By extending tillage, the great landlords sought to squeeze more labor from their serfs rather than greater productivity from the soil. Eastern European landlords, like their western counterparts, sought to increase their profits, but they were much less ambitious and successful. The only significant nutritional gain achieved through their efforts was the introduction of maize and the potato. Livestock production did not increase significantly.

Population Expansion

The population explosion with which the entire world must contend today had its origins in the eighteenth century. Before this time, Europe's population had experienced dramatic increases, but plagues, wars, or famine had redressed the balance. Beginning in the second quarter of the eighteenth century, the population began to increase steadily. The need to feed this population caused food prices to rise, which spurred agricultural innovation. The need to provide everyday consumer goods for the expanding numbers of people fueled the demand side of the Industrial Revolution.

Our best estimates are that in 1700 Europe's population, excluding the European provinces of the Ottoman Empire, was between 100 million and 120 million people. By 1800 the figures had risen to almost 190 million, and by 1850 to 260 million. The population of England and Wales rose from 6 million in 1750 to more than 10 million in 1800. France grew from 18 million in 1715 to about 26 million in 1789. Russia's population increased from 19 million in 1722 to 29 million in 1766. Such extraordinary, sustained growth put new demands on all resources and considerable pressure on existing social organization.

The population expansion occurred across the Continent in both the country and the cities. Only a limited consensus exists among scholars about the causes of this growth. There was a clear decline in the death rate. There were fewer wars and somewhat fewer epidemics in the eighteenth century. Hygiene and sanitation also improved. Better medical knowledge and techniques were once thought to have contributed to the decline in deaths. This factor is now discounted because the more important medical advances came after the initial population explosion or would not have contributed directly to it.

Rather, changes in the food supply itself may have allowed population growth to be sustained. Improved and expanding grain production made one contribution. Another and even more important change was the cultivation of the potato. This tuber was a product of the New World and came into widespread European production during the eighteenth century. On a single acre enough potatoes could be raised to feed one peasant's family for an entire year. This more certain food supply enabled more children to survive to adulthood and rear children of their own.

The impact of the population explosion can hardly be overestimated. It created new demands for food, goods, jobs, and services. It provided a new pool of labor. Traditional modes of production and living had to be revised. More people lived in the countryside than could find employment there. Migration increased. There were also more people who might become socially and politically discontented. And because the population growth fed on itself, these pressures and demands continued to increase. The society and the social practices of the Old Regime literally outgrew their traditional bounds.

The Industrial Revolution of the Eighteenth Century

The second half of the eighteenth century witnessed the beginning of the industrialization of the European economy. The Industrial Revolution constituted the achievement of sustained economic growth. Previously, production had been limited. The economy of a province or a country might grow, but growth soon reached a plateau. Since the late eighteenth century, however, the economy of Europe has managed to expand almost uninterrupted. Depressions and recessions have been temporary, and even during such economic downturns, the Western economy has continued to grow.

At considerable social cost, industrialization made possible the production of more goods and more services than ever before in human history. Industrialization in Europe eventually overcame the economy of scarcity. The new means of production demanded new kinds of skills, new discipline in work, and a large labor force. The goods produced met immediate consumer demand and also created new demands. In the long run, industrialization clearly raised the standard of living and overcame the poverty that most Europeans who lived during the eighteenth century and earlier had taken for granted. It gave human beings greater control over the forces of nature than they had ever known before; yet industrialism would also by the middle of the nineteenth century cause new and unanticipated problems with the environment.

During the eighteenth century, people did not call these economic developments a *revolution*. That term came to be applied to the British economic phenomena only after the French Revolution. Then continental writers observed that what had taken place in Britain was the economic equivalent of the political events in France, hence an *Industrial Revolution*. It was revolutionary less in its speed, which was on the whole rather slow, than in its implications for the future of European society.

A Revolution in Consumption

The most familiar side of the Industrial Revolution was the invention of new machinery, the establishment of factories, and the creation of a new kind of workforce. Recent studies, however, have emphasized the demand side of the Industrial Revolution

Consumption of all forms of consumer goods increased greatly in the eighteenth century. This engraving illustrates a shop, probably in Paris. Here women, working apparently for a woman manager, are making dresses and hats to meet the demands of the fashion trade. As the document on page 558 demonstrates, some women writers urged more such employment opportunities for women. [Bildarchiv Preussischer Kulturbesitz]

and the vast increase in both the desire and the possibility of consuming goods and services that arose in the early eighteenth century.

The inventions of the Industrial Revolution increased the supply of consumer goods as never before in history. The supply of goods was only one side of the economic equation, however. The supply had been called forth by an unprecedented demand for humble goods of everyday life. Those goods included everyday consumer items such as clothing of all kinds, buttons, toys, china, furniture, rugs, kitchen utensils, candlesticks, brassware, silverware, pewterware, glassware, watches, jewelry, soap, beer, wines, and foodstuffs. It was the ever-increasing demand for these goods that sparked the ingenuity of designers and inventors. Furthermore, there seemed to be no limits to consumer demand.

Many social factors came into play to establish the markets for these consumer goods. During the seventeenth century, the Dutch had enjoyed enormous prosperity and had led the way in new forms of both everyday consumption and that of luxury goods. For reasons that are still not clear, during the eighteenth century, increasing numbers first of the English and then of people living on the Continent came to have more disposable income. This wealth may have resulted from the improvements in agriculture. Those incomes allowed people to buy consumer goods that previous generations had inher-

ited or did not possess. What is key to this change in consumption is that it depended primarily upon expanding the various domestic markets in Europe.

This revolution, if that is not too strong a term, in consumption was not automatic. People became persuaded that they needed or wanted new consumer goods. Often, entrepreneurs caused it to happen by developing new methods of marketing. An enterprising manufacturer such as the porcelain manufacturer Josiah Wedgwood (1730–1795) first attempted to find customers among the royal family and the aristocracy. Once he had gained their business with luxury goods, he would then produce a somewhat less expensive version of the chinaware for middle-class customers. He also used advertising. He opened showrooms in London and had salespeople traveling all over England with samples and catalogs of his wares. On the Continent, he equipped salespeople with bilingual catalogs. There seemed to be no limit to the markets for different kinds of consumer goods that could be stimulated by social emulation on the one hand and advertising on the other.

Furthermore, the process of change in style itself became institutionalized. New fashions and inventions were always better than old ones. If new kinds of goods could be produced, there usually was a market for them. If one product did not find a market, its failure provided a lesson for the development of a different new product.

This expansion of consumption quietly but steadily challenged the social assumptions of the day. Fashion publications made all levels of society aware of new styles. Clothing fashions could be copied. Servants could begin to dress well if not luxuriously. There were changes in the consumption of food and drink that also called forth demand for new kinds of dishware for the home. Tea and coffee became staples. The brewing industry became fully commercialized. Those developments entailed the need for new kinds of cups and mugs and many more of them.

There would always be critics of this consumer economy. The vision of luxury and comfort it offered contrasted with the asceticism of ancient Sparta and contemporary Christian ethics. Yet ever-increasing consumption and production of the goods of everyday life became a hallmark of modern Western society from the eighteenth century to our own day. It would be difficult to overestimate the importance of the desire for consumer goods and the increasing material standard of living that they made possible in Western history after the eighteenth century. The presence and accessibility of such goods became the hallmark of a nation's prosperity. It is perhaps relevant to note that it was the absence of such consumer goods as well as of civil liberties that during the 1980s led to such deep discontent with the communist regimes in Eastern Europe and the former Soviet Union.

Industrial Leadership of Great Britain

Great Britain was the home of the Industrial Revolution and, until the middle of the nineteenth century, maintained the industrial leadership of Europe. Several factors contributed to the early start in Britain.

Great Britain took the lead in the consumer revolution that expanded the demand for goods that could be efficiently supplied. London was by far the largest city in Europe. It was the center of a world of fashion and taste to which hundreds of thousands if not millions of British citizens were exposed each year. In London, these people learned to want the consumer goods they saw on visits for business and pleasure. Newspapers thrived in Britain during the eighteenth century, allowing for advertising that increased consumer wants. The social structure of Britain allowed and even encouraged people to imitate the lifestyles of their social superiors. It seems to have been in Britain that a world of fashion first

developed that led people to want to accumulate goods. In addition to the domestic consumer demand, the British economy benefitted from demand from the colonies in North America.

Britain was also the single largest free-trade area in Europe. The British had good roads and waterways without internal tolls or other trade barriers. The country was endowed with rich deposits of coal and iron ore. Its political structure was stable, and property was absolutely secure. The sound systems of banking and public credit established a stable climate for investment. Taxation in Britain was heavy, but it was efficiently and fairly collected, largely from indirect taxes. Furthermore, British taxes received legal approval through Parliament with all social classes and all regions of the nation paying the same taxes. In contrast to the Continent, there was no pattern of privileged tax exemptions.

Finally, British society was mobile by the standards of the time. Persons who had money or could earn money could rise socially. The British aristocracy would receive into its midst people who had amassed large fortunes. Even persons of wealth not admitted to the aristocracy could enjoy their riches, receive social prominence, and exert political influence. No one of these factors preordained the British advance toward industrialism. Together, however, when added to the progressive state of British agriculture, they provided the nation with the marginal advantage to create a new mode of economic production.

New Methods of Textile Production

The industry that pioneered the Industrial Revolution and met growing consumer demand was the production of textiles for clothing. It provides the key example of industrialism emerging to supply the demands of an ever-growing market for everyday goods. Furthermore, it illustrates the surprising fact that much of the earliest industrial change took place not in cities but in the countryside.

Although eighteenth-century society was primarily agricultural, manufacturing also permeated rural areas. The peasant family living in a one- or two-room cottage was the basic unit of production rather than the factory. The same peasants who tilled the land in spring and summer often spun thread or wove textiles in the winter.

Under what is termed the domestic, or putting-out, system, agents of urban textile merchants took wool or other unfinished fibers to the homes of peasants, who spun it into thread. The agent then transported the thread to other peasants, who wove it into the finished product. The merchant sold the wares. In thousands of peasant cottages from Ireland to Austria, there stood a spinning wheel or a handloom. Sometimes the spinners or weavers owned their own equipment, but more often than not by the middle of the century, the merchant capitalist owned the machinery as well as the raw material.

The domestic system of textile production was a basic feature of this family economy and would continue to be so in Britain and on the Continent well into the nineteenth century. By mid-century, however, a series of production bottlenecks had developed within the domestic system. The demand for cotton textiles was growing more rapidly than production, especially in Great Britain, which had a large domestic and North American market for cotton textiles. Inventors devised some of the most famous machines of the early Industrial Revolution in response to this consumer demand for cotton textiles.

THE SPINNING JENNY   Cotton textile weavers had the technical capacity to produce the quantity of fabric demanded. The spinners, however, did not have the equipment to produce as much thread as the weavers needed. James Kay's invention of the flying shuttle, which increased the productivity of the weavers, had created this imbalance during the 1730s. Thereafter, various groups of manufacturers and merchants offered prizes for the invention of a machine to eliminate this bottleneck.

About 1765 James Hargreaves (d. 1778) invented the spinning jenny. Initially, this machine allowed 16 spindles of thread to be spun, but by the close of the century its capacity had been increased to as many as 120 spindles.

THE WATER FRAME   The spinning jenny broke the bottleneck between the productive capacity of the spinners and the weavers, but it was still a piece of machinery used in the cottage. The invention that took cotton textile manufacture out of the home and put it into the factory was Richard Arkwright's (1732–1792) water frame, patented in 1769. This was a water-powered device designed to permit the production of a purely cotton fabric rather than a cotton fabric containing linen fiber for durability. Eventually Arkwright lost his patent rights, and other manufacturers could use his invention freely. As a result, many factories sprang up in the coun-

tryside near streams that provided the necessary waterpower. From the 1780s onward, the cotton industry could meet an ever-expanding demand. Cotton output increased by 800 percent between 1780 and 1800. By 1815 cotton composed 40 percent of the value of British domestic exports, and by 1830 just over 50 percent.

The Industrial Revolution had commenced in earnest by the 1780s, but the full economic and social ramifications of this unleashing of human productive capacity were not really felt until the early nineteenth century. The expansion of industry and the incorporation of new inventions often occurred rather slowly. For example, Edmund Cartwright (1743–1822) invented the power loom for machine weaving in the late 1780s. Yet not until the 1830s were there more power-loom weavers than handloom weavers in Britain. Nor did all the social ramifications of industrialism appear immediately. The first cotton mills used water power, were located in the country, and rarely employed more than two dozen workers. Not until the late-century application of the steam engine, perfected by James Watt (1736–1819) in 1769, to the running of textile machinery could factories easily be located in or near existing urban centers. The steam engine not only vastly increased and regularized the available energy but also made possible the combination of urbanization and industrialization.

The Steam Engine

More than any other invention, the steam engine permitted industrialization to grow on itself and to expand into one area of production after another. This machine provided for the first time in human history a steady and essentially unlimited source of inanimate power. Unlike engines powered by water or the wind, the steam engine, driven by the burning of coal, provided a portable source of industrial power that did not fail or falter as the seasons of the year changed. Unlike human or animal power, the steam engine depended on mineral energy that did not tire during a day. Finally, the steam engine could be applied to many industrial and, eventually, transportation uses.

The first practical engine using steam power had been the invention of Thomas Newcomen (1663–1729) in the early eighteenth century. The piston of this device was moved when the steam that had been induced into the cylinder condensed, causing

the piston to fall. The Newcomen machine was large, inefficient in its use of energy because both the condenser and the cylinder were heated, and practically untransportable. Despite these problems, English mine operators used the Newcomen machines to pump water out of coal and tin mines. By the third quarter of the eighteenth century, almost 100 Newcomen machines were operating in the mining districts of England.

During the 1760s, James Watt, a Scottish engineer and machine maker, began to experiment with a model of a Newcomen machine at the University of Glasgow. He gradually understood that separating the condenser from the piston and the cylinder would achieve much greater efficiency. In 1769 he patented his new invention, but transforming his idea into application presented difficulties. His design required precise metalwork. Watt soon found a partner in Matthew Boulton (1728–1809), a successful toy and button manufacturer in Birmingham, the city with the most skilled metalworkers in Britain. Watt and Boulton, in turn, consulted with John Wilkinson (1728–1808), a cannon manufacturer, to find ways to drill the precise metal cylinders required by Watt's design. In 1776 the Watt steam engine found its first commercial application pumping water from mines in Cornwall.

The use of the steam engine spread slowly because until 1800 Watt retained the exclusive patent rights. He was also reluctant to make further changes in his invention that would permit the engine to operate more rapidly. Boulton eventually persuaded him to make modifications and improvements. These allowed the engines to be used not only for pumping but also for running cotton mills. By the early nineteenth century, the steam engine had become the prime mover for all industry. With its application to ships and then to wagons on iron rails, the steam engine also revolutionized transportation.

Iron Production

The manufacture of high-quality iron has been basic to modern industrial development. It is the chief element of all heavy industry and land or sea transport. Iron has also been the material out of which most productive machinery itself has been manufactured. During the early eighteenth century, British ironmakers produced somewhat less than 25,000 tons annually. Three factors held back the production of the metal. First, charcoal rather than coke was used to smelt the ore. Charcoal, derived from wood, was becoming scarce and does not burn at as high a temperature as coke, derived from coal. Second, until the perfection of the steam engine, insufficient blasts could be achieved in the furnaces. Finally, the demand for iron was limited. The elimination of the first two problems also eliminated the third.

Eventually, British ironmakers began to use coke, and the steam engine provided new power for the blast furnaces. Coke was an abundant fuel because of Britain's large coal deposits. The existence of the steam engine both improved iron production and increased the demand for iron.

In 1784 Henry Cort (1740–1800) introduced a new puddling process, that is, a new method for melting and stirring the molten ore. Cort's process allowed more slag (the impurities that bubbled to the top of the molten metal) to be removed and a purer iron to be produced. Cort also developed a rolling mill that continuously shaped the still-molten metal into bars, rails, or other forms. Previously the metal had to be pounded into these forms.

All these innovations achieved a better, more versatile product at a lower cost. The demand for iron grew as its price became lower. By the early nineteenth century, the British produced over a million tons annually. The lower cost of iron, in turn, lowered the cost of steam engines and allowed them to be used more widely.

Cities

Remarkable changes occurred in the pattern of city growth between 1500 and 1800. In 1500 within Europe (excluding Hungary and Russia) there were 156 cities with a population greater than 10,000. Only 4 of those cities—Paris, Milan, Venice, and Naples—had populations larger than 100,000. By 1800, 363 cities had 10,000 or more inhabitants, and 17 of them had populations larger than 100,000. The percentage of the European population living in urban areas had risen from just over 5 percent to just over 9 percent. There had also occurred a major shift in urban concentration from southern, Mediterranean Europe to the north.

Patterns of Preindustrial Urbanization

The eighteenth century witnessed a considerable growth of towns, closely related to the tumult of the day and the revolutions with which the century closed. London grew from about 700,000 inhabitants in 1700 to almost 1 million in 1800. By the time of the French Revolution, Paris had more than 500,000 inhabitants. Berlin's population tripled during the century, reaching 170,000 in 1800. Warsaw had 30,000 inhabitants in 1730, but almost 120,000 in 1794. Saint Petersburg, founded in 1703, numbered more than 250,000 inhabitants a century later. In addition to the growth of these capitals, the number of smaller cities of 20,000–50,000 people increased considerably. This urban growth must, however, be kept in perspective. Even in France and Great Britain, probably somewhat less than 20 percent of the population lived in cities. And the town of 10,000 inhabitants was much more common than the giant urban center.

These raw figures conceal significant changes that took place in how cities grew and how the population distributed itself. The major urban development of the sixteenth century had been followed by a leveling off and even a decline in the seventeenth. New growth began in the early eighteenth century and accelerated during the late eighteenth and the early nineteenth centuries. Between 1500 and 1750 the major urban expansion took place within already established and generally already large cities. After 1750 the pattern changed with the birth of new cities and the rapid growth of older smaller cities.

GROWTH OF CAPITALS AND PORTS   In particular, between 1600 and 1750, the cities that grew most vigorously were capitals and ports. This situation reflects the success of monarchical state building during those years and the consequent burgeoning of bureaucracies, armies, courts, and other groups who lived in the capitals. The growth of port cities, in turn, reflects the expansion of European overseas trade and most especially that of the Atlantic routes. Except for Manchester in England and Lyons in France, the new urban conglomerates were nonindustrial cities.

Furthermore, between 1600 and 1750, cities with populations of fewer than 40,000 inhabitants declined. These included older landlocked trading centers, medieval industrial cities, and ecclesiastical centers. They contributed less to the new political regimes, and the expansion of the putting-out system transferred to the countryside much production that had once occurred in medieval cities. Rural labor was cheaper than urban labor, and cities with concentrations of labor declined as production was moved from the urban workshop into the country.

EMERGENCE OF NEW CITIES AND GROWTH OF SMALL TOWNS In the middle of the eighteenth century, a new pattern emerged. The rate of growth of existing large cities declined, while new cities began to emerge and existing smaller cities began to grow. Several factors were at work in the process, which Jan De Vries has termed "an urban growth from below."[2] First, there was the general overall population increase. Second, the early stages of the Industrial Revolution, particularly in Britain, occurred in the countryside and fostered the growth of smaller towns and cities located near factories. Factory organization itself led to new concentrations of population.

Cities also grew as a result of the new prosperity of European agriculture even where there was little industrialization. Improved agricultural production promoted the growth of nearby market towns and other urban centers that served agriculture or allowed more prosperous farmers to have access to the consumer goods and recreation they wanted. This new pattern of urban growth—new cities and the expansion of smaller existing ones—would continue into the nineteenth century.

Urban Classes

Social divisions were as marked in the cities of the eighteenth century as they were in the industrial centers of the nineteenth. Visible segregation often existed between the urban rich and the urban poor. The nobles and the upper middle class lived in fashionable town houses, often constructed around newly laid-out green squares. The poorest town dwellers usually congregated along the rivers. Small merchants and artisans lived above their shops. Whole families might live in a single room. Modern sanitary facilities were still unknown. There was little pure water. Cattle, pigs, goats, and other animals walked the streets with the people. All reports on the cities of Europe during this period emphasize both the striking grace and beauty of the dwellings of the wealthy and the dirt, filth, and stench that filled the streets.

Poverty was not just an urban problem; it was usually worse in the countryside. In the city, however, poverty was more visible in the form of crime, prostitution, vagrancy, begging, and alcoholism.

[2]Jan De Vries, "Patterns of Urbanization in Pre-Industrial Europe, 1500–1800," in H. Schmal, ed., *Patterns of Urbanization Since 1500* (London: Croom Helm, 1981), p. 103.

The socially astute English artist William Hogarth (1697–1764) created a series of engravings and etchings in which he commented on the evils of city life. This picture, from "A Harlot's Progress, Plate One" is entitled "Ensnared by a Procuress" (1732). [The Trustees of the Weston Park Foundation/The Bridgeman Art Library, London]

Many a young man or woman from the countryside migrated to the nearest city to seek a better life, only to discover poor housing, little food, disease, degradation, and finally death. It did not require the Industrial Revolution and the urban factories to make the cities into hellholes for the poor and the dispossessed. The full darkness of London life during the mid-century "gin age," when consumption of that liquor blinded and killed many poor people, is evident in the engravings of William Hogarth (1697–1764).

Also contrasting with the serenity of the aristocratic and upper-commercial-class lifestyle were the public executions that took place all over Europe, the breaking of men and women on instruments of torture in Paris, and the public floggings in Russia. Brutality condoned and carried out by the ruling classes was simply a fact of everyday life.

THE UPPER CLASSES At the top of the urban social structure stood a generally small group of nobles, large merchants, bankers, financiers, clergy, and government officials. These upper-classmen controlled the political and economic affairs of the town. Nor-

Manchester's Calico Printers Protest the Use of New Machinery

The introduction of the new machines associated with the Industrial Revolution stirred much protest. With machines able to duplicate the skills of laborers, workers feared the loss of jobs and the resulting loss of status when their chief means of livelihood lay in their possession of those displaced and now mechanized skills. The following letter was sent anonymously to a Manchester manufacturer by English workers. It shows the outrage of those workers, the intimidation they were willing to use as threats, and their own economic fears.

✦ *How might new machines adversely affect the livelihood of workers? Did the workers have other complaints against Mr. Taylor in addition to the introduction of new machinery? How have these workers reached an agreement to protect the interests of James Hobson? How do the workers combine the threat of violent actions with claims that other actions they have taken are legal?*

Mr. Taylor, If you dont discharge James Hobson from the House of Correction we will burn your House about your Ears for we have sworn to stand by one another and you must immediately give over any more Mashen Work for we are determined there shall be no more of them made use of in the Trade and it will be madness for you to contend with the Trade as we are combined by Oath to fix Prices we can afford to pay him a Guinea Week and not hurt the fund if you was to keep him there till Dumsday therefore mind you comply with the above or by God we will keep our Words with you we will make some rare Bunfires in this Countey and at your Peril to call any more Meetings mind that we will make the Mosney Pepel shake in their Shoes we are determined to destroy all Sorts of Masheens for Printing in the Kingdom for there is more hands then is work for so no more from the ingerd Gurnemen Rember we are a great number sworn nor you must not advertise the Men that you say run away from you when your il Usage was the Cause of their going we will punish you for that our Meetings are legal for we want nothing but what is honest and to work for selvs and familers and you want to starve us but it is better for you and a few more which we have marked to die then such a Number of Pore Men and their famerles to be starved.

London Gazette, 1786, p. 36, as reprinted in Douglas Hay, ed., Albion's Fatal Tree (New York: Pantheon Books, 1975), p. 318.

mally, they constituted a self-appointed and self-electing oligarchy that governed the city through its corporation or city council. These rights of self-government had normally been granted by some form of royal charter that gave the city corporation its authority and the power to select its own members. In a few cities on the Continent, artisan guilds controlled the corporations, but more generally the councils were under the influence of the local nobility and the wealthiest commercial people.

THE MIDDLE CLASS   Another group in the city was the prosperous but not always immensely wealthy merchants, tradespeople, bankers, and professional people. They were the most dynamic element of the urban population and constituted the persons traditionally regarded as the middle class, or bourgeoisie. The concept of the middle class was much less clear-cut than that of the nobility. The middle class itself was and would remain diverse and divided with persons employed in the professions often resentful of those who drew their incomes from commerce. Less wealthy members of the middle class of whatever occupation resented wealthier members who might be connected to the nobility through social or business relationships.

This engraving illustrates a metalworking shop such as might have been found in almost any town of significance in Europe. Most of the people employed in the shop probably belonged to the same family. Note that two women are also working. The wife may very well have been the person in charge of keeping the accounts of the business. The two younger boys might be children of the owner or apprentices in the trade, or both. [Bildarchiv Preussischer Kulturbesitz]

The middle class had less wealth than most nobles but more than urban artisans. Middle-class people lived in the cities and towns, and their sources of income had little or nothing to do with the land. In one way or another, they all benefitted from expanding trade and commerce whether as merchants, as lawyers, or as small factory owners. Theirs was a world in which the earning and saving of money allowed for rapid social mobility and change in lifestyle. They saw themselves as people willing to use their capital and energy to work, while they portrayed the nobility as idle. The members of the middle class tended to be economically aggressive and socially ambitious. People often made fun of them for these characteristics and were jealous of their success. The middle class normally supported reform, change, and economic growth. The bourgeoisie also wanted more rational regulations for trade and commerce, as did some of the more progressive aristocrats.

The middle class was made up of people whose lives fostered the revolution in consumption. On one hand, as owners of factories and of wholesale and retail businesses, they produced and sold goods for the expanding consumer market; on the other hand, members of the middle class were also among the chief consumers. It was to their homes that the vast array of new consumer goods made their way. They were also the people whose social values clearly embraced most fully the commercial spirit. They might not enjoy the titles or privileges of the nobility, but they could enjoy considerable material comfort and prosperity. It was this style of life that less well-off people could still emulate as they sought to acquire consumer goods for themselves.

During the eighteenth century, the relationship between the middle class and the aristocracy was complicated. On one hand, the nobles, especially in England and France, increasingly embraced the commercial spirit associated with the middle class by improving their estates and investing in cities. On the other hand, wealthy members of the middle class often tried to imitate the lifestyle of the nobility by purchasing landed estates. The aspirations of the middle class for social mobility, however, conflicted with the determination of the nobles to maintain and reassert their own privileges and to protect their own wealth. The middle-class commercial figures—traders, bankers, manufacturers, and lawyers—often found their pursuit of both profit and prestige blocked by the privileges of the nobility and its social exclusiveness, by the inefficiency of monarchical bureaucracies dominated by the nobility, or by aristocrats who controlled patronage and government contracts.

The bourgeoisie was not rising to challenge the nobility; rather, both were seeking to add new dimensions to their existing political power and social prestige. The tensions that arose between the nobles and the middle class during the eighteenth century normally involved issues of power sharing or access to political influence rather than clashes over values or goals associated with class.

The middle class in the cities also feared the lower urban classes as much as they envied the nobility. The lower orders were a potentially violent element in society, a potential threat to property, and, in their poverty, a drain on national resources. The lower classes, however, were much more varied than either the city aristocracy or the middle class cared to admit.

ARTISANS   Shopkeepers, artisans, and wage earners were the single largest group in any city. They were grocers, butchers, fishmongers, carpenters, cabinet-makers, smiths, printers, handloom weavers, and tailors, to give a few examples. They had their own culture, values, and institutions. Like the peasants of the countryside, they were in many respects conservative. Their economic position was highly vulnerable. If a poor harvest raised the price of food, their own businesses suffered. These urban classes also contributed to the revolution in consumption, however. They could buy more goods than ever before, and many of them sought to the extent their incomes permitted to copy the domestic consumption of the middle class.

The lives of these artisans and shopkeepers centered on their work and their neighborhoods. They usually lived near or at their place of employment. Most of them worked in shops with fewer than a half dozen other artisans. Their primary institution had historically been the guild, but by the eighteenth century, the guilds rarely had the influence of their predecessors in medieval or early modern Europe.

Nevertheless, the guilds were not to be ignored. They played a conservative role. Rather than seeking economic growth or innovation, they tried to preserve the jobs and skills of their members. The guilds were still able in many countries to determine who could pursue a particular craft. To lessen competition, they attempted to prevent too many people from learning a particular skill.

The guilds also provided a framework for social and economic advancement. At an early age, a boy might become an apprentice to learn a craft or trade. After several years he would be made a journeyman. Still later, if successful and sufficiently competent, he might become a master. The artisan could also receive certain social benefits from the guilds. These might include aid for his family during sickness or the promise of admission for his son. The guilds were the chief protection for artisans against the operation of the commercial market. They were particularly strong in central Europe.

The Urban Riot

The artisan class, with its generally conservative outlook, maintained a rather fine sense of social and economic justice. These ideals were based largely on traditional practices. If the collective sense of what was economically "just" was offended, arti-

sans frequently manifested their displeasure by rioting. The most sensitive area was the price of bread, the staple food of the poor. If a baker or a grain merchant announced a price that was considered unjustly high, a bread riot might well ensue. Artisan leaders would confiscate the bread or grain and sell it for what the urban crowd considered a "just price." They would then give the money paid for the grain or bread to the baker or merchant.

The potential for bread riots restrained the greed of merchants. Such disturbances represented a collective method of imposing the "just price" in place of the price set by the commercial marketplace. Thus, bread and food riots, which occurred throughout Europe, were not irrational acts of screaming hungry people but highly ritualized social phenomena of the Old Regime and its economy of scarcity.

Other kinds of riots also characterized eighteenth-century society and politics. The riot was a way in which people who were excluded in every other way from the political processes could make their will known. Sometimes urban rioters were incited by religious bigotry. For example, in 1753 London Protestant mobs compelled the government ministry to withdraw an act to legalize Jewish naturalization. In 1780 the same rabidly Protestant spirit manifested itself in the Gordon riots. Lord George Gordon (1751–1793) had raised the specter of an imaginary Catholic plot after the government relieved military recruits from having to take specifically anti-Catholic oaths.

In these riots and in food riots, violence was normally directed against property rather than against people. The rioters themselves were not "riff-raff" but usually small shopkeepers, freeholders, artisans, and wage earners. They usually wanted only to restore a traditional right or practice that seemed endangered. Nevertheless, considerable turmoil and destruction could result from their actions.

During the last half of the century, urban riots increasingly involved political ends. Though often simultaneous with economic disturbances, the political riot always had nonartisan leadership or instigators. In fact, the "crowd" of the eighteenth century was often the tool of the upper classes. In Paris, the aristocratic *Parlement* often urged crowd action in their disputes with the monarchy. In Geneva, middle-class citizens supported artisan riots against the local urban oligarchy. In Great Britain in 1792, the government incited mobs to attack English sympathizers of the French Revolution. Such outbursts of popular unrest suggest that the crowd or mob first entered the European political and social arena well before the revolution in France.

The Jewish Population: The Age of the Ghetto

Although the small Jewish communities of Amsterdam and other western European cities became famous for their intellectual life and financial institutions, the vast majority of European Jews lived in eastern Europe. In the eighteenth century and thereafter, the Jewish population of Europe was concentrated in Poland, Lithuania, and the Ukraine, where no fewer than three million Jews dwelled. There were perhaps as many as 150,000 Jews in the Habsburg lands, primarily Bohemia, around 1760. Fewer than 100,000 Jews lived in Germany. There were approximately 40,000 Jews in France. Much smaller Jewish populations resided in England and Holland, each of which had a Jewish population of fewer than 10,000. There were even smaller groups of Jews elsewhere.

In 1762 Catherine the Great of Russia specifically excluded Jews from a manifesto that welcomed foreigners to settle in Russia. She somewhat relaxed the exclusion a few years later. After the first partition of Poland of 1772, to be discussed in Chapter 18, Russia included a large Jewish population. There were also larger Jewish communities in Prussia and under Austrian rule.

Jews dwelled in most nations without enjoying the rights and privileges of other subjects of the monarchs unless such rights were specifically granted to them. They were regarded as a kind of resident alien whose residence might well be temporary or changed at the whim of local rulers or the monarchical government.

No matter where they dwelled, the Jews of Europe under the Old Regime lived apart in separate communities from non-Jewish Europeans. These communities might be distinct districts of cities known as ghettos or in primarily Jewish villages in the countryside. Jews were also treated as a distinct people religiously and legally. In Poland for much of the century, they were virtually self-governing. In other areas, they lived under the burden of discriminatory legislation. Except in England, Jews could not and did not mix in the mainstream of the societies in which they dwelled. This period, which really may be said to have begun with the expulsion of the Jews from Spain at the end of the fifteenth century, is known as the age of the ghetto or separate community.

During the seventeenth century, a few Jews had helped finance the wars of major rulers. These financiers often became close to the rulers and were known as "court Jews." Perhaps the most famous was Samuel Oppenheimer (1630–1703), who helped the Habsburgs finance their struggle against the Turks and the defense of Vienna. Even these privileged Jews, including Oppenheimer, however, often failed to have their loans repaid. The court Jews and their financial abilities became famous. They tended to marry among themselves.

The overwhelming majority of the Jewish population of Europe, however, lived in poverty. They occupied the most undesirable sections of cities or poor rural villages. They pursued money-lending in some cases, but often worked at the lowest occupations. Their religious beliefs, rituals, and community set them apart. Virtually all laws and social institutions kept them apart from their Christian neighbors in situations of social inferiority.

Under the Old Regime, it is important to emphasize, all of this discrimination was based on religious separateness. Jews who converted to Christianity were welcomed, even if not always warmly, into the major political and social institutions of gentile European society. Until the last two decades of the eighteenth century, in every part of Europe, however, those Jews who remained loyal to their faith were subject to various religious, civil, and social disabilities. They could not pursue the professions freely; often they could not change residence freely; and they stood outside the political structures of the nations in which they lived. Jews could be expelled from the cities where they lived, and their property could be confiscated. They were regarded as socially and religiously inferior. They could be required to listen to sermons that insulted them and their religion. Jews might find their children taken away from them and given Christian instruction. They knew that their non-Jewish neighbors might suddenly turn against them and kill them or their fellow religious believers.

As will be seen in subsequent chapters, the end of the Old Regime brought major changes in the lives of these Jews and in their relationship to the larger culture.

✦

Near the close of the eighteenth century, European society was on the brink of a new era. That society had remained traditional and corporate largely because of the economy of scarcity. Beginning in the eighteenth century, the commercial spirit and the values of the marketplace, although not new, were permitted fuller play than ever before in European history. The newly unleashed commercial spirit led increasingly to a conception of human beings as individuals rather than as members of communities. In particular that spirit manifested itself in agricultural and industrial revolutions, as well as in the drive toward greater consumption. Together those two vast changes in production overcame most of the scarcity that had haunted Europe and the West generally. The accompanying changes in landholding and production would bring major changes to the European social structure.

The expansion of population provided a further stimulus for change. More people meant more labor, more energy, and more minds contributing to the creation and solution of social difficulties. Cities had to accommodate themselves to expanding populations. Corporate groups, such as the guilds, had to confront the existence of a larger labor force. New wealth meant that birth would eventually become less and less a determining factor in social relationships, except in regard to the social roles assigned to the two sexes. Class structure and social hierarchy remained, but the boundaries became somewhat blurred.

Finally, the conflicting ambitions of monarchs, the nobility, and middle class generated innovation. In the pursuit of new revenues, the monarchs interfered with the privileges of the nobles. In the name of ancient rights, the nobles attempted to secure and expand their existing social privileges. The middle class, in all of its diversity, was growing wealthier from trade, commerce, and the practice of the professions. Its members wanted social prestige and influence equal to their wealth. They resented privileges, frowned on hierarchy, and rejected tradition.

All these factors meant that the society of the eighteenth century stood at the close of one era in European history and at the opening of another.

Review Questions

1. Describe the life of an English aristocrat at the beginning of the eighteenth century and toward its close. How did the English aristocrat differ from the French aristocrat in this regard? What

kind of privileges separated European aristocrats from other social groups?
2. How would you define the term *family economy*? What were some of the particular characteristics of the northwestern European household as opposed to that in eastern Europe? In what ways were the lives of women constrained by the family economy in preindustrial Europe?
3. What caused the Agricultural Revolution? How did technological innovations help change European agriculture? To what extent did the English aristocracy contribute to the Agricultural Revolution? What were some of the reasons for peasant revolts in Europe in the eighteenth century?
4. What factors explain the increase in Europe's population in the eighteenth century? What were the effects of the population explosion? How did population growth contribute to changes in consumption?
5. What caused the Industrial Revolution of the eighteenth century? What were some of the technological innovations and why were they important? Why did Great Britain take the lead in the Industrial Revolution? How did the consumer contribute to the Industrial Revolution?
6. Describe city life during the eighteenth century. Were all European cities of the same character? What changes had taken place in the distribution of population in cities and towns? Compare the lifestyle of the upper class with that of the middle and lower classes. What were some of the causes of urban riots?

Suggested Readings

I. T. Berend and G. Ranki, *The European Periphery and Industrialization, 1780–1914* (1982). Examines the experience of eastern and Mediterranean Europe.

J. Blum, *Lord and Peasant in Russia from the Ninth to the Nineteenth Century* (1961). A thorough and wide-ranging discussion.

J. Blum, *The End of the Old Order in Rural Europe* (1978). The most comprehensive treatment of life in rural Europe, especially central and eastern, from the early eighteenth through the mid-nineteenth centuries.

F. Braudel, *The Structures of Everyday Life: The Limits of the Possible*, trans. by M. Kochan (1982). A magisterial survey by the most important social historian of our time.

J. Brewer and R. Porter, *Consumption and the World of Goods* (1993). A large, wide-ranging collection of essays.

J. Cannon, *Aristocratic Century: The Peerage of Eighteenth-Century England* (1985). A useful treatment based on the most recent research.

P. Deane, *The First Industrial Revolution*, 2nd ed. (1979). A well-balanced and systematic treatment.

J. De Vries, *The Economy of Europe in an Age of Crisis, 1600–1750* (1976). An excellent overview that sets forth the main issues.

J. De Vries, *European Urbanization 1500–1800* (1984). The most important and far-ranging recent treatment of the subject.

W. Doyle, *The Old European Order: 1660–1800* (1992). The best one-volume treatment.

P. Earle, *The Making of the English Middle Class: Business, Community, and Family Life in London, 1660–1730* (1989). The most careful study of the subject.

M. W. Flinn, *The European Demographic System, 1500–1820* (1981). A major summary.

R. Forster and O. Ranum, *Deviants and Abandoned in French Society* (1978). This and the following volume contain important essays from the French journal *Annales*.

R. Forster and O. Ranum, *Medicine and Society in France* (1980).

D. V. Glass and D. E. C. Eversley (eds.), *Population in History: Essays in Historical Demography* (1965). Fundamental for understanding the eighteenth-century increase in population.

P. Goubert, *The Ancien Régime: French Society, 1600–1750*, trans. by S. Cox (1974). A superb account of the peasant social order.

D. Hay (ed.), *Albion's Fatal Tree: Crime and Society in Eighteenth-Century England* (1975). Separate essays on a previously little explored subject.

O. H. Hufton, *The Poor of Eighteenth-Century France, 1750–1789* (1975). A brilliant study of poverty and the family economy.

R. M. Isherwood, *Farce and Fantasy: Popular Entertainment in Eighteenth-Century Paris* (1986). A study that concentrates primarily on the theater and related spectacles.

C. Jones, *Charity and Bienfaisance: The Treatment of the Poor in the Montpellier Region, 1740–1815* (1982). An important local French study.

E. L. Jones, *Agriculture and Economic Growth in England, 1650–1815* (1968). A good introduction to an important subject.

A. Kahan, *The Plow, the Hammer, and the Knout: An Economic History of Eighteenth-Century Russia* (1985). An extensive and detailed treatment.

H. Kamen, *European Society, 1500–1700* (1985). The best one-volume treatment.

R. K. McClure, *Coram's Children: The London Foundling Hospital in the Eighteenth Century* (1981).

A moving work that deals with the plight of all concerned with the problem.

N. McKenderick (ed.), *The Birth of a Consumer Society: The Commercialization of Eighteenth-Century England* (1982). Deals with several aspects of the impact of commercialization.

F. E. Manuel, *The Broken Staff: Judaism Through Christian Eyes* (1992). An important discussion of Christian interpretations of Judaism.

M. A. Meyer, *The Origins of the Modern Jew: Jewish Identity and European Culture in Germany, 1749–1824* (1967). A general introduction organized around individual case studies.

P. B. Munsche, *Gentlemen and Poachers: The English Game Laws, 1671–1831* (1981). An excellent analysis of these laws.

S. Pollard, *The Genesis of Modern Management: A Study of the Industrial Revolution in Great Britain* (1965). Treats the issue of industrialization from the standpoint of factory owners.

S. Pollard, *Peaceful Conquest: The Industrialization of Europe, 1760–1970* (1981). A useful survey.

A. Ribeiro, *Dress in Eighteenth Century Europe, 1715–1789* (1985). An interesting examination of the social implication of style in clothing.

G. Rudé, *The Crowd in History 1730–1848* (1964). A pioneering study.

S. Schama, *The Embarrassment of Riches: An Interpretation of Dutch Culture in the Golden Age* (1987). A broad examination of the impact of wealth on the Dutch.

H. Schmal (ed.), *Patterns of European Urbanization Since 1500* (1981). Major revisionist essays.

L. Stone, *The Family, Sex and Marriage in England 1500–1800* (1977). A pioneering study of a subject receiving increasing interest from historians.

L. Stone, *An Open Elite?* (1985). Raises important questions about the traditional view of open access to social mobility in England.

T. Tackett, *Priest and Parish in Eighteenth-Century France: A Social and Political Study of the Curés in a Diocese of Dauphiné, 1750–1791* (1977). An important local study that displays the role of the church in the fabric of social life in the Old Regime.

R. Wall (ed.), *Family Forms in Historic Europe* (1983). Essays that cover the entire continent.

E. A. Wrigley and R. S. Schofield, *The Population History of England, 1541–1871: A Reconstruction* (1982). One of the most ambitious demographic studies ever undertaken.

E. A. Wrigley, *Continuity, Chance and Change: The Character of the Industrial Revolution in England* (1988). A major conceptual reassessment.

The trade and empires of the eighteenth century were held together and protected by navies. These navies patrolled sea lanes to protect ships from pirates and smugglers and from attacks by hostile forces. In this painting, "The British Fleet Sailing into Lisbon Harbour", (1735) by Peter Monamy (1689–1749), ships from the British sailing fleet rest in Lisbon harbor where they may well have stopped to take on supplies. Britain and Portugal were major trading partners, with British wool being exchanged for Portuguese wine. [Ackermann and Johnson Ltd., London/The Bridgeman Art Library, London]

Empire, War, and Colonial Rebellion

K E Y   T O P I C S

- Europe's mercantilist empires
- Spain's vast colonial empire in the Americas
- The wars of the mid-eighteenth century in Europe and the colonies
- The struggle for independence in Britain's North American colonies

The middle of the eighteenth century witnessed a renewal of European warfare on a worldwide scale. The conflict involved two separate but interrelated rivalries. Austria and Prussia fought for dominance in central Europe, while Great Britain and France dueled for commercial and colonial supremacy. The wars were long, extensive, and costly in both effort and money. They resulted in a new balance of power on the Continent and on the high seas. Prussia emerged as a great power, and Great Britain gained a world empire.

Moreover, the expense of these wars led every major European government after the Peace of Paris of 1763 to reconstruct its policies of taxation and finance. These revised fiscal programs produced internal conditions for the monarchies of Europe that had most significant results for the rest of the century. These included the American Revolution, enlightened absolutism on the Continent, a continuing financial crisis for the French monarchy, and reform of the Spanish Empire in South America.

Periods of European Overseas Empires

Since the Renaissance, European contacts with the rest of the world have gone through four distinct stages. The first was that of the European discovery, exploration, initial conquest, and settlement of the New World. This period had closed by the end of the seventeenth century.

The second era, which is largely the concern of this chapter, was one of colonial trade rivalry among Spain, France, and Great Britain. The Anglo-French side of the contest has often been compared to a second Hundred Years' War. During this second period, both the British colonies of the North American seaboard and the Spanish colonies of

Mexico and Central and South America emancipated themselves from European control. This era may be said to have closed during the 1820s.

The third stage of European contact with the non-European world occurred in the nineteenth century. During that period, European governments carved new formal empires involving the European administration of indigenous peoples in Africa and Asia. Those nineteenth-century empires also included new areas of European settlement, such as Australia, New Zealand, and South Africa. The bases of these empires were trade, national honor, and military strategy.

The last period of European empire occurred during the mid-twentieth century, with the decolonization of peoples who had previously lived under European colonial rule.

During the four-and-one-half centuries before decolonization, Europeans exerted political dominance over much of the rest of the world that was far disproportional to the geographical size or population of Europe. Europeans frequently treated other peoples as social, intellectual, and economic inferiors. They ravaged existing cultures because of greed, religious zeal, or political ambition. These actions are major facts of European history and significant factors in the contemporary relationship of Europe and its former colonies. What allowed the Europeans to exert such influence and domination for so long over so much of the world was not any innate cultural superiority but a technological supremacy related to naval power and gunpowder. Ships and guns allowed the Europeans to exercise their will almost wherever they chose.

Eighteenth-Century Empires

Eighteenth-century European empires existed primarily to enrich trade. They were empires based on commerce, and the trade of these empires helped to establish the consumer revolution discussed in the previous chapter. Extensive trade rivalries sprang up around the world. Consequently, the protection of these empires required extensive naval power. Spain dominated the largest of these empires and constructed elaborate naval, commercial, and political structures to exploit and govern it. Finally, these empires depended largely upon slave labor. Indeed, the Atlantic slave trade itself represented one of the major ways in which European merchants enriched themselves. That trade in turn forcibly brought the peoples of Africa into the life and culture of the New World.

Mercantile Empires

Navies and merchant shipping were the keystones of the mercantile empires that were meant to bring profit to a nation rather than to provide areas for settlement. The Treaty of Utrecht (1713) established the boundaries of empire during the first half of the century.

Except for Brazil, which was governed by Portugal, Spain controlled all of mainland South America. In North America, it ruled Florida, Mexico, California, and the Southwest. The Spanish also governed the islands of Cuba, Puerto Rico, and half of Hispaniola.

The British Empire consisted of the colonies along the North Atlantic seaboard, Nova Scotia, Newfoundland, Jamaica, and Barbados. Britain also possessed a few trading stations on the Indian subcontinent.

The French domains covered the Saint Lawrence River valley and the Ohio and Mississippi river valleys. They included the West Indian islands of Saint Domingue, Guadeloupe, and Martinique and also stations in India. To the French and British merchant communities, India appeared as a vast potential market for European goods as well as the source of calicos and spices that were much in demand in Europe.

The Dutch controlled Surinam, or Dutch Guiana, in South America, and various trading stations in Ceylon and Bengal. Most important, they controlled the trade with Java in what is now Indonesia. The Dutch had opened these markets largely in the seventeenth century and had created a vast trading empire far larger in extent, wealth, and importance than the geographical size of the United Netherlands would have led one to expect. The Dutch had been daring sailors and had made important technological innovations in sailing.

All of these powers also possessed numerous smaller islands in the Caribbean. So far as eighteenth-century developments were concerned, the major rivalries existed among the Spanish, the French, and the British.

MERCANTILIST GOALS   Where any formal economic theory lay behind the conduct of these empires, it was *mercantilism*, that practical creed of hardheaded businesspeople. The terms *mercantilism*

and *mercantile system* were invented by opponents of the system whereby governments heavily regulated trade and commerce in hope of increasing national wealth. Economic writers believed it necessary for a nation to gain a favorable trade balance of gold and silver bullion. They regarded bullion as the measure of a country's wealth, and a nation was truly wealthy only if it amassed more bullion than its rivals.

The mercantilist statesmen and traders regarded the world as an arena of scarce resources and economic limitation. The attitudes associated with mercantilist thinking assumed very modest levels of economic growth. Such thinking pre-dated the expansion of agricultural and later industrial productivity discussed in the previous chapter. Prior to the beginning of such sustained economic growth, the wealth of one nation was assumed to grow or to be increased largely at the direct cost of another nation. That is to say, the wealth of one state might expand only if its armies or navies conquered the domestic or colonial territory of another state and thus gained the productive capacity of that area or if a state expanded its trading monopoly over new territory or if, by smuggling, it could intrude upon the trading monopoly of another state.

From beginning to end, the economic well-being of the home country was the primary concern of mercantilist writers. Colonies were to provide markets and natural resources for the industries of the home country. In turn, the home country was to furnish military security and political administration for the colonies. For decades both sides assumed that the colonies were the inferior partner in the relationship. The home country and its colonies were to trade exclusively with each other. To that end, they tried to forge trade-tight systems of national commerce through navigation laws, tariffs, bounties to encourage production, and prohibitions against trading with the subjects of other monarchs. National monopoly was the ruling principle.

Mercantilist ideas had always been neater on paper than in practice. By the early eighteenth century, mercantilist assumptions were far removed from the economic realities of the colonies. The colonial and home markets simply did not mesh. Spain could not produce enough goods for South America. Economic production in the British North American colonies challenged English manufacturing and led to British attempts to limit certain colonial industries, such as iron and hat making.

Colonists of different countries wished to trade with each other. English colonists could buy sugar more cheaply from the French West Indies than from English suppliers. The traders and merchants of one nation always hoped to break the monopoly of another. For all these reasons the eighteenth century became the "golden age of smugglers."[1] The governments could not control the activities of all their subjects. Clashes among colonists could and did bring about conflict between governments.

[1]Walter Dorn, *Competition for Empire, 1740–1763* (New York: Harper, 1940), p. 266.

The Mercantilist Position Stated

One of the earliest discussions of the economic theory of mercantilism appeared in England's Treasure by Forraign Trade *(1664) by Thomas Mun (1571–1641). In this passage from that work, Mun explained why it was necessary to the prosperity of the nation for more goods to be exported than imported. Although mercantilist theory later became more sophisticated, all writers in the eighteenth century emphasized the necessity of a favorable balance of trade.*

◆ *Why does Mun emphasize foreign trade rather than the development of a domestic market? Why might persons of Mun's day have put so much stress on the possession of gold and silver bullion? How does the outlook of this passage assume a world of scarce goods rather than one in which economies might grow through the production of new kinds of products?*

The ordinary means therefore to increase our wealth and treasure is by Forraign Trade wherein wee must ever observe this rule; to sell more to strangers yearly than wee consume of theirs in value. For suppose that when this Kingdom is plentifully served with the Cloth, Lead, Tinn, Iron, Fish and other native commodities, we doe yearly export the overplus to forraign countries to the value of twenty two hundred thousand pounds; by which means we are enabled beyond the Seas to buy and bring in forraign wares for our use and Consumptions, to the value of twenty hundred thousand pounds; By this order duly kept in our trading, we may rest assured that the Kingdom shall be enriched yearly two hundred thousand pounds, which must be brought to us in so much Treasure; because that part of our stock which is not returned to us in wares must necessarily be brought home in treasure [i.e., gold or silver bullion].

Thomas Mun, England's Treasure by Forraign Trade, *as quoted in Charles Wilson,* England's Apprenticeship, 1603–1763 *(London: Longman, 1965), p. 60.*

FRENCH–BRITISH RIVALRY Major flash points existed between France and Britain in North America. Their colonists quarreled endlessly with each other. Both groups of settlers coveted the lower Saint Lawrence River valley, upper New England, and later the Ohio River valley. There were other rivalries over fishing rights, fur trade, and alliances with Native American tribes.

India was another area of French-British rivalry. On the Indian subcontinent, both France and Britain traded through privileged, chartered companies that enjoyed a legal monopoly. The East India Company was the English institution; the French equivalent was the *Compagnie des Indes.* The trade of India and Asia figured only marginally in the economics of empire. Nevertheless, enterprising Europeans always hoped to develop profitable commerce with India. Others regarded India

as a springboard into the even larger potential market of China. The original European footholds in India were trading posts called *factories.* They existed through privileges granted by various Indian governments.

Two circumstances in the middle of the eighteenth century changed this situation in India. First, the indigenous administration and government of several Indian states had decayed. Second, Joseph Dupleix (1697–1763) for the French and Robert Clive (1725–1774) for the British saw this developing power vacuum as opportunities for expanding the control of their respective companies. To maintain their own security and to expand their privileges, each of the two companies began in effect to take over the government of some regions. Each group of Europeans hoped to checkmate the other.

The Spanish Colonial System

Spanish control of its American Empire involved both a system of government and one of monopolistic trade regulation. Both were more rigid in appearance than in practice. Actual government was often informal, and the trade monopoly was frequently breached.

COLONIAL GOVERNMENT   Because Queen Isabella of Castile (r. 1474–1504) had commissioned Columbus, the technical legal link between the New World and Spain was the crown of Castile. Its powers both at home and in America were subject to few limitations. The Castilian monarch assigned the government of America to the Council of the Indies, which, with the monarch, nominated the viceroys of New Spain (Mexico) and Peru. These viceroys served as the chief executives in the New World and carried out the laws promulgated by the Council of the Indies.

Each of the viceroyalties was divided into several subordinate judicial councils, known as *audiencias*. There was also a variety of local officers, the most important of which were the *corregidores*, who presided over municipal councils. All of these offices provided the monarchy with a vast array of patronage, usually bestowed on persons born in Spain. Virtually all power flowed from the top of this political structure downward; in effect, local initiative or self-government scarcely existed.

TRADE REGULATION   The colonial political structures functioned largely to support Spanish commercial self-interest. The *Casa de Contratación* (House of Trade) in Seville regulated all trade with the New World. Cadiz was the only port authorized for use in the American trade. The Casa de Contratación was the most influential institution of the Spanish Empire. Its members worked closely with the *Consulado* (Merchant Guild) of Seville and other groups involved with the American commerce in Cadiz.

A complicated system of trade and bullion fleets administered from Seville was the key for maintaining the trade monopoly. Each year, a fleet of commercial vessels (the flota) controlled by Seville merchants, escorted by warships, carried merchandise from Spain to a few specified ports in America. These included Portobello, Veracruz, and Cartagena. There were no authorized ports on the Pacific Coast.

Areas far to the south, such as Buenos Aires on the Rio de la Plata, received goods only after the shipments had been unloaded at one of the authorized ports. After selling their wares, the ships were loaded with silver and gold bullion, usually wintered in heavily fortified Caribbean ports, and then sailed back to Spain. The flota system always worked imperfectly, but trade outside it was illegal. Regulations prohibited the Spanish colonists within the American Empire from establishing direct trade with each other and from building their own shipping and commercial industry. Foreign merchants were also forbidden to breach the Spanish monopoly.

COLONIAL REFORM UNDER THE SPANISH BOURBON MONARCHS   A crucial change occurred in the Spanish colonial system in the early eighteenth century. The War of the Spanish Succession (1701–1714) and the Treaty of Utrecht (1713) replaced the Spanish Habsburgs with the Bourbons of France on the Spanish throne. Philip V (r. 1700–1746) and his successors tried to use French administrative skills to reassert the imperial trade monopoly, which had decayed under the last Spanish Habsburgs, and thus to improve the domestic economy and revive Spanish power in European affairs.

Under Philip V, Spanish coastal patrol vessels tried to suppress smuggling in American waters. An incident arising from this policy (to be discussed later in this chapter) led to war with England in 1739. In 1739 Philip established the viceroyalty of New Granada in the area that today includes Venezuela, Colombia, and Ecuador. The goal was to increase direct royal government in the area.

During the reign of Ferdinand VI (r. 1746–1759), the great mid-century wars exposed the vulnerability of the empire to naval attack and economic penetration. As an ally of France, Spain emerged as one of the defeated powers in 1763. Government circles became convinced that further changes in the colonial system had to be undertaken.

Charles III (r. 1759–1788), the most important of the royal imperial reformers, attempted to reassert Spain's control of the empire. Like his two Bourbon predecessors, Charles III emphasized royal ministers rather than councils. Thus, the role of both the Council of the Indies and the Casa de Contratación diminished. After 1765 Charles abolished the monopolies of Seville and Cadiz and permitted other Spanish cities to trade with America. He also opened more South American and Caribbean ports

Visitors Describe the Portobello Fair

The Spanish tried to restrict all trade within their Latin American empire to a few designated ports. Each year a fair was held in certain of these ports. The most famous of these was Portobello on the Isthmus of Panama. In the 1730s, two visitors saw the event and described it. This fair was the chief means of facilitating trade between the western coast of South America and Spain.

✦ *What products were sold at this fair? How might the actual sale of gold bullion at this fair have led to attitudes such as were seen in the earlier document by Thomas Mun? How does this passage illustrate the inefficiency of monopoly trade in the Spanish empire and the many chances for smuggling?*

The town of Portobello, so thinly inhabited, by reason of its noxious air, the scarcity of provisions, and the soil, becomes, at the time of the [Spanish] galleons one of the most populous places in all South America. . . .

The ships are no sooner moored in the harbour, than the first work is, to erect, in the square, a tent made of the ship's sails, for receiving its cargo; at which the proprietors of the goods are present, in order to find their bales, by the marks which distinguish them. These bales are drawn on sledges, to their respective places by the crew of every ship, and the money given them is proportionally divided.

Whilst the seamen and European traders are thus employed, the land is covered with droves of mules from Panama, each drove consisting of above an hundred, loaded with chests of gold and silver, on account of the merchants of Peru. Some unload them at the exchange, others in the middle of the square; yet, amidst the hurry and confusion of such crowds, no theft, loss, or disturbance, is ever known. He who has seen this place during the tiempo muerto, or dead time, solitary, poor, and a perpetual silence reigning everywhere; the harbour quite empty, and every place wearing a melancholy aspect; must be filled with astonishment at the sudden change, to see the bustling multitudes, every house crowded, the square and streets encumbered with bales and chests of gold and silver of all kinds; the harbour full of ships and vessels, some bringing by the way of Rio de Chape the goods of Peru, such as cacao, quinquina, or Jesuit's bark, Vicuña wool, and bezoar stones; others coming from Carthagena, loaded with provisions; and thus a spot, at all times detested for its deleterious qualities, becomes the staple of the riches of the old and new world, and the scene of one of the most considerable branches of commerce in the whole earth.

The ships being unloaded, and the merchants of Peru, together with the president of Panama, arrived, the fair comes under deliberation. And for this purpose the deputies of the several parties repair on board the commodore of the galleons, where, in the presence of the commodore, and the president of Panama, . . . the prices of the several kinds of merchandizes are settled. . . . The purchases and sales, as likewise the exchanges of money, are transacted by brokers, both from Spain and Peru. After this, every one begins to dispose of his goods; the Spanish brokers embarking their chests of money, and those of Peru sending away the goods they have purchased, in vessels called chatas and bongos, up the river Chagres. And thus the fair of Portobello ends.

George Juan and Antonio de Ulloa, A Voyage to South America, vol. 1 (London, 1772), pp. 103–110, as quoted in Benjamin Keen, ed., Readings in Latin-American Civilization 1492 to the Present (New York: Houghton Mifflin, 1955), pp. 107–108.

to trade and authorized some commerce between Spanish ports in America. In 1776 he organized a fourth viceroyalty in the region of Rio de la Plata, which included much of present-day Argentina, Uruguay, Paraguay, and Bolivia. (See Map 17–1.)

While relaxing Spanish trade with and in America, Charles III attempted to increase the efficiency of tax collection and to end bureaucratic corruption. To achieve those ends, he introduced the institution of the intendent into the Spanish Empire. These loyal, royal bureaucrats were patterned on the French intendants made so famous and effective as agents of the absolutism of Louis XIV.

These late-eighteenth-century Bourbon reforms did stimulate the imperial economy. Trade expanded and became more varied. These reforms, however, also brought the empire more fully under direct Spanish control. Many *peninsulares* (persons born in Spain) entered the New World to fill new posts. Expanding trade brought more Spanish merchants to Latin America. The economy remained export oriented, and economic life was still organized to benefit Spain. As a result of these policies, the *creoles* (persons of European descent born in the Spanish colonies) came to feel that they were second-class subjects. In time their resentment would provide a major source of the discontent leading to the wars of independence in the early nineteenth century. The imperial policies of Charles III were the Spanish equivalent of the new colonial measures undertaken by the British government after 1763, which led to the American Revolution.

Black African Slavery, the Plantation System, and the Atlantic Economy

The heart of the eighteenth-century colonial rivalry lay in the West Indies. These islands, close to the American continents, were the jewels of empire. The West Indies raised tobacco, cotton, indigo, coffee, and, above all, sugar, for which there existed strong markets in Europe. These commodities were becoming part of daily life especially in western Europe; they represented one aspect of those major changes in consumption that marked eighteenth-century European culture. Sugar in particular had become a staple rather than a luxury. It was used in coffee, tea, and cocoa, for making candy and preserving fruits, and in the brewing industry. There seemed no limit to its uses, and no limit to consumer demand for it.

Slavery was basic to the economies of the West Indies, the Spanish and Portuguese settlements in South America, and the British colonies on the South Atlantic seaboard of North America. The major source of slaves was black West Africans.

Slavery had existed in various parts of Europe since ancient times. Before the eighteenth century, little or no moral or religious stigma attached to slave owning or slave trading. It had had a continuous existence in the Mediterranean world, where only the sources of slaves changed over the centuries. After the conquest of Constantinople in the mid-fifteenth century, the Ottoman Empire forbade the exportation of white slaves from regions under its control. The Portuguese had then begun to import African slaves into the Iberian Peninsula from the Canary Islands and West Africa. Black slaves from Africa were also not uncommon in other parts of the Mediterranean, and a few found their way into northern Europe. There they might be used as personal servants or displayed because of the novelty of their color in the courts of royalty or homes of the wealthy.

THE PLANTATION SYSTEM Once the New World was discovered and settled, the conquering Spanish and Portuguese faced a severe shortage of labor. They and most of the French and English settlers who came later had no intention of undertaking manual work themselves. At first, they used Native Americans as laborers, but during the sixteenth and seventeenth centuries, disease killed hundreds of thousands of Native Americans. As a result labor soon became scarce. The Spanish and Portuguese then turned to the labor of imported African slaves. By the late sixteenth century, in the islands of the West Indies and the major cities of South America, black slaves equaled or surpassed the numbers of white European settlers.

On much of the South American continent dominated by Spain, the numbers of slaves declined during the late seventeenth century, and the institution became less fundamental there than elsewhere. Slavery continued to prosper, however, in Brazil and in the Caribbean. Later, slavery spread into the British North American colonies. The first slaves were brought to Jamestown in 1619. They soon became a fundamental institution in North American colonial life, where at one time or another slaves were held in all the colonies.

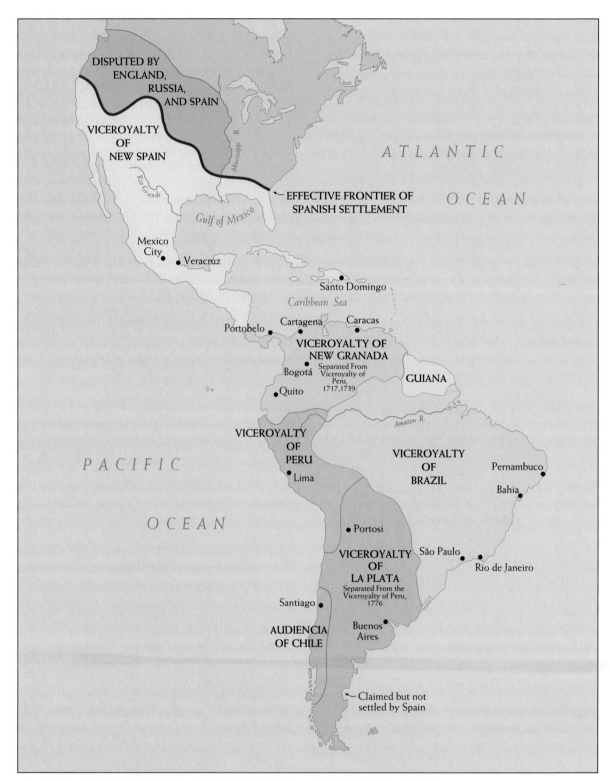

MAP 17–1 VICEROYALTIES IN LATIN AMERICA IN 1780 *The late-eighteenth century viceroyalties in Latin America display the effort of the Spanish Bourbon monarchy to establish more direct control of the continent. They sought this control through the introduction of more royal officials and by establishing more governmental districts.*

One of the forces that led to the spread of slavery in Brazil and the West Indies was the cultivation of sugar. Small landowners could not cultivate sugar because it required a large investment in land and equipment. Only slave labor could provide enough workers for the extremely large and profitable sugar plantations. By the close of the seventeenth century, the Caribbean islands were the world center for the production of sugar and the chief supplier for the ever growing consumer demand for the product. As the production of sugar expanded, so also did the demand for slaves and their consequent importation. By 1725, it has been estimated, almost 90 percent of the population of Jamaica was black slaves. The situation was similar throughout the West Indies. There and elsewhere, in Brazil and the southern British colonies, prosperity and slavery went hand in hand. The wealthiest and most prized of the colonies were those that raised staples such as sugar, rice, tobacco, or cotton by slave labor. In Brazil, slave labor sustained first sugar production and then late in the eighteenth century gold mining and coffee cultivation.

The plantation to which the slaves eventually arrived was always in a more or less isolated rural setting, but its products rapidly entered a larger integrated transatlantic economy. The plantation might raise food for its owners and their slaves, but the main production, whether sugar, tobacco, or later cotton and coffee, was intended for export. The production of the plantations was thus drawn into the world of transatlantic trade, manufacture, and consumption. In turn, the plantation owners imported virtually all the finished or manufactured goods used or consumed on the plantation from Europe.

Colonial trade followed roughly a geographic triangle. European goods were carried to Africa to be exchanged for slaves, who were then taken to the West Indies, where they were traded for sugar and other tropical products, which were then shipped to Europe. Not all ships covered all three legs of the triangle. Another major trade pattern existed between New England and the West Indies with New England fish or ship stores being traded for sugar.

Slavery and the slave trade touched most of the economy of the transatlantic world. The prosperity of such cities as Newport, Rhode Island, Liverpool, England, and Nantes, France, rested almost entirely on the slave trade. Cities in the British North American colonies profited from slavery sometimes by trading in slaves but more often by supplying other goods to the West Indian market. It was not the New World planters and slave traders alone, however, who were involved in the trade. Slavery touched most of the economy of the transatlantic world. All the shippers who handled cotton, tobacco, and sugar depended on slavery, though they might not have had direct contact with the institution, as did all the manufacturers and merchants who produced the finished products for the consumer market.

SLAVE EXPERIENCE The Spanish, Portuguese, Dutch, French, and English traders who participated in the slave trade forcibly transported several million (perhaps more than nine million) Africans to the New World. During the first four centuries of settlement, far more black slaves came involuntarily to the New World than did free European settlers. The conditions of their passage across the Atlantic were wretched. Quarters were unspeakably cramped; food was bad; disease was rampant. Many Africans died on the crossing. Yet the trade persisted because of the demand for labor in America, where it was cheaper to import new slaves than it was to rear slave children to adulthood. The mortality rate of slaves in the West Indies and elsewhere was very high. More and more new Africans had to be bought into slavery simply to keep a steady supply.

The life conditions of plantation slaves differed from colony to colony. Black slaves living in Portuguese areas had the fewest legal protections. In the Spanish colonies, the church attempted to provide some protection for black slaves but devoted more effort toward protecting the Native Americans. Slave codes were developed in the British and the French colonies during the seventeenth century, but they provided only the most limited protection. Virtually all slaveowners feared a slave revolt, and legislation and other regulations were intended to prevent one. All slave laws favored the master rather than the slave. Slave masters were permitted to whip slaves and inflict other exceedingly harsh corporal punishment. Furthermore, slaves were often forbidden to gather in large groups lest they plan a revolt. In most of these slave societies, the marriages of slaves were not recognized by law. The children of slaves continued to be slaves and were owned by the owner of their parents.

The daily life of most slaves during these centuries was one of hard agricultural labor, poor diet, and inadequate housing. Slave families could be

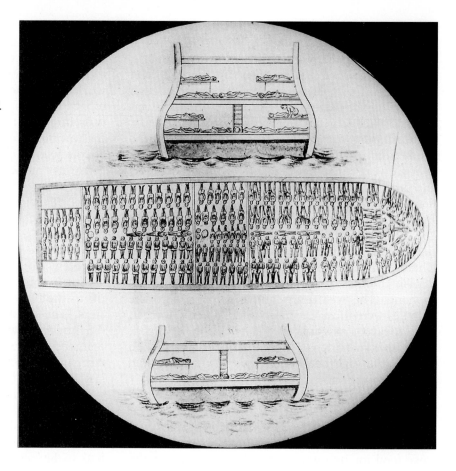

African captives imported into the Americas were carried across the Atlantic in unspeakable conditions on ships designed to maximize the number of human beings carried as cargo. This cross-section illustrates how the human cargo was arranged. The following document describes the Atlantic passage. [Bildarchiv Preussischer Kulturbesitz]

separated by the owner during his life or sold separately after his death. Their welfare and their lives were sacrificed to the continuing expansion of the sugar, rice, and tobacco plantations that made their owners wealthy and that produced goods for European consumers. Scholars have sometimes concluded that slaves in one area lived better than in another. Today, it is generally accepted that all the slaves in plantation societies led exposed and difficult lives with little variation among them.

The African slaves who were transported to the Americas, were, like the Native Americans, converted to Christianity. In the Spanish, French, and Portuguese domains, they became Roman Catholics, and in the English colonies they became Protestants of one denomination or another. In either case, although some African practices survived in muted forms, these practices were gradually separated from African religious belief. Although slaves did manage to mix Christianity with their previous African religions, their conversion to Christianity was nonetheless another exam-

ple, like that of the Native Americans, of the crushing of a set of non-European cultural values in the context of the New World economies and social structures.

The European settlers in the Americas and the slave traders also carried with them prejudices against black Africans. Many Europeans considered Africans to be savages or less than civilized. Still others looked down on them simply because they were slaves. Both Christians and Muslims had shared these attitudes in the Mediterranean world, where European slavery had for so long existed. Furthermore, many European languages and cultures attached negative connotations to the idea and image of blackness. In virtually all these plantation societies, race was an important element in keeping black slaves in a position of marked subservience. Although racial thinking in regard to slavery became important primarily in the nineteenth century, the fact of slaves being differentiated from the rest of the population by race as well as by their being chattel property was fundamental to the

A Slave Trader Describes the Atlantic Passage

During 1693 and 1694, Captain Thomas Phillips carried slaves from Africa to Barbados on the ship Hannibal. *The financial backer of the voyage was the Royal African Company of London, which held an English crown monopoly on slave trading. Phillips sailed to the west coast of Africa, where he purchased the Africans who were sold into slavery by an African king. Then he set sail westward.*

✦ *Who are the various people described in this document who in one way or another were involved in or profited from the slave trade? What dangers did the Africans face on the voyage? What contemporary attitudes could have led this ship captain to treat and think of his human cargo simply as goods to be transported? What are the grounds of his self-pity for the difficulties he met?*

Having bought my complement of 700 slaves, 480 men and 220 women, and finish'd all my business at Whidaw [on the Gold Coast of Africa], I took my leave of the old king and his cappasheirs [attendants], and parted, with many affectionate expressions on both sides, being forced to promise him that I would return again the next year, with several things he desired me to bring from England. . . . I set sail the 27th of July in the morning, accompany'd with the East-India Merchant, who had bought 650 slaves, for the Island of St. Thomas . . . from which we took our departure on August 25th and set sail for Barbadoes.

We spent in our passage from St. Thomas to Barbadoes two months eleven days, from the 25th of August to the 4th of November following: in which time there happened such sickness and mortality among my poor men and Negroes. Of the first we buried 14, and of the last 320, which was a great detriment to our voyage, the Royal African Company losing ten pounds by every slave that died, and the owners of the ship ten pounds ten shillings, being the freight agreed on to be paid by the charter-party for every Negro delivered alive ashore to the African Company's agents at Barbadoes. . . . The loss in all amounted to near 6500 pounds sterling.

The distemper which my men as well as the blacks mostly died of was the white flux, which was so violent and inveterate that no medicine would in the least check it, so that when any of our men were seized with it, we esteemed him a dead man, as he generally proved. . . .

The Negroes are so incident to the small-pox that few ships that carry them escape without it, and sometimes it makes vast havock and destruction among them. But tho' we had 100 at a time sick of it, and that it went thro' the ship, yet we lost not above a dozen by it. All the assistance we gave the diseased was only as much water as they desir'd to drink, and some palm-oil to annoint their sores, and they would generally recover without any other helps but what kind nature gave them. . . .

But what the small pox spar'd, the flux swept off, to our great regret, after all our pains and care to give them their messes in due order and season, keeping their lodgings as clean and sweet as possible, and enduring so much misery and stench so long among a parcel of creatures nastier than swine, and after all our expectations to be defeated by their mortality. . . .

No gold-finders can endure so much noisome slavery as they do who carry Negroes; for those have some respite and satisfaction, but we endure twice the misery; and yet by their mortality our voyages are ruin'd, and we pine and fret ourselves to death, and take so much pains to so little purpose.

Thomas Phillips, "Journal," A Collection of Voyages and Travels, *vol. VI, ed. by Awnsham and John Churchill (London, 1746), as quoted in Thomas Howard, ed.,* Black Voyage: Eyewitness Accounts of the Atlantic Slave Trade *(Boston: Little, Brown and Company, 1971), pp. 85–87.*

TO BE SOLD on board the Ship *Bance-Island*, on tuesday the 6th of *May* next, at *Afhley-Ferry*; a choice cargo of about 250 fine healthy NEGROES, juft arrived from the Windward & Rice Coaft. —The utmoft care has already been taken, and fhall be continued, to keep them free from the leaft danger of being infected with the SMALL-POX, no boat having been on board, and all other communication with people from *Charles-Town* prevented.

Aufin, Laurens, & Appleby.

N. B. Full one Half of the above Negroes have had the SMALL-POX in their own Country.

Those Africans who survived the voyage across the Atlantic were immediately sold into slavery in the Americas. This slave-auction notice relates to a group of slaves whose ship had stopped at Charleston, South Carolina, and then landed elsewhere in the region to auction its human cargo. Notice the concern to assure potential buyers that the slaves were healthy. [The Bettmann Archive]

system. All of these factors formed the racial prejudice that continues to plague society in the former slave-owning regions.

The plantations that stretched from the middle Atlantic colonies of North America through the West Indies and into Brazil constituted a vast corridor of slave societies in which social and economic subordination was based on both involuntary servitude and race. It had not existed before the European discovery and exploitation of the resources of the Americas. This kind of society in its extent and totality of dependence on slave labor and racial differences was novel in both European and world history. As already noted, its social and economic influence touched not only the plantation societies themselves but West Africa, western Europe, and New England. It existed from the sixteenth century through the second half of the nineteenth century, when slave emancipation had been completed through the Slave revolt of Saint Domingue (1794), British outlawing of the slave trade

(1807), the Latin American Wars of Independence, the Emancipation Proclamation of 1863 in the United States, and Brazilian emancipation of 1888. To the present day, every society where this form of plantation slavery once existed still contends with the long-term effects of that institution.

Mid-Eighteenth-Century Wars

From the standpoint of international relations the state system of the middle of the eighteenth century was quite unstable and tended to lead the major states of Europe into periods of prolonged warfare. The statesmen of the period generally assumed that warfare could be used to further national interests. There were essentially no forces or set of powers who saw it in their interest to prevent war or to maintain peace. Because eighteenth-century wars before the French Revolution were fought by professional armies and navies, civilian populations were rarely drawn deeply into the conflicts. Wars were not associated with domestic political or social upheaval, and peace was not associated with the achievement of international stability. Consequently, periods of peace at the conclusion of a war were often viewed simply as times when a nation might become strong enough to recommence warfare at a later period for the purpose of seizing another nation's territory or of invading another empire's area of trading monopoly.

There were two fundamental areas of great power rivalry: the overseas empires and central and eastern Europe. Alliances and general strategic concerns repeatedly interrelated these regions of conflict.

The War of Jenkins's Ear

In the middle of the eighteenth century, the West Indies had become a hotbed of trade rivalry. Spain attempted to tighten its monopoly, and English smugglers, shippers, and pirates attempted to pierce it. Matters came to a climax in the late 1730s.

The Treaty of Utrecht (1713) gave two special privileges to Great Britain in the Spanish Empire. The British received a thirty-year *asiento*, or contract, to furnish slaves to the Spanish. Britain also gained the right to send one ship each year to the trading fair at Portobello, a major Caribbean seaport on the Panamanian coast. These two privileges allowed British traders and smugglers potential inroads into the Spanish market. Little but friction

Slaves in Brazil washing diamond ore to isolate gems. Notice the ratio of white overseers with whips to black slaves. [Bildarchiv Preussischer Kulturbesitz]

arose from these rights. During the night offshore, British ships often resupplied the annual legal Portobello ship with additional goods as it lay in port. Much to the chagrin of the British, the Spanish government took its own alleged trading monopoly seriously and maintained coastal patrols, which boarded and searched English vessels to look for contraband.

In 1731, during one such boarding operation, there was a fight, and the Spaniards cut off the ear of an English captain named Robert Jenkins. Thereafter he carried about his severed ear preserved in a jar of brandy. This incident was of little importance until 1738, when Jenkins appeared before the British Parliament, reportedly brandishing his ear as an example of Spanish atrocities to British merchants in the West Indies. The British merchant and West Indies interests put great pressure on Parliament to relieve Spanish intervention in their trade. Sir Robert Walpole (1676–1745), the British prime minister, could not resist these pressures. In late 1739, Great Britain went to war with Spain. This war might have been a relatively minor incident, but because of developments in continental Euro-

pean politics, it became the opening encounter to a series of European wars fought across the world until 1815.

The War of the Austrian Succession (1740–1748)

In December 1740, after being king of Prussia for less than seven months, Frederick II seized the Austrian province of Silesia in eastern Germany. The invasion shattered the provisions of the Pragmatic Sanction (see Chapter 15) and upset the continental balance of power as established by the Treaty of Utrecht. The young king of Prussia had treated the House of Habsburg simply as another German state rather than as the leading power in the region. Silesia itself rounded out Prussia's possessions, and Frederick was determined to keep his ill-gotten prize.

MARIA THERESA PRESERVES THE HABSBURG EMPIRE The Prussian seizure of Silesia could have marked the opening of a general hunting season on Habsburg holdings and the beginning of revolts by Habsburg subjects. Instead it led to new political allegiances. Maria Theresa's great achievement was not

Maria Theresa of Austria provided the leadership that saved the Habsburg Empire from possible disintegration after the Prussian invasion of Silesia in 1740. [Kunsthistorisches Museum, Vienna]

the reconquest of Silesia, which eluded her, but the preservation of the Habsburg Empire as a major political power.

Maria Theresa was then only twenty-three and had succeeded to the Habsburg realms only two months before the invasion. She won loyalty and support from her various subjects not merely through her heroism but more specifically by granting new privileges to the nobility. Most significant, the empress recognized Hungary as the most important of her crowns and promised the Magyars considerable local autonomy. She thus preserved the Habsburg state, but at considerable cost to the power of the central monarchy.

Hungary would continue to be, as it had been in the past, a particularly troublesome area in the Habsburg Empire. When the monarchy enjoyed periods of strength and security, guarantees made to Hungary could be ignored. At times of weakness, or when the Magyars could stir enough opposition, the monarchy promised new concessions.

FRANCE DRAWS GREAT BRITAIN INTO THE WAR   The war over the Austrian succession and the British–Spanish commercial conflict could have remained separate disputes. What quickly united them was the role of France. Just as British merchant interests had pushed Sir Robert Walpole into war, a group of aggressive court aristocrats compelled the elderly Cardinal Fleury (1653–1743), first minister of Louis XV, to abandon his planned naval attack on British trade and instead to support the Prussian aggression against Austria, the traditional enemy of France. This was among the more fateful decisions in French history.

In the first place, aid to Prussia consolidated a new and powerful state in Germany. That new power could, and indeed later did, endanger France. Second, the French move against Austria brought Great Britain into the Continental war, as Britain sought to assure that the Low Countries remained in the friendly hands of Austria, not France. In 1744 the British–French conflict expanded beyond the Continent, as France decided to support Spain against Britain in the New World. As a result, French military and economic resources were badly divided. France could not bring sufficient strength to the colonial struggle. Having chosen to continue the old struggle with Austria, France lost the struggle for the future against Great Britain. The war ended in stalemate in 1748 with the Treaty of Aix-la-Chapelle. Prussia retained Silesia, and Spain renewed the *asiento* agreement with Great Britain. Most observers rightly thought the treaty was a truce rather than a permanent peace.

The "Diplomatic Revolution" of 1756

Before the rivalries again erupted into war, a dramatic shift of alliances took place. In January 1756 Prussia and Great Britain signed the Convention of Westminster, a defensive alliance aimed at preventing the entry of foreign troops into the Germanies. Frederick II feared invasions by both Russia and France. The convention meant that Great Britain, the ally of Austria since the wars of Louis XIV, had now joined forces with Austria's major eighteenth-century enemy.

Maria Theresa was despondent over this development. It delighted her foreign minister, Prince Wenzel Anton Kaunitz (1711–1794), however. He had long hoped for an alliance with France to help dismember Prussia. The Convention of Westminster made possible this alliance, which would have been unthinkable a few years earlier. France was agreeable because Frederick had not consulted with its ministers before coming to his understanding with Britain. So, later in May 1756, France and Austria signed a defensive alliance. Kaunitz had succeeded in completely reversing the direction that French foreign policy had followed since the sixteenth century. France would now fight to restore Austrian supremacy in central Europe.

The Seven Years' War (1756–1763)

Although the Treaty of Aix-la-Chapelle had brought peace in Europe, France and Great Britain continued to struggle unofficially on the colonial front. There were continual clashes between their settlers in the Ohio River valley and in upper New England. These were the prelude to what is known in American history as the French and Indian War. Once again, however, Frederick II precipitated a European war that extended into a colonial theater.

FREDERICK THE GREAT OPENS HOSTILITIES   In August 1756, Frederick II opened what would become the Seven Years' War by invading Saxony. Frederick considered this to be a preemptive strike against a conspiracy by Saxony, Austria, and France to destroy Prussian power. He regarded this invasion as a continuation of the defensive strategy of the Convention of Westminster. The invasion itself,

William Pitt the Elder guided Great Britain to a stunning victory in the Seven Years' War. [National Portrait Gallery, London]

however, created the very destructive alliance that Frederick feared. In the spring of 1757, France and Austria made a new alliance dedicated to the destruction of Prussia. They were eventually joined by Sweden, Russia, and many of the smaller German states.

Two factors in addition to Frederick's stubborn leadership (it was after this war that he came to be called Frederick the Great) saved Prussia. First, Britain furnished considerable financial aid. Second, in 1762 Empress Elizabeth of Russia died. Her successor was Tsar Peter III (he was murdered the same year), whose admiration for Frederick was boundless. He immediately made peace with Prussia, thus relieving Frederick of one enemy and allowing him to hold off Austria and France. The Treaty of Hubertusburg of 1763 ended the continental conflict with no significant changes in prewar borders. Silesia remained Prussian, and Prussia clearly stood among the ranks of the great powers.

WILLIAM PITT'S STRATEGY FOR WINNING NORTH AMERICA   The survival of Prussia was less impressive to the rest of Europe than the victories of Great Britain in every theater of conflict. The architect of these victories was William Pitt the Elder (1708–1778). Pitt was a person of colossal ego and administrative genius who had grown up in a commercial family. Although he had previously criticized British involvement with the Continent, once he became secretary of state in charge of the war in 1757, he reversed himself and pumped huge financial subsidies to Frederick the Great. He regarded the German conflict as a way to divert French resources and attention from the colonial struggle. He later boasted of having won America on the plains of Germany.

North America was the center of Pitt's real concern. Put quite simply, he wanted all of North America east of the Mississippi for Great Britain, and that was exactly what he won. He sent more than 40,000 regular English and colonial troops against the French in Canada. Never had so many soldiers been devoted to a field of colonial warfare. He achieved unprecedented cooperation with the American colonies, whose leaders realized that they might finally defeat their French neighbors.

The French government was unwilling and unable to direct similar resources against the English in America. Their military administration was corrupt; the military and political command in Canada were divided; and France could not adequately provision its North American forces. In September 1759, on the Plains of Abraham overlooking the valley of the Saint Lawrence River at Quebec City, the British army under General James Wolfe defeated the French under Lieutenant General Louis Joseph de Montcalm. The French Empire in Canada was ending.

Pitt's colonial vision, however, extended beyond the Saint Lawrence Valley and the Great Lakes Basin. The major islands of the French West Indies fell to British fleets. Income from the sale of captured sugar helped finance the British war effort. British slave interests captured the bulk of the French slave trade. Between 1755 and 1760 the value of the French colonial trade fell by more than 80 percent. In India, the British forces under the command of Robert Clive defeated the French in 1757 at the Battle of Plassey. This victory opened the way for the eventual conquest of Bengal in northeast India and later of all India by the British East India Company. Never had Great Britain or any other European power experienced such a complete worldwide military victory.

THE TREATY OF PARIS OF 1763   The Treaty of Paris of 1763 reflected somewhat less of a victory than Britain had won on the battlefield. Pitt was no longer in office. George III (r. 1760–1820) and Pitt had quarreled over policy, and the minister had departed. His replacement was the earl of Bute (1713–1792), a favorite of the new monarch. Bute was responsible for the peace settlement. Britain received all of Canada, the Ohio River valley, and the eastern half of the Mississippi River valley. Britain returned Pondicherry and Chandernagore in India and the West Indian sugar islands of Guadeloupe and Martinique to the French.

The Seven Years' War had been a vast conflict. Tens of thousands of soldiers and sailors had been killed or wounded. Major battles had been fought around the globe. At great internal sacrifice, Prussia had permanently wrested Silesia from Austria and had turned the Holy Roman Empire into an empty shell. Habsburg power now depended largely on the Hungarian domains. France, though still having sources of colonial income, was no longer a great colonial power. The Spanish Empire remained largely intact, but the British were still determined to penetrate its markets.

On the Indian subcontinent, the British East India Company was able to continue to impose its own authority on the decaying indigenous governments. The results of that situation would be felt until the middle of the twentieth century. In North America, the British government faced the task of organizing its new territories. From this time until World War II, Great Britain was a world power, not just a European one.

The quarter century of warfare also caused a long series of domestic crises among the European powers. The French defeat convinced many people in that nation of the necessity for political and administrative reform. The financial burdens of the wars had astounded all contemporaries. Every power had to begin to find ways to increase revenues to pay its war debt and to finance its preparation for the next combat. Nowhere did this search for revenue lead to more far-ranging consequences than in the British colonies in North America.

The American Revolution and Europe

The revolt of the British colonies in North America was an event in both transatlantic and European history. It erupted from problems of revenue collection common to all the major powers after the Seven Years' War. The War of the American Revolution also continued the conflict between France and Great Britain. The French support of the Americans deepened the existing financial and administrative difficulties of the French monarchy.

Resistance to the Imperial Search for Revenue

After the Treaty of Paris of 1763, the British government faced two imperial problems. The first was the sheer cost of empire, which the British felt they could no longer carry alone. The national debt had risen considerably, as had domestic taxation. Since the American colonies had been the chief beneficiaries of the conflict, the British felt that it was rational for the colonies henceforth to bear part of the cost of their protection and administration. The second problem was the vast expanse of new territory in North America that the British had to organize. This included all the land from the mouth of the Saint Lawrence River to the Mississippi River, with its French settlers and, more importantly, its Native American possessors. (See Map 17–2.)

The British drive for revenue began in 1764 with the passage of the Sugar Act under the ministry of George Grenville (1712–1770). The measure attempted to produce more revenue from imports into the colonies by the rigorous collection of what was actually a lower tax. Smugglers who violated the law were to be tried in admiralty courts without juries. The next year, Parliament passed the

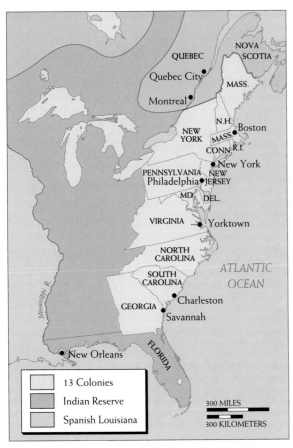

MAP 17–2 NORTH AMERICA IN 1763 *In the year of the victory over France, the English colonies lay along the Atlantic seaboard. The difficulties of organizing authority over the previous French territory in Canada and west of the Appalachian Mountains would contribute to the coming of the American Revolution.*

Stamp Act, which put a tax on legal documents and certain other items such as newspapers. The British considered these taxes legal because the decision to collect them had been approved by Parliament. They regarded them as just because the money was to be spent in the colonies.

The Americans responded that they alone through their assemblies had the right to tax themselves and that they were not represented in Parliament. Furthermore, the expenditure in the colonies of the revenue levied by Parliament did not reassure the colonists. They feared that if colonial government were financed from outside, they would lose control over it. In October 1765, the Stamp Act Congress met in America and drew up a protest to the crown. There was much disorder in the colonies, particularly in Massachusetts, roused by groups known as the Sons of Liberty. The colonists agreed to refuse to import British goods. In 1766 Parliament repealed the Stamp Act, but through the Declaratory Act said that it had the power to legislate for the colonies.

The Stamp Act crisis set the pattern for the next ten years. Parliament, under the leadership of a royal minister, would approve revenue or administrative legislation. The Americans would then resist by reasoned argument, economic pressure, and violence. Then the British would repeal the legislation, and the process would begin again. Each time, tempers on both sides became more frayed and positions more irreconcilable. With each clash the Americans more fully developed their own thinking about political liberty.

"The Horse America throwing his Master," an eighteenth-century cartoon mocking George III about the rebellion of the American colonies. Although he tried to reassert some of the monarchical influence on Britain's politics that had eroded under George I and George II, the first two Hanoverian kings, George III never sought to make himself a tyrant as his critics charged. [The Granger Collection]

The Stamp Act Congress Addresses George III

In 1765 the Stamp Act Congress met to protest the British imposition of taxes on the colonies. The resolutions of the Congress made it very clear that American leaders believed that Great Britain had no right to impose such taxation.

✦ *What are the rights of English citizens that the Americans claim? How has the Stamp Act violated them? Why do they believe the British Parliament has no right to tax them? Do the colonists believe it possible for themselves to be represented in Parliament?*

The Members of this Congress, sincerely devoted, with the warmest sentiments of affection and duty to His Majesty's person and government . . . and with minds deeply impressed by a sense of the present and impending misfortunes of the British colonies on this continent; having considered as maturely as time will permit, the circumstances of the said colonies, esteem it our indispensable duty to make the following declarations of our humble opinion, respecting the most essential rights and liberties of the colonists, and of the grievances under which they labor, by reason of several late acts of Parliament.

I. That His Majesty's subjects in these colonies, own the same allegiance to the crown of Great Britain, that is owing from his subjects born within the realm, and all due subordination to that august body the Parliament of Great Britain.

II. That His Majesty's liege subjects in these colonies are entitled to all the inherent rights and liberties of his natural born subjects, within the kingdom of Great Britain.

III. That it is inseparably essential to the freedom of a people, and the undoubted right of Englishmen, that no taxes be imposed on them but with their own consent, given personally, or by their representatives.

IV. That the people of these colonies are not, and cannot, be represented in the House of Commons in Great Britain.

V. That the only representatives of the people of these colonies are persons chosen therein by themselves, and that no taxes ever have been, or can be constitutionally imposed on them, but by their respective legislatures.

VI. That all supplies to the crown being free gifts of the people, it is unreasonable and inconsistent with the principles and spirit of the British constitution, for the people of Great Britain to grant to His Majesty the property of the colonists.

VII. That trial by jury, is the inherent and invaluable right of every British subject in these colonies.

VIII. That the late act of Parliament entitled, An act for granting and supplying certain stamp duties, and other duties, in the British colonies and plantations, in America, etc. by imposing taxes on the inhabitants of these colonies, and the said act, and several other acts, by extending the jurisdiction of the courts of admiralty beyond its ancient limits, have a manifest tendency to subvert the rights and liberties of the colonists.

Journal of the First Congress of the American Colonies . . . 1765 (New York, 1845), pp. 27–29, as quoted in Oscar Handlin, ed., Readings in American History (New York: Alfred A. Knopf, 1957), pp. 116–117.

The Crisis and Independence

In 1767 Charles Townshend (1725–1767), as Chancellor of the Exchequer, the British finance minister, led Parliament to pass a series of revenue acts relating to colonial imports. The colonists again resisted. The ministry sent over its own customs agents to administer the laws. To protect these new officers, the British sent troops to Boston in 1768. The obvious tensions resulted. In March 1770, the Boston Massacre, in which British troops killed five citizens, took place. That same year, Parliament

This view of the "Boston Massacre" of March 5, 1770 by Paul Revere owes more to propaganda than fact. There was no order to fire and the innocent citizens portrayed here were really an angry, violent mob. [New-York Historical Society]

repeated all of the Townshend duties except the one on tea.

In May 1773, Parliament passed a new law relating to the sale of tea by the East India Company. The measure permitted the direct importation of tea into the American colonies. It actually lowered the price of tea while retaining the tax imposed without the colonists' consent. In some cities, the colonists refused to permit the unloading of the tea; in Boston, a shipload of tea was thrown into the harbor.

The British ministry of Lord North (1732–1792) was determined to assert the authority of Parliament over the resistant colonies. During 1774 Parliament passed a series of laws known in American history as the *Intolerable Acts*. These measures closed the port of Boston, reorganized the government of Massachusetts, allowed troops to be quartered in private homes, and removed the trials of royal customs officials to England. The same year, Parliament approved the Quebec Act for the future administration of Canada. It extended the boundaries of Quebec to include the Ohio River valley. The Americans regarded the Quebec Act as an attempt to prevent the extension of their mode of self-government westward beyond the Appalachian Mountains.

During these years, citizens critical of British policy had established committees of correspondence throughout the colonies. They made the various sections of the eastern seaboard aware of common problems and aided united action. In September 1774, these committees organized the gathering of the First Continental Congress in Philadelphia. This body hoped to persuade Parliament to restore self-government in the colonies and to abandon its attempt at direct supervision of colonial affairs. Conciliation, however, was not forthcoming. By April 1775, the Battles of Lexington and Concord had been fought. In June, the colonists suffered defeat at the Battle of Bunker Hill. Despite that defeat, the colonial assemblies soon began to meet under their own authority rather than under that of the king.

The Second Continental Congress gathered in May 1775. It still sought conciliation with Britain, but the pressure of events led it to begin to conduct the government of the colonies. By August 1775, George III had declared the colonies in rebellion. During the winter, Thomas Paine's (1737–1809) pamphlet *Common Sense* galvanized public opinion in favor of separation from Great Britain. A colonial army and navy were organized. In April 1776, the Continental Congress opened American ports to the trade of all nations. And on July 4, 1776, the Continental Congress adopted the Declaration of Independence. Thereafter, the War of the American Revolution continued until 1781, when the forces of George Washington defeated those of Lord Cornwallis at Yorktown. Early in 1778, however, the war had widened into a European conflict when Benjamin Franklin (1706–1790) persuaded the French government to support the rebellion. In 1779 the Spanish also came to the aid of the colonies. The 1783 Treaty of Paris concluded the conflict, and the thirteen American colonies had established their independence.

American Political Ideas

The political ideas of the American colonists had largely arisen out of the struggle of seventeenth-century English aristocrats and gentry against the absolutism of the Stuart monarchs. The American colonists looked to the English Revolution of 1688 as having established many of their own fundamental political liberties as well as those of the English. The colonists claimed that, through the measures imposed from 1763 to 1776, George III and the British Parliament were attacking those liberties and dissolving the bonds of moral and political allegiance that had formerly united the two peoples. Consequently, the colonists employed a theory that had developed to justify an aristocratic rebellion to support their own popular revolution.

These Whig political ideas, largely derived from the writings of John Locke, were, however, only a part of the English ideological heritage that affected the Americans. Throughout the eighteenth century, they had become familiar with a series of British political writers called the *Commonwealthmen*. These writers held republican political ideas that had their intellectual roots in the most radical thought of the Puritan revolution. During the early eighteenth century, these writers, the most influential of whom were John Trenchard (1662–1723) and Thomas Gordon (d. 1750) in *Cato's Letters* (1720–1723), had relentlessly criticized the government patronage and parliamentary management of Sir Robert Walpole and his successors. They argued that such government was corrupt and that it

Thomas Paine was the author of Common Sense, *a political pamphlet published early in 1776 that helped galvanize American opinion in favor of independence. [Bildarchiv Preussischer Kulturbesitz]*

undermined liberty. They regarded much parliamentary taxation as simply a means of financing political corruption. They also considered standing armies instruments of tyranny. In Great Britain, this republican political tradition had only a marginal impact. The writers were largely ignored because most British subjects regarded themselves as the freest people in the world. Three thousand miles away, however, colonists read these radical books and pamphlets and often accepted them at face value. The policy of Great Britain toward America following the Treaty of Paris of 1763 and certain political events in Britain had made many colonists believe that the worst fears of the Commonwealthmen were coming true. All of these events coincided with the accession of George III to the throne.

Events in Great Britain

George III (r. 1760–1820) believed that a few powerful Whig families and the ministries that they controlled had bullied and dominated his two immediate royal predecessors. George III also believed that he should have ministers of his own choice and that Parliament should function under royal rather than aristocratic management. When William Pitt resigned after a disagreement with George over war policy, the king appointed the earl of Bute as his first minister. In doing so, he ignored the great Whig families that had run the country since 1715. The king sought the aid of politicians whom the Whigs hated. Moreover, he tried to use the same kind of patronage techniques developed by Walpole to achieve royal control of the House of Commons.

Between 1761 and 1770, George tried one minister after another, but each in turn failed to gain enough support from the various factions in the House of Commons. Finally, in 1770 he turned to Lord North, who remained the king's first minister until 1782. The Whig families and other political spokespersons claimed that George III was attempting to impose a tyranny. What they meant was that the king was attempting to curb the power of a particular group of the aristocracy. George III certainly was seeking to restore more royal influence to the government of Great Britain, but he was not attempting to make himself a tyrant.

THE CHALLENGE OF JOHN WILKES Then, in 1763, began the affair of John Wilkes (1725–1797). This

This satirical portrait of John Wilkes is by William Hogarth. It depicts Wilkes with unattractive personal characteristics and questions the sincerity of his calls for liberty. [Library of Congress]

London political radical and member of Parliament published a newspaper called *The North Briton*. In issue Number 45 of this paper, Wilkes strongly criticized Lord Bute's handling of the peace negotiations with France. Wilkes was arrested under the authority of a general warrant issued by the secretary of state. He pleaded the privileges of a member of Parliament and was released. The courts also later ruled that the vague kind of general warrant by which he had been arrested was illegal. The House of Commons, however, ruled that issue Number 45 of *The North Briton* constituted libel, and expelled Wilkes. He soon fled the country and was outlawed. Throughout these procedures there was widespread support for Wilkes, and many popular demonstrations were held in his cause.

In 1768 Wilkes returned to England and again stood for election to Parliament. He won the election, but the House of Commons, under the influence of George III's friends, refused to seat him. He was elected three more times. After the fourth elec-

tion, the House of Commons simply ignored the results and seated the government-supported candidate. As had happened earlier in the decade, large, popular, unruly demonstrations of shopkeepers, artisans, and small property owners supported Wilkes. He also received aid from some aristocratic politicians who wished to humiliate George III. Wilkes himself contended during all his troubles that his was the cause of English liberty. "Wilkes and Liberty" became the slogan of all political radicals and many noble opponents of the monarch. Wilkes was finally seated in 1774, after having become the lord mayor of London.

The American colonists closely followed these developments. Events in Britain confirmed their fears about a monarchical and parliamentary conspiracy against liberty. The king, as their Whig friends told them, was behaving like a tyrant. The Wilkes affair displayed the arbitrary power of the monarch, the corruption of the House of Commons, and the contempt of both for popular electors. That same monarch and Parliament were attempting to overturn the traditional relationship of Great Britain to its colonies by imposing parliamentary taxes. The same government had then landed troops in Boston, changed the government of Massachusetts, and undermined the traditional right of jury trial. All of these events fulfilled too exactly the portrait of political tyranny that had developed over the years in the minds of articulate colonists.

MOVEMENT FOR PARLIAMENTARY REFORM   The political influences between America and Britain operated both ways. The colonial demand for no taxation without representation and the criticism of the adequacy of the British system of representation struck at the core of the eighteenth-century British political structure. British subjects at home who were no more directly represented in the House of Commons than were the Americans could adopt the colonial arguments. The colonial questioning of the taxing authority of the House of Commons was related to the protest of John Wilkes. Both the Americans and Wilkes were challenging the power of the monarch and the authority of Parliament. Moreover, both the colonial leaders and Wilkes appealed over the head of legally constituted political authorities to popular opinion and popular demonstrations. Both were protesting the power of a largely self-selected aristocratic political body. The British ministry was fully aware of these broader political implications of the American troubles.

Major Cartwright Calls for the Reform of Parliament

During the years of the American Revolution, there were many demands in England itself for a major reform of Parliament. In this pamphlet of 1777, Major John Cartwright (1740–1824) demanded that many more English citizens be allowed to vote for members of the House of Commons.

✦ *What does Cartwright mean by "deep parliamentary corruption"? Does it extend beyond Parliament itself? Why are annual parliaments and equal representation a solution? Why are the claims of the few who now send representatives to Parliament rejected by Cartwright?*

Suffering as we do, from a deep parliamentary corruption, it is no time to tamper with silly correctives, and trifle away the life of public freedom: but we must go to the bottom of the stinking sore and cleanse it thoroughly: we must once more infuse into the constitution the vivifying spirit of liberty and expel the very last dregs of this poison. Annual parliaments with an equal representation of the commons are the only specifics in this case: and they would effect a radical cure. That a house of commons, formed as ours is, should maintain septennial elections, and laugh at every other idea is no wonder. The wonder is, that the British nation which, but the other day, was the greatest nation on earth, should be so easily laughed out of its liberties. . . .

Those who now claim the exclusive right of sending to parliament the 513 representatives for about six million souls (amongst whom are one million five hundred thousand males, competent as electors) consist of about two hundred and fourteen thousand persons; and 254 of these representatives are elected by 5,723. . . . Their pretended rights are many of them, derived from royal favour; some from ancient usage and prescription; and some indeed from act of parliament; but neither the most authentic acts of royalty, nor precedent, nor prescription, nor even parliament can establish any flagrant injustice; much less can they strip one million two hundred and eighty six thousand of an inalienable right, to vest it in a number amounting to only one seventh of that multitude. . . .

John Cartwright, Legislative Rights of the Commonality Vindicated *(1777), cited in S. Maccoby,* The English Radical Tradition, 1763–1914 *(London: Adam and Charles Black, 1966), pp. 32–33.*

The American colonists also demonstrated to Europe how a politically restive people in the Old Regime could fight tyranny and protect political liberty. They established revolutionary but orderly political bodies that could function outside the existing political framework: the congress and the convention. These began with the Stamp Act Congress of 1765 and culminated in the Constitutional Convention of 1787. The legitimacy of those congresses and conventions lay not in existing law but in the alleged consent of the governed. This approach represented a new way to found a government.

Toward the end of the War of the American Revolution, calls for parliamentary reform arose in Britain itself. The method proposed for changing the system was the extralegal Association Movement.

THE YORKSHIRE ASSOCIATION MOVEMENT By the close of the 1770s, many in Britain resented the mismanagement of the American war, the high taxes, and Lord North's ministry. In northern England in 1778, Christopher Wyvil (1740–1822), a landowner and retired clergyman, organized the Yorkshire Association Movement. Property owners, or freeholders, of Yorkshire met in a mass meeting to demand rather moderate changes in the corrupt system of parliamentary elections. They organized corresponding societies elsewhere. They intended that the association examine—and suggest reforms for—the entire government. The Association Movement was thus a popular attempt to establish an extralegal institution to reform the government.

The movement collapsed during the early 1780s because its supporters, unlike Wilkes and the American rebels, were not willing to appeal for broad popular support. Nonetheless, the agitation of the Association Movement provided many people with experience in political protest. Several of its younger figures lived to raise the issue of parliamentary reform after 1815.

Parliament was not insensitive to the demands of the Association Movement. In April 1780, the Commons passed a resolution that called for lessening the power of the crown. In 1782 Parliament adopted a measure for "economical" reform, which abolished some patronage at the disposal of the monarch. These actions, however, did not prevent George III from appointing a minister of his own choice. In 1783 shifts in Parliament obliged Lord North to form a ministry with Charles James Fox (1749–1806), a long-time critic of George III. The monarch was most unhappy with the arrangement.

In 1783 the king approached William Pitt the Younger (1759–1806), son of the victorious war minister, to manage the House of Commons. During the election of 1784, Pitt received immense patronage support from the crown and constructed a House of Commons favorable to the monarch. Thereafter, Pitt sought to formulate trade policies that would give his ministry broad popularity. He attempted in 1785 one measure of modest parliamentary reform. When it failed, the young prime minister, who had been only twenty-four at the time of his appointment, abandoned the cause of reform.

By the mid-1780s, George III had achieved a part of what he had sought since 1761. He had reasserted the influence of the monarchy in political affairs. It proved a temporary victory because his own mental illness, which would eventually require a regency, weakened the royal power. The cost of his years of dominance had been high, however. On both sides of the Atlantic, the issue of popular sovereignty had been raised and widely discussed. The American colonies had been lost. Economically, this loss did not prove disastrous. British trade with America after independence actually increased.

The Americans—through the state constitutions, the Articles of Confederation, and the federal Constitution adopted in 1788—had demonstrated to Europe the possibility of government without kings

Events in Britain and America Relating to the American Revolution	
1760	George III becomes king
1763	Treaty of Paris concludes the Seven Years' War
1763	John Wilkes publishes issue Number 45 of *The North Briton*
1764	Sugar Act
1765	Stamp Act
1766	Sugar Act repealed and Declaratory Act passed
1767	Townshend Acts
1768	Parliament refuses to seat John Wilkes after his election
1770	Lord North becomes George III's chief minister
1770	Boston Massacre
1773	Boston Tea Party
1774	Intolerable Acts
1774	First Continental Congress
1775	Second Continental Congress
1776	Declaration of Independence
1778	France enters the war on the side of America
1778	Yorkshire Association Movement founded
1781	British forces surrender at Yorktown
1783	Treaty of Paris concludes War of the American Revolution

and hereditary nobilities. They had established the example of a nation in which written documents based on popular consent and popular sovereignty—rather than on divine law, natural law, tradition, or the will of kings—were the highest political and legal authority. The political novelty of these assertions should not be ignored.

As the crisis with Britain unfolded during the 1760s and 1770s, the American colonists had come to see themselves as first preserving traditional English liberties against the tyrannical crown and corrupt Parliament and then as developing a whole new sense of liberty. By the mid-1770s, the colonists had rejected monarchical government and embraced republican political ideals. They would govern themselves through elected assemblies without any presence of a monarchical authority. Once a constitution was adopted, they would insist on a bill of rights specifically protecting a whole series of civil liberties. The Americans would reject the aristocratic social hierarchy that had existed in the colonies. They would embrace democratic ideals even if the franchise remained limited. They would assert the equality of white male citizens not only before the law but in ordinary social relations. They would reject social status based on birth and inheritance and assert the necessity of the liberty for all citizens to improve their social standing and economic lot by engaging in free commercial activity. They did not free their slaves nor did they address issues of the rights of women or of Native Americans, but the American colonists of the eighteenth century in making their revolution produced a society more free than any the world had seen and one that would eventually expand the circle of political and social liberty. In all these respects, the American Revolution was a genuinely radical movement, whose influence would widen as Americans moved across the continent and as other peoples began to question traditional modes of European government.

◆

Throughout the eighteenth century, the great European powers fought in two major arenas—their overseas commercial empires and central Europe.

In the New World, Britain, France, and Spain battled for commercial dominance. France and Britain also clashed over their spheres of influence in India. By the third quarter of the century, Britain had succeeded in ousting France from most of its major holdings in North America and from any significant presence in India. Spain, though no longer a military power of the first order, had managed to maintain its vast colonial empire in Latin America and a large measure of its monopoly over the region's trade.

On the Continent, France, Austria, and Prussia collided over conflicting territorial and dynastic ambitions. Britain became involved to protect its continental interests and to use the continental wars to divert France from the colonial arena. Prussia with British aid had emerged in 1763 as a major continental power. Austria had lost considerable territory to Prussia. France had accumulated a vast debt.

The mid-century conflicts in turn led to major changes in all the European states. Each of the monarchies needed more money and tried to govern itself more efficiently. This problem led Britain to attempt to tax the North American colonies, which led to a revolution and the colonies' independence. Already deeply in debt, the French monarchy aided the Americans, fell into a deeper financial crisis, and soon sharply clashed *with the nobility as royal ministers tried to find new revenues. That clash eventually unleashed the French Revolution. Spain moved to administer its Latin American empire more efficiently, which increased revolutionary discontent in the early nineteenth century. In preparation for future wars, the rulers of Prussia, Austria, and Russia pursued a mode of activist government known as Enlightened Absolutism. This will be examined in the next chapter. In that regard, the mid-eighteenth-century wars set in motion most of the major political developments of the next half century.*

Review Questions

1. What were the fundamental ideas associated with mercantile theory? Did they work? Which European country was most successful in establishing a mercantile empire? Least successful? Why?

2. What were the main points of conflict between Britain and France in North America, the West Indies, and India? How did the triangles of trade function between the Americas, Europe, and Africa?

3. How was the Spanish colonial empire in the Americas organized and managed? What changes did the Bourbon monarchs institute in the Spanish Empire?

4. What was the nature of slavery in the Americas? How was it linked to the economies of the Americas, Europe, and Africa? What was the plantation system and how did it contribute to the inhumane treatment of slaves?

5. The Seven Years' War was a major conflict with battles fought around the globe. What were the results of this war? Which countries emerged in a stronger position and why?

6. Discuss the American Revolution in the context of European history. To what extent were the colonists influenced by European ideas and political developments? To what extent did their actions in turn influence Europe?

Suggested Readings

B. BAILYN, *The Ideological Origins of the American Revolution* (1967). An important work illustrating the role of English radical thought in the perceptions of the American colonists.

B. Bailyn, *The Peopling of British North America: An Introduction* (1988). A study of the immigrants to the British colonies on the eve of the Revolution.

C. A. Bayly, *Imperial Meridian: The British Empire and the World, 1780–1830* (1989). A major study of the empire after the loss of America.

C. Becker, *The Declaration of Independence: A Study in the History of Political Ideas* (1922). Remains an important examination of the political and imperial theory of the Declaration.

L. Bethell (ed.), *The Cambridge History of Latin America*, vols. 1 and 2 (1984). Excellent essays on the colonial era.

J. Black, *Pitt the Elder* (1992). The most recent biography.

J. Black, *European Warfare, 1660–1815* (1994). A major, wide-ranging synthesis.

C. Bonwick, *English Radicals and the American Revolution* (1977). Explores the relationship between English radical politics and events in America.

D. Brading, *The First America* (1991). A major study of colonial Latin America.

J. Brewer, *Party Ideology and Popular Politics at the Accession of George III* (1976). An important series of essays on popular radicalism.

J. Brewer, *The Sinews of Power: War, Money, and the English State, 1688–1783* (1989). A study that emphasizes the financial power behind British military success.

J. Brooke, *King George III* (1972). The best biography.

K. N. Chaudhuri, *The Trading World of Asia and the English East India Company* (1978). Examines the impact of trade on both Asians and Europeans.

L. Colley, *Britons: Forging the Nation, 1707–1837* (1992). A major work with important discussions of the recovery from the loss of America.

P. Curtin, *The Atlantic Slave Trade* (1969). The best work on the subject.

D. B. Davis, *The Problem of Slavery in Western Culture* (1966). A brilliant and far-ranging discussion.

D. B. Davis, *The Problem of Slavery in the Age of Revolution, 1770–1823* (1975). A major work on both European and American history.

R. Davis, *The Rise of the Atlantic Economies* (1973). A major synthesis.

W. Dorn, *Competition for Empire, 1740–1763* (1940). Still one of the best accounts of the mid-century struggle.

C. Gibson, *Spain in America* (1966). A splendidly clear and balanced discussion.

P. Langford, *A Polite and Commercial People: England 1717–1783* (1989). An excellent survey of mid-century Britain based on the most recent scholarship covering social history as well as politics, the overseas wars, and the American Revolution.

J. Lockhardt and S. B. Schwartz, *Early Latin America: A History of Colonial Spanish America and Brazil* (1983). The new standard work.

J. R. McNeil, *Atlantic Empires of France and Spain: Louisbourg and Havana, 1700–1763* (1985). An examination of imperial policies for two key overseas outposts.

S. W. Mintz, *Sweetness and Power: The Place of Sugar in Modern History* (1985). Traces the role of sugar in the world economy and how sugar has had an impact on world culture.

A. Pagden, *Lords of All the World: Ideologies of Empire in Spain, Britain, and France, 1492–1830* (1995). One of the few comparative studies of empire during this period.

J. H. Parry, *Trade and Dominion: The European Overseas Empires in the Eighteenth Century* (1971). A comprehensive account with attention to the European impact on the rest of the world.

J. G. A. Pocock, *The Machiavellian Moment: Florentine Political Thought and the Atlantic Republican Tradition* (1975). An important book that traces the origins of Anglo-American radicalism to Renaissance Florence.

C. D. Rice, *The Rise and Fall of Black Slavery* (1975). An excellent survey of the subject with careful attention to the numerous historiographical controversies.

J. C. Riley, *The Seven Years' War and the Old Regime in France: The Economic and Financial Toll* (1986). A useful analysis of pressures that would undermine the French monarchy.

G. Rudé, *Wilkes and Political Liberty* (1962). A close analysis of popular political behavior.

K. W. Schweizer, *Frederick the Great, William Pitt, and Lord Bute: The Anglo-Prussian Alliance, 1756–1763* (1991). The most recent study of this complex diplomacy.

I. K. Steele, *The English Atlantic, 1675–1740: An Exploration of Communication and Community* (1986). An exploration of culture and commerce in the transatlantic world.

R. L. Stein, *The French Sugar Business in the Eighteenth Century* (1988). A study that covers all aspects of the French sugar trade.

J. Thornton, *Africa and Africans in the Making of the Atlantic World, 1400–1680* (1992). A discussion of the role of Africans in the emergence of the transatlantic economy.

J. West, *Gunpower, Government, and War in the Mid-Eighteenth Century* (1991). A study of how warfare touched much of government.

G. Wills, *Inventing America: Jefferson's Declaration of Independence* (1978). An important study that challenges much of the analysis in the Becker volume.

G. S. Wood, *The Creation of the American Republic, 1776–1787* (1969). A far-ranging work dealing with Anglo-American political thought.

G. S. Wood, *The Radicalism of the American Revolution* (1991). A major interpretation.

Enlightenment and Revolution

Between approximately 1750 and 1850, certain extraordinary changes occurred in Western civilization. Although of immediate significance primarily for the nations of Europe and the Americas, these developments in the long run had an immense worldwide impact. Eventually, all civilizations were to feel the influence of the European intellectual ferment and political turmoil of these years. Most of the intellectual, political, economic, and social characteristics associated with the modern world came into being during this era. Europe became the great exporter of ideas and technologies that in time transformed one area after another of human experience.

An intellectual movement known as the *Enlightenment*, characterized by ideals of reform and challenge to traditional cultural authority, captured the imagination of the reading public. The Enlightenment drew confidence from the scientific worldview that had emerged during the seventeenth century. Its exponents urged the application of the spirit of critical rationalism in one area of social and political life after another. They posed serious historical and moral questions to the Christian faith. They contended that laws of society and economics could be discovered and could then be used to improve the human condition. They embraced the idea of economic growth and development. They called for political reform and more efficient modes of government. They upheld the standard of rationality in order to cast doubt on traditional modes of thought and behavior that seemed to them less than rational. As a result of their labors, initially in Europe and ultimately throughout the world, the idea of change as a positive value, which has played so important a role in modern life, emerged for the first time.

For many people, however, change seemed to come too rapidly and violently when revolution erupted in France in 1789. Beginning as an aristocratic revolt against the monarchy, the revolution rapidly spread to every corner of French political and social life. The rights of man and citizen displaced those of the monarchy, the aristocracy, and the church. By 1792 the revolution had become a genuinely popular movement and had established a French republic whose armies challenged the other major European monarchies. The reign of terror that saw the execution of the French king unleashed civil violence unlike anything witnessed in Europe since the age of the religious wars. By the end of the 1790s, to restore order, French political leaders turned themselves over to the leadership of Napoleon. Thereafter, for more than a decade, his armies uprooted institutions of the Old Regime across the Continent. Only in 1815, after the Battle of Waterloo, was the power of France and Napoleon finally contained.

The French Revolution in one way or another served as a model for virtually all later popular revolutions. It unleashed new forces and political creeds in one area of the world after another. The French Revolution, with its broad popular base, brought the *people* to the forefront of world political history. In defining the early goals of the revolution—to establish a legal framework of limited monarchical power, secure citizen rights, and make possible relatively free economic activity—its supporters developed the political creed of *liberalism*.

The wars of the French Revolution and of Napoleon, stretching from 1792 to 1815, awakened the political force of *nationalism*, which has proved to be the single most powerful ideology of the modern world. Loyalty to the nation defined in ethnic terms of a common language, history, and culture replaced loyalty to dynasties. As a political ideology, nationalism could be used both to liberate a people from the domination of another nation and to justify wars of aggression. Nationalism was put to both uses in Europe and throughout the rest of the world in the two centuries following the revolution in France. Nationalism became a kind of secular religion that aroused a degree of loyalty and personal self-sacrifice previously prompted only by the great religious traditions.

Finally, between 1750 and 1850, Europe became not only an exporter of reform and revolution but also of manufactured commodities. The technology and the society associated with industrialism took root throughout the western portion of the Continent. Europeans achieved a productive capacity that, in cooperation with their naval power, permitted them to dominate the markets of the world. Thereafter, to be strong, independent, and modern seemed to require industrialization and imitation of the manufacturing techniques of Europe and, later, of the United States.

Industrialism and its society, however, fostered immense social problems, dislocations, and injustices. The major intellectual and political response to these was *socialism*, several varieties of which emerged from the European social and economic turmoil of the 1830s and 1840s. History eventually proved the most significant of these to be that espoused by Karl Marx, whose *Communist Manifesto* appeared in 1848.

Remarkable ironies are attached to the European achievements of the late eighteenth and the early nineteenth centuries. Enlightenment, revolution, and industrialism contributed to an awakening of European power that permitted the Continent to dominate the world for a time at the end of the nineteenth century. Yet those same movements produced various intellectual critiques, political ideas, and economic skills that twentieth-century non-European peoples would turn against their temporary European masters. It is for that reason that the Age of Enlightenment and revolution in the West proved so important, not only for Europe, but for the history of the entire modern world. ✦

	POLITICS AND GOVERNMENT	SOCIETY AND ECONOMY	RELIGION AND CULTURE
1700–1789	1713 Peace of Utrecht 1713–1740 Frederick William I builds Prussian military 1720–1740 Walpole in England, Fleury in France 1739 War of Jenkins's Ear 1740 Maria Theresa succeeds to Habsburg throne 1740–1748 War of the Austrian Succession	1715–1763 Colonial rivalry in the Caribbean 1733 James Kay's flying shuttle	1721 Montesquieu, *Persian Letters* 1733 Voltaire, *Letters on the English* 1738 Voltaire, *Elements of the Philosophy of Newton* 1739 Wesley begins field preaching 1748 Hume, *Inquiry into Human Nature* 1748 Montesquieu, *Spirit of the Laws*

Voltaire

	POLITICS AND GOVERNMENT	SOCIETY AND ECONOMY	RELIGION AND CULTURE
	1756–1763 Seven Years' War 1767 Legislative Commission in Russia 1772 First Partition of Poland 1775–1783 American Revolution 1785 Catherine the Great of Russia issues Charter of Nobility	1750s Agricultural Revolution in Britain 1750–1840 Growth of new cities 1763 British establish dominance in India 1763–1789 Enlightened absolutist rulers seek to spur economic growth 1765 James Hargreaves's spinning jenny 1769 Richard Arkwright's waterframe 1771–1775 Pugachev's Rebellion 1780 Gordon riots in London 1787 Edmund Cartwright's power loom	1750 Rousseau, *Discourse on the Moral Effects of the Arts and Sciences* 1751 First volume of Diderot's *Encyclopedia* 1762 Rousseau, *Social Contract and Émile* 1763 Voltaire, *Treatise on Toleration* 1774 Goethe, *Sorrows of Young Werther* 1776 Smith, *Wealth of Nations* 1779 Lessing, *Nathan the Wise* 1781 Joseph II adopts toleration in Austria 1781 Kant, *Critique of Pure Reason*
1789–1815	1789 Gathering of the Estates General at Versailles; fall of the Bastille; Declaration of the Rights of Man and Citizen 1791 French monarchy abolished 1793 Louis XVI executed 1793–1794 Reign of Terror	1789–1802 Revolutionary legislation restructures French economic life	1789 Blake, *Songs of Innocence* 1790 Civil Constitution of the Clergy; Burke, *Reflections on the Revolution in France* 1792 Wollstonecraft, *Vindication of the Rights of Woman* 1793 France proclaims Cult of Reason

	POLITICS AND GOVERNMENT	SOCIETY AND ECONOMY	RELIGION AND CULTURE
1789–1815 (cont.)	1795 The Directory established in France	1794–1824 Wars of independence in Latin America break the colonial system	1794 France proclaims Cult of the Supreme Being
	1799 Napoleon named First Consul in France		1798 Wordsworth and Coleridge, *Lyrical Ballads*; Malthus, *Essay on the Principle of Population*
	1803 War resumes between Britain and France		
	1804 Napoleonic Code; Napoleon crowned emperor		1799 Schleiermacher, *Speeches on Religion to Its Cultured Despisers*
	1805 Third Coalition formed against France; battles of Trafalgar and Austerlitz		1802 Chateaubriand, *Genius of Christianity*
	1806 Napoleon establishes the Continental System		1802 Napoleon, Concordat with the Papacy
	1807 Treaty of Tilsit between France and Russia		1806 Hegel, *Phenomenology of Mind*
	1808 Spanish resistance to Napoleon stiffens		1807 Fichte, *Addresses to the German Nation*
			1808 Goethe, *Faust*, Part I
	1812 Napoleon invades Russia; meets defeat	1810 Abolition of serfdom in Prussia	1812 Byron, *Childe Harold's Pilgrimage*
	1814 Napoleon abdicates; Congress of Vienna opens; Louis XVIII restored in France		
1815–1850	1815 Napoleon defeated at Waterloo		
	1819 Carlsbad Decrees in Germanies; Peterloo Massacre and the Six Acts, Britain	1800–1850 British industrial dominance	1817 Ricardo, *Principles of Political Economy*
		1825 Stockton and Darlington Railway opens	1819 Byron, *Don Juan*
	1820 Spanish Revolution begins	1828–1850 First European police departments	1829 Catholic Emancipation Act in Great Britain
	1821 Greek Revolution begins	1830–1850 Railway building in western Europe	1830–1842 Comte, *The Positive Philosophy*
	1823 France intervenes in Spanish Revolution	1833 English Factory Act to protect children	1830 Lyell, *Principles of Geology*
	1825 Decembrist Revolt in Russia	1834 German *Zollverein* established	1833 Russia begins "Official Nationality" policy
	1829 Catholic Emancipation Act in Great Britain	1842 Chadwick, *Report on the Sanitary Condition of the Labouring Population*	1835 Strauss, *Life of Jesus*
	1830 Revolution in France, Belgium, and Poland; Serbia gains independence	1846 Corn Laws repealed in Britain	1840 Villermé, *Catalogue of the Physical and Moral State of Workers*
	1832 Great Reform Bill in Britain	1847 Ten Hour Act passed in Britain	1843 Kierkegaard, *Fear and Trembling*
	1848 Revolutions sweep across Europe	1848 Serfdom abolished in Austria and Hungary	1848 Marx and Engels, *Communist Manifesto*

Napoleon Bonaparte

*Philosopher, dramatist, poet, historian, and popularizer of scientific ideas, Voltaire
(1694–1778) was the most famous and influential of the eighteenth-century philosophes.
His sharp satire and criticism of religious institutions opened the way for a more general
critique of the European political and social status quo. [Private Collection, Musee de la
Ville de Paris, Musee Carnavalet, Paris, France. Giraudon/Art Resource]*

The Age of Enlightenment: Eighteenth-Century Thought

Formative Influences
Ideas of Newton and Locke
The Example of British Toleration and Stability
Need for Reform in France
The Emergence of a Print Culture

The *Philosophes*
Voltaire's Agenda of Intellectual Reform
The *Encyclopedia*

The Enlightenment and Religion
Deism
Toleration
Radical Enlightenment Criticism of Religion

The Enlightenment and Society
Beccaria and Reform of Criminal Law

The Physiocrats and Economic Freedom
Adam Smith and *The Wealth of Nations*

Political Thought of the *Philosophes*
Montesquieu and *Spirit of the Laws*
Rousseau: A Radical Critique of Modern Society
Women in the Thought and Practice of the Enlightenment

Enlightened Absolutism
Frederick the Great of Prussia
Joseph II of Austria
Catherine the Great of Russia
The Partition of Poland
The End of the Eighteenth Century in Central and Eastern Europe

K E Y   T O P I C S

- The intellectual and social background of the Enlightenment
- The *philosophes* of the Enlightenment and their agenda of intellectual and political reform
- Efforts of "enlightened" monarchs in central and eastern Europe to increase the economic and military strength of their domains
- The partition of Poland by Prussia, Russia, and Austria

During the eighteenth century, the conviction began to spread throughout the literate sectors of European society that change and reform were both possible and desirable. This attitude is now commonplace, but it came into its own only after 1700. It represents one of the primary intellectual inheritances from that age. The movement of people and ideas that fostered such thinking is called the Enlightenment.

Its leading voices combined confidence in the human mind inspired by the Scientific Revolution and faith in the power of rational criticism to challenge the intellectual authority of tradition and the Christian past. These writers stood convinced that human beings could comprehend the operation of physical nature and mold it to the ends of material and moral improvement, economic growth, and political reform. The rationality of the physical universe became a standard against which the customs and traditions of society could be measured and criticized. Such criticism penetrated every corner of contemporary society, politics, and religious opinion. As a result, the spirit of innovation and improvement came to characterize modern Europe and Western society.

Some of the ideas and outlooks of the Enlightenment had a direct impact on several rulers in central and eastern

Europe. These rulers, whose policies became known by the term enlightened absolutism, *sought to centralize their authority so as to reform their countries. They often attempted to restructure religious authority and to sponsor economic growth. Although they were often associated with the writers of the Enlightenment, many of their policies were in direct opposition to enlightened ideals. Nonetheless, both the Enlightenment writers and these monarchs were forces for modernization in European life.*

Formative Influences

The Newtonian worldview, the stability and prosperity of Great Britain after 1688, the need for reform in France after the wars of Louis XIV, and the consolidation of what is known as a *print culture* were the chief factors that fostered the ideas of the Enlightenment and the call for reform throughout Europe.

Ideas of Newton and Locke

Isaac Newton (1642–1727) and John Locke (1632–1704) were the major intellectual forerunners of the Enlightenment. Newton's formulation of the law of universal gravitation exemplified the power of the human mind. By example and in his writing, he encouraged Europeans to approach the study of nature directly and to avoid metaphysics and supernaturalism. Newton had always insisted on empirical support for his general laws and constantly used empirical experience to check his rational speculations. This emphasis on concrete experience became a key feature of Enlightenment thought.

Newton also seemed to have revealed a pattern of rationality in the physical world. During the eighteenth century, thinkers began to apply this insight to society. If nature was rational, they reasoned, society too should be organized rationally.

As noted in Chapter 14, Newton's success in physics inspired his countryman John Locke to explain human psychology in terms of experience. In *An Essay Concerning Human Understanding* (1690), Locke argued that all humans enter the world a *tabula rasa*, or blank page. Personality is the product of the sensations that impinge on an individual from the external world throughout his or her life. Thus, experience, and only experience, shapes character. The implication of this theory

This elaborate eighteenth-century engraving pays homage to Isaac Newton. Newton was a major intellectual influence on the Enlightenment. This engraving is in the collection of the British Museum. [Corbis-Bettmann]

was that human nature is changeable and can be molded by modifying the surrounding physical and social environment. Locke's was a reformer's psychology. It suggested the possibility of improving the human condition. Locke's psychology also, in effect, rejected the Christian doctrine that human beings are permanently flawed by sin. Human beings need not wait for the grace of God or other divine aid to better their lives. They could take charge of their own destiny.

The Example of British Toleration and Stability

Newton's physics and Locke's psychology provided the theoretical basis for a reformist approach to society. The domestic stability of Great Britain after the Revolution of 1688 furnished a living example of a society in which enlightened reforms appeared to function for the benefit of all. England permitted religious toleration to all except Unitarians and Roman Catholics, and even they were not actually persecuted. Relative freedom of the press and free speech prevailed. The authority of the monarchy was limited, and political sovereignty resided in Parliament. The courts protected citizens from arbitrary government action. The army was small. In the view of reformist observers on the Continent, these liberal policies had produced not disorder and instability but prosperity, stability, and a loyal citizenry. This view may have been idealized, but England was nonetheless significantly freer than any other European nation at the time.

Need for Reform in France

If the example of Great Britain suggested that change and freedom need not be disastrous, France seemed to illustrate those aspects of European politics and society that most demanded reform. Its legacy from Louis XIV was absolute monarchy, a large standing army, heavy taxation, and religious persecution. Louis's policies had ultimately brought defeat in war and left his people so miserable that many celebrated when he died. His successors continued to curb liberties. The regime restricted freedom of worship and censored the press and literary expression. Authors often had their works printed in Switzerland to avoid these restraints. Critics of the regime were subject to arbitrary arrest, although some of them reached accommodations with the authorities. State regulations hampered economic growth. Many aristocrats, regarding themselves as part of a military class, upheld traditional militaristic values.

Yet France, because it confronted its political thinkers so sharply with the need for reform, became a major center for the Enlightenment.

The Emergence of a Print Culture

The Enlightenment was the first major intellectual movement of European history to flourish in a print culture, a culture in which books, journals, newspapers, and pamphlets had achieved a status of their own. Although printed books and pamphlets played a significant role during the Reformation and Counter-Reformation, the powerful messages of those movements were spread mostly by preaching. During the eighteenth century, the volume of printed material—books, journals, magazines, and daily newspapers—increased sharply throughout Europe, most notably in Britain. Prose came to be valued as highly as poetry and the novel emerged as a distinct genre. The printed word had become the chief vehicle for the communication of ideas and would remain so until the electronic revolution of our own day.

A growing concern with everyday life and material concerns—with secular as opposed to religious issues—accompanied this expansion of printed forms. Toward the end of the seventeenth century, half the books published in Paris were religious; by the 1780s, only about 10 percent were.

Books were not inexpensive in this era, but they, and the ideas they conveyed, circulated in a variety of ways to reach a broad public. Private and public libraries grew in number, allowing single copies to reach many readers. Authors might also publish the same material in different formats. The English essayist, critic, and dictionary author Samuel Johnson (1709–1784), for example, published as books collections of essays that had first appeared in newspapers or journals.

Familiarity with books and secular ideas came increasingly to be expected within aristocratic and middle-class society. Popular publications, such as *The Spectator*, begun in 1711 by Joseph Addison (1672–1719) and Richard Steele (1672–1729), fostered the value of polite conversation and the reading of books. Coffee houses became centers for the discussion of writing and ideas. The lodges of Freemasons, the meeting places for members of a movement that began in Britain and spread to the Continent, provided another site for the consideration of secular ideas in secular books.

The expanding market for printed matter allowed writers to earn a living from their work for the first time, making authorship an occupation. Parisian ladies sought out popular writers for their fashionable salons. Some writers, notably Alexander Pope (1688–1744) and Voltaire, grew wealthy, providing an example for their aspiring young colleagues. In a challenge to older aristocratic values, status for authors in this new print culture was based on merit and commercial competition, not heredity and patronage.

A division, however, soon emerged between high and low literary culture. Successful authors of the Enlightenment addressed themselves to monarchs, nobles, the upper middle classes, and professional groups and were read and accepted in these upper levels of society. Other authors found social and economic disappointment. They lived marginally,

The world of the Enlightenment has often been portrayed as entirely optimistic. Such was hardly the case. Some people feared that the expansion of knowledge might bring danger as well as liberation. In this famous painting of a bird in an air pump, Joseph Wright of Derby captures some of that uncertainty. The scene is suffused in light, a metaphor for scientific enlightenment, but the bird will probably die as a result of the experiment. The people gathered around it are clearly having varied reactions to what they are witnessing. [Joseph Wright of Derby, "Experiment with an Air Pump". National Gallery, London, Great Britain. Bridgeman/Art Resource, N.Y.]

writing professionally for whatever newspaper or journal would pay for their pages. Many of these lesser writers grew resentful, blaming a corrupt society for their lack of success. From their anger, they often espoused radical ideas or carried Enlightenment ideas to radical extremes, transmitting them in this embittered form to their often lower-class audience. The new print culture thus circulated the ideas of the Enlightenment to virtually all literate groups in society.

An expanding literate public and the growing influence of secular printed materials created a new and increasingly influential social force called *public opinion*. This force—the collective effect on political and social life of views circulated in print and discussed in the home, the workplace, and centers of leisure—seems not to have existed as a vital force before the middle of the eighteenth century. Books and newspapers could have thousands of readers, who in effect supported the writers whose works they bought, discussing their ideas and circulating them widely. The writers, in turn, had to answer only to their readers. The result changed the cultural and political climate in Europe. In 1775 a new member of the French Academy declared:

A tribunal has arisen independent of all powers and that all powers respect, that appreciates all talents, that pronounces on all people of merit. And in an enlightened century, in a century in which each citizen can speak to the entire nation by way of print, those who have a talent for instructing men and a gift for moving them—in a word, men of letters—are, amid the public dispersed, what the orators of Rome and Athens were in the middle of the public assembled.[1]

Governments could no longer operate wholly in secret or with disregard to the larger public sphere. They, as well as their critics, had to explain and discuss their views and policies openly.

Continental European governments sensed the political power of the new print culture. They regulated the book trade, censored books and newspapers, confiscated offending titles, and imprisoned offending authors. The eventual expansion of freedom of the press represented also an expansion of the print culture—with its independent readers, authors, and publishers—and the challenge it represented to traditional intellectual, social, and political authorities.

The *Philosophes*

The writers and critics who forged the new attitudes favorable to change, who championed reform, and who flourished in the emerging print culture

[1]Chrétien-Guillaume Malesherbes, as quoted in Roger Chartier, *The Cultural Origins of the French Revolution*, trans. by Lydia G. Cochran (Durham, N.C.: Duke University Press, 1991), pp. 30–31.

were the *philosophes*. Not usually philosophers in a formal sense, they sought rather to apply the rules of reason and common sense to nearly all the major institutions and social practices of the day. The most famous of their number included Voltaire, Montesquieu, Diderot, Rousseau, Hume, Gibbon, Smith, Lessing, and Kant.

A few of these *philosophes* occupied professorships in universities. Most, however, were free agents who might be found in London coffee houses, Edinburgh drinking spots, the salons of fashionable Parisian ladies, the country houses of reform-minded nobles, or the courts of the most powerful monarchs on the Continent. In eastern Europe, they were often to be found in the royal bureaucracies. They were not an organized group; they disagreed on many issues. Their relationship with each other and with lesser figures of the same turn of mind has quite appropriately been compared with that of a family, in which despite quarrels and tensions a basic unity still remains.[2]

The chief bond among the *philosophes* was their common desire to reform thought, society, and government for the sake of human liberty. As Peter Gay has suggested, this goal included "freedom from arbitrary power, freedom of speech, freedom of trade, freedom to realize one's talents, freedom of aesthetic response, freedom, in a word, of moral man to make his way in the world."[3] No other single set of ideas has done so much to shape the modern world. The literary vehicles through which the *philosophes* delivered their message included books, pamphlets, plays, novels, philosophical treatises, encyclopedias, newspapers, and magazines. During the Reformation and the religious wars, writers had used the printed word to debate the proper mode of faith in God. The *philosophes* of the Enlightenment employed the printed word to proclaim a new faith in the capacity of humankind to improve itself without the aid of God.

Many of the *philosophes* were of middle-class origins. The bulk of their readership was also drawn from the prosperous commercial and professional people of the eighteenth-century towns and cities. These people discussed the reformers' writings and ideas in local philosophical societies, Freemason lodges, and clubs. They had enough income and leisure time to buy and read the *philosophes'* works.

[2]Peter Gay, *The Enlightenment: An Interpretation*, vol. 1 (New York: Knopf, 1967), p. 4.
[3]Gay, p. 3.

Although the writers of the Enlightenment did not consciously champion the goals or causes of the middle class, they did provide an intellectual ferment and a major source of ideas that could be used to undermine existing social practices and political structures. They taught their contemporaries how to pose pointed, critical questions. Moreover, the *philosophes* generally supported the economic growth, the expansion of trade, and the improvement of transport, which were transforming the society and the economy of the eighteenth century and enlarging the middle class.

The Enlightenment evolved over the course of the century and involved writers living at different times in various countries. Its early exponents popularized the rationalism and scientific ideas of the seventeenth century. (See Chapter 14.) They worked to expose contemporary social and political abuses and argued that reform was necessary and possible. Their progress in this cause was anything but steady. Among the obstacles they met were vested interests, political oppression, and religious condemnation.

Yet, by mid-century, they had brought enlightened ideas to the European public in a variety of formats. The *philosophes'* "family" had come into being. They corresponded with each other, wrote for each other as well as for the public, and defended each other against the political and religious authorities.

By the second half of the century, they were sufficiently safe to quarrel among themselves on occasion. They had stopped talking in generalities, and their major advocates were addressing specific abuses. Their books and articles had become more specialized and more practical. They had become more concerned with politics than with religion. Having convinced Europeans that change was a good idea, they began to suggest exactly what changes were most desirable. They had become honored figures.

Voltaire's Agenda of Intellectual Reform

One of the earliest and by far the most influential of the *philosophes* was François Marie Arouet, known to posterity as Voltaire (1694–1778). During the 1720s, Voltaire had offended the French authorities by certain of his writings. He was arrested and put in prison for a brief time.

Later Voltaire went to England, visiting its best literary circles, observing its tolerant intellectual and religious climate, relishing the freedom he felt in its moderate political atmosphere, and admiring its science and economic prosperity. In 1733 he published *Letters on the English*, which appeared in French the next year. The book praised the virtues of the English and indirectly criticized the abuses of French society. In 1738 he published *Elements of the Philosophy of Newton*, which popularized the thought of the great scientist. Both works were well received and gave Voltaire a reputation as an important writer.

Thereafter Voltaire lived part of the time in France and part near Geneva, just across the French border, where the royal authorities could not bother him. He wrote essays, history, plays, stories, and letters that made him the literary dictator of Europe. He used the bitter venom of his satire and sarcasm against one evil after another in French and European life. In his most famous satire, *Candide* (1759), he attacked war, religious persecution, and what he regarded as unwarranted optimism about the human condition.

Like most *philosophes*, Voltaire believed that improvement of human society was necessary and possible. But he was never certain that reform, if achieved, would be permanent. The optimism of the Enlightenment was a tempered hopefulness rather than a glib certainty. An undercurrent of pessimism characterized most of the works of the period.

The Encyclopedia

The mid-century witnessed the publication of the *Encyclopedia*, one the greatest monuments of the Enlightenment. Under the heroic leadership of Denis Diderot (1713–1784), and Jean le Rond d'Alembert (1717–1783), the first volume appeared in 1751. Numbering seventeen volumes of text and eleven of plates (illustrations), the project reached completion in 1772.

The *Encyclopedia*, in part a collective plea for freedom of expression, reached fruition only after many attempts to censor it and to halt its publication. It was the product of the collective effort of more than 100 authors, and its editors had at one time or another solicited articles from all the major French *philosophes*. It included the most advanced critical ideas of the time on religion, government, and philosophy. To avoid official censure, these ideas often had to be hidden in obscure articles or under the cover of irony. The *Encyclopedia* also

included important articles and illustrations on manufacturing, canal building, ship construction, and improved agriculture, making it an important source of knowledge about eighteenth-century social and economic life.

Between 14,000 and 16,000 copies of various editions of the *Encyclopedia* were sold before 1789. The project had been designed to secularize learning and to undermine intellectual assumptions that lingered from the Middle Ages and the Reformation. The articles on politics, ethics, and society ignored divine law and concentrated on humanity and its immediate well-being. The Encyclopedists looked to antiquity rather than to the Christian centuries for their intellectual and ethical models. For them, the future welfare of humankind lay not in pleasing God or following divine commandments but rather in harnessing the power and resources of the Earth and in living at peace with one's fellow human beings. The good life lay here and now and was to be achieved through the application of reason to human relationships. With the publication of the *Encyclopedia*, Enlightenment thought became more fully diffused over the Continent, penetrating German and Russian intellectual and political circles.

The Enlightenment and Religion

For many but not all *philosophes* of the eighteenth century, ecclesiastical institutions were the chief impediment to human improvement and happiness. Voltaire's cry, "Crush the Infamous Thing," summed up the attitude of a number of *philosophes* toward the church and Christianity. Almost all varieties of Christianity, but especially Roman Catholicism, felt their criticism.

The critical *philosophes* complained that the churches hindered the pursuit of a rational life and the scientific study of humanity and nature. The clergy taught that humans were basically depraved, becoming worthy only through divine grace. According to the doctrine of original sin, Protestant or Catholic, meaningful improvement in human nature on Earth was impossible. Religion thus turned attention away from this world to the world to come. For example, the *philosophes* argued that the Calvinist doctrine of predestination denied a relationship between virtuous actions in this life and the fate of the soul after death. Mired in conflicts over obscure doctrinal differences, the churches promoted intolerance and bigotry, inciting torture, war, and other forms of human suffering.

With this attack, the *philosophes* were challenging not only a set of ideas but also some of Europe's most powerful institutions. The churches were deeply enmeshed in the power structure of the old regime. They owned large amounts of land and collected tithes from peasants before any secular authority collected its taxes. Most clergy were legally exempt from taxes and made only annual voluntary grants to the government. The upper clergy in most countries were relatives of aristocrats. Clerics were actively involved in politics, serving in the British House of Lords and advising princes on the Continent. In Protestant countries, the leading local landowner usually appointed the clergyman of a particular parish. Across the Continent, membership in the predominant denomination of the kingdom gave certain subjects political advantages. Nonmembership often excluded other subjects from political participation. Clergy of all faiths preached the sinfulness of political disobedience. They provided intellectual justification for the social and political status quo, and they were active agents of religious and literary censorship.

Deism

The *philosophes*, although critical of many religious institutions and frequently anticlerical, were not opposed to all religion. In Scotland, for example, the enlightened historian William Robertson (1721–1793) was the head of the Scottish Kirk. In England, clergy of the established church did much to popularize the thought of Newton. What the *philosophes* sought, however, was religion without fanaticism and intolerance, a religious life that would not substitute church authority for the authority of human reason. The Newtonian worldview had convinced many writers that nature was rational. Therefore, the God who had created nature must also be rational, and the religion through which that God was worshiped should be rational. Most of them believed that the life of religion and of reason could be combined, giving rise to a movement known as *deism*.

The title of one of the earliest deist works, *Christianity Not Mysterious* (1696) by John Toland (1670–1722), indicates the general tenor of this religious outlook. Toland and later deist writers promoted religion as a natural and rational, rather than a supernatural and mystical, phenomenon. In this respect they differed from Newton and Locke, both

of whom regarded themselves as distinctly Christian. Newton believed God could interfere with the natural order, whereas the deists regarded God as a kind of divine watchmaker who had created the mechanism of nature, set it in motion, and then departed. Most of the deist writers were also strongly anticlerical and for that reason regarded as radical.

There were two major points in the deists' creed. The first was a belief in the existence of God, which they thought could be empirically justified by the contemplation of nature. Joseph Addison's poem on the spacious firmament (1712) illustrates this idea:

The spacious firmament on high,
With all the blue ethereal sky,
And spangled heav'n, a shining frame,
Their great Original proclaim:
Th' unwearied Sun, from day to day,
Does his Creator's power display,
And publishes to every land
The work of an Almighty hand.

Because nature provided evidence of a rational God, that deity must also favor rational morality. So the second point in the deists' creed was a belief in life after death, when rewards and punishments would be meted out according to the virtue of the lives people led on this Earth.

Deism was empirical, tolerant, reasonable, and capable of encouraging virtuous living. Voltaire declared:

The great name of Deist, which is not sufficiently revered, is the only name one ought to take. The only gospel one ought to read is the great book of Nature, written by the hand of God and sealed with his seal. The only religion that ought to be professed is the religion of worshiping God and being a good man.[4]

Deists hoped that wide acceptance of their faith would end rivalry among the various Christian sects and with it religious fanaticism, conflict, and persecution. They also felt deism would remove the need for priests and ministers, who, in their view, were often responsible for fomenting religious differences and denominational hatred.

Toleration

According to the *philosophes*, religious toleration was a primary social condition for the virtuous life. Again Voltaire took the lead in championing this cause. In 1762 the Roman Catholic political author-

[4]Quoted in J. H. Randall, *The Making of the Modern Mind*, rev. ed. (New York: Houghton Mifflin, 1940), p. 292.

ities in Toulouse ordered the execution of a Huguenot named Jean Calas. He stood accused of having murdered his son to prevent him from converting to Roman Catholicism. Calas was viciously tortured and publicly strangled without ever confessing his guilt. The confession would not have saved his life, but it would have given the Catholics good propaganda to use against Protestants.

Voltaire learned of the case only after Calas's death. He made the dead man's cause his own. In 1763 he published his *Treatise on Tolerance* and hounded the authorities for a new investigation. Finally, in 1765 the judicial decision against the unfortunate man was reversed. For Voltaire, the case illustrated the fruits of religious fanaticism and the need for rational reform of judicial processes. Somewhat later in the century, the German playwright and critic Gotthold Lessing (1729–1781) wrote *Nathan the Wise* (1779), a plea for toleration not only of different Christian sects but also of religious faiths other than Christianity.

The premise behind all of these calls for toleration was, in effect, that life on Earth and human relationships should not be subordinated to religion. Secular values and considerations were more important than religious ones.

Radical Enlightenment Criticism of Religion

Some *philosophes* went beyond the formulation of a rational religious alternative to Christianity and the advocacy of toleration to attack the churches and the clergy with great vehemence. Voltaire repeatedly questioned the truthfulness of priests and the morality of the Bible. In his *Philosophical Dictionary* (1764) he humorously pointed out inconsistencies in biblical narratives and immoral acts of the biblical heroes. The Scottish philosopher David Hume (1711–1776), in "Of Miracles," a chapter in his *Inquiry into Human Nature* (1748), argued that no empirical evidence supported the belief in divine miracles central to much of Christianity. For Hume, the greatest miracle was that people believed in miracles. In *The Decline and Fall of the Roman Empire* (1776), Edward Gibbon (1737–1794), the English historian, explained the rise of Christianity in terms of natural causes rather than the influence of miracles and piety.

A few *philosophes* went further. Baron d'Holbach (1723–1789) and Julien Offray de La Mettrie (1709–1751) embraced positions very near to atheism and materialism. Theirs was distinctly a minority position, however. Most of the *philosophes* sought not the abolition of religion but its transformation into a humane force that would encourage virtuous living.

The *philosophes'* criticisms of traditional religion nonetheless often reflected an implicit contempt not only for Christianity but also, and sometimes more vehemently, for Judaism. Their attack on the veracity of biblical miracles and biblical history undermined the authority of the Hebrew scriptures as well as the Christian, and their satirical barbs were aimed most often at personalities from the Hebrew scriptures. Some *philosophes* characterized Judaism as a more primitive faith than Christianity. The Enlightenment view of religion thus served in some ways to further stigmatize Jews and Judaism in the eyes of non-Jewish Europeans.

The Enlightenment and Society

Although the *philosophes* wrote much on religion, humanity was the center of their interest. As one writer in the *Encyclopedia* observed, "Man is the unique point to which we must refer everything,

David Hume (1711–1776), the Scottish philosopher, argued against belief in miracles and, by implication, against belief in Christianity itself. [The Bettmann Archive]

Voltaire Attacks Religious Fanaticism

The chief complaint of the philosophes *against Christianity was that it bred a fanaticism that led people to commit crimes in the name of religion. In this passage from Voltaire's* Philosophical Dictionary *(1764), he directly reminds his readers of the intolerance of the Reformation era and indirectly referred to examples of contemporary religious excesses. He argues that the philosophical spirit can overcome fanaticism and foster toleration and more humane religious behavior. Shocking many of his contemporaries, he praises the virtues of Confucianism over those of Christianity.*

✦ *What concrete examples of religious fanaticism might Voltaire have had in mind? Why does Voltaire contend that neither religion nor laws can contain religious fanaticism? Why does Voltaire admire the Chinese?*

Fanaticism is to superstition what delirium is to fever and rage to anger. The man visited by ecstasies and visions, who takes dreams for realities and his fancies for prophecies, is an enthusiast; the man who supports his madness with murder is a fanatic. . . .

The most detestable example of fanaticism was that of the burghers of Paris who on St. Bartholomew's Night [1572] went about assassinating and butchering all their fellow citizens who did not go to mass, throwing them out of windows, cutting them in pieces.

Once fanaticism has corrupted a mind, the malady is almost incurable. . . .

The only remedy for this epidemic malady is the philosophical spirit which, spread gradually, at last tames men's habits and prevents the disease from starting; for once the disease has made any progress, one must flee and wait for the air to clear itself. Laws and religion are not strong enough against the spiritual pest; religion, far from being healthy food for infected brains, turns to poison in them. . . .

Even the law is impotent against these attacks of rage; it is like reading a court decree to a raving maniac. These fellows are certain that the holy spirit with which they are filled is above the law, that their enthusiasm is the only law they must obey.

What can we say to a man who tells you that he would rather obey God than men, and that therefore he is sure to go to heaven for butchering you?

Ordinarily fanatics are guided by rascals, who put the dagger into their hands; these latter resemble that Old Man of the Mountain who is supposed to have made imbeciles taste the joys of paradise and who promised them an eternity of the pleasures of which he had given them a foretaste, on condition that they assassinated all those he would name to them. There is only one religion in the world that has never been sullied by fanaticism, that of the Chinese men of letters. The schools of philosophy were not only free from this pest, they were its remedy; for the effect of philosophy is to make the soul tranquil, and fanaticism is incompatible with tranquility. If our holy religion has so often been corrupted by this infernal delirium, it is the madness of men which is at fault.

Voltaire, Philosophical Dictionary, *trans. by P. Gay (New York: Basic Books, 1962), pp. 267–269.*

---

if we wish to interest and please amongst considerations the most arid and details the most dry."[5]

[5]Quoted in F. L. Baumer, *Main Currents of Western Thought,* 4th ed. (New Haven, Conn.: Yale University Press, 1978), p. 374.

The *philosophes* believed that the application of human reason to society would reveal laws in human relationships similar to those found in physical nature. At the same time, the use of the word *man* in this passage was not simply an accident of language. Most *philosophes* were thinking primarily of men, not women, when they framed their reformist ideas. With a few exceptions, as will be seen later in this chapter, they had little interest in expanding women's intellectual and social opportunities.

Although the term did not appear until later, the idea of social science originated with the Enlightenment. *Philosophes* hoped to end human cruelty by discovering social laws and making people aware of them. These concerns are most evident in the *philosophes'* work on law and prisons.

Beccaria and Reform of Criminal Law

In 1764 Cesare Beccaria (1738–1794), an Italian *philosophe*, published *On Crimes and Punishments*, in which he applied critical analysis to the problem of making punishments both effective and just. He wanted the laws of monarchs and legislatures—that is, positive law—to conform with the rational laws of nature. He rigorously and eloquently attacked both torture and capital punishment. He thought that the criminal justice system should ensure speedy trial and certain punishment, and that the intent of punishment should be to deter further crime. The purpose of laws was not to impose the will of God or some other ideal of perfection; its purpose was to secure the greatest good or happiness for the greatest number of human beings. This utilitarian philosophy based on happiness in this life permeated most of Enlightenment writing on practical reforms.

The Physiocrats and Economic Freedom

Economic policy was another area where the *philosophes* saw existing legislation and administration preventing the operation of natural social laws. They believed that mercantilist legislation (designed to protect a country's trade from external competition) and the regulation of labor by governments and guilds actually hampered the expansion of trade, manufacture, and agriculture. In France, these economic reformers were called the *physiocrats*. Their leading spokespeople were François Quesnay (1694–1774) and Pierre Dupont de Nemours (1739–1817).

The physiocrats believed that the primary role of government was to protect property and to permit its owners to use it freely. They particularly felt that all economic production depended on sound agriculture. They favored the consolidation of small peasant holdings into larger, more efficient farms. Here as elsewhere there was a close relationship between the rationalism of the Enlightenment and the spirit of improvement at work in eighteenth-century European economic life.

Adam Smith and The Wealth of Nations

The most important economic work of the Enlightenment was Adam Smith's (1723–1790) *Inquiry into the Nature and Causes of the Wealth of Nations* (1776). Smith, who was for a time a professor at Glasgow, believed that economic liberty was the foundation of a natural economic system. As a result, he urged that the mercantile system of England—including the navigation acts, the bounties, most tariffs, special trading monopolies, and the domestic regulation of labor and manufacture—be abolished. These regulations were intended to preserve the wealth of the nation, to capture wealth from other nations, and to maximize the work available for the nation's laborers. Smith argued, however, that they hindered the expansion of wealth and production. The best way to encourage economic growth, he maintained, was to unleash individuals to pursue their own selfish economic interest. As self-interested individuals sought to enrich themselves by meeting the needs of others in the marketplace, the economy would expand. Consumers would find their wants met as manufacturers and merchants competed for their business.

It was a basic assumption of mercantilism that the Earth's resources are limited and scarce, so that one nation can only acquire wealth at the expense of others. Smith's book challenged this assumption. He saw the resources of nature—water, air, soil, and minerals—as boundless. To him, they demanded exploitation for the enrichment and comfort of humankind. In effect, Smith was saying that the nations and peoples of Europe need not be poor.

The idea that humans should exploit nature's infinite bounty for their benefit, which dominated Western economic activity until recently, thus stemmed directly from the Enlightenment. When Smith wrote, the population of the world was smaller, its people poorer, and the quantity of undeveloped resources per capita much greater than now. For people of the eighteenth century, true improvement of the human condition seemed to lie in the uninhibited exploitation of natural resources.

Smith is usually regarded as the founder of *laissez-faire* economic thought and policy, which favors a limited role for the government in economic life. The *Wealth of Nations* was, however, a complex book. Smith was no simple dogmatist. For example, he did not oppose all government activity touching the economy. The state, he argued, should provide schools, armies, navies, and roads. It should also undertake certain commercial ventures, such as the opening of dangerous new trade routes that were economically desirable but too expensive or risky for private enterprise.

Political Thought of the *Philosophes*

Nowhere was the *philosophes'* appreciation of the complexity of the problems of contemporary society clearer than their political thought. Nor did any other area of their reformist enterprise so clearly illustrate the tension and conflict within the "family" of the Enlightenment. Most *philosophes* were discontented with certain political features of their countries, but they were especially discontented in France. There the corruptness of the royal court, the blundering of the bureaucracy, the less than glorious mid-century wars, and the power of the church compounded all problems. Consequently, the most important political thought of the Enlightenment occurred in France. The French *philosophes*, however, stood quite divided as to the proper solution to their country's problems. Their attitudes spanned a wide political spectrum from aristocratic reform to democracy to absolute monarchy.

Montesquieu and Spirit of the Laws

Charles Louis de Secondat, Baron de Montesquieu (1689–1755), was a lawyer, noble of the robe, and a member of a provincial *parlement*. He also belonged to the Bordeaux Academy of Science, before which he presented papers on scientific topics.

Although living comfortably within the bosom of French society, he saw the need for reform. In 1721 he published *The Persian Letters* to satirize contemporary institutions. The book consisted of letters purportedly written by two Persians visiting Europe. They explained to friends at home how European behavior contrasted with Persian life and customs. Behind the humor lay the cutting edge of criticism and an exposition of the cruelty and irrationality of much contemporary European life.

In his most enduring work, *Spirit of the Laws* (1748), Montesquieu held up the example of the British constitution as the wisest model for regulating the power of government. With his interest in science, his hope for reform, and his admiration for Britain, he embodied all the major elements of the Enlightenment mind.

Montesquieu's *Spirit of the Laws*, perhaps the single most influential book of the century, exhibits the internal tensions of the Enlightenment. In it, Montesquieu pursued an empirical method, taking illustrative examples from the political experience of both ancient and modern nations. From these he concluded there could be no single set of political laws that applied to all peoples at all times and in all places. The good political life depended rather on the relationship among many political variables. Whether the best form of government for a country was a monarchy or a republic, for example, depended on its size, population, social and reli-

Charles de Secondat, Baron de Montesquieu (1689–1755), was the author of Spirit of the Laws, *possibly the most influential work of political thought of the eighteenth century. [Bettmann/Hulton]*

Montesquieu Defends the Separation of Powers

Spirit of the Laws (1748) was probably the most influential political work of the Enlightenment. In this passage Montesquieu explains how the division of powers within a government would make that government more moderate and would protect the liberty of its subjects. This idea was adopted by the writers of the United States Constitution when they devised the checks and balances of the three branches of government.

◆ *What did Montesquieu mean by "moderate governments," and why did he associate political liberty with such governments? What might he have seen as such a government in his own day? How does Montesquieu define the liberty of a subject? Why does he regard a situation where the power of government is not divided as one where there can be no liberty?*

Democratic and aristocratic states are not in their own nature free. Political liberty is to be found only in moderate governments; and even in these it is not always found. It is there only when there is no abuse of power. But constant experience shows us that every man invested with power is apt to abuse it, and to carry his authority as far as it will go. . . .

To prevent this abuse, it is necessary from the very nature of things that power should be a check to power. . . .

In every government there are three sorts of power: the legislative; the executive in respect to things dependent on the law of nations; and the executive in regard to matters that depend on the civil law [the realm of the judiciary]. . . .

The political liberty of the subject is a tranquillity of mind arising from the opinion each person has of his safety. In order to have this liberty, it is requisite that government be so constituted as one man need not be afraid of another.

When the legislative and executive powers are united in the same person, or in the same body of magistrates, there can be no liberty; because apprehensions may arise, lest the same monarchy or senate should enact tyrannical laws, to execute them in a tyrannical manner.

Again, there is no liberty, if the judiciary power be not separated from the legislative and executive. Were it joined with the legislative, the life and liberty of the subject would be exposed to arbitrary control; for the judge would be then the legislator. Were it joined to the executive power, the judge might behave with violence and oppression.

There would be an end of everything, were the same man or the same body, whether of the nobles or of the people, to exercise those three powers, that of enacting laws, that of executing the public resolutions, and of trying the causes of individuals.

Baron de Montesquieu, Spirit of the Laws, trans. by Thomas Nugent, (New York: Hafner Press, 1949), pp. 150–152.

gious customs, economic structure, traditions, and climate. Only a careful examination and evaluation of these elements could reveal what mode of government would prove most beneficial to a particular people.

So far as France was concerned, Montesquieu had some definite ideas. He believed in a monarchical government tempered and limited by various sets of intermediary institutions. These included the aristocracy, the towns, and the other corporate bodies that enjoyed liberties the monarch had to respect. These corporate bodies might be said to represent various segments of the general population and thus of public opinion. In France, he regarded the aristocratic courts, or *parlements*, as the major example of an intermediary association. Their role was to limit the power of the monarchy and thus to preserve the liberty of its subjects.

In championing these aristocratic bodies and the general role of the aristocracy, Montesquieu was a political conservative. He adopted this conservatism in the hope of achieving reform, however, for he believed the oppressive and inefficient absolutism of the monarchy accounted for the degradation of French life.

One of Montesquieu's most influential ideas was that of the division of power in government. For his model of a government with authority wisely separated among different branches, he took contemporary Great Britain. There, he believed, executive power resided in the king, legislative power in the Parliament, and judicial power in the courts. He thought any two branches could check and balance the power of the other. His perception of the eighteenth-century British constitution was incorrect because he failed to see how patronage and electoral corruption allowed a handful of powerful aristocrats to dominate the government. Moreover, he was also unaware of the emerging cabinet system, which was slowly making the executive power a creature of the Parliament.

Nevertheless, Montesquieu's analysis illustrated his strong sense that monarchs should be subject to constitutional limits on their power and that a separate legislature, not the monarch, should formulate laws. For this reason, although he set out to defend the political privileges of the French aristocracy, Montesquieu's ideas had a profound and still-lasting effect on the constitutional form of liberal democracies of the next two centuries.

Rousseau: A Radical Critique of Modern Society

Jean-Jacques Rousseau (1712–1778) held a view of the exercise and reform of political power quite different from Montesquieu's. Rousseau was a strange, isolated genius who never felt particularly comfortable with the other *philosophes*. His own life was troubled. He could form few close friendships. He sired numerous children whom he abandoned to foundling hospitals. Yet perhaps more than any other writer of the mid-eighteenth century, he transcended the political thought and values of his own time. Rousseau had a deep antipathy toward the world and the society in which he lived. It seemed to him impossible for human beings living according to contemporary commercial values to achieve moral, virtuous, or sincere lives. In 1750, in his *Discourse on the Moral Effects of the Arts and Sci-*

ences, he contended that the process of civilization and enlightenment had corrupted human nature. In 1755, in his *Discourse on the Origin of Inequality*, Rousseau blamed much of the evil in the world on the uneven distribution of property.

In both works Rousseau brilliantly and directly challenged the social fabric of the day. He drew into question the concepts of material and intellectual progress and the morality of a society in which commerce and industry were regarded as the most important human activities. He felt that the real purpose of society was to nurture better people. In this respect Rousseau's vision of reform was much more radical than that of other contemporary writers. The other *philosophes* believed that life would improve if people could enjoy more of the fruits of the Earth or could produce more goods. Rousseau raised the more fundamental question of what constitutes the good life. This question has haunted European social thought ever since the eighteenth century.

Jean-Jacques Rousseau (1712–1778) raised some of the most profound social and ethical questions of the Enlightenment. This portrait is by Maurice Quentin. [Bildarchiv Preussischer Kulturbesitz]

Rousseau carried these same concerns into his political thought. His most extensive discussion of politics appeared in *The Social Contract* (1762). Although the book attracted rather little immediate attention, by the end of the century it was widely read in France. The *Social Contract*, compared with Montesquieu's *Spirit of the Laws*, is a very abstract book. It does not propose specific reforms but outlines the kind of political structure that Rousseau believed would overcome the evils of contemporary politics and society.

In the tradition of John Locke, most eighteenth-century political thinkers regarded human beings as individuals and society as a collection of individuals pursuing personal, selfish goals. These writers wished to liberate individuals from the undue bonds of government. Rousseau picked up the stick from the other end. His book opens with the declaration, "All men are born free, but everywhere they are in chains."[6] The rest of the volume is a defense of the chains of a properly organized society over its members.

Rousseau suggested that society is more important than its individual members, because they are what they are only because of their relationship to the larger community. Independent human beings living alone can achieve very little. Through their relationship to the larger community, they become moral creatures capable of significant action. The question then becomes what kind of community allows people to behave morally. In his two previous discourses, Rousseau had explained that contemporary European society was not such a community. It was merely an aggregate of competing individuals whose chief social goal was to preserve selfish independence in spite of all potential social bonds and obligations.

Rousseau envisioned a society in which each person could maintain personal freedom while behaving as a loyal member of the larger community. Drawing on the traditions of Plato and Calvin, he defined *freedom* as obedience to law. In his case, the law to be obeyed was that created by the general will. In a society with virtuous customs and morals in which citizens have adequate information on important issues, the concept of the general will is normally equivalent to the will of a majority of voting citizens. Democratic participation in decision making would bind the individual citizen to the community. Rousseau believed that the general will, thus understood, must always be right and that to obey the general will is to be free. This argument led him to the notorious conclusion that under certain circumstances some people must be forced to be free. Rousseau's politics thus constituted a justification for radical direct democracy and for collective action against individual citizens.

Rousseau had in effect launched an assault on the eighteenth-century cult of the individual and the fruits of selfishness. He stood at odds with the commercial spirit that was transforming the society in which he lived. Rousseau would have disapproved of the main thrust of Adam Smith's *Wealth of Nations*, which he may or may not have read, and would no doubt have preferred a study on the virtue of nations. Smith wanted people to be prosperous; Rousseau wanted them to be good even if being good meant that they might remain poor. He saw human beings not as independent individuals but as creatures enmeshed in necessary social relationships. He believed that loyalty to the community should be encouraged. As one device to that end, he suggested a civic religion based on the creed of deism. Such a shared religious faith would help unify a society.

Rousseau's chief source of intellectual inspiration was Plato and the ancient Greek *polis*. Especially in Sparta, he thought he had discovered human beings dwelling in a moral society inspired by a common purpose. He hoped that modern human beings might also create such a moral commonwealth in which virtuous living would be valued over commercial profit.

Rousseau had only a marginal impact on his own time. The other *philosophes* questioned his critique of material improvement. Aristocrats and royal ministers could hardly be expected to welcome his proposal for radical democracy. Too many people were either making or hoping to make money to appreciate his criticism of commercial values. He proved, however, to be a figure to whom later generations returned. Many leaders in the French Revolution were familiar with his writing, and he influenced most writers in the nineteenth and twentieth centuries who were critical of the general tenor and direction of Western culture. Rousseau hated much about the emerging modern society in Europe, but he contributed much to modernity by exemplifying for later generations the critic who dared to call into question the very foundations of social thought and action.

[6]Jean-Jacques Rousseau, *The Social Contract and Discourses*, trans. by G. D. H. Cole (New York: Dutton, 1950), p. 3.

Women in the Thought and Practice of the Enlightenment

Women, especially in France, helped significantly to promote the careers of the *philosophes*. In Paris, the salons of women such as Marie-Thérèse Geoffrin (1699–1777), Julie de Lespinasse (1733–1776), and Claudine de Tencin (1689–1749) gave the *philosophes* access to useful social and political contacts and a receptive environment in which to circulate their ideas. Association with a fashionable salon brought *philosophes* increased social status and added luster and respectability to their ideas. They clearly enjoyed the opportunity to be the center of attention that a salon provided, and their presence at them could boost the sales of their works. The women who organized the salons were well-connected to major political figures who could help protect the *philosophes* and secure them pensions. The marquise de Pompadour, the mistress of Louis XV (1721–1764), played a key role in overcoming efforts to censor the *Encyclopedia*. She also helped block the circulation of works attacking the *philosophes*. Other salon hostesses purchased the writings of the *philosophes* and distributed them among their friends. Madame de Tencin was responsible for promoting Montesquieu's *Spirit of the Laws* in this way.

Despite this help and support from the learned women of Paris, the *philosophes* were on the whole not strong feminists. Many urged better and broader education for women. They criticized the education women did receive as overly religious, and they tended to reject ascetic views of sexual relations. But in general they displayed rather traditional views toward women and advocated no radical changes in the social condition of women.

Montesquieu, for example, illustrates some of these tensions in the views of Enlightenment writers toward women. He maintained in general that the status of women in a society was the result of climate, the political regime, culture, and women's physiological nature. He believed women were not naturally inferior to men and should have a wider role in society. He showed himself well aware of the kinds of personal, emotional, and sexual repression European women endured in his day. He sympathetically observed the value placed on women's appearance and the prejudice women met as they aged. In *The Persian Letters*, he included a long exchange about the repression of women in a Persian harem, condemning by implication the restrictions on women in European society. Yet there were limits to Montesquieu's willingness to consider social change in regard to the role of women in European life. Although in the *Spirit of the Laws* he indicated a belief in the equality of the sexes, he still retained a traditional view of marriage and family and expected men to dominate those institutions. Furthermore, although he supported the right of women to divorce and opposed laws directly oppressive of women, he upheld the ideal of female chastity.

The salon of Mme. Marie-Thérèse Geoffrin (1699–1777) was one of the most important gathering spots for Enlightenment writers during the middle of the eighteenth century. Well-connected women such as Mme. Geoffrin were instrumental in helping the philosophes *they patronized to bring their ideas to the attention of influential people in French society and politics. [Giraudon/Art Resource, N.Y.]*

Rousseau Argues for Separate Spheres for Men and Women

Rousseau published Émile, *a novel about education, in 1762. In it he made one of the strongest and most influential arguments of the eighteenth century for distinct social roles for men and women. Furthermore, he portrayed women as fundamentally subordinate to men. In the next document, Mary Wollstonecraft, a contemporary, presents a rebuttal.*

✦ *How does Rousseau move from the physical differences between men and women to an argument for distinct social roles and social spheres? What would be the proper kinds of social activities for women in Rousseau's vision? What kind of education would he think appropriate for women?*

There is no parity between the two sexes in regard to the consequences of sex. The male is male only at certain moments. The female is female her whole life or at least during her whole youth. Everything constantly recalls her sex to her; and, to fulfill its functions well, she needs a constitution which corresponds to it. She needs care during her pregnancy; she needs rest at the time of childbirth; she needs a soft and sedentary life to suckle her children; she needs patience and gentleness, a zeal and an affection that nothing can rebuff in order to raise her children. She serves as the link between them and their father; she alone makes him love them and gives him the confidence to call them his own. How much tenderness and care is required to maintain the union of the whole family! And, finally, all this must come not from virtues but from tastes, or else the human species would soon be extinguished.

The strictness of the relative duties of the two sexes is not and cannot be the same. When woman complains on this score about unjust man-made inequality, she is wrong. This inequality is not a human institution—or, at least, it is the work not of prejudice but of reason. It is up to the sex that nature has charged with the bearing of children to be responsible for them to the other sex. Doubtless it is not permitted to any one to violate his faith, and every unfaithful husband who deprives his wife of the only reward of the austere duties of her sex is an unjust and barbarous man. But the unfaithful woman does more; she dissolves the family and breaks all the bonds of nature. . . .

Once it is demonstrated that man and woman are not and ought not be constituted in the same way in either character or temperament, it follows that they ought not to have the same education. In following nature's directions, man and woman ought to act in concert, but they ought not to do the same things. The goal of their labors is common, but their labors themselves are different, and consequently so are the tastes directing them. . . .

The good constitution of children initially depends on that of their mothers. The first education of men depends on the care of women. Men's morals, their passions, their tastes, their pleasures, their very happiness also depend on women. Thus the whole education of women ought to relate to men. To please men, to be useful to them, to make herself loved and honored by them, to raise them when young, to care for them when grown, to counsel them, to console them, to make their lives agreeable and sweet—these are the duties of women at all times, and they ought to be taught from childhood. So long as one does not return to this principle, one will deviate from the goal, and all the precepts taught to women will be of no use for their happiness or for ours.

Jean-Jacques Rousseau, Émile; or, On Education, *trans. by Allan Bloom (New York: Basic Books, Inc., 1979), pp. 361, 363, 365.*

The views about women expressed in the *Encyclopedia* were less generous than those of Montesquieu. It suggested some ways to improve women's lives, but in general it did not include the condition of women as a focus of reform. The editors, Diderot and d'Alembert, recruited men almost exclusively as contributors, and there is no indication they saw a need to include many articles by women. Most of the articles that dealt with women specifically or that discussed women in connection with other subjects often emphasized their physical weakness and inferiority, usually attributed to menstruation or childbearing. Contributors disagreed on the social equality of women. Some favored it, others opposed it, and still others were indifferent. The articles conveyed a general sense that women were reared to be frivolous and unconcerned with important issues. The Encyclopedists discussed women primarily in a family context—as daughters, wives, and mothers—and presented motherhood as their most important occupation. And on sexual behavior, the Encyclopedists upheld an unquestioned double standard.

In contrast to the articles, however, illustrations in the *Encyclopedia* showed women deeply involved in the economic activities of the day. The illustrations also showed the activities of lower- and working-class women, about whom the articles have little to say.

One of the most surprising and influential analyses of the position of women came from Jean-Jacques Rousseau. This most radical of all Enlightenment political theorists urged a very traditional and conservative role for women. In his novel *Émile* (1762) (discussed again in Chapter 20), he set forth a radical version of the view that men and women occupy separate spheres. He declared that women should be educated for a position subordinate to men, emphasizing especially women's function in bearing and rearing children. In his vision there was little else for women to do but make themselves pleasing to men. He portrayed them as weaker and inferior to men in virtually all respects except perhaps for their capacity for feeling and giving love. He excluded them from political life. The world of citizenship, political action, and civic virtue was to be populated by men. Women were assigned the domestic sphere alone. Many of these attitudes were not new—some have roots as ancient as Roman law—but Rousseau's powerful presentation and the influence of his other writings gave them

Major Works of the Enlightenment and Their Publication Dates

1687	Newton's *Principia Mathematica*
1690	Locke's *Essay Concerning Human Understanding*
1696	Toland's *Christianity Not Mysterious*
1721	Montesquieu's *Persian Letters*
1733	Voltaire's *Letters on the English*
1738	Voltaire's *Elements of the Philosophy of Newton*
1748	Montesquieu's *Spirit of the Laws*
1748	Hume's *Inquiry into Human Nature*, with the chapter "Of Miracles"
1750	Rousseau's *Discourse on the Moral Effects of the Arts and Sciences*
1751	First volume of the *Encyclopedia*, edited by Diderot
1755	Rousseau's *Discourse on the Origin of Inequality*
1759	Voltaire's *Candide*
1762	Rousseau's *Social Contract* and *Émile*
1763	Voltaire's *Treatise on Toleration*
1764	Voltaire's *Philosophical Dictionary*
1764	Beccaria's *On Crimes and Punishments*
1776	Gibbon's *Decline and Fall of the Roman Empire*
1776	Smith's *Wealth of Nations*
1779	Lessing's *Nathan the Wise*
1792	Wollstonecraft's *Vindication of the Rights of Woman*

new life in the late eighteenth century. Rousseau deeply influenced many leaders of the French Revolution, who, as will be seen in the next chapter, often incorporated his view on gender roles in the policies they implemented.

Paradoxically, in spite of these views and in spite of his own ill treatment of the many women who bore his many children, Rousseau achieved a vast following among women in the eighteenth century. He is credited with persuading thousands of upper-class women to breast-feed their own children rather than putting them out to wet nurses. One explanation for this influence is that his writings, although they did not advocate liberating women or expanding their social or economic roles, did stress the importance of their emotions and subjective feelings. He portrayed the domestic life and the role of wife and mother as a noble and fulfilling vocation, giving middle- and upper-class women

Mary Wollstonecraft Criticizes Rousseau's View of Women

Mary Wollstonecraft published A Vindication of the Rights of Woman *in 1792, thirty years after Rousseau's* Émile *had appeared. In this pioneering feminist work, she criticizes and rejects Rousseau's argument for distinct and separate spheres for men and women. She portrays that argument as defending the continued bondage of women to men and as hindering the wider education of the entire human race.*

◆ *What specific criticisms does Wollstonecraft direct against Rousseau's views? Why does Wollstonecraft put so much emphasis on a new kind of education for women?*

The most perfect education . . . is such an exercise of the understanding as is best calculated to strengthen the body and form the heart. Or, in other words, to enable the individual to attain such habits of virtue as will render it independent. In fact, it is a farce to call any being virtuous whose virtues do not result from the exercise of its own reason. This was Rousseau's opinion respecting men: I extend it to women. . . .

I may be accused of arrogance; still I must declare what I firmly believe, that all the writers who have written on the subject of female education and manners from Rousseau to Dr. Gregory [a Scottish physician], have contributed to render women more artificial, weak characters, than they would other wise have been; and, consequently, more useless members of society. . . .

. . . Strengthen the female mind by enlarging it, and there will be an end to blind obedience; but, as blind obedience is ever sought for by power, tyrants and sensualists are in the right when they endeavour to keep women in the dark, because the former only wants slaves, and the latter a play-thing. The sensualist, indeed, has been the most dangerous of tyrants, and women have been duped by their lovers, as princes by their ministers, whilst dreaming that they reigned over them.

a sense that their daily occupations had purpose. He assigned them a degree of influence in the domestic sphere that they could not have competing with men outside it.

In 1792, in *A Vindication of the Rights of Woman*, Mary Wollstonecraft (1759–1797) brought Rousseau before the judgment of the rational Enlightenment ideal of progressive knowledge. The immediate incentive for this essay was her opposition to certain policies of the French Revolution, unfavorable to women, which were inspired by Rousseau. Wollstonecraft (who, like so many women of her day, died of puerperal fever shortly after childbirth) accused Rousseau and others after him who upheld traditional roles for women of attempting to narrow women's vision and limit their experience. She argued that to confine women to the separate domestic sphere because of supposed limitations of their physiological nature was to make them the sensual slaves of men. Confined in this separate sphere, they were the victims of male tyranny, their obedience was blind, and they could never achieve their own moral or intellectual identity. Denying good education to women would impede the progress of all humanity. With these arguments, Wollstonecraft was demanding for women the kind of liberty that male writers of the Enlightenment had been championing for men for more than a century. In doing so, she placed herself among the *philosophes* and broadened the agenda of the Enlightenment to include the rights of women as well as those of men.

. . . Rousseau declares that a woman should never, for a moment, feel herself independent, that she should be governed by fear to exercise her natural cunning, and made a coquetish slave in order to render her a more alluring object of desire, a sweeter companion to man, whenever he chooses to relax himself. He carries the arguments, which he pretends to draw from the indications of nature, still further, and insinuates that truth and fortitude, the corner stones of all human virtue, should be cultivated with certain restrictions, because, with respect to the female character, obedience is the grand lesson which ought to be impressed with unrelenting rigour.

What nonsense! when will a great man arise with sufficient strength of mind to put away the fumes which pride and sensuality have thus spread over the subject! If women are by nature inferior to men, their virtues must be the same in quality, if not in degree, or virtue is a relative idea; consequently, their conduct should be founded on the same principles, and have the same aim.

Connected with man as daughters, wives, and mothers, their moral character may be estimated by their manner of fulfilling those simple duties; but the end, the grand end of their exertions should be to unfold their own faculties and acquire the dignity of conscious virtue. . . .

But avoiding . . . any direct comparison of the two sexes collectively, or frankly acknowledging the inferiority of women, according to the present appearance of things, I shall only insist that men have increased that inferiority till women are almost sunk below the standard of rational creatures. Let their faculties have room to unfold, and their virtues to gain strength, and then determine where the whole sex must stand in the intellectual scale. . . .

. . . I . . . will venture to assert, that till women are more rationally educated, the progress of human virtue and improvement in knowledge must receive continual checks. . . .

The mother, who wishes to give true dignity of character to her daughter, must, regardless of the sneers of ignorance, proceed on a plan diametrically opposite to that which Rousseau has recommended with all the deluding charms of eloquence and philosophical sophistry: for his eloquence renders absurdities plausible, and his dogmatic conclusions puzzle, without convincing, those who have not ability to refute them.

Mary Wollstonecraft, A Vindication of the Rights of Woman, ed. by Carol H. Poston (New York: W. W. Norton & Co., Inc., 1975), pp. 21, 22, 24–26, 35, 40, 41.

Enlightened Absolutism

Most of the *philosophes* favored neither Montesquieu's reformed and revived aristocracy nor Rousseau's democracy as a solution to contemporary political problems. Like other thoughtful people of the day in other stations and occupations, they looked to the existing monarchies. Voltaire was a very strong monarchist. He and others—such as Diderot, who visited Catherine II of Russia, and the physiocrats, some of whom were ministers to the French kings—did not wish to limit the power of monarchs. Rather, they sought to redirect that power toward the rationalization of economic and political structures and the liberation of intellectual life. Most *philosophes* were not opposed to power if they could find a way of using it for their own purposes.

During the last third of the century, it seemed to some observers that several European rulers had actually embraced many of the reforms set forth by the *philosophes*. *Enlightened absolutism* is the term used to describe this phenomenon. The phrase indicates monarchical government dedicated to the rational strengthening of the central absolutist administration at the cost of other lesser centers of political power. The monarchs most closely associated with it are Frederick II of Prussia, Joseph II of Austria, and Catherine II of Russia.

Frederick II corresponded with the *philosophes*, for a time provided Voltaire with a place at his court, and even wrote history and political tracts. Catherine II, adept at what would later be called *public relations*, consciously sought to create the image of being enlightened. She read the works of the *philosophes*, became a friend of Diderot and Voltaire, and made frequent references to their ideas, all in the hope that her nation might seem more modern and Western. Joseph II continued numerous initiatives begun by his mother, Maria Theresa. He imposed a series of religious, legal, and social reforms that contemporaries believed he had derived from suggestions of the *philosophes*.

The relationship between these rulers and the writers of the Enlightenment was, however, more complicated than these appearances suggest. The humanitarian and liberating zeal of the Enlightenment writers was only part of what motivated the policies of the rulers. Frederick II, Joseph II, and Catherine II were also determined that their nations would play major diplomatic and military roles in Europe. In no small measure, they adopted Enlightenment policies favoring the rational economic and social integration of their realms because these policies also increased their military strength. As explained in Chapter 17, all the states of Europe had emerged from the Seven Years' War knowing they would need stronger armies for future wars and increased revenue to finance those armies. The search for new revenues and internal political support was one of the incentives prompt-

ing the "enlightened" reforms of the monarchs of Russia, Prussia, and Austria. Consequently, they and their advisers used rationality to pursue many goals admired by the *philosophes* but also to further what the *philosophes* considered irrational militarism.

Frederick the Great of Prussia

Frederick II, the Great (r. 1740–1786) sought the recovery and consolidation of Prussia in the wake of its suffering and near defeat in the mid-century wars. He succeeded, at great military and financial cost, in retaining Silesia, which he had seized from Austria in 1740, and worked to promote it as a manufacturing district. Like his Hohenzollern forebears, he continued to import workers from outside Prussia. He directed new attention to Prussian agriculture. Under state supervision, swamps were drained, new crops introduced, and peasants encouraged and sometimes compelled to migrate where they were needed. For the first time in Prussia, potatoes and turnips came into general production. Frederick also established a land-mortgage credit Association to help landowners raise money for agricultural improvements.

The impetus for these economic policies came from the state. The monarchy and its bureaucracy were the engine for change. Most Prussians, however, did not prosper under Frederick's reign. The

Frederick II, the Great (r. 1740–1786), sought to create prosperity for all parts of the Prussian economy and would make personal visits to factories and shops to inspect the goods being made and sold in his kingdom. Here he visits a fashionable shop. [Gemalde von Albert Baur, ca. 1901 "Frederick II, the Great House von der Leyen in Krefeld, on June 10, 1763." Bildarchiv Preussischer Kulturbesitz]

burden of taxation continued to fall disproportionally on peasants and townspeople.

Frederick's noneconomic policies met with somewhat more success. Continuing the Hohenzollern policy of toleration, he allowed Catholics and Jews to settle in his predominantly Lutheran country, and he protected the Catholics living in Silesia. This policy permitted the state to benefit from the economic contribution of foreign workers. Frederick, however, virtually always appointed Protestants to major positions in the government and army.

Frederick also ordered a new codification of Prussian law, completed after his death. His object was to rationalize the existing legal system, making it more efficient, eliminating regional peculiarities, and reducing aristocratic influence. Frederick shared this concern for legal reform with the other enlightened monarchs, who saw it as a means of extending and strengthening royal power.

Reflecting an important change in the European view of the ruler, Frederick liked to describe himself as "the first servant of the State." The impersonal state was beginning to replace the personal monarchy. Kings might come and go, but the apparatus of government—the bureaucracy, the armies, the laws, the courts, and the combination of power, service, and protection that compelled citizen loyalty—remained. The state as an entity separate from the personality of the ruler came into its own after the French Revolution, but it was born in the monarchies of the old regime.

Joseph II of Austria

No eighteenth-century ruler so embodied rational, impersonal force as the emperor Joseph II of Austria. He was the son of Maria Theresa and co-ruler with her from 1765 to 1780. During the next ten years he ruled alone. He was an austere and humorless person. During much of his life, he slept on straw and ate little but beef. He prided himself on a narrow, passionless rationality, which he sought to impose by his own will on the various Habsburg domains. Despite his eccentricities and the coldness of his personality, Joseph II sincerely wished to improve the lot of his people. He was much less a political opportunist and cynic than either Frederick the Great of Prussia or Catherine the Great of Russia. The ultimate result of his well-intentioned efforts was a series of aristocratic and peasant rebellions extending from Hungary to the Austrian Netherlands.

Joseph II of Austria (r. 1765–1790), shown here in the center, with his brother Leopold (later Leopold II) on his right, attempted to impose exceedingly rational policies on the Habsburg Empire. Joseph urged religious toleration and confiscated church lands. His attempts to tax the nobility stirred up a revolt that Leopold settled after Joseph's death by rescinding his policies. [Kunsthistorisches Museum, Vienna]

CENTRALIZATION OF AUTHORITY   As explained in Chapter 15, of all the rising states of the eighteenth century, Austria was the most diverse in its people and problems. Robert Palmer likened it to "a vast holding company."[7] The Habsburgs never succeeded in creating either a unified administrative structure or a strong aristocratic loyalty. To preserve the monarchy during the War of the Austrian Succession (1740–1748), Maria Theresa had guaranteed the aristocracy considerable independence, especially in Hungary.

[7]Robert R. Palmer, *The Age of Democratic Revolution*, vol. 1 (Princeton, N.J.: Princeton University Press, 1959), p. 103.

Maria Theresa and Joseph II of Austria Debate the Question of Toleration

In 1765 Joseph, the eldest son of the Empress Maria Theresa, had become co-regent with his mother. He began to believe that some measure of religious toleration should be introduced into the Habsburg realms. Maria Theresa, whose opinions on many political issues were quite advanced, adamantly refused to consider adopting a policy of toleration. This exchange of letters sets forth their sharply differing positions. The toleration of Protestants in dispute related only to Lutherans and Calvinists. Maria Theresa died in 1780; the next year Joseph issued an edict of toleration.

◆ How does Joseph define toleration, *and why does Maria Theresa believe it is the same as religious indifference? Why does Maria Theresa fear that toleration will bring about political as well as religious turmoil? Why does Maria Theresa think the belief in toleration has come from Joseph's acquaintance with wicked books?*

Joseph to Maria Theresa, July 20, 1777

It is only the word "toleration" which has caused the misunderstanding. You have taken it in quite a different meaning [from mine expressed in an earlier letter]. God preserve me from thinking it a matter of indifference whether the citizens turn Protestant or remain Catholic, still less, whether they cleave to, or at least observe, the cult which they have inherited from their fathers! I would give all I possess if all the Protestants of your states would go over to Catholicism.

The word "toleration," as I understand it, means only that I would employ any persons, without distinction of religion, in purely temporal matters, allow them to own property, practice trades, be citizens, if they were qualified and if

---

During and after the conflict, however, Maria Theresa took steps to strengthen the power of the crown outside of Hungary, building more of a bureaucracy than had previous Habsburg rulers. In Austria and Bohemia, through major administrative reorganization, she imposed a much more efficient system of tax collection that extracted funds even from the clergy and the nobles. She also established several central councils to deal with governmental problems. To assure her government a sufficient supply of educated officials, she sought to bring all educational institutions into the service of the crown. She also expanded primary education on the local level.

Maria Theresa was concerned about the welfare of the peasants and serfs. She brought them some assistance by extending the authority of the royal bureaucracy over local nobles and decreeing limits on the amount of labor, or *robot*, landowners could demand from peasants. Her concern was not par-

ticularly humanitarian; rather, it arose from her desire to assure a good pool from which to draw military recruits. In all these policies and in her general desire to stimulate prosperity and military strength by royal initiative, Maria Theresa anticipated the policies of her son.

Joseph II was more determined than his mother and his projected reforms were more wide-ranging. He aimed to extend the borders of his territories in the direction of Poland, Bavaria, and the Ottoman Empire. His greatest ambition, however, was to increase the authority of the Habsburg emperor over his various realms. He sought to overcome the pluralism of the Habsburg holdings by imposing central authority in areas of political and social life where Maria Theresa had wisely chosen not to exert authority.

In particular, Joseph sought to reduce Hungarian autonomy. To avoid having to guarantee Hungary's existing privileges or extend new ones at the time of

this would be of advantage to the State and its industry. Those who, unfortunately, adhere to a false faith, are far further from being converted if they remain in their own country than if they migrate into another, in which they can hear and see the convincing truths of the Catholic faith. Similarly, the undisturbed practice of their religion makes them far better subjects and causes them to avoid irreligion, which is a far greater danger to our Catholics than if one lets them see others practice their religion unimpeded.

Maria Theresa to Joseph, Late July, 1777
Without a dominant religion? Toleration, indifference are precisely the true means of undermining everything, taking away every foundation; we others will then be the greatest losers. . . . He is no friend of humanity, as the popular phrase is, who allows everyone his own thoughts. I am speaking only in the political sense, not as a Christian; nothing is so necessary and salutary as religion. Will you allow everyone to fashion his own religion as he pleases? No fixed cult, no subordination to the Church—what will then become of us? The result will not be quiet and contentment; its outcome will be the rule of the stronger and more

unhappy times like those which we have already seen. A manifesto by you to this effect can produce the utmost distress and make you responsible for many thousands of souls. And what are my own sufferings, when I see you entangled in opinions so erroneous? What is at stake is not only the welfare of the State but your own salvation. . . . Turning your eyes and ears everywhere, mingling your spirit of contradiction with the simultaneous desire to create something, you are ruining yourself and dragging the Monarchy down with you into the abyss. . . . I only wish to live so long as I can hope to descend to my ancestors with the consolation that my son will be as great, as religious as his forebears, that he will return from his erroneous views, from those wicked books whose authors parade their cleverness at the expense of all that is most holy and most worthy of respect in the world, who want to introduce an imaginary freedom which can never exist and which degenerates into license and into complete revolution.

As quoted in C. A. Macartney, ed., The Habsburg and Hohenzollern Dynasties in the Seventeenth and Eighteenth Centuries (New York: Walker, 1970), pp. 151–153.

his coronation, he refused to have himself crowned king of Hungary and even had the Crown of Saint Stephen sent to the Imperial Treasury in Vienna. He reorganized local government in Hungary to increase the authority of his own officials. He also required the use of German in all governmental matters. The Magyar nobility resisted these measures, and in 1790 Joseph had to rescind most of them.

ECCLESIASTICAL POLICIES   Another target of Joseph's assertion of royal absolutism was the church. From the reign of Charles V in the sixteenth century to that of Maria Theresa, the Habsburgs had been the most important dynastic champion of Roman Catholicism. Maria Theresa was devout, but she had not allowed the church to limit her authority. Although she had attempted to discourage certain of the more extreme modes of Roman Catholic popular religious piety, such as public flagellation, she adamantly opposed toleration.

Joseph II was also a practicing Catholic, but from the standpoint of both enlightenment and pragmatic politics, he favored a policy of toleration. In October 1781, Joseph issued a toleration patent or decree, that extended freedom of worship to Lutherans, Calvinists, and the Greek Orthodox. They were permitted to have their own places of worship, to sponsor schools, to enter skilled trades, and to hold academic appointments and positions in the public service. From 1781 through 1789, Joseph issued a series of patents and other enactments that relieved the Jews in his realms of certain taxes and signs of personal degradation. He also extended to them the right of private worship. Although these actions benefitted the Jews, they did not grant them full equality with other Habsburg subjects.

Joseph also sought to bring the various institutions of the Roman Catholic Church directly under royal control. He forbade direct communication between the bishops of his realms and the pope.

Viewing religious orders as unproductive, he dissolved more than 600 monasteries and confiscated their lands. He excepted, however, certain orders that ran schools or hospitals. He dissolved the traditional Roman Catholic seminaries, which instilled in priests too great a loyalty to the papacy and too little concern for their future parishioners. In their place he sponsored eight general seminaries where the training emphasized parish duties. He also issued decrees creating new parishes in areas with a shortage of priests, funding them with money from the confiscated monasteries. In effect, Joseph's policies made Roman Catholic priests the employees of the state, ending the influence of the Roman Catholic Church as an independent institution in Habsburg lands. In many respects the ecclesiastical policies of Joseph II, known as *Josephinism*, prefigured those of the French Revolution.

ECONOMIC AND AGRARIAN REFORM   Like Frederick of Prussia, Joseph sought to improve the economic life of his domains. He abolished many internal tariffs and encouraged road building and the improvement of river transport. He went on personal inspection tours of farms and manufacturing districts. Joseph also reconstructed the judicial system to make laws more uniform and rational and to lessen the influence of local landlords. National courts with power over the landlord courts were established. All of these improvements were expected to bring new unity to the state and more taxes into the imperial coffers in Vienna.

Joseph's policies toward serfdom and the land were a far-reaching extension of those Maria Theresa had initiated. Over the course of his reign he introduced a series of reforms that touched the very heart of the rural social structure. He did not seek to abolish the authority of landlords over their peasants, but he did seek to make that authority more moderate and subject to the oversight of royal officials. He abolished serfdom as a legally sanctioned state of servitude. He granted peasants a wide array of personal freedoms, including the right to marry, to engage in skilled work, and to have their children trained in skilled work without the landlord's permission.

Joseph reformed the procedures of the manorial courts and opened avenues of appeal to royal officials. He also encouraged landlords to change land leases so it would be easier for peasants to inherit them or to transfer them to other peasants. His goal in all of these efforts to reduce traditional burdens on peasants was to make them more productive and industrious farmers.

Near the end of his reign, Joseph proposed a new and daring system of land taxation. He decreed in 1789 that all proprietors of the land were to be taxed regardless of social status. No longer were the peasants alone to bear the burden of taxation. He abolished *robot* and commuted it into a monetary tax, only part of which was to go to the landlord, the rest reverting to the state. Resistant nobles blocked the implementation of this decree, and after Joseph died in 1790 it did not go into effect. This and other of Joseph's earlier measures, however, brought turmoil throughout the Habsburg realms. Peasants revolted over disagreements about the interpretation of their newly granted rights. The nobles of the various realms protested the taxation scheme. The Hungarian Magyars resisted Joseph's centralization measures and forced him to rescind them.

On Joseph's death, the crown went to his brother Leopold II (r. 1790–1792). Although sympathetic to Joseph's goals, Leopold found himself forced to repeal many of the most controversial decrees, such as that on taxation. In other areas, Leopold thought his brother's policies simply wrong. For example, he returned much political and administrative power to local nobles because he thought it expedient for them to have a voice in government. Still, he did not repudiate his brother's policies wholesale. He retained, in particular, Joseph's religious policies and maintained political centralization to the extent he thought possible.

Catherine the Great of Russia

Joseph II never grasped the practical necessity of forging political constituencies to support his policies. Catherine II (r. 1762–1796), who had been born a German princess but who became empress of Russia, understood only too well the fragility of the Romanov dynasty's base of power.

After the death of Peter the Great in 1725, the court nobles and the army repeatedly determined the Russian succession. As a result, the crown fell primarily into the hands of people with little talent. Peter's wife, Catherine I, ruled for two years (1725–1727) and was succeeded for three years by Peter's grandson, Peter II. In 1730 the crown devolved on Anna, a niece of Peter the Great. During 1740 and 1741, a child named Ivan VI, who was less than a year old, was the nominal ruler. Finally, in 1741 Peter the Great's daughter Eliza-

Catherine the Great, here portrayed as a young princess, ascended to the Russian throne after the murder of her husband. She tried initially to enact major reforms but she never intended to abandon absolutism. She assured nobles of their rights and by the end of her reign had imposed press censorship. [The Bettmann Archive]

beth came to the throne. She held the title of empress until 1762, but her reign was not notable for new political departures or sound administration. Her court was a shambles of political and romantic intrigue. Much of the power possessed by the tsar at the opening of the century had vanished.

At her death in 1762, Elizabeth was succeeded by Peter III, one of her nephews. He was a weak ruler whom many contemporaries considered mad. He immediately exempted the nobles from compulsory military service and then rapidly made peace with Frederick the Great, for whom he held unbounded admiration. That decision probably saved Prussia from military defeat in the Seven Years' War. The one positive feature of this unbalanced creature's life was his marriage in 1745 to a young German princess born in Anhalt Zerbst. This was the future Catherine the Great.

For almost twenty years Catherine lived in misery and frequent danger at the court of Elizabeth. During that time she befriended important nobles and read widely in the books of the *philosophes*. She was a shrewd person whose experience in a court crawling with rumors, intrigue, and conspiracy had taught her how to survive. She exhibited neither love nor fidelity toward her demented husband. A few months after his accession as tsar, Peter was deposed and murdered with Catherine's approval, if not her aid, and she was immediately proclaimed empress.

Catherine's familiarity with the Enlightenment and the general culture of western Europe convinced her that Russia was very backward and that it must make major reforms if it was to remain a great power. She understood that any major reform must have a wide base of political and social support, especially since she had assumed the throne through a palace coup. In 1767 she summoned a legislative commission to advise her on revisions in the law and government of Russia. There were more than 500 delegates, drawn from all sectors of Russian life. Before the commission convened, Catherine issued a set of instructions, partly written by herself. They contained many ideas drawn from the political writings of the philosophes. The commission considered the instructions as well as other ideas and complaints raised by its members.

The revision of Russian law, however, did not occur for more than half a century. In 1768 Catherine dismissed the commission before several of its key committees had reported. Yet the meeting had not been useless, for a vast amount of information had been gathered about the conditions of local administration and economic life throughout the realm. The inconclusive debates and the absence of programs from the delegates themselves suggested that most Russians saw no alternative to an autocratic monarchy. For her part, Catherine had no intention of departing from absolutism.

Alexander Radishchev Attacks Russian Censorship

Alexander Radishchev (1749–1802) was an enlightened Russian landowner who published A Journey from Saint Petersburg to Moscow *in 1790. The book criticized many aspects of Russian political and social life, including the treatment of serfs. Shortly after its publication, Catherine the Great, fearing that the kind of unrest associated with the French Revolution might spread to Russia, had Radishchev arrested. He was tried and sentenced to death, but Catherine commuted the sentence to a period of Siberian exile. All but eighteen copies of his book were destroyed. It was not published in Russia again until 1905. These passages criticizing censorship illustrate how a writer filled with the ideas of the Enlightenment could question some of the fundamental ways in which an enlightened absolutist ruler, such as Catherine, governed.*

✦ *How does Radishchev satirize censorship and the censors? Why does he contend that public opinion rather than the government will act as an adequate censor? Would work censored by public opinion be truly free from censorship? Why might Catherine the Great or other enlightened absolutist rulers have feared opinions like these?*

Having recognized the usefulness of printing, the government has made it open to all; having further recognized that control of thought might invalidate its good intention in granting freedom to set up presses, it turned over the censorship or inspection of printed works to the Department of Public Morals. Its duty in this matter can only be the prohibition of the sale of objectionable works. But even this censorship is superfluous. A single stupid official in the Department of Public Morals may do the greatest harm to enlightenment and may for years hold back the progress of

---

LIMITED ADMINISTRATIVE REFORM Catherine proceeded to carry out limited reforms on her own authority. She gave strong support to the rights and local power of the nobility. In 1777 she reorganized local government to solve problems brought to light by the legislative commission. She put most local offices in the hands of nobles rather than creating a royal bureaucracy. In 1785 Catherine issued the Charter of the Nobility, which guaranteed many noble rights and privileges. In part, the empress had no choice but to favor the nobles. They had the capacity to topple her from the throne. There were too few educated subjects in her realm to establish an independent bureaucracy, and the treasury could not afford an army strictly loyal to the crown. So Catherine wisely made a virtue of necessity. She strengthened the stability of her crown by making convenient friends with her nobles.

ECONOMIC GROWTH Part of Catherine's program was to continue the economic development begun under Peter the Great. She attempted to suppress internal barriers to trade. Exports of grain, flax, furs, and naval stores grew dramatically. She also favored the expansion of the small Russian urban middle class so vital to trade. And through all of these departures Catherine tried to maintain ties of friendship and correspondence with the *philosophes*. She knew that if she treated them kindly, they would be sufficiently flattered to give her a progressive reputation throughout Europe.

TERRITORIAL EXPANSION Catherine's limited administrative reforms and her policy of economic growth had a counterpart in the diplomatic sphere. The Russian drive for warm-water ports continued. (See

reason: he may prohibit a useful discovery, a new idea, and may rob everyone of something great. Here is an example on a small scale. A translation of a novel is brought to the Department of Public Morals for its imprimatur. The translator, following the author in speaking of love calls it "the tricky god." The censor in uniform and in the fullness of piety strikes out the expression saying, "It is improper to call a divinity tricky." He who does not understand should not interfere. . . .

Let anyone print anything that enters his head. If anyone finds himself insulted in print, let him get his redress at law. I am not speaking in jest. Words are not always deeds, thoughts are not crimes. These are the rules in the Instruction for a New Code of Laws. But an offense in words or in print is always an offense. Under the law no one is allowed to libel another, and everyone has the right to bring suit. But if one tells the truth about another, that cannot, according to the law, be considered a libel. What harm can there be if books are printed without a police stamp? Not only will there be no harm; there will be an advantage, an advantage from the first to the last, from the least to the greatest, from the Tsar to the last citizen. . . .

I will close with this: the censorship of what is printed belongs properly to society, which gives the author a laurel wreath or uses his sheets for wrapping paper. Just so, it is the public that gives its approval to a theatrical production, and not the director of the theater. Similarly the Censor can give neither glory nor dishonor to the publication of a work. The curtain rises, and every one eagerly watches the performance. If they like it, they applaud; if not, they stamp and hiss. Leave what is stupid to the judgment of public opinion, stupidity will find a thousand censors. The most vigilant policy cannot check worthless ideas as well as a disgusted public. They will be heard just once; they will die, never to rise again. But once we have recognized the uselessness of the censorship, or, rather, its harmfulness in the realm of knowledge, we must also recognize the vast and boundless usefulness of freedom of the press.

Alexander Radishchev, A Journey from Saint Petersburg to Moscow *(Cambridge, Mass.: Harvard University Press, 1958), pp. 9–19, as quoted in Thomas Riha, ed.*, Readings in Russian Civilization, *2nd ed., rev., vol. II (Chicago: The University of Chicago Press, 1969), pp. 269–271.*

Map 18–1, on page 636.) This goal required warfare with the Turks. In 1769, as a result of a minor Russian incursion, the Ottoman Empire declared war on Russia. The Russians responded in a series of strikingly successful military moves.

During 1769 and 1770, the Russian fleet sailed all the way from the Baltic Sea into the eastern Mediterranean. The Russian army won several major victories that by 1771 gave Russia control of Ottoman provinces on the Danube River and the Crimean coast of the Black Sea. The conflict dragged on until 1774, when it was closed by the Treaty of Kuchuk-Kainardji. The treaty gave Russia a direct outlet on the Black Sea, free navigation rights in its waters, and free access through the Bosporus. Moreover, the province of the Crimea became an independent state, which Catherine painlessly annexed in 1783.

The Partition of Poland

These Russian military successes obviously brought Catherine much domestic political support, but they made the other states of eastern Europe uneasy. These anxieties were overcome by an extraordinary division of Polish territory known as the First Partition of Poland.

The Russian victories along the Danube River were most unwelcome to Austria, which also harbored ambitions of territorial expansion in that direction. At the same time, the Ottoman Empire was pressing Prussia for aid against Russia. Frederick the Great made a proposal to Russia and Austria that would give each something it wanted, prevent conflict among the powers, and save appearances. After long, complicated, secret negotiations the three powers agreed that Russia would

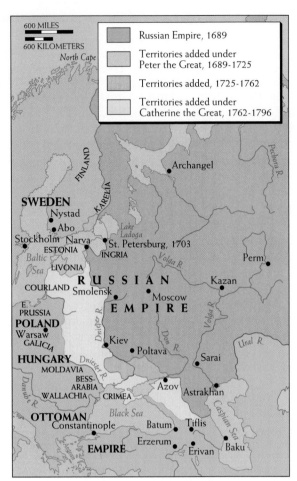

MAP 18–1 EXPANSION OF RUSSIA 1689–1796 *The overriding territorial aim of Peter the Great in the first quarter and of Catherine the Great in the latter half of the eighteenth century was to secure year-round navigable outlets to the sea for the vast Russian Empire, hence Peter's push to the Baltic Sea and Catherine's to the Black Sea. Catherine also managed to acquire large areas of Poland through the partitions of that country.*

abandon the conquered Danubian provinces. In compensation Russia received a large portion of Polish territory with almost two million inhabitants. As a reward for remaining neutral, Prussia annexed most of the territory between East Prussia and Prussia proper. This land allowed Frederick to unite two previously separate sections of his realm. Finally, Austria took Galicia, with its important salt mines, and other Polish territory with more than two and one-half million inhabitants. (See Map 18–2.)

In September 1772, the helpless Polish aristocracy, paying the price for maintaining internal liberties at the expense of developing a strong central government, ratified this seizure of nearly one-third of Polish territory. The loss was not necessarily fatal to Poland's continued existence, and it inspired a revival of national feeling. Real attempts were made to adjust the Polish political structures to the realities of the time. These proved, however, to be too little and too late. The political and military strength of Poland could not match that of its stronger, more ambitious neighbors. The partition of Poland clearly demonstrated that any nation that had not established a strong monarchy, bureaucracy, and army could no longer compete within the European state system. It also demonstrated that the major powers in eastern Europe were prepared to settle their own rivalries at the expense of such a weak state. But if such territory from a weaker state had not been available, the tendency of the international rivalries would have been to warfare.

Russia and Prussia partitioned Poland again in 1793, and Russia, Prussia, and Austria partitioned it a third time in 1795, removing it from the map of Europe for more than a century. Each time, the great powers contended that they were saving themselves, and by implication the rest of Europe, from

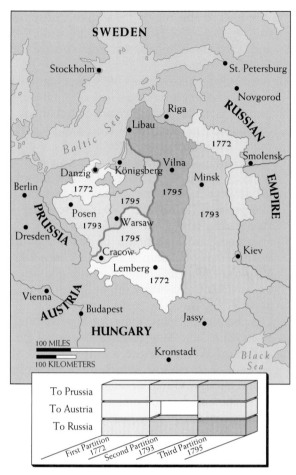

MAP 18–2   PARTITIONS OF POLAND, 1772; 1793; 1795   *The callous eradication of Poland from the map displayed eighteenth-century power politics at its most extreme. Poland, without strong central governmental institutions, fell victim to those states in central and eastern Europe that had developed such institutions.*

Polish anarchy. The fact of the matter was that Poland's political weakness left it vulnerable to plunderous aggression. The partitions of 1793 and 1795 took place in the shadow of the French Revolution, which left the absolute monarchies of eastern Europe concerned for their own stability. As a result, they reacted harshly even to minor attempts at reform by the Polish nobles, fearing they might infect their own domains.

The End of the Eighteenth Century in Central and Eastern Europe

During the last two decades of the eighteenth century, all three regimes based on enlightened abso-lutism became more conservative and politically repressive. In Prussia and Austria, the innovations of the rulers stirred resistance among the nobility. In Russia, fear of peasant unrest was the chief factor.

Frederick the Great of Prussia grew remote during his old age, leaving the aristocracy to fill important military and administrative posts. A reaction to Enlightenment ideas also set in among Prussian Lutheran writers.

In Austria, Joseph II's plans to restructure society and administration in his realms provoked growing frustration and political unrest, with the nobility calling for an end to innovation. In response, Joseph turned increasingly to censorship and his secret police.

Russia faced a peasant uprising, the Pugachev Rebellion, between 1773 and 1775, and Catherine the Great never fully recovered from the fears of social and political upheaval it raised. Once the French Revolution broke out in 1789, the Russian empress censored books based on Enlightenment thought and sent offensive authors into Siberian exile.

By the close of the century, fear of and hostility to change permeated the ruling classes of central and eastern Europe. This reaction had begun before 1789, but the events in France bolstered and sustained it for almost half a century. Paradoxically, nowhere did the humanity and liberalism of the Enlightenment encounter greater rejection than in those states that had been governed by "enlightened" rulers.

Although the enlightened absolute monarchs lacked the humanity of the *philosophes*, they had embraced the Enlightenment spirit of innovation. They wanted to change the political, social, and economic structures of their realms. From the close of the Seven Years' War (1763) until the opening of the French Revolution in 1789, the monarchies of both western and eastern Europe had been the major agents of institutional change. In every case they provoked aristocratic, and sometimes popular, resistance and resentment. George III of Britain fought for years with Parliament and lost the colonies of North America in the process. Frederick II of Prussia succeeded with his program of reform only because he accepted new aristocratic influence over the bureaucracy and the army. Catherine II of Russia had to come to terms with Russia's nobility. Joseph II, who did not consult with the nobility of his domains, left those domains in turmoil.

These monarchs pushed for innovations from a desire for increased revenue. In France also, the royal drive for adequate fiscal resources led to aristocratic resistance. In France, however, neither the monarchy nor the aristocracy could control the social and political forces their quarrel unleashed.

✦

The writers of the Enlightenment, known as philosophes, *charted a major new path in modern European and Western thought. They operated within a print culture that made public opinion into a distinct cultural force. Admiring Newton and the achievements of physical science, they tried to apply reason and the principles of science to the cause of social reform. They believed also that passions and feelings were essential parts of human nature. Throughout their writings they championed reasonable moderation in social life. More than any other previous group of Western thinkers, they strongly opposed the authority of the established churches and especially of Roman Catholicism. Most of them championed some form of religious toleration. They also sought to achieve a science of society that could discover how to maximize human productivity and material happiness. The great dissenter among them was Rousseau, who also wished to reform society but in the name of virtue rather than material happiness.*

The political influence of these writers went in several directions. The founding fathers of the American republic looked to them for political guidance, as did moderate liberal reformers throughout Europe, especially within royal bureaucracies. The autocratic rulers of eastern Europe consulted the philosophes *in the hope that Enlightenment ideas might allow them to rule more efficiently. The revolutionaries in France would honor them. This diverse assortment of followers illustrates the diverse character of the* philosophes *themselves. It also shows that Enlightenment thought cannot be reduced to a single formula. Rather it should be seen as an outlook that championed change and reform, giving central place to humans and their welfare on Earth rather than to God and the hereafter.*

Review Questions

1. How did the Enlightenment change basic Western attitudes toward reform, faith, and reason?

What were the major formative influences on the *philosophes*? How important were Voltaire and the *Encyclopedia* in the success of the Enlightenment?

2. Why did the *philosophes* consider organized religion to be their greatest enemy? Discuss the basic tenets of deism. What criticism might a deist direct at traditional Christianity and how might she or he improve it?

3. What were the attitudes of the *philosophes* toward women? What was Rousseau's view of women? What were the separate spheres he imagined men and women occupying? What were Mary Wollstonecraft's criticisms of Rousseau's view?

4. Compare the arguments of the mercantilists with those of Adam Smith in his book, *The Wealth of Nations*. How did both sides view the Earth's resources? Why might Smith be regarded as an advocate of the consumer?

5. Discuss the political views of Montesquieu and Rousseau. Was Montesquieu's view of England accurate? Was Rousseau a child of the Enlightenment or its enemy? Which did Rousseau value more, the individual or society?

6. Were the enlightened monarchs true believers in the ideal of the *philosophes* or was their enlightenment a mere veneer? Were they really absolute in power? What motivated their reforms? What does the partition of Poland indicate about the spirit of enlightened absolutism?

Suggested Readings

G. J. BARKER-BENFIELD, *The Culture of Sensibility: Sex and Society in Eighteenth-Century Britain* (1992). A broad exploration of the role of women in society and literature in the age of enlightenment.

R. P. BARTLETT, *Human Capital: The Settlement of Foreigners in Russia, 1762–1804* (1979). Examines Catherine's policy of attracting farmers and skilled workers to Russia.

D. BEALES, *Joseph II: In the Shadow of Maria Theresa, 1741–1780* (1987). The best treatment in English of the early political life of Joseph II.

C. BECKER, *The Heavenly City of the Eighteenth Century Philosophers* (1932). An influential but very controversial discussion.

C. B. A. BEHRENS, *Society, Government, and the Enlightenment: The Experiences of Eighteenth-Century France and Prussia* (1985). A wide-ranging comparative study.

D. D. BIEN, *The Calas Affair: Persecution, Toleration, and Heresy in Eighteenth-Century Toulouse* (1960). The standard treatment of the famous case.

R. Chartier, *The Cultural Origins of the French Revolution* (1991). A wide-ranging discussion of the emergence of the public sphere and the role of books and the book trade during the Enlightenment.

H. Chisick, *The Limits of Reform in the Enlightenment: Attitudes Toward the Education of the Lower Classes in Eighteenth-Century France* (1981). An attempt to examine the impact of the Enlightenment on nonelite classes.

R. Darnton, *The Literary Underground of the Old Regime* (1982). Essays on the world of printers, publishers, and booksellers.

R. Darnton, *The Forbidden Best-Sellers of Pre-Revolutionary France* (1995). An exploration of what books the French read and the efforts of the government to control the book trade.

T. S. Dock, *Women in the* Encyclopédie: *A Compendium* (1983). An analysis of the articles from the *Encyclopedia* that deal with women.

J. Gagliardo, *Enlightened Despotism* (1967). A discussion of the subject in its European context.

P. Gay, *The Enlightenment: An Interpretation*, 2 vols. (1966, 1969). The most important and far-reaching treatment.

P. Gay, *Voltaire's Politics* (1988). A wide-ranging discussion.

C. C. Gillispie, *Science and Polity in France at the End of the Old Regime* (1980). A major survey of the subject.

D. Goodman, *The Republic of Letters: A Cultural History of the French Enlightenment* (1994). Concentrates on the role of salons.

N. Hampson, *A Cultural History of the Enlightenment* (1969). A useful introduction.

M. C. Jacob, *The Radical Enlightenment: Pantheists, Freemasons, and Republicans* (1981). A treatment of frequently ignored figures in the Age of Enlightenment.

M. C. Jacob, *Living the Enlightenment: Freemasonry and Politics in Eighteenth-Century Europe* (1991). The best treatment in English of Freemasonry.

A. Kernan, *Printing Technology, Letters, and Samuel Johnson* (1987). A discussion of print culture and its impact on English letters.

R. Kreiser, *Miracles, Convulsions, and Ecclesiastical Politics in Early Eighteenth-Century Paris* (1978). An important study of the kind of religious life that the philosophes opposed.

J. B. Landes, *Women and the Public Sphere in the Age of the French Revolution* (1988). An extended essay on the role of women in public life during the eighteenth century.

C. A. Macartney, *The Habsburg Empire, 1790–1918* (1971). Provides useful coverage of major mid-eighteenth century developments.

I. de Madariaga, *Russia in the Age of Catherine the Great* (1981). The best discussion in English.

J. M. McManners, *Death and the Enlightenment: Changing Attitudes to Death Among Christians and Unbelievers in Eighteenth-Century France* (1982). Explores a wide spectrum of religious beliefs.

G. Ritter, *Frederick the Great* (trans. 1968). A useful biography.

R. O. Rockwood (ed.), *Carl Becker's Heavenly City Revisited* (1958). Important essays qualifying Becker's thesis.

J. Schwartz, *The Sexual Politics of Jean-Jacques Rousseau* (1984). A controversial reading of Rousseau's political thought organized around gender issues.

R. B. Sher, *Church and University in the Scottish Enlightenment: The Moderate Literati of Edinburgh* (1985). A major study that examines the role of religious moderates in aiding the goals of the Enlightenment.

J. N. Shklar, *Men and Citizens, a Study of Rousseau's Social Theory* (1969). A thoughtful and provocative overview of Rousseau's political thought.

D. Spadafora, *The Idea of Progress in Eighteenth Century Britain* (1990). A recent major study that covers many aspects of the Enlightenment in Britain.

S. I. Spencer, *French Women and the Age of Enlightenment* (1984). An outstanding collection of essays that cover the political, economic, and cultural roles of women.

J. Starobinski, *Jean-Jacques Rousseau: Transparency and Obstruction* (1971). A powerful analysis of Rousseau.

R. E. Sullivan, *John Toland and the Deist Controversy: A Study in Adaptation* (1982). An important and informative discussion.

A. M. Wilson, *Diderot* (1972). A splendid biography of the person behind the *Encyclopedia* and other major Enlightenment publications.

L. Wolff, *Inventing Eastern Europe: The Map of Civilization on the Mind of the Enlightenment* (1994). A remarkable study of the manner in which Enlightenment writers recast the understanding of this part of the continent.

The Declaration of the Rights of Man and Citizen promulgated by the National Assembly in August, 1789, constituted the cornerstone of the new political order being established by the French Revolution. It declared equality of civil rights, protected property, and recognized the political sovereignty of the nation. It was published repeatedly in a wide variety of formats surrounded by symbols of the nation and of the revolution [Giraudon/Art Resource]

The French Revolution

K E Y   T O P I C S

- The financial crisis that impelled the French monarchy to call the Estates
  General
- The transformation of the Estates General into the National Assembly,
  the Declaration of the Rights of Man and Citizen, and the reconstruction
  of the political and ecclesiastical institutions of France
- The second revolution, the end of the monarchy, and the turn to more
  radical reforms
- The war between France and the rest of Europe
- The Reign of Terror, the Thermidorian Reaction, and the establishment of
  the Directory

In the spring of 1789, the long-festering conflict between the French monarchy and the aristocracy erupted into a new political crisis. This dispute, unlike earlier ones, quickly outgrew the issues of its origins and produced the wider disruption known as the French Revolution. Before the turmoil settled, small-town provincial lawyers and Parisian street orators exercised more influence over the fate of the Continent than did aristocrats, royal ministers, or monarchs. Armies commanded by people of low birth and filled by conscripted village youths emerged victorious over forces composed of professional soldiers led by officers of noble birth. The very existence of the Roman Catholic faith in France was challenged. Politically and socially neither France nor Europe would ever be the same after these events.

The Crisis of the French Monarchy

Although the French Revolution was a turning point in modern European history, it grew out of the tensions and problems that characterized practically all late-eighteenth-century states. The French monarchy emerged from the Seven Years' War (1756–1763) both defeated and in debt and was unable afterward to put its finances on a sound basis. French support of the American revolt against Great Britain further deepened the financial difficulties of the government. On the eve of the revolution, the interest and payments on the royal debt amounted to just over one-half of the entire budget. Given the economic vitality of the nation, the debt was neither overly large nor disproportionate to the debts of other European powers. The problem lay with the inability of the royal government to tap the wealth of the French nation through taxes to service and repay the debt. Paradoxically France was a rich nation with an impoverished government.

The Monarchy Seeks New Taxes

The debt was symptomatic of the failure of the late eighteenth-century French monarchy to come to terms with the resurgent social and political power of aristocratic institutions and in particular the *parlements*. For twenty-five years after the Seven Years' War there was a stand-off between them as one royal minister after another attempted to devise new tax schemes that would tap the wealth of the nobility, only to be confronted by the opposition of both the Parlement of Paris and provincial *parlements*. Both Louis XV (r. 1715–1774) and Louis XVI (r. 1774–1792) lacked the character and the resolution to carry the dispute to a successful conclusion. The moral and political corruption of both their courts and the indecision of Louis XVI meant that the monarchy could not rally the French public to its side. In place of a consistent policy to deal with the growing debt and aristocratic resistance to change, the monarchy gave way to hesitancy, retreat, and even duplicity.

In 1770 Louis XV appointed René Maupeou (1714–1792) as chancellor. The new minister was determined to break the *parlements* and increase taxes on the nobility. He abolished the *parlements* and exiled their members to different parts of the country. He then began an ambitious program of reform and efficiency. What ultimately doomed Maupeou's policy was less the resistance of the

nobility than the death of Louis XV in 1774. His successor, Louis XVI, in an attempt to regain what he conceived to be popular support, restored all the *parlements* and confirmed their old powers.

France's successful intervention on behalf of the American colonists against the British did nothing to relieve the government's financial difficulties. By 1781, as a result of the aid to America, its debt was larger and its sources of revenues were unchanged. The new director-general of finances, Jacques Necker (1732–1804), a Swiss banker, then produced a public report that suggested that the situation was not so bad as had been feared. He argued that if the expenditures for the American war were removed, the budget was in surplus. Necker's report also revealed that a large portion of royal expenditures went to pensions for aristocrats and other royal court favorites. This revelation angered court aristocratic circles, and Necker soon left office. His financial sleight of hand, nonetheless, made it more difficult for later government officials to claim a real need to raise new taxes.

The monarchy hobbled along until 1786. By this time, Charles Alexandre de Calonne (1734–1802) was the minister of finance. Calonne proposed to encourage internal trade, to lower some taxes, such as the *gabelle* on salt, and to transform peasants' services to money payments. More important, Calonne urged the introduction of a new land tax that would require payments from all landowners regardless of their social status. If this tax had been imposed, the monarchy could have abandoned other indirect taxes. The government would also have had less need to seek additional taxes that required approval from the aristocratically dominated *parlements*. Calonne also intended to establish new local assemblies to approve land taxes; in these assemblies the voting power would have depended on the amount of land owned rather than on the social status of the owner. All these proposals would have undermined both the political and the social power of the French aristocracy.

The Aristocracy and the Clergy Resist Taxation

Calonne's policies and the country's fiscal crisis made a new clash with the nobility unavoidable, and the monarchy had very little room to maneuver. The creditors were at the door; the treasury was nearly empty. In 1787 Calonne met with an Assembly of Notables drawn from the upper ranks

This late-eighteenth-century cartoon satirizes the French social structure. It shows a poor man in chains, who represents the vast majority of the population, supporting an aristocrat, a bishop, and a noble of the robe. The aristocrat is claiming feudal rights, the bishop holds papers associating the church with religious persecution and clerical privileges, and the noble of the robe holds a document listing the rights of the noble-dominated parlements. *[The Bettmann Archive]*

of the aristocracy and the church to seek support and approval for his plan. The assembly adamantly refused any such action; rather, it demanded that the aristocracy be allowed a greater share in the direct government of the kingdom. The notables called for the reappointment of Necker, who they believed had left the country in sound fiscal condition. Finally, they claimed that they had no right to consent to new taxes and that such a right was vested only in the medieval institution of the Estates General of France, which had not met since 1614. The notables believed that calling the Estates General, which had been traditionally organized to allow aristocratic and church dominance, would produce a victory for the nobility over the monarchy.

Again Louis XVI backed off. He dismissed Calonne and replaced him with Étienne Charles Loménie de Brienne (1727–1794), archbishop of Toulouse and the chief opponent of Calonne at the Assembly of Notables. Once in office Brienne found, to his astonishment, that the situation was as bad as his predecessor had asserted. Brienne himself now sought to impose the land tax. The *Parlement* of Paris, however, took the new position that it lacked authority to authorize the tax and said that only the Estates General could do so. Shortly thereafter Brienne appealed to the Assembly of the Clergy to approve a large subsidy to allow funding of that part of the debt then coming due for payment. The clergy, like the *Parlement* dominated by aristocrats, not only refused the subsidy but also reduced their existing contribution, or *don gratuit*, to the government.

As these unfruitful negotiations were taking place at the center of political life, local aristocratic *parlements* and estates in the provinces were making their own demands. They wanted a restoration of the privileges they had enjoyed during the early seventeenth century, before Richelieu and Louis XIV had crushed their independence. Consequently, in July 1788, the king, through Brienne,

agreed to convoke the Estates General the next year. Brienne resigned and Necker replaced him. The institutions of the aristocracy—and to a lesser degree, of the church—had brought the French monarchy to its knees. In the country of its origin, royal absolutism had been defeated.

The Revolution of 1789

The year 1789 proved to be one of the most remarkable in the history of both France and Europe. The French aristocracy had forced Louis XVI to call the Estates General into session. Yet the aristocrats' triumph proved to be quite brief. From the moment the monarch summoned the Estates General, the political situation in France drastically changed. Social and political forces that neither the nobles nor the king could control were immediately unleashed.

From that calling of the Estates General to the present, historians have heatedly debated the meaning of the event and the turmoil that followed over the next decade. Many historians long believed that the calling and gathering of the Estates General unleashed a clash between the bourgeoisie and the aristocracy that had been building in the decades before 1789. More recently other historians have countered that the two groups actually had much in common by 1789 and that many members of both the bourgeoisie and the aristocracy resented and opposed the clumsy absolutism of the late-eighteenth-century monarchy. This second group of historians contends that the fundamental issue of 1789 was the determination of various social groups to reorganize the French government to assure the future political influence of all forms of wealth.

As this complicated process was being worked out, the argument goes, distrust arose between the aristocracy and increasingly radical middle-class leaders. The latter then turned to the tradespeople of Paris, building alliances with them to achieve their goals. That alliance radicalized the revolution. When in the mid-1790s revolutionary policies and actions became too radical, aristocratic and middle-class leaders once again cooperated to reassert the security of all forms of private wealth and property. According to this view, there did exist conflict among different social groups during the years of the revolution, but its causes were immediate, not hidden in the depths of French economic and social development.

Other historians also look to the influence of immediate rather than long-term causes. They believe that the faltering of the monarchy and the confusion following the calling, election, and organization of the Estates General created a political vacuum. Various leaders and social groups, often using the political vocabulary of the Enlightenment, stepped into that vacuum, challenging each other for dominance. The precedent for such public debate had been set during the years of conflict between the monarchy and the *parlements* when the latter had begun to challenge the former as the true representative of the nation. These debates and conflicts over the language, and hence values, of political life and activity had been made possible by the emergence of the new print culture with its reading public and numerous channels for the circulation of books, pamphlets, and newspapers. Emerging from this culture were a large number of often-unemployed authors who were resentful of their situation and ready to use their skills to radicalize the discussion. The result was a political debate wider than any before in European history. The events of the era represented a continuing effort to dominate public opinion about the future course of the nation. The French Revolution, according to this view, thus illustrates the character of a new political culture created by changes in the technology and distribution of print communication.

Yet another group of historians maintains that the events of 1789 through 1795 are only one chapter in a longer-term political reorganization of France following the paralysis of monarchical government, a process that was not concluded until the establishment of the Third Republic in the 1870s. According to this interpretation, the core accomplishment of the revolution of the 1790s was to lay the foundations for a republic that could assure both individual liberty and the safety of property. It was not until the last quarter of the nineteenth century, however, that such a republic actually came into existence.

To some extent, how convincing one finds each of these interpretations depends on which years or even months of the revolution one examines. The various interpretations are not, in any case, always mutually exclusive. Certainly, the weakness and ultimate collapse of the monarchy influenced events more than was once acknowledged. All sides did indeed make use of the new formats and institutions of the print culture. Individual leaders shifted their positions and alliances quite frequently, sometimes out of principle, more often for political expediency. Furthermore, the actual political situation differed from city to city and from region to region. The controversial and divisive religious policies of the revolutionary government itself were often determining factors in the attitudes that French citizens assumed toward the revolution. What does seem clear is that much of the earlier consensus—that the revolution arose almost entirely from conflict between the aristocracy and bourgeoisie—no longer stands except with many qualifications. The interpretive situation is now much more complicated, and a new consensus has yet to emerge.

The Estates General Becomes the National Assembly

Almost immediately after the Estates General was called, the three groups, or Estates, represented within it clashed with each other. The First Estate was the clergy, the Second Estate the nobility, and the Third Estate theoretically everyone else in the kingdom, although its representatives were drawn primarily from wealthy members of the commercial and professional middle classes. All the representatives in the Estates General were men. During the widespread public discussions preceding the meeting of the Estates General, representatives of the Third Estate made it clear that they would not permit the monarchy and the aristocracy to decide the future of the nation.

A comment by the Abbé Siéyès (1748–1836) in a pamphlet published in 1789 captures the spirit of the Third Estate's representatives: "What is the Third Estate? Everything. What has it been in the political order up to the present? Nothing. What does it ask? To become something."[1]

DEBATE OVER ORGANIZATION AND VOTING   The initial split between the aristocracy and the Third Estate occurred before the Estates General gathered. The public debate over the proper organiza-

---

[1]Quoted in Leo Gershoy, *The French Revolution and Napoleon* (New York: Appleton-Century-Crofts, 1964), p. 102.

The Estates General opened at Versailles in 1789 with much pomp and splendor. This print shows the representatives of the three estates seated in the hall and Louis XVI on a throne at its far end. [Giraudon/Art Resource, N.Y.]

tion of the body drew the lines of basic disagreement. The aristocracy made two moves to limit the influence of the Third Estate. First, they demanded an equal number of representatives for each estate. Second, in September 1788, the *Parlement* of Paris ruled that voting in the Estates General should be conducted by order rather than by head—that is, each estate, or order, should have one vote, rather than each member. This procedure would ensure that the aristocratic First and Second Estates could always outvote the Third. Both moves exposed the hollowness of the aristocracy's alleged concern for French liberty and revealed it as a group determined to maintain its privileges. Spokespeople for the Third Estate denounced the arrogant claims of the aristocracy. Although the aristocracy and the Third Estate shared many economic interests and goals and some intermarriage had occurred throughout the country between nobles and the elite of the Third Estate, a fundamental social distance separated the members of the two orders. There were far more examples of

enormous wealth and military experience among the nobility than among the Third Estate; the latter also had experienced various forms of political and social discrimination from the nobility. The resistance of the nobility to voting by head simply confirmed the suspicions and resentments of the members of the Third Estate, who were overwhelmingly lawyers of substantial but not enormous economic means.

The royal council eventually decided that the cause of the monarchy and fiscal reform would best be served by a strengthening of the Third Estate. In December 1788, the council announced that the Third Estate would elect twice as many representatives as either the nobles or the clergy. This so-called doubling of the Third Estate meant that it could easily dominate the Estates General if voting were allowed by head rather than by order. It was correctly assumed that liberal nobles and clergy would support the Third Estate, confirming that despite social differences these groups shared important interests and reforming goals. The method of voting was settled by the king only after the Estates General had gathered at Versailles in May 1789.

THE CAHIERS DE DOLÉANCES   When the representatives came to the royal palace, they brought with them *cahiers de doléances*, or lists of grievances, registered by the local electors, to be presented to the king. Many of these have survived and provide considerable information about the state of the country on the eve of the revolution. These documents recorded criticisms of government waste, indirect taxes, church taxes and corruption, and the hunting rights of the aristocracy. They included calls for periodic meetings of the Estates General, more equitable taxes, more local control of administration, unified weights and measures to facilitate trade and commerce, and a free press. The overwhelming demand of the *cahiers* was for equality of rights among the king's subjects.

These complaints and demands could not, however, be discussed until the questions of organization and voting had been decided. From the beginning, the Third Estate, whose members consisted largely of local officials, professionals, and other persons of property, refused to sit as a separate order as the king desired. For several weeks there was a stand-off. Then, on June 1, the Third Estate invited the clergy and the nobles to join them in organizing a new legislative body. A few members of the lower clergy did so. On June 17, that body declared itself the National Assembly.

THE TENNIS COURT OATH   Three days later, finding themselves accidentally locked out of their usual meeting place, the National Assembly moved to a nearby tennis court. There its members took an oath to continue to sit until they had given France a constitution. This was the famous Tennis Court Oath. Louis XVI ordered the National Assembly to

This painting of the Tennis Court Oath, June 20, 1789, is by Jacques-Louis David (1748–1825). In the center foreground are members of different Estates joining hands in cooperation as equals. The presiding officer is Jean-Sylvain Bailly, soon to become mayor of Paris. [Giraudon/Art Resource, N.Y.]

The Third Estate of a French City Petitions the King

The cahiers de doléances *were the lists of grievances brought to Versailles in 1789 by members of the Estates General. This particular* cahier *originated in Dourdan, a city of central France, and reflects the complaints of the Third Estate. The first two articles refer to the organization of the Estates General. The other articles ask that the king grant various forms of equality before the law and in matters of taxation. These demands for equality appeared in practically all the* cahiers *of the Third Estate.*

✦ *Which of the following petitions relate to political rights and which to economic equality? The slogan most associated with the French Revolution was "Liberty, Equality, Fraternity." Which of these petitions represents each of those values?*

The order of the third estate of the City . . . of Dourdan . . . supplicates [the king] to accept the grievances, complaints, and remonstrances which it is permitted to bring to the foot of the throne, and to see therein only the expression of its zeal and the homage of its obedience.

It wishes:

1. That his subjects of the third estate, equal by such status to all other citizens, present themselves before the common father without other distinction which might degrade them.

2. That all the orders, already united by duty and common desire contribute equally to the needs of the State, also deliberate in common concerning its needs.

3. That no citizen lose his liberty except according to law: that, consequently, no one be arrested by virtue of special orders, or, if imperative circumstances necessitate such orders, that the prisoner be handed over to regular courts of justice within forty-eight hours at the latest.

. . . .

12. That every tax, direct or indirect, be granted only for a limited time, and that every collection beyond such term be regarded as peculation, and punished as such.

. . . .

15. That every personal tax be abolished; that thus the *capitation* [a poll tax] and the *taille* [tax from which nobility and clergy were exempt] and its accessories be merged with the *vingtièmes* [an income tax] in a tax on land and real or nominal property.

16. That such tax be borne equally, without distinction, by all classes of citizens and by all kinds of property, even feudal . . . rights.

17. That the tax substituted for the *corvée* be borne by all classes of citizens equally and without distinction. That said tax, at present beyond the capacity of those who pay it and the needs to which it is destined, be reduced by at least one-half.

John Hall Stewart, A Documentary Survey of the French Revolution *(New York: Macmillan, 1951), pp. 76–77.*

desist from their actions, but shortly afterward a majority of the clergy and a large group of nobles joined the assembly.

On June 27, the king capitulated and formally requested the First and Second Estates to meet with the National Assembly, where voting would occur by head rather than by order. Had nothing further occurred, the government of France would have been transformed. Government by privileged orders had ended. The National Assembly, which renamed itself the National Constituent Assembly, was composed of people from all three orders, who shared liberal goals for the administrative, constitutional, and economic reform of the country. The revolution in France against government by privileged hereditary orders had begun.

Fall of the Bastille

Two new forces soon intruded on the scene. The first was Louis XVI himself, who attempted to regain the political initiative by mustering royal troops near Versailles and Paris. It appeared that he might, following the advice of Queen Marie Antoinette (1755–1793), his brothers, and the most conservative nobles, be contemplating disruption of the National Constituent Assembly. On July 11, without consulting assembly leaders, Louis abruptly dismissed his minister of finance, Necker. These actions marked the beginning of a steady, but consistently poorly executed, royal attempt to undermine the assembly and halt the revolution. Most of the National Constituent Assembly wished to establish some form of constitutional monarchy, but from the start Louis's refusal to cooperate thwarted that effort. The king fatally decided to throw his lot in with the conservative aristocracy against the emerging forces of reform drawn from across the social and political spectrum.

The second new factor to impose itself on the events at Versailles was the populace of Paris. The mustering of royal troops created anxiety in the city, where throughout the winter and spring of 1789 there had been several bread riots. The Parisians who had elected their representatives to the Third Estate had continued to meet after the elections. By June they were organizing a citizen militia and collecting arms. They regarded the dismissal of Necker as the opening of a royal offensive against the National Constituent Assembly and the city.

On July 14, somewhat more than 800 people, most of them small shopkeepers, tradespeople, artisans, and wage earners, marched to the Bastille in search of weapons for the militia. This great fortress, with ten-foot-thick walls, had once held political prisoners. Through miscalculations and ineptitude on the part of the governor of the fortress, the troops in the Bastille fired into the crowd, killing ninety-eight people and wounding many others. Thereafter the crowd stormed the fortress and eventually gained entrance. They released the seven prisoners, none of whom was there for political reasons, and killed several troops and the governor. They found no weapons.

On July 15, the militia of Paris, by then called the National Guard, offered its command to the marquis de Lafayette (1757–1834). This hero of the American Revolution gave the guard a new insignia: the red and blue stripes of Paris separated by the white stripe of the king. This emblem became the revolutionary *cockade* (badge) and eventually the flag of revolutionary France.

The attack on the Bastille marked the first of many crucial *journées*, days on which the populace of Paris redirected the course of the revolution. The fall of the fortress signaled that the National Constituent Assembly alone would not decide the political future of the nation. As the news of the taking of the Bastille spread, similar disturbances took place in provincial cities. A few days later, Louis XVI again bowed to the force of events and personally visited Paris, where he wore the revolutionary *cockade* and recognized the organized electors as the legitimate government of the city. The king also recognized the National Guard. The citizens of Paris were, for the time being, satisfied. They also had established themselves as an independent political force with which other political groups might ally for their own purposes.

The "Great Fear" and the Surrender of Feudal Privileges

Simultaneous with the popular urban disturbances, a movement known as the "Great Fear" swept across much of the French countryside. Rumors had spread that royal troops would be sent into the rural districts. The result was an intensification of the peasant disturbances that had begun during the spring. The Great Fear saw the burning of *châteaux*, the destruction of records and documents, and the

On July 14, 1789, crowds stormed the Bastille, a prison in Paris. This event, whose only practical effect was to free a few prisoners, marked the first time the populace of Paris redirected the course of the revolution. [France, 18th c., "Seige of the Bastille, 14 July, 1789." Obligatory mention of the following: Musee de la Ville de Paris, Musee Carnavalet, Paris, France. Giraudon/Art Resource, N.Y.]

refusal to pay feudal dues. The peasants were determined to take possession of food supplies and land that they considered rightfully theirs. They were reclaiming rights and property that they had lost through the aristocratic resurgence of the last quarter century, as well as venting their general anger against the injustices of rural life.

On the night of August 4, 1789, aristocrats in the National Constituent Assembly attempted to halt the spreading disorder in the countryside. By prearrangement, several liberal nobles and clerics rose in the assembly and renounced their feudal rights, dues, and tithes. In a scene of great emotion, hunt-

ing and fishing rights, judicial authority, and special exemptions were surrendered. These nobles gave up what they had already lost and what they could not have regained without civil war in the rural areas. Later they would also, in many cases, receive compensation for their losses. Nonetheless, after the night of August 4, all French citizens were subject to the same and equal laws. That dramatic session of the assembly paved the way for the legal and social reconstruction of the nation. Without those renunciations, the constructive work of the National Constituent Assembly would have been much more difficult.

Both the attack on the Bastille and the Great Fear displayed characteristics of the rural and urban riots that had occurred often in eighteenth-century France. Louis XVI first thought that the turmoil over the Bastille was simply another bread riot. Indeed, the popular disturbances were only partly related to the events at Versailles. A deep economic downturn had struck France in 1787 and continued into 1788. The harvests for both years had been poor, and food prices in 1789 were higher than at any time since 1703. Wages had not kept up with the rise in prices. Throughout the winter of 1788–1789, an unusually cold one, many people suffered from hunger. Several cities had experienced wage and food riots. These economic problems helped the revolution reach the vast proportions it did.

The political, social, and economic grievances of many sections of the country became combined. The National Constituent Assembly could look to the popular forces as a source of strength against the king and the conservative aristocrats. When the

---

The National Assembly Decrees Civic Equality in France

These famous decrees of August 4, 1789, in effect created civic equality in France. The special privileges previously possessed or controlled by the nobility were removed.

✦ *What institutions and privileges are included in "the feudal regime"? How do these decrees recognize that the abolition of some privileges and former tax arrangements will require new kinds of taxes and government financing to support religious, educational, and other institutions?*

1. The National Assembly completely abolishes the feudal regime. It decrees that, among the rights and dues . . . all those originating in real or personal serfdom, personal servitude, and those which represent them, are abolished without indemnification; all others are declared redeemable, and that the price and mode of redemption shall be fixed by the National Assembly. . . .

2. The exclusive right to maintain pigeon-houses and dove-cotes is abolished. . . .

3. The exclusive right to hunt and to maintain unenclosed warrens is likewise abolished. . . .

4. All manorial courts are suppressed without indemnification.

5. Tithes of every description and the dues which have been substituted for them . . . are abolished, on condition, however, that some other method be devised to provide for the expenses of divine worship, the support of the officiating clergy, the relief of the poor, repairs and rebuilding of churches and parsonages, and for all establishments, seminaries, schools, academies, asylums, communities, and other institutions, for the maintenance of which they are actually devoted. . . .

. . . .

7. The sale of judicial and municipal offices shall be suppressed forthwith. . . .

8. Pecuniary privileges, personal or real, in the payment of taxes are abolished forever. . . .

. . . .

11. All citizens, without distinction of birth, are eligible to any office or dignity, whether ecclesiastical, civil or military. . . .

Frank Maloy Anderson, ed. and trans., The Constitutions and Other Select Documents Illustrative of the History of France, 1789–1907, 2nd. ed., rev. and enl. (Minneapolis: H. W. Wilson, 1908), pp. 11–13.

various elements of the assembly later fell into quarrels among themselves, the resulting factions appealed for support to the politically sophisticated and well-organized shopkeeping and artisan classes. They, in turn, would demand a price for their cooperation.

The Declaration of the Rights of Man and Citizen

In late August 1789, the National Constituent Assembly decided that before writing a new constitution, it should set forth a statement of broad political principles. On August 27, the assembly issued the Declaration of the Rights of Man and Citizen. This declaration drew upon much of the political language of the Enlightenment and was also influenced by the Declaration of Rights adopted by Virginia in America in June 1776.

Civic equality was one of the hallmarks of the revolutionary era. This figure of Equality holds in her hand a copy of the Declaration of the Rights of Man and Citizen. [The Bettmann Archive]

The French declaration proclaimed that all men were "born and remain free and equal in rights." The natural rights so proclaimed were "liberty, property, security, and resistance to oppression." Governments existed to protect those rights. All political sovereignty resided in the nation and its representatives. All citizens were to be equal before the law and were to be "equally admissible to all public dignities, offices, and employments, according to their capacity, and with no other distinction than that of their virtues and talents." There were to be due process of law and presumption of innocence until proof of guilt. Freedom of religion was affirmed. Taxation was to be apportioned equally according to capacity to pay. Property constituted "an inviolable and sacred right."[2]

Although these statements were rather abstract, almost all of them were directed against specific abuses of the old aristocratic and absolutist regime. If any two principles of the future governed the declaration, they were civic equality and protection of property. The Declaration of the Rights of Man and Citizen has often been considered the death certificate of the Old Regime.

It was not accidental that the Declaration of the Rights of Man and Citizen specifically applied to men and not to women. As discussed in the previous chapter, much of the political language of the Enlightenment, and most especially that associated with Rousseau, separated men and women into distinct gender spheres. According to this view, which influenced the legislation of the revolutionary era, men were suited for citizenship, women for motherhood and the domestic life. Nonetheless, in the charged atmosphere of the summer of 1789, many politically active and informed French women hoped the guarantees of the declaration would be extended to them. Their issues of particular concern related to property, inheritance, family, and divorce. Some people saw in the declaration a framework within which women might eventually enjoy the rights and protection of citizenship.

The Royal Family Forced to Return to Paris

Louis XVI stalled before ratifying both the declaration and the aristocratic renunciation of feudalism.

[2]Quoted in Georges Lefebvre, *The Coming of the French Revolution*, trans. by R. R. Palmer (Princeton, N.J.: Princeton University Press, 1967), pp. 221–223.

The women of Paris marched to Versailles on October 5, 1789. The following day the royal family was forced to return to Paris with them. Henceforth, the French government would function under the constant threat of mob violence. [Giraudon/Art Resource]

The longer he hesitated, the stronger grew suspicions that he might again try to resort to the use of troops. Moreover, bread continued to be scarce. On October 5, a crowd of as many as 7,000 Parisian women armed with pikes, guns, swords, and knives marched to Versailles demanding more bread. They milled about the palace, and many stayed the night. Intimidated by these Parisian women, the king agreed to sanction the decrees of the assembly. The next day he and his family appeared on a balcony before the crowd. The Parisians, however, were deeply suspicious of the monarch and believed that he must be kept under the watchful eye of the people. They demanded that Louis and his family return to Paris. The monarch had no real choice in the matter. On October 6, 1789, his carriage followed the crowd into the city, where he and his family settled in the palace of the Tuileries.

The march of the women of Paris was the first example of a popular insurrection employing the language of popular sovereignty directed against the monarch. The National Constituent Assembly also soon moved into Paris. Thereafter, both Paris and France remained relatively stable and peaceful until the summer of 1792.

The Reconstruction of France

Once established in Paris, the National Constituent Assembly set about reorganizing France. In government, it pursued a policy of constitutional monarchy; in administration, rationalism; in economics, unregulated freedom; and in religion, anticlericalism. Throughout its proceedings the assembly was determined to protect property in all its forms. In those policies the aristocracy and the middle-class elite stood united. The assembly also sought to limit the impact on national life of the unpropertied elements of the nation and even of possessors of small amounts of property. Although championing civic equality before the law, the assembly spurned social equality and extensive democracy. In all these ways the assembly charted a general course that, to a greater or lesser degree, nineteenth-century liberals across Europe would follow.

Political Reorganization

The Constitution of 1791, the product of the National Constituent Assembly's deliberations, established a constitutional monarchy. The major political authority of the nation would be a unicameral Legislative Assembly, in which all laws would originate. The monarch was allowed a suspensive veto that could delay but not halt legislation. Powers of war and peace were vested in the assembly.

ACTIVE AND PASSIVE CITIZENS   The constitution provided for an elaborate system of indirect elections intended to thwart direct popular pressure on the government. The citizens of France were divided into active and passive categories. Only active citizens—that is, men paying annual taxes equal to three days of local labor wages—could vote. They chose electors, who then in turn voted for the members of the legislature. At the level of electors or members, still further property qualifications were imposed. Only about fifty thousand citizens of a population of about twenty-five million could qualify as electors or members of the Legislative Assembly. Women could neither vote nor hold office.

These constitutional arrangements effectively transferred political power from aristocratic wealth to all forms of propertied wealth in the nation. Political authority would no longer be achieved through hereditary privilege or through purchase of titles, but through the accumulation of land and commercial property. These new political arrangements based on property rather than birth recognized the new complexities of French society that had developed over the past century and allowed more social and economic interests to have a voice in the governing of the nation.

The laws that excluded women from both voting and holding office did not pass unnoticed. In 1791 Olympe de Gouges (d. 1793), a butcher's daughter from Montauban who became a major revolutionary radical in Paris, composed a *Declaration of the Rights of Woman*, which she ironically addressed to Queen Marie Antoinette. Much of the document

reprinted the Declaration of the Rights of Man and Citizen adding the word *woman* to the various original clauses. That strategy demanded that women be regarded as citizens and not merely as daughters, sisters, wives, and mothers of citizens. Olympe de Gouges further outlined rights that would permit women to own property and require men to recognize the paternity of their children. She called for equality of the sexes in marriage and improved education for women. She declared, "Women, wake up; the tocsin of reason is being heard throughout the whole universe; discover your rights."[3] Her declaration illustrated how the simple listing of rights in the Declaration of the Rights of Man and Citizen created a structure of universal civic expectations even for those it did not cover. The National Assembly had established a set of values against which it was itself to be measured. It provided criteria for liberty, and those to whom it had not extended full liberties could demand to know why and could claim that the revolution was incomplete until they enjoyed those freedoms.

DEPARTMENTS REPLACE PROVINCES   In reconstructing the local and judicial administration, the National Constituent Assembly applied the rational spirit of the Enlightenment. It abolished the ancient French provinces, such as Burgundy and Brittany, and established in their place eighty-three departments, or "*départements*," of generally equal size named after rivers, mountains, and other geographical features. (See Map 19–1.) The departments in turn were subdivided into districts, cantons, and communes. Most local elections were also indirect. The departmental reconstruction proved to be a permanent achievement of the assembly. The departments exist to the present day.

All the ancient judicial courts, including the seigneurial courts and the *parlements*, were also abolished. Uniform courts with elected judges and prosecutors were organized in their place. Procedures were simplified, and the most degrading punishments were removed from the books.

Economic Policy

In economic matters the National Constituent Assembly continued the policies formerly advo-

---

[3]Quoted in Sara E. Melzer and Leslie W. Rabine, eds., *Rebel Daughters: Women and the French Revolution* (New York: Oxford University Press, 1992), p. 88.

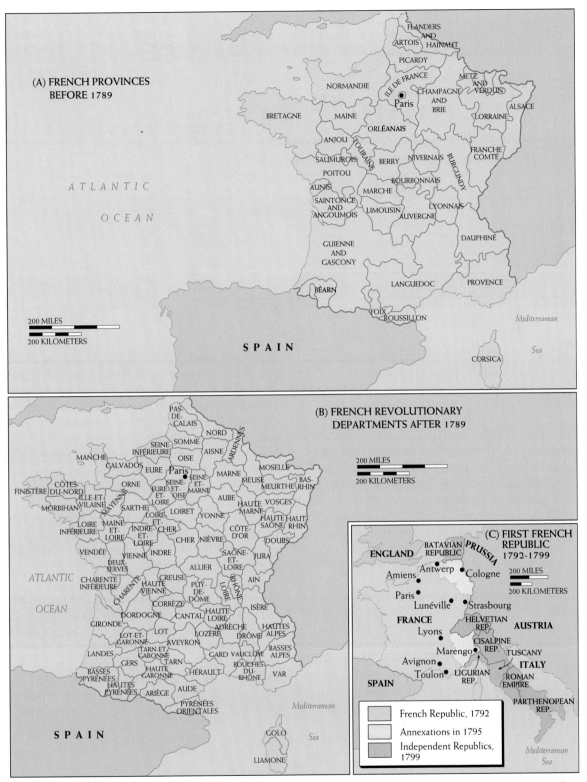

MAP 19–1   FRENCH PROVINCES AND THE REPUBLIC   *In 1789 the National Constituent Assembly redrew the map of France. The ancient provinces (A) were replaced with a larger number of new, smaller departments (B). This redrawing of the map was part of the assembly's effort to impose greater administrative rationality in France. The borders of the republic (C) changed as the French army conquered new territory.*

The assignats *were government bonds that were backed by confiscated church lands. They circulated as money. When the government printed too many of them, inflation resulted and their value fell. [Bildarchiv Preussischer Kulturbesitz]*

cated by Louis XVI's reformist ministers. It suppressed the guilds and liberated the grain trade. The assembly established the metric system to provide the nation with uniform weights and measures.

WORKERS' ORGANIZATIONS FORBIDDEN   These policies of economic freedom and uniformity disappointed both peasants and urban workers caught in the cycle of inflation. By decrees in 1789, the assembly placed the burden of proof on the peasants to rid themselves of the residual feudal dues for which compensation was to be paid. On June 14, 1791, the assembly crushed the attempts of urban workers to protect their wages by enacting the Chapelier Law, which forbade workers' associations. Peasants and workers were henceforth to be left to the freedom and mercy of the marketplace.

CONFISCATION OF CHURCH LANDS   While these various reforms were being put into effect, the original financial crisis that had occasioned the calling of the Estates General persisted. The assembly did not repudiate the royal debt, because it was owed to the bankers, the merchants, and the commercial traders of the Third Estate. The National Constituent Assembly had suppressed many of the old, hated indirect taxes and had substituted new land taxes, but these proved insufficient. Moreover, there were not enough officials to collect them. The continuing financial problem led the assembly to take what

may well have been, for the future of French life and society, its most decisive action. The assembly decided to finance the debt by confiscating and then selling the land and property of the Roman Catholic Church in France. The results were further inflation, religious schism, and civil war. In effect, the National Constituent Assembly had opened a new chapter in the relations of church and state in Europe.

THE ASSIGNATS   Having chosen to plunder the land of the church, in December 1789 the assembly authorized the issuance of *assignats*, or government bonds. Their value was guaranteed by the revenue to be generated from the sale of church property. Initially a limit was set on the quantity of *assignats* to be issued. The bonds, however, proved so acceptable to the public that they began to circulate as currency. The assembly decided to issue an ever larger number of them to liquidate the national debt and to create a large body of new property owners with a direct stake in the revolution. Within a few months, however, the value of the *assignats* began to fall and inflation increased, putting new stress on the lives of the urban poor.

The Civil Constitution of the Clergy

The confiscation of church lands required an ecclesiastical reconstruction. In July 1790, the National

The Revolutionary Government
Forbids Worker Organizations

The Chapelier Law of June 14, 1791, was one of the most important pieces of revolutionary legislation. It abolished the kinds of labor organizations that had protected skilled workers under the Old Regime. The principles of this legislation prevented effective labor organization in France for well over half a century.

♦ *Why are workers' organizations declared to be contrary to the principles of liberty? Why were guilds seen as one of the undesirable elements of the Old Regime? What are the coercive powers that are to be brought to bear against workers' organizations? In light of this legislation, what courses of actions were left open to workers as they confronted the operation of the market economy?*

1. Since the abolition of all kinds of corporations of citizens of the same occupation and profession is one of the fundamental bases of the French Constitution, reestablishment thereof under any pretext or form whatsoever is forbidden.

2. Citizens of the same occupation or profession, entrepreneurs, those who maintain open shop, workers, and journeymen of any craft whatsoever may not, when they are together, name either president, secretaries, or trustees, keep accounts, pass decrees or resolutions, or draft regulations concerning their alleged common interests.

. . . .

4. If, contrary to the principles of liberty and the Constitution, some citizens associated in the same professions, arts, and crafts hold deliberations or make agreements among themselves tending to refuse by mutual consent or to grant only at a determined price the assistance of their industry or their labor, such deliberations and agreements, whether accompanied by oath or not, are declared unconstitutional, in contempt of liberty and the Declaration of the Rights of Man, and noneffective; administrative and municipal bodies shall be required so to declare them. . . .

. . . .

8. All assemblies composed of artisans, workers, journeymen, day laborers, or those incited by them against the free exercise of industry and labor appertaining to every kind of person and under all circumstances arranged by private contract, or against the action of police and the execution of judgments rendered in such connection, as well as against public bids and auctions of divers enterprises, shall be considered as seditious assemblies, and as such shall be dispersed by the depositories of the public force, upon legal requisitions made thereupon, and shall be punished according to all the rigor of the laws concerning authors, instigators, and leaders of the said assemblies, and all those who have committed assaults and acts of violence.

John Hall Stewart, A Documentary Survey of the French Revolution *(New York: Macmillan, 1951), pp. 165–166.*

Constituent Assembly issued the Civil Constitution of the Clergy, which transformed the Roman Catholic Church in France into a branch of the secular state. This legislation reduced the number of bishoprics from 135 to 83 and brought the borders of the dioceses into conformity with those of the new departments. It also provided for the election of priests and bishops, who henceforth became salaried employees of the state. The assembly consulted neither the pope nor the French clergy about these broad changes. The king approved the measure only with the greatest reluctance.

The Civil Constitution of the Clergy was the major blunder of the National Constituent Assembly. It created embittered relations between the French church and state that have persisted to the present day. The measure immediately created immense opposition within the French church even from bishops who had long championed Gallican liberties over papal domination. In the face of this resistance, the assembly unwisely ruled that all clergy must take an oath to support the Civil Constitution. Only seven bishops and about half the clergy did so. In reprisal, the assembly designated the clergy who had not taken the oath as "refractory" and removed them from their clerical functions.

Further reaction was swift. Refractory priests attempted to celebrate mass. In February 1791, the pope condemned not only the Civil Constitution of the Clergy but also the Declaration of the Rights of Man and Citizen. That condemnation marked the opening of a Roman Catholic offensive against liberalism and the revolution that continued throughout the nineteenth century. Within France itself, the pope's action created a crisis of conscience and political loyalty for all sincere Catholics. Religious devotion and revolutionary loyalty became incompatible for many people. French citizens were divided between those who supported the constitutional priests and those who resorted to the refractory clergy. Louis XVI and his family favored the refractory clergy.

Counterrevolutionary Activity

The revolution had other enemies besides the pope and the devout Catholics. As it became clear that the old political and social order was undergoing fundamental and probably permanent change, many aristocrats left France. Known as the *émigrés*, they settled in countries near the French border, where they sought to foment counterrevolution. Among the most important of their number was the king's younger brother, the count of Artois (1757–1836). In the summer of 1791, his agents and the queen persuaded Louis XVI to attempt to flee the country.

FLIGHT TO VARENNES   On the night of June 20, 1791, Louis and his immediate family, disguised as servants, left Paris. They traveled as far as Varennes on their way to Metz. At Varennes the king was recognized, and his flight was halted. On June 24, a company of soldiers escorted the royal family back to Paris. The leaders of the National Constituent Assembly, determined to save the constitutional monarchy, announced that the king had been abducted from the capital. Such a convenient public fiction could not cloak the realities that the chief counterrevolutionary in France now sat on the throne and that the constitutional monarchy might not last long.

DECLARATION OF PILLNITZ   Two months later, on August 27, 1791, under pressure from a group of *émigrés*, Emperor Leopold II of Austria, who was the brother of Marie Antoinette, and Frederick William II (r. 1786–1797), the king of Prussia, issued the Declaration of Pillnitz. The two monarchs promised to intervene in France to protect the royal family and to preserve the monarchy if the other major European powers agreed. This provision rendered the statement meaningless because at the time Great Britain would not have given its consent. The declaration was not, however, so read in France, where the revolutionaries saw the nation surrounded by aristocratic and monarchical foes.

The National Constituent Assembly drew to a close in September 1791. Its task of reconstructing the government and the administration of France had been completed. One of its last acts was the passage of a measure that forbade any of its own members to sit in the Legislative Assembly then being elected. The new body met on October 1 and had to confront the immense problems that had emerged during the earlier part of the year. Within the Legislative Assembly major political divisions also soon developed over the future course of the nation and the revolution. Those groups whose

In the image banner:
AVARENNE · LE 22 · JUIN 1791 ·

A CORDÉE A M.
50 MILLE LIVRE
20 MILLE LIVRE

Gardes nationaux qui ont bravé les menaces d'un détachement de huffards, qui avoit été commandé par le traître Bouillé! M. Sauce, Procureur de la Commune, a invité le Roi d'entrer chez lui, & de s'y repofer lui & fa famille. Le généreux citoyen de Varennes n'a point accepté les offres du Roi, difant qu'il devoit tout à fa patrie.

In June 1791, Louis XVI and his family attempted to flee France. They were recognized in the town of Varennes, where their flight was halted and they were returned to Paris. This ended any realistic hope for a constitutional monarchy. [The Bettmann Archive]

members had been assigned to passive citizenship began to demand full political participation in the nation.

A Second Revolution

By the autumn of 1791, the government of France had been transformed into a constitutional monarchy. Virtually all the other administrative and religious structures of the nation had also been reformed. The situation both inside and outside France, however, remained unstable. Louis XVI had reluctantly accepted the constitution on July 14, 1790. French aristocrats resented their loss of position and plotted to overthrow the new order. In the west of France, peasants resisted the revolutionary changes especially as they affected the church. In Paris, many groups of workers believed the revolution had not gone far enough. Furthermore, during these same months women's groups in Paris began to organize both to support the revolution and to demand a wider civil role and civic protection for women. Radical members of the new Legislative Assembly also believed the revolution should go further. The major foreign powers saw the French Revolution as dangerous to their own domestic political order. By the spring of 1792, all these unstable elements had begun to overturn the first revolutionary settlement and led to a second series of revolutionary changes far more radical and democratically extensive than the first.

End of the Monarchy

The issues raised by the Civil Constitution of the Clergy and Louis XVI's uncertain trustworthiness undermined the unity of the newly organized nation. Factionalism plagued the Legislative Assembly throughout its short life (1791–1792). Ever since the original gathering of the Estates General, deputies from the Third Estate had organized themselves into clubs composed of politically like-minded persons. The most famous and best organized of these were the Jacobins, whose name derived from the fact that Dominican friars were called Jacobins, and the group met in a Dominican monastery in Paris. The Jacobins had also established a network of local clubs throughout the provinces. They had been the most advanced political group in the National Constituent Assembly and had pressed for a republic rather than a constitutional monarchy. Their political language and rhetoric were drawn from the most radical thought of the Enlightenment. That thought and language became all the more effective because the events of 1789–1791 had destroyed the old political framework and the old monarchical political vocabulary was less and less relevant. The political language and rhetoric of a republic filled that vacuum and for a time supplied the political values of the day. The events of the summer of 1791 led to the reassertion of demands for establishing a republic.

In the Legislative Assembly, a group of Jacobins known as the Girondists (because many of them came from the department of the Gironde) assumed

French Women Petition to Bear Arms

The issue of women serving in the revolutionary French military appeared early in the revolution. In March 1791, Pauline Léon presented a petition to the National Assembly on behalf of more than 300 Parisian women asking the right to bear arms and train for military service for the revolution. Similar requests were made during the next two years. Some women did serve in the military, but in 1793 legislation specifically forbade women from participating in military service. The ground for that refusal was the argument that women belonged in the domestic sphere and military service would lead them to abandon family duties.

♦ Citoyenne *is the feminine form of the French word for* citizen. *How does this petition seek to challenge the concept of citizenship in the Declaration of the Rights of Man and Citizen? How do these petitioners relate their demand to bear arms to their role as women in French society? How do the petitioners relate their demands to the use of all national resources against the enemies of the revolution?*

Patriotic women come before you to claim the right which any individual has to defend his life and liberty.

. . . We are *citoyennes,* [female citizens], and we cannot be indifferent to the fate of the fatherland.

. . . Yes, Gentlemen, we need arms, and we come to ask your permission to procure them. May our weakness be no obstacle; courage and intrepidity will supplant it, and the love of the fatherland and hatred of tyrants will allow us to brave all dangers with ease. . . .

No, Gentlemen, We will [use arms] only to defend ourselves the same as you; you cannot refuse us, and society cannot deny the right nature gives us, unless you pretend the Declaration of Rights does not apply to women and that they

leadership.[4] They were determined to oppose the forces of counterrevolution. They passed one measure ordering the *émigrés* to return or suffer loss of property and another requiring the refractory clergy to support the Civil Constitution or lose their state pensions. The king vetoed both acts.

Furthermore, on April 20, 1792, the Girondists led the Legislative Assembly to declare war on Austria, by this time governed by Francis II (r. 1792–1835) and allied to Prussia. The Girondists believed that the pursuit of the war would preserve the revolution from domestic enemies and bring the most advanced revolutionaries to power. Paradoxically, Louis XVI and other monarchists also favored the war. They thought that the conflict would

strengthen the executive power (the monarchy). The king also entertained the hope that foreign armies might defeat French forces and restore the Old Regime. Both sides were playing dangerously foolish politics.

The war radicalized the revolution and led to what is usually called the *second revolution*, which overthrew the constitutional monarchy and established a republic. Both the country and the revolution seemed in danger. As early as March 1791, a group of women led by Pauline Léon had petitioned the Legislative Assembly for the right to bear arms and to fight for the protection of the revolution. Earlier she had led an effort to allow women to serve in the National Guard. These demands to serve, voiced in the universal language of citizenship, illustrated how the words and rhetoric of the revolution could be used to challenge traditional social roles and the concept of separate social spheres for

[4]The Girondists are also frequently called the Brissotins after Jacques-Pierre Brissot (1754–1793), their chief spokesperson in early 1792.

---

should let their throats be cut like lambs, without the right to defend themselves. For can you believe the tyrants would spare us? . . . Why then not terrorize aristocracy and tyranny with all the resources of civic effort and the pure zeal, zeal which cold men can well call fanaticism and exaggeration, but which is only the natural result of a heart burning with love for the public weal? . . .

. . . If, for reasons we cannot guess, you refuse our just demands, these women you have raised to the ranks of *citoyennes* by granting that title to their husbands, these women who have sampled the promises of liberty, who have conceived the hope of placing free men in the world, and who have sworn to live free or die—such women, I say, will never consent to concede the day to slaves; they will die first. They will uphold their oath, and a dagger aimed at their breasts will deliver them from the misfortunes of slavery! They will die, regretting not life, but the uselessness of their death; regretting moreover, not having been able to drench their hands in the impure blood of the enemies of the fatherland and to avenge some of their own!

But, Gentlemen, let us cast our eyes away from these cruel extremes. Whatever the rages and plots

of aristocrats, they will not succeed in vanquishing a whole people of united brothers armed to defend their rights. We also demand only the honor of sharing their exhaustion and glorious labors and of making tyrants see that women also have blood to shed for the service of the fatherland in danger.

Gentlemen, here is what we hope to obtain from your justice and equity:

1. Permission to procure pikes, pistols, and sabres (even muskets for those who are strong enough to use them), within police regulations.

2. Permission to assemble on festival days and Sundays on the *Champ de la Fédération*, or in other suitable places, to practice maneuvers with these arms.

3. Permission to name the former French Guards to command us, always in conformity with the rules which the mayor's wisdom prescribes for good order and public calm.

From Pauline Léon, Adresse individuelle à l'Assemblée nationale, par des citoyennes de la Capitale, le 6 mars 1791 (Paris, n.d.), as quoted and translated in Darline Gay Levy, Harriet Branson Applewhite, and Mary Durham Johnson, eds., Women in Revolutionary Paris, 1789–1795 (Urbana: University of Illinois Press, 1979), pp. 72–73.

men and women. Furthermore, the pressure of war raised the possibility that the military needs of the nation could not be met if the ideal of separate spheres were honored. Once the war began, some French women did enlist in the army and served with distinction.

Initially the war effort went quite poorly. In July 1792, the duke of Brunswick, commander of the Prussian forces, issued a manifesto promising the destruction of Paris if harm came to the French royal family. This statement stiffened support for the war and increased the already significant distrust of the king.

Late in July, under radical working-class pressure, the government of Paris passed from the elected council to a committee, or *commune,* of representatives from the sections (municipal wards) of the city. On August 10, 1792, a very large Parisian crowd invaded the Tuileries palace and forced Louis XVI and Marie Antoinette to take refuge in the Legislative Assembly itself. The crowd fought with the royal Swiss guards. When Louis was finally able to call off the troops, several hundred of them and many Parisian citizens lay dead. The monarchy itself was also a casualty of that melee. Thereafter the royal family was imprisoned in comfortable quarters, but the king was allowed to perform none of his political functions. The recently established constitutional monarchy no longer had a monarch.

The Convention and the Role of the Sans-culottes

Early in September the Parisian crowd again made its will felt. During the first week of the month, in what are known as the September Massacres, the Paris Commune summarily executed or murdered about 1,200 people who were in the city jails. Many of these people were aristocrats or priests, but the majority were simply common criminals. The crowd had assumed that the prisoners were all counterrevolutionaries.

The Paris Commune then compelled the Legislative Assembly to call for the election by universal male suffrage of a new assembly to write a democratic constitution. That body, called the *Convention* after its American counterpart of 1787, met on September 21, 1792. The previous day the French army had halted the Prussian advance at the Battle of Valmy in eastern France. The victory of democratic forces at home had been confirmed by victory on the battlefield. As its first act, the Convention declared France a republic, that is, a nation governed by an elected assembly without a monarch.

GOALS OF THE *SANS-CULOTTES* The second revolution had been the work of Jacobins more radical than the Girondists and of the people of Paris known as the *sans-culottes*. The name of this group means "without breeches" and derived from the long trousers that, as working people, they wore instead of aristocratic knee breeches. The *sans-culottes* were shopkeepers, artisans, wage earners, and, in a few cases, factory workers. The persistent food shortages and the revolutionary inflation had made their difficult lives even more burdensome. The politics of the Old Regime had ignored them, and the policies of the National Constituent Assembly had left them victims of unregulated economic liberty. The government, however, required their labor and their lives if the war was to succeed. From the summer of 1792 until the summer of 1794, their attitudes, desires, and ideals were the primary factors in the internal development of the revolution.

The *sans-culottes* generally knew what they wanted. The Parisian tradespeople and artisans sought immediate relief from food shortages and rising prices through price controls. They believed that all people had a right to subsistence and profoundly resented most forms of social inequality. This attitude made them intensely hostile to the aristocracy and the original leaders of the revolution of 1789, who they believed simply wanted to share political power, social prestige, and economic security with the aristocracy. The *sans-culottes'* hatred of inequality did not take them so far as to demand the abolition of property. Rather, they advocated a community of small property owners who would also participate in the political nation.

In politics they were antimonarchical, strongly republican, and suspicious even of representative government. They believed that the people should make the decisions of government to as great an extent as possible. In Paris, where their influence was most important, the *sans-culottes* had gained their political experience in meetings of the Paris sections. Those gatherings exemplified direct community democracy and were not unlike a New England town meeting. The economic hardship of their lives made them impatient to see their demands met.

THE POLICIES OF THE JACOBINS The goals of the *sans-culottes* were not wholly compatible with those of the Jacobins. The latter were republicans who sought representative government. Jacobin hatred of the aristocracy and hereditary privilege did not extend to a general suspicion of wealth. Basically, the Jacobins favored an unregulated economy. From the time of Louis XVI's flight to Varennes onward, however, the more extreme Jacobins began to cooperate with leaders of the Parisian *sans-culottes* and the Paris Commune for the overthrow of the monarchy. Once the Convention began its deliberations, these Jacobins, known as the *Mountain* because of their seats high in the assembly hall, worked with the *sans-culottes* to carry the revolution forward and to win the war. This willingness to cooperate with the forces of the popular revolution separated the Mountain from the Girondists, who were also members of the Jacobin Club.

EXECUTION OF LOUIS XVI By the spring of 1793, several issues had brought the Mountain and its *sans-culottes* allies to domination of the Convention and the revolution. In December 1792, Louis XVI was put on trial as mere "Citizen Capet," the family name of extremely distant forebears of the royal family. The Girondists looked for some way to spare his life, but the Mountain defeated the effort. Louis was convicted, by a very narrow majority, of conspiring against the liberty of the people and the security of the state. He was condemned to death and was beheaded on January 21, 1793.

The next month the Convention declared war on Great Britain, Holland, and Spain. Soon thereafter

On August 10, 1792, the Swiss Guards of Louis XVI fought Parisians who attacked the Tuileries Palace. Several hundred troops and citizens were killed, and Louis XVI and his family were forced to take refuge with the Legislative Assembly. After this event, the monarch virtually ceased to influence events in France. [Giraudon/Art Resource, N.Y.]

A Pamphleteer Describes a Sans-culotte

This pamphlet is a 1793 description of a sans-culotte *written either by one or by a sympathizer. It describes the* sans-culotte *as a hard-working, useful, patriotic citizen who bravely sacrifices himself to the war effort. It contrasts those virtues to the lazy and unproductive luxury of the noble and the personally self-interested plottings of the politician.*

✦ *What social resentments appear in this description? How could these social resentments be used to create solidarity among the* sans-culottes *to defend the revolution? How does this document relate civic virtue to work? Do you see any relationship between the social views expressed in this document and the abolition of workers' organizations in a previous document? Where does this document suggest the* sans-culotte *may need to confront enemies of the republic?*

A *sans-culotte* you rogues? He is someone who always goes on foot, who has no millions as you would all like to have, no chateaux, no valets to serve him, and who lives simply with his wife and children, if he has any, on a fourth or fifth story.

He is useful, because he knows how to work in the field, to forge iron, to use a saw, to use a file, to roof a house, to make shoes, and to shed his last drop of blood for the safety of the Republic.

And because he works, you are sure not to meet his person in the Café de Chartres, or in the gaming houses where others conspire and game; nor at the National theatre . . . nor in the literary clubs. . . .

In the evening he goes to his section, not powdered or perfumed, or smartly booted in the hope of catching the eye of the citizenesses in the galleries, but ready to support good proposals with all his might, and to crush those which come from the abominable faction of politicians.

Finally, a *sans-culotte* always has his sabre sharp, to cut off the ears of all enemies of the Revolution; sometimes he even goes out with his pike; but at the first sound of the drum he is ready to leave for the Vendée, for the army of the Alps or for the army of the North. . . .

"Reply to an Impertinent Question: What is a Sans-culotte?" April 1793. Reprinted in Walter Markov and Albert Soboul, eds., Die Sansculotten von Paris, and republished trans. by Clive Emsley in Merryn Williams, ed., Revolutions: 1775–1830 (Baltimore: Penguin Books, in association with the Open University, 1971), pp. 100–101.

---

the Prussians renewed their offensive and drove the French out of Belgium. To make matters worse, General Dumouriez (1739–1823), the Girondist victor of Valmy, deserted to the enemy. Finally, in March 1793, a royalist revolt led by aristocratic officers and priests erupted in the Vendée in western France and roused much popular support. Thus, the revolution found itself at war with most of Europe and much of the French nation. The Girondists had led the country into the war but had proved themselves incapable either of winning it or of suppressing the enemies of the revolution at home. The

Mountain stood ready to take up the task. Every major European power was now hostile to the revolution.

Europe at War with the Revolution

Initially the rest of Europe had been ambivalent toward the revolutionary events in France. Those people who favored political reform regarded the revolution as wisely and rationally reorganizing a

Louis XVI was executed on January 21, 1793. [Giraudon/Art Resource, N.Y.]

corrupt and inefficient government. The major foreign governments thought that the revolution meant that France would cease to be an important factor in European affairs for several years.

Edmund Burke Attacks the Revolution

In 1790, however, the Irish-born writer and British statesman Edmund Burke (1729–1799) argued a different position in *Reflections on the Revolution in France*. Burke regarded the reconstruction of French administration as the application of a blind rationalism that ignored the historical realities of political development and the complexities of social relations. He also forecast further turmoil as people without political experience tried to govern France. As the revolutionaries proceeded to attack the church, the monarchy, and finally the rest of Europe, Burke's ideas came to have many admirers. His *Reflections* became the handbook of European conservatives for decades.

By the outbreak of the war with Austria in April 1792, the other European monarchies recognized the danger of both the ideas and the aggression of revolutionary France. The ideals of the Rights of Man and Citizen were highly exportable and applicable to the rest of Europe. In response, one government after another turned to repressive domestic policies.

Suppression of Reform in Britain

In Great Britain, William Pitt the Younger (1759–1806), the prime minister, who had unsuccessfully supported moderate reform of Parliament during the 1780s, turned against both reform and popular movements. The government suppressed the London Corresponding Society, founded in 1792 as a working-class reform group. In Birmingham, the government sponsored mob action to drive Joseph Priestley (1733–1804), a famous chemist and a radical political thinker, out of the country. In early

Edmund Burke (1729–1799) published Reflections on the Revolution in France *in 1790. It became the most famous of all conservative denunciations of the revolution. [National Portrait Gallery, London]*

Burke Denounces the Extreme Measures of the French Revolution

Edmund Burke was undoubtedly the most important and articulate foreign critic of the French Revolution. His first critique Reflections on the Revolution in France *appeared in 1790. He continued to attack the revolution in later years. In 1796 he published* Letters on a Regicide Peace *which opposed a peace treaty between Great Britain and revolutionary France. In that work he enumerated what he regarded as the most fundamental evils of the revolutionary government: the execution of the king, the confiscation of property of the church and nobles, and the policy of dechristianization.*

✦ *To which of the major events in the French Revolution does Burke make reference? Why by 1796 would Burke and others have attached so much importance to the religious policies of the revolution? Did Burke exaggerate the evils of the revolution? Who might have been persuaded by Burke's condemnation?*

A government of the nature of that set up at our very door has never been hitherto seen, or even imagined in Europe. . . . France, since her revolution, is under the sway of a sect, whose leaders have deliberately, at one stroke, demolished the whole body of that jurisprudence which France had pretty nearly in common with other civilized countries. . . .

Its foundation is laid in regicide, in Jacobinism, and in atheism, and it has joined to those principles a body of systematic manners, which secures their operation. . . .

I call a commonwealth *regicide*, which lays it down as a fixed law of nature, and a fundamental right of man, that all government, not being a democracy, is an usurpation. That all kings, as

1793, Pitt secured parliamentary approval for acts suspending habeas corpus and making it possible to commit treason in writing. With less success Pitt attempted to curb freedom of the press. All political groups who dared oppose the government faced being associated with revolutionary sedition.

The End of Enlightened Absolutism in Eastern Europe

In eastern Europe, the revolution brought an end to enlightened absolutism. The aristocratic resistance to the reforms of Joseph II in the Habsburg lands led his brother, Leopold II, to come to terms with the landowners. Leopold's successor, Francis II (r. 1792–1835), became a major leader of the counterrevolution. In Prussia, Frederick William II (r. 1786–1797), the nephew of Frederick the Great, looked to the leaders of the Lutheran church and the aristocracy to discourage any potential popular uprisings, such as those of the downtrodden Silesian weavers. In Russia, Catherine the Great burned the works of her one-time friend Voltaire. She also exiled Alexander Radishchev (1749–1802) to Siberia for publishing his *Journey from Saint Petersburg to Moscow*, a work critical of Russian social conditions. (See the document in Chapter 18, Alexander Radishchev Attacks Russian Censorship.)

In 1793 and 1795, the eastern powers once again combined against Poland. In that unhappy land, aristocratic reformers had finally achieved the abolition of the *liberum veto* and had organized a new constitutional monarchy in 1791. Russia and Prussia, which already had designs on Polish territory, saw or pretended to see a threat of revolution in the new Polish constitution. In 1793 they annexed large sections of the country; in 1795 Austria joined the two other powers in a final partition that removed Poland from the map of Europe until after World War I. The governments of eastern Europe had used the widely

such, are usurpers; and for being kings may and ought to be put to death, with their wives, families, and adherents. That commonwealth which acts uniformly upon those principles . . .—this I call regicide by establishment.

Jacobinism is the revolt of the enterprising talents of a country against its property. When private men form themselves into associations for the purpose of destroying the pre-existing laws and institutions of their country; when they secure to themselves an army, by dividing amongst the people of no property the estates of the ancient and lawful proprietors, when a state recognizes those acts; when it does not make confiscations for crimes, but makes crimes for confiscations; when it has its principal strength, and all its resources, in such a violation of property . . .—I call this *Jacobinism by establishment*.

I call it *atheism by establishment*, when any state, as such, shall not acknowledge the existence of God as a moral governor of the world; . . .—when it shall abolish the Christian religion by a regular decree;—when it shall persecute with a cold, unrelenting, steady cruelty, by every mode of confiscation, imprisonment, exile, and death, all its ministers; —when it shall generally shut up or pull down churches; when the few buildings which remain of this kind shall be opened only for the purpose of making a profane apotheosis of monsters, whose vices and crimes have no parallel amongst men . . . When, in the place of that religion of social benevolence, and of individual self-denial, in mockery of all religion, they institute impious, blasphemous, indecent theatric rites, in honour of their vitiated, perverted reason, and erect altars to the personification of their own corrupted and bloody republic; . . . when wearied out with incessant martyrdom, and the cries of a people hungering and thirsting for religion, they permit it, only as a tolerated evil—I call this *atheism by establishment*.

When to these establishments of regicide, of Jacobinism, and of atheism, you add the *correspondent system of manners*, no doubt can be left on the mind of a thinking man concerning their determined hostility to the human race.

The Works of the Right Honourable Edmund Burke (London: Henry G. Bohn, 1856), 5: 206–208.

shared fear of further revolutionary disorder to justify old-fashioned eighteenth-century aggression.

War with Europe

In a paradoxical fashion the very success of the revolution in France brought a rapid close to reform movements in the rest of Europe. The French invasion of the Austrian Netherlands and the revolutionary reorganization of that territory roused the rest of Europe to the point of active hostility. In November 1792, the Convention declared that it would aid all peoples who wished to cast off the burdens of aristocratic and monarchical oppression. The Convention had also proclaimed the Scheldt River in the Netherlands open to the commerce of all nations and thus had violated a treaty that Great Britain had made with Austria and Holland. The British were on the point of declaring war on France over this issue when the Convention in February 1793 issued its own declaration of hostilities.

By April 1793, when the Mountain began to direct the French government, the nation was at war with Austria, Prussia, Great Britain, Spain, Sardinia, and Holland. The governments of those nations, allied in what is known as the *First Coalition*, were attempting to protect their social structures, political systems, and economic interests against the aggression of the revolution.

The Reign of Terror

The outbreak of war in the winter and spring of 1793 brought new, radical political actions within France. The government mobilized both itself and the nation for conflict. Throughout the nation there was the sense that a new kind of war had erupted. In this war the major issue was not protection of national borders as such but rather the defense of the bold new republican political and social order that had emerged during the past four years. The French people understood that the achievements of the revolution were in danger. To protect those achievements the government took extraordinary actions that touched almost every aspect of national life.

The Republic Defended

To mobilize for war, the revolutionary government organized a collective executive in the form of pow-

erful committees. These in turn sought to organize all French national life on a wartime footing. The result was an immense military effort dedicated to both the protection and advance of revolutionary ideals. Ironically, this war effort brought the suppression of many liberties within France itself and led ultimately to a destructive search for internal enemies of the revolution.

THE COMMITTEE OF PUBLIC SAFETY   In April 1793, the Convention established a Committee of General Security and a Committee of Public Safety to perform the executive duties of the government. The latter committee became more important and eventually enjoyed almost dictatorial power. The most prominent leaders of the Committee of Public Safety were Jaques Danton (1759–1794), who had provided heroic leadership in September 1792; Maximilien Robespierre (1758–1794), who became for a time the single most powerful member of the committee; and Lazare Carnot (1753–1823), who was in charge of the military. All of these men and the other figures on the committee were strong republicans who had opposed the weak policies of the Girondists. They conceived of their task as saving the revolution from mortal enemies at home and abroad. They enjoyed a working political relationship with the *sans-culottes* of Paris, but this was an alliance of expediency on the part of the committee.

THE LEVÉE EN MASSE   The major problem for the Convention was to wage the war and at the same time to secure domestic support for the effort. In early June 1793, the Parisian *sans-culottes* invaded the Convention and successfully demanded the expulsion of the Girondist members. That action further radicalized the Convention and gave the Mountain complete control. On June 22, the Convention approved a fully democratic constitution but delayed its implementation until the conclusion of the war emergency. In point of fact, it was never implemented. On August 23, Carnot began a mobilization for victory by issuing a *levée en masse*, a military requisition on the entire population, conscripting males into the army and directing economic production to military purposes. On September 17, a ceiling on prices was established in accord with *sans-culotte* demands. During these same months the armies of the revolution also successfully crushed many of the counterrevolutionary disturbances in the provinces.

The French Convention Calls Up the Entire Nation

This proclamation of the levée en masse, *August 23, 1793, marked the first time in European history that all citizens of a nation were called to contribute to a war effort. The decree set the entire nation on a wartime footing under the centralized direction of the Committee of Public Safety.*

✦ *How did this declaration put the entire nation on a wartime footing? How does this remarkable call to patriotism and opposition to the enemies of the revolution turn extraordinary power over to the revolutionary government? How could the government believe it would receive the wartime support of the workers whose organizations it had forbidden (see the document entitled "The Revolutionary Government Forbids Worker Organizations," earlier in this chapter)?*

1. From this moment until that in which the enemy shall have been driven from the soil of the Republic, all Frenchmen are in permanent requisition for the service of the armies.

The young men shall go to battle; the married men shall forge arms and transport provisions; the women shall make tents and clothing and shall serve in the hospitals; the children shall turn old linen into lint; the aged shall betake themselves to the public places in order to arouse the courage of the warriors and preach the hatred of kings and the unity of the Republic.

2. The national buildings shall be converted into barracks, the public places into workshops for arms, the soil of the cellars shall be washed in order to extract therefrom the saltpetre.

3. The arms of the regulation calibre shall be reserved exclusively for those who shall march against the enemy; the service of the interior shall be performed with hunting pieces and side arms.

4. The saddle horses are put in requisition to complete the cavalry corps; the draught-horses, other than those employed in agriculture, shall convey the artillery and the provisions.

5. The Committee of Public Safety is charged to take all the necessary measures to set up without delay an extraordinary manufacture of arms of every sort which corresponds with the ardor and energy of the French people.

. . . .

8. The levy shall be general. . . .

Frank Maloy Anderson, ed. and trans., The Constitutions and Other Select Documents Illustrative of the History of France, 1789–1907, 2nd ed., rev. and enl. *(Minneaspolis: H. W. Wilson, 1908), pp. 184–185.*

Never before had Europe seen a nation organized in this way nor one defended by a citizen army. Other events within France astounded Europeans even more. The Reign of Terror had begun. Those months of quasi judicial executions and murders stretching from the autumn of 1793 to the mid-summer of 1794 are probably the most famous or infamous period of the revolution. They can be understood only in the context of the war on one hand and the revolutionary expectations of the Convention and the *sans-culottes* on the other.

The "Republic of Virtue"

The presence of armies closing in on the nation made it easy to dispense with legal due process. The people who sat in the Convention and composed the Committee of Public Safety, however, did not see their actions simply in terms of expediency made necessary by war. They also believed they had created something new in world history, a "republic of virtue". In this republic, civic virtue would flourish in place of aristocratic and monarchical corruption. The republic of virtue manifested itself in many ways: in the renaming of streets from the egalitarian vocabulary of the revolution; in republican dress copied from that of the *sans-culottes* or the Roman Republic; in the absence of powdered wigs; in the suppression of plays that were insufficiently republican; and in a general attack against crimes, such as prostitution, that were supposedly characteristic of aristocratic society.

THE SOCIETY OF REVOLUTIONARY REPUBLICAN WOMEN Revolutionary women established their own distinct institutions during these months. In May 1793, Pauline Léon and Claire Lacombe founded the Society of Revolutionary Republican Women. Their purpose was to fight the internal enemies of the revolution. They saw themselves as militant citizens. Initially the Jacobin leaders welcomed the organization. Its members and other women filled the galleries of the Convention to hear the debates and cheer their favorite speakers. The Society became increasingly radical, however. Its members sought stricter

Maximilien Robespierre (1758–1794) emerged as the most powerful revolutionary figure in 1793 and 1794, dominating the Committee of Public Safety. He considered the Terror essential for the success of the revolution. [Giraudon/Art Resource, N.Y.]

controls on the price of food and other commodities, worked to ferret out food hoarders, and brawled with working market women thought to be insufficiently revolutionary. The women of the Society also demanded the right to wear the revolutionary cockade usually worn only by male citizens. By October 1793, the Jacobins in the Convention had begun to fear the turmoil the Society was causing and banned all women's clubs and societies. The debates over these decrees show that the Jacobins believed the Society opposed many of their economic policies, but the deputies used the Rousseauian language of separate spheres for men and women to justify their exclusion of women from active political life.

There were other examples of repression of women in 1793. Olympe de Gouges, author of the *Declaration of the Rights of Woman*, opposed the Terror and accused certain Jacobins of corruption. She was tried and guillotined in November 1793. The same year, women were formally excluded from serving in the French army. They were also excluded from the galleries of the Convention. In a very real sense the exclusion of women from public political life was a part of the establishment of the Jacobin republic of virtue, because in such a republic men would be active citizens in the military and political sphere and women would be active in the domestic sphere.

DECHRISTIANIZATION   The most dramatic departure of the republic of virtue, and one that illustrates the imposition of political values that would justify the Terror, was an attempt by the Convention to dechristianize France. In November 1793, the Convention proclaimed a new calendar dating from the first day of the French Republic. There were twelve months of thirty days with names associated with the seasons and climate. Every tenth day, rather than every seventh, was a holiday. Many of the most important events of the next few years became known by their dates on the revolutionary calendar.[5] In November 1793, the convention decreed the Cathedral of Notre Dame to be a "Temple of Reason." The legislature then sent trusted members, known as *deputies on mission*, into the provinces to enforce dechristianization by closing churches, persecuting clergy and believers,

and occasionally forcing priests to marry. This religious policy roused much opposition and deeply separated the French provinces from the revolutionary government in Paris.

ROBESPIERRE   During the crucial months of late 1793 and early 1794, the person who emerged as the chief figure on the Committee of Public Safety was Robespierre. This complex figure has remained controversial to the present day. He was utterly selfless and from the earliest days of the revolution had favored a republic. The Jacobin Club provided his primary forum and base of power. A shrewd and sensitive politician, Robespierre had opposed the war in 1792 because he feared it might aid the monarchy. He largely depended on the support of the *sans-culottes* of Paris, but he continued to dress as he had before the revolution and opposed dechristianization as a political blunder. For him, the republic of virtue meant wholehearted support of republican government and the renunciation of selfish gains from political life. He once told the Convention:

If the mainspring of popular government in peacetime is virtue, amid revolution it is at the same time virtue and terror: virtue, without which terror is fatal; terror, without which virtue is impotent. Terror is nothing but prompt, severe, inflexible justice; it is therefore an emanation of virtue.[6]

Robespierre and those who supported his policies were among the first of a succession of secular ideologues of the left and the right who, in the name of humanity, would bring so much suffering to Europe in the following two centuries.

Progress of the Terror

The Reign of Terror manifested itself through a series of revolutionary tribunals established by the Convention during the summer of 1793. The mandate of these tribunals was to try the enemies of the republic, but the definition of *enemy* was uncertain and shifted as the months passed. It included those who might aid other European powers, those who endangered republican virtue, and finally good republicans who opposed the policies of the domi-

---

[5]From summer to spring the months on the revolutionary calendar were *Messidor, Thermidor, Fructidor, Vendémiaire, Brumaire, Frimaire, Nivose, Pluviose, Ventose, Germinal, Floreal,* and *Prairial.*

[6]Quoted in Richard T. Bienvenu, *The Ninth of Thermidor: The Fall of Robespierre* (New York: Oxford University Press, 1968), p. 38.

nant faction of the government. In a very real sense the Terror of the revolutionary tribunals systematized and channeled the popular resentment that had manifested itself in the September Massacres of 1792.

The first victims of the Terror were Marie Antoinette, other members of the royal family, and some aristocrats, who were executed in October 1793. They were followed by certain Girondist politicians who had been prominent in the Legislative Assembly. These executions took place in the same weeks that the Convention had moved against the Society of Revolutionary Republican Women, whom it had also seen as endangering Jacobin control.

By the early months of 1794, the Terror had moved to the provinces, where the deputies on mission presided over the summary execution of thousands of people who had allegedly supported inter-

nal opposition to the revolution. One of the most infamous incidents occurred in Nantes, where several hundred people were simply tied to rafts and drowned in the river. The victims of the Terror were now coming from every social class, including the *sans-culottes*.

REVOLUTIONARIES TURN AGAINST THEMSELVES   In Paris during the late winter of 1794, Robespierre began to orchestrate the Terror against republican political figures of the left and right. On March 24, he secured the execution of certain extreme *sans-culottes* leaders known as the *enragés*. They had wanted further measures regulating prices, securing social equality, and pressing dechristianization. Robespierre then turned against more conservative republicans, including Danton. They were accused of being insufficiently militant on the war, profiting

On the way to her execution in 1793, Marie Antoinette was sketched from life by Jacques-Louis David as she passed his window. [Giraudon/Art Resource, N.Y.]

The Girondists on the way to the Guillotine. The reign of terror commenced with the execution of aristocrats and members of the French royal family, but soon supporters of the revolution also became victims of the Terror. In October, 1793, a number of Girondist politicians were sentenced to death. [Archive Photos]

monetarily from the revolution, and rejecting any link between politics and moral virtue. Danton was executed during the first week in April. In this fashion, Robespierre exterminated the leadership from both groups that might have threatened his position. Finally, on June 10, he secured passage of the Law of 22 *Prairial*, which permitted the revolutionary tribunal to convict suspects without hearing substantial evidence. The number of executions was growing steadily.

FALL OF ROBESPIERRE   In May 1794, at the height of his power, Robespierre, considering the worship of "Reason" too abstract for most citizens, abolished it and established the "Cult of the Supreme Being." This deistic cult reflected Rousseau's vision of a civic religion that would induce morality among

citizens. Robespierre, however, did not long preside over his new religion.

On July 26, he made an ill-tempered speech in the Convention declaring that other leaders of the government were conspiring against himself and the revolution. Such accusations against unnamed persons had usually preceded his earlier attacks. On July 27—the Ninth of *Thermidor*—members of the Convention, by prearrangement, shouted him down when he rose to make another speech. That night Robespierre was arrested, and the next day he was executed. The revolutionary *sans-culottes* of Paris would not save him because he had deprived them of their chief leaders. The other Jacobins turned against him because after Danton's death they feared becoming the next victims. Robespierre had destroyed rivals for leadership without creating sup-

The Convention Establishes the Worship of the Supreme Being

On May 7, 1794, the Convention passed an extraordinary piece of revolutionary legislation. It established the worship of the Supreme Being as a state cult. Although the law drew on the religious ideas of deism, the point of the legislation was to provide a religious basis for the new secular French state. The reader should pay particular attention to Article 7, which outlines the political and civic values that the Cult of the Supreme Being was supposed to nurture.

✦ *How does this declaration reflect the ideas of the Enlightenment? Why has it been seen as establishing a* civil *religion? What personal and social values was this religion supposed to nurture?*

1. The French people recognize the existence of the Supreme Being and the immortality of the soul.

2. They recognize that the worship worthy of the Supreme Being is the observance of the duties of man.

3. They place in the forefront of such duties detestation of bad faith and tyranny, punishment of tyrants and traitors, succoring of unfortunates, respect of weak persons, defence of the oppressed, doing to others all the good that one can, and being just towards everyone.

4. Festivals shall be instituted to remind man of the concept of the Divinity and of the dignity of his being.

5. They shall take their names from the glorious events of our Revolution, or from the virtues most dear and most useful to man, or from the greatest benefits of nature.

· ·

7. On the days of *décade* [the name given to a particular day in each month of the revolutionary calendar] it shall celebrate the following festivals:

To the Supreme Being and to nature; to the human race; to the French people; to the benefactors of humanity; to the martyrs of liberty; to liberty and equality; to the Republic; to the liberty of the world; to the love of the Patrie [Fatherland]; to the hatred of tyrants and traitors; to truth; to justice; to modesty; to glory and immortality; to friendship; to frugality; to courage; to good faith; to heroism; to disinterestedness; to stoicism; to love; to conjugal love; to paternal love; to maternal tenderness; to filial piety; to infancy; to youth; to manhood; to old age; to misfortune; to agriculture; to industry; to our forefathers; to posterity; to happiness.

John Hall Stewart, A Documentary Survey of the French Revolution *(New York: Macmillan, 1951), pp. 526–527.*

porters for himself. In that regard, he was the selfless creator of his own destruction.

The fall of Robespierre might simply have been one more shift in the turbulent politics of the revolution. Instincts of self-preservation rather than major policy differences motivated those who brought about his demise. They had generally supported the Terror and the executions. Yet within a

short time the Reign of Terror, which ultimately claimed more than 25,000 victims, came to a close. The largest number of executions had involved peasants and *sans-culottes* who had joined rebellions against the revolutionary government. By the late summer of 1794, those provincial uprisings had been crushed, and the war against foreign enemies was also going well. Those factors, combined with

The Festival of the Supreme Being, which took place in June 1794, inaugurated Robespierre's new civic religion. Its climax occurred when a statue of Atheism was burned and another statue of Wisdom rose from the ashes. [Pierre–Antoine Demachy, "Festival of the Supreme Being at the Champ de Mars on June 8, 1794." Obligatory mention: Musee de la Ville de Paris, Musee Carnavalet, Paris, France. Giraudon/Art Resource NY.]

the feeling in Paris that the revolution had consumed enough of its own children, brought the Terror to an end.

The Thermidorian Reaction

This tempering of the revolution, called the *Thermidorian Reaction*, began in July 1794. It consisted of the destruction of the machinery of terror and the institution of a new constitutional regime. It was the result of a widespread feeling that the revolution had become too radical. In particular, it displayed a weariness of the Terror and a fear that the *sans-culottes* were exerting far too much political influence.

The End of the Terror

The influence of generally wealthy middle-class and professional people soon replaced that of the *sans-culottes*. Within days and weeks of Robespierre's execution, the Convention allowed the Girondists who had been in prison or hiding to return to their seats. There was a general amnesty for political prisoners. The Convention restructured the Committee of Public Safety and gave it much less power. The Convention also repealed the notorious Law of 22 *Prairial*. Some, though by no means all, of the people responsible for the Terror were removed from public life. Leaders of the Paris Commune and certain deputies on mission were executed. The Paris Commune itself was outlawed. The Paris Jacobin Club was closed, and Jacobin clubs in the provinces were forbidden to correspond with each other.

The executions of former terrorists marked the beginning of "the white terror." Throughout the country, people who had been involved in the Reign of Terror were attacked and often murdered. Jacobins were executed with little more due process than they had extended to their victims a few months earlier. The Convention itself approved some of these trials. In other cases, gangs of youths who had aristocratic connections or who had avoided serving in the army roamed the streets beating known Jacobins. In Lyons, Toulon, and Mar-

The closing of the Jacobin Club in November 1794 was a major event in the Thermidorean Reaction that began with the fall of Robespierre. [Roger-Viollet, © Collection Violett]

seilles, these "bands of Jesus" dragged suspected terrorists from prisons and murdered them much as alleged royalists had been murdered during the September Massacres of 1792.

The republic of virtue gave way, if not to one of vice, at least to one of frivolous pleasures. The dress of the *sans-culottes* and the Roman Republic disappeared among the middle class and the aristocracy. New plays appeared in the theaters, and prostitutes again roamed the streets of Paris. Families of victims of the Reign of Terror gave parties in which they appeared with shaved necks like the victims of the guillotine and red ribbons tied about them. Although the Convention continued to favor the Cult of the Supreme Being, it allowed Catholic services to be held. Many refractory priests returned to the country. One of the unanticipated results of the

Thermidorian Reaction was a genuine revival of Catholic worship.

The Thermidorian Reaction also saw the repeal of legislation that had been passed in 1792 making divorce more equitable for women. As this suggests, the reaction did not result in any extension of women's rights or an improvement in women's education. The Thermidorians and their successors had seen enough attempts at political and social change. They sought to return family life to its status before the outbreak of the revolution. Political authorities and the church articulated a firm determination to reestablish separate spheres for men and women and to reinforce traditional gender roles. As a result, French women may have had somewhat less freedom after 1795 than before 1789.

The French Revolution

1789
May 5	The Estates General opens at Versailles
June 17	The Third Estate declares itself the National Assembly
June 20	The National Assembly takes the Tennis Court Oath
July 14	Fall of the Bastille in the city of Paris
Late July	The Great Fear spreads in the countryside
August 4	The nobles surrender their feudal rights in a meeting of the National Constituent Assembly
August 27	Declaration of the Rights of Man and Citizen
October 5–6	Parisian women march to Versailles and force Louis XVI and his family to return to Paris

1790
July 12	Civil Constitution of the Clergy adopted
July 14	A new political constitution is accepted by the king

1791
June 14	Chapelier Law
June 20–24	Louis XVI and his family attempt to flee France and are stopped at Varennes
August 27	The Declaration of Pillnitz
October 1	The Legislative Assembly meets

1792
April 20	France declares war on Austria
August 10	The Tuileries palace is stormed, and Louis XVI takes refuge with the Legislative Assembly
September 2–7	The September Massacres
September 20	France wins the Battle of Valmy
September 21	The Convention meets, and the monarchy is abolished

1793
January 21	King Louis XVI is executed
February 1	France declares war on Great Britain
March	Counterrevolution breaks out in the Vendée
April	The Committee of Public Safety is formed
June 22	The Constitution of 1793 is adopted but not implemented
July	Robespierre enters the Committee of Public Safety
August 23	*Levée en masse* proclaimed
September 17	Maximum prices set on food and other commodities
October 16	Queen Marie Antoinette is executed
October 30	Women's societies and clubs banned
November 10	The Cult of Reason is proclaimed; the revolutionary calendar, beginning on September 22, 1792, is adopted

1794
March 24	Execution of the leaders of the *sans-culottes* known as the *enragés*
April 6	Execution of Danton
May 7	Cult of the Supreme Being proclaimed
June 8	Robespierre leads the celebration of the Festival of the Supreme Being
June 10	The Law of 22 *Prairial* is adopted
July 27	The Ninth of *Thermidor* and the fall of Robespierre
July 28	Robespierre is executed

1795
August 22	The Constitution of the Year III is adopted, establishing the Directory

Establishment of the Directory

The Thermidorian Reaction involved further political reconstruction. The fully democratic constitution of 1793, which had never gone into effect, was abandoned. The Convention issued in its place the Constitution of the Year III, which reflected the Thermidorian determination to reject both constitutional monarchy and democracy. The new document provided for a legislature of two houses. Members of the upper body, or Council of Elders, were to be men over forty years of age who were either husbands or widowers. The lower Council of Five Hundred was to consist of men of at least thirty who were either married or single. The executive body was to be a five-person Directory chosen by the Elders from a list submitted by the Council of Five Hundred. Property qualifications limited the franchise, except for soldiers, who even without property were permitted to vote.

The term *Thermidor* has come to be associated with political reaction. If the French Revolution had originated in political conflicts characteristic of the eighteenth century, however, it had by 1795 become something very different. A society and a political structure based on rank and birth had given way to one based on civic equality and social status based on property ownership. People who had never been allowed direct, formal access to political power had, to different degrees, been granted it. Their entrance in political life had given rise to questions of property distribution and economic regulations that could not again be ignored. Representation had been established as a principle of politics. Henceforth the question before France and eventually before all of Europe would be which new groups would be permitted representation. In the *levée en masse* the French had demonstrated to Europe the power of the secular ideal of nationhood.

The post-Thermidorian course of the French Revolution did not void these stunning changes in the political and social contours of Europe. What triumphed in the Constitution of the Year III was the revolution of the holders of property. For this reason the French Revolution has often been considered a victory of the bourgeoisie, or middle class. The property that won the day, however, was not industrial wealth but the wealth stemming from commerce, the professions, and from land. The largest new propertied class to emerge from the revolutionary turmoil was the peasantry, who, as a result of the destruction of aristocratic privileges, now owned their land. And unlike peasants liberated from traditional landholding in other parts of Europe during the next century, French peasants had to pay no monetary compensation.

Removal of the Sans-culottes from Political Life

The most decisively reactionary element in the Thermidorian Reaction and the new constitution was the removal of the *sans-culottes* from political life. With the war effort succeeding, the Convention severed its ties with the *sans-culottes*. True to their belief in an unregulated economy, the Thermidorians repealed the ceiling on prices. As a result, the winter of 1794–1795 brought the worst food shortages of the period. There were many food riots, which the Convention put down with force to prove that the era of the *sans-culottes journées* had come to a close. Royalist agents, who aimed to restore the monarchy, tried to take advantage of their discontent. On October 5, 1795–13 *Vendémiaire*—the sections of Paris led by the royalists rose up against the Convention. The government turned the artillery against the royalist rebels. A general named Napoleon Bonaparte (1769–1821) commanded the cannon, and with a "whiff of grapeshot" he dispersed the crowd.

By the Treaty of Basel in March 1795, the Convention concluded peace with Prussia and Spain. The legislators, however, feared a resurgence of both radical democrats and royalists in the upcoming elections for the Council of Five Hundred. Consequently, the Convention ruled that at least two-thirds of the new legislature must have been members of the older body. The Thermidorians did not even trust the property owners as voters.

The next year, the newly established Directory again faced social unrest. In Paris, Gracchus Babeuf (1760–1797) led the Conspiracy of Equals. He and his followers called for more radical democracy and for more equality of property. They declared at one point, "The aim of the French Revolution is to destroy inequality and to re-establish the general welfare. ... The Revolution is not complete, because the rich monopolize all the property and govern exclusively, while the poor toil like slaves, languish in misery, and count for nothing in the *state.*"[7] They were in a sense correct. The Directory fully intended to resist any further social changes in France that might endanger property. Babeuf was arrested, tried, and executed. This minor plot became famous many decades later when European socialists attempted to find their historical roots in the French Revolution.

The suppression of the *sans-culottes*, the narrow franchise of the constitution, the rule of the two-thirds, and the Catholic royalist revival presented the Directory with problems that it never suc-

---

[7]Quoted in John Hall Stewart, *A Documentary Survey of the French Revolution* (New York: Macmillan, 1966), pp. 656–657.

ceeded in overcoming. It lacked any broad base of meaningful political support. It particularly required active loyalty because France remained at war with Austria and Great Britain. Consequently, the Directory came to depend on the power of the army rather than on constitutional processes for governing the country. All the soldiers could vote. Moreover, within the army, created and sustained by the revolution, were officers who were eager for power and ambitious for political conquest. The results of the instability of the Directory and the growing role of the army held profound consequences not only for France but for the entire Western world.

◆

The French Revolution is the central political event of modern European history. It unleashed political and social forces that shaped events in Europe and much of the rest of the world for the next two centuries. The revolution began with a clash between the monarchy and the nobility. Once the Estates General gathered, however, discontent could not be contained within the traditional boundaries of eighteenth-century political life. The Third Estate, in all of its diversity, demanded real influence in government. Initially, that meant the participation of middle-class members of the Estates General, but quite soon the people of Paris and the peasants of the countryside made their demands known. Thereafter, popular nationalism exerted itself on French political life and the destiny of Europe.

Revolutionary legislation and popular uprisings in Paris, the countryside, and other cities transformed the social as well as the political life of the nation. Nobles surrendered traditional social privileges. The church saw its property confiscated and its operations brought under state control. For a time there was an attempt to dechristianize the nation. Vast amounts of landed property changed hands, and France became a nation of peasant landowners. Urban workers lost much of the protection they had enjoyed under the guilds and became much more subject to the forces of the marketplace.

Great violence accompanied many of the revolutionary changes. The Reign of Terror took the lives of thousands. France also found itself at war with virtually all of the rest of Europe. Resentment, fear, and a new desire for stability brought the Terror to an end. That desire for stability, com-

bined with a determination to defeat the foreign enemies of the revolution and to carry it abroad, would in turn work to the advantage of the army. Eventually Napoleon Bonaparte would claim leadership in the name of stability and national glory.

Review Questions

1. It has been said that France was a rich nation with an impoverished government. Explain this statement. How did the financial weaknesses of the French monarchy lay the foundations of the revolution of 1789?

2. Discuss the role of Louis XVI in the French Revolution. What were some of Louis XVI's most serious mistakes? Had Louis been a more able ruler, could the French Revolution have been avoided, or might a constitutional monarchy have succeeded? Or did the revolution ultimately have little to do with the competence of the monarch?

3. How was the Estates General transformed into the National Assembly? How does the Declaration of the Rights of Man and Citizen reflect the social and political values of the eighteenth-century Enlightenment? What were the chief ways in which France and its government were reorganized in the early years of the revolution? Why has the Civil Constitution of the Clergy been called the greatest blunder of the National Assembly?

4. Why were some political factions dissatisfied with the constitutional settlement of 1791? What was the revolution of 1792 and why did it occur? Who were the *sans-culottes* and how did they become a factor in the politics of the period? How influential were they during the Terror in particular? Why did the *sans-culottes* and the Jacobins cooperate at first? Why did that cooperation end?

5. Why did France go to war with Austria in 1792? What were the benefits and drawbacks for France of fighting an external war while in the midst of a domestic political revolution? What were the causes of the Terror? How did the rest of Europe react to the French Revolution and the Terror?

6. A motto of the French Revolution was "equality, liberty and fraternity." How did the revolution both support and violate this motto? Did French women benefit from the revolution? Did French peasants benefit from it?

Suggested Readings

K. M. Baker and C. Lucas (eds.), *The French Revolution and the Creation of Modern Political Culture*, 3 vols. (1987). A splendid collection of important original articles on all aspects of politics during the revolution.

K. M. Baker, *Inventing the French Revolution: Essays on French Political Culture in the Eighteenth Century* (1990). Influential essays on political thought before and during the revolution.

T. C. W. Blanning (ed.), *The Rise and Fall of the French Revolution* (1996). A wide-ranging collection of essays illustrating the recent interpretive debates.

C. Blum, *Rousseau and the Republic of Virtue: The Language of Politics in the French Revolution* (1986). An exploration of the role of Rousseau's political ideals in the debates of the French Revolution.

R. Cobb, *The Police and the People: French Popular Protest, 1789–1820* (1970). An interesting and imaginative treatment of the question of social control during the revolution.

R. Cobb, *The People's Armies* (1987). The best treatment in English of the revolutionary army.

J. Egret, *The French Pre-Revolution, 1787–88* (1978). A useful survey of the coming crisis for the monarchy.

K. Epstein, *The Genesis of German Conservatism* (1966). A major study of antiliberal forces in Germany before and during the revolution.

F. Fehér, *The French Revolution and the Birth of Modernity* (1990). A wide-ranging collection of essays on political and cultural facets of the revolution.

A. Forrest, *The French Revolution and the Poor* (1981). A study that expands consideration of the revolution beyond the standard social boundaries.

F. Furet, *Interpreting the French Revolution* (1981). A collection of controversial revisionist essays that cast doubt on the role of class conflict in the revolution.

F. Furet, *Revolutionary France, 1770–1880* (1988). An important survey by an historian who argues the revolution must be seen in the perspective of an entire century.

J. Godechot, *The Taking of the Bastille, July 14, 1789* (1970). The best modern discussion of the subject and one that places the fall of the Bastille in the context of crowd behavior in the eighteenth century.

J. Godechot, *The Counter-Revolution: Doctrine and Action, 1789–1803* (1971). An examination of opposition to the revolution.

A. Goodwin, *The Friends of Liberty: The English Democratic Movement in the Age of the French Revolution* (1979). A major work that explores the impact of the French Revolution on English radicalism.

C. Hesse, *Publishing and Cultural Politics in Revolutionary Paris* (1991). Probes the world of print culture during the French Revolution.

L. Hunt, *Politics, Culture, and Class in the French Revolution* (1986). A series of essays that focus on the modes of symbolic expression for revolutionary values and political ideals.

E. Kennedy, *A Cultural History of the French Revolution* (1989). An important examination of the role of the arts, schools, clubs, and intellectual institutions.

M. Kennedy, *The Jacobin Clubs in the French Revolution: The First Years* (1982). A careful scrutiny of the organizations chiefly responsible for the radicalizing of the revolution.

M. Kennedy, *The Jacobin Clubs in the French Revolution: The Middle Years* (1988). A continuation of the previously listed study.

G. Lefebvre, *The French Revolution*, 2 vols. (1962–1964). The leading study of the scholar noted for his subtle class interpretation of the revolution.

D. G. Levy, H. B. Applewhite, and M. D. Johnson (eds. and Trans.), *Women in Revolutionary Paris, 1789–1795* (1979). A remarkable collection of documents on the subject.

G. Lewis and C. Lucas (eds.), *Beyond the Terror: Essays in French Regional and Social History, 1794–1815* (1983). Explorations of the counter-terror that followed in the wake of the Thermidorian Reaction.

M. Lyons, *France Under the Directory* (1975). A brief survey of the post-Thermidorian governmental experiment.

T. W. Margadant, *Urban Rivalries in the French Revolution* (1992). Examines the political tensions between the central government in Paris and the cities and towns of the provinces.

S. E. Melzer and L. W. Rabine (eds.), *Rebel Daughters: Women and the French Revolution* (1992). A collection of essays exploring various aspects of the role and image of women in the French Revolution.

C. C. O'Brien, *The Great Melody: A Thematic Biography of Edmund Burke* (1992). The best recent biography.

M. Ozouf, *Festivals and the French Revolution* (1988). A pioneering study of the role of public festivals in the revolution.

R. R. Palmer, *Twelve Who Ruled: The Committee of Public Safety During the Terror* (1941). A clear narrative and analysis of the policies and problems of the committee.

R. R. Palmer, *The Age of Democratic Revolution: A Political History of Europe and America, 1760–1800*, 2 vols. (1959, 1964). An impressive survey of the political turmoil in the transatlantic world.

C. Proctor, *Women, Equality, and the French Revolution* (1990). An examination of how the ideas of the Enlightenment and the attitudes of revolutionaries affected the legal status of women.

W. J. Sewell, Jr., *A Rhetoric of Bourgeois Revolution: The Abbé Siéyès and What is the Third Estate* (1994). An important study of the political thought of Siéyès.

A. SOBOUL, *The Parisian Sans-Culottes and the French Revolution, 1793–94* (1964). The best work on the subject.

A. SOBOUL, *The French Revolution* (trans., 1975). An important work by a Marxist scholar.

B. S. STONE, *The French Parlements and the Crisis of the Old Regime* (1988). A study that considers the role of the aristocratic courts in bringing on the collapse of monarchical government.

D. G. SUTHERLAND, *France, 1789–1815: Revolution and Counterrevolution* (1986). A major synthesis based on recent scholarship in social history.

T. TACKETT, *Religion, Revolution, and Regional Culture in Eighteenth-Century France: The Ecclesiastical Oath of 1791* (1986). The most important study of this topic.

T. TACKETT, *Becoming a Revolutionary: The Deputies of the French National Assembly and the Emergence of a Revolutionary Culture (1789-1790)* (1996). The best study of the early months of the revolution.

J. M. THOMPSON, *Robespierre*, 2 vols. (1935). The best biography.

C. TILLY, *The Vendée* (1964). A significant sociological investigation.

D. K. VAN KLEY, *The Religious Origins of the French Revolution: From Calvin to the Civil Constitution, 1560–1791* (1996). Examines the manner in which debates within French Catholicism influenced the coming of the revolution.

M. WALZER (ED.), *Regicide and Revolution: Speeches at the Trial of Louis XVI* (1974). An important and exceedingly interesting collection of documents with a useful introduction.

The Napoleonic Wars spread savage destruction across Europe. The Spanish artist Francisco Goya (1794–1828) was horrified by the atrocities perpetrated by both sides during the guerrilla warfare that followed Napoleon's occupation of Spain in 1808. This painting, entitled "The Third of May" depicts French troops executing Spanish insurgents. Events such as this roused popular resistance in Spain where the British soon began to assist the insurgency. [Museo del Prado, Madrid, Spain. Scala/Art Resource, N.Y.]

The Age of Napoleon and the Triumph of Romanticism

KEY TOPICS

- Napoleon's rise, his coronation as emperor, and his administrative reforms
- Napoleon's conquests, the creation of a French Empire, and Britain's enduring resistance
- The invasion of Russia and Napoleon's decline
- The reestablishment of a European order at the Congress of Vienna
- Romanticism and the reaction to the Enlightenment

By the late 1790s, there existed a general wish for stability in France, especially among property owners, who now included the peasants. The government of the Directory was not providing this stability. The one force that was able to take charge of the nation as a symbol of both order and popular national will was the army. The most politically astute of the army generals was Napoleon Bonaparte. He had been a radical during the early revolution, a victorious general in Italy, and a supporter of the attempt to suppress revolutionary disturbances after Thermidor. Furthermore, as a general, he was a leader in the French army, the institution seen most clearly to embody the popular values of the nation and the revolution.

Once in power, Napoleon consolidated many of the achievements of the revolution. He also repudiated much of it by establishing an empire. Thereafter, his ambitions drew France into wars of conquest and liberation throughout the continent. For over a decade Europe was at war, with only brief periods of armed truce. In leading the French armies across the Continent, Napoleon spread many of the ideas and institutions of the revolution and overturned much of the old political and social order. He also provoked popular nationalism in opposition to his conquest. This new force and the great diplomatic alliances that arose against France eventually defeated Napoleon.

Throughout these Napoleonic years, new ideas and sensibilities, known by the term romanticism, *grew across Europe. Many of the ideas had originated in the eighteenth century, but they flourished in the turmoil of the French Revolution and the Napoleonic Wars. The events and values of the revolution spurred the imagination of poets, painters, and philosophers. Some romantic ideas, such as romantic nationalism, supported the revolution; others, such as the emphasis on history and religion, opposed the values of the revolution.*

The Rise of Napoleon Bonaparte

The chief danger to the Directory came from the royalists, who hoped to restore the Bourbon monarchy by legal means. Many of the *émigrés* had returned to France. Their plans for a restoration drew support from devout Catholics and from those citizens disgusted by the excesses of the revolution. Monarchy seemed to promise stability. The spring elections of 1797 replaced most incumbents with constitutional monarchists and their sympathizers, thus giving them a majority.

To preserve the republic and prevent a peaceful restoration of the Bourbons, the antimonarchist Directory staged a coup d'état on 18 *Fructidor* (September 4, 1797). They put their own supporters into the legislative seats won by their opponents. They then imposed censorship and exiled some of their enemies. At the request of the Directors, Napoleon Bonaparte, the general in charge of the Italian campaign, had sent one of his subordinates to Paris to guarantee the success of the coup. In 1797, as in 1795, the army and Bonaparte had saved the day for the government installed in the wake of the Thermidorian Reaction.

Napoleon Bonaparte was born in 1769 to a poor family of lesser nobles at Ajaccio, Corsica. Because France had annexed Corsica in 1768, he went to French schools, pursued a military career, and in 1785 obtained a commission as a French artillery officer. He strongly favored the revolution and was a fiery Jacobin. In 1793 he played a leading role in recovering the port of Toulon from the British. In reward for his service, he was appointed a brigadier general. His previous radical associations threatened his career during the Thermidorian Reaction, but his defense of the new regime on 13 *Vendémiaire* won him another promotion and a command in Italy.

Early Military Victories

By 1795 French arms and diplomacy had shattered the enemy coalition, but France's annexation of Belgium guaranteed continued fighting with Britain and Austria. The attack on Italy aimed at depriving Austria of the provinces of Lombardy and Venetia. In a series of lightning victories, Bonaparte crushed the Austrian and Sardinian armies. On his own initiative, and in many ways against the wishes of the government in Paris, he concluded the Treaty of Campo Formio in October 1797. The treaty took Austria out of the war and crowned Napoleon's campaign and independent policy with success. Before long, all of Italy and Switzerland had fallen under French domination.

In November 1797, the triumphant Bonaparte returned to Paris to be hailed as a hero and to confront France's only remaining enemy, Britain. He judged it impossible to cross the channel and invade England at that time. Instead, he chose to attack British interests through the eastern Mediterranean. He set out to capture Egypt from the Ottoman Empire. By this strategy he hoped to drive the British fleet from the Mediterranean, cut off British communications with India, damage British trade, and threaten the British Empire.

Even though Napoleon overran Egypt, the invasion was a failure. Admiral Horatio Nelson (1758–1805) destroyed the French fleet at Abukir on August 1, 1798. Cut off from France, the French army could then neither accomplish anything of importance in the Near East nor get home. To make matters worse, the situation in Europe was deteriorating. The invasion of Egypt had alarmed Russia, which had its own ambitions in the Near East. The Russians, the Austrians, and the Ottomans soon

Napoleon Bonaparte used his military successes to consolidate his political leadership as First Consul and later as Emperor of France. In this heroic portrait Jacques-Louis David portrays Napoleon as a force of nature conquering not only the armies of the enemies of France but also the Alps. On the rocks in the foreground his name follows those of Hannibal and Charlemagne, other great generals who had led armies over the Alps. [Bildarchiv Preussischer Kulturbesitz]

joined Britain to form the Second Coalition. In 1799 the Russian and Austrian armies defeated the French in Italy and Switzerland and threatened to invade France.

The Constitution of the Year VIII

Economic troubles and the dangerous international situation eroded the already fragile support of the Directory. One of the Directors, the Abbé Siéyès, proposed a new constitution. The author of the pamphlet *What Is the Third Estate?* (1789) wanted to establish a vigorous executive body independent of the whims of electoral politics, a government based on the principle of "confidence from below, power from above." The change would require another coup d'état with military support. News of France's diplomatic misfortunes had reached Napoleon in Egypt. Without orders and leaving his doomed army

behind, he returned to France in October 1799. Although some people thought that he deserved a court-martial for desertion, he received much popular acclaim. He soon joined Siéyès. On 19 Brumaire (November 10, 1799), his troops drove out the legislators and ensured the success of the coup.

Siéyès appears to have thought that Napoleon could be used and then dismissed, but if so, he badly misjudged his man. The proposed constitution divided executive authority among three consuls. Bonaparte quickly pushed it aside, as he did Siéyès, and in December 1799, he issued the Constitution of the Year VIII. Behind a screen of universal male suffrage that suggested democratic principles, a complicated system of checks and balances that appealed to republican theory, and a Council of State that evoked memories of Louis XIV, the new constitution in fact established the rule of one man—the First Consul, Bonaparte. To find an appro-

In this early-nineteenth-century cartoon, England, personified by a caricature of Williams Pitt, and France, personified by a caricature of Napoleon, are carving out their areas of interest around the globe. [Bildarchiv Preussischer Kulturbesitz]

priate historical analogy, one must go back to Caesar and Augustus and the earlier Greek tyrants. The career of Bonaparte, however, pointed forward to the dictators of the twentieth century. He was the first modern political figure to use the rhetoric of revolution and nationalism, to back it with military force, and to combine those elements into a mighty weapon of imperial expansion in the service of his own power and ambition.

The Consulate in France (1799–1804)

Establishing the Consulate, in effect, closed the revolution in France. The leading elements of the Third Estate—that is, officials, landowners, doctors, lawyers, and financiers—had achieved most of their goals by 1799. They had abolished hereditary privilege, and the careers thus opened to talent allowed them to achieve the wealth, status, and security for their property they sought. The peasants were also satisfied. They had gained the land they had always wanted and had destroyed oppressive feudal privileges as well. The newly established dominant classes were profoundly conservative. They had little or no desire to share their new privileges with the lower social orders. Bonaparte seemed just the person to give them security. When he submitted his constitution to the voters in a plebiscite, they overwhelmingly approved it.

Suppressing Foreign Enemies and Domestic Opposition

Bonaparte quickly justified the public's confidence by making peace with France's enemies. Russia had already quarreled with its allies and left the Second Coalition. A campaign in Italy brought another victory over Austria at Marengo in 1800. The Treaty of Luneville early in 1801 took Austria out of the war and confirmed the earlier settlement of Campo Formio. Britain was now alone and, in 1802, concluded the Treaty of Amiens, which brought peace to Europe.

Bonaparte also restored peace and order at home. He used generosity, flattery, and bribery to win over some of his enemies. He issued a general amnesty and employed in his own service persons from all political factions. He required only that they be loyal to him. Some of the highest offices were occupied by persons who had been extreme radicals during the Reign of Terror, others by persons who had fled the Terror and favored constitutional monarchy, and still others by former high officials of the old monarchical government.

On the other hand, Bonaparte was ruthless and efficient in suppressing opposition. He established a highly centralized administration in which prefects directly responsible to the central government in Paris managed all departments. He employed secret police. He stamped out once and for all the royalist rebellion in the west and made the rule of

Napoleon Describes Conditions Leading to the Consulate

In late 1799 various political groups in France became convinced that the constitution that had established the Directory could not allow France to achieve military victory. They also feared domestic unrest and new outbreaks of the radicalism that had characterized the French Revolution during the mid-1790s. With the aid of such groups Napoleon Bonaparte seized power in Paris in November, 1799. Thereafter, under various political arrangements he governed France until 1814. He later gave his own version of the situation that brought him to power.

◆ *What are the factors that Napoleon outlines as having created a situation in which the government of France required change? In his narration how does he justify the use of military force? How does he portray himself as a savior of political order and liberty?*

On my return to Paris I found division among all authorities, and agreement upon only one point, namely, that the Constitution was half destroyed and was unable to save liberty.

All parties came to me, confided to me their designs, disclosed their secrets, and requested my support; I refused to be the man of a party.

The Council of Elders summoned me; I answered its appeal. A plan of general restoration had been devised by men whom the nation has been accustomed to regard as defenders of liberty, equality, and property; this plan required an examination, calm, free, exempt from all influence and all fear. Accordingly, the Council of Elders resolved upon the removal of the Legislative Body to Saint-Cloud; it gave me the responsibility of disposing the force necessary for its independence. I believed it my duty to my fellow citizens, to the soldiers perishing in our armies, to the national glory acquired at the cost of their blood, to accept the command. . . .

I presented myself to the Council of Five Hundred, alone, unarmed, my head uncovered, just as the Elders had received and applauded me; I came to remind the majority of its wishes, and to assure it of its power.

The stilettos which menaced the deputies were instantly raised against their liberator; twenty assassins threw themselves upon me and aimed at my breast. The grenadiers of the Legislative Body whom I had left at the door of the hall ran forward, placed themselves between the assassins and myself. One of these brave grenadiers had his clothes pieced by a stiletto. They bore me out.

At the same moment cries of "Outlaw" were raised against the defender of the law. It was the fierce cry of assassins against the power destined to repress them.

They crowded around the president, uttering threats, arms in their hands; they commanded him to outlaw me. I was informed of this; I ordered him to be rescued from their fury, and six grenadiers of the Legislative Body secured him. Immediately afterwards some grenadiers of the Legislative Body charged into the hall and cleared it.

The factions, intimidated, dispersed and fled. . . .

Frenchmen, you will doubtless recognize in this conduct the zeal of a soldier of liberty, a citizen devoted to the Republic. Conservative, tutelary, and liberal ideas have been restored to their rights through the dispersal of the rebels who oppressed the Councils. . . .

J. H. Stuart, A Documentary Survey of the French Revolution *(New York: Macmillan, 1951),* pp. 763–765.

Paris effective in Brittany and the Vendée for the first time in many years.

Napoleon also used and invented opportunities to destroy his enemies. When a bomb plot on his life surfaced in 1804, the event provided an excuse to attack the Jacobins, though the bombing was the work of the royalists. In 1804 his forces violated the sovereignty of the German state of Baden to seize the Bourbon duke of Enghien (1772–1804). The duke was accused of participation in a royalist plot and put to death, though Bonaparte knew him to be innocent. The action was a flagrant violation of international law and of due process. Charles Maurice de Talleyrand-Périgord (1754–1838), Bonaparte's foreign minister, later termed the act "worse than a crime—a blunder," because it helped to provoke foreign opposition. On the other hand, it was popular with the former Jacobins, for it seemed to preclude the possibility of a Bourbon restoration. The executioner of a Bourbon was hardly likely to restore the royal family. The execution also seems to have put an end to royalist plots.

Concordat with the Roman Catholic Church

A major obstacle to internal peace was the steady hostility of French Catholics. Refractory clergy continued to advocate counterrevolution. The religious revival that dated from the Thermidorian Reaction increased discontent with the secular state created by the revolution. Bonaparte regarded religion as a political matter. He approved its role in preserving an orderly society but was suspicious of any such power independent of the state.

In 1801, to the shock and dismay of his anticlerical supporters, Napoleon concluded a concordat with Pope Pius VII (r. 1800–1823). The settlement gave Napoleon what he most wanted. The agreement required both the refractory clergy and those who had accepted the revolution to resign. Their replacements received their spiritual investiture from the pope, but the state named the bishops and paid their salaries and the salary of one priest in each parish. In return, the church gave up its claims on its confiscated property.

The concordat declared, "Catholicism is the religion of the great majority of French citizens." This was merely a statement of fact and fell far short of what the pope had wanted: religious dominance for the Roman Catholic Church. The clergy had to swear an oath of loyalty to the state. The Organic Articles of 1802, which were actually distinct from the concordat, established the supremacy of state over church. Similar laws were applied to the Protestant and Jewish communities as well, reducing still further the privileged position of the Catholic Church.

The Napoleonic Code

In 1802 a plebiscite ratified Napoleon as consul for life, and he soon produced another constitution that granted him what amounted to full power. He thereafter set about reforming and codifying French law. The result was the Civil Code of 1804, usually known as the *Napoleonic Code*.

The Napoleonic Code safeguarded all forms of property and tried to make French society secure against internal challenges. All the privileges based on birth that had marked the Old Regime and that had been overthrown during the revolution remained abolished. Employment of salaried officials chosen on the basis of merit replaced the purchase of offices.

The conservative attitudes toward labor and women that had emerged during the revolutionary years, however, received full support. Workers' organizations remained forbidden, and workers had fewer rights than their employers. Within families, fathers were granted extensive control over their children and husbands over their wives. At the same time, laws of primogeniture remained abolished, and property was distributed among all children, males and females. Married women could only dispose of their own property with the consent of their husbands. Divorce remained more difficult for women than for men. French law before this code had been a patchwork that differed from region to region. Within that confused set of laws, women had had opportunities to assert and protect their interests. The universality of the Napoleonic Code ended those possibilities.

Establishing a Dynasty

In 1804 Bonaparte seized on the bomb attack on his life to make himself emperor. He argued that establishing a dynasty would make the new regime secure and make further attempts on his life useless. Another new constitution was promulgated in which Napoleon Bonaparte was called Emperor of the French, instead of First Consul of the Republic. This constitution was also overwhelmingly ratified in a plebiscite.

The coronation of Napoleon, December 2, 1804, as painted by Jacques-Louis David. Having first crowned himself, the emperor is shown about to place the crown on the head of Josephine. Napoleon instructed David to paint Pope Pius VII with his hand raised in blessing. [Giraudon/Art Resource, N.Y.]

To conclude the drama, Napoleon invited the pope to Notre Dame to take part in the coronation. At the last minute, however, the pope agreed that Napoleon should place the crown on his own head. The emperor had no intention of allowing anyone to think that his power and authority depended on the approval of the church. Henceforth, he was called Napoleon I.

Napoleon's Empire (1804–1814)

Between his coronation as emperor and his final defeat at Waterloo (1815), Napoleon conquered most of Europe in a series of military campaigns that astonished the world. France's victories changed the map of Europe. The wars put an end to the Old Regime and its feudal trappings throughout western Europe and forced the eastern European states to reorganize themselves to resist Napoleon's armies.

Everywhere Napoleon's advance unleashed the powerful force of nationalism. His weapon was the militarily mobilized French nation, one of the achievements of the revolution. Napoleon could put as many as 700,000 men under arms at one time, risk as many as 100,000 troops in a single battle, endure heavy losses, and return to fight again. He could conscript citizen soldiers in unprecedented numbers, thanks to their loyalty to the nation and to their remarkable leader. No single enemy could match such resources. Even coalitions were unsuccessful until Napoleon finally overreached himself and made mistakes that led to his own defeat.

Conquering an Empire

The Peace of Amiens (1802) between France and Great Britain was merely a truce. Napoleon's unlimited ambitions shattered any hope that it might last. He sent an army to restore the rebellious colony of Haiti to French rule. This move

Admiral Viscount Horatio Nelson (1758–1805) was the greatest naval commander of his age. From the battle of Abukir in 1798 to his death at the battle of Trafalgar in 1805, he won a series of brilliant victories that gave Britain mastery of the seas. [Bettmann Newsphotos]

aroused British fears that he was planning the renewal of a French empire in America, because Spain had restored Louisiana to France in 1800. More serious were his interventions in the Dutch Republic, Italy, and Switzerland and his role in the reorganization of Germany. The Treaty of Campo Formio had required a redistribution of territories along the Rhine River, and the petty princes of the region engaged in a shameful scramble to enlarge their holdings. Among the results were the reduction of Austrian influence in Germany and the emergence of a smaller number of larger German states in the west, all dependent on Napoleon.

BRITISH NAVAL SUPREMACY   The British found these developments alarming enough to justify an ultimatum. When Napoleon ignored it, Britain declared war in May 1803. William Pitt the Younger

returned to office as prime minister in 1804 and began to construct the Third Coalition. By August 1805, he had persuaded Russia and Austria to move once more against French aggression. A great naval victory soon raised the fortunes of the allies. On October 21, 1805, the British admiral Horatio, Lord Nelson, destroyed the combined French and Spanish fleets at the Battle of Trafalgar just off the Spanish coast. Nelson died in the battle, but the British lost no ships. The victory of Trafalgar put an end to all French hope of invading Britain and guaranteed British control of the sea for the rest of the war.

NAPOLEONIC VICTORIES IN CENTRAL EUROPE   On land the story was different. Even before Trafalgar, Napoleon had marched to the Danube River to attack his continental enemies. In mid-October he forced a large Austrian army to surrender at Ulm and soon occupied Vienna. On December 2, 1805, in perhaps his greatest victory, Napoleon defeated the combined Austrian and Russian forces at Austerlitz. The Treaty of Pressburg that followed won major concessions from Austria. The Austrians withdrew from Italy and left Napoleon in control of everything north of Rome. He was recognized as king of Italy.

Napoleon also made extensive political changes in Germany. In July 1806, he organized the Confederation of the Rhine, which included most of the western German princes. The withdrawal of these princes from the Holy Roman Empire led Francis II of Austria to dissolve that ancient political body and henceforth to call himself Emperor of Austria.

Prussia, which had carefully remained neutral up to this point, was now provoked into war against France. Napoleon's forces quickly crushed the famous Prussian army at the battles of Jena and Auerstädt on October 14, 1806. Two weeks later, Napoleon was in Berlin. There, on November 21, he issued the Berlin Decrees forbidding his allies from importing British goods. On June 13, 1807, Napoleon defeated the Russians at Friedland and went on to occupy Königsberg, the capital of East Prussia. The French emperor was master of all Germany.

TREATY OF TILSIT   Unable to fight another battle and unwilling to retreat into Russia, Tsar Alexander I (r. 1801–1825) was ready to make peace. He and Napoleon met on a raft in the middle of the Niemen River while the two armies and the nervous king of Prussia watched from the bank. On

Napoleon's victory at the battle of Austerlitz is considered his most brilliant. A French army of 73,000 crushed an Austro-Russian army of 86,000 under the command of the tsar and the emperor of Austria. [Giraudon/Art Resource, N.Y.]

July 7, 1807, they signed the Treaty of Tilsit, which confirmed France's gains. Moreover, the treaty reduced the Prussian state to half its previous size, and only the support of Alexander saved it from extinction. Prussia openly and Russia secretly became allies of Napoleon in his war against Britain.

Napoleon organized conquered Europe much like the domain of a Corsican family. The great French Empire was ruled directly by the head of the clan, Napoleon. On its borders lay several satellite states carved out as the portions of the several family members. His stepson ruled Italy for him, and three of his brothers and his brother-in-law were made kings of other conquered states. Napoleon denied a kingdom only to his brother Lucien, of whose wife he disapproved. The French emperor expected his relatives to take orders without question. When they failed to do so, he rebuked and even punished them. This establishment of the Napoleonic family as the collective sovereigns of Europe was unpopular and provoked political opposition that needed only encouragement and assistance to flare up into serious resistance.

The Continental System

After the Treaty of Tilsit, such assistance could come only from Britain, and Napoleon knew that he must defeat the British before he could feel safe. Unable to compete with the British navy, he continued the economic warfare begun by the Berlin Decrees. He planned to cut off all British trade with the European continent and thus to cripple British commercial and financial power. He hoped to cause

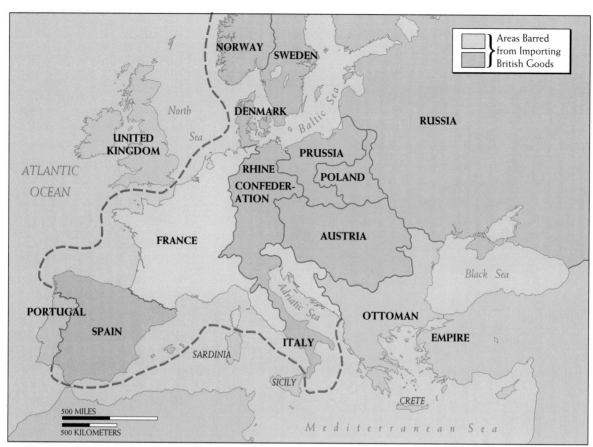

MAP 20–1   THE CONTINENTAL SYSTEM, 1806–1810   *Napoleon hoped to cut off all British trade with the European continent and thereby drive the British from the war.*

Napoleon and the Continental System

1806	Napoleon establishes the Continental System prohibiting all trade with England
1807	The peace conference at Tilsit results in Russia joining the Continental System and becoming an ally of Napoleon
1809 and 1810	Napoleon at the peak of his power
1810	Russia withdraws from the Continental System and resumes relations with Britain; Napoleon plans to crush Russia militarily
1812	Napoleon invades Russia; the Russians adopt a scorched-earth policy and burn Moscow; the thwarted Napoleon deserts his dwindling army and rushes back to Paris

domestic unrest and revolution, and thus to drive the British from the war. The Milan Decree of 1807 went further and attempted to stop neutral nations from trading with Britain.

Despite initial drops in exports and domestic unrest, the British economy survived. British control of the seas assured access to the growing markets of North and South America and of the eastern Mediterranean. At the same time, the Continental System did badly hurt the European economies. (See Map 20–1.) Napoleon rejected advice to turn his empire into a free-trade area. Such a policy would have been both popular and helpful. Instead, his tariff policies favored France, increased the resentment of foreign merchants, and made them less willing to enforce the system and more ready to engage in smuggling. It was in part to prevent smuggling that Napoleon invaded Spain in 1808. The resulting peninsular campaign in Spain and Portugal helped to bring on his ruin.

Napoleon Advises His Brother to Rule Constitutionally

As Napoleon conquered Europe, he set his relatives on the thrones of various conquered kingdoms and then imposed written constitutions on them. In this letter of November 1807, Napoleon sent his brother Jerome (1784–1860) a constitution for the Kingdom of Westphalia in Germany. The letter provides a good description of how Napoleon spread the political ideas and institutions of the French Revolution across Europe. Napoleon ignored, however, the possibility of nationalistic resentment that French conquest aroused even when that conquest brought more liberal political institutions. Such nationalism would be one of the causes of his downfall.

✦ *What are the benefits that Napoleon believes his conquest and subsequent rule by his brother will bring to their new subjects? How does he believe these rather than military victory will achieve new loyalty? How does Napoleon suggest playing off the resentment of the upper classes to consolidate power? What is the relationship between having a written constitution such as Napoleon is sending his brother and the power of public opinion that he mentions toward the close of the letter?*

I enclose the constitution for your Kingdom. You must faithfully observe it. I am concerned for the happiness of your subjects, not only as it affects your reputation, and my own, but also for its influence on the whole European situation.

Don't listen to those who say that your subjects are so accustomed to slavery that they will feel no gratitude for the benefits you give them. There is more intelligence in the Kingdom of Westphalia than they would have you believe; and your throne will never be firmly established except upon the trust and affection of the common people. What German opinion impatiently demands is that men of no rank, but of marked ability, shall have an equal claim upon your favour and your employment, and that every trace of serfdom, or of a feudal hierarchy between the sovereign and the lowest class of his subjects shall be done away with. The benefits of the Code Napoleon, public trial, and the introduction of juries, will be the leading features of your Government. And to tell you the truth, I count more upon their effects, for the extension and consolidation of your rule, than upon the most resounding victories. I want your subjects to enjoy a degree of liberty, equality, and prosperity hitherto unknown to the German people. ... Such a method of government will be a stronger barrier between you and Prussia than the Elbe, the fortresses, and the protection of France. What people will want to return under the arbitrary Prussian rule, once it has tasted the benefits of a wise and liberal administration? In Germany, as in France, Italy, and Spain, people long for equality and liberalism. I have been managing the affairs of Europe long enough now to know that the burden of the privileged classes was resented everywhere. Rule constitutionally. Even if reason, and the enlightenment of the age, were not sufficient cause, it would be good policy for one in your position; and you will find that the backing of public opinion gives you a great natural advantage over the absolute kings who are your neighbors.

J. M. Thompson, ed., Napoleon's Letters (London: Dent, 1954), pp. 190–191, as quoted in Maurice Hutt, ed., Napoleon (Englewood Cliffs, N.J.: Prentice Hall, 1972), p. 34.

European Response to the Empire

Napoleon's conquests stimulated the two most powerful political forces in nineteenth-century Europe: liberalism and nationalism. The export of his version of the French Revolution directly and indirectly spread the ideas and values of the Enlightenment and the principles of 1789. Wherever Napoleon ruled, the Napoleonic Code was imposed, and hereditary social distinctions were abolished. Feudal privileges disappeared, and the peasants were freed from serfdom and manorial dues. In the towns, the guilds and the local oligarchies that had been dominant for centuries were dissolved or deprived of their power. New freedom thus came to serfs, artisans, workers, and entrepreneurs outside the privileged circles. The established churches lost their traditional independence and were made subordinate to the state. Church monopoly of religion was replaced by general toleration.

These reforms were not undone by the fall of Napoleon. Along with the demand for representative, constitutional government, they remained the basis of later liberal reforms. It also became clear, however, that Napoleon's policies were intended first for his own glory and that of France. The Continental System demonstrated that France, rather than Europe generally, was to be enriched by Napoleon's rule. Consequently, before long the conquered states and peoples grew restive.

German Nationalism and Prussian Reform

The German response to Napoleon's success was particularly interesting and important. There had never been a unified German state. The great German writers of the Enlightenment, such as Immanuel Kant, Friedrich von Schiller, and Gotthold Lessing, were neither deeply politically engaged nor nationalistic.

At the beginning of the nineteenth century, the romantic movement had begun to take hold. One of its basic features in Germany was the emergence of nationalism. Nationalism went through two distinct stages. Initially, nationalistic writers emphasized the unique and admirable qualities of German culture, which, they argued, arose from the peculiar history of the German people. Such cultural nationalism prevailed until Napoleon's humiliation of Prussia at Jena in 1806.

At that point many German intellectuals began to urge resistance to Napoleon on the basis of German nationalism. The French conquest endangered the independence and achievements of all German-speaking people. Many nationalists were also critical of the German princes, who ruled selfishly and inefficiently and who seemed ever ready to lick the boots of Napoleon. Only a people united through its language and culture could resist the French onslaught. No less important in forging a German national sentiment was the example of France itself, which had attained greatness by enlisting the active support of the entire people in the patriotic cause. Henceforth many Germans sought to solve their internal political problems by attempting to establish a unified German state, reformed to harness the energies of the entire people.

After Tilsit, only Prussia could arouse such patriotic feelings. Elsewhere German rulers were either under Napoleon's thumb or actively collaborating with him. Defeated, humiliated, and diminished, Prussia continued to resist, however feebly. To Prussia fled German nationalists from other states, calling for reforms and unification that were, in fact, feared and hated by Frederick William III (r. 1797–1840) and the Junker nobility. Reforms came about despite such opposition because the defeat at Jena had made clear the necessity of new departures for the Prussian state.

The Prussian administrative and social reforms were the work of Baron vom Stein (1757–1831) and Count von Hardenberg (1750–1822). Neither of these reformers intended to reduce the autocratic power of the Prussian monarch or to put an end to the dominance of the Junkers, who formed the bulwark of the state and of the army officer corps. Rather, they aimed at fighting French power with their own version of the French weapons. As Hardenberg declared:

Our objective, our guiding principle, must be a revolution in the better sense, a revolution leading directly to the great goal, the elevation of humanity through the wisdom of those in authority. ... Democratic rules of conduct in a monarchical administration, such is the formula ... which will conform most comfortably with the spirit of the age.[1]

[1]Quoted in Geoffrey Brunn, *Europe and the French Imperium* (New York: Harper & Row, 1938), p. 174.

Fichte Calls for the Regeneration of Germany

Johann Gottlieb Fichte (1762–1814) began to deliver his famous Addresses to the German Nation *late in 1807 as a series of Sunday lectures in Berlin. Earlier that year Prussia had been crushed by Napoleon's armies. In this passage from Fichte's concluding lecture, presented in early 1808, he challenged the younger generation of Germans to recognize the national duty that historical circumstances had placed on their shoulders. They might either accept their defeat and the consequent slavery or revive the German nation and receive the praise and gratitude of later generations. It is important to note that Fichte saw himself speaking to all Germans as citizens of a single cultural nation rather than as the subjects of various monarchs and princes.*

✦ *What are the conditions that Fichte portrays as the consequences of inaction? What do you think he meant by viewing Germany as "the regenerator and re-creator of the world"? To what extent do you think he is hoping that Germany may exert power and influence on the European scene similar to what France had exerted since 1792?*

Review in your own minds the various conditions between which you now have to make a choice. If you continue in your dullness and helplessness, all the evils of serfdom are awaiting you; deprivations, humiliations, the scorn and arrogance of the conqueror; you will be driven and harried in every corner, because you are in the wrong and in the way everywhere; until, by the sacrifice of your nationality and your language, you have purchased for yourselves some subordinate and petty place, and until in this way you gradually die out as a people. If, on the other hand, you bestir yourselves and play the man, you will continue in a tolerable and honorable existence, and you will see growing up among and around you a generation that will be the promise for you and for the Germans of most illustrious renown. You will see in spirit the German name rising by means of this generation to be the most glorious among all peoples; you will see this nation the regenerator and re-creator of the world.

It depends on you whether you want to be the end, and to be the last of a generation unworthy of respect and certain to be despised by posterity even beyond its due—a generation of whose history . . . your descendants will read the end with gladness, saying its fate was just; or whether you want to be the beginning and the point of development for a new age glorious beyond all your conceptions, and the generation from whom posterity will reckon the year of their salvation. Reflect that you are the last in whose power this great alteration lies.

Johann Gottlieb Fichte, Addresses to the German Nation, *ed. by George Armstrong Kelly (New York: Harper Torchbooks, 1968), pp. 215–216.*

Although the reforms came from the top, they wrought important changes in Prussian society.

Stein's reforms broke the Junker monopoly of landholding. Serfdom was abolished. The power of the Prussian Junkers, however, did not permit the total end of the system in Prussia as was occurring in the western principalities of Germany. In Prussia, peasants remaining on the land were forced to continue manorial labor, although they were free to leave the land if they chose. They could obtain the ownership of the land they worked only if they forfeited a third of it to the lord. The result was that

Junker holdings grew larger. Some peasants went to the cities to find work, others became agricultural laborers, and some did actually become small free-holding farmers. In Prussia and elsewhere, serfdom had ended, but new social problems had been created as a landless labor force was enlarged by the population explosion.

Military reforms sought to increase the supply of soldiers and to improve their quality. Jena had shown that an army of free patriots commanded by officers chosen on merit rather than by birth could defeat an army of serfs and mercenaries commanded by incompetent nobles. To remedy the situation, the Prussian reformers abolished inhumane military punishments, sought to inspire patriotic feelings in the soldiers, opened the officer corps to commoners, gave promotions on the basis of merit, and organized war colleges that developed new theories of strategy and tactics.

These reforms soon enabled Prussia to regain its former power. Because Napoleon strictly limited the size of the Prussian army to 42,000 men, however, universal conscription could not be introduced until 1813. Before that date, the Prussians evaded the limit by training one group each year, putting them into the reserves, and then training a new group the same size. Prussia could thus boast an army of 270,000 by 1814.

The Wars of Liberation

SPAIN   In Spain more than elsewhere in Europe, national resistance to France had deep social roots. Spain had achieved political unity as early as the sixteenth century. The Spanish peasants were devoted to the ruling dynasty and especially to the Roman Catholic Church. France and Spain had been allies since 1796. In 1807, however, a French army came into the Iberian Peninsula to force Portugal to abandon its traditional alliance with Britain. The army stayed in Spain to protect lines of supply and communication. When a revolt broke out in Madrid in 1808, Napoleon used it as a pretext to depose the Spanish Bourbons and to place his brother Joseph (1768–1844) on the Spanish throne. Attacks on the privileges of the church increased public outrage. Many members of the upper classes were prepared to collaborate with Napoleon, but the peasants, urged on by the lower clergy and the monks, rose in a general rebellion.

In Spain, Napoleon faced a new kind of warfare. Guerilla bands cut lines of communication, killed stragglers, destroyed isolated units, and then disappeared into the mountains. The British landed an army under Sir Arthur Wellesley (1769–1852), later the duke of Wellington, to support the Spanish insurgents. Thus began the long peninsular campaign that would drain French strength from elsewhere in Europe and play a critical role in Napoleon's eventual defeat.

AUSTRIA   The French troubles in Spain encouraged the Austrians to renew the war in 1809. Since their defeat at Austerlitz, they had sought a war of revenge. The Austrians counted on Napoleon's distraction in Spain, French war weariness, and aid from other German princes. Napoleon was fully in command in France, however; and the German princes did not move. The French army marched swiftly into Austria and won the Battle of Wagram. The resulting Peace of Schönbrunn deprived Austria of much territory and three and a half million subjects.

Another spoil of victory was the Austrian archduchess Marie Louise (1791–1847), daughter of the emperor. Napoleon's wife, Josephine de Beauharnais (1763–1814), was forty-six and had borne him no children. His dynastic ambitions, as well as the desire for a marriage matching his new position as master of Europe, led him to divorce his wife and to marry the eighteen-year-old Austrian princess. Napoleon had also considered marrying the sister of Tsar Alexander but had received a polite rebuff.

The Invasion of Russia

The failure of Napoleon's marriage negotiations with Russia emphasized the shakiness of the Franco-Russian alliance concluded at Tilsit. The alliance was unpopular with Russian nobles because of the liberal politics of France and because the Continental System prohibited timber sales to Britain. Only French aid in gaining Constantinople could justify the alliance in their eyes, but Napoleon gave them no help against the Ottoman Empire. The organization of the Grand Duchy of Warsaw as a Napoleonic satellite on the Russian doorstep and its enlargement in 1809 after the Battle of Wagram angered Alexander. Napoleon's annexation of Holland in violation of the Treaty of Tilsit, his recognition of the French Marshal Bernadotte (1763–1844) as the future King Charles XIV of Sweden, and his marriage to an Austrian princess further disturbed the tsar. At the end of 1810, Russia withdrew from the Continental

When their marriage failed to produce a male heir, Napoleon divorced his first wife, Josephine de Beauharnais (1763–1814). Many considered the action one aspect of Napoleon's betrayal of the Revolution, especially because he then married a daughter of the Habsburg emperor. This portrait is by F. P. Gerard. [Chateau, Fontainebleau, France. Giraudon/Art Resource]

Napoleon's second wife, Marie Louise (1791–1847), bore him a son. It was clear that Napoleon hoped to establish a new imperial dynasty in France. This portrait is by J. B. Isabey. [Francois–Pascal–Simon Gerard (1770–1837), "Marie Louise and the King of Rome" (1811–1873) (oil on canvas), Chateau de Versailles, France. The Bridgeman Art Library]

System and began to prepare for war. (See Map 20-2.)

Napoleon was determined to end the Russian military threat. He amassed an army of more than 600,000 men, including a core of Frenchmen and more than 400,000 other soldiers drawn from the rest of his empire. He intended the usual short campaign crowned by a decisive battle, but the Russians disappointed him by retreating before his advance. His vast superiority in numbers—the Russians had only about 160,000 troops—made it foolish for them to risk a battle. Instead they followed a "scorched-earth" policy, destroying all food and supplies as they retreated. The so-called Grand Army of Napoleon could not live off the country, and the expanse of Russia made supply lines too

long to maintain. Terrible rains, fierce heat, shortages of food and water, and the courage of the Russian rear guard eroded the morale of Napoleon's army. Napoleon's advisers urged him to abandon the venture, but he feared that an unsuccessful campaign would undermine his position in the empire and in France. He pinned his faith on the Russians' unwillingness to abandon Moscow without a fight.

In September 1812, Russian public opinion forced the army to give Napoleon the battle he wanted despite the canny Russian General Kutuzov's (1745–1813) wish to avoid the fight and to let the Russian winter defeat the invader. At Borodino, not far west of Moscow, the bloodiest battle of the Napoleonic era cost the French 30,000 casualties

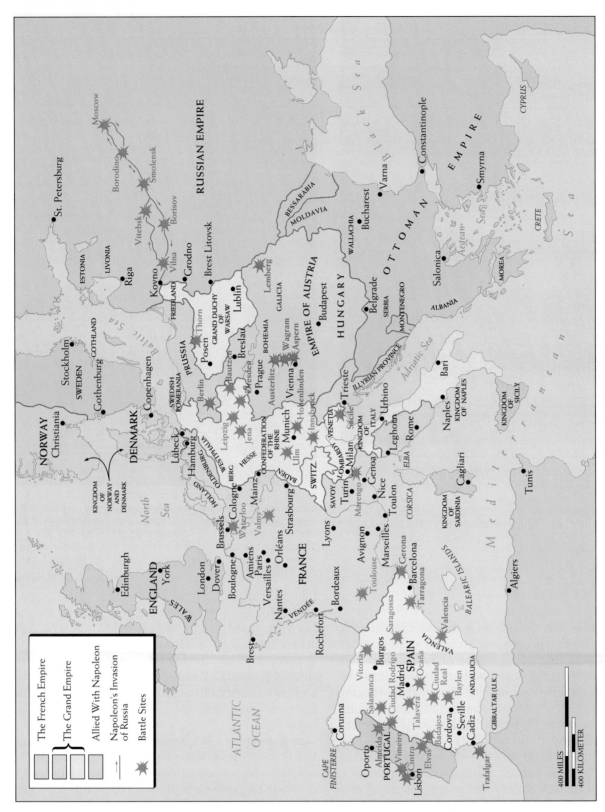

MAP 20–2 NAPOLEONIC EUROPE IN LATE 1812 *By mid-1812 the areas shown in peach were incorporated into France, and most of the rest of Europe was directly controlled by or allied with Napoleon. But Russia had withdrawn from the failing Continental System, and the decline of Napoleon was about to begin.*

and the Russians almost twice as many. Yet the Russian army was not destroyed. Napoleon won nothing substantial, and the battle was regarded as a defeat for him.

Fires, set by the Russians, soon engulfed Moscow and left Napoleon far from home with a badly diminished army lacking adequate supplies as winter came to a vast and unfriendly country. Napoleon, after capturing the burned city, addressed several peace offers to Alexander, but the tsar ignored them. By October, what was left of the Grand Army was forced to retreat. By December, Napoleon realized that the Russian fiasco would encourage plots against him at home. He returned to Paris, leaving the remnants of his army to struggle westward. Perhaps only as many as 100,000 of the original army of more than 600,000 lived to tell the tale of their terrible ordeal.

European Coalition

Even as the news of the disaster reached the West, the final defeat of Napoleon was far from certain. He was able to put down his opponents in Paris and raise another 350,000 men. Neither the Prussians nor the Austrians were eager to risk another bout with Napoleon, and even the Russians hesitated. The Austrian foreign minister, Prince Klemens von Metternich (1773–1859), would have been glad to make a negotiated peace that would leave Napoleon on the throne of a shrunken and chastened France rather than see Europe dominated by Russia. Napoleon might have won a reasonable settlement by negotiation had he been willing to make concessions that would have split his jealous opponents. He would not consider that solution, however. As he explained to Metternich:

Your sovereigns born on the throne can let themselves be beaten twenty times and return to their capitals. I cannot do this because I am an upstart soldier. My domination will not survive the day when I cease to be strong, and therefore feared.[2]

In 1813 patriotic pressure and national ambition brought together the last and most powerful coalition against Napoleon. The Russians drove westward, and Prussia and then Austria joined them. All were assisted by vast amounts of British money. From the west Wellington marched his

[2]Quoted in Felix Markham, *Napoleon and the Awakening of Europe* (New York: Macmillan, 1965), pp. 115–116.

peninsular army into France. Napoleon's new army was inexperienced and poorly equipped. His generals had lost confidence and were tired. The emperor himself was worn out and sick. Still he waged a skillful campaign in central Europe and defeated the allies at Dresden. In October, however, he was decisively defeated by the combined armies of the enemy at Leipzig in what the Germans called the Battle of the Nations. At the end of March 1814, the allied army marched into Paris. A few days later, Napoleon abdicated and went into exile on the island of Elba, off the coast of northern Italy.

The Congress of Vienna and the European Settlement

Fear of Napoleon and hostility to his ambitions had held the victorious coalition together. As soon as he was removed, the allies pursued their separate ambitions. The key person in achieving eventual agreement among them was Robert Stewart, Viscount Castlereagh (1769–1822), the British foreign secretary. Even before the victorious armies had entered Paris, he brought about the signing of the Treaty of Chaumont on March 9, 1814. It provided for the restoration of the Bourbons to the French throne and the contraction of France to its frontiers of 1792. Even more important was the agreement by Britain, Austria, Russia, and Prussia to form a Quadruple Alliance for twenty years to guarantee the peace terms and to act together to preserve whatever settlement they later agreed on. Remaining problems—and there were many—and final details were left for a conference to be held at Vienna.

Territorial Adjustments

The Congress of Vienna assembled in September 1814 but did not conclude its work until November 1815. Although a glittering array of heads of state attended the gathering, the four great powers conducted the important work of the conference. The only full session of the congress met to ratify the arrangements made by the big four. The easiest problem facing the great powers was France. All the victors agreed that no single state should be allowed to dominate Europe, and all were determined to see

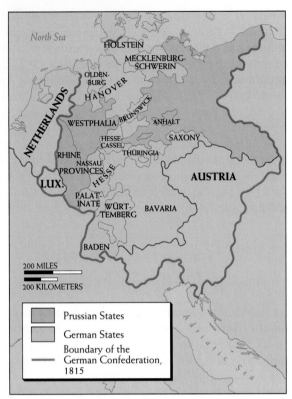

MAP 20–3   THE GERMAN STATES AFTER 1815   *As noted, the German states were also reorganized.*

that France should be prevented from doing so again. The restoration of the French Bourbon monarchy, which was temporarily popular, and a nonvindictive boundary settlement were designed to keep France calm and satisfied.

The powers also built up a series of states to serve as barriers to any new French expansion. (See Political Transformations, page 702.) They established the kingdom of the Netherlands, including Belgium, in the north and added Genoa to Piedmont in the south. Prussia, whose power was increased by accessions in eastern Europe, was given important new territories along the Rhine River to deter French aggression in the west. Austria was given full control of northern Italy to prevent a repetition of Napoleon's conquests there. As for the rest of Germany, most of Napoleon's arrangements were left untouched. The venerable Holy Roman Empire, which had been dissolved in 1806, was not revived. In all these areas, the congress established the rule of legitimate monarchs and rejected any hint of the republican and democratic politics that had flowed from the French Revolution.

On these matters agreement was not difficult, but the settlement of eastern Europe sharply divided the victors. Alexander I of Russia wanted all Poland under his rule. Prussia was willing to give it to him in return for all of Saxony. Austria, however, was unwilling to surrender its share of Poland or to see Prussian power grow or Russia penetrate deeper into central Europe. The Polish–Saxon question brought the congress to a standstill and almost caused a new war among the victors. But defeated France provided a way out. The wily Talleyrand, now representing France at Vienna, suggested that the weight of France added to that of Britain and Austria might bring Alexander to his senses. When news of a secret treaty among the three leaked out, the tsar agreed to become ruler of a smaller Poland, and Frederick William III of Prussia accepted only part of Saxony. (See Map 20–3.) Thereafter, France was included as a fifth great power in all deliberations.

The Hundred Days and the Quadruple Alliance

Unity among the victors was further restored by Napoleon's return from Elba on March 1, 1815. The French army was still loyal to the former emperor, and many of the French people thought that their fortunes might be safer under his rule than under that of the restored Bourbons. The coalition seemed to be dissolving in Vienna. Napoleon seized the opportunity, escaped to France, and was soon restored to power. He promised a liberal constitution and a peaceful foreign policy. The allies were not convinced. They declared Napoleon an outlaw (a new device under international law) and sent their armies to crush him. Wellington, with the crucial help of the Prussians under Field Marshal von Blücher (1742–1819), defeated Napoleon at Waterloo in Belgium on June 18, 1815. Napoleon again abdicated and was sent into exile on Saint Helena, a tiny Atlantic island off the coast of Africa, where he died in 1821.

The Hundred Days, as the period of Napoleon's return is called, frightened the great powers and made the peace settlement harsher for France. In addition to some minor territorial adjustments, the victors imposed a war indemnity and an army of occupation on France. Alexander proposed a Holy Alliance, whereby the monarchs promised to act together in accordance with Christian principles.

Arthur Wellesley, the duke of Wellington, first led troops against Napoleon in Spain and later defeated him at the battle of Waterloo, June 18, 1815. Unlike his great naval contemporary, Nelson, he survived to become an elder statesman of Britain. [Bildarchiv Preussischer Kulturbesitz]

Austria and Prussia signed; but Castlereagh thought it absurd and England abstained. The tsar, who was then embracing mysticism, believed his proposal a valuable tool for international relations. The Holy Alliance soon became a symbol of extreme political reaction.

The Quadruple Alliance among England, Austria, Prussia, and Russia was renewed on November 20, 1815. Henceforth, it was as much a coalition for the maintenance of peace as for the pursuit of victory over France. A coalition with such a purpose had not previously existed in European international relations. Its existence and later operation represented an important new departure in European affairs. Unlike the situation in the eighteenth century certain powers were determined to prevent the outbreak of future war. The experiences of the statesmen at Vienna were very different from those of their eighteenth century counterparts. They had seen the armies of the French Revolution change

major frontiers of the European states. They had witnessed Napoleon overturning the political and social order of much of the continent. They had seen their nations experience unprecedented military organization and destruction. They knew that war affected not a relatively few people in professional armies and navies but civilian populations and the entire social and political life of the continent. They were determined to prevent such upheavel and destruction from repeating itself.

Consequently, the chief aims of the Congress of Vienna were to prevent a recurrence of the Napoleonic nightmare and to arrange an acceptable settlement for Europe that might produce lasting peace. The leaders of Europe had learned that the previous peace treaties of the revolutionary era had failed and that the purpose of a treaty should be not to secure victory but to secure future peace. The shared purpose of the diplomats was to establish a framework for future stability not to punish a defeated France. The great powers through the Vienna Settlement framed international relations in such a manner that the major powers would respect that settlement and not as in the eighteenth century use military force to change it.

The Congress of Vienna succeeded remarkably in achieving these goals. France accepted the new situation without undue resentment in part because it was recognized as a great power in the new international order as well as the defeated enemy of the revolutionary and Napoleonic eras. The victorious powers settled difficult problems among themselves and lesser states reasonably. They established a new legal framework among states whereby treaties were made between states rather than between or among monarchs. The treaties remained in place when a monarch died. Furthermore, during the quarter century of warfare European leaders had come to calculate the nature of political and economic power in new ways that went beyond the simple vision of gaining a favorable balance of trade that had caused so many eighteenth-century wars. They took into account their natural resources, the technological structure of their economies, their systems of education, and the possibility of a general growth in agriculture, commerce, and industry whereby all states could prosper economically and not one at the expense of others.

The work of the congress has been criticized for failing to recognize and provide for the great forces that would stir the nineteenth century—nationalism

POLITICAL TRANSFORMATIONS

500 MILES

500 KILOMETERS

FINLAND
RUSSIA, 1809

St. Petersburg

Novgorod

Bergen

NORWAY AND SWEDEN
1814

Christiania

Stockholm

Pskov

Tv

Riga

RUSSIA

North

SCOTLAND

Belfast

Edinburgh

DENMARK

SCHLESWIG

Vitebsk

Smoler

EMPIR

Sea

IRELAND

Dublin

Manchester

Liverpool

HOLSTEIN

Danzig

LITHUANIA

WALES

ENGLAND

FORMER
DUTCH
REPUBLIC

FORMER
AUSTRIAN
NETHERLANDS

HANOVER

Berlin

Warsaw

KINGDOM
OF
POLAND

VOLHYNIA

Kiev

Zhitomir

London

NETHERLANDS

Cologne

Breslau

Cracow

UKRAIN

ATLANTIC

Brussels

Prague

BOHEMIA
MORAVIA

OCEAN

Rouen

BAVARIA

Brest

Reims

Munich

AUSTRIA

HUNGARY

Khers

Odessa

Rennes

Paris

Strasbourg

Vienna

Budapest

MOLDAVIA

Orléans

Nantes

FRANCE

Lyons

Berne

TYROL

Trieste

Agram

AUSTRIAN EMPIRE

TRANSYLVANIA

WALLACHIA

Bucharest

SAVOY

LOMBARDY

VENETIA

CROATIA

Bordeaux

PIEDMONT

NICE

PAR.
MOD.

Bologna

Belgrade

Oviedo

Montpellier

Marseilles

TUSCANY

STATES
OF THE
CHURCH

Sarajevo

MONTENEGRO

Sofia

OTTOMAN

Adrianopl

ANDORRA

KINGDOM
OF
SARDINIA

Rome

ITALY

Naples

Ochrida

Salonica

Constantino

PORTUGAL

SPAIN

Barcelona

Janina

Br

Lisbon

Valencia

BALEARIC ISLANDS
(SP.)

SARDINIA

KINGDOM OF
TWO SICILIES

Cosenza

Athens

Smyr

Córdoba

Seville

Mediterranean

SICILY

RHODES

CRETE

Tangier

GIBRALTAR (U.K.)

Ceuta

THE BARBARY STATES

Algiers

Tunis

Sea

MOROCCO

Fez

ALGERIA (TURK. TO 1830)

TUNISIA
(TURK.)

	Prussia		France		Russian Empire
	Sardinia		Austrian Empire		German States
——	Boundary of German Confederation				

MAP 20–4

The Congress of Vienna Redraws the Map of Europe

The Congress of Vienna redrew the map of Europe in 1815, following a period of continuous warfare that had begun in 1792. Those wars had flowed from the political turmoil of the French Revolution followed by Napoleon's attempt to dominate the Continent. And indeed, several of Napoleon's military campaigns had redrawn the ancient boundaries of Europe, replacing ruling dynasties with members of Napoleon's family on thrones in Spain and the Italian peninsula.

The goals of the statesmen who gathered at Vienna were conservative in the sense that they hoped to restore legitimate dynasties to the thrones of Europe. Their goals were novel in that they hoped to establish a system of international relations that would sustain peace rather than foster the kinds of wars that had marked eighteenth-century state relations. A permanent peace would require monarchs to believe that they had more to gain by supporting each other's governments than by attacking each other.

France was restored to its traditional borders with virtually no recognition of its various conquests since 1792. The Dutch republic and former Austrian Netherlands were united into a single state known as the Netherlands. The German Confederation replaced the now defunct Holy Roman Empire, with power in the Confederation primarily divided between Prussia and Austria. England had been determined to maintain a relatively strong Prussia as a buffer against possible future Russian aggression into Europe as well as against an overly strong Austrian Empire. Poland remained partitioned among Prussia, Austria, and Russia with the last power dominating most of the formerly independent kingdom. The Austrian Empire continued to include a vast number of nationalities. The Congress of Vienna left Italy divided among a number of small local states with Austria dominating the northeast and Piedmont the northwest. Spain and Portugal were restored to their former dynasties. The Ottoman Empire continued to govern southeastern Europe but with a very weak grip that permitted Russia, England, and France to establish spheres of influence.

The boundary decisions of the Congress of Vienna gave virtually no recognition to the principle of nationality. Yet except for the revolutions in Greece in 1821 and in Belgium in 1830 and the achievement of serbian independence in 1830, the borders established by the Congress of Vienna held until the mid-1850s. In the following passage Metternich expresses his views on the obligation of monarchs to maintain political stability, and to resist forces of political change.

The first principle to be followed by the monarchs, united as they are by the coincidence of their desires and opinions, should be that of maintaining the stability of political institutions against the disorganized excitement which has taken possession of men's minds; the immutability of principles against the madness of their interpretation; and respect for laws actually in force against a desire for their destruction.

. . . .

Let [the Governments] in these troublous times be more than usually cautious in attempting real ameliorations, not imperatively claimed by the needs of the moment, to the end that good itself may not turn against them—which is the case whenever a Government measure seems to be inspired by fear.

Let them not confound concessions made to parties with the good they ought to do for their people, in modifying, according to their recognized needs, such branches of the administration as require it.

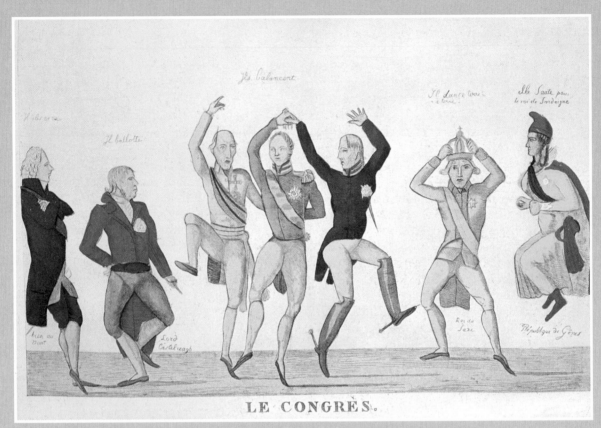

In this political cartoon of the Congress of Vienna, Tallyrand simply watches which way the wind is blowing, Castlereagh hesitates, while the monarchs of Russia, Prussia, and Austria form the dance of the Holy Alliance. The king of Saxony holds onto his crown and the republic of Geneva pays homage to the Kingdom of Sardinia. [Bildarchiv Preussischer Kulturbesitz]

. . . .

Let them give minute attention to the financial state of their kingdoms, so that their people may enjoy, by the reduction of public burdens, the real, not imaginary, benefits of a state of peace.

Let them be just, but strong; beneficent, but strict.

Let them maintain religious principles in all their purity, and not allow the faith to be attacked and morality interpreted according to the *social contracts* or visions of foolish sectarians. . . .

In short, let the great monarchs strengthen their union, and prove to the world that if it exists, it is beneficent, and ensures the political peace of Europe: that it is powerful only for the maintenance of tranquillity at a time when so many

attacks are directed against it; that the principles which they profess are paternal and protective, menacing only the disturbers of public tranquillity. . . .

To every great State determined to survive the storm there still remain many chances of salvation, and a strong union between the States on the principles we have announced will over come the storm itself.

Prince Klemons von Metternich, Memoirs of Prince Metternich, 1815–1829, *ed. Prince Richard Metternich (New York: Howard Fertig, 1970; photoreprint of a Scribner and Sons 1881 edition), vol. 3, pp. 473–476, as quoted in Brian Tierney and Joan Scott, eds.,* Western Societies: A Documentary History *(New York: Alfred A. Knopf, 1984), 2: 242.*

1797	Napoleon concludes the Treaty of Campo Formio
1798	Nelson defeats the French navy in the harbor of Abukir in Egypt
1799	Consulate established in France
1801	Concordat between France and the papacy
1802	Treaty of Amiens
1803	War renewed between France and Britain
1804	Execution of Duke of Enghien
1804	Napoleonic Civil Code issued
1804	Napoleon crowned as emperor
1805 (October 21)	Nelson defeats French fleet at Trafalgar
1805 (December 2)	Austerlitz
1806	Jena
1806	Continental System established by Berlin Decrees
1807	Friedland
1807	Treaty of Tilsit
1808	Beginning of Spanish resistance to Napoleonic domination
1809	Wagram
1809	Napoleon marries Archduchess Marie Louise of Austria
1812	Invasion of Russia and French defeat at Borodino
1813	Leipzig (Battle of the Nations)
1814	Treaty of Chaumont (March) establishes Quadruple Alliance
1814 (September)	Congress of Vienna convenes
1815 (March 1)	Napoleon returns from Elba
1815 (June 18)	Waterloo
1815 (September 26)	Holy Alliance formed at Congress of Vienna
1815 (November 20)	Quadruple Alliance renewed at Congress of Vienna
1821	Napoleon dies on Saint Helena

and democracy. Such criticism is inappropriate, however. At the time there were relatively few nationalist pressures; the general desire across the continent was for peace. The settlement, like all such agreements, was aimed at solving past ills, and in that it

succeeded. The powers would have had to have been more than human to have anticipated future problems or to have yielded to forces of which they disapproved and which they believed threatened international peace and stability. It was unusual enough, indeed virtually unprecedented, to produce an international settlement that remained essentially intact for almost half a century and that allowed Europe to suffer no general war for a hundred years.

The Romantic Movement

The years of the French Revolution and the conquests of Napoleon saw the emergence of a new and important intellectual movement throughout Europe. *Romanticism* in its various manifestations was a reaction against much of the thought of the Enlightenment. Romantic writers opposed what they considered the excessive scientific narrowness of the eighteenth-century *philosophes*. They accused the latter of subjecting everything to geometrical and mathematical models and thereby demeaning feelings and imagination. Romantic thinkers refused to conceive of human nature as primarily rational. They wanted to interpret both physical nature and human society in organic rather than mechanical terms and categories. The Enlightenment *philosophes* had often criticized religion and faith; the romantics, in contrast, saw religion as basic to human nature and faith as a means to knowledge.

Some historians, most notably Arthur O. Lovejoy, have warned against speaking of a single European-wide romantic movement. They have pointed out that a variety of such movements—occurring almost simultaneously in Germany, England, and France—arose independently and had their own particular courses of development. Such considerations have not, however, prevented the designation of a specific historical period, dated roughly from 1780 to 1830, as the *Age of Romanticism*, or the *romantic movement*.

Despite national differences, a shared reaction to the Enlightenment marked all of these writers and artists. They saw the imagination or some such intuitive intellectual faculty supplementing reason as a means of perceiving and understanding the world. Many of these writers urged a revival of Christianity, such as had permeated Europe during the Middle Ages. And unlike the *philosophes*, the romantics liked the art, literature, and architecture of medieval times. They were also deeply interested in folklore, folk songs, and fairy tales. The romantics were fascinated by dreams, hallucinations, sleepwalking, and other phenomena that suggested the existence of a world beyond that of empirical observation, sensory data, and discursive reasoning.

Romantic Questioning of the Supremacy of Reason

Several historical streams fed the romantic movement. These included the individualism of the Renaissance and the Reformation, the pietism of the seventeenth century, and the eighteenth-century English Methodist movement. The latter influence encouraged a heartfelt, practical religion in place of dogmatism, rationalism, and deism. The sentimental novels of the eighteenth century, such as Samuel Richardson's (1689–1761) *Clarissa* (1747),

also paved the way for thinkers who would emphasize feeling and emotion. The so-called *Sturm und Drang*, "storm and stress," period of German literature and German idealist philosophy were important to the romantics. Two writers who were also closely related to the Enlightenment, however, provided the immediate intellectual foundations for romanticism. They were Jean-Jacques Rousseau and Immanuel Kant, both of whom raised questions about the sufficiency of the rationalism so dear to the *philosophes*.

Rousseau and Education

It has already been pointed out in Chapter 18 that Jean-Jacques Rousseau, though sharing in the reformist spirit of the Enlightenment, opposed many of its other facets. What romantic writers especially drew from Rousseau was his conviction that society and material prosperity had corrupted

In A Philosopher in a Moonlit Churchyard, *the British artist Philip James de Loutherbourg captured many of the themes of the Romantic movement. The painting suggests a sense of history, a love of Gothic architecture, a sense of the importance of religion, and a belief that the world is essentially mysterious. [Philip James de Loutherbourg (RA) (1740–1812), "A Philosopher in a Moonlit Churchyard", signed and dated 1790. Oil on canvas, 34 x 27 in. (86.3 x 68.5 cm). B1974.3.4. Yale Center for British Art, Paul Mellon Collection.]*

human nature. In his works, Rousseau had portrayed humankind as happy and innocent by nature and originally living in a state of equilibrium, able to do what it desired and desiring only what it was able to do. To become happy again, humankind must remain true to its natural being while still attempting to realize the new moral possibilities of life in society. In his *Social Contract* (1762), Rousseau had provided his prescription for the reorganization of political life that would achieve that goal.

Rousseau set forth his view on the individual's development toward the good and happy life in his novel *Émile* (1762), discussed in Chapter 19 in regard to his views on gender. Initially this treatise on education was far more influential than the *Social Contract*. In *Émile*, Rousseau stressed the difference between children and adults. He distinguished the stages of human maturation and urged that children be raised in maximum individual freedom. Each child should be allowed to grow freely, like a plant, and to learn by trial and error what reality is and how best to deal with it. The parent or teacher would help most by providing the basic necessities of life and warding off what was manifestly harmful. Beyond that, the adult should stay completely out of the way, like a gardener who waters and weeds a garden but otherwise lets nature take its course. As noted in Chapter 19, Rousseau thought that men and women because of their physical differences would naturally grow into social roles with different spheres of activity.

Rousseau thought that the child's sentiments as well as its reason should be permitted to flourish. To romantic writers, this concept of human development vindicated the rights of nature over those of artificial society. They thought that such a form of open education would eventually lead to a natural society. In its fully developed form, this view of life led the romantics to value the uniqueness of each individual and to explore childhood in great detail. Like Rousseau, the romantics saw humankind, nature, and society as organically interrelated.

Kant and Reason

Immanuel Kant (1724–1804) wrote the two greatest philosophical works of the late eighteenth century: *The Critique of Pure Reason* (1781) and *The Critique of Practical Reason* (1788). He sought to accept the rationalism of the Enlightenment and still to preserve a belief in human freedom, immortality, and the existence of God. Against Locke and other philosophers who saw knowledge rooted in sensory experience alone, Kant argued for the subjective character of human knowledge. For Kant, the human mind did not simply reflect the world around it like a passive mirror; rather, the mind actively imposed on the world of sensory experience "forms of sensibility" and "categories of understanding." The mind itself generated these categories. In other words, the human mind perceives the world as it does because of its own internal mental categories. This meant that human perceptions were as much the product of the mind's own activity as of sensory experience.

Kant found the sphere of reality that was accessible to pure reason to be quite limited. He believed, however, that beyond the phenomenal world of sensory experience, over which "pure reason" was master, there existed what he called the "noumenal" world. This world was a sphere of moral and aesthetic reality known by "practical reason" and conscience. Kant thought that all human beings possessed an innate sense of moral duty or an awareness of what he called a *categorical imperative*. This term referred to an inner command to act in every situation as one would have all other people always act in the same situation. Kant regarded the existence of this imperative of conscience as incontrovertible proof of humankind's natural freedom. On the basis of humankind's moral sense, Kant postulated the existence of God, eternal life, and future rewards and punishments. He believed that these transcendental truths could not be proved by discursive reasoning. Still, he was convinced that they were realities to which every reasonable person could attest.

To many romantic writers, Kantian philosophy constituted a decisive refutation of the narrow rationality of the Enlightenment. Whether they called it "practical reason," "fancy," "imagination," "intuition," or simply "feeling," the romantics believed in the presence of a special power in the human mind that could penetrate beyond the limits of largely passive human understanding as set forth by Hobbes, Locke, and Hume. Most of them also believed that poets and artists possessed these powers in abundance. Other romantic writers appealed to the limits of human reason to set forth new religious ideas or political thought that was often at odds with Enlightenment writers.

Romantic Literature

The term *romantic* appeared in English and French literature as early as the seventeenth century. Neoclassical writers then used the word to describe literature that they considered unreal, sentimental, or excessively fanciful. In the eighteenth century, the English writer Thomas Warton (1728–1790) associated romantic literature with medieval romances. In Germany, a major center of the romantic literary movement, Johann Gottfried Herder (1744–1803) used the terms *romantic* and *Gothic* interchangeably. In both England and Germany, the term came to be applied to all literature that did not observe classical forms and rules and that gave free play to the imagination.

As an alternative to such dependence on the classical forms, August Wilhelm von Schlegel (1767–1845) praised the "romantic" literature of Dante, Petrarch, Boccaccio, Shakespeare, the Arthurian legends, Cervantes, and Calderón. According to Schlegel, romantic literature was to classical literature what the organic and living were to the merely mechanical. He set forth his views in *Lectures on Dramatic Art and Literature* (1809–1811).

The romantic movement had peaked in Germany and England before it became a major force in France under the leadership of Madame de Staël (1766–1817) and Victor Hugo (1802–1885). So influential was the classical tradition in France that not until 1816 did a French writer openly declare himself a romantic. That was Henri Beyle (1783–1842), who wrote under the pseudonym Stendhal. He praised Shakespeare and Lord Byron and criticized his own countryman, the seventeenth-century classical dramatist Jean Racine (1639–1699).

The English Romantic Writers

The English romantics believed that poetry was enhanced by freely following the creative impulses of the mind. In this belief, they directly opposed Lockean psychology, which regarded the mind as a passive receptor and poetry as a mechanical exercise of "wit" following prescribed rules. For William Blake and Samuel Taylor Coleridge, the artist's imagination was God at work in the mind. As Coleridge expressed his views, the imagination was "a repetition in the finite mind of the eternal act of creation in the infinite I AM." So conceived of, poetry could not be considered idle play. It was the highest of human acts, humankind's self-fulfillment in a transcendental world.

BLAKE William Blake (1757–1827) considered the poet a seer and poetry to be translated vision. He thought it a great tragedy that so many people understood the world only rationally and could perceive no innocence or beauty in it. In the 1790s, he went through a deep personal depression that seems to have been related to his own inability to perceive the world as he believed it to be. The better one got to know the world, the more the life of the imagination and its spiritual values seemed to recede. Blake saw this problem as evidence of the materialism and injustice of English society. He was deeply impressed by the strong sense of contradiction between a true childlike vision of the world and conceptions of it based on experience.

COLERIDGE Samuel Taylor Coleridge (1772–1834) was the master of Gothic poems of the supernatural, such as "Christabel," "The Ancient Mariner," and "Kubla Khan." "The Ancient Mariner" relates the story of a sailor cursed for killing an albatross. The poem treats the subject as a crime against nature and God and raises the issues of guilt, punishment, and the redemptive possibilities of humility and penance. At the end of the poem, the mariner discovers the unity and beauty of all things. Having repented, he is delivered from his awful curse, which has been symbolized by the dead albatross hung around his neck:

O happy living things! no tongue
Their beauty might declare:
A spring of love gushed from my heart,
And I blessed them unaware . . .
The self-same moment I could pray;
And from my neck so free
The Albatross fell off, and sank
Like lead into the sea.

Coleridge also made major contributions to romantic literary criticism in his lectures on Shakespeare and in *Biographia Literaria* (1817), which presents his theories of poetry.

WORDSWORTH William Wordsworth (1770–1850) was Coleridge's closest friend. Together they published *Lyrical Ballads* in 1798 as a manifesto of a new poetry that rejected the rules of eighteenth-century criticism. Among Wordsworth's most important later poems is his "Ode on Intimations of Immortality" (1803), written in part to console Coleridge, who was suffering a deep personal crisis. Its subject is the loss of poetic vision, something Wordsworth also keenly felt then in himself. Nature, which he had worshiped, no longer spoke freely to him, and he feared that it might never speak to him again:

There was a time when meadow, grove, and
  stream,
The earth, and every common sight,
To me did seem
Appareled in celestial light,
The glory and the freshness of a dream.
It is not now as it hath been of yore—
Turn whereso'er I may,
By night or day,
The things which I have seen I now can
  see no more.

He had lost what he believed that all human beings lose in the necessary process of maturation: their childlike vision and closeness to spiritual reality. For both Wordsworth and Coleridge, childhood was the bright period of creative imagination. Wordsworth held a theory of the soul's preexistence in a celestial state before its creation. The child, being closer in time to its eternal origin and undistracted by worldly experience, recollects the supernatural world much more easily. Aging and urban living corrupt and deaden the imagination, making one's inner feelings and the beauty of nature less important. In his book-length poem *The Prelude* (1850), Wordsworth presented a long autobiographical account of the growth of the poet's mind.

LORD BYRON   A true rebel among the romantic poets was Lord Byron (1788–1824). In Britain, even most of the other romantic writers distrusted and disliked him. He had little sympathy for their views of the imagination. Outside England, however, Byron was regarded as the embodiment of the new person of the French Revolution. He rejected the old traditions (he was divorced and famous for his paramours) and championed the cause of personal liberty. Byron was outrageously skeptical and mocking, even of his own beliefs. In *Childe Harold's Pilgrimage* (1812), he created a brooding, melancholy romantic hero. In *Don Juan* (1819), he wrote with

Lord Byron may well have been the most famous European poet of the first quarter of the nineteenth century. This portrait by the contemporary artist Géricault captures the poet in a brooding, introspective mood. [Bildarchiv Preussischer Kulturbesitz]

ribald humor, acknowledged nature's cruelty as well as its beauty, and even expressed admiration for urban life.

The German Romantic Writers

Much romantic poetry was also written on the Continent, but almost all major German romantics wrote at least one novel. Romantic novels often were highly sentimental and borrowed material from medieval romances. The characters of romantic novels were treated as symbols of the larger truth of life. Purely realistic description was avoided. The first German romantic novel was Ludwig Tieck's (1773–1853) *William Lovell* (1793–1795). It contrasts the young Lovell, whose life is built on love and imagination, with those who live by cold reason alone and who thus become an easy

Johann Wolfgang von Goethe (1749–1832), perhaps the greatest German writer of modern times, is portrayed here in the garb of a pilgrim against a Romantic background of classical ruins in the fields outside Rome. [Städelisches Kunstinstitut, Frankfurt/Artothek]

prey to unbelief, misanthropy, and egoism. As the novel rambles to its conclusion, Lovell is ruined by a mixture of philosophy, materialism, and skepticism, administered to him by two women whom he naïvely loves.

SCHLEGEL   Friedrich Schlegel (1767–1845) wrote a progressive early romantic novel, *Lucinde* (1799), which attacked contemporary prejudices against women as capable of being little more than lovers and domestics. Schlegel's novel reveals the ability of the romantics to become involved in the social issues of their day. He depicted Lucinde as the perfect friend and companion, as well as the unsurpassed lover, of the hero. Like other early romantic novels, the work shocked contemporary morals by frankly discussing sexual activity and by describing Lucinde as equal in all ways to the male hero.

GOETHE   Towering above all of these German writers stood the figure of Johann Wolfgang von Goethe (1749–1832). Perhaps the greatest German writer of modern times, Goethe defies any easy classification. Part of his literary production fits into the romantic mold, and part of it was a condemnation of romantic excesses. The book that made his early reputa-

tion was *The Sorrows of Young Werther*, published in 1774. This novel, like many others in the eighteenth century, is composed of a series of letters. The hero falls in love with Lotte, who was married to another man. The letters explore this relationship and display the emotional sentimentalism that was characteristic of the age. Eventually Werther and Lotte part, but in his grief over his abandoned love, Werther takes his own life. This novel became popular throughout Europe. Virtually all later romantic authors, and especially those in Germany, admired it because of its emphasis on feeling and on living outside the bounds of polite society.

Much of Goethe's early poetry was also erotic in nature. As he became older, however, Goethe became much more serious and self-consciously moral. He published many other works, including *Iphigenia at Tauris* (1787) and *Wilhelm Meister's Apprenticeship* (1792–1800) that explored how human beings come to live moral lives while still acknowledging the life of the senses.

Goethe's greatest masterpiece was *Faust*, a long dramatic work of poetry in two parts. Part I was published in 1808. It tells the story of Faust, who, weary of life, makes a pact with the Devil—he will exchange his soul for greater knowledge than other human beings possess. As the story progresses, Faust seduces a young woman named Gretchen. She dies but is received into heaven as the grief-stricken Faust realizes that he must continue to live.

In Part II, completed in the year of Goethe's death (1832), Faust is taken through a series of strange adventures involving witches and various mythological characters. This portion of the work has never been admired as much as Part I. At the conclusion, however, Faust dedicates his life, or what remains of it, to the improvement of humankind. In this dedication he feels that he has found a goal that will allow him to overcome the restless striving that first induced him to make the pact with the Devil. That new knowledge breaks the pact. Faust then dies and is received by angels.

In this great work, Goethe obviously was criticizing much of his earlier thought and that of contemporary romantic writers. He was also attempting to portray the deep spiritual problems that Europeans would encounter as the traditional moral and religious values of Christianity were abandoned. Yet Goethe himself could not reaffirm those values. In that respect, both he and his characters symbolized the spiritual struggle of the nineteenth century.

Religion in the Romantic Period

During the Middle Ages, the foundation of religion had been the church. The Reformation leaders had appealed to the authority of the Bible. Then, later Enlightenment writers had attempted to derive religion from the rational nature revealed by Newtonian physics. Romantic religious thinkers, on the other hand, appealed to the inner emotions of humankind for the foundation of religion. Their forerunners were the mystics of Western Christianity. One of the first great examples of a religion characterized by romantic impulses—Methodism—arose in England.

Methodism

Methodism originated in the middle of the eighteenth century as a revolt against deism and rationalism in the Church of England. The Methodist revival formed an important part of the background of English romanticism. The leader of the Methodist movement was John Wesley (1703–1791). His education and religious development had been carefully supervised by his remarkable mother, Susan-

John Wesley (1703–1791) was the founder of Methodism. He emphasized the role of emotional experience in Christian conversion. [The Bettmann Archive]

nah Wesley, who bore eighteen children in addition to John.

While at Oxford, Wesley organized a religious group known as the "Holy Club." He soon left England for missionary work in Georgia in America, where he arrived in 1735. While crossing the Atlantic, a group of German Moravians on the ship had deeply impressed him. These German pietists exhibited unshakable faith and confidence during a violent storm at sea, while Wesley despaired of his life. Wesley concluded that they knew far better than he the meaning of justification by faith. When he returned to England in 1738 after an unhappy missionary career, Wesley began to worship with Moravians in London. There, in 1739, he underwent a conversion experience that he described in the words, "My heart felt strangely warmed." From that point on, he felt assured of his own salvation.

Wesley discovered that he could not preach his version of Christian conversion and practical piety in Anglican Church pulpits. Therefore, late in 1739, he began to preach in the open fields near the cities and towns of western England. Thousands of humble people responded to his message of repentance and good works. Soon he and his brother Charles (1707–1788), who became famous for his hymns, began to organize Methodist societies. By the late eighteenth century, the Methodists had become a separate church. They ordained their own clergy and sent missionaries to America, where they eventually achieved their greatest success and most widespread influence.

Methodism stressed inward, heartfelt religion and the possibility of Christian perfection in this life. John Wesley described Christianity as "an inward principle . . . the image of God impressed on a created spirit, a fountain of peace and love springing up into everlasting life." True Christians were those who were "saved in this world from all sin, from all unrighteousness . . . and now in such a sense perfect as not to commit sin and . . . freed from evil thoughts and evil tempers."[3]

Many people, weary of the dry rationalism that derived from deism, found Wesley's ideal relevant to their own lives. The Methodist preachers emphasized the role of enthusiastic emotional experience as part of Christian conversion. After Wesley, reli-

Friedrich Schleiermacher (1768–1834) was the most important protestant theologian of the first half of the nineteenth century. He stressed the importance of feelings in religious experience. [Bildarchiv Preussischer Kulturbesitz]

gious revivals became highly emotional in style and content.

New Directions in Continental Religion

Similar religious developments based on feeling appeared on the Continent. After the Thermidorian Reaction, a strong Roman Catholic revival took place in France. Its followers disapproved of both the religious policy of the revolution and the anticlericalism of the Enlightenment. The most important book to express these sentiments was *The Genius of Christianity* (1802) by Viscount François René de Chateaubriand (1768–1848). In this work, which became known as the "Bible of romanticism," Chateaubriand argued that the essence of religion was "passion." The foundation of faith in the church was the emotion that its teachings and sacraments inspired in the heart of the Christian.

Against the Newtonian view of the world and of a rational God, the romantics found God immanent in nature. No one stated the romantic religious ideal more eloquently or with greater impact on the modern world than Friedrich Schleiermacher

[3]Quoted in Albert C. Outler, ed., *John Wesley: A Representative Collection of His Writings* (New York: Oxford University Press, 1964), p. 220.

Chateaubriand Describes the Appeal of a Gothic Church

Throughout most of the eighteenth century, writers had harshly criticized virtually all aspects of the Middle Ages, then considered an unenlightened time. One of the key elements of romanticism was a new appreciation of all things medieval. In this passage from The Genius of Christianity, *Chateaubriand praises the beauty of the Middle Ages and the strong religious feelings produced by stepping into a Gothic church. The description exemplifies the typically romantic emphasis on feelings as the chief foundation of religion.*

✦ *Why does the capacity of a Gothic church to carry Chateaubriand back in time add to its power of inducing a religious feeling? How does Chateaubriand unite the church with nature to emphasize its religious character? Is this vision of religion dependent upon the authority of an organized church or of sacred writings, such as the Bible?*

You could not enter a Gothic church without feeling a kind of awe and a vague sentiment of the Divinity. You were all at once carried back to those times when a fraternity of cenobites [a particular order of monks], after having meditated in the woods of their monasteries, met to prostrate themselves before the altar and to chant the praises of the Lord, amid the tranquility and the silence of the night. . . .

Everything in a Gothic church reminds you of the labyrinths of a wood; everything excites a feeling of religious awe, of mystery, and of the Divinity.

The two lofty towers erected at the entrance of the edifice overtop the elms and yew trees of the church yard, and produce the most picturesque effect on the azure of heaven. Sometimes their twin heads are illumined by the first rays of dawn; at others they appear crowned with a capital of clouds or magnified in a foggy atmosphere. The birds themselves seem to make a mistake in regard to them, and to take them for the trees of the forests; they hover over their summits, and perch upon their pinnacles. But, lo! confused noises suddenly issue from the tops of these towers and scare away the affrighted birds. The Christian architect, not content with building forests, has been desirous to retain their murmurs; and, by means of the organ and of bells, he has attached to the Gothic temple the very winds and thunders that roar in the recesses of the woods. Past ages, conjured up by these religious sounds, raise their venerable voices from the bosom of the stones, and are heard in every corner of the vast cathedral. The sanctuary reechoes like the cavern of the ancient Sibyl; loud-tongued bells swing over your head, while the vaults of death under your feet are profoundly silent.

Viscount François René de Chateaubriand, The Genius of Christianity, *trans. by C. I. White (Baltimore: J. Murphy, 1862), as quoted in Howard E. Hugo, ed.,* The Romantic Reader *(New York: Viking, 1957), pp. 341–342.*

Publication Dates of Major Romantic Works

1762	Rousseau's *Émile*
1774	Goethe's *Sorrows of Young Werther*
1781	Kant's *Critique of Pure Reason***
1788	Kant's *Critique of Practical Reason***
1789	Blake's *Songs of Innocence*
1794	Blake's *Songs of Experience*
1798	Wordsworth and Coleridge's *Lyrical Ballads*
1799	Schlegel's *Lucinde*
1799	Schleiermacher's *Speeches on Religion to Its Cultured Despisers*
1802	Chateaubriand's *Genius of Christianity*
1806	Hegel's *Phenomenology of Mind*
1808	Goethe's *Faust*, Part I
1812	Byron's *Childe Harold's Pilgrimage*
1819	Byron's *Don Juan*

*Kant's books were not themselves part of the Romantic Movement, but they were fundamental to later Romantic writers.

Romantic Views of Nationalism and History

A distinctive feature of romanticism, especially in Germany, was its glorification of both the individual person and individual cultures. Behind these views lay the philosophy of German idealism, which understood the world as the creation of subjective egos. J. G. Fichte (1762–1814), an important German philosopher and nationalist, identified the individual ego with the Absolute that underlies all existing things. According to him and similar philosophers, the world is truly the creation of humankind. The world is as it is because especially strong persons conceive of it in a particular way and impose their wills on the world and other people. Napoleon served as the contemporary example of such a great person. This philosophy has ever since served to justify the glorification of great persons and their actions in overriding all opposition to their will and desires.

Herder and Culture

In addition to this philosophy, the influence of new historical studies lay behind the German glorification of individual cultures. German romantic writers went in search of their own past in reaction to the copying of French manners in eighteenth-century Germany, the impact of the French Revolution, and the imperialism of Napoleon. An early leader in this effort was Johann Gottfried Herder (1744–1803). Herder had early resented the French cultural preponderance in Germany. In 1778 he published an influential essay entitled "On the Knowing and Feelings of the Human Soul." In it, he vigorously rejected the mechanical explanation of nature so popular with Enlightenment writers. He saw human beings and societies as developing organically, like plants, over time. Human beings were different at different times and places.

Herder revived German folk culture by urging the collection and preservation of distinctive German songs and sayings. His most important followers in this work were the Grimm brothers, Jakob (1785–1863) and Wilhelm (1786–1859), famous for their collection of fairy tales. Believing that each language and culture were the unique expression of a people, Herder opposed both the concept and the use of a "common" language, such as French, and "universal" institutions, such as those imposed on

(1768–1834). In 1799 he published *Speeches on Religion to Its Cultured Despisers*. It was a response to Lutheran orthodoxy, on the one hand, and to Enlightenment rationalism, on the other. The advocates of both were the "cultured despisers" of real, or heartfelt, religion. According to Schleiermacher, religion was neither dogma nor a system of ethics. It was an intuition or feelings of absolute dependence on an infinite reality. Religious institutions, doctrines, and moral activity expressed that primal religious feeling only in a secondary, or indirect, way.

Although Schleiermacher considered Christianity the "religion of religions," he also believed that every world religion was unique in its expression of the primal intuition of the infinite in the finite. He thus turned against the universal natural religion of the Enlightenment, which he termed "a name applied to loose, unconnected impulses," and defended the meaningfulness of the numerous world religions. Every such religion was seen to be a unique version of the emotional experience of dependence on an infinite being. In so arguing, Schleiermacher interpreted the religions of the world in the same way that other romantic writers interpreted the variety of unique peoples and cultures.

Hegel Explains the Role of Great Men in History

Hegel believed that behind the development of human history from one period to the next lay the mind and purpose of what he termed the "World-Spirit," a concept somewhat resembling the Christian God. Hegel thought particular heroes from the past (such as Caesar) and in the present (such as Napoleon) were the unconscious instruments of that Spirit. In this passage from his lectures on the philosophy of history, Hegel explained how these heroes could change the course of history. All these concepts are characteristic of the romantic belief that human beings and human history are always intimately connected with larger, spiritual forces at work in the world. The passage also reflects the widespread belief of the time that the world of civic or political action pertained to men and that of the domestic sphere belonged to women.

✦ How might the career of Napoleon have inspired this passage? What are the antidemocratic implications of this passage? In this passage, do great men make history or do historical developments make great men? Why do you think Hegel does not associate this power of shaping history with women as well as men? In that regard, note how he relates history with political developments rather than with those of the private social sphere.

Such are all great historical men—whose own particular aims involve those large issues which are the will of the World-Spirit. They may be called Heroes, inasmuch as they have derived their purposes and their vocation, not from the calm, regular course of things, sanctioned by the existing order, but from a concealed fount—one which has not attained to phenomenal, present existence—from that inner Spirit, still hidden beneath the surface, which, impinging on the outer world as on a shell, bursts it in pieces, because it is another kernel than that which belonged to the shell in question. They are men, therefore, who appear to draw the impulse of their life from themselves; and whose deeds have produced a condition of things and a complex of historical relations which appear to be only their interest, and their work.

Such individuals had no consciousness of the general Idea they were unfolding, while prosecuting those aims of theirs; on the contrary, they were practical, political men. But at the same time they were thinking men, who had an insight into the requirements of the time—what was ripe for development. This was the very Truth for their age, for their world; the species next in order, so to speak, and which was already formed in the womb of time. It was theirs to know this nascent principle; the necessary, directly sequent step in progress, which their world was to take; to make this their aim, and to expend their energy in promoting it. World-historical men—the Heroes of an epoch—must, therefore, be recognized as its clear-sighted ones; their deeds, their words are the best of that time.

G. W. F. Hegel, The Philosophy of History, trans. by J. Sibree (New York: Dover, 1956), pp. 30–31.

The philsopher J. G. Fichte (1762–1814), shown here in the uniform of a Berlin home guard. Fichte glorified the role of the great individual in history. [Bildarchiv Preussischer Kulturbesitz]

Europe by Napoleon. These, he believed, were forms of tyranny over the individuality of a people. Herder's writings led to a broad revival of interest in history and philosophy. Although initially directed toward the identification of German origins, such work soon expanded to embrace other world cultures as well. Eventually the ability of the romantic imagination to be at home in any age or culture spurred the study of non-Western religion, comparative literature, and philology.

Hegel and History

The most important philosopher of history in the Romantic Period was the German, Georg Wilhelm Friedrich Hegel (1770–1831). He is one of the most difficult and significant philosophers in the history of Western civilization.

Hegel believed that ideas develop in an evolutionary fashion that involves conflict. At any given time, a predominant set of ideas, which he termed the *thesis*, holds sway. The thesis is challenged by other conflicting ideas, which Hegel termed the *antithesis*. As these patterns of thought clash, a *synthesis* emerges that eventually becomes the new thesis. Then the process begins all over again. Periods of world history receive their character from the patterns of thought predominating during them.

Several important philosophical conclusions followed from this analysis. One of the most significant was the belief that all periods of history have been of almost equal value because each was, by definition, necessary to the achievements of those that came later. Also, all cultures are valuable because each contributes to the necessary clash of values and ideas that allows humankind to develop. Hegel discussed these concepts in *The Phenomenology of Mind* (1806), *Lectures on the Philosophy of History* (1822–1831), and other works, many of which were published only after his death. During his lifetime, his ideas became widely known through his university lectures at Berlin.

◆

These various romantic ideas made a major contribution to the emergence of nationalism, which proved to be one of the strongest motivating forces of the nineteenth and twentieth centuries. The writers of the Enlightenment had generally championed a cosmopolitan outlook on the world. The romantic thinkers, however, emphasized the individuality and worth of each separate people and culture. A people or a nation was defined by a common language, a common history, a homeland that possessed historical associations, and common customs. This cultural nationalism gradually became transformed into a political creed. It came to be widely believed that every people, ethnic group, or nation should constitute a separate political entity, and that only when it so existed could the nation be secure in its own character.

The example of France under the revolutionary government and then Napoleon had demonstrated

This colored lithograph of G. W. F. Hegel shows him attired in the robes of a university professor. Hegel was the most important philosopher of history in the Romantic period. [Bildarchiv Preussischer Kulturbesitz]

the power of nationhood. Other peoples came to desire similar strength and confidence. Napoleon's toppling of ancient political structures, such as the Holy Roman Empire, proved the need for new political organization in Europe. By 1815 these were the aspirations of only a few Europeans, but as time passed, such yearnings came to be shared by scores of peoples from Ireland to Ukraine. The Congress of Vienna could ignore such feelings, but for the rest of the nineteenth century, as will be seen in subsequent chapters, statesmen had to confront the growing reality of the power these feelings unleashed.

Review Questions

1. How did Napoleon rise to power? What groups supported him? What were the stages by which he eventually made himself emperor? What were his major domestic achievements? Did his rule more nearly fulfill or betray the ideals of the French Revolution?

2. What regions made up Napoleon's realm and what status did each region have within it? How did Napoleon rule his empire? Did his administration show foresight or did the empire ultimately become a burden he could not afford?

3. Why did Napoleon decide to invade Russia? Why did the operation fail? Can Napoleon be considered a "military genius"? Why or why not? To what extent was his brilliance dependent on the ineptitude of his enemies?
4. Who were the principal personalities and what were the most significant problems of the Congress of Vienna? What were the results of the Congress and why were they significant?
5. Compare the role of feelings for romantic writers with the role of reason for Enlightenment writers. What questions did Rousseau and Kant raise about reason?
6. Why did poetry become important to romantic writers? How did the romantic concept of religion differ from Reformation Protestantism and Enlightenment deism? How did romantic writers use the idea of history?

Suggested Readings

M. H. ABRAMS, *The Mirror and the Lamp: Romantic Theory and the Critical Tradition* (1958). A standard text on romantic literary theory that looks at English romanticism in the context of German romantic idealism.

M. H. ABRAMS, *Natural Supernaturalism: Tradition and Revolution in Romantic Literature* (1971). A brilliant survey of romanticism across western European literature.

J. S. ALLEN, *Popular French Romanticism: Authors, Readers, and Books in the Nineteenth Century* (1981). Relates romanticism to popular culture.

F. C. BEISER, *Enlightenment, Revolution, and Romanticism: The Genesis of Modern German Political Thought, 1790–1800* (1992). The best recent study of the subject.

L. BERGERON, *France Under Napoleon* (1981). An in-depth examination of Napoleonic administration.

J. F. BERNARD, *Talleyrand: A Biography* (1973). A useful account.

E. CASSIRER, *Kant's Life and Thought* (1981). A brilliant work by one of the major philosophers of this century.

D. G. CHANDLER, *The Campaigns of Napoleon* (1966). A good military study.

D. G. CHARLTON, *New Images of the Natural in France* (1984). An examination of the changing attitude toward nature in France during the romantic era.

K. CLARK, *The Romantic Rebellion* (1973). A useful discussion that combines both art and literature.

O. CONNELLY, *Napoleon's Satellite Kingdoms* (1965). The rule of Napoleon and his family in Europe.

A. D. CULLER, *The Victorian Mirror of History* (1985). Studies in the writing of the nineteenth century with emphasis on romantic influences.

J. ENGELL, *The Creative Imagination: Enlightenment to Romanticism* (1981). An important book on the role of the imagination in romantic literary theory.

M. GLOVER, *The Peninsular War, 1807–1814: A Concise Military History* (1974). An interesting account of the military campaign that so drained Napoleon's resources in western Europe.

F. W. J. HEMMINGS, *Culture and Society in France: 1789–1848* (1987). Discusses French romantic literature, theater, and art.

H. HONOUR, *Romanticism* (1979). The best introduction to the subject in terms of the fine arts.

G. N. IZENBERG, *Impossible Individuality: Romanticism, Revolution, and the Origins of Modern Selfhood, 1787–1802* (1992). Explores the concepts of individualism in Germany, England, and France.

H. KISSINGER, *A World Restored: Metternich, Castlereagh and the Problems of Peace, 1812–1822* (1957). A provocative study by an author who became an American Secretary of State.

S. KÖRNER, *Kant* (1955). A clear introduction to a difficult thinker.

M. LEBRIS, *Romantics and Romanticism* (1981). A lavishly illustrated work that relates politics and romantic art.

G. LEFEBVRE, *Napoleon*, 2 vols., trans. by H. Stockhold (1969). The fullest and finest biography.

F. MARKHAM, *Napoleon and the Awakening of Europe* (1954). Emphasizes the growth of nationalism.

H. NICOLSON, *The Congress of Vienna* (1946). A good, readable account.

Z. A. PELCZYNSKI, *The State and Civil Society: Studies in Hegel's Political Philosophy* (1984). An important series of essays.

R. PLANT, *Hegel: An Introduction* (1983). Emphasis on his political thought.

R. PORTER AND M. TEICH (EDS.), *Romanticism in National Context* (1988). Essays on the phenomenon of romanticism in the major European nations.

B. M. G. REARDON, *Religion in the Age of Romanticism: Studies in Early Nineteenth-Century Thought* (1985). The best introduction to this important subject.

P. W. SCHROEDER, *The Transformation of European Politics, 1763–1848* (1994). A major synthesis of the diplomatic history of the period emphasizing the new departures of the Congress of Vienna.

S. B. SMITH, *Hegel's Critique of Liberalism: Rights in Context* (1989). An excellent introduction to Hegelian political thought.

C. TAYLOR, *Hegel* (1975). The best one-volume introduction.

J. M. THOMPSON, *Napoleon Bonaparte: His Rise and Fall* (1952). A sound biography.

A. WALICKI, *Philosophy and Romantic Nationalism: The*

Case of Poland (1982). Examines how philosophy influenced the character of Polish nationalism.

W. R. WARD, *The Protestant Evangelical Awakening* (1992). Examines the religious revivals of the eighteenth and nineteenth century from a transatlantic perspective.

B. YACK, *The Longing for Total Revolution: Philosophic Sources of Social Discontent from Rousseau to Marx and Nietzsche* (1986). A major exploration of the political philosophy associated with romanticism.

T. ZIOLKOWSKI, *German Romanticism and Its Institutions* (1990). An exploration of how institutions of intellectual life influenced creative literature.

INDEX

The alphabetical arrangement is letter-by-letter. Page numbers in italic refer to illustrations.

Asquith, Henry, 855
Asquith, Herbert, 862, 981
Assembly, in Roman Republic, 118
Assembly of Notables, 642–43
Assignats, 656
Assyria/Assyrians, 3, 8, 25, 27, 168
Aston, Louise, 770
Astrology, 15
Astronomy, Hellenistic, 108–9
Atahualpa, 359
Ataraxia, 105
Athanasius, 190, 218
Athena, 58
Athenian Constitution (Aristotle), 54–55
Athens. *See* Ancient Greece
Atlantic Charter, 1065
Atomic bomb, 1058, 1072
Atomists, 89
Aton, 2, 24
Attalus, King, 135
Attic tragedy, 87
Attila the Hun, 203, 204
Attlee, Clement, 1066, 1106, 1129
Auburn system, 774
Auclert, Hubertine, 856
Audiencias, 583
Auerstädt, Battle of, 690
Augsburg
    Diet of, 387
    League of, 474
    Peace of, 306, 378, 387–89, 415, 438, 439, 440
        Ecclesiastical Reservation of, 440–41
Augsburg Confession, 306, 387
Augustan Age. *See* Roman Empire
Augustine, Saint, 5, 192, 198, 217
Augustinus (Jansen), 469
Augustus (Octavian), 5, 156–62
Aurelius, Marcus, 164, 172, 179
Ausculta fili, 323
Ausgleich of 1876, 819

Austerlitz, Battle of, 607, 690
Australia, 580
Austrasia, 223
Austria, 426, 445, 552. *See also* World War I
    aristocracy, 548
    Austro-Prussian War, 810
    Habsburgs and, 529–31
    Hitler's annexation of, 1038
    Italy and, 806
    Napoleonic wars, 696
    post-WWI, 987
    revolution of 1848 in, 787–88
    War of Austrian Succession, 591–92
Austria-Hungary
    Congress of Berlin and, 922
    Dual Alliance and, 923
Austrian Succession, War of, 307, 591–92
Austro-Hungarian Empire, end of, 949
Austro-Prussian War, 810
Avars, 225
Averröes, 216
Avicenna, 216
Avignon papacy, 306, 323–28
Ayacucho, Battle of, 740
Azerbaijan, 1153
Azov, 541
Aztec civilization, 306, 359, 398

B

Babeuf, Gracchus, 678
Babington, Anthony, 438
Babington plot, 438
Babylon, 12, 26, 101
Babylonia, 63
Babylonian Captivity of the Church (Luther), 377
Babylonian dynasty, 2, 13–14
Bacchus, 126
Bacon, Francis, 307, 499–501

Bactrians, 103
Badoglio, Pietro, 1052
Bagehot, Walter, 815
Baghdad, 213
Bakewell, Robert, 563
Baldwin, 251
Baldwin, Stanley, 981, 983
Balearic Islands, 121
Balfour Declaration, 947, 1081
Balkans
    Congress of Berlin and, 922–23
    wars in, 922, 928
Ball, John, 313
Ballot Act of 1872, 828
Balzac, Honoré de, 890
Banalités, 549
Banhoeffer, Dietrich, 1140
Bao Dai, 1098
Barbarian invasions, 168, 179, 185, 192, 202–4
Barca, Pedro Calderon de la, 494
Bardi banking house, 336, 364
Bar-Kochba Rebellion, 169
Barnabites, 394
Baroque art/architecture, 417
Barshchina, 549
Barth Karl, 1141
Basel
    Council of, 328, 329
    Treaty of, 678
Basilica of the Sacred Heart, 842
Basil the Great, 218
Bastille, fall of, 606, 649
Batista, Fulgencio, 1091
Battle of the Nations, 699
Batu Khan, 267
Bavaria/Bavarians, 224, 242, 441, 445, 464
Bay of Sluys, Battle of, 312
Beatles, 1137
Beauharnais, Josephine de, 696
Beaulieu, Peace of, 422
Beaverbrook, Lord, 1061
Bebel, August, 863

Beccaria, Cesare, 618
Becket, Thomas à, 259
Becquerel, Henri, 890
Beghards, 255, 371
Begin, Menachem, 1103
Beguines, 255, 371
Behaim, Martin, 357
Being and Time (Heidegger), 1135
Belgium, 700
    independence of, 747–48
    WWI, 932, 933
Bell, Vanessa, 892, 893
Benedetti, Count Vincent, 811
Benedict XI, Pope, 323
Benedict XII, Pope, 324
Benedictine monasticism, 218–19, 244
Benedict of Nursia, 198, 218, 244
Benefices, 223, 235, 236, 237, 320, 324, 373, 384
Benes, Eduard, 1077
Benezet, Anthony, 756
Ben-Gurion, David, 1082
Bentham, Jeremy, 776
Berchtold, Leopold von, 929
Berengar of Friuli, 242
Berengar of Tours, 294
Berlin, 570, 1056
    blockade, 1079
    Wall, 1090, 1147–48
Berlin, Congress of, 922
Berlin Decrees, 691
Berlinguer, Enrico, 1133
Bern, 384, 385
Bernard, Claude, 891
Bernard of Clairvaux, Saint, 251, 291
Bernini, Gianlorenzo, 417
Bernstein, Eduard, 865, 868
Berri, Duke of, 734
Bessemer, Henry, 837
Bessus, 101, 103
Bethlen, Stephen, 986–87
Bethmann-Hollweg, Theobald von, 930, 932
Beveridge, William B., 1129
Beyle, Henri, 708

civil rights movement
and, 1117–18
Eastern Europe,
1120–21
Latin America, 1119
Mediterranean area,
1118
postwar world and,
1116–17
South Africa, 1120
Democritus of Abdera,
89, 105, 159
Demosthenes, 32, 99, 100
Denmark
Danish War, 810
Protestant Reformation
in, 387
Thirty Years' War, 443
Department stores, 839
Deputies on mission, 671
De Rerum Natura
(Lucretius), 159
Deroin, Jeanne, 786
Descartes, René, 307,
486, 501–2
Descent of Man, The
(Darwin), 881,
903
Desiderius, King, 225
Dessalines, Jean-Jacques,
757
De Valera, Eamon, 984
Deventer, 372
Devolution, War of,
470–71
De Witt, Cornelius, 471
De Witt, Jan, 471
*Dialogue on the Two
Chief Systems of
the World*
(Galileo), 485,
488
Dias, Bartholomew, 357,
361
Dickens, Charles, 890
Dictator, in ancient
Rome, 117
Dictatores, 291
Diderot, Denis, 307, 614,
627
Dien Bien Phu, Battle of,
1098–99
*Digest (Corpus juris
civilis)*, 207
Dimitri of Moscow,
Grand Duke, 267
Dioceses, 184

Diocletian, 5, 173, 182,
184, 189, 202
Diogenes of Sinope, 4, 94
Dionysus, 3, 54, 126
Directory (French
Revolution), 606,
677–79, 684
Discourse on Method
(Descartes), 488,
501
*Discourse on the Moral
Effects of the
Arts and
Sciences*
(Rousseau), 621
*Discourse on the Origin
of Inequality*
(Rousseau), 621
Discovery, voyages of,
356–65
impact on Europe,
364–65
Disraeli, Benjamin, 828,
829–30, 915, 922
Divine Comedy (Dante),
306, 338, 482
Divine right, king by,
466–67
Divorce laws, late 19th
century, 847
Dollfuss, Engelbert, 987
Doll's House, A (Ibsen),
891
Domesday Book, 199,
257
Dominic, Saint, 255
Dominican order, 199,
255, 256, 275,
276
Domitian, 163, 164
Domus, 170
Donation of Constantine,
198, 225, 306,
341, 355
Donatism, 326
Donatus, 289
Don gratuit, 643
Don Juan (Byron), 709
Don Quixote (Cervantes),
307, 494, 498
Dorian invasion, 40
Doric column, 88
Dover, Treaty of, 459,
471
Dr. Zhivago (Pasternak),
1085
Draco, 53

Drake, Francis, 436, 438
Drama
early Greek, 3, 86–87
sixteenth and
seventeenth
century, 494–95
Dresden, Battle of, 699
Dreyfus, Alfred, 816–17
Dreyfus Affair, 816–17,
858, 862, 891,
901
Dromos, 38
Drusus, M. Livius,
136–37
Dual Alliance, 923
Dubcek, Alexander, 1092,
1151
Dubois, Pierre, 323
Duma, 870
Dumouriez, General,
664
Dupleix, Joseph, 582
Durkheim, Émile, 898
Dutch Revolt, 427–32

E

Early Middle Ages
agrarian
economy/society,
198, 229–30
Byzantine Empire,
205–11
Charlemagne, 225–31
Christianity, 216–22,
224–25, 230
fall of Rome and,
202–5
feudalism, 234–37
Franks, 222–34
Islam, 211–16
East India Company, 582,
594, 597
Ebert, Friedrich, 992
Ebro River, 123, 124
Ecclesiastical History
(Eusebius), 192
Ecclesiastical Reservation
of Peace of
Augsburg,
440–41
Eck, John, 377
*Economic Consequences
of the Peace, The*
(Keynes), 950
Economics
classical, 775–76

government policies
based on, 775–76
Malthus, 775
Ricardo, 775
mercantilism, 470,
580–82
Eden, Anthony, 1087
Edessa, 251
Edinburgh, Treaty of, 437
Education
High Middle Ages,
285–94
in late 19th century
advances in, 878–79
women and, 847–48
Protestant Reformation
and, 400–403
Roman Republic, 126,
128–30, 132
Rousseau and, 706–7
Education Acts
1870, 828, 886
1902, 886
Education of the Orator
(Quintilian), 340
Edward I, King of
England, 322,
323, 389
Edward III, King of
England, 310,
312
Edward IV, King of
England, 352
Edward VI, King of
England, 391,
393, 432
Edward the Confessor,
256
Egmont, Count of, 427,
428, 429
Egypt
Napoleon's invasion of,
684
under Sadat, 1103
Six Days' War, 1103
Suez Canal, 915, 922
Suez crisis, 1087–88
Yom Kippur War, 1103
Eiffel Tower, 842
Eighteenth century
Europe, 545–77
agricultural revolution,
561–65
aristocracy, 547–49
cities, 570–75
empires, 580–90
mercantile, 580–82

H

Habsburgs, 351, 364, 376, 378, 418, 426, 443, 445, 474
dual monarchy, 818, 819
dynastic integrity, 728–29
Jews and, 575
Maria Theresa and, 591–92
pragmatic sanction and, 530–31
revolutions of 1848 and, 786–90, 818
Roman Catholicism and, 631–32, 817–18
unrest of nationalities under, 819–23
Habuba Kabirah, 12
Hacienda system, 362
Hadrian, 164, 168, 173, 206
Haeckel, Ernst, 880
Hagia Sophia, 198, 210
Hagia Triada, 37
Haiti, 689–90
slave revolt, 737, 739, 757
Halle University, 534
Hamilcar Barca, 123
Hamlet (Shakespeare), 495
Hammer of Witches, The (Krämer and Sprenger), 492
Hammurabi, 2, 13
Hampden, John, 455
Hannibal, 123–24
Hanoverian dynasty, 475, 518
Hansemann, David, 791
Hardenberg, Count von, 694
Hardie, Keir, 861
Harding, Warren G., 966
Hargreaves, James, 307, 568, 570, 606
Harmodius, 56
Harun-al-Rashid, 227
Harvey, William, 504
Hasdrubal, 123
Hastings, Battle of, 199, 256
Hathaway, Anne, 494

Hattusas, 25
Haussmann, Georges, 841
Havel, Vaclav, 1150, 1162–63
Hawaii, 920
Hawkins, John, 436
Hedio, Caspar, 382
Hegel, Georg Wilhelm Friedrich, 607, 715, 716, 727, 779
Hegira, 211
Heidegger, Martin, 1135
Heidelberg University, 287
Heisenberg, Werner, 890
Hektemoroi, 82, 151
Helena (Euripides), 92
Heliocentric theory, 108–9
Helladic period, 37, 38
Hellenistic Greece
Alexander the Great, 100–103
successors of, 103–4
culture architecture, 106
literature, 106
mathematics/science, 106, 108–9
philosophy, 104–6
sculpture, 106
Macedonian conquest, 98–100
Roman conquest, 124–26
Hellespont, 66, 67, 74, 75, 100
Helots, 49, 50, 51, 75, 82, 85, 151
Helsinki Accords, 1110, 1146–47
Henlein, Konrad, 1038
Henry I, King of England, 257
Henry I, King of Germany, 199, 242
Henry II, King of England, 257–58
Henry II, King of France, 418
Henry III, Holy Roman Emperor, 245
Henry III, King of England, 261, 322

Henry III, King of France, 421–23
Henry IV, Holy Roman Emperor, 245–47
Henry IV, King of France, 423–25, 451, 463, 469. *See also* Henry of Navarre
Henry V, Holy Roman Emperor, 247–48
Henry V, King of England, 313
Henry VI, Holy Roman Emperor, 251, 259, 265
Henry VI, King of England, 352
Henry VII, King of England, 350, 352–53, 390
Henry VIII, King of England, 306, 352, 356, 389–93, 434
Henry of Guise, 421
Henry of Navarre, 418, 421–23, 436
Henry the Lion, 251, 264, 265
Henry the Navigator, 357
Henry Tudor, King of England, 284
Hephaestus, 58
Hera, 58
Heraclidae, 40
Heraclides of Pontus, 108
Heraclitus, 88
Heraclius, 209, 213, 216
Herder, Johann Gottfried, 708, 714, 716
Hermandad, 351
Hermes, 58
Herodotus, 4, 52, 90–91
Herriot, Edouard, 981
Herrmann (Arminius), 157
Herzen, Alexander, 825
Herzl, Theodor, 901–3
Hesiod, 3, 57, 59, 161
Hesse, 378, 387, 420
Hestia, 58
Hidalgo y Costilla, Miguel, 740
Hiero, 121
Hieroglyphics, 20, 37
Higglers, 552

High Commission, Court of, 456
High Middle Ages
clergy, 274–77
Cluny reform movement, 243–45
Crusades, 248–53
England in, 256–59
Fourth Lateran Council, 253–54
France in, 259–62, 280, 284
Innocent III, 252–54
investiture struggle, 245–48
nobles, 272–74
Ottonian kings, 242–43
peasants, 277–79
schools/universities, 285–94
towns/townspeople, 279–85
Himmler, Heinrich, 1012, 1050
Hindenburg, Paul von, 934, 992, 1006, 1009
Hipparchus of Nicea, 55, 109
Hippias, 55, 64, 65
Hippocrates of Cos, 32, 91, 216, 297
Hippodamus of Miletus, 106
Hirohito, Emperor of Japan, 1058
History of Rome (Livy), 161, 191
History of the Persian War (Herodotus), 4, 90–91
Hitler, Adolf, 822, 986
annexation of Austria, 1038
anti-semitism, 989
consolidation of power, 1009
Czechoslovakia and, 1038–39
early career, 989–92
European plans of, 1048–49
goals of, 1034
remilitarization of Rhineland by, 1036

Mesoamerica/Mesoamericans, 10, 358–59
Mesopotamia, 8, 10, 168, 179
  Alexander's conquest of, 101
  dynasties, 12–14
  government, 15
  key events/people, 17
  religion, 15–16
  slavery, 150
  society, 16–17
  Sumerian city states, 12
Messana, 121
Messiah, 28, 174
Mesta, 351
Metamorphoses (Ovid), 161
Metaxas, John, 987
Metayer system, 563
Methodism, 711–12, 755
Metternich, Klemens von, 699, 728–31, 735, 786
Mettrie, Offray de La, 616
Mexico
  Aztecs in, 359
  French invasion of, 812
  independence of, 740–41
Michelangelo Buonarroti, 332, 342, 343–44, 345
Middle Ages. *See* Early Middle Ages; High Middle Ages; Late Middle Ages
Middle classes
  18th century, 573–75
  ascendancy of, 838–40
Middle Comedy, 92
Middle Kingdom, ancient Egypt, 21, 23
Migrations
  ancient Greece, 40
  external, 1127
  internal, 1128
Milan, 182, 202, 264, 335, 346, 570
Milan Decree, 692
Militia Ordinance, 457
Mill, John Stuart, 855
Millenary Petition, 452
Millerand, Alexander, 862
Millets, 526

Milos, 737
Milosevic, Slobodan, 1159
Miltiades, 66, 75, 90
Milton, John, 496–97
Mindszenty, Cardinal, 1078
Mining, in Latin America, 362
Minoans, 2, 36–38
Mirandola, Pico della, 340
Mississippi Bubble, 307, 516–17
Mississippi Company, 516–17
Mitannians, 8, 25
Mithraism, 217
Mithridates, 137, 139
Mitterand, François, 1107
Modern Devotion, 353, 371–74
Modernism, 892–94
Modern Man in Search of a Soul (Jung), 897
Mohacs, Battle of, 378
Moldboard plow, 198, 229–30
Molotov, Vyacheslav, 1073
Molyke, Helmuth von, 934
Mona Lisa (Da Vinci), 343
Monarchy
  absolute, 450, 463–76
  northern European revival of, 350–53
  parliamentary, 450, 451–63
Monasticism, 217–19, 243–44
Mongols, 199
Monnet, Jean, 1108
Monophysitism, 206, 207, 221
Monotheism, 3, 27–28, 30
Monroe Doctrine, 920
Montagu, Mary Wortley, 520
Montaigne, Michel de, 365, 417
Montcalm, Joseph de, 593
Monte Cassino, 218

Montenegro, 923, 928
Montesquieu, Charles de, 307, 606, 619–21, 623, 755, 756
Montezuma, 359
Montfort, Simon de, 253
Montgomery, Bernard, 1052
Montmorency-Chatillons, 418
Moravia, 552
More, Thomas, 306, 356, 389–90, 391
Morelos y Pavón, José, 740
Moriscos, 352
Mornay, Philip du Plessis, 421
Moro, Ludovico il, 346, 347
Moroccan crises, 926, 928
Moses, 27
Mosley, Oswald, 1003
Mothers Protection League, 904
Mountain, Girondists *vs.*, 663, 668
Mozambique, 1095
Mrs. Dalloway (Woolf), 893
Mrs. Warren's Profession (Shaw), 892
Muhammad, 211–12
Mun, Thomas, 582
Munda, Battle of, 141
Munich agreement, 1039
Municipia, 104
Münster, 383, 445
Müntzer, Thomas, 383
Muslims, 211
Mussolini, Benito, 975–79, 1034–36, 1039
Mycale, battle at, 68
Mycenaeans, 2, 37, 38–40
  culture, 38
  Dorian invasion, 40
  rise and fall of, 38–40

N

Nagy, Imre, 1089, 1146
Namibia, 915
Nana (Zola), 891
Nancy, Battle of, 351
Nantes, Edict of, 306, 424–25, 461

revocation of, 461, 464, 471–74
Naples, 335, 346, 351, 570
Napoleonic Code, 607, 688, 726, 847
Napoleon III, 786, 802, 803, 806, 810, 812, 841, 859
Narbonese Gaul, 141
Narva, Battle of, 526
Naseby, Battle of, 457
Nasser, Gamal Abdel, 1087, 1102
Nathan the Wise (Lessing), 616
National Assembly, 647, 648, 651, 782, 812–14
National Constituent Assembly, 649–50, 652–54, 656
National Council of French Women (CNFF), 856
National Government, 1001–3
National Insurance Act, 862
Nationalism, 604–5. *See also* specific countries
  emergence of, 722–23
  language and, 722–23, 820
  liberalism and, 727
  nationhood and, 723
  Romantic Movement and, 714, 716
National Liberation Front, 1100
National Socialist German Workers' Party (Nazis), 989–91, 1006–17
National Union of Women's Suffrage Societies, 855
Nationhood, 723
Native Americans
  Columbus and, 357
  economy of exploitation, 362, 364

Constitution, 117–19
consuls, 117
culture
  history, 159
  law, 159, 160
  poetry, 159–60
education, 126, 128–30,
  132
fall of, 139–47
First Triumvirate,
  140–41
Gracchi, 132–36
Greek influences, 126,
  128–29, 158, 159
Punic Wars, 121–24
religion, 126
Second Triumvirate, 5,
  144–47
slavery, 132
struggle of the orders,
  118–19
Twelve Tables, 119
Romantic movement/
  Romanticism,
  705–17
history and, 716
intellectual foundations
  for, 706–7
literature, 708–11
nationalism and, 714,
  716
religion, 711–14
Romantic republicanism,
  803–4
Rome, 182
  early Church in, 178
Rome, Treaty of, 1108
Rome-Berlin Axis Pact,
  1037
Romeo and Juliet
  (Shakespeare),
  495
Rommel, Erwin, 1046–47,
  1052
Romulus, 115
Room of One's Own, A
  (Woolf), 905–7
Roosevelt, Franklin D.,
  1045, 1058,
  1065, 1066, 1072
Rossi, Count Pelligrino,
  790
Rota Romana, 320
Rotten boroughs, 750
Roundheads, 457
Rousseau, Jean-Jacques,
  307, 606, 621–22,

624, 625–26,
  706–7
Roxane, wife of
  Alexander the
  Great, 103
Rubens, Peter Paul, 417
Rubicon River, 141, 145
Rudolf II, Holy Roman
  Emperor, 441
Ruhr, 981, 989, 992, 998
Rule for Monasteries
  (St.Benedict),
  218, 228, 244,
  276
Rule of St. Augustine,
  276
Rump Parliament, 458
Runciman, Steven, 221
Russell, Lord John, 828
Russia, 199
  agricultural
    improvements,
    eighteenth
    century, 564
  Alexander II, reforms
    of, 823–25
  Alexander III, 827
  aristocracy, 548–49
  Bolshevism, rise of,
    867–72
  Catherine the Great,
    548, 551, 575,
    627, 628, 632–35,
    637
  Crimean War, 801–3
  Decembrist Revolt,
    742–44
  Great Northern War,
    526
  industrial
    development,
    865–67
  Jews in, 575
  major turn-of-century
    dates, 872
  Medieval, 267–68
  Napoleon's invasion of,
    696–99
  Official Nationality
    policy, 607, 744
  Peter the Great,
    536–41
  Revolution of 1905,
    869–72, 926
  Romanov dynasty, 536
  Russo-Japanese War,
    926

Serbia and, 737
serfdom, 549–50
  abolition of, 823–24
territorial expansion,
  634–35
Russian Orthodox
  Church, 539
Russian Revolution,
  939–44
communist
  dictatorship,
  942–44
Lenin/Bolsheviks and,
  941–42, 943
outbreak of, 940–41
provisional
  government,
  939–40
Russo-Japanese War, 869,
  926
Russo-Turkish War, 922
Rutherford, Ernest, 890
Ryswick, Peace of, 474

S

Sabbats, 488
Sacred Mount, 119
Sacrosancta, 329
Saeculum, 244, 275
Saguntum, 123
Saint Bartholomew's Day
  Massacre, 306,
  421, 427, 436
Saint-Germain-en-Laye,
  Peace of, 420
Saint Helena, 700
Saint Petersburg, 538,
  541, 570
Saint-Simon, Claude
  Henri de, 777,
  778, 779
Saisset, Bernard, 323
Sakharov, Andrei, 1110,
  1144
Saladin, 199, 251
Salamis, 67
Salian Franks, 203, 222
Salisbury, Lord, 830
Sallust, 5, 138, 159
Salutati, Colluccio, 342
Samarkand, 103
Samnites, 121
Samos, 68, 77
Samson Agonistes
  (Milton), 496–97
Sand, Karl, 730

San Martín, José de,
  739–40
San Salvador, 357
Sans-culottes, 662–63,
  664, 668, 672,
  673
  suppression of, 678–79
San Stefano, Treaty of,
  922
Santorini, 39
Sappho, 61
Sarajevo, 929
Sardinia, 121, 124, 126
Sargon, 2, 12
Sartre, Jean-Paul, 1132,
  1134, 1135
Sassanians, 179
Satires (Horace), 161
Satraps, 64
Satyricon, The
  (Petronius), 173
Satyr plays, 87
Saul of Tarsus, 176
Savonarola, Girolamo,
  347
Savoy, House of, 418
Saxons, 205, 224, 225,
  233
Saxony, 242, 246, 378,
  384, 387, 443,
  445, 592, 700
Schacht, Hjalmar, 992
Scheidmann, Philipp, 950
Schism, 199
Schlegel, August Wilhelm
  von, 708
Schlegel, Friedrich, 710
Schleicher, Kurt von,
  1007, 1009
Schleiermacher,
  Friedrich, 607,
  712, 714
Schleitheim Confession,
  383
Schleswig-Holstein
  problem, 810
Schlieffen, Alfred von,
  933
Schlieffen Plan, 931, 932,
  934
Schmalkaldic
  Articles, 387
  League, 387
Scholasticism, 290, 337
  Aristotle and, 292–94
  critics of, 291–92,
    293

Solomon, King, 3, 27
Solon, 53–54, 55, 356
Solway process, 837
Solzhenitsyn, Alexandr, 1085, 1158–59
Somaschi, 394
Some Condiderations on the Keeping of Negroes (Benezet), 756
Somme, Battle of, 938
Sons of Liberty, 595
Sophists, 4, 89, 93, 94
Sophocles, 87
Sophrosyne, 60
Soranus of Ephesus, 297
Sorbon, Robert de, 289
Sorbonne, 847
Sorel, Georges, 863, 898, 899
Sorrows of Young Werther, The (Goethe), 710
South Africa, 580
  democratization in, 1120
Southeast Asia Treaty Organization (SEATO), 1099
Southern Society, 742
South Sea Company, 519
Soviets, 939–40
Soviet Union. *See also* Cold War
  Brezhnev era, 1110–11, 1113
  collectivization, 1019–22
  foreign reactions/ repurcussions, 1022–23
  Great Purges, 1023–25
  industrialization, 1018–19
  Khruschev era, 1084–87
  Nazi-Soviet pact, 1042
  New Economic Policy (NEP), 969
  War Communism, 968–69
  World War II, 1045–48, 1052, 1063–64
Sozzini, Faustus, 383
Spaak, Paul-Henri, 1108

Spain
  ancient Rome and, 5, 121, 123, 124, 125, 126, 140
  Bismarck and, 811–12
  Civil War, 1036–38
  in 18th century aristocracy, 547
  colonial system, 583–85
  Empire in Americas, 307, 357–65, 736
  Catholic Church and, 396–98
  England and, 432–38, 454
  expulsion of Jews from, 306, 352
  France and, 463–64
  humanism in, 356
  Islam in, 351–52
  as maritime power, 514
  Muslim armies in, 213
  Napoleonic wars, 696
  Philip II, 425–32
  revival of monarchy in, 351–52
  Revolution of 1820, 735–36
Spanish-American War, 920
Spanish Armada, 306, 423, 432, 438
Spanish Civil War, 1036–38
Spanish Fury, 430
Spanish Revolution, 607
Spanish Succession, War of, 307, 470, 474–75, 514, 534, 583
Sparta. *See* Ancient Greece
Spartacus, 139, 153
Speeches on Religion to Its Cultured Despisers (Schleiermacher), 714
Speer, Albert, 1059
Spencer, Herbert, 882, 904
Speyer, Diet of, 378
Spinning jenny, 307, 568, 606
Spinoza, Baruch, 504

Spirit of the Laws (Montesquieu), 619–21, 623, 755
Spiritual Exercises (Ignatius of Loyola), 394–95, 401
Spiritual Franciscans, 256, 323, 324
Spiritualists, 383
Sportsmen, in Middle Ages, 273
Sri Lanka, 1094
Staël, Madame de, 708
Stafford, Earl of, 455, 456
Stalin, Joseph, 969, 970–71, 986, 1020, 1022–23, 1024, 1025, 1063, 1065, 1073, 1077, 1084
Stalingrad, Battle of, 1052
Stamp Act, 595
Stamp Act Congress, 595, 596, 600
Star Chamber, Court of, 306, 456
Statutes of Provisors, 389
Stavisky, Serge, 1003
Stavisky affair, 1003, 1004
Steam engine, 568–69
Steele, Richard, 611
Steffens, Lincoln, 1022
Stein, Baron vom, 694
Stendhal, 708
Stephen II, Pope, 222, 225
Stephen IX, Pope, 245
Stoa, 106
Stoa poikile, 105
Stockton and Darlington Railway, 607, 763
Stoecker, Adolf, 901
Stoics, 104, 105–6
Stolypin, P.A., 870, 872
Stopes, Marie, 905
Storm troopers (SA), 1006, 1009
Strachey, Lytton, 892
Stranger, The (Camus), 1135
Strasbourg, 385, 399, 441
Strauss, 607
Strauss, David Friedrich, 884
Streltsy, 536, 537, 539

Stresemann, Gustav, 992
Struggle of the orders, 4, 118–19
Strymon Valley, 98
Stuart monarchies, 451, 458–61
Students
  popular music and, 1136–37
  university, expanding population of, 1136
Studia humanitatis, 337, 403
Studies in Hysteria (Freud and Breuer), 896
Sturm und Drang, 706
Subjection of Women, The (Mill and Taylor), 855
Suburbs, 842
Subways, 841
Successor states, 985–87
Sudetenland, 986, 1038–39
Suetonius, 144
Suez Canal, 915, 922
Suez crisis, 1087–88
Suffragettes, 855
Sugar, slavery and, 587
Sugar Act, 594
Suger, Abbot, 261
Sulla, L. Cornelius, 5, 136, 137–39
Sully, Duke of, 463
Sumer/Sumerians, 2, 8, 11–12, 15, 25
  language, 13
Summa, 290
Summa Theologiae (Thomas Aquinas), 199, 290, 292
Sunni muslims, 213
Supremacy, Acts of, 390, 434
Swabia, 242
Sweden
  in eighteenth century, 525–26
  Protestant Reformation in, 387
  Thirty Years' War, 443, 445
Swiss Brethren, 383
Swiss Confederacy, 445

Tull, Jethro, 562
Turgot, Robert, 562–63
Turkey, 927, 928
  mandate system and, 953
  WWI and, 936, 937, 942
Turks, 427
  fall of Constantinople to, 183
Turner, Nat, 757
Tutankhamen, 2, 6, 24–25
Twelfth Dynasty, ancient Egypt, 21
Twelve Tables, 4, 119, 126
Twelve Years' Truce, 432
Twenty-five points, 989
Two Sicilies, 735
Two Treatises of Government (Locke), 462, 498, 507
Tyler, Wat, 313
Tyndale, William, 389, 393
Tyrants/tyranny, in ancient Greece, 3, 45–48, 54, 64
Tyre, 101, 121

U

Ukraine, Jews in, 575
Ulema, 212
Ulster, 984–85
Ulyanov, Vladimir Ilyich. *See* Lenin, Vladimir Ilyich
Ulysses (Joyce), 893
Umar, Caliph, 213, 215
Umayyad dynasty, 213
Unam Sanctam, 306, 323
Uncertainty principle, 890
Unemployment, late 19th century, 838
Unfree serfs, 229
Uniformity, Acts of, 393, 434
Union, Act of, 749
Union of German Women's Organizations (BDFK), 857
Unions, 859

United Nations, 1074–75
United States
  antislavery movement, 758
  collapse of Soviet Union and, 1156
  détente and, 1111
  Great Depression, 998–99
  Vietnam War, 1098, 1099–1102
  WWI, 939
  WWII, 1050–52, 1056–58
Ur, 12, 13, 28
Urban II, Pope, 247, 248, 249
Urban IV, Pope, 320
Urban VI, Pope, 328
Urbanization. *See* Cities and towns
Ursalines, 394
Uruguay, 739
Uruk, 12
Urukagina of Lagash, King, 14
Uthman, Caliph, 213, 215
Utilitarianism, 776
Utnapishtim, 29
Utopia (More), 356
Utopian socialism, 777–78
Utrecht, Treaty of, 307, 475, 514, 529, 580, 583, 590, 606
Utrecht, Union of, 431, 432
Uvarov, Count S.S., 744

V

Vaihinger, Hans, 890
Valens, 184–85, 202
Valentinian, 184–85
Valerian, 5, 179, 189
Valla, Lorenzo, 225, 306, 340–42
Valmy, Battle of, 662
Valois dynasty, 378
Van Artevelde, Jacob, 312
Vandals, 198, 202–3, 204, 205
Varennes, 658
Vassalage, 235–36
Vassi, 235
Vassy massacre, 419
Vatican II, 1141

Vauban, Sebastien, 469, 470
Vega, Lope de, 494
Veii, 119, 120
Velvet revolution, 1150–51
Venice, 251, 316, 335, 346, 570
Ventadorn, Bernart de, 258
Veracruz, 583
Verdun, Battle of, 938
Verdun, Treaty of, 198, 231, 232–33
Vergerio, Pietro Paolo, 339
Vergil, 5, 146, 158, 161, 960
Vergina, 100
Vermuyden, Cornelius, 562
Verona, Congress of, 735–36
Versailles, 467–68
  Treaty of, 945–50, 989, 993, 1013
Vervins, Treaty of, 424
Vesey, Denmark, 757
Vespasian, 163, 164, 169
Vespucci, Amerigo, 357
Vesteras, Diet of, 387
Vesuvians, 786
Viceroys, 583
Vichy government, 1060–61
Victor Emmanuel II, King of Italy, 790, 804, 808
Victor Emmanuel III, King of Italy, 978
Victor III, Pope, 247
Vienna uprising, 787
Viet Cong, 1100, 1102
Viet Minh, 1095, 1099
Vietnamization policy, 1101
Vietnam War, 1095, 1098–1102
Vikings, 198, 234
Villa, 184, 185
Villafranca, Treaty of, 806
Villermé, Louis René, 607, 843, 844
Vindication of the Rights of Woman, A (Wollstonecraft), 626, 855

Vingtième, 548
Virchow, Rudolf, 843
Virgin Mary, 230, 253, 294
Virtù, 348
Visconti family, 324
Visigoths, 5, 184, 185, 192, 198, 202, 204, 205, 222
Vita Nuova (Dante), 338
Vladimir of Kiev, Prince, 267
Vogt, Karl, 903
Voix des Femmes, 786
Voltaire, 307, 606, 611, 613–14, 615–16, 617, 627
Voting Rights Act (1965), 1118
Vulgate, 192

W

Wagram, Battle of, 696
Wakefield, Priscilla, 558
Waldeck-Rousseau, Pierre, 886
Waldeck-Rousseau, René, 862
Waldensians, 255, 321, 371
Walesa, Lech, 1113, 1145
Wallace, Alfred Russel, 880
Wallas, Graham, 861, 898
Walpole, Robert, 307, 518–25, 591, 598, 606
Walsingham, Francis, 437–38
Wanax, 38
War Communism, 968–69
Warriors in Middle Ages, 272
Warsaw, 570
Warsaw Pact, 1080
Wars of the Roses, 306, 352
Warton, Thomas, 708
Washington, George, 597
Water frame, 307, 568, 606
Watergate scandal, 1111
Waterloo, Battle of, 604, 607, 700
Watlings Island, 357